Sociology

Fourth Edition

Sociology
Changing Societies in a Diverse World

George J. Bryjak
University of San Diego

Michael P. Soroka
University of San Diego

Allyn and Bacon
Boston   London   Toronto   Sydney   Tokyo   Singapore

Series Editor: Jeff Lasser
Editor-in-Chief, Social Sciences: Karen Hanson
Editorial Assistant: Sue Hutchinson
Marketing Manager: Judeth Hall
Production Administrator: Joe Sweeney
Editorial-Production Service: Colophon
Text Designer: Glenna Collett
Cover Administrator: Linda Knowles
Composition Buyer: Linda Cox
Manufacturing Buyer: Suzanne Lanear
Photo Research: Sue C. Howard
Text Composition: Omegatype, Inc.

Library of Congress Cataloging-in-Publication Data
Bryjak, George J.
    Sociology: changing societies in a diverse world /
George J. Bryjak, Michael P. Soroka.—4th ed.
        p.   cm
    Includes bibliographical references and index.
    ISBN 0–205–29463-4 (alk. paper)
    1. Sociology.   I. Soroka, Michael P.   II. Title.
    HM586 .B896   2000
301—dc21   00-055833

Printed in the United States of America
10 9 8 7 6 5 4 3 2 1 04 03 02 01 00

Photo Credits

p. 2, © Patrick Ward/ CORBIS; p. 7, left, © Mike Ya-
mashita/Woodfin Camp & Associates; p. 7, right, © Geof-
frey Clifford/Woodfin Camp & Associates; p. 13, © Frank
Johnston/Woodfin Camp & Associates; p. 24, © AP/Wide
World Photos; p. 30, © Liaison Agency; p. 34, © B & C
Alexander; p. 38, © AP/Wide World Photos; p. 45, ©
Bettmann/CORBIS; p. 47, © A. Ramey/Stock Boston;
p. 52, © Ted Streshinsky/CORBIS; p. 56, © Owne
Franken/Stock Boston; p. 62, © Richard Pasley/Stock
Boston; p. 69, © Robert Maass/CORBIS; p. 73, © CORBIS;
p. 82, © Betty Press/Woodfin Camp & Associates; p. 84, ©
Tomas van Houtryve/Liaison Agency; p. 85, © Eastcott/
Momatiuk/Liaison Agency; p. 91, © Catherine Karnow/
CORBIS; p. 97, © Dilip Mehta/Woodfin Camp & Associ-
ates; p. 102, © Dilip Mehta/Woodfin Camp & Associates;
p. 104, © S. Moorani/Woodfin Camp & Associates; p. 110,
© AP/Wide World Photos; p. 114, © AP/Wide World Pho-
tos; p. 118, © Stephanie Maze/CORBIS; p. 124, © AFP/
CORBIS; p. 132, © AP/Wide World Photos; p. 137, © AP/
Wide World Photos; p. 144, © Charles Gupton/Stock
Boston; p. 151, © Noel-Figaro/Liaison Agency; p. 153,
© AP/Wide World Photos; p. 160, © Todd Robertson;

Photo credits continued on page 400, which constitutes a continuation of the copyright page.

Contents

4 / *Socialization* 73

5 / *Inequality and Stratification* 91

6 / *Race and Ethnicity* 114

7 Gender and Gender Issues 137

8 Crime, Deviance, and Social Control 160

9 Marriage and the Family 192

14 / Sociology and the Future   341

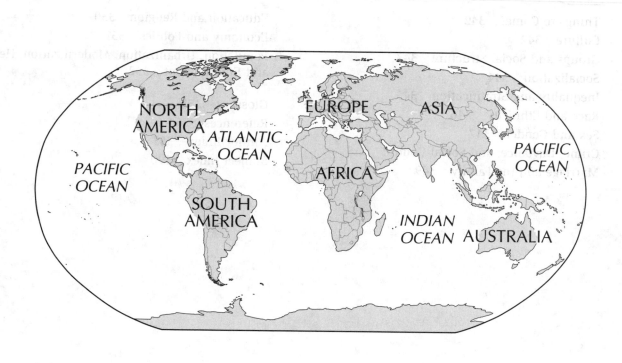

Preface

THEMES AND RATIONALE

At the recent annual meetings of the American Sociological Association, more than three dozen introductory sociology texts were on display at the publishers' book exhibit—and these were only the offerings of the handful of companies that comprise the "major" academic publishing houses. An equal or larger number were available from the many smaller companies who also were displaying their wares to the assembled multitudes. Like the legendary swamp-drainers who were up to their ears (or some other portion of their anatomies) in alligators, it seems that introductory sociology instructors are up to their own ears in possible texts for that course. Most, if not all, of these books are well-written; they all pretty much cover the same basic or core topics; and many appear virtually indistinguishable from one another, making the final selection of a text for one's course a more difficult task than it need be ("So many textbooks, so little time"). Why, then, are we adding yet another log to a fire that is already well ablaze?

In spite of the abundance of very good introductory texts, our many years of combined experience teaching introductory sociology have shown us that existing texts do not completely fulfill our vision of what the first course in this field could and should accomplish. The primary objective of any introductory course is to infuse students with the sociological perspective—to help them develop, in C. Wright Mills' famous and oft-quoted phrase, a "sociological imagination." In this regard, introductory texts (including this one) commonly expose students to the theoretical and methodological tools of the discipline, using them to interpret the students' surrounding social environment. But, although a thorough understanding of one's own society may be a necessary condition for attaining a sociological imagination, it is not sufficient for reaching that goal. To comprehend and appreciate fully the dynamics and effects of social and cultural forces in the contemporary world, students must be provided with a far broader perspective than many existing texts typically offer.

A Cross-Cultural Perspective

It is abundantly clear that the forces affecting our daily lives are not confined to the internal dynamics of the United States. International trade agreements and political alliances influence much more than just the cost of imported and exported consumer goods. They also partially determine the nation's employment picture and occupational structure as well as the rate and consequences of some forms of criminal behavior (such as the use of illegal drugs). Although the global marketplace and political arena have always had some effect on people in the United States, the frequency and magnitude of changes in these areas have never been greater. The ascendancy of newly industrialized nations such as South Korea, Taiwan, Singapore, and Hong Kong, and the sweeping changes taking place throughout the former Soviet Union and the Eastern European countries have already profoundly influenced our lives, and will continue to do so in the foreseeable future.

One goal of this text is to acquaint students with the concept of modernization, the ongoing process of change that transforms traditional agricultural or pastoral societies into industrial (and now, postindustrial) nation-states. Although modernization cannot explain all the momentous events and processes occurring in the world today, it is a very useful—and, in many introductory texts, overlooked—perspective for examining globalization and other contemporary phenomena. Because modernization significantly affects virtually all aspects of contemporary societies, we believe an understanding of this concept is vital to developing a true sociological imagination. Today, the first course in sociology is an appropriate setting for introducing students to this key force in our world. We are convinced that students will intuitively recognize that in addition to such fundamental sociological phenomena as culture, social structure, socialization, and stratification, the process of modernization plays a central role in their lives.

An exploration of this key social process obviously calls for a cross-cultural framework, and this text is replete with examples and statistics from numerous countries, especially developing nations. However, we have attempted to avoid the danger of presenting a bewildering array of "strange but true" facts drawn from too large an assortment of societies and cultures from around the world. Such a display may make for entertaining reading, but it can confuse rather than enlighten students taking their first course in sociology.

To provide students with insight into the workings of other societies as they relate to one or more of the central themes developed within chapters, Chapters 2–13 contain "Focus on" segments. Each of these segments highlights a particular society or region and offers a detailed analysis of a significant facet of life or pressing issue facing its population members—in Chapter 2, for example, the focus is on the People's Republic of China and changing cultural beliefs and values as that society marks its 50th anniversary under communist rule. In Chapter 7, the focus is on Afghanistan, where the current Taliban-ruled government has imposed on women restrictions that may be the most oppressive in the world. Combining historical background with current sociological trends, these "Focus on" segments give students the opportunity to compare and contrasts familiar elements of their own lives with similar yet unfamiliar elements of other peoples' lives. It is from such comparisons and contrasts that students can best see and extract those common patterns and concerns that truly make for a global society.

An Exploration of Cultural Diversity in U.S. Society

In addition to devoting a significant portion of the text to the people, processes, and structures of other societies, *Sociology: Changing Societies in a Diverse World* consistently explores the many social groups and cultural patterns coexisting within contemporary U.S. society. The social, economic, and political consequences of the rapidly changing composition of the U.S. population, and changing conceptions of gender roles are examined throughout. For example, in Chapter 2, on culture, we explore the influence of race, ethnicity, and social class on "traditional" core values of U.S. society. What constitutes the essence of being an American? The attempt by members of the majority group to preserve "American" culture by legislating English as the official language of the United States is one facet of this controversial ques-

tion explored in the chapter. In Chapter 5, on inequality and stratification, we investigate subgroup memberships and the effects of racial, ethnic, and gender differences on individuals' experiences within the socioeconomic class system. The theme of cultural diversity is similarly threaded through separate chapters on race and ethnicity, sex and gender, five key social institutions (marriage and family, politics, economy, education, and religion), and population and urbanization.

A Basic Foundation

Notwithstanding the important themes introduced so far, the primary function of any introductory text in sociology must be the clear and theoretically balanced presentation of the discipline's most important core concepts. *Sociology: Changing Societies in a Diverse World* is first and foremost a sound introduction to the discipline of sociology. Theory, culture, socialization, groups and social structure, stratification, race and ethnicity, sex and gender, and deviance and social control are presented in a lively and comprehensive manner. Chapters on population, urbanization, and modernization build on core concepts and inform students about crucial areas of sociological study. The fourteen-chapter format allows instructors the option of supplementing the text with other readings; however, *Sociology: Changing Societies in a Diverse World* was created to stand alone as a firm foundation for the introductory course.

CHANGES TO THE FOURTH EDITION

"May you live in interesting times"—the Irish toast that is as much a curse as a blessing—could very well have been raised to the population of the world at the beginning of the third millennium. We are, indeed, living in interesting times—a period of dramatic and rapid societal, international, and global changes that have shaken many nations and overwhelmed some others altogether. In parts of the former Soviet Union, continuing economic and political problems have led to a merry-go-round of governments, ethnic secessionist movements, and an unparalleled growth of criminal behavior and criminal organizations. Economic crises that began in east and southeast Asia have reverberated throughout Europe and the Americas, staggering Mexico, Brazil and other Latin American societies that were just beginning to recover from earlier economic recessions. Under the banner of the United Nations, U.S. troops were deployed to Kosovo to prevent the sort of "ethnic cleansing" that had earlier shocked the world as the historically explosive Balkans once again ignited. In Africa, AIDS, starvation, and civil wars continued to decimate the populations of sub-Saharan nations, already among the poorest people on earth. Throughout the world, people waited anxiously to see if life as they knew it would come to a sudden and dramatic end as a result of the so-called "Y2K" problem that threatened to bring down the computer-driven informational and transactional network on which the planet had become so dependent.

Perhaps more than ever before, the members of this and other societies are beset by rapid and often unexpected changes; and any sociology text that would hope to offer its readers an accurate, up-to-date picture of the human social world must be prepared to keep up with those changes. Towards this end, in this fourth edition (now titled, *Sociology: Changing Societies in a Diverse World*) we have made a number of significant additions and deletions.

First—and possibly foremost—in response to comments and suggestions from many of the instructors who used previous editions of what was then titled *Sociology: Cultural Diversity in a Changing World*, we have completely redone the "Focus on" chapter segments that have been a hallmark of the text since its inception. In past editions, those pieces were devoted exclusively to Japan and Mexico, two societies we believed to be of particular interest and relevance in examining the modernization process and in providing important points of comparison and contrast to United States society. While our belief was shared by a large number of instructors who initially chose the text at least in part because of this feature, a growing number of other users found the chapter-by-chapter focusing on these two societies a bit too restrictive for their own purposes. Some continued to use the text in spite of its emphasis on Japan and Mexico; others opted for one of the number of other cross-cultural or "global" texts that by then had begun to appear. We have thus attempted to address their concerns by developing new "Focus on" essays that effectively discuss specific sociological principles and patterns while exposing students to a larger array of "foreign" societies and cultures. Appearing in Chapters 2–13, these "Focus on" segments deal with such diverse countries and regions as China, South Korea, South Africa, Yugoslavia, Afghanistan, Canada, Europe, and the Latin America/Caribbean Basin, among others. Each of these "Focus on" segments selects an issue discussed at length in the given chapter (changing cultural values; building and maintaining societal cohesion; ethnic tensions; the rights of women; crime and deviance in the aftermath of fundamental structural changes; and problems of population aging, to name just a few), showing students how the phenomenon is played out in a society other than their own and giving them the basis for interpreting and understanding similar events as they impinge on U.S. society.

Second, in addition to drawing on the most recent available empirical data and statistics to illustrate and support chapter topics, this new edition contains new global, regional, and country maps to give students a better sense of the geographic locations and significant physical features of the individual societies discussed in the "Focus on" segments throughout the text. The "Focus on" segment is accompanied by a map of the particular society or area under examination, helping students toward a more global context.

Finally, we end the text with a brief "Sociology and the Future" chapter in which, drawing on and extrapolating from contemporary social, cultural, economic, political, and other trends, we offer students a series of projections as to what the first few decades of the 21st century may bring to (or take from) their lives. Though making forecasts about even the short-term future is fraught with hazards, we believe that students should be exposed to such efforts—particularly as such projections, when made by "professional" social scientists, become the basis for domestic and foreign policy decisions that will impact their lives.

FEATURES OF THE TEXT

"Focus on" Segments

As described, these sections provide students with an in-depth look into many significant aspects of societies and cultures outside the United States. Each "Focus on" section investigates how the core concepts introduced in that chapter manifest themselves in some other society, providing students with meaningful points of comparison and contrast to their own lives.

Other Pedagogical Features

Questions to Consider Directly following each chapter's brief introductory overview, students are presented with focusing questions to alert them to the important concepts and issues to be introduced and developed in the chapter. These questions have been created to develop students' analytical skills by encouraging them to critically evaluate, rather than simply memorize, what they are learning.

Key Terms   Key terms are defined throughout the text in boldface, easily identifiable type. These terms provide students with a working definition of the most important sociological concepts as they are introduced and applied.

Extensive Chapter Summaries   Numbered chapter summaries review, highlight, and reinforce the most important concepts and issues discussed in each chapter. They are linked to the chapter-opening Questions to Consider.

Comprehensive Glossary   A comprehensive glossary brings together all important concepts and terms introduced throughout the text into a single, accessible format.

Features of the Supplements Package

Supplements for Instructors

Instructor's Manual/Test Bank (Lee Frank, Community College of Allegheny County)   This supplement provides chapter outlines and summaries, learning objectives, key terms, and classroom lecture and discussion suggestions. The Test Bank includes multiple choice, true-false, fill-in, and essay questions for each chapter.

Computerized Testing   Allyn and Bacon Test Manager is an integrated suite of testing and assessment tools for Windows and Macintosh. You can use Test Manager to create professional-looking exams in just minutes by selecting from the existing database of questions, editing questions, or writing your own. Course management features include a class roster, gradebook, and item analysis. Test Manager also has everything you need to create and administer online tests.

Allyn and Bacon Interactive Video for Introductory Sociology, and **Video User's Guide**   This custom video features television news footage on both national and global topics. The up-to-the-minute video segments are great for launching lectures, sparking classroom discussion, and encouraging critical thinking. A user's guide provides detailed descriptions of each video segment, specific tie-ins to the text, and suggested discussion questions.

A&B Video Library   Qualified adopters may select from a wide variety of high quality videos from such sources as Films for the Humanities and Sciences and Annenberg/CPB.

Allyn & Bacon Transparencies for Introductory Sociology   Revised for this edition, this package includes over 100 color acetates featuring illustrations from a variety of sources.

Digital Media Archive for Sociology   This CD-ROM for Windows and Macintosh contains a variety of media elements that you can use to create electronic presentations in the classroom. It includes hundreds of original images, as well as selected art from Allyn and Bacon sociology texts, providing instructors with a broad selection of graphs, charts, maps, and figures that illustrate key sociological concepts. For classrooms with full multimedia capability, it also contains digitized video segments and links to sociology Web sites.

The Blockbuster Approach: A Guide to Teaching Sociology with Video (Casey Jordan, Western Connecticut State University)   This manual describes hundreds of commercially available videos that represent sociological ideas and themes, and provides sample assignments.

Supplements for Students

Global Societies (Grant Farr, Portland State University)   This supplement, new to the Fourth Edition, can be packaged with the text upon request. It focuses on contemporary social life in eight countries: Japan, Mexico, Brazil, China, Poland, Iran, South Africa, and Indonesia. The author provides a brief factual profile of each society, a discussion of the main issues facing it now and in the future, a recent newspaper or magazine article, and a list of suggested resources for further study.

Study Guide (Lee Frank, Community College of Allegheny County)   This supplement, available for student purchase, includes learning objectives, chapter summaries and outlines, lists of key terms and people, and self-test questions in a variety of formats.

Sociology on the Net (Joseph Jacoby, Bowling Green University, and Doug Gotthoffer, California State University-Northridge)   This reference guide, updated annually, introduces students to the basics of the Internet and the World Wide Web, and lists hundreds of URLs for sites that are useful for the study of sociology.

Acknowledgments

We would like to thank the reviewers who offered their thoughtful comments about this text over all four editions:

Louis Clunk, Golden West College

Mary Kirby Diaz, State University of New York-Farmingdale

Susan Dvorak, New Mexico State University

Len England, Brigham Young University

Robert Fiala, University of New Mexico

Clyde W. Franklin, Ohio State University

Debbie Franzman, Allan Hancock College

James A. Glynn, Bakersfield College

Gary Kiger, Utah State University

Ted Kraus, University of Toledo, Community and Technical Campus

Ivy Lee, California State University-Sacramento

Patrick McNamara, University of New Mexico

Gwendolyn E. Nyden, Oakton Community College

David L. Preston, San Diego State University

Helaine Prince-Aubrey, New Mexico State University

Donald Ratcliffe, Toccoa Falls College

Andres Rindon, California State University-Sacramento

Edward Silva, El Paso Community College

Paul Star, Auburn University

Ron Stewart, State University of New York-Buffalo

Barbara Strassberg, Aurora University

Leslie Wang, University of Toledo, Community and Technical Campus

Ed Wesnofske, State University of New York-Oneonta

Jim Williams, Weber State University

Herb Ziegler, Chesapeake College

Sociology

1

The World According to Sociology

In a Department of Motor Vehicles office in South Florida, a group of excited, nervous teenaged girls and boys wait for the big moment. Clutching their learner's permits and perhaps whispering one last heartfelt prayer, they are ready to begin a final series of written and road examinations. If they pass, they will earn the first badge of their impending adulthood—their driver's license—and the adult-like freedom and independence that accompany the legal right to operate a motor vehicle in this society. If they fail, they must remain dependent on the willingness of parents and friends to transport them to and from school, work, and other important destinations.

Less than two hundred miles away, just outside of Havana, Cuba, in a scene replayed throughout Latin America, an excited, nervous teenaged girl waits for the big moment. Clothed in an elegant dress and surrounded by family and friends, she is about to begin her *quinceañera,* the formal celebration marking her fifteenth birthday and her entry into the world of female adulthood. As elaborate and lavish as a wedding ceremony, the *quinceañera* can easily match or exceed a wedding in financial expenses. But, even though the girl's coming-of-age festivities may well end up costing her working-class family as much as three months' wages, they are willing and happy to make the sacrifice. They would not dream of denying their daughter the once-in-a-lifetime experience that is so much a part of their traditional world.

More than six thousand miles away, in Tanzania, East Africa, an excited, nervous Masai teenaged boy waits for the big moment. He is about to undergo the painful rite of circumcision that will make him a man in the eyes of his people, and he knows that he must be brave under their watchful gaze. As his father has told him of the coming ordeal: "You must not budge; don't move a muscle or even blink. You can face only one direction until the operation is completed. The slightest movement on your part will mean you are a coward, incompetent and unworthy to be a Masai man" (Saitoti in Nanda and Warms, 1998, p. 93). Though he may dread what lies immediately ahead, the boy nonetheless relishes the prospect of assuming the honor, respect, and responsibilities accorded only to full-fledged adults in his society.

These three examples of what are called *rites of initiation* or *rites of passage* involve activities that are very much unlike one another, yet in some respects are quite similar. In spite of the vast differences in their degree of formality and in their specific details, each event defines and symbolizes a significant change in the life situation of its main participants. And, though undoubtedly strange and perhaps even incomprehensible to an outside observer (for example, a Miami Beach teenager witnessing a Masai coming-of-age public circumcision ritual), each is familiar and understandable to those who are involved in it. That is because the behaviors of all participants are patterned. They take place according to a logical system that is known and that makes sense to all the members of the local population.

In this text, we examine a large array of human activities from the perspective of **sociology,** the academic discipline that attempts to describe, explain, and predict human social patterns from a scientific orientation. Sociology is one of a number of academic fields known collectively as the *social sciences,* which also include anthropology, economics, political science, and psychology. But sociology differs from these other disciplines in its emphasis on social groups as both its primary unit of analysis and as phenomena whose organization and operations serve as significant factors in the shaping of human thoughts and actions. In keeping with this approach, our attention throughout the text is on different groups or kinds of people—college students, career women, and government employees, among others—rather than on particular individual persons.

For example, in modern societies such as the United States, many young adults expend enormous amounts of time, effort, and money to earn advanced educational degrees, whereas many others do not. In attempting to understand why some, but not all, people of a given age successfully complete college or university studies, psychologists typically focus on personal attributes such as intelligence, dedication, and motivation, that vary from one individual to another. From the psychological perspective, those people who are brighter or harder-working or more motivated (or all three) are much more likely to start and complete an advanced educational degree than those people who lack one, some, or all of these characteristics.

In contrast, when addressing the same phenomenon (as we do in Chapter 5 on Inequality and Stratification and in Chapter 10 on Education and Religion), sociologists typically examine group or structural factors that lie outside and beyond the personal attributes—and personal control—of individuals. One such factor is the extent to which formal educational degrees and credentials can help people in a given society achieve or attain better lives. In a society in which an advanced education serves as an important means to upward social mobility, many people will be led to acquire this valuable tool. However, in a society in which no amount of formal education will improve the social standing and social fortunes of population members, very few people will seek a higher education, since it will have no appreciable impact on their life situations. A second important factor is the extent to which formal education—and especially higher education—is accessible to members of all the different racial, ethnic, social class, and other recognizable groups that make up the populations of most contemporary societies. In a society in which a truly open public or mass educational system exists, people from all population segments will be represented among the ranks of the highly educated. In a society in which various population subgroups are formally or informally restricted or excluded from the educational system, formal education degrees will be limited to members of select groups.

The United States is a society in which a college-level education is widely viewed as a springboard, if not an absolute requirement, for better jobs and higher incomes. Consequently, many people—perhaps most people—feel that they need to complete a college or university degree in order to improve their life situations. However, as you may already be painfully aware, pursuing an advanced-level education in this society is a very expensive proposition. The high costs of tuition, room and board, books, and other educational incidentals make it much less likely that certain kinds of people—poor whites, as well as many members of racial and ethnic minority groups, who tend to have lower levels of income and much higher rates of poverty than do whites—will be able to start, much less complete, college. Regardless of how intelligent or hard-working or motivated they may be as individuals, their lack of financial resources significantly hinders their collective chances of attaining higher-level educational degrees. From the sociological perspective, it is hardly coincidental that, in this society, white young adults from middle-class, upper-middle-class, and upper-class backgrounds have much higher rates of college and university completion than do minorities in general and whites from working-class and lower-class backgrounds. In effect, many members of these latter groups have been priced out of the advanced education market.

Our goal in this text is to bring you to an understanding of how human social patterns such as the distribution of college and university degrees in modern societies are created, maintained, and changed over time. We also explore the important consequences that particular social patterns have for the people who carry them out. In addition to marking our movement from one stage of social life to another, these patterns also define the kinds of lives we can expect to lead at each stage of our journey.

Questions to Consider

1. What is the subject matter of sociology?
2. When did the two phases of modernization begin?
3. In what sense is sociology a debunking science?
4. What is globalization and how is this phenomenon affecting societies throughout the world?
5. What is positivism?
6. What are social facts, and how do they differ from individual/psychological phenomena?
7. What is a theory? What is the difference between grand theories and middle-range theories?
8. What is the problem of order, and how is it solved, according to functionalist sociologists?
9. What are the functional requirements that all societies must meet if they are to survive?
10. What are manifest and latent functions?
11. What basic assumptions do conflict sociologists make about the nature of society?
12. Can conflict be beneficial for society?
13. According to symbolic interactionism, in what sense do people create the world they live in?
14. What is the difference between the independent and dependent variables in a scientific experiment?
15. What is survey research, and what are some of the problems associated with this investigative technique?
16. What is participant observation, and what are some of the problems surrounding this strategy?

The Modernization of Sociology: A Growing International Perspective

When we think of social scientists doing **cross-cultural research**—that is, gathering comparable data from different human populations—the discipline of anthropology usually comes to mind. As a result of watching Indiana Jones–type movies, people often think of cross-cultural research as a continuing adventure with investigators studying strange and sometimes dangerous people in the far reaches of the globe. **Cultural anthropologists** typically study the social organization and patterns of behavior of premodern people throughout the world, but their days are more likely to be filled with hard work and careful observation than with adventure.

A sister discipline of anthropology, sociology focuses on the social organization and patterns of behavior in large, complex, modern, industrial societies. Although interested in modern societies as a whole, sociologists have traditionally attempted to understand and explain social phenomena in their own countries and have not spent as much time carefully examining patterns of behavior in other nations. For example, to the extent that American and French sociologists have looked beyond their own borders, they have been inclined to see whether what was happening in the United States and France was similar to the social structures and patterns of behavior in other industrial nations as a whole.

This tendency to peer inward at one's own society as well as to look outward at the broader picture can be traced to sociology's inception in mid-nineteenth-century Europe. By this time, the Industrial Revolution was well underway, and societies that had been relatively stable for hundreds of years were changing rapidly. As new machines and sources of power enhanced humans' ability to produce a growing list of products, people left farms and small towns by the tens of thousands and moved to the cities for a life of factory work. This heretofore unprecedented rural-to-urban migration resulted in the growth of hundreds of cities in Europe and in North America. With this growth came many of the social problems (like higher rates of violent crime) that accompany urbanization and that increasingly plague cities today. Population increase, the beginning of mass education, and the fall of aristocracies in favor of increasingly democratic forms of government were transforming the face of Europe. The old rural, feudal, agrarian way of life was giving way to urban, capitalist, industrial societies.

Some intellectuals of this period realized that although the disciplines of psychology and economics helped them understand these changes, their focus of study was too narrow. Psychologists studied individual behavior and were more likely to shed light on how people were affected by these changes than on what brought the changes about in the first place. Economists studied the production, distribution, exchange, and consumption of goods and services in society. Although the transformation of economies was a vital component of the Industrial Revolution, societies are composed of other crucial institutions such as the family, religion, and government. A new science that would take into account the interrelation and interdependence of all the institutions in society was required to explain the scope, direction, and duration of these changes. French philosopher Auguste Comte (1798–1857) coined the term *sociology* for the discipline he believed would eventually become the "queen of the sciences."

The question of how and under what conditions societies change has been the most important sociological question since the days of Comte over 150 years ago. In the post–World War II era, more and more sociologists have attempted to understand the process of modernization, or the Second Industrial Revolution, as developing nations attempt to abandon traditional institutions and emulate societies like the United States and Japan. Today, sociologists from many nations study the interrelation of political and economic institutions of societies that make up the so-called global village. They also are taking a closer look at the day-to-day lives of people who live in these nations. The proliferation of social science research in many countries and the amount of this material available in English and other international languages make in-depth, cross-cultural research possible today.

In this book we draw from the rich store of cross-cultural sociological data that have greatly enhanced our discipline's understanding of human social phenomena. Not only does this research strategy enable us to comprehend better the workings of other societies, it gives us a look at ourselves from another vantage point. This view of the United States from the outside looking in could provide us with additional insights as we assess the strengths and weaknesses of this society and attempt to correct the latter.

The Modernization of the World

You don't have to be a seasoned traveler to realize that a country such as the United States is more prosperous than Mexico and thousands of times wealthier than some of the poorest nations in Africa and Asia. Not only is the United States more economically advanced than these nations, the people in this and other rich countries have a different world view or mind-set from that of individuals who struggle to survive on a day-to-day basis. To alleviate the suffering and misery that affect 85 percent of the earth's population, almost every poor nation is attempting to increase its economic productivity, reduce death and disease, and improve the quality of life for its citizens. They are all trying to leave the world of the "have nots" and join the world of the "haves." In short, they desperately want to modernize. Hundreds of millions of people in poor countries realize that they have been left out of the modernization process (see Table 1.1 for terminology used in this section) and want to acquire a share of the planet's wealth before they are left hopelessly behind.

At the risk of an oversimplification, we may think of modernization as occurring in two broad stages.

The first stage began with the Industrial Revolution and resulted in the modernization of numerous European countries, the United States, Canada, Australia, and New Zealand. The second phase started in the aftermath of World War II and continues to unfold at different speeds and under widely different circumstances in the developing world.

Social scientists use classification schemes to categorize nations according to their degree of modernity. Although these systems are quite useful and permit us to speak in general terms of now-rich countries and less developed countries, in reality the approximately 200 independent states of the world cannot be so neatly divided. More accurately, they might be thought of as falling along a lengthy continuum from very poor to very rich, all at various stages or levels of development. It is also somewhat misleading to speak of stages of development, since there is no single path to modernization with a specified number and sequence of stages that all nations

TABLE 1.1
Modernization Terminology

Term	Definition
Modernization	This rather slippery, often vague concept is used by journalists, politicians, and social scientists to describe the transformation from a traditional, usually agrarian, society to a contemporary, industrial state. According to Black (1966), modernization is the general process of change across five major dimensions of society: intellectual, political, economic, social, and psychological. In this text, the terms *modernization* and *development* are used synonymously.
First World	The modern, industrial, capitalist countries of North America and Europe. Japan, Israel, Australia, New Zealand, and South Africa are also in this group. Almost all these nations have democratic political institutions.
Second World	Until events beginning in 1989–1990, this term referred to the totalitarian, industrial countries of eastern Europe and the Soviet Union. Most eastern European nations and the republics that once formed the Soviet Union are in the process of changing to market economies and more democratic political institutions. These countries are moving toward capitalism or possibly a mixed (socialist and capitalist) economic system with more political freedom and less government control over the day-to-day lives of their citizens. It remains to be seen how long this transformation will take and how successful it will be.
Third World	Coined by the French intellectual Alfred Sauvy in 1952, the term *Third World* is a translation of the expression *le tiers monde*. Sauvy made a comparison between the inhabitants of poor, post–World War II nations struggling to rid themselves of colonial rule and the common people in France—the Third Estate—at the time of the French Revolution. The term is widely used to refer to the poor nations of the world collectively. A problem with this characterization is that it includes desperately poor countries like the Sudan and Bangladesh, as well as increasingly prosperous nations like Argentina and South Korea. Another difficulty with this term is that many individuals who reside in these countries consider it condescending, that is, third implies inferiority to whatever is first and second.
Less Developed Countries (LDCs)	This more neutral term refers to the less *economically* developed countries of the world and is often used interchangeably with *Third World* and *traditional societies*. Typically, between 40 and 90 percent of the labor force in LDCs work in agriculture. As Toffler (1990) noted, *less developed* is really an "arrogant misnomer," as many LDCs including Mexico, Peru, India, and China have highly developed cultures dating back hundreds (and in some cases thousands) of years.
Now-Rich Countries (NRCs)	The rich, industrialized countries of the world taken as a whole. This includes societies with capitalist as well as mixed (capitalist and socialist) economies.

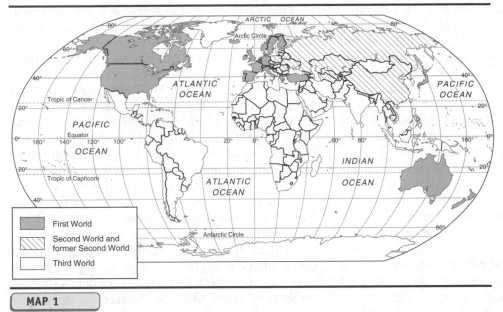

MAP 1

First, Second, and Third World Countries

Legend:
- First World
- Second World and former Second World
- Third World

will inevitably follow. For example, First World countries like the United States and Japan developed with capitalist economic systems, whereas the former Soviet Union (until recently a Second World nation) industrialized under a socialist system. Each country, because of its own history and culture, takes a somewhat different path. However, a set of problems shared by most Third World nations (rapidly increasing populations, food shortages, large foreign debt, etc.) allows us to think of them as a whole to a certain extent. Regardless of which path of development individual nations follow, they will have to solve these problems, and the range of possible solutions may be quite limited.

The study of modernization, according to Paul Harrison (1984, p. 17), is the "central story of our time," a story affecting the lives of more than three-fourths of humanity. Social scientists began studying modernization seriously in the years after World War II, when people in now-rich countries became aware of the enormous discrepancies of wealth between rich nations and poor nations (Larkin and Peters, 1983). This was also a period of revolutionary activity as many colonial Third World nations demanded

Virtually all large societies are a combination of modern and traditional characteristics. The woman talking on the cell phone in a busy Hanoi neighborhood may be working on an international business deal or confirming an appointment. Perhaps no more than an hour's drive from the largest city in northern Vietnam, peasants work the land in much the same manner their ancestors did hundreds of years ago.

and fought for independence. As an increasing number of poor countries were successful in their struggle for freedom, government officials watched and waited to see whether they would align themselves with the communist world or the "free" world and what impact these new countries would have on Cold War politics. In the aftermath of World War II, policy-oriented researchers were primarily interested in how to increase the economic output of poor nations. As a result, they measured modernization almost exclusively in terms of economic indicators such as the gross national product and per capita income.

Today, modernization is a much broader concept that focuses on the positive social changes accompanying industrialization and economic growth. Some researchers assert that, ideally, modernization should include an equitable distribution of the wealth that comes from economic progress. As a result, people in the developing world will share a "higher standard of living in terms of income, food and other forms of consumption, health, housing, education and increased freedom of choice in all aspects of life" (Welsh and Butorin, 1990, p. 310).

Globalization

Upon the chance meeting of a neighborhood acquaintance in a distant country, one is likely to think that it really is a "small world." Although planet Earth is not shrinking in a literal sense, it is getting smaller regarding a number of dimensions of human activity. **Globalization** refers to the migration of jobs, capital, industry, and people as well as the movement of values and other aspects of culture across societies. It also alludes to the growing interrelation and interdependence of human societies.

In business and industry this phenomenon is hardly new as nations have been trading with each other for hundreds of years. However, in the post–World War II era, the volume, scope, and interpenetration of global commerce has increased significantly. For example, Ford and General Motors not only sell their products in Europe, but they also have substantial manufacturing operations on that continent. Likewise the "big three" Japanese automakers (Toyota, Honda, and Nissan) both sell and manufacture cars and trucks in the United States (Graham, 1993). Inasmuch as these vehicles are designed by Japanese engineers, use both American and Japanese components, and are assembled by workers in this country, it is difficult to determine if the cars and trucks that roll off of these assembly lines are American or Japanese. In addition, people from all over the world own stock in these giant auto manufacturing corporations.

When European and Japanese automobiles began appearing en masse in this country in the mid- to late-1950s, it forced domestic car manufacturers to improve their products if they were going to compete successfully with the cheaper and more reliable imports. Edward Graham (1993, p. 9) argues that the "true winner" of this aspect of globalization has been "the buyer of any automobile." Much the same could be said for a variety of other industries and their globalization strategies that have resulted in low-priced products such as computers assembled in Mexico and dress shoes constructed in Brazil.

Globalization has also ushered in an era of increased business mergers and takeovers. In 1998, the German company Daimler-Benz (the maker of Mercedes Benz automobiles) merged with the Chrysler Corporation (Smith, 1998). The new company known as Daimler-Chrysler will ostensibly result in a stronger corporation more likely to succeed in the highly competitive international automobile marketplace. Consumers benefit by having access to high-quality cars that will ultimately force other manufacturers to upgrade the quality of their products.

However, there is a dark side to globalization, especially in the business sector. The slowdown of the Japanese economy in the 1990s coupled with the near collapse of the Indonesian and South Korean economies has affected the financial well-being of countries around the world. Slower growth in the United States because of the Asian situation could significantly undermine Latin America's economic future inasmuch as 75 percent of the money invested in this region comes from the United States (Olms, 1998). We would add that slower or stalled economic growth in Central and South America will have a boomerang effect as people from these countries (now with reduced purchasing power) curtail their spending on goods made in the United States.

Whereas the Daimler-Chrysler merger may be a win/win situation for both companies, globalization, according to its critics, has certainly contributed to the growing number of losers in the world economy. In her book *L'Horreur Economique* (*The Economic Horror*), French novelist and social critic Viviane Forrester argues that we are witnessing "a transformation of society and civilization" ("We Are Witnessing," 1997, p. 47). For Forrester, economic globalization has turned into the "globalization of poverty" as multinational corporations have discovered that it is cheaper to exploit women, children, and prisoners in developing countries rather than automate their production facilities in the rich nations.

As companies seek out the lowest cost of labor in poor nations of the world, we will see the formation of "hyperghettos" as a new class of urban poor emerges—those individuals working for survival wages as well as the "uneeded," superfluous masses who are not even worth exploiting ("We Are Witnessing," 1997; Van Kempen and Marcuse, 1997). Collectively these people will be characterized by intractable poverty, the absence of decent paying jobs, deplorable living conditions, and "no realistic hope of change" (Van Kempen and Marcuse, 1997, p. 294). Simply put, some areas of the world will profit from the economic forces of globalization whereas others will not. While it is evident that this has always been an (undesirable) aspect of international commerce, the economic gap between the very rich and the very poor of the world today is enormous and growing larger. In 1996, 41 of the approximately 200 independent nations were designated "heavily indebted poor nations" by the World Bank; states whose debt is never likely to be repaid in full. An Oxfam report noted that these countries were in a "vicious circle" of social and economic decline (Callaghy, 1997).

Perhaps the biggest losers in the globalization game have been the world's estimated 300 to 600 million indigenous (native) people. In the Ecuadorian Amazon, oil companies have spilled approximately 17 million gallons of crude oil into rivers (one and a half times the amount spilled in the Alaska/Exxon *Valdez* disaster) ravaging the environment and all but destroying the traditional way of life of the local Indians (Watson, 1997). In search of raw material for new medicine and pharmaceutical products, corporate "gene hunters" have combed jungles and mountains in some of the remotest areas of the planet. Utilizing the help and knowledge of native people, these forays have been successful to the amount of $43 *billion* in sales. Ethnobiologist Darrell Posey (in Watson, 1997, p. 390) estimates that as of 1990, a mere .001 percent of the profits from this highly lucrative industry was returned to indigenous tribes.

Advancements in communications and transportation have also made the world a much more interrelated community. Within minutes of the automobile accident that claimed the life of Princess Diana in 1997, individuals all over the world were aware of the tragedy. A few days later, hundreds of millions of people witnessed the royal funeral via television in perhaps the single most watched event in history. No doubt some of these viewers resided in the Andes mountains of South America where homes equipped with satellites dishes have access to 40 or more television stations. Owners of these dishes (and their poorer neighbors) can watch local programming as well as news, sports events, and a variety of shows from numerous countries in Spanish, English, French, and German. While global information heightens peoples' awareness, it can also make them dissatisfied with the status quo. Their "reference groups" can change from other villagers to more affluent urban residents, or even people in distant countries (the United States, for example). For better or worse, this rejection of existing conditions can lead to social and political instability as people move to already overcrowded cities (and illegally to the United States) in search of increased economic opportunities (see Chapter 12), and/or become involved in radical political movements.

While modern transportation makes for the rapid movement of people and goods, it also substantially increases the chances that individuals infected with contagious diseases can spread their maladies to people across the planet in a matter of hours. Assuming that almost every urban center with 500,000 people or more has an airport, a resident of any one of these locations is no more than 20 to 24 hours away from any other city in the world. In a time of "emerging diseases" (see Chapter 12) such as AIDS and the Ebola Virus, the health and health risks of all six billion inhabitants of planet Earth are much more tightly intertwined. No longer is the outbreak of a communicable disease in Asia, Africa, or the United States simply a local problem.

As rapid as the pace of globalization has been in the second half of the twentieth century, it will undoubtedly accelerate in the first 50 years of the new millennium. In this text we will comment on the impact (and likely impact) of globalization wherever applicable, especially in the chapters dealing with the economy, crime, population, urbanization, and modernization.

The Debunking Science

Before proceeding with our introduction to the science of sociology and subsequent examination of the United States and other societies, a few words about the sociological perspective are in order. It is the nature of sociology to look at the various structures and patterns of behavior with a critical eye. One aspect of this critical examination is what sociologist Peter Berger (1963) referred to as **debunking**—looking for levels of reality other than those given in the official interpretations. However, this unmasking of the hidden but very real facets of societal life is in no way meant to denigrate or belittle those people and institutions that are the subjects of inquiry. As Danish criminologist Karl Otto Christiansen (1977) stated, "It is the object of criminology to describe and explain criminality, not to condemn it or defend it." We take the same position in this book. Like most sociologists, we are attempting to explain what is and not what should or ought to be, and we are not passing judgment on the values and behavior of others.

It is imperative that students keep this perspective in mind, especially when reading the *Focus On* sections devoted to other countries as well as the numerous cross-cultural examples used throughout the book. For example, like other modernizing nations, Mexico is faced with a host of social, political, and economic problems. However, our critical analysis of these difficulties should not be construed as an indictment of the Mexican people. On the contrary, during the course of our research (as well as residing in San Diego only minutes from the Mexican border) it soon became apparent that they are an extremely proud, hard-working people who will do just about anything for the well-being of their families. In a typical year, over one and a half million Mexicans seeking employment in the United States will be caught illegally crossing the border. Many of them will try again and again (often risking their lives) until they are successful. The mostly young males who make up this growing "army of the poor" are not headed for high-paying jobs. Usually, and for very low wages, they do the dirty, boring, backbreaking, and sometimes dangerous work that other people will not even consider. So much for the stereotypical lazy Mexican. Millions of poor people in Mexico and hundreds of millions of impoverished individuals throughout the developing world live with the physical hardships and psychological pain of poverty each and every day of their existence. The overwhelming majority do so with courage and dignity, and as such they are worthy of our understanding and compassion. Most of all, they deserve our respect. We hope our presentation of countries in the *Focus On* sections gives students an accurate, although limited, view of these societies.

THE SOCIOLOGICAL STYLE: UNRAVELING HUMAN SOCIAL PATTERNS

Prescientific and Nonscientific Interpretations of Social Reality

The development of the scientific perspective has given humans the tools to analyze their world in a comprehensive way. Long before there were sciences and scientists, however, large numbers of thoughtful people had tried to make sense out of the natural and social realities that surrounded them. Some, such as political rulers, did so for practical reasons. The physical survival of the people under their leadership depended on their ability to read the world correctly and adjust to it accordingly. Others, such as

theologians and philosophers, perhaps did so for less tangible reasons. Their attempts to explain the world were reflections of the same intellectual curiosity that had led them into their respective fields in the first place. In any event, a variety of world interpretations predated scientific models by thousands of years and guided the social behaviors of the millions of humans who lived during those times.

Auguste Comte, the founder of sociology, claimed that the method employed by people to understand their world was perhaps the single most significant factor shaping the course of societal development. Different kinds of knowledge systems, he argued, did a better or worse job of providing an accurate picture of how the world worked. In turn, people's ability to know the true nature of reality was crucial to their collective well-being. It determined whether or not they could organize social and cultural patterns that would promote their survival and comfort. The better the understanding of the world provided by the available knowledge base, the more elaborate and successful the social structure that was possible.

According to Comte (1877), societies evolved through three historical stages or epochs, each of which was characterized by a distinctive way of explaining the world. In the **theological stage,** *imagination* dominated as the principle of understanding. People interpreted events in terms of supernatural beings (spirits of good and evil) and their activities. Social patterns consequently were structured to reflect these relations and obligations to the supernatural world, and the patterns remained very simple. For example, in a traditional farming society, crop failure might be interpreted as a sign of the gods' displeasure with the people. The required response would be an appropriate sacrificial offering to atone for the offense and restore the gods' goodwill.

As time passed and humans began to exercise their capacity for abstract thought, societies advanced into what Comte called the **metaphysical stage** of development. *Observation* of specific events led to rational *speculation* as to the nature of general events. Through the power of the mind and the application of accepted principles of logic, people could derive sophisticated theoretical explanations of real-world phenomena. They no longer had to rely on imagined supernatural forces to interpret what was happening around them. The enhanced grasp of reality that was made possible by this change in their way of knowing allowed for the development of larger and more sophisticated social arrangements.

One example of this type of prescientific knowledge comes from historical attempts to explain social deviance. During the Middle Ages, Europeans believed that people who engaged in behaviors that violated established moral or legal rules were possessed by evil spirits (a theological explanation). However, with the age of enlightenment that swept through European societies during the eighteenth century, philosophers and other intellectuals began to reject this doctrine. Instead, they developed what has since become known as the classical perspective or model of crime and deviancy (Pfohl, 1994).

According to this interpretation, criminal and deviant behaviors, like other kinds of human behaviors, represented the outcome of rational calculation and free decision. People chose to break the law and violate social rules when they believed it was in their best interest to do so. For example, a student confronted by a surprise sociology exam and the likelihood of a failing grade might decide to copy answers from a classmate who seemed to be prepared, even though such cheating was a violation of university policy. In this case (at least from the cheating student's standpoint), the cost of failing the examination would be greater than any benefit to be derived from taking the test honestly.

The only way in which people like the student might be deterred from rule-breaking behaviors was to make the costs of those actions so high that they would outweigh any potential benefits. The penalty for cheating on college examinations is almost always a failing grade in the course and often expulsion as well. In modified form, this principle still underpins the criminal justice system in this society. (Crime and deviance are examined in Chapter 8.)

Despite the ability of rational, calculated thought to provide people a more successful interpretation of the world, Comte believed that metaphysical knowledge still was not a satisfactory basis for societal development. Complex social and cultural arrangements, he theorized, could be created and sustained only by the kind of understanding generated through the adoption of the scientific method of analysis and the movement of society into the final, **positivistic stage** of development. To this end, he sought to create a new field of inquiry that would be devoted specifically to the *scientific analysis* of the human social world.

The Sociological View of the World: Comte and Durkheim and the Development of Scientific Sociology

Auguste Comte Auguste Comte believed that the task of his new discipline was to discover the underlying forces in society responsible for *social statics* (stability) and *social dynamics* (change and progress). He argued that just as natural laws governed the biological and physical world, social laws were responsible for the patterns of social integration and change present in all human societies. The philosophical foundation of sociology is based on a way of understanding the social and physical environment called positivism—the belief that knowledge can be derived only from people's sensory experience. In other words, human beings can know something of the world only to the extent that they can see, hear, feel, touch, and taste it. Positivism is a rejection of intuition, speculation, or any purely logical analysis for attaining knowledge (Theodorson and Theodorson, 1969).

Influenced by the success of the natural sciences (biology, chemistry, etc.), Comte introduced the methodology of these disciplines to his scientific analysis of society (Coser, 1971). Guided by theory, sociologists would observe social facts in the environment, determine how these facts are related to one another, and explain their meaning. Whenever possible, some form of experimentation would be used to test these explanations. Next, sociologists would engage in cross-cultural research and compare societies at different stages of their evolutionary development. Finally, Comte called for an overarching historical analysis that would put the evolution of societies in their proper chronological context. The father of sociology believed that historical comparison was at "the very core of sociological inquiry" (Coser, 1971, p. 6).

This emphasis on observation and experimentation was an important step in establishing sociology as the scientific study of society. As such, it was distinct from the writings of social philosophers who speculated on the nature of society and the causes of human behavior without conducting any firsthand, systematic research in the social world. However, Comte's belief that social laws determined the inevitable progression of human societies through a number of stages was erroneous and unwarranted. This evolutionary theory contributed to sociology's misunderstanding of societal change and modernization for over a hundred years. Collins and Makowsky (1984) noted that sociologists are finally beginning to realize "the so-called developing nations show few signs of creating our kind of politics, stratification, or even economy in the foreseeable future . . . " (p. 29). Ironically, the man who emphasized the collection, organization, and comparison of facts in his new science of society could not himself overcome speculation and conjecture in his theories of social change.

Emile Durkheim For most of his career, the great French sociologist Emile Durkheim (1858–1919) defended sociology against the reductionism of psychologists (especially) and biologists who claimed that any social phenomena could ultimately be reduced to, and explained in, psychological and biological terms. Reductionists stated that although society is a collection of interacting individuals, in the final analysis any form of social behavior is individual behavior and can be explained only in terms of each person's personality, motivation, and overall state of consciousness. Therefore the emerging science of sociology is basically irrelevant.

Durkheim countered by persuasively arguing that social phenomena exist *sui generis* (in and of themselves) and cannot be reduced, effectively studied, or interpreted at the individual level of analysis. He presented a "definitive critique of reductionist explanations of social behavior" by demonstrating that social facts were the primary subject matter of sociology (Coser, 1971). According to Durkheim (in Johnson, 1981, pp. 172–173), social facts have three characteristics that distinguish them from individual and psychological phenomena: (1) they exist *external* to individuals (e.g., language, laws, and institutions such as the family); (2) they *constrain* or influence a person independent of his or her will; and (3) they are *shared* by a significant number of people.

Let's examine a social fact that Durkheim considered to be of utmost importance, the collective conscience—those beliefs and sentiments common to the average member of a group or society. The collective conscience is easily recognized and experienced by members of emotionally charged groups. As Collins and Makowsky (1984) stated, "It is a feeling of contact with something outside yourself that does not depend precisely on any one person there, but which everyone participates in together" (p. 108). For example, consider the sentiments and excitement at a big football game just before kickoff as the crowd anticipates a close, competitive match—and a home-team victory. The excitement in the air is external to individuals and independent of any individual who moves in or out of the stadium. The sentiment of the crowd would no doubt change dramatically if the home team were losing by forty-two points at halftime. Some disgruntled fans could become rowdy and start picking fights. The majority, however, would resist any temptation to engage in violence, being *constrained* by *shared* rules of civility, as well as by the sight of security personnel with nightsticks. (Social facts can have physical consequences.)

Durkheim argued that social facts could be explained only in terms of other social facts. To do otherwise was to slide back into reductionism. He used a basic research strategy that is still widely practiced in sociology—*controlled comparison.* To determine the cause of something, "look for *the conditions under which it occurs* and compare them with *the conditions*

under which it does not occur" (Collins and Makowsky, 1984, p. 110). Durkheim used this method effectively in his landmark study of suicide, as described later.

Emile Durkheim almost single-handedly made Comte's dream of a legitimate science of society a reality. Whereas Comte struggled for recognition most of his life, Durkheim had a long and fruitful career in the French university system. In 1913, sociology was formally recognized at the Sorbonne (University of Paris), the most prestigious university in France. The title of Durkheim's academic chair was changed to Science of Education and Sociology.

THINKING SOCIOLOGICALLY: THEORETICAL PARADIGMS

Theories and Science

In everyday conversation, *theory* is used synonymously with the words *guess* or *hunch.* For example, when someone says, "My theory is that John just doesn't like Marsha," he or she usually means "My guess is that . . . " Theory also is thought of as something at a high level of abstraction not grounded in observation and factual experience. Typical reactions are "Don't give me your theories, I just want the facts," and "Theories are one thing, the real world is something else."

For a scientist, a **theory** is a set of logically coherent, interrelated concepts that attempts to explain some observable phenomena or group of facts. As such, it is not a wild, off-the-cuff guess, but rather a carefully thought-out explanation grounded in observable (and usually repeatable) phenomena. In sociology, there are two types of theories. A **grand theory** deals with universal aspects of social life and is usually grounded in basic assumptions (as opposed to data) concerning the nature of humans and society. The grand theories of Comte and Karl Marx explained the workings of all types of societies as they progressed through evolutionary stages. These theories tend to be at a rather high level of abstraction and are difficult, if not impossible, to test. They could be considered world views from a sociological perspective.

Middle-range theories focus on relatively specific problems in the social world. For example, in the United States, the rate of divorce tends to be higher in the lower classes than in the upper classes. Also, people who marry at an early age have higher divorce rates than those who marry when they are older. A theory of the middle range would explain these specific, observable facts of one component of social life—marriage and divorce. Ultimately, a number of middle-range theories could be incorporated into some larger theoretical framework (Johnson, 1981), perhaps a grand theory.

Theories are necessary because facts do not speak for themselves. Knowing that as social class goes up divorce goes down is very different from knowing why this relationship exists. In a sense, a theory is like a story, weaving together all the available data about a particular phenomenon, forming a coherent, integrated explanation. Without theory, science would be nothing more than an ever-increasing mass of facts completely devoid of any understanding of how and why those facts are related. Theory is the life blood of science. In the case of sociology, it organizes and explains observable facts and relationships, as well as guides the course of research.

The Organic Analogy: Classic and Contemporary Functionalist Theory

Pioneer sociologists such as Comte and Herbert Spencer (1820–1903) constructed theories on a grand scale. They wanted to explain the structure, internal dynamics, and historical development of societies. As was previously noted, Comte was heavily influenced by the success of the natural sciences, especially biology. He believed that biology and sociology were similar in that both had living beings as their focus of study. Just as a human organism was made up of a number of systems, organs, and tissues, the social organism was made up of various parts. Societies had institutions (e.g., the family), classes, and cities that were interrelated and interdependent. Turner and Maryanski (1979) noted that

this vision of society as a complex social body with numerous parts contributing to the well-being and survival of the whole was an important moment in sociological theorizing: "When society is seen as an organism, it is a short analytical step to asking: What does this or that structure 'do for' or 'contribute to' the society" (p. 7)? In other words, what is the function of each of the constituent parts for the whole? This is the beginning of functional analysis and *functionalist* theories of society.

Early functionalist sociologists were concerned with the problem of order. Recall that sociology was born in the midst of major social, economic, and political transformations sweeping across Europe as a result of the Industrial Revolution. The question of how societies endure and maintain order even though they were changing rapidly was uppermost in the minds of these theorists. For that matter, what keeps societies from breaking up into thousands of groups or hundreds of thousands of families with everyone behaving in their own self-interest even during periods of tranquility? For both Comte and Durkheim, the answer was the same—the foundation of society and social stability is moral order (Collins and Makowsky, 1984). People reach a consensus on laws, religious beliefs, and the basic rules that govern everyday life. This consensus makes for a shared world view that binds people to their families and various communal organizations, as well as to larger economic and political institutions. Governments exist because individuals agree to the principles they are founded on; people even agree to the manner in which those governments resort to force when necessary. Social solidarity and stability are impossible without this shared moral order.

In 1978, over 900 dedicated followers of the Reverend Jim Jones committed mass suicide in the South American country of Guyana. Primarily from the San Francisco area, the mostly poor, Black residents of Jonestown were physically and psychologically isolated in a remote jungle area. Believing that the United States government was about to destroy his organization, Jones ordered his followers to drink Kool Aid laced with cyanide. Intensely involved in one group to the exclusion of the others, the people who took their lives in Jonestown committed what Durkheim called obligatory altruistic suicide.

Suicide: The Sociology of Self-Destruction

Suicide is the final act of people who have decided they must end their lives. Since self-destructive behavior is committed by individuals, suicide is typically analyzed from a psychological or psychiatric perspective. Its causes are thought to be lodged in the depths of the individual's personality. However, nineteenth-century statisticians discovered that these were not purely individual events, randomly distributed in the population. On the contrary, suicides followed predictable patterns. For example, Durkheim found the following in his examination of suicide rates in France and some central European countries in the 1800s:

1. Soldiers have a higher suicide rate than civilians.
2. Protestants have higher rates than Catholics.
3. The rate is higher among single, widowed, and divorced people than among the married.
4. Older people have a higher rate than younger people.
5. Rates rise in times of economic crisis and fall during times of political crisis.

In *Suicide* (1951/1897), Durkheim argued that these patterns of behavior clearly indicate that the root causes of the "intensely individual" act of suicide must be external to the individual (Douglas, 1967). For each group in society, a "collective force of a definite amount of energy" (Durkheim, 1951/1897, p. 299) impels people to self-destruction. In other words, although the individual pulls the trigger of the gun that ends his life, a number of social factors determine the likelihood of his putting the gun to his head.

Durkheim theorized that there were four types of suicide in society. *Altruistic* and *egoistic suicides* are one related pair, and *anomic* and *fatalistic suicides* form another. **Altruistic suicide** is committed by individuals who are overinvolved in and therefore overcommitted to a particular group or society as a whole. Durkheim subdivided this category into two types, *obligatory altruistic* and *optional altruistic.* In obligatory altruistic suicide, the self-destructive act is viewed as an obligation or duty. Failure to perform it results in dishonor or punishment. This form of suicide can be institutionalized, as it was in Japan during World War II when *kamikaze* pilots and *raiden* (suicide submarine pilots) crashed their vessels into American ships. These acts were redefined so that individuals who committed them considered their behavior "other-destructive" and not "self-destructive" (Lebra, 1976).

The death of 39 Heaven's Gate members in 1997 was a collective form of obligatory altruistic suicide by people whose lives only had meaning within the parameters of that organization. Although not physically isolated or constrained, members interacted almost exclusively within the confines of a closed community where they reinforced each other's world (and extraterrestrial) view. When Heaven's Gate leader Marshall Applewhite decided it was time to move to the "next level" via collective suicide, they felt obliged to follow his directive (Bryjak, 1997).

In optional altruistic suicide, society does not demand that the individual take his or her life, although social prestige is often attached to doing so. For example, in feudal Japan the *samurai* (warrior class) code of honor stated that it was honorable for an individual to kill himself rather than run the risk of being captured and disgraced by the enemy. Durkheim concluded that, as a whole, soldiers are taught to devalue their sense of self and think in terms of the group. Life itself becomes less important to them, and suicide no longer has the same meaning that it does to civilians. Consequently, it becomes easier for military personnel to take their own lives.

In modern Japan, there is social pressure on company presidents disgraced by a major financial setback—especially bankruptcy—to avoid additional humiliation by way of self-destruction. The first major indignity one must endure is the *dogeza,* a meeting with creditors wherein the now destitute company owner "sits on the floor, bows deeply and begs forgiveness while his creditors scream abuses" (Desmond, 1998, p. 28). In addition, there is a financial incentive/obligation to take one's life. Japanese life insurance companies pay full benefits to the beneficiaries of suicide victims as long as the policy is at least one year old. These suicides can be interpreted as optional altruistic in that individuals were overly involved with work and family and felt they had to kill themselves for not living up to the expectations of others, or for subjecting them (the family) to public humiliation. As a Japanese attorney stated, "The way people here see it, going bankrupt is like committing a crime" (Desmond, 1998 p. 28).

Whereas altruistic suicide is a function of overinvolvement with and commitment to the group, **egoistic suicide** is caused by lack of involvement with and commitment to others. If individuals do not share beliefs common to a social group, they will not be integrated into that body or be involved regularly with people who share a common world view. Durkheim (1951/1897) argued that a strongly integrated group or society "holds individuals under its control" (p. 209) and forbids them from taking their own lives. Conversely, when people are not well integrated into groups, they cannot help but realize that all their efforts in life will finally end in nothingness, since they will die and disappear—alone.

Durkheim reasoned that Protestants have a higher suicide rate (egoistic) than Catholics because they are less integrated and involved in group activity. For Catholics, salvation comes *through* the church, which serves as an intermediary between the individual and God. In Protestant sects, individuals have a more direct relationship with God, and the church is a less necessary link between the two.

Married individuals are less likely to take their own lives than nonmarried individuals because they become involved in a family network. This network gives additional meaning to their lives and binds them to spouses and children both emotionally and by way of mutual obligations. Elderly people have higher suicide rates than younger individuals because they are not as involved in groups as a result of retirement, death of a spouse, and physical impairments that prevent them from fully participating in group activities.

Group involvement (but not overinvolvement) binds people together, provides a system of shared beliefs, and, as such, tends to protect them from suicide. Conversely, lack of shared beliefs and social attachments increases the likelihood of suicide. For Durkheim, the level of association or involvement people have with groups such as the church and family are social facts available for positivistic, sociological analysis.

Anomic and fatalistic suicides are polar opposites on a continuum of social regulation. Durkheim observed that people cannot be happy unless their desires and the means for achieving these desires are in harmony. Since human beings have no natural "psychological constitution," these desires are held in check by society. For example, during periods of economic stability, means and ends (desires) are in balance as people

keep their wants in line with existing mechanisms for satisfying them. In times of economic prosperity, however, desires increase to the point that they are unlimited and, by definition, cannot be satisfied. During periods of rapid economic growth, people often move from one economic class to another in a short period of time, but even this newfound wealth fails to satisfy them. "Inextinguishable thirst is constantly renewed torture" (Durkheim, 1951/1897, p. 247) and leads to **anomic suicide.**

The "torture" of never having one's escalating desires satisfied is complicated by the fact that people are now in social positions that are unfamiliar to them. Norms and rules that formerly regulated their behavior have been replaced by rules they do not understand or accept. These individuals are free-floating in society, devoid of regulations that might anchor them in a familiar social reality. This lack of stability also contributes to anomic suicide.

Durkheim found that people in less developed countries tend to have lower suicide rates than those in developed nations. He observed that poverty protects against suicide because it is a restraint in and of itself. Prolonged poverty keeps people's longing for wealth, status, and power in check. Individuals do not passionately desire things that they have virtually no chance of acquiring.

Whereas economic upheavals increase the rate of suicide, political crises such as wars tend to reduce the number of self-destructive acts. During periods of external conflict, society is more integrated as the population stands behind an effort to survive and defeat a common enemy. People may also experience a shift away from personal troubles as they increasingly focus on the nation's war effort. One's individual problems may appear rather insignificant in comparison to the

fighting and dying taking place on the battlefield.

At the other end of the social regulation continuum, people's desires can be choked off by excessive control. Their lives are so closely regulated that they have little if any freedom to do even the most basic things in life. Durkheim suggested that excessive restraint results in **fatalistic suicide** such as that committed by slaves. Farberow (1989) noted that thousands of Indians in Mexico and Central America who were enslaved by Spanish Conquistadors took their own lives. More recently, an Indian rights group in Brazil reported 74 suicides over a two-year period on the Guarani-Kaiowa reservation. Anthropologists said the victims—all between 14 and 21 years of age—took their lives as a result of the loss of tribal identity and land to white cattle ranchers. Depressed by the destruction of their culture, these young suicide victims get drunk on sugar cane rum before hanging themselves (Kepp, 1991).

In northeast Colombia, the Occidental Petroleum Company along with Royal/Dutch Shell were preparing to undertake full-scale oil production in that region. Fearing that their centuries-old way of life and "sacred" lands will be destroyed once the drilling begins, the roughly 5,000 members of the U'wa tribe have threatened to commit mass suicide if the project is not halted (Chelala, 1998). According to Durkheim (1951/1897), victims of moral and physical despotism often choose to die rather than lead lives over which they have no control. As of mid-1998 Royal/Dutch Shell was considering abandoning drilling in this region of Colombia.

Fatalistic suicide may also explain a significant number of the approximately 350,000 self-destructive acts that occur in China each year. Comprising 21 percent of planet Earth's female population, Chinese women and girls account for 56 percent of all female suicides worldwide (Macleod, 1998). With the rate of suicide in rural areas three times that of the cities, many of the already poor women who reside here have seen their lives take a turn for the worse. One observer noted (in Macleod, 1998, p. 63), "It's these women who do over 70 percent of the work in the fields nowadays, while their men go off to earn money in the cities. Many simply find it hard to cope with lives that are overburdened, poor and lonely with little support. Worse still, they are not treated with any respect." While poverty protects against suicide because it serves as a built-in restraint, the relatively sudden loss of significant others (husbands), status, and respect, may well have plunged many of these women into the depths of despair and hopelessness from which they could see no way out; no improvement whatsoever in their lives in the foreseeable future.

In Durkheim's fourfold typology, each of the forms of self-destructive behavior is associated with a different state of mind (Madge, 1962). The altruistic suicide has strong inner convictions, and death by one's own hand is in line with them. The egoistic suicide is in a state of resignation, having made the choice to opt out of society. The anomic suicide is a person whose desire for pleasure is out of control. Finally, the fatalistic suicide's passion for life has been crushed by overregulation.

While Durkheim's *Suicide* is a complex and valuable piece of research, it does not fully explain self-destructive behavior. As Collins and Makowsky (1984) pointed out, not everyone who is elderly, unmarried, and Protestant commits suicide. To determine why many people who fit into Durkheim's classification do not kill themselves, psychological factors would have to be taken

into consideration. However, Durkheim was not particularly interested in psychology; rather, he wanted to account for varying rates of suicide in different groups over time, and toward this end he was quite successful. Although the official statistics he used were not completely reliable, as ours are not completely reliable today (Douglas, 1967), and he made analytical mistakes, his theory is still a powerful tool for understanding different rates of suicide both within and among countries.

Suicide in the United States

In the United States, the suicide rate is at the low end of the continuum of now-rich countries, although it is much higher than the rates of poorer nations like Guatemala and Azerbaijan. The national rate in 1996 was 10.8 (per 100,000), a figure that included data for African Americans whose suicide rate was in line with rates in some developing nations. Kastenbaum and Kastenbaum (1989) believe that the rate for black Americans is low because historically this group has been the target of systematic discrimination in the marketplace. As a result, their desire for economic success has been held in check. Hence they have a low rate of anomic suicide. Strong support from the family, church, and black community means that egoistic suicide would be low. Similar arguments could be made for the low rate of Hispanic suicide in the United States. We would predict that economic and social equality for these groups will be accompanied by higher rates.

The suicide rate for teenagers between 15 and 19 years of age increased dramatically from 3.3 per 100,000 in 1959, to 10.9 in 1993 (Freeman, 1998). Suicide is now the third leading cause of death in this age group, behind accidents and homicides. The actual rate in undoubtedly higher

TABLE 1.2	
Suicide Rates (per 100,000) for Selected Countries, 1984–1995	
Country	**Rate**
Russia	41.8
Hungary	32.9
Finland	27.3
France	20.8
China	17.6
Japan	16.7
Norway	13.7
Canada	12.8
U.S.A.	12.0
Ireland	10.0
South Korea	9.5
Zimbabwe	8.2
Israel	7.7
Costa Rica	4.5
Ecuador	4.4
Colombia	3.1
Mexico	2.6
Dominican Republic	2.1
Azerbaijan	0.6
Guatemala	0.5

Source: 1995 Demographic Yearbook (New York: United Nations, 1997).

inasmuch as an unknown number of teen suicides are recorded as accidental deaths (Douglas, 1991). Psychiatrist Keith Hawton (1986) associated the loss of family support systems resulting from a high rate of divorce with the trend for young people to face the pressures involved with assuming adult roles earlier in life. "Evidence is accumulating concerning the importance of supportive relationships at such times, and how, if they are lacking, depression is a likely consequence" (p. 44). This may be a major cause of teenage suicide, in view of the "well-established linkage between depression and suicide" (p. 44). The loss of religious faith that leads to the abandonment of church-affiliated groups may be another contributing factor. These phenomena would promote egoistic suicide. According to at least one observer, suicide rates among the 15-to-19-year-old age group will continue to increase (Freeman, 1998).

In the United States, as in other countries, suicide rates are highest among the elderly, especially among males over 70 years of age. Although suicide occurs in other age groups, three types of self-destructive behavior appear to be especially prevalent among the aged (Sorenson, 1991): (1) suicide associated with depression, (2) suicide associated with extreme stress, and (3) suicide as a deliberate act. Whereas most suicide attempts among teenagers and young adults appear to be impulsive acts following a significant "external stressor," elderly people are prone to carefully plan their own deaths.

Durkheim's contribution to our understanding of suicide is that he focused on the individual's decision to forfeit life (arguably the most agonizing decision anyone ever makes) and demonstrated that it was in some way the result of social factors (Douglas, 1967). His book also helped to put sociology on the academic and intellectual map in Europe. If something as seemingly personal and individual as suicide could be explained in part by sociology, then virtually any aspect of human behavior could be analyzed from a sociological perspective.

Twentieth-century functionalist theorists have been interested in more than the problem of order and social solidarity. Talcott Parsons (1902–1979) outlined four basic functional requirements that all social systems (from small groups to societies) must meet if they are to survive.

Adaptation Social systems must adapt to their social and physical environment. For example, modern societies are choking (figuratively and literally) as a result of the wholesale pollution of their air and water. If significant changes are not made, failure to adapt to the natural environment could result in the deaths of millions of people worldwide, as well as the production of a greenhouse effect threatening the entire planet.

Goal Attainment All social systems must provide their members with goals (or ends) and the means necessary to achieve them. If instructors were not motivated to teach and pursue knowledge and the public did not see fit to fund schools, the entire system of education would collapse.

Integration Like their nineteenth-century predecessors, modern functionalists realize that all of the components of society must be coordinated into a cohesive whole if the social system is to function effectively.

Pattern Maintenance Members of a social system must be provided with occasional periods of rest. This is especially true in fast-paced, modern societies in which people are subject to considerable pressure and tension. However, rest periods cannot result in reduced commitment to one's duties. The current emphasis on engaging in regular exercise and sports provides people with a psychological break from work, helps keep them in physical shape, yet reinforces basic values such as working hard, getting ahead, and continually striving to better oneself.

Sociologist Robert Merton (1968) refined the tools of functional analysis by introducing concepts that permitted investigators to examine the *multiple consequences* of patterns of behavior and institutions. **Manifest functions** are consequences that contribute to the system and are intended and/or recognized by participants in the system. **Latent functions** are consequences that are neither intended nor recognized. For example, let's look at the manifest and latent functions of professional basketball in the United States. Owners of teams in the National Basketball Association (NBA) became involved in this enterprise to make money by way of providing entertainment to the American public. Because of the popularity of the sport, the average NBA player earns almost $2 million a year, with superstars like Shaquille O'Neal and Glenn Robinson making much more between their salaries and lucrative commercial endorsements. The *intent* of the owners was to make money (for themselves) and the *consequence* of their efforts is a financially successful business for all concerned.

However, the latent function or unintended consequence of their action was to provide unrealistic career goals in the form of rich role models for tens of thousands of adolescent males. Whereas the NBA employs about 375 players (collectively the four major team sports in the United States, baseball, basketball, football, and hockey have no more than 3,750 athletes on their payrolls), over 525,000 boys played high school basketball in 1998–1999. To the extent that many high school athletes devote most of their time and effort to sport at the expense of being successful academically, they are severely limiting their chances for earning more than the minimum wage when they fail to make it to college, much less the professional ranks. This is especially problematic for African-American inner-city youths who already have a more limited opportunity structure. A nationwide poll (*Los Angeles Times,* 1990) found that 43 percent of black high school athletes surveyed said they could make it in professional sports. The corresponding number for white high school athletes was 16 percent. Realistically, the odds of a black male between the ages of 20 and 39 years of age becoming a professional basketball player are 1 in 153,800. Sport sociologist Jay J. Coakley (1998, p. 313) noted that "if some other business organization tried to encourage all young blacks, especially black males, in the United States and Canada to dedicate their childhood and adolescence to developing highly specialized skills useful in only 3,500 jobs, it would be accused of fraud."

The latent (unintended) function of a successful sports league is a decline in academic motivation and in eventual economic success for a significant number of young men. Whereas the existence of the NBA is beneficial (functional) for owners, players, and most fans, it is dysfunctional for thousands of high school student athletes. A dysfunctional phenomenon is one that undermines the stability or survival of the system.

Contemporary functionalism has been criticized for being ahistorical, concentrating on how present-day events are functional in helping to maintain the social system. As we will see in the next section, conflict theorists (especially Marxists) argue that any form of social theorizing and analysis that ignores the social, political, and economic forces instrumental in creating any society is all but useless. Critics also contend that inasmuch as functionalism focuses on integration, stability, and consensus, it is inherently conservative and supportive of the status quo. They contend that competition, conflict, and social change are almost totally ignored by functionalist theory and analysis. According to Turner and Maryanski (1979), although much functional analysis has been ahistorical, conservative, and tending to ignore conflict and change, it is inherently none of

these. There is a difference between what a theory is capable of and how it is used.

Conflict Sociology: The Zero-Sum Game

Whereas functionalist sociologists view society as a rather harmonious, well-integrated social system held together by shared values and common goals, conflict theorists look at the social world and see strife at virtually every level of group existence. For them, society is not held together by value consensus but by the exercise of power. Institutions, organizations, and individuals simply force people with less power than themselves to conform to their values and standards of conduct.

For conflict theorists, dissension (and sometimes open combat) is everywhere. Examples in the United States include blacks versus whites, labor versus management, students versus faculty and administrators, prochoice versus prolife groups, and gangs versus the community, the police, and other gangs. Even the sacred institution of the family is not immune from strife. The United States has one of the highest rates of divorce in the world and each year records hundreds of thousands of cases of spousal and child abuse. For some sociologists, conflict is as much a part of social life as breathing is a part of our physical existence. To be alive is to struggle and fight. Although the roots of conflict sociology can be traced back to many theorists, the most influential writer in this tradition was Karl Marx (1818–1883). Keep in mind that although all Marxists are conflict theorists, not all conflict theorists are Marxists. As we will see, the world of conflict sociology is quite diverse.

Like other evolutionary thinkers, Marx believed that societies progress through various stages. The driving force in history (the force responsible for movement from one stage to another) is the way people relate to one another in the workplace. Some individuals own and control the means of production—those things used to create material objects and wealth—and others have only their labor to trade for wages. In an industrial society, the means of production include land, machines, buildings, and technological know-how. Under capitalism, these resources are used to further the private fortunes of their owners.

The owners of the means of production in a capitalist society are the **bourgeoisie,** and those who exist by selling their labor power in the market Marx called the **proletariat.** The bourgeoisie systematically exploit the proletariat and, in doing so, become increasingly wealthier and more politically powerful. Meanwhile, the lives of the working class become more and more wretched. However, in time, the significantly more numerous proletariat realize that liberty, justice, and equality are nothing more than empty words and stage a successful revolution against their bourgeois masters. With class conflict between the haves and have nots at an end, capitalism gives way to socialism, an economic system in which the means of production are owned by all the people and the wealth is distributed equitably. For Marx, the end of capitalism was also the end of centuries of class conflict in the historical stages preceding and including capitalism. Socialism signaled the final stage of our economic evolution, at which class conflict ceased and humans could realize their maximum potential.

Ralf Dahrendorf German sociologist Ralf Dahrendorf constructed a theory of conflict that is more general than the Marxist perspective. According to Dahrendorf, conflict is not limited to the dispute between the bourgeoisie and the proletariat regarding ownership of the means of production. In more advanced capitalist states, ownership is no longer a crucial factor in disputes between the haves and the have nots, which center on who should *control* the means of production. The conflict is now between managers and executives (who are not owners) and workers. As such, this is not a struggle over possession but over authority—who will make and implement policy. Dahrendorf posited that virtually all social conflict is a struggle between those who exercise authority and those who are subject to that authority.

These struggles can be intense and are often violent because authority (and power) relationships are examples of a zero-sum game. This means that in any relationship there is a fixed amount of power (100 percent) and that any increase in power made by some individuals comes at the expense or loss of this commodity on the part of others. For example, four production managers in an aircraft company supervise 250 employees and have total power regarding the day-to-day operation of their department. In other words, they have 100 percent of the authority and power. If the employees go on strike and eventually win the right to participate in decision making, the managers will no longer have total control. A gain of power of 25 percent by the employees would translate to a loss of 25 percent on the part of the managers, who would now have 75 percent of the decision-making power.

For Dahrendorf (1959), authority relations exist wherever people are subject to legitimate sanctions that originate *outside* of themselves but *inside* a social structure. For example, on entering college, you became subject to the rules of that institution, rules over which you had absolutely no input. A moment's reflection will reveal that most people are in a number of such authority relations at school, at work, and in voluntary organizations such as clubs. It is important to note that the conflict between those with and those without authority is rooted in the "very nature of the authority structure" (Johnson, 1981, p. 472) and is not a consequence of individual personalities. Working in the Durkheimian tradition, Dahrendorf argued that the ubiquitous conflict over authority is a social fact and, as such, cannot be explained by psychological variables like anger or aggression.

Lewis Coser The word *conflict* typically brings to mind thoughts of a struggle or battle, perhaps a violent confrontation between opposing parties. In this sense, it is to be avoided or entered into with extreme care, inasmuch as the consequences can be dysfunctional and deadly. However, Lewis Coser (1964) maintained that conflict both *internal* and *external* to the group can have positive benefits. At Marine Corps boot camp in Parris Island, South Carolina, a drill instructor tells recruits, "I want you to dedicate all this training to one very special person. To your enemy: the reason being so he can die for his country. So who are we going to dedicate all this training to, privates?" And the recruits shout enthusiastically, "The enemy, Sir! The enemy, Sir!" (Dyer, 1985, p. 124). The threat of the enemy (in peacetime or during war) is continually held up to the recruits, binding them together and reinforcing their commitment to each other, their unit, and, in this example, the Marine Corps. As Coser (1964) described it, "'searching for the outside enemy' (or exaggeration of the danger which an actual enemy presents) serves not only to maintain the structure of the group, but also to strengthen its cohesion when threatened by a relaxation of energies or by internal dissension" (p. 106). Conflict within a group can act as a safety valve when the differences and hostilities between members are openly expressed and then negotiated. If these feelings are suppressed, they can intensify, to explode at some later date and seriously damage or destroy the group. This is especially true of groups such as the family that are characterized by strong emotional feelings.

Conflict theorists are criticized by functionalists for viewing the world almost entirely in terms of strife and disorder. They are preoccupied with class antagonisms and the struggle for wealth, status, and power and thus fail to recognize the harmonious, integrative, and stabilizing aspects of group life that are a product of shared religious, moral, and political values. Dahrendorf (1968) believed that neither conflict theory nor functionalist theory can make a "claim to comprehensive and exclusive applicability. . . . As far as I can see we need both models for the explanation of social problems . . . one of stability, harmony, and consensus, and one of change, conflict, and constraint" (p. 128).

Symbolic Interactionism: The Subjectivist Approach

As we have seen, functionalist and conflict theorists stand poles apart in their portrayals of social groupings and interactions. Functionalists stress the cohesiveness and collective benefits of organized social life. In sharp contrast, conflict proponents focus on the power struggles and other forces that pull people apart and create exploitive social relations. In at least two respects, however, the approaches share common ground.

First, structural-functional theory and conflict theory represent what are called **macro-level** paradigms or models (Collins, 1988b). Both are concerned primarily with large-scale social phenomena such as societies (e.g., Russia) and the major structural elements within those societies (e.g., the Russian political system). Their analyses of social processes also are directed at assessing the impact of various forces on maintaining or changing the structures and operations of these units.

Second, both approaches are essentially **objectivistic** in orientation. That is, they begin with the assumption that the tangible, objective facts of social reality, such as the structure of the political system in Russian society, are of primary importance in shaping events and lives within that society. Both perspectives then proceed to identify and examine those objective social phenomena from substantially different viewpoints.

In contrast, a third major sociological paradigm, **symbolic interactionism,** takes a quite different approach. This theory is concerned primarily with small-scale, **micro-level** social phenomena and analyzes them from a **subjectivistic** perspective (Collins, 1994). In these respects, symbolic interactionism represents more of a social psychological than a purely sociological perspective.

Cooley, Mead, and Thomas   Although the term *symbolic interactionism* did not appear until the mid-1930s (Collins, 1994), the roots of this approach can be traced to the work of a trio of scholars at the University of Chicago in the beginning of this century. Charles H. Cooley and George Herbert Mead (whose works are examined in detail in Chapter 4) were both concerned with the process by which individuals acquire a set of human personal and social char-

acteristics, especially a self-identity. They concluded that people are not born with this sense of self. It is a social product created and maintained through the individual's interaction with other human beings. Mead went even further, arguing that the human mind itself was a product of the same social interaction, as was the language that provided the mind with the means to think.

William Isaac Thomas, the third member of this founding trio, perhaps is best known in sociology for his massive study (conducted with a colleague, Florian Znaniecki) of the adjustment of Polish peasant immigrants to big-city life in the United States of the early 1900s. From this work, he derived his assertion that human behavior ultimately is subjective. Thomas (1967/1923) claimed that, before people respond to an objective event, they engage in what he called a **definition of the situation,** a personal interpretation. They then respond in terms of this subjective reading, whether or not it is accurate and valid. In Thomas's famous and often-quoted words, "If men define situations as real, they are real in their consequences" (Thomas and Thomas, 1928, p. 572).

In other words, social patterns can be understood only in terms of peoples' subjective picture of their world and not by examining that world's objective properties. For example, someone who is dying of cancer but is not aware of the seriousness of her disease may act carefree, as though she had all the time in the world to live, when in fact she may have only six months. Conversely, someone who is quite healthy but is convinced that she has an advanced terminal illness may begin to give away prized possessions and otherwise close out her affairs, even though in fact she has all the time in the world. In each case, knowledge of the objective health of the person, terminally ill or healthy, would not help us explain or understand the behavior. Rather, we would have to know what the individual thought about her state of health in order to make sense out of her behavior.

Together, the contributions of these three pioneers formed the foundation for the modern symbolic interactionist perspective. This particular way of looking at social relations focuses on the millions of small-scale social encounters or interactions that take place between individuals every single day and that are the building blocks for larger-scale social units. It attempts to understand the process by which the participants are able to structure these interactions in a way that allows them normally to take place without great friction or conflict. As part of this effort, symbolic interactionists are led to examine the role of human communication in the construction of the subjective meanings that shape people's responses to their world.

Symbolic interactionists argue that human communication is unique among the animal world because of its use of **significant symbols** or stimuli that have attached meanings and values. These meanings and values are created through social interaction, and people respond to objects in terms of their symbolic content rather than their physical properties (Blumer, in Collins, 1994).

For example, in early 1999, police were called in to the "Little Saigon" area of Westminster, California, to protect a Vietnamese-American merchant who was under physical attack from other Vietnamese immigrants for displaying a photograph of the late communist leader Ho Chi Minh and a North Vietnamese flag in his shop window. His actions had infuriated his neighbors, most of whom had fled South Vietnam involuntarily, some after spending years in prison camps following the capture of Saigon by the North Vietnamese (Breznican, 1999). The point of contention was not the physical objects (the photograph and the flag) themselves but, rather, what those objects stood for in the eyes of the local immigrant population—a repressive political regime responsible for the end of life as they had known it. In a similar vein, the continuing controversy over legislation concerning the desecration of the U.S. flag has nothing at all to do with the fact that an inexpensive, multicolored cloth rectangle is being burned, ripped, or otherwise mutilated. The real source of the controversy is symbolic. One side views the flag's destruction as a desecration of the United States itself, an assault on core American beliefs and values. The other side sees the same behavior as an expression of one of our most cherished values, the freedom of speech. For this group, the right to burn the American flag is an affirmation of what the United States and its flag represent.

Social patterns must therefore be understood in terms of the symbolic contexts in which they occur, and these contexts are always subject to negotiation. For symbolic interactionists, human societies are continuing processes rather than finished structures. They are always dependent on the subjective perceptions and interpretations of their members, and these subjective readings are never simply automatic or permanent responses to objective conditions in the external world. Herbert Blumer, the sociologist who is generally credited as being the creator of contemporary symbolic interaction theory, summarized what he called the basic ideas or "root images" of the perspective (Blumer, 1969):

1. People respond to things (objects, events, actions, other people, circumstances) on the basis of the meanings those things have for them.

2. These meanings do not exist in the things themselves but are created through the process of social interaction.

3. Individuals interpret these meanings as they apply in specific circumstances. The assignment of meaning to a given thing by a particular individual can and will vary with the situation.

In its more extreme versions, symbolic interactionism denies the existence of any sort of recognizable objective social reality, effectively making integration of this approach with either functionalism or conflict theory impossible. In more moderate form, however, this perspective complements and supplements these other theories. It permits sociologists to understand the linkage between external social realities and human social patterns that may vary significantly from one group to another (each of these groups is interpreting the objective event in a different way, attaching a different subjective meaning to it). Like each of the other two perspectives, symbolic interactionism provides a different and productive view of our social world. As in the case of the functionalist and conflict models, however, that view, by itself, is incomplete.

DOING SOCIOLOGY: IS THERE A METHOD TO THIS MADNESS?

Problems in Social Scientific Research

Comte and other early sociologists believed that it was possible and desirable for this new field to duplicate the methodology of the natural sciences in its study of social patterns. Contemporary sociologists, however, are more likely to acknowledge that whereas the employment of scientific methodology in sociological analysis might be desirable (although not all sociologists would agree on this point), it is not really possible. The differences between the natural and social worlds make such a simple one-to-one translation out of the question.

As applied to the study of the natural physical world, the scientific approach is characterized by a number of distinctive features that set it apart from other possible techniques for understanding and explaining reality. (See Table 1.3 for some important methodological terminology.) Scientific research begins with the systematic observation of empirical phenomena of some sort and the formulation of a problem or question for study. This problem is stated as one or more hypotheses about how two or more variables are related to each other. Generally, these hypotheses are offered in the form of **causal relationships,** asserting that one of the factors under

TABLE 1.3

Important Methodological Terms

Term	Definition
Empirical	Existing in or relating to the physical world.
Variable	An empirical object or phenomenon that can assume a number of different values; for example, individual yearly income.
Independent variable	A factor that is assumed to be responsible for causing or bringing about the value of some other factor. For example, the number of hours worked by a person in a given year might be a major factor shaping that individual's income for the year.
Dependent variable	A factor whose value is assumed to be caused or brought about by the operation of an independent variable. Yearly income, in the preceding example, depends on the number of hours worked during the year.
Hypothesis	The statement of a relationship between independent and dependent variables. The greater the number of hours worked during the year, the higher the yearly income level.
Reliability	The ability of a measurement instrument to give the same results when repeated; that is, its consistency. The time clock in a factory would be a reliable measure of the passage of units of work time.
Validity	The ability of an instrument to measure what it is supposed to. The use of time card records is likely to be a valid measure of the number of hours worked by a person in a factory.

examination (the independent variable) is somehow responsible for bringing about the observed value of the other factor (the dependent variable). These hypotheses must be stated in such a way as to allow for the possibility of empirical disconfirmation; that is, it must be possible to find physical evidence that would disprove the hypotheses. This requirement means that the phenomena under study must be capable of being measured accurately. Scientific research thus is restricted to verifiable phenomena in the empirical world.

Scientific testing of hypotheses ideally involves some sort of experiment in which the variables are subjected to a series of controlled conditions according to a systematic plan developed by the researcher. The objective of these controlled experiments is to observe whether changes in the value of the independent variable from one experimental condition to another will lead to changes in the dependent variable as predicted or implied by the hypothesis. If the predicted changes do in fact take place, the hypothesis can be accepted tentatively (subject to further empirical testing). If the predicted changes do not occur, the hypothesis will be rejected.

If all this sounds a little too abstract, consider the following example. Suppose that, after spending two weeks' vacation at a beach resort observing the passing array of body shapes and sizes, I notice that there seems to be a distinct and strong relationship between people's height and their weight. By and large, taller people appear to weigh significantly more than shorter people. Believing that these two phenomena are linked in a causal relationship and that the former (height) is somehow the result of the latter (weight), I conduct an experiment involving a group of students of the same initial height and weight. Over the next six months, I treat the students to calorie-rich meals designed to increase their weight. At the end of the six months, I again measure the height and weight of each student, expecting to find that they will now all be taller (since they have all gained weight), and that those who have gained the most weight will also have grown the tallest. To my surprise, I find that this has not happened. In some instances, the now-heavier students have indeed grown taller, but, in other cases, they have not. In some cases, the largest weight gains have been accompanied by the largest height gains, but, in some other instances, just the opposite has occurred. In fact, the only consistent relationship I can observe is that between food intake and weight gain. Those students who have indulged most enthusiastically in the unlimited free meals have gained the most weight, but they have not necessarily gotten any taller. So much for the hypothesis that weight causes height.

Although the scientific testing procedure might sound fairly straightforward, several inherent features of the human social world make its direct application in the social sciences problematic.

Nonempirical Variables One basic problem involves the fact that the social world inhabited by human beings is not simply or entirely empirical. It also consists of many significant nonphysical components including religious beliefs (a supreme being), political values (individual freedom), and emotional states of being (love) that reflect our human characteristics and capacities. Scientists refer to these nonempirical components as **constructs** (Black and Champion, 1976). Because constructs are not directly measurable, they are not, strictly speaking, proper subjects for scientific inquiry. But because they are so significant and so distinctively human, they cannot be ignored by any discipline such as sociology that hopes to understand social realities.

The attempted solution to this problem involves social scientists in the creation and application of often ingenious (and sometimes bizarre) **operational definitions** that specify how a phenomenon that has no direct empirical basis (e.g., intelligence) is to be measured empirically: Intelligence is that which is measured by an intelligence test. The question of how validly or correctly these operational definitions capture the commonly accepted idea of a phenomenon is a critical one in the social sciences. Very often, social and political policies have been constructed on the basis of scientific measures of human characteristics that did not at all accomplish what they claimed. According to some observers, this is especially true of traditional intelligence tests, which have incorrectly defined particular groups of people as mentally inferior to others and thus deserving of unequal treatment. Stephen Jay Gould (1981) called these tests "the mismeasure of man" (p. 25).

Ethical Constraints   A second basic impediment to the direct application of the scientific method to the study of social patterns lies in the nature of sociology's subject matter—human beings. For a number of reasons, we just do not make ideal subjects for scientific research.

People have basic moral and legal rights that include the recognition and protection of their physical and psychological well-being. Consequently, they cannot be used as guinea pigs in a sociological experiment in the same way that real guinea pigs could be used in a natural experiment. For example, earlier in the chapter, we examined a theory of suicide developed by Durkheim. Durkheim was able to find support for his hypotheses by observing specific social circumstances in which suicide rates were unusually high or unusually low. To test this theory, however, he would have had to conduct controlled experiments in which groups of people who were otherwise equal in all important respects were subjected to different social pressures structured to generate suicidal forces (the independent variable). If people

who were exposed to these experimental conditions then committed suicide (the dependent variable) and those who were not exposed did not, the theory would have received very strong empirical support. But you can imagine the justifiable public outrage and the deep trouble that Durkheim would have been in once the nature of this research became known.

Social scientists must take great care not to jeopardize in any way the people who serve as the subjects in their research efforts, and this often means that crucial kinds of analyses have to be abandoned. Recognizing this obligation, most universities and research organizations maintain a research subjects committee that evaluates proposed studies involving humans to ensure that no harm comes to them. As the authors of this text can verify from personal experience, such committees take their work very seriously and scrutinize research proposals rigorously. Even apparently harmless attitude surveys may have to be redesigned or scrapped if they contain any hint that certain questions will result in any psychological, social, or economic harm to respondents. These committees may be discouraging to researchers, but they are essential to speak up for people whose rights and needs might otherwise be ignored or compromised.

The Hawthorne Effect   An additional difficulty presented by the use of human beings in social science research lies in the fact that these subjects often react to the study itself in ways that nonhuman subjects of natural science experiments cannot. Knowing that they are participating in a scientific investigation, subjects may change their behaviors or attitudes in ways not fully known to the researcher, thus invalidating the results of the study. Known as the **Hawthorne effect** after the 1930s-era study of an industrial plant where the phenomenon was first documented, this response most often involves attempts by individuals to be "good" subjects; that is, to live up (or down) to the researcher's expectations. Efforts by social scientists to deal with this problem led to the creation of "unobtrusive measures" (Webb et al., 1966) that allow researchers to study people without the subjects being aware they are being studied. Even so, the problem remains serious in many types of sociological research. Sociologists and other social scientists must work hard for their money, but with persistence and creativity they can and do get the job done.

Nonexperimental Research Designs in Sociology

A large number of sociological studies involve what is called **nonexperimental** or **descriptive research.**

They follow some format other than the controlled experiment and normally are not concerned with trying to establish the existence of causal relationships among a specific set of variables. Rather, their primary objective is to provide accurate information about some aspect of social reality that can be used as the basis for more elaborate research or for policy development. For example, imagine that you are the owner of a fast-food restaurant chain and you are trying to put together a long-range plan for your company. As part of the preparation stage, you will need to assess how well your chain currently is doing. To do this, you have to know how many people are eating in your restaurants, which individual restaurants are drawing the largest (and the smallest) numbers of customers, and which menu items are the most (and the least) popular. You may also want to know how your customers feel about your food, your prices, and the "total dining experience" being served up in your restaurants. Before you can begin to plan effectively for the future, you must know the present, and this is what nonexperimental or descriptive research is all about.

To gather this necessary information, you will probably take advantage of an assortment of data collection techniques at your disposal. For instance, it is likely that a number of departments within your organization already possess pertinent information about operating costs and revenues for the individual restaurants that make up your chain. A quick telephone call or visit to the accounting, marketing, and operations departments may give you a set of figures describing customer flow, peak service hours, and menu item sales figures, from which you can calculate trends. In the larger world of sociological research, many private and public organizations collect similar information as part of their daily activities and routinely make it available to social scientists. For example, the United States Bureau of the Census is a gold mine of such data, and you will note the many references to Census Bureau publications throughout this text.

Although the use of existing data (information collected by some group or agency other than oneself) has many appealing advantages, the technique has one serious potential problem. Information is only as good as the methods used to gather it, and using data that were collected and analyzed by someone else does not usually allow the researcher to directly assess their validity or reliability. This is especially true when the information comes from a society or culture other than one's own.

Sociological Research Methods Sociologists do not claim to have a monopoly when it comes to perceptive and accurate understanding of social realities. But we do claim a special way of conceptualizing and examining human social relations that sensitizes us to certain phenomena that may be missed or dismissed by observers employing different perspectives. One can certainly acquire a store of valuable knowledge by direct experiences such as living in another culture and talking extensively with local people who have an insider's knowledge of it. But these experiences are not really complete substitutes for the basic world view that one develops through deep immersion and involvement in a particular discipline. For these reasons, sociologists prefer, whenever possible, to gather information themselves or, if necessary, to use data collected by other social scientists. Fortunately, a number of ways exist in which this can be accomplished.

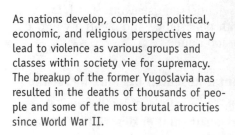

As nations develop, competing political, economic, and religious perspectives may lead to violence as various groups and classes within society vie for supremacy. The breakup of the former Yugoslavia has resulted in the deaths of thousands of people and some of the most brutal atrocities since World War II.

One such method involves what is called **survey research.** In this technique, the social scientist attempts to learn about people's behaviors or attitudes (or some other social phenomenon) by asking them to respond to a series of questions. These questions may be asked verbally in the course of an **interview** or posed in writing in a **questionnaire.** In some cases, it will be possible to survey the entire **population** (all the members of the particular group being studied). More often, however, the sociologist will have to limit the survey to a smaller segment or **representative sample** that is assumed to be reflective of the larger population (all the members of the target population must have an equal chance of being selected for the sample).

Again, imagining that you are the owner of that fast-food restaurant chain, consider how you might apply survey research techniques to find out how people feel about your restaurants and your food. If time and resources permit, you could attempt to interview personally every customer served by your chain. Given your volume of business, however, it is much more likely that you will find it necessary to put together a series of questions to be distributed to all the customers in your various restaurants. These questions will be designed in such a way as to elicit customers' feelings about the quality and quantity of your food, prices, the friendliness and efficiency of your staff, and other relevant issues.

If you do find you have too many customers to make surveying each and every one feasible, you might draw a representative sample of customers to respond to the questionnaires. This sample can be constructed so that customers in each individual restaurant and during each peak meal time are included in the survey—for example, people eating during breakfast and lunch hours in restaurant A, during lunch and dinner hours in restaurant B, during dinner and breakfast hours in restaurant C, and so on. In this way, you are maximizing the likelihood that the answers you receive from your respondents will be typical of those that customers who are not included in the sample would give if asked the same questions.

Survey research is probably the most popular and widespread form of nonexperimental methodology in sociology today. It is a straightforward technique, inexpensive, relatively easy to conduct, and the large amount of data generated can be coded and computer-analyzed very quickly. However, a number of problems are inherent in this type of research that can often limit its utility to social scientists.

Some of these problems are mechanical; that is, they revolve around the technical difficulties in drawing samples that really are representative of larger populations and developing questions that ask what they are supposed to while being clear enough for respondents to understand. Although troublesome, these problems can be resolved, if necessary, through simple trial and error. But a deeper problem in survey research is not mechanical or so easily resolved. That is the problem of truthfulness.

The logic of survey research is based on the assumption that people know why they are behaving (or thinking) in a certain way and that they are willing to share that knowledge with the researcher. Very often, however, this assumption turns out to be invalid. Subjects in both oral and written surveys can and do provide less than truthful information with great frequency. The researcher who is not careful can be duped by respondents (Douglas, 1976).

Sometimes this lack of truthfulness reflects the fact that respondents are asked to admit to illegal or deviant behaviors; for example, questions about spouse abuse or "abnormal" sexual practices. At other times, the behaviors being studied are not in themselves illegal or deviant but are nonetheless embarrassing, such as failing to vote in a society like the United States where that right is considered a central value. Finally, respondents might hedge on their answers if they feel that what they say could jeopardize them. For many reasons, the fact remains that responses to survey questions cannot and should not be taken entirely at face value.

Observation Studies   Faced with these difficulties, many sociologists prefer to conduct a more immediate form of research, known as the **observation study.** As the name might imply, the technique involves the researcher directly observing the subjects' behaviors or expressions of attitudes, rather than relying on their reporting of what they do or think. The principle might be summed up as "believe what I do, not what I say." The two main varieties of these studies are distinguished from one another on the basis of the degree of the researcher's involvement with the observed groups.

In the **neutral observation** study, the researcher remains removed (in terms of participation in group activities, if not in actual physical distance) from the group being studied, while the subjects go about their normal activities. As the fast-food restaurant owner, for example, you might observe customers and staff through a one-way mirror or an audio-video device installed in your office for that purpose. In other instances, you might visit one of your restaurants and observe events from a table or booth. However, either case, especially the latter, is likely to generate the Hawthorne effect discussed earlier. Knowing that they are being observed by the big boss, your employees may work doubly hard to be friendly and efficient. Their unusually positive attitudes and behaviors could, in turn, change those of your customers, creating a climate that is anything but business as usual.

A possible solution to this problem lies in what is termed **participant observation** research. Here, the researcher does not remain an outsider but, rather, joins the group being studied and participates in its activities. In some cases, the researcher's identity may be known to the group members (**overt participant observation**), but, more commonly, the researcher engages in **covert participant observation.** That is, the researcher is not known as such to group members. As far as they are concerned, the researcher is no more nor less than one of them.

To continue our ongoing example, you, our hypothetical restaurant owner, are probably too well known to be able to go undercover as a worker or as a customer. But you may bring in some other trained, trustworthy person to conduct the observations from the inside by joining the staff as a new employee or by posing as a customer and visiting various restaurants in you chain during peak breakfast, lunch, and dinner hours. (In point of fact, many restaurants, department stores, airlines, and other businesses routinely employ "professional customers" for exactly this purpose.) Not being known either by customers or by your employees, this observer could look at the stores as they really are being operated. As part of the group, the observer could also develop a greater sense of why your employees and your customers engage in certain behaviors and not in others. Such close involvement allows for an understanding of the group's definition of the situation and its consequent subjective structuring of the world. For these reasons, participant observation is a favored research technique of sociologists in the symbolic interactionist theoretical perspective.

Problems in Observation Studies In spite of its many potential advantages, significant problems are associated with participant observation research, especially the covert variety. To maintain cover, the researcher must deceive or lie to the subjects, thus depriving them of what social scientists call *informed consent*, the option of choosing not to participate in the study. This can become especially problematic if the research could in any way cause harm to the subjects as a result of something they did or said in the presence of the researcher whose existence was unknown to them.

Suppose, for instance, that an employee of one of your fast-food restaurants made some extremely negative comments about the chain's owner (you)

while having coffee with the covert observer, and these comments later were reported to you. This is roughly equivalent of having someone tape other people's telephone conversations without their knowledge. Believing that they were speaking in confidence, the unknowing parties might say things that could prove highly embarrassing and possibly damaging if they were to go beyond that particular time and place.

In this society, at least, people in the ordinary social world now are legally required to inform others that their conversation is being taped. In similar fashion, social scientists are required by human subjects protection committees to acquire the informed consent of subjects before the start of the research. The objective, of course, is to avoid these kinds of compromising conditions. Although the restrictions accomplish that objective, they also place severe limits on the possibility of successfully conducting this type of research. Sociologists who do covert participation observation argue that, without this technique, we would never be able to study deviant and criminal subcultures or any organization that for some reason or other does not want to be scrutinized.

By this time, we hope the message is clear. Sociologists have a variety of descriptive research techniques to draw on in their attempts to understand the human social world. Whereas most of these procedures can generate important information when and if properly employed, none is cost free or without significant weaknesses. For this reason, it is always a wise move not to rely on any one methodology in carrying out even descriptive research in this field. Whenever and wherever possible, sociologists try to cross-check the results of any single piece of research with another, different technique. Survey results, for example, may be verified through a series of observational studies. Observational studies may be compared to results of research conducted by other social scientists or sources outside academia. If the results of these different procedures are consistent, we have some assurance that our descriptions of that portion of the social world under study are accurate. If they are not consistent, we have a problem whose resolution may require more sophisticated types of analyses.

Experimental Research Designs in Sociology

Whereas the purpose of nonexperimental research in sociology is to describe social patterns, the objective of **experimental research** is to *explain* these observed patterns or *predict* future ones. To put it a little differently, nonexperimental research generates the information to construct hypotheses, and experimental research provides the data to test hypotheses. These research designs can take a large variety of different forms (Campbell and Stanley, 1963), but several common elements cut across individual versions.

All true experimental designs involve the systematic comparison of at least two groups of subjects who initially are equivalent in all characteristics relevant to the study, especially the dependent variable. The **control group** consists of subjects who will not be exposed to the experimental condition (some deliberate change in the independent variable). This group essentially serves as the baseline against which the second or **experimental group** will be measured. Members of the latter group will be exposed to the experimental condition that is the focus of the research. After that exposure, the two groups again will be measured on the dependent variable. Any changes that now are observed between them will be attributed to the effects of the experimental condition, since that is the only characteristic of the groups that is now different.

For example, suppose that Professor X has developed a hypothesis that students' performances on introductory sociology examinations can be improved by the application of what behavioral psychologists call a "negative reinforcement agent," in this case, physical pain. To test her hypothesis, she sets up an experiment using the students in her freshman Sociology 101 classes. These students all complete one ordinary midterm examination and then are grouped on the basis of their test scores into different pools—*A* students, *B* students, *C* students, and so on. From within each pool, students are randomly assigned to either the control group or the experimental group. After the second midterm exam has been given, individual members of each group meet with their instructor to go over the test answers. Members of the control group will be advised of their correct and incorrect answers, receive their grade, and be sent on their way.

For members of the experimental group, however, the experience will be a bit different. They will be seated in a special chair and have electrodes attached to their wrists and ankles. The other end of the electrodes will be attached to a portable generator. As long as the students' exam answers are correct, nothing happens. The first time an incorrect answer is detected, however, they receive a negative reinforcement (15 volts of electric shock). The second incorrect answer prompts a second reinforcement (30 volts this time). The application of these reinforcement stimuli continues until the entire examination has been scored. The students are then allowed to go.

At the end of the semester, the third and final examination is given, and the scores of the control and the experimental groups are compared. The performance of each student on the third test also is compared to his or her performances on the previous two so that the improvement (or lack of it) can be charted. The scores of the experimental group—those who received the electric shocks—show a dramatic rise between the second and third exams. They also are substantially higher than both the scores and the increase in scores of the control group. The researcher thus concludes that the application of the negative reinforcers had the predicted effect. On the basis of her findings, Professor X submits a large grant application to her university's research and development department.

The Milgram Experiment If this example sounds a bit farfetched, you might be surprised to learn that it is based loosely on a real social science experiment that took place a number of years ago (Milgram, 1963, 1965), although nobody actually received electric shocks. The study generated the same type of response from the academic community as the preceding example perhaps did from you when you read it.

In this experiment, Stanley Milgram, a psychologist at Yale University, placed an ad in the local newspapers requesting paid volunteers for participation in the study of a new learning technique. When the people who answered the ad arrived at the psychology labs, they joined a group of other people who they thought also were there in response to the ad. In fact, this other group consisted of people who were working for Milgram.

The group was split up into smaller groups of two, a "teacher" and a "student." In each case, the real subjects of the experiment served as the teachers, and the researcher's assistants were the students. The instructions called for the application of electric shocks to students who were unable to repeat a sequence of words after learning them from the teacher. Each additional incorrect response or a refusal by the student to respond called for a higher level of electric shock. Milgram had instructed his assistants to give incorrect responses (and had disconnected all the electrical wiring), since the true purpose of the experiment was to discover the extent to which the real subjects would be willing to comply with an order to administer what they might think was a dangerous electric shock to a stranger. As the experiment progressed, Milgram was surprised and disturbed to discover that a large number of subjects were so willing, although many did so under protest.

When Milgram published the results of his study of "obedience," he was criticized severely (for a review of some of these criticisms, see Miller, 1986). Among other things, he was accused of causing harm to his research subjects—not the "students" (remember, they did not really receive any electric shocks), but to the "teachers" who were the real subjects. At the end of the experiment, Milgram explained the study to them and assured them that his assistants ("students") had not been hurt in any way. Nonetheless, the subjects had discovered something very disturbing about themselves during this experiment. They had learned that they were capable of doing harmful things to other humans just because they had been ordered to do so by someone in authority who had agreed to take responsibility for the consequences. Critics claimed that, without being fully aware of what he had done, Milgram perhaps had caused these subjects psychological trauma by forcing them to see a side of themselves they would prefer not to know. It was partially because of controversies like the one generated by this experiment that such great concern is expressed today for the rights of human research subjects. Like the covert participation study, the possibility of conducting experiments in sociology has been greatly reduced by the restrictions on social science that are currently in place.

Even without these considerations, a number of other factors limit the application of the experimental method in sociology. This particular type of research is suitable only for micro-level social phenomena; that is, for small-group research. It would be impossible, for instance, to assign entire societies to control or experimental groups and then manipulate their environments to test the validity of some hypothesis. In addition, most social phenomena occur in a real-world setting where the simultaneous effects of what may be hundreds of individual variables make systematic control and manipulation all but impossible.

Nevertheless, experimental methodologies have contributed a significant body of information to the store of sociological knowledge, particularly in that subfield known as group dynamics. A great deal of what sociologists know about the formation and development of small social groups, friends or co-workers, for example, has come from experimental studies. These findings perhaps are not directly transferable to larger, macro-level social phenomena, but they have often served as the starting point for that type of larger-scale research.

SUMMARY AND REVIEW

Theme of the Text

1. *What is sociology?*

Sociology is the academic discipline that attempts to describe, explain, and predict human social patterns from a scientific orientation. It is one of the social sciences—disciplines that study human behavior scientifically. Other social sciences are anthropology, psychology, political science, and economics. (P. 3)

2. *What is the subject matter of sociology?*

Sociology typically focuses on the social organization and patterns of behavior of large, complex, modern industrial states. However, in recent years, sociologists have started investigating patterns of behavior and change in developing or Third World nations. (P. 3)

3. *When and where did sociology originate?*

Sociology originated in the mid-nineteenth century, when the Industrial Revolution was rapidly transforming European societies. Early sociologists sought to understand the cause of these changes and the consequences they had on societies' major institutions as well as on people's behavior. (P. 5)

4. *What is globalization?*

Globalization refers to the migration of jobs, capital, industry, and people as well as the movement of values and other aspects of culture across societies. It also alludes to the growing interrelation and interdependence of human societies. The globalization phenomenon will accelerate as we move into the twenty-first century. (Pp. 8–9)

5. *In what sense is sociology a "debunking" science?*

Sociology is a debunking science; that is, it looks for levels of reality other than those presented in official interpretations of society and people's "commonsense" explanations of the social world. Sociologists seek to understand and explain what is and are not interested in passing judgment on people, their behavior, or entire societies. (Pp. 9–10)

The Sociological Style: Unraveling Human Social Patterns

6. *Who was the founder of sociology, and what is positivism?*

Auguste Comte, the founding father of sociology, believed that some nations were moving into the positivistic stage, the third and final phase of societal development. Positivism is the belief that reliable knowledge of the world can be gained only through people's five senses. Scientific analysis, with its emphasis on observation and experimentation, is grounded in positivism. (Pp. 10–11)

7. *What are social facts?*

Emile Durkheim argued against the reductionist position that social phenomena could be reduced or explained in biological and psychological terms. According to Durkheim, social facts exist *sui generis* (in and of themselves) and cannot be interpreted at the individual psychological level. Social facts such as laws exist external to the individual, constrain or influence a person's behavior, and are shared by a significant number of people. (P. 12)

Thinking Sociologically: Theoretical Paradigms

8. *What is a theory?*

A theory is a set of logically coherent, interrelated concepts that explains some observable phenomenon or group of facts. Grand theories explain "the big picture," that is, the progression or development of societies over long periods of time. Middle-range theories focus on a much narrower range of events in the social world; for example, Durkheim's explanation of suicide in different social groups and societies. (P. 12)

9. *What is functionalism?*

Influenced by the biological sciences, early functionalist theorists thought of society as a social organism made up of interrelated and interdependent parts of institutions. Each of these parts performed a certain useful function for society. Modern functionalists such as Talcott Parsons examined the functional requirements that all societies must fulfill if they are to survive. (Pp. 13, 17)

10. *What are manifest and latent function?*

Robert Merton introduced the concepts of manifest and latent functions. Manifest functions are the recognized and/or intended consequences of a group or organization. For example, a manifest function of universities is to provide young adults the skills necessary for productive employment. However, in the 1960s universities became recruiting grounds and headquarters for a significant amount of antiestablishment behavior. This was a latent or unintended consequence of higher education. (Pp. 17–18)

11. *How did conflict theorist Karl Marx view capitalist societies?*

In contrast to the group consensus orientation or functionalist theorists, conflict sociologists see turmoil as the fundamental reality of social life. Karl Marx argued that capitalist societies such as the United States consist of two classes locked in struggle. The ruling class, or bourgeoisie, owns and controls the means of production—land, factories, machinery, and capital. With few if any resources, the proletariat must sell its labor (for whatever the ruling class will pay them) in order to survive. This struggle between the haves and have nots will eventually give way to revolution and a socialist society. (Pp. 18–19)

12. *What is symbolic interactionism?*

Symbolic interactionists focus on micro-level rather than macro-level social phenomena and reject the objectivist approach of both functionalist and conflict sociologists. From this perspective, sociologists must strive to understand the world from the individual's subjective point of view. People define a particular situation and then act on the basis of that subjective definition. Symbolic interactionists maintain that human beings communicate by significant symbols to which they have attached meaning. (Pp. 20–21)

Doing Sociology: Is There a Method to This Madness?

13. *What are dependent and independent variables?*

Much scientific research is an attempt to determine whether there is a causal relationship between variables. The independent variable is the factor that is thought to be a cause of, or bring about change in, something. The dependent variable is a measure of the observed change caused by the independent variable. (P. 22)

14. *What is a hypothesis?*

A scientific problem is usually stated in terms of a hypothesis—an educated guess concerning the relationship between two or more variables. An example of a hypothesis would be: As education goes up (independent variable), racial prejudice goes down (dependent variable). To test this hypothesis, the researcher would devise some way of measuring each of the variables. (P. 22)

15. *What is survey research?*

Using survey research, sociologists ask people a series of questions regarding their attitudes and behavior. This may be done directly during the course of an interview or indirectly with a questionnaire. Sociologists rarely survey all the members of a given population. Rather, they take a representative sample of the population and generalize their findings to this larger group. For a sample to be truly representative, all members of the population must have an equal chance of being represented or selected. (P. 25)

16. *Is there a difference between overt and covert participant observation?*

One type of observational study frequently used by sociologists is participant observation. In overt participant observation, the researcher informs members of the group being observed that he or she is a sociologist. In covert studies, group members do not realize they are being observed. Rather, they believe the researcher is one of them. (P. 26)

17. *What are the major components of an experiment?*

A true experiment involves the comparison of at least two groups of subjects who are identical across all characteristics that are relevant to the study. One or more experimental groups receives or is exposed to the independent variable. The control group does not receive the independent variable and is used as a baseline or comparison group to the experimental group(s). In the absence of a control group, we would not know whether changes in the experimental group (dependent variable) were caused by the independent variable or were the result of some other factor. (P. 27)

2 *Culture*

embers of any given social group have much in common; that is, they share the same basic "world view." However, even in highly integrated, homogeneous societies, individuals may have fundamental disagreements regarding what they believe and how they should behave. In the United States, consider the contentious views people hold on issues such as abortion, gun control, drug use, and various aspects of sexuality. Conflict over "the good, the true, and the beautiful" among people from different societies can be so vast that they disagree on almost everything but the most trivial concerns.

In recent years the clash of values over a practice called female circumcision (FC) or female genital mutilation (FGM) has taken center stage in the world community. FC/FGM is the partial or total removal of the external female genitalia or the mutilation of genital organs for cultural or religious reasons (Hamilton, 1997). More specifically, this procedure is undertaken to substantially reduce a female's sexual desire and pleasure toward the end of ensuring that she remains a virgin until marriage. One advocate of FC/FGM in Egypt stated that if a woman's genitals are not surgically reduced, wearing tight clothes "will make her want any man, any boy for sex" (in Cooperman and Carey, 1997, p. 51). In some societies the pretense for FC/FGM is to remove the "unhealthy" portions of a woman's body that will harm her husband and children (Woolard and Edwards, 1997).

Although FC/FGM is associated primarily with Islamic countries, it predates the religion of Mohammed by more than a thousand years, and at one time or another has been performed in Africa, Asia, Australia, Latin America, North America, and Europe. Guesstimates on the number of females alive today who have experienced this ritual range from 60 to 140 million. FC/FGM is performed in 27 of 54 African nations as well as on the Arabian peninsula (Yemen, Oman, and the United Arab Emirates). In a recent survey, 97 percent of Egyptian women between the ages of 15 and 49 reported being subjected to this practice (Chelala, 1998). According to one estimate, as of 1990, approximately 36,000 females had undergone genital mutilation while living in the United States (Hollander, 1997).

While FC/FGM can be performed on a female as early as one month old, or as late as age 18, the most frequent period of occurrence is between 7 and 12 years of age. In a number of societies older women with no medical training do the cutting (without the benefit of anesthesia) using a variety of (unsterilized) implements including razor blades, kitchen knives, scissors, even broken glass (Hamilton, 1997; Woolard and Edwards, 1997). Short-term effects of this crude surgery include severe pain, shock, and ulceration of the genital region while some girls die as a result of severe hemorrhaging (blood loss). Long-term consequences include urinary incontinence, urinary tract infections (antibiotics are rarely used), infertility, and complications during childbirth (Hamilton, 1997).

The World Health Organization (WHO), the United Nations International Children's Fund (UNICEF), and the United Nations Population Fund have condemned FC/FGM as an "unsafe and unjustifiable traditional practice" and called for a "major decline" in this procedure within the next ten years, and worldwide abolishment within three generations (Hamilton, 1997). Article five of the Universal Declaration of Human Rights states that "No one shall be subjected to torture, or to cruel, inhuman degrading treatment or punishment" (Obiora, 1997, p. 277). From this essentially universalistic position, there are "categories and constructions" of dignity and integrity that apply to all people, in all societies, at all times.

A recent U.S. law mandates that individuals arriving in this country from regions where FC/FGM is practiced be warned that if these procedures are performed here the perpetrator is subject to fines as well as a prison sentence of up to five years. In 1997, U.S. government representatives of international financial institutions were instructed to oppose loans to any country where FC/FGM is practiced unless local authorities have begun an educational campaign to prevent its occurrence (Woolard and Edwards, 1997).

Supporters of genital mutilation strongly resent the international community interfering in their affairs. They argue that religious freedom gives them the right to raise and socialize their children as they see fit; adding that citizens of nations practicing FC/FGM should not be subjected to the values and morals of people who live on the other side of the world. From this perspective, what outsiders see as torture, advocates of genital mutilation consider a vitally important, time-honored component of their socio-religious heritage. Universal standards of right and wrong are rejected in favor of local autonomy and cultural uniqueness.

The controversy of FC/FGM is a powerful, albeit extreme example of the importance of culture in all of our lives. **Culture** is a people's way of life or social heritage and includes values, norms, institutions, and artifacts that are passed from generation to generation by learning alone (Hoult, 1974). Culture provides a "world-taken-for-granted" that most people accept most of the time. Even seemingly basic biological functions are not free of cultural imperatives. "Humans cannot eat, breathe, defecate, mate, reproduce, sit, move about, sleep, or lie down without following or expressing some aspect of their culture" (Harris, 1989, p. 27).

Culture sets boundaries for behavior and provides standards for good and bad, right and wrong, beauty and ugliness, and so on. However, it would be a serious mistake to view culture as some all-powerful irresistible force that compels people to conform slavishly to an ideal standard of behavior. Culture not only helps to shape and determine our behavior, but in turn is altered by human beings as they adapt to a changing social and physical environment.

Questions to Consider

both

1. Is human behavior a function of instincts, biological drives, or both?
2. What are the main arguments of the proponents and opponents of sociobiology?
3. What is language, and how does it differ from nonverbal communication?
4. What is the relation between material and nonmaterial culture?
5. What is popular culture, and why do sociologists study this aspect of culture?
6. What are some of the core values of American society? Are they changing?
7. What are mores, and why must they be obeyed? What are some mores in American society?
8. What is the difference between ethnocentrism and cultural relativism?
9. What is the difference between subcultures and countercultures? Are countercultures always destructive elements in society?
10. What is cultural lag? Is cultural lag inevitable in modern industrial societies? In Third World societies?

THE ROOTS OF HUMAN CULTURE

The Biological Basis

In everyday explanations of behavior, the term "human nature" is often mentioned or alluded to. This catch-all phrase has been used to explain everything from a mother's love for her child to a group of adolescent males fighting. As we will see in Chapter 7, many of the attributes and patterns of behavior we associate with men are thought of as natural or somehow rooted in the male physiology. Biological explanations for female behavior are just as common in hundreds of societies. The question of whether human behavior as a whole, as well as more gender-specific acts, is a function of "nature or nurture" is one of the oldest and most controversial riddles in the biological and social sciences. Are human cultures a result of some biological programming that predisposes our species to act and evolve socially in a certain way, or are they a function of our ability to learn and adapt to a varied and changing environment?

By the 1920s, this question was answered in terms of **instincts**—an unlearned, complex behavioral response or set of responses in a species that are biologically programmed and triggered by environmental stimuli. Almost every aspect of human behavior was thought to be the result of some instinct or other. However, as scientists began to realize that they were not coming any closer to explaining the tremendous diversity in human behavior and cultural variation by labeling everything an instinct, this line of research was abandoned. But failing to discover a core group of instincts responsible for much if not most of our behavior does not mean that human beings are free of biological constraints.

Many social scientists are of the opinion that human beings have **biological drives** experienced as a bodily imbalance or tension leading to activity that restores balance and reduces tension. For example, drives such as hunger, thirst, and sex are influenced by stimuli that originate inside the body. The fact that drives can be satisfied in a variety of ways makes cultural variation possible. Consider for a moment the sex drive and the myriad ways in which it can be satisfied: males with females, males with males, females with females, males and animals, females and animals, males and inanimate objects, females and inanimate objects, males by themselves, and females by themselves. This list not only demonstrates the malleability of the human sex drive, but illustrates that important cultural values (especially religious values) are associated with sexual behavior. In our society, all but "normal" male and female sexual relations are considered unnatural, even wrong, by a significant number of people.

Biological drives influence our behavior in yet another important way. For example, human beings have to eat and drink on a regular basis, optimally a number of times each day. This means that hunting, gathering, fishing, and cultivating various forms of food are essential activities in every human society. Since we cannot fly or run as fast as a cheetah and lack innate, predatory skills, we had to learn to acquire food and adapt to a changing environment. This satisfaction of biological drives through learned behavior not only permitted our species to survive and prosper, but also accounts for human cultural diversity. Humans have successfully adapted to a changing physical and social world because they are flexible and "not pre-programmed to a particular way of life" (*Economist,* 1987, p. 83).

Although human beings are not "pre-programmed" to behave in a specified manner, research indicates that between 30 and 70 percent of the IQ (intelligence quotient) variation among individuals, as well as some personality traits (extroversion, neuroticism, authoritarianism, and so forth), appear to have a genetic component (J. Scott, 1992). Regarding personality characteristics, genes may lead people to certain friends, jobs, and lifestyles that complement inherited predispositions. If this "soft" biological determinism is correct, some of our preferences in life (concerning work and leisure activities, for example) are a combination of both inherited characteristics *and* choices that are available to us in the social world. This means that "we are not just passive recipients of environmental effects. We are active agents in how we structure our situations" (Segal in J. Scott, 1992).

In the 1970s, some researchers in the emerging discipline of *sociobiology* offered a "hard" biological determinism to explain a significant amount of human behavior. These individuals noted that, although human beings do not have instincts, some forms of behavior such as altruism, aggression, and homosexuality were biologically based and transmitted genetically from one generation to another. Sociobiologists reasoned that because these behaviors are found in virtually every human society, they must have a biological base. They argued that just as our bodies prevented us from flying, for example, our genetic makeup predisposes us to various types of behavior that we simply cannot escape. Even though we have highly developed brains and are capable of an almost endless assortment of behavior, we are still prisoners of our physiology and heredity.

Pioneer sociobiologist Edward O. Wilson (1988) noted that whereas we do not inherit an instinct that directs us to engage in specific types and quantities of aggression, our capacity and tendency to engage in violent behavior is hereditary. Wilson argued further "that it is entirely possible for all known components of the mind, including will, to have a neurophysiological basis subject to genetic evolution by natural selection" (p. 13). Although humans are highly adaptable creatures, learning and adaptability evolved and were naturally selected. The flexibility that distinguishes us from other animals is part of our genetic makeup.

Although sociobiology has its adherents, most scientists are hostile to the biological determinism that is such an important component of this perspective. Paleontologist Stephen Jay Gould (1976) believes that sociobiologists have overstated the biological basis of human behavior. For Gould, the fact that human beings are animals "does not imply that our specific patterns of behavior and social arrangements are in any way directly determined by our genes" (p. 12). He believes that sociobiologists have erred by confusing the concepts of "potential" and "determinism." The "brain's enormous flexibility" gives us the potential to engage in a wide variety of behavior but directs us toward none in particular. Leeds and Dusek (1981/1982, pp. xxxv) stated that some critics of sociobiology deny any biological component to human behavior beyond "eating, sleeping, and defecating." When pressed by their adversaries, sociobiologists claim that culture is 10 percent biological and 90 percent social, "which is hardly informative." Critics note that because biological constraints on culture are too weak to be significant, "models of genetic evolution will be of little use in understanding variation in human behavior" (Rogers, 1988, p. 819).

Anthropologist Ashley Montagu (1980) argued that above all, human beings are creatures of learning: "If there is one trait more than any other that distinguishes *Homo sapiens* from all other living creatures it is educability . . . the species trait of mankind. Humans are polymorphously educable, which is to say they are capable of learning everything it is possible to learn" (p. 11). For Montagu and others, we are not predisposed to any type of behavior, and we have the capacity to make and continually change our cultures virtually without limit. Biological drives require that we continually satisfy a number of bodily needs and functions, but the fact that we choose how to meet these drives is what distinguishes us from the other animals. Although the sociobiological position cannot be dismissed, it has yet to demonstrate that there is a link between some aspect of our genetic endowment and significant specieswide patterns of behavior.

By way of summary, although sociologists do not deny that biological processes (drives) affect human conduct, they stress that these processes *interact* with social and cultural forces to produce behavior. What

As members of a given culture, we become aware of standards of behavior, including appropriate attire for different occasions. This Sami woman from Norway is being outfitted in a traditional wedding costume.

is not completely understood, however, is where biological factors end and sociocultural forces begin.

Language, Thought, and Culture

As linguists Fromkin and Rodman (1988) pointed out, language more than anything else separates humans from the other animals. According to the philosophy, myths, and religions of numerous cultures, it is the source of our humanity and power. The spoken language developed approximately 40,000 years ago, and a written form of symbolic communication is about 4,000 years old. The written word, coupled with the language-assisted ability for more complex thought, was a crucial feature in human evolution and is closely linked to our modern "cultural take-off" (Harris, 1983, p. 29).

The development of language was important for at least three reasons. First, human beings acquired the ability to transmit culture from one generation to another. This meant that much information gained from experience would not be lost, making it unnecessary for subsequent generations to learn these things anew. Second, language makes possible an ever-expanding repository of knowledge and tradition. It has been estimated that in the modern world, the accumulated knowledge of our species doubles approximately every ten years, with much of this information stored in written form. Finally, with language we have achieved what Greenberg (1968) called semantic universality, the ability to transcend the here and now and speak of people, places, and events in the past, present, and future, be they near or far, real or imaginary.

This last aspect of language is a major difference between human and nonhuman communication. Other animals communicate by sound, odor, movement, and touch, with these signals having meaning for their immediate environment or emotional state. Some species are also capable of communicating aggressiveness and superordination and subordination, especially as they relate to sexual activity. Inasmuch as the basic vocabulary of animals is limited to the present, however, communication is primarily an emotional response to particular situations (Fromkin and Rodman, 1988). In other words, animals have no way of relating the hunger they felt the day before yesterday or expressing anticipation for next week's hunt.

By contrast, human communication relies to a great extent on sounds that have *arbitrary* meanings and can be arranged into an almost infinite number of combinations to convey information about any subject imaginable. For example, by age 3 years, speakers of English generally know what the word *cat* signifies. But "cat" is an arbitrary sound with no inherent meaning. Children in Mexico learn the furry little animal that goes "meow" is a *gato,* whereas speakers of Japanese call the same creature a *neko.* Speaking a language, therefore, means knowing that particular sounds signify specific meanings.

There are a number of theories of how children learn to speak (Fromkin and Rodman, 1988). According to the **imitation perspective,** children simply repeat what they hear spoken by those around them. No doubt, imitation is involved in language acquisition to some extent, but from whom would a child hear "boat big wow uh-huh," or "Mommy already eated"? The **reinforcement theory** suggests that children are positively reinforced when they say something correctly and negatively reinforced when they say something wrong. However, one study indicated that when children are corrected, it is usually for pronunciation or the incorrect reporting of facts and not for ungrammatical sentences (Brown, 1973). Even if they are corrected for grammatical mistakes, children do not know what they are doing wrong and are typically unable to make appropriate changes.

Linguist Noam Chomsky offered the now widely held explanation of language acquisition that has been labeled the **innateness hypothesis.** Human beings learn to speak because our cerebral cortex is "prewired" to acquire language. In other words, the ability to speak is "a distinct piece of the biological makeup of our brains" (Pinker in Brownlee, 1998, p. 48). We learn language naturally, with little if any formal introduction, because humans inherit a deep-seated "universal grammar" that serves as a foundation underlying the grammar of the world's approximately 6,000 languages. Research indicates that the brain has distinct areas and procedures for handling different forms of language. For example, Steven Pinker (in LaFee, 1992) found that in native English speakers with normal language skills, regular verbs such as "walk" and "climb" are filed in the brain's "internal dictionary." Learned rules of language state that the past tense is formed by adding "ed" to create "walked" and "climbed." However, with an irregular verb such as "bring/brought," the brain must individually memorize each and every form (LaFee, 1992). Therefore, when a child utters a sentence such as "I holded the cat," he/she has not yet learned that "to hold" is one of the almost 200 commonly used irregular verbs in English. Recent work indicates that not only do infants begin to memorize words (without knowing their meaning) within the first few months of life, but that very young children internalize and apply rules of grammar long before they have the slightest notion of what grammar is and under what circumstances specific rules should be utilized. Approximately 90 percent of the sentences spoken by a typical three-year-old are grammatically correct (Brownlee, 1998).

The innateness hypothesis may explain why all the attempts to teach other primates language have resulted in only limited success and why no animal has acquired the linguistic skills normally found in a three-year-old human (Harris, 1995). Perhaps the innateness hypothesis also explains why young children so easily learn two languages at the same time and achieve literacy in both (Graham, 1995).

Children also learn a language faster if they are exposed to more words at an early age. One study found that by age 20 months children of more talkative mothers had 131 more words in their vocabulary than children of women who were less vocal. By age two years the vocabulary gap had increased to 295 words (in Brownlee, 1998).

The Sapir–Whorf Hypothesis   As noted, acquisition of language was the key ingredient in humankind's cultural takeoff. Although it is easy to see how language unleashed our creative abilities in virtually every human endeavor, we do not usually think of it as something that limits our ability to think and therefore to act. However, anthropologist Edward Sapir and his student, linguist Benjamin Whorf, argued that language is more than just a means of communication. Languages are like so many pairs of colored glasses, and the people who wear these glasses see and interpret the world around them differently; that is, they furnish the categories by which we think, divide up, and make sense of the social world.

For example, in the English language, the color black has more negative connotations and associations than positive ones. It represents death, sickness, evil, villains, crime, gloom, and despair. It is also associated with the occult, devils, and vampires. We have expressions such as "Black Death," "black arts," "black magic," "black-listed," "black mark," "blackmail," "black market," "black cat," "black sheep," and "black heart." Conversely, white is associated with birth, purity, holiness, goodness, and innocence. This linguistic color coding of things and attributes as either good and desirable (white) or bad and undesirable (black) may function as a cultural backdrop in which racial prejudice can thrive.

The Sapir–Whorf hypothesis goes beyond suggesting that language merely influences the way in which people relate to the world around them. Rather, it functions as a kind of mental straitjacket that actually forces people to perceive the social and physical environment in terms that are built into the language (Howard and McKim, 1986). For example, in English the two major classifications of words are nouns and verbs, a system that leads to a bipolar view of nature. People, animals, and plants (nouns) run, walk, and grow (verbs). Lightning, flame, waves, and a puff of smoke are events (nouns). In the Hopi language, however, lightning, flame, and so on are verbs, "events of brief duration cannot be anything but verbs" (Whorf, 1939, in Carroll, 1961, p. 44). In other words, the Hopi language uses what we would call events (nouns) as verbs and classifies them by their duration, from short to long. Whereas English draws our attention to the thing or event (e.g., flame), the Hopi language focuses on motion and change.

The way in which a society is organized can significantly influence the development and use of language and, ultimately, how members of that society view their surroundings. The Agta (a fishing people in the Philippines whose livelihood depends to a great extent on the success of their catch) have thirty-one verbs meaning "to fish," each word referring to a particular type of fishing. An all-inclusive verb "to fish" (which is not specific enough for their needs) does not exist in the Agta language. Similarly, people in preliterate societies who "live off the land," so to speak, can typically identify and name between 500 and 1,000 different plant species. Conversely, big-city residents of industrial nations who spend much more time in "urban jungles" than tropical jungles can usually recognize and name no more than 50–100 separate species (Harris, 1989).

Language also reflects the orientation and world view of a particular group of people. For example, the use and number of personal pronouns in the Japanese language indicate the importance of status and hierarchical arrangements. Japanese uses a number of first-person pronouns—*watakushi, boku, ore,* and the like—that help to distinguish power differences and gradations of social distance between the speaker and the person being addressed. Suzuki (in Lebra and Lebra, 1986, pp. 142–157) referred to this process as "speaker's linguistic self-identification" and noted that in Japanese, "one actually alters the linguistic definition of self to accord with changed conditions." As you might expect, a number of second-person pronouns are also used on the basis of power differences and social distance. Conversely, in languages like English and Spanish, the speaker uses only one personal pronoun to identify herself or himself (I and *yo*). Spanish uses the formal *(usted)* and informal *(tú)* second-person pronouns, but speakers of English employ the pronoun "you" regardless of whether they are speaking to a dog or to the president of the United States.

Language as Social Control   From the example of pronoun usage in Japan, we can see that language can be a continuing and not very subtle mechanism of social control. Superordinate and subordinate positions in virtually every aspect of Japanese society are verbalized and reinforced hundreds of millions of times each day. British novelist and social critic George Orwell was deeply concerned with how language can be used not only to influence but also to diminish people's thought processes. Recall the basic premise of the Sapir—Whorf hypothesis, that the structure of language determines how people view the world around them. In Orwell's most famous novel, *1984,* the totalitarian government of Big Brother invented a language called Newspeak with a very limited vocabulary. The idea behind Newspeak

was that the fewer words and categories people had at their disposal, the less capable they were of complex, abstract thought and therefore the easier they would be to control. Words such as *honor, justice, democracy,* and *science* were abolished and replaced by the single word *crimethink.*

Although words in American English have not disappeared as a result of some sinister plot, government officials and other bureaucrats routinely use *doublespeak* to convey messages. Doublespeak is a combination of Orwell's Newspeak and "double-think." According to William Lutz (1989, p. 1), it is "language which pretends to communicate but really doesn't. It is language which makes the bad seem good, the something negative appear positive, something unpleasant appear positive (or at least tolerable). It is language which avoids responsibility. . . ." Doublespeak illustrates how the use of language is shaped by power relations in society. Those in power invent a distorted language that obscures reality. From a conflict perspective, doublespeak keeps the masses ignorant and confused, less likely to understand that they are being exploited by the ruling class.

Corporations that cut jobs as a result of moving facilities to a developing nation or merging with another company do not fire workers; rather, they engage in "work reengineering," "employee repositioning" and "proactive downsizing" ("Doublespeak Awards," 1994). Colleges and universities also engage in doublespeak. Faculty and staff are never fired or laid off, instead they are "seasonally adjusted," "dehired," "selected out," "repositioned," "restructured," or "subjected to negative personpower adjustment." At one university, students do not live in dormitories but reside in "campus venues," while at another college students eat, sleep, and keep their belongings in "living learning centers." Teenage sexual intercourse has been described as "penile insertive behavior." In at least one police department officers do not shoot fleeing suspects but "neutralize" them (Kehl, 1994). Buses have become "motorized transportation modules," and a U.S. government agency refers to an airplane crash as an "unanticipated impact with the terrain."

As these examples illustrate, language can be used to influence how people perceive the world, the way they think, and ultimately how they behave. Language is also important because it is a central component of a people's identity and is often linked with intense feelings of patriotism and nationalism. Prior to gaining independence from Great Britain in 1947, the leaders of the Indian Congress Party promised that when the British finally "quit" (left) India, the country would be reorganized along linguistic lines. What the leaders failed to consider is that in a country with

200 languages and 630 local dialects, regional loyalties would severely weaken nationalism. With the Constitution of 1950, the new Indian government changed course and said that local languages would be used until 1965 when Hindi was to become the national language. However, the plan was scrapped after language riots broke out in many parts of the country as the deadline approached (Warshaw, 1992).

Language can also help to preserve a group's identity under the most difficult circumstances. Partitioned by Prussia, Russia, and Austria in the latter part of the eighteenth century, Poland disappeared from the map of Europe until the Treaty of Versailles (1918) redrew its borders after World War I. For over 100 years, Polish identity persisted because people tenaciously held on to their culture primarily through the use of the Polish language. Linguistic pride may also prove to be a key issue in the partition of Canada. Since the 1960s, Canada has been trying to deal with the conflict between its English-speaking and its French-speaking citizens and the possible independence of the province of Quebec. Although many of the problems between Quebec and the rest of the country revolve around economic and political issues, the future of the French language and culture is a key component. The nearly one million French Canadians living outside the province of Quebec worry that their descendants will eventually lose their "Francophone" identity and be assimilated into the English mainstream (Chipello, 1998). A people's cultural heritage anchored in their language will stir the passions and give them the will and energy to fight like few other things in this world.

A battle of language has also been taking place in the United States. Two groups, U.S. English and English First, want English to be the official language of this country. Twenty-five states (mostly in the West and South) have such legislation in place, and a number of other states are considering English-only laws. Advocates of this position argue that in a society as pluralistic as ours, the government should do everything possible to unite the many diverse segments of the population in order to foster a national identity. They note that we are currently in a period of the largest immigration to this country since the early 1900s, and 32 million Americans speak a language other than English at home (Phillips, 1997). Advocates of English-only typically oppose any form of bilingual education and cite Canada as a nation that has wasted billions of dollars trying to create a dual language system and Canadians are currently more divided than ever over the language issue (Phillips, 1997).

Opponents of the English-only movement note that these organizations play into deeply held fears of the majority population—fears of minority groups and change. They reject the comparison of the United States to Canada concerning the language issue arguing that Spanish speakers are not a majority in any state, nor is there any movement for separation/independence (as there is in Quebec) based on language and ethnicity (Phillips, 1997). Census data showing that 97 percent of Americans over the age of five are fluent in English is evidence that the problem of non-English speakers has been greatly exaggerated. Arturo Madrid (1990) believes that the imposition of an official English-only policy will limit "civic assimilation and participation" (p. 62) of non-English-speaking people. Just as so-called literacy tests were used to keep many non-whites from voting until the Voting Rights Act of 1963, English-only laws would effectively disenfranchise hundreds of thousands of people. Madrid notes that the framers of the Declaration of Independence and the Constitution "wisely chose not to single out English as the national or official Language" (p. 62). Some opponents of English-only laws note that if these statutes were ever rigidly enforced, even communicating with deaf people via sign language would be barred because this language is not English ("Whose Language Is It?," 1996).

Material and Nonmaterial Culture

The concept of culture comes from anthropology and is that discipline's most important contribution to the social sciences. Whereas culture represents the complete social heritage and way of life of a society or group of people, sociologists generally make a distinction between its material and nonmaterial parts. **Material culture** comprises those things people make and use. In other words, features of the material culture have our handprint, since they were created and fashioned by human beings. The building you are sitting in, the clothes on your back, as well as computers, airplanes, and the Styrofoam boxes hamburgers used to come in are all examples of material culture. **Nonmaterial culture** does not have physical substance, although it, too, was created by human beings. Ideas, religions, beliefs, customs, laws, and economic systems such as capitalism and socialism are all examples.

As you may have guessed, aspects of material and nonmaterial culture are almost always intertwined, as the latter give meaning to the former. Consider an airplane loaded with baseball bats that crashes in a country where nobody ever heard of the infield fly rule. The bats are likely to be thought of as fence posts, clubs, fancy firewood, or whatever, but not as implements with which Babe Ruth, Hank Aaron, and Mark McGwire hit home runs. In the absence of knowledge of baseball and the rules of the game (nonmaterial culture), bats are just so many evenly proportioned pieces of timber. Children in any society spend a good deal of time learning how features of their material and nonmaterial cultures fit together. One of the questions most frequently asked by 2-, 3-, and 4-year-olds is "What's this?" Older siblings and adults then name the object and give some explanation regarding how, when, and why the thing is used.

Popular Culture

A society's material and nonmaterial culture are not limited to economic, political, and religious spheres of life. Much that we see, hear, appreciate, and become obsessed with is part of **popular culture**; that is, the culture of everyday life as expressed through sport, films, television, books, magazines, comic books, music, automobiles, hobbies (especially collecting), and other channels. Popular culture is also a medium for connecting with our past and helps people celebrate a time, place, person, or thing that is important to them.

Perhaps the individual who has had the greatest continuing impact on popular culture in the United States is Elvis Presley, the enormously popular entertainer who died at age 42 in 1977. Not only have sales of his music remained strong, but individuals all over the world see Elvis as a personification of a romanticized, more carefree, rock-and-roll era of their youth. Elvis sightings appear on a regular basis, and just over 8 percent of Americans between 35 and 44 years of age think it is likely that "the King" is still alive. Each year approximately 700,000 fans pay $15 to visit Elvis' Graceland home in Memphis, Tennessee, where

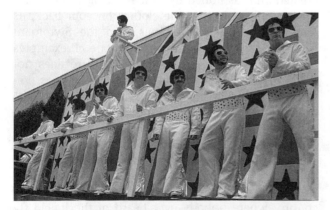

Elvis Presley, Michael Jordan, and Madonna are some of the most well known names and images in the world. These Elvis impersonators ride on a float in the annual Elvis Day Parade in downtown Kansas City. Almost 25 years after his death, "The King" still has tens of millions of fans in scores of countries around the world.

they purchase over $150 million worth of souvenirs (Edmondson, 1998). Some religious scholars view this phenomenon as being akin to the faithful making a pilgrimage to Rome, Jerusalem, or Mecca (Di Sabatino, 1997). There is even an official (satirical) First *Presleytarian* Church of Elvis the Divine. Its founder, who views pop star Michael Jackson as a false idol or the "anti-Elvis" (the "evil one-gloved one"), wants to "put the fun back into fundamentalism" (in Di Sabatino, 1997, p. 38). Academic conferences on "Elvisology" are common, with the theme of one such recent event titled "Are You Lonesome Tonight?: Elvis and the Dysfunctional Family."

The many critics of popular culture (as discussed in Gans, 1983) have argued that this manifestation of contemporary culture is not so much a form of artistic expression as it is an industry organized for profit. For example, the success or failure of Hollywood films is more often measured in terms of box-office revenues rather than cinematic merit. Similarly, "bestseller" books become so because of multimillion-dollar sales figures, and not the quality of their literary content. Television shows are renewed or canceled on the basis of their share of the viewing audience, not their ability to inform or to educate. Critics argue further that, in order for this popular culture industry to be profitable, it must create a homogeneous and standardized product that appeals to a mass audience, as witness the endless sequels and "spinoffs" that follow just about every successful (that is, profitable) film, novel, or television program. In contrast to other, "higher" forms of culture, popular culture appeals to the least common denominator of public taste (in Gans, 1983).

Whether or not these criticisms are valid, popular culture is the vehicle of mass consumption by which we continually reinterpret the past, evaluate the present, and speculate on the future. As such, it can exercise a great deal of influence on shaping, as well as reflecting, public beliefs and behaviors. For example, African Americans were rarely featured in motion pictures between 1920 and 1950. When they did appear, they were typically stereotyped as happy-go-lucky, simple-minded servants (of white people), and occasionally as entertainers and athletes. African Americans were portrayed as childlike individuals, completely dependent on good, benevolent white folk for their well-being.

Sportswriters of that period offer a vivid description of how African Americans were conceptualized by a significant portion of the population. Even a figure as popular as boxer Joe Louis was routinely characterized as a "jungle killer," "the chocolate chopper," "the coffee-colored kayo king," and the "shufflin' shadow;" a savage, animalistic, fighter who destroyed his opponents instinctively. After Louis defeated the Italian "giant" Primo Carnera, one columnist wrote that "Something sly and sinister and perhaps not quite human came out of the African jungle last night . . . " (in Mead, 1985, p. 62).

By the 1960s, and the civil rights movement, Hollywood often featured independent, no-nonsense black tough guys in the *Super Fly* mold. In the 1980s and 1990s, African Americans on television ("The Cosby Show," "The Fresh Prince of Bel-Air," "Martin," "Living Single" and the "Cosby Mysteries") were depicted as upwardly mobile, successful professionals in a more tolerant society.

THE NORMATIVE ORDER

Core Values and National Character

Every society has a set of values that establishes which forms of behavior and beliefs are desirable and which are undesirable. In the United States, cleanliness is an important part of our culture (Spradley and McCurdy, 1989). As children, we are taught to bathe regularly, practice personal hygiene, and wash our hands before every meal. However, cleanliness is valued to some extent in virtually every modern society. In contrast, **core values** are especially promoted by a particular culture (Haviland, 1990) and are often important identifying characteristics of that culture. They provide the basis for social behavior and some of the goals pursued by members of society (Howard and McKim, 1986).

On the basis of core values, anthropologists and sociologists sometimes generalize about the personality characteristics and patterns of behavior of an entire tribe or society. Critics of this approach believe it is impossible to assess accurately the national character of a group in this manner. But anthropologist Francis Hsu (1979) maintained that studies of national character are important if we are to understand what motivates the leaders and civil servants of nations in the modern world. This is especially true of developing nations. However, virtually every society places some value on duty, loyalty, honor, and the like. Our discussion focuses on the relative importance of these concepts and how they shape a people's national character. (Core values in China will be discussed in the Focus on China section at the end of this chapter.)

American Values

Sociologist Robin M. Williams (1970) attempted to identify the major values in U.S. society. Although he listed twenty core values, twelve appear to be the most important. They are placed in groups of four, including the identifying value of that cluster.

Certainly one of the cornerstones of U.S. life is the tremendous emphasis placed on success and related values of work, achievement, and material comfort. Success and upward mobility have been part of both the fact and fiction of life in the United States since the days of its founding. The dream of making it big has attracted millions of people, beginning with the huge migration of European settlers in the middle of the nineteenth century. In a society that placed much more emphasis on what an individual can do than on who one is or where one comes from, for many people the dream came true.

Rags-to-riches stories were celebrated in the nation's popular culture as early as the nineteenth century. Young boys read the adventures of Horatio Alger's (1834–1899) heroes as they overcame poverty and adversity on the road to fame and fortune. Sports have come to reflect the hard work—achievement—success theme, and movies such as *The Knute Rockne Story* and *The Lou Gehrig Story* reinforced the idea that anyone can have success if they want it badly enough. More recently, films such as *Rocky, The Natural,* and *Field of Dreams* have done much the same. Television has also been an important vehicle for the success motif. Todd Gitlin (1985, pp. 268–269) noted that many programs, especially the soap operas, feature characters who are preoccupied with ambition. "Personal ambition and consumerism are the driving forces of their lives. The sumptuous and brightly lit settings of most series amount to advertisements for a consumption-centered version of the good life. . . ."

If the quest for success has been a prime ingredient in this country's economic achievements, hard work has always been viewed as the road to prosperity. Williams (1970) noted that work has been a core value in U.S. culture for at least three reasons. First, in the days of frontier settlements and westward expansion, work was necessary for group survival. Second, the majority of people who initially came to this country were from the working classes in Britain and Europe. We might add that the experience of blacks from the earliest days of slavery was certainly one of hard physical labor. Latinos, Chinese Americans, and other non-European minorities also have a history of very demanding work. Finally, the Puritan ethic linked work and success with a state of grace and eternal salvation. Robert Bellah et al. (1996) stated that work is the basis not only for success, but for self-esteem as well. In a society that measures people in terms of what they do, what they have, and what they have accomplished, unemployment is particularly painful.

A second cluster of values revolves around *progress*, efficiency, rationality, and applied science. Since Alexis de Tocqueville visited this country in the 1830s, foreign observers have been impressed with America's faith in progress and high expectations of the future. A fundamental component of progress is the acceptance of change for the good of society. For generations of Americans, the benefits of technological change surrounded them as they lived longer, more prosperous lives. There was nothing that ingenuity and hard work could not accomplish. Even failures were viewed as temporary setbacks. When the Soviet Union sent *Sputnik* to orbit around the earth in 1956, the U.S. space program went into high gear and put a man on the moon by 1969. In the 1940s and 1950s, outbreaks of poliomyelitis crippled and killed thousands of children. The disease was almost wiped out by the development of the Salk and Sabin vaccines.

Progress is closely linked to our belief and faith in *technology* and *applied science*. Whereas most people may be indifferent to science as it relates to questions concerning the origin of life or understanding black holes in deep space, they are enthusiastic about scientific applications that will make their lives easier, healthier, and longer. Williams (1970) noted that Americans are much more receptive to events in the here and now that make an immediate impact in our lives. As a nation, we are more "manipulative than contemplative" (p. 502). Applied science is so highly valued because it permits us to control nature to a significant degree.

Science and progress also go hand in hand with *efficiency* and *practicality*. They are important in a society concerned with getting things done quickly and economically, with a minimal amount of wasted time, energy, and money. People oriented toward these values are constantly looking to the future, searching for time- and labor-saving means for doing more things faster. Traditionalism and a strong attachment to the past are the antithesis of a "Let's do it better, cheaper, and faster" ethos. For example, although France is a modern industrial state, practicality and efficiency are not nearly as important to the French as to Americans. Most shops and government offices in France are closed from noon until 2 or 3 P.M.—precisely the time when people on lunch breaks could use their services. The majority of stores are closed on Sundays and holidays, and the nation's economy shifts into low gear during August, when a significant number of French people are on vacation. It is still quite common for people to spend an hour or two eating the evening meal, whereas Americans are more likely to be hurrying through supper and mentally preparing for some upcoming activity.

The final cluster of core American values is *freedom*, individualism, equality, and patriotism. Bellah et al. (1996) argued that freedom is perhaps the most deeply held American value. To be free "is not simply to be left alone by others; it is also somehow to be your own person . . . free as much as possible from the demands of conformity to family, friends, or community" (p. 23). Freedom gives each person a sense and a measure of power to strive for whatever he or she desires.

A corollary of freedom is individualism, which "lies at the very core of American culture" (Bellah et al., 1996, p. 142). The dignity of the individual is sacred, and any threat to limit a person's right to act and think for himself or herself is sacrilegious. The Bill of Rights outlines more individual safeguards than perhaps any other political document in the world. We enjoy thinking of ourselves as a nation of rugged individuals, made from the same mold as the pioneers who tamed the land on their own initiative without the help or hindrance of the government or anybody else. Americans have had a continuing love affair with the mythical individual hero—the cowboy—since at least the turn of the century. Be it Alan Ladd in the classic movie *Shane* or the Lone Ranger (Bellah et al., 1996), the cowboy-hero saves the town from some terrible injustice, kisses his horse, and rides off into the sunset. Private detectives, loner cops, and people who persevere and win against all odds possess the unconventionality, stubbornness, and personal toughness that Americans associate with success and moral righteousness.

Fairness and equality, especially equality of opportunity, have been persistent themes in this society for most of our history as a nation (Williams, 1970). If a person's eventual success or failure is to be a function of his or her abilities and hard work, then society must provide an opportunity structure that is free of any individual or group favoritism or discrimination. It is precisely at this juncture of freedom, individualism, and equality that inconsistencies related to these values as they are translated into behavior by both individuals and institutions have been the most evident. The history of the United States is rife with examples of discrimination based on race, ethnicity, gender, religion, sexual preference, age, and language that have effectively prohibited people from participating politically, economically, and socially to one degree or another.

The final value in this cluster is patriotism. Despite the waning confidence Americans express in their elected officials and public institutions, they have a "degree of patriotism that is remarkable when compared to most other industrial societies" (Bellah et al., 1996, pp. 221–222). We continue to rally around the flag even though the percentage of people voting in local and national elections is low and dropping in many parts of the country. President Carter's inability to free the American hostages in Iran may have cost him the 1980 election as a significant number of voters interpreted this crisis as indicative of the country's political and military decline. The ensuing military buildup in the Reagan years occurred with the support of much of the nation.

It would be naive to think that everyone in the United States accepts and adheres to these values with the same level of intensity. The extent to which core values are held is related to a number of factors, including race, ethnicity, and social class and the experiences people have had as individuals and in groups as a result of these factors. Madsen and Meyer (1978, p. 244) argued that the "central character of the value system" of Mexican Americans "comes from their long history of feudalism from Spain, oppression in Mexico, and discrimination in the United States." William Madsen (1964) noted that Mexican Americans temper the core value of progress with an acceptance and understanding of things as they are. He summarized this aspect of the Mexican-American world view as follows:

> We are not very important in the universe. We are here because God sent us and we must leave when God calls us. God has given us a good way to live and we should try to see the beauty of His commands. We often fail for many are weak but we should try. There is much suffering; we should accept it for it comes from God. Life is sad but beautiful. (p. 17)

If Madsen is correct, Mexican Americans are not interested in progress and change in the sense that these terms mean a mastery of the physical environment and a better life through science and technology. Because God controls events, Mexican Americans plan less for the future than do people in Anglo cultures; one cannot control or predict what is ultimately in God's hands.

Culture of Poverty   The culture of poverty thesis put forth by anthropologist Oscar Lewis (1966) and others states that the core values of poor people are different from those of more economically successful individuals. These values are passed down from generation to generation and contribute to a cycle of poverty from which they cannot escape. The poor are thought to lack the drive, desire, and discipline to be successful, as well as to condone a good deal of behavior the rest of society regards as deviant. Hyman Rodman (1963) rejected this interpretation, arguing that lower-status people develop an alternative set of values without abandoning the core value of success.

They "stretch" these values so that lesser degrees of success become desirable—and attainable. For example, whereas middle-class families simply assume their children will finish high school and go on to college or find good jobs, families living in poverty have internalized the core value of success but have scaled it down to be realistic and therefore attainable. For them, having their children finish high school and gain steady employment in neighborhoods with high rates of unemployment is considered success.

In a participant observation study of working and nonworking black men who frequented a local bar and liquor store, Elijah Anderson (1978) found that these men did not stretch a set of given values as much as they created their own standards of social conduct in line with the opportunities available to them. When certain individuals could not find jobs and conduct their lives on values based on decency, they could gain the esteem of their peers by being "good" hoodlums.

Although core values are not likely to be completely abandoned, they can be modified. Heightened awareness of environmental pollution and destruction has already called into question fundamental values of progress in a society that has come to realize the affluence of a throw-away industrial society.

Norms, Folkways, Mores, and Laws

Every society has codes of conduct that regulate the behavior of its members. These standards tell what demeanor is appropriate in the classroom, in the boardroom, and even in the bedroom. In other words, in no society are individuals completely free to do whatever they please, whenever they please. **Norms** are rules that state "what human beings should or should not think, say or do under given circumstances" (Blake and Davis, 1964, p. 456). Marshall Clinard (1974) observed that people are not usually aware of the arbitrary nature of the norms they live by, as these rules of conduct become part of an individual's world-taken-for-granted from an early age. A moment's reflection will reveal that we are bound by norms virtually every time we interact with other people. We are also subject to the normative standards of various organizations and institutions to which we belong. Not all norms are of equal importance, however, or carry equal punishment or reward. The hierarchy of rules from least to most important is usually defined as folkways, mores, and laws (Wickman, 1974).

Coined by the American sociologist and anthropologist William Graham Sumner (1840–1910), the term **folkways** refers to the customary, habitual way a group does things—simply stated, the ways of the folks. Folkways should be followed because they represent proper etiquette, manners, and the generally acceptable and approved way in which people behave in social situations. For example, in the United States, as in most other countries, people eat soup with a spoon or drink it out of a cup or bowl. Someone dining in a restaurant who dipped his hands in a soup bowl and then slurped it out of his palms would probably be stared at in amazement (and disgust), laughed at, and possibly asked to leave. People who violate folkways may be thought of as immature or strange, but they are not considered evil or wicked. Similarly, if your sociology instructor came to class wearing a tuxedo and a top hat or a flowing formal evening gown, he or she would probably get some stares and no doubt would be greeted with a good deal of laughter. Such attire, totally inappropriate to the college classroom, would be a clear violation of folkways.

Whereas the folkways of a group or larger society should be followed, **mores** must be obeyed. Continuing with the preceding example, if a male sociology instructor began wearing an evening gown to class on a regular basis, he would have to deal with more than laughter. In many institutions, he would surely be dismissed. Mores are important because they are grounded in deep-seated cultural values. People are likely to believe (rightly or wrongly) that if they are violated, something bad will happen to the group. In this instance, many individuals would be incensed because in their view, a man wearing a dress is condoning or flaunting a deviant sexual lifestyle and poses a serious threat to the morality of students.

Incest taboos (from the Polynesian *tapu*) are good examples of mores. No society permits either marriage or sexual intercourse between mother and son, father and daughter, or brother and sister. Anthropologist Bronislaw Malinowski (1927) believed that these liaisons were forbidden and punished because they would produce so much tension, rivalry, and competition that the family could not function properly and might even be destroyed (Ember and Ember, 1988). Evidence from psychologists and family therapists suggests that family harmony and stability are certainly threatened where incest exists.

As societies modernize, some of the most important norms are codified, or formally written into a legal code. They become **laws** and are legally binding for people who reside in a specific political jurisdiction. **Proscriptive laws** state what behavior is prohibited or forbidden. Laws against taking another's life, robbing people, or burglarizing their homes are proscriptive and carry some form of punishment administered by the state. **Prescriptive laws** spell out what must be done. Income tax laws, traffic laws, draft registration laws, and licensing laws require people to do things at specific times, in specific places, and under given circumstances. These two types of laws are not limited to the legal system. The Ten Commandments are a combination of prescriptive ("Honor thy father and thy mother") and proscriptive ("Thou shall not kill") rules that ostensibly govern the lives of Christians.

When people violate norms and their nonconforming behavior is observed or later discovered, they are likely to be punished or sanctioned for their transgression. This sanction can be either mild or severe, formal or informal. An informal sanction may be administered by a relative or friend by way of a frown, an angry word, or even a slap in the face. Some occasions of child abuse and wife beating can be thought of as severe informal sanctions. Formal sanctions are handed out by organizations and institutions when rules (usually written ones) are violated. These groups typically have specific procedures for determining that a rule has been broken and what sanction applies in a given situation.

In one sense, norms (and their implementation) constitute the backbone of society. Without them, human groups would fly apart or degenerate into a kind of free-for-all in which everyone did as he or she pleased and the powerful ravaged the powerless. Most people would agree that norms and laws are necessary to maintain stability; however, many questions remain concerning a society's normative order. Who should make and administer the laws? Should everyone in society have input into the formation of group norms, or should this important job be left to a select few "wise" individuals? Should a society's laws be grounded in religious "truths" or secular values? Should laws be designed to safeguard individual freedoms or be made with the welfare of the group in mind, even if individual freedoms are jeopardized?

Functionalist and conflict theorists disagree sharply concerning the manner in which norms are created and implemented (social control). The former are more likely to see norms originating as a result of group consensus, and the latter argue that laws are a product of power relations. For example, in a society like the United States, the capitalist class (bourgeoisie) makes laws to exploit and control the proletariat or working class. We will have more to say about norms and social control in the chapters on socialization and deviance.

Ethnocentrism and Cultural Relativism

The world-taken-for-granted that culture provides is often synonymous with the view that one's way of life is best. **Ethnocentrism** is the tendency to believe that the norms and values of one's own culture are superior to those of others and to use these norms as a standard in evaluating all other cultures. The "ugly American" tourist in another country who continually notes that in the United States everything is bigger, better, and more expensive and who cannot figure out why the natives act the way they do is being ethnocentric.

It is commonplace for people to believe their own way of life is of value, and a certain amount of ethnocentrism is, in fact, beneficial, as it facilitates social cohesion and a sense of "we-ness." Solidarity and pride in one's group are necessary if an organization or political state is to survive and prosper. More extreme levels, however, result in the unwarranted rejection and condemnation of other people and their ways of life. When expressed in terms of fanatical patriotism and nationalism, ethnocentrism can set the stage for war.

People can be ethnocentric and not even realize they are offending another group. Residents of the United States think of themselves as, and call themselves, Americans. This term is used by the person in the street, news commentators, and the authors of this text with no intention of slighting or demeaning anyone. Unfortunately, in the eyes of Mexicans and Latin Americans, that is exactly what we are doing. Residents of these nations are quick to point out that they too are Americans, and they resent the fact that people from the United States reserve this term exclusively for themselves (Broom and Selznick, 1970). The Americans of these other nations refer to us as, and wish we would call ourselves, North Americans. Because we have been using the word Americans for over 200 years and there is no identifiable, easily used alternative, this form of self-identification will no doubt remain.

Views concerning the superiority of one's group lead to stereotyping the values, attitudes, and behavior of others. A **stereotype** is a preconceived (not based on experience), standardized, group-shared idea about the alleged essential nature of a whole category of people without regard to individual differences within the category (Hoult, 1974). Stereotypes often focus on the supposed negative or humorous attributes of a group. In the nineteenth century, they were routinely used by businesses to sell products to largely Anglo-American consumers. Advertising stereotypes consisted of "lively Latins, thrifty Scots, clean Dutch, Italian fruit peddlers, Mexican bandits, and pigtailed Chinese" (Westerman, 1989, p. 29). Blacks were subservient domestics and "hired help," like the Cream of Wheat chef and the plantation mammy, Aunt Jemima.

Since the mid-1970s or so, such stereotyping on the part of the business community has disappeared to a significant extent. Unfortunately, this practice did not subside because people realized that it was often harmful and cruel and categorized entire groups of people as one-dimensional, but for political and economic reasons. The civil rights movement of the 1950s and 1960s resulted in more minorities voting, thus creating a political pressure group. More sophisticated marketing research indicated that minorities had increasing amounts of buying power. For example, in the mid-1990s, African Americans, Hispanic Americans, and Asian Americans—some 70 million people altogether—had over $60 *billion* in spending power. It appears the days of the Aunt Jemima lookalike and the Frito Bandito are just about over. However, stereotypes are still firmly rooted in the nation's humor as is evidenced by the number of jokes about Italians, Poles, Jews, Mexicans, Irish, and every other nationality and cultural group under the sun.

Whereas ethnocentrism is the practice of using one's culture as a basis for judging the way of life of others, **cultural relativism** is the belief that there is no universal standard of good and bad or right and wrong and that an aspect of any given culture can be judged only within its own context. In other words, the values, laws, and religious practices of society A cannot be evaluated by using the standards of society B. Every culture is a special entity and must be dealt with as such. For example, Mexicans seem to have a preoccupation with death that culminates with a celebration on November 2, the Day of the Dead ("El Día De Los Muertos"). Although children playing with death-related toys and people eating cookies shaped like skulls may seem bizarre and macabre to an outsider, within the context of the Mexican value system this behavior loses its sinister connotations and makes sense.

When the Japanese women's volleyball team was defeated at the Tokyo Olympics in 1964, the athletes all burst into tears. From a Western perspective, this could easily be interpreted as poor sportsmanship on the part of an immature group of sore losers. But the Tokyo Olympics marked Japan's return to respectability in the aftermath of World War II, and the crying women were expressing a profound sense of shame after failing to win a gold medal in front of their fellow citizens (Tasker, 1987). In the context of a so-called shame culture, this incident can be understood for what it really meant.

The problem with cultural relativism is that any behavior can be accepted, rationalized, and justified. Amnesty International reports that human rights violations and torture occur in approximately one-third of the world's nations. Under the Pol Pot regime in Cambodia in the 1970s, one million or more people were murdered by the state or died from hardships inflicted by the government. Idi Amin's reign of terror in Uganda in the 1970s resulted in the brutal deaths of approximately 300,000 people. In a bloody civil war in Rwanda (1994), fighting between Hutu and Tutsi tribesmen resulted in the deaths of between 500,000 and one million people, many of them innocent men, women, and children who were indiscriminately slaughtered.

Few individuals would condone this behavior or accept cultural relativism as a justification for torture and murder. The question, therefore, is how far can we push the cultural relativism perspective? Is behavior always "relative" to the situation, or is there some absolute standard of right and wrong? If so, what is it, and how do we know this value is correct? For Klaus-Friedrich Koch (1974), the answer to these questions is simple and straightforward: "Notions of dignity, honor, and cooperation are as universal as the taboo against the indiscriminate killing of fellow men, notwithstanding cultural differences in the definition of these ideas" (p. 67).

Culture Shock

In the popular television program "Star Trek: The Next Generation," the crew of the *USS Enterprise* travels to distant galaxies on its mission to "seek out and explore" new civilizations. Often these beings from alien societies engage in a wide variety of behavior that leaves crew members bewildered and confused. **Culture shock** is the experience of encountering people who do not share one's world view that leads to feelings of disorientation, frustration, and, on some occasions, revulsion.

It is unlikely that any of us will ever experience culture shock at the intergalactic level, but the emotional upheaval of observing and dealing with people from other nations (and even different parts of our own country) can be profound. The greater the difference between our way of life and that of the people we are interacting with, the more intense the shock is likely to be. For example, imagine you are dining in an elegant restaurant in China. How would you react to the following as reported by *O* correspondent Nury Vittachi (1995, p. 343)? Human fetuses "just a few weeks old are eaten shredded in soup by diners who believe that the concentration of human hormones and other chemicals are good for health. One hospital employee boasted that her skin was so good because she had eaten a hundred."

One aspect of culture shock, as the preceding example vividly points out, revolves around the culinary habits of people across cultures. The delicacies of one group are often seen as abhorrent to outsiders. Whereas people in the United States are apt to think

of dogs as faithful companions, millions of South Koreans (who also keep these animals as pets) consume as many as two million canines a year that are raised in rural "dog farms" and sold by the country's estimated 20,000 dog meat sellers. As one man stated concerning this popular food, "I love dog meat. It is sweeter than beef or pork. When sweltering summer sets in, I go to the market and buy a dog. My wife boils it for a whole day in a big pot and we eat the meat with sprinkles of salt" (Hun-Choe, 1997, p. A23). Ancient medical texts recommend dog meat for a variety of conditions including enhancing male sexual prowess and a speedy recovery from major surgery and long illnesses (Hun-Choe, 1997).

While walking down a busy street in Bombay, one of us suddenly came upon and old, blind beggar with no arms and legs, lying on a tattered blanket in the middle of the sidewalk. Some of the many passersby gave him a few coins, although most adroitly stepped around the pitiful figure without looking at the man. On another occasion, a woman whose face, arms, and hands were grotesquely disfigured by leprosy was also asking for money. Coming from a society in which people with such deformities are institutionalized (some would say warehoused), seeing people in this condition, struggling to survive, is quite disturbing. So, too, was the fact that the majority of people paid no attention to these individuals. Roman Catholic nuns from other nations working in India are often instructed that when walking in the streets they should keep their arms close to their bodies so that some poor, distraught woman does not slip her newborn baby under the sister's arm and then disappear into the crowd.

Lepers begging in the streets and the people who routinely ignore them, as well as women who will give their babies to nuns knowing these children will be cared for are all manifestations of extreme poverty. After only a few days in India it became clear that in a densely populated country with so many suffering and needy people, one could not possibly give even a meager amount of money to the hundreds of beggars and disfigured individuals that are routinely encountered. The shock of seeing lepers in the street began to wear off in the same way that one is less likely to be frightened by even the scariest movie after watching it three or four times.

CULTURAL DIVERSITY AND CHANGE

Subcultures and Countercultures

What do a Polish-American steelworker in Pittsburgh, a Vietnamese-American fisherman in Galveston,

Texas, a Mexican-American cattle rancher in Colorado, and a Japanese-American computer operator in San Francisco have in common? Outside of the fact that they all live and work in the United States and share some of the core values discussed earlier, the answer is probably little or nothing, because they come from different cultural traditions. All of us belong to numerous **subcultures**—groups that hold norms, values, and patterns of behavior in common with the larger society but also have their own design for living and world view.

Subcultures are especially numerous in heterogeneous societies like the United States, a nation settled by people from all over the world. In fact, one might argue that we have no dominant culture, inasmuch as we are a nation of such diverse racial and ethnic backgrounds. From this perspective, the country is a collection of racial and ethnic groups sharing a geographic location, living in a loosely agreed-on political state. Subcultures are composed not only of people from various racial and ethnic groups, but also of individuals from different religions, geographical locations, occupations, political affiliations, and recreational interests.

For example, soldiers have specialized training in the use of sophisticated weapons, wear distinctive uniforms, and have jobs as well as a set of values and norms that requires them to kill people and give up their own lives if necessary. They are typically young males known for their he-man attitudes and frequent use of profanity. There are even subcultures within subcultures. The life of an infantryman is different from that of someone in an armored division. These individuals train and fight with different technologies and have their own work-related language or argot.

Perhaps the most culturally diverse society in the world, India is made up of people from 3,000 *jati,* or subcastes, who speak almost 200 languages and 630 regional dialects (Warshaw, 1992). India's Hindu majority (83 percent) has been at odds with people from different religious subcultures for hundreds of years. Since group identification and pride are so often rooted in language, religion, and geographical residence, societies with subcultural divisions along these lines are prone to conflict and violence.

Subcultures like those consisting of people who share the same hobby (e.g., stamp or coin collecting) may have little impact on any group or institution in society. Others, however, have significant consequences for a nation's political, economic, and social institutions. Hundreds of thousands of military men and women served in Vietnam during the 1960s. On returning to the United States, thousands of them joined the Vietnam Veterans Against the War, a subculture committed to pressuring the government to end the fighting in Southeast Asia. In the past few years, subcultures of individuals for and against the right of women to legally have an abortion have clashed (often violently) over this important and deeply emotional issue.

Some cultures are not only different from, but also in opposition to, mainstream society. **Countercultures** are groups whose members share values, norms, and ways of life that contradict the fundamental beliefs and lifestyles of the larger, more dominant culture. These members reject some or all of the core values and institutions of society and may or may not engage in criminal behavior (often criminal violence). For example, founded in Tennessee just after the Civil War by ex–Confederate Army officers, the Ku Klux Klan (KKK) rejects the core value of freedom, liberty, and justice for all, and has engaged in violence against African Americans, Hispanics, Asians, Catholics, and Jews. Beginning in the late 1980s, young males with shaved heads (in the United

One of the oldest countercultures in the United States, the Ku Klux Klan was founded just after the Civil War by ex-Confederate Army officers. While the KKK has always been an anti-Black movement, in recent years, the Klan has also focused on legal and illegal immigrants from Mexico, Latin America, and Asia. Most of the Klan's support comes from lower-class Whites who feel economically threatened in an increasingly heterogeneous society. The young child in this photo is learning counterculture values from his or her parents.

Focus on
China

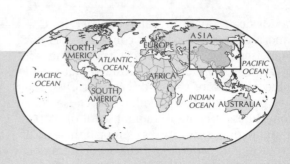

Population: 1,246,871,951
Life Expectancy at Birth (years): Male—68.57; Female—
71.48
Form of Government: Communist Party-led State
Major Religions: Officially atheist; Buddhism; Taoism;
some Muslims
Major Racial and Ethnic Groups: Han Chinese (92%); Tibetan;
Mongul; Korean; Manchu
Population Doubling Time: 73 years
Per Capita GNP (1997 U. S. dollars): $860
Principal Economic Activities: Agriculture; Heavy Industries
Colonial Experience: Never a Colony
Adult Literacy Rate: 82% Male—90%; Female—73%

Changing Values, the Youth Culture, and Chairman Mao

With the victory of Mao Zedong's armies in 1949, the Chinese Communist Party (CCP) took control of the country. The party's official ideology was grounded in the political/economic philosophies of Marx and Lenin, and to a great extent, the writings of Mao himself. Communism called for the public ownership of the **modes of production** (factories, machinery, and technology), the elimination of wealth-based class differences, as well as Mao's emphasis on simple living, self-sacrifice, and altruism (Kwong, 1994).

Upon Mao Zedong's death in 1976 and the rise to power of Deng Xiaoping, Chinese communism underwent a dramatic revision. According to "reform socialism" or "socialism with a Chinese character," egalitarianism had significantly slowed the nation's economic progress. Deng advocated a more individualistic ethos, a rekindling of the entrepreneurial spirit, and material incentives to spur economic growth. In a phrase that would have been viewed as nothing less than heresy just a few years earlier, Deng proclaimed that "To get rich is glorious" (Kwong, 1994, p. 116).

As a result of information gathered from six trips to China, sociologist Julia Kwong (1994, pp. 252–260) offers a "snapshot"

of the changing values (in the Mao and post-Mao eras) of young people on a number of dimensions.

Individualism

Prior to the 1980s, Chinese youth accepted the fact that their destiny was in the hands of government officials. They followed career paths that were most needed by the country, and typically worked wherever they were assigned. In the post-1980 era, young people "abandoned the altruistic Maoist philosophy" (p. 253) and were more apt to follow a course of individual preferences and goals.

Personal Aspirations

In a 1981 survey, 37 percent of students polled wanted to "have a high salary and secure life," while 36 percent chose "to make our motherland rich and powerful" as their top priority in life. When the same questions were posed to students in 1989, 62 percent opted for salary and security, and only 21 percent placed national interests above personal goals.

Growing Alienation

During the Cultural Revolution (1966–1976) China's young people were more than willing to defer gratification and personal happiness toward the end of cre-

ating a better society for future generations. However, in a climate of rising unemployment in the mid- to late 1980s, Chinese youth became increasingly alienated from the larger society as they faced a lifetime of work that was "monotonous, unchallenging, and meaningless."

Individual Qualities

As people's values change so do their role models. In 1963 people all over China learned of the dedication and self-sacrifice of a young soldier, Lei Feng, who died in a freak accident. Lei Feng campaigns were organized by the Communist Youth League complete with a slogan penned by Chairman Mao: "Learn from Lei Feng" (Dietrich, 1998, p. 167). Portions of a fictitious diary (written by Communist Party officials) were published so the nation could read of his unswerving allegiance to Chairman Mao and "my beloved party" (Spence, 1991; MacFarquhar, 1997, p. 338). While Lei Feng the individual was of little consequence, the values he extolled were of the utmost importance.

Today, there is not much left of Lei Feng's blind obedience and devotion to the CCP and country. A 1991 survey conducted by the Communist Youth League found that almost one out of two respondents reported that helping a fellow student was the right thing to do as long as it did not interfere with their own work.

With approximately 300 million people between the ages of 15 and 24 (a number greater than the entire population of the

United States) the youth generation accounts for about a quarter of the nation's population and represents a major segment of the consumer market. As such they are prime targets for marketing strategists (both local and foreign) in China's rapidly expanding economy. Advertisers in turn are sensitive to the values, fads, and desires of young people. These individuals are very much intrigued with Western science, technology, and popular culture, especially things from the United States, a nation that many in this age bracket view as their "dream country" (Kwong, 1994).

Attempting to capitalize on people's infatuation with Western culture, department stores and malls in major cities are promoting Christmas as a shopping/gift-giving occasion in a country with a minuscule Christian population. According to an article in the *China News Digest* (in Kang, 1997, p. 100), stores "are working hard to promote the idea of Christmas as a gift-sharing holiday among the young people in their 20s." To the extent that the sentiments of one young man, who noted that "we young people in Shanghai like to copy Western Habits" (p. 100), are widespread, merchants will have successful sales campaigns.

Advertising both promotes goods and services as well as creates a desire for such things. Magazines, television, and billboards in the world's most populous country are replete with ads designed to appeal to young people looking for Christmas gifts or products at any other time of the year. Ads from multinational corporations like Nike and Sony are almost as common in urban China as they are in more affluent societies. Young, glamorous models are shown wearing trendy clothing, sitting on motorbikes, and sipping expensive drinks (Hooper, 1991). Both young men and (especially) women participate in the "appearance revolution," with their mode of attire

Hardly reminiscent of the Mao era, these young Chinese women show off the latest attire at a Shanghai fashion show. Slightly more than a generation ago, such a display of "decadent" Western materialism would have been unimaginable. Twenty years from now, will a youth culture in China have anything more than a rudimentary knowledge of Mao and what he stood for?

often in stark contrast to more conservative, older generations.

When the government approved the release of up to 10 foreign films annually in 1996, it is unlikely that CCP officials contemplated the popularity of a movie like "Titanic." Beijing and other cities were awash in advertising as people lined up to pay $10 to see the film—about a week's wages for most urban dwellers. Ticket scalpers commanded even higher prices, and there was a brisk business in pirated videocassette copies of the film (Platt, 1998). If party leaders are worried about the impact blockbuster Western films will have on their citizens (especially young people) Orville Schell (in Platt, 1998) of the University of California at Berkeley can understand their concern. According to Schell the "American entertainment complex is one of the strongest forces in the world, and probably has greater global influence than the U.S. military" (p. 6).

In addition to state-sponsored MTV, karaoke sing-alongs, dance parties, and contests are popular forms of entertainment. Karaoke has caught on with trade unions

and Communist Youth League groups as they celebrate holidays and special occasions (Kang, 1997). Even the *China Cultural Gazette,* the official publication of the Ministry of Culture, succumbed to a changing economic climate. So far in debt that it was in danger of folding, the once dull "stronghold of hard-line" party members began publishing photos of nude and semi-nude women. With feature articles on women, sex, and the local "pop" culture scene, the gazette soon became "the coolest paper in Beijing" (Zha, 1995).

In 1993, *The Abandoned Capital,* a novel with some 60 sexually explicit scenes, sold over 500,000 thousand copies in a few months. Hailed as a "monument of contemporary Chinese literature" by some, others viewed this novel as nothing more than a compilation of "unbearably vulgar sex scenes" and "despicable male sexual psychology" (Zha, 1995, p. 129). In January 1994, after selling perhaps millions of official and pirated copies, the government announced a ban on the novel. Perhaps the most remarkable aspect of this piece of literature was that it was published at all, and upon the official ban, the author was not arrested and prosecuted.

A trip to most college campuses in the United States will find both young men and women watching soap operas in the student union. In the early 1990s, a 50-part serial entitled *Kewang* (translated to "Yearning" or "a desire like thirst") captured the imagination of tens of millions of Chinese. The story follows the increasingly intertwined lives of a simple working family (the Luis), and a more sophisticated intellectual family (the Wangs) during the Cultural Revolution (1966 to 1976) and the 1980s reforms (Zha, 1995). The *"Yearning craze"* was so intense that in some cities 98 percent of the television viewing audience regularly tuned in to watch the show. When a scheduled power blackout in the city of Wuhan interrupted *Yearning* during the middle of an episode, angry townspeople surrounded the power plant and pressured the mayor until he ordered the power

back on. *Yearning*'s cast and crew received a reception in Nanking that rivaled the greeting Chairman Mao received many years ago (Zha, 1995).

In any period of rapid social and cultural change, there are, so to speak, winners and losers. Perhaps the biggest loser in China's transition to a more liberal, capitalist economy has been Mao himself. The once revered face of the Great Helmsman now adorns T-shirts, buttons, banners, coffee cups, and just about anything else one can imagine. The Shanghai Tang department store sells Mao jackets in a variety of colors including hot-pink and chartreuse (Schell, 1997). Even worse than being forgotten, Mao and much of what he stood for have been trivialized, existing at the same level of popular culture (for tens of millions of people, although not everyone) as Disney characters and the latest rock star. The manager of a factory that made 10,000 Mao watches (on the occasion of the former leader's 100 birthday) that sold for $350 each stated, "Who now cares about Mao or

Marx? We're only concerned about making money" (in Li, 1997, p. 45). Speaking of Mao's symbolism, Chinese historian Jonathan Spence (in Pappas and Levine, 1998, p. 39) noted, "I do not think there is much political meaning to the icon anymore." Mao's "great leap forward" has come full circle with a giant step backward.

In her book *China Pop,* Jianying Zha (1995) argues that the system of social control so evident in the Mao Zedong years has been weakened. Today, people are acutely aware of the "boundaries of freedom" and realize that if you "don't engage in overt political protest, the state will more or less leave you alone" (p. 202). Will an increasingly affluent, young, urban populace remain satisfied with life in a political straitjacket, or as was the case in South Korea and Taiwan, will economic success eventually lead to demands for democratic reforms? If a concerted push for political change does occur, China's young people will undoubtedly be a vital segment of that movement.

States and Europe) calling themselves Skinheads started harassing and beating up some of the same people the KKK targeted.

In the aftermath of the Oklahoma City bombing in 1995, Americans became aware of the "patriot" movement in this country. Individuals in these organizations share a deep hatred of the federal government and typically have a "virulently anti-Semitic and racist theology" ("The Patriot Movement," 1998, p. 6). As a Georgia Identity minister noted in a recent speech, these groups view violence as a legitimate means to achieve their political/religious goals: "I want to tell you the war rages in America. The enemy is not coming. The enemy is here." "God has ordained that his people be a warring people . . . Lord of Hosts means a mass of people organized for war" (*"The Patriot Movement,"* 1998, p. 6). As of mid-1998, there were an estimated 523 of these counterculture groups in the United States with pa-

triot activity most pronounced in Arizona, California, Florida, Michigan, Ohio, and Texas.

Occasionally, a counterculture is incorporated into the larger society. In Poland during most of the 1980s, the Solidarity (*Solidarnosc*) Union was considered a counterculture from the point of view of the ruling Communist Party. Solidarity demanded better pay for workers and wanted an open, more democratic government. Union members engaged in demonstrations, work stoppages, and prolonged strikes in an effort bring about a more open society. Their leaders were routinely harassed, jailed, and tortured by a government that refused to make major concessions. With the collapse of the Communist regime in Poland, however, Solidarity and its members became part of the legitimate power structure. In a somewhat similar but less successful manner, the African National Congress (outlawed for many years by the South African government) was recognized by the government in the months after the release of Nelson Mandela from prison. As the winner of the nationwide democratic election, Mandela became president of South African in 1994.

Integration and Change

To a certain extent all cultures are integrated, meaning that the major material and nonmaterial components of a society fit together and form a consistent, workable whole. However, no culture is completely integrated, if for no other reason than societies are continually changing, and this change in not always predictable or easily controlled by a society's major institution (the family, the polity, and religion, for example). Change occurs because societies must adapt to the internal and external demands of the social and physical environment. The way of life of some Australian aborigines has changed relatively little over hundreds of years. On the other hand, both the material and nonmaterial cultures changed rapidly in the 1960s and 1970s. One need only consider the impact of the civil rights movement, the women's movement, the gay liberation movement, the environment movement, the drug culture, and the rise of Christian fundamentalism to realize the tremendous changes that occurred during this period.

More recently, the proliferation of information available on the Internet has dramatically changed formal education in developed countries from the primary through university levels. Between "surfing the Net" and communicating with people in chat rooms, many individuals spend more time interacting with other human beings via computers than they do in face-to-face interaction. Furthermore, some researchers have concluded that a significant number of people would rather communicate by way of a computer than talk to a living, breathing human being standing right in front of them. Obviously, the implications of this alteration in the way people interact with one another are profound.

Rapid and continuous cultural change can put enormous pressure on people who are trying to determine the extent to which they should modify their values and behavior in accord with such transformations. Young people coming of age in the 1960s and 1970s raised in conservative, religious families saw friends and classmates experiment with alcohol, drugs, casual sex, and alternative lifestyles that ran contrary to the middle-class norm of going to school, getting a job, getting married, and settling down to raise a family. They had to decide whether to accept the values and standards of behavior they had been taught, or go along with the new lifestyle of an emerging youth culture.

Cultural Lag Whereas technology has developed at an extremely rapid pace in the twentieth century, not all aspects of culture have changed at a steady pace over the same period of time. Sociologist William Ogburn (1950) referred to this phenomenon as **cultural lag**—the process whereby one aspect of culture changes faster than another aspect of culture to which it is related. Ogburn noted that the social customs, patterns of organizations, and levels of technology that exist within a given society change at different rates. In modern societies, material culture (especially technology) typically changes faster than associated values, norms, and laws (nonmaterial culture).

This lag or gap means that modern humans live in a state of perpetual "maladjustment" (Ogburn, 1950). For example, medical technology now makes it possible for people to remain alive indefinitely although they may have been pronounced "brain dead" with no hope of recovery. This has resulted in a number of complex legal and ethical questions. Who should decide if and when "the plug is pulled" from a life support system? the family? doctors? one's church? the state? If an individual's head injury is the result of a crime should the "killer" of a brain dead person be tried for murder? If found guilty, should the convicted offender receive the death penalty? The fact that people are making living wills and leaving instructions about what should be done if they are rendered brain dead (regarding the donation of organs, for example) is indicative of the lag time between technological change and our adaptation to it.

After a Scottish researcher cloned a sheep in 1997, the inevitable question of how long it would take to successfully clone human beings was raised. The implications of such a possibility and the legal and moral difficulties associated with routinely reproducing people in this manner are staggering. Once again the major question, as Arthur Zucker (1997, p. 319) points out, is "How would we choose to clone and who would do the choosing?" For example, should some or all people be cloned at birth producing a genetically identical person to be used for spare parts in the event of future medical problems? How about cloning a dozen Michael Jordans, Mark McGwires, or Sammy Sosas to make a real "dream team?" Hundreds of thousands of individuals with strong backs and weak minds could be cloned to do the dirty, dangerous, and boring work that most people shun. What would the future of international war and conflict be if a subcaste of disposable soldiers could be cloned? Perhaps it was scenarios such as these that prompted the German newspaper *Die Welt* to state "The cloning of human beings would fit precisely into Adolph Hitler's plans" (in Harris, 1997, p. 354). While these possibilities may seem completely unrealistic, so, too, was the prospect of cloning any living creature only a few years ago. As one prominent biologist stated "Absolutely we're going to have the cloning of humans" (in Lampman, 1998, p. B3).

With the increasing pace and sophistication of advances in medicine, genetics, and other areas of applied science, we can expect to see more examples of nonmaterial culture (laws, values, ethical and religious systems) lagging behind. The maladjustment Ogburn spoke of appears to be a permanent condition of modern industrial societies.

Human ingenuity has been responsible for advances in technology from the production of stone tools to the launching of space probes that explore distant planets. Within the context of various political, economic, and social institutions, people ultimately decide how that technology is to be used. However, we tend to view some of these inventions as things beyond our control. In a sense, they have a life of their own, with human beings *reacting* to them rather than *determining* how they will be used. For example, many people seem to have accepted the notion that an unfortunate (yet inevitable) consequence of modernization is environmental pollution. Politicians typically speak in terms of economic growth (jobs) versus environmental protection, as though the two were inherently mutually exclusive.

SUMMARY AND REVIEW

The Roots of Human Culture

1. *From a sociological standpoint, what is culture?*
Culture is a people's way of life or social heritage that includes values, norms, institutions, and artifacts that are passed from generation to generation by learning alone. Culture provides members of a society with a world-taken-for-granted. (P. 31)

2. *Is there a difference between instincts and biological drives?*
Instincts are biologically inherited predispositions that cause members of a species to react to a given stimulus in a given, specific way. Human beings have biological drives that are experienced as bodily tensions leading to activity that restores balance. These drives can be satisfied in a variety of ways, a fact that makes cultural diversity possible and inevitable. (P. 32)

3. *How do sociobiologists explain a significant amount of human behavior?*
Sociobiologists argue that although human beings do not have instincts, some forms of behavior such as altruism and aggression are transmitted genetically from one generation to another. (P. 33)

4. *What is language?*
Human beings communicate through language—a set of sounds and symbols that have arbitrary meanings. These meanings can be arranged into an almost infinite number of combinations to convey information. (P. 34)

5. *What are the three major explanations of language acquisition?*
The three major theories of how children learn to speak are the imitation perspective, the reinforcement theory, and the innateness hypothesis. (Pp. 34–35)

6. *What is the Sapir–Whorf hypothesis?*
According to the Sapir–Whorf hypothesis, language furnishes the categories by which people interpret and make sense of the physical and social world in which they live. (P. 35)

7. *What is the relationship between language and power?*
Language also reflects and helps reinforce power relationships in society. George Orwell noted that it can diminish people's thought processes by hiding and misinterpreting information. In this sense, language is an important mechanism of social control in society. (P. 36)

8. *What is popular culture?*
Popular culture is the culture of everyday life as expressed through sport, movies, television, books, magazines, and so on. Sociologists use it as a vehicle for understanding the values, norms, and patterns of behavior of subcultures and the larger society. Popular culture also reflects a society's changing values and attitudes. (Pp. 38–39)

The Normative Order

9. *List some of the core values in the United States.*
Core values are values especially promoted by and central to the life of a given culture. Some of the most important ones in the United States are success, progress, freedom, and patriotism. The extent to which people adhere to these values is a function of race and ethnicity, social class, and individual experience. People in the lower class may stretch or modify success values so they can be more easily achieved. (Pp. 39–41)

10. *Why are norms important?*
All societies regulate people's behavior through a system of norms. The hierarchy of norms from least to most important is folkways, mores, and laws. Whereas folkways should be followed, mores must be obeyed. (Pp. 41–42)

11. *How do functionalist and conflict sociologists differ regarding the origin of norms in society?*
Functionalist sociologists see norms originating as a result of group consensus, whereas conflict theorists think that norms are created by the most powerful groups in society and used to dominate politically and exploit economically the lower classes. (P. 42)

12. *What are ethnocentrism and cultural relativism?*

Ethnocentrism is the tendency to view one's group and way of life as superior to the values and behavior of others. Ethnocentrism promotes social cohesion and a sense of "we-ness." In extreme forms, it can result in prejudice, discrimination, and even war. According to cultural relativism, any aspect of a culture can be judged only within the context of that culture. The problem with this perspective is that any behavior (genocide, for example) can be rationalized and justified. (Pp. 42–44)

13. *What is culture shock? Give an example of this phenomenon.*

Culture shock is the experience of initially encountering people who do not share one's core values and overall world view. The shock of such an experience is usually a painful reminder that values and norms can vary considerably from one culture to another. (P. 44)

Cultural Diversity and Change

14. *What is the difference between a subculture and a counterculture?*

All of us belong to a number of subcultures, groups that have norms and values in common with the larger society but also have some of their own patterns of behaviors. Countercultures reject some or all aspects of the larger, more dominant culture. Because they are opposed to some core values of the larger society, they are often associated with violence as either perpetrators or victims. (Pp. 45, 48)

15. *Are human societies culturally integrated?*

The values, norms, patterns of behavior, and institutions of individual societies are integrated to a certain extent. However, this integration is far from complete, as societies are continually changing and often experience internal strife. (P. 49)

16. *What is the pace or speed of cultural change in society?*

Some primitive groups change very slowly, whereas modern, industrial states do so much more rapidly. Change is typically uneven in industrial nations as some aspects of a society (such as technology) develop at a faster rate than people's values and behavior. According to William Ogburn, cultural lag is the process whereby one aspect of the culture changes faster than another aspect of the culture to which it is related. (Pp. 49–50)

3

Groups and Social Structure

Every year, hundreds of thousands of students graduating from all levels and all types of schools across the United States order copies of their respective alma maters' yearbooks or "annuals." When the much-awaited books finally arrive, these outgoing students, with varying degrees of delight or dismay, will relive the highlights and lowlights of their educational careers by poring through the pages of these keepsake volumes. Perhaps they will get teachers and fellow students to autograph their books and to add some appropriate (or inappropriate) written comments about shared past experiences and possible future plans. In later years, long after graduation, these now-vintage books may be periodically retrieved from garage and attic storage spaces, dusted off, and once again pored through as their now-vintage owners reminisce about their old school friends and their old school days, when life was simpler and the possibilities for their futures seemed almost endless.

Regardless of whether the particular school in question happens to be an elementary school, a junior or senior high school, or a college or university, these yearbooks follow a very familiar and remarkably similar format. At heart, they consist of collections of photographs that provide a visual chronicle of the different groups—academic classes, faculty members and administrative staff, athletic teams, campus clubs, service and social organizations—and the different group events—new student orientation, midterm and final examination weeks, homecoming dances, intramural and intermural sports contests, graduation ceremonies—that define the typical American school. This group-oriented theme is repeated in the snapshot biographies that appear beneath the individual portraits of the members of the graduating class. Besides listing each person's name and perhaps offering a few other bits of personal information, these little sketches also summarize each student's membership in various teams, clubs, and organizations, giving the reader a quick overview of that individual's participation (or lack of participa-

tion) in the life of the school community. In so doing, they offer valuable clues as to what the people behind the smiling faces are—or at least were—really like. Without really knowing particular students very well or at all, we can nonetheless gain some sense of whether they were leaders or followers, introverted or extroverted, achievers or slackers, party-minded or sports-minded or studious, by examining their history of involvement in the groups and group activities available at their school.

Our adult lives following our completion of formal education are not ordinarily likely to involve the purchase of yearbooks as we "graduate" from one occupational or residential or marital and family situation to another. But these aspects of our lives, too, are largely defined in terms of our participation in an array of groups and group experiences. For better or worse, whether by nature or by necessity, most of us spend the bulk of each day working, playing, praying, and, in general, being with other people. We are part of groups such as families, work teams, basketball squads, and church or temple congregations. In turn, these groups are part of larger social organizations such as clans, corporations, sports leagues, and religions that, together, constitute a social structure. By forming the boundaries and the contours of our surrounding society, these groups and structures are tremendously important in shaping the conditions of our individual everyday lives. They are equally important in shaping the outlines of our personal and social identities as well. To a large extent, they help us tell ourselves and others just who and what we are. In many respects, we are, quite literally, judged by the company we keep.

In this chapter, we examine groups and other types of social collectivities that, in combination with shared cultural values, beliefs, and norms, are the building blocks of human societies. We also examine societies themselves, charting their development from small and simple to incredibly large and complex human undertakings.

Questions to Consider

1. How do social groups differ from aggregates and categories?
2. What is the difference between an ascribed status and an achieved status?
3. What is a master status?
4. How does role strain differ from role conflict?
5. What is the difference between a membership group and a reference group?
6. Why do primary groups have such lasting impacts on their members?
7. What factors make the social dyad the most fragile of all social groups?
8. How does increasing group size affect relations among group members?
9. What is the difference between a utilitarian organization and a coercive organization?

Continued

10. What are the distinguishing features of bureaucratic organization?
11. What is an informal organization?
12. In what ways does the Japanese formal organization differ from traditional bureaucracy?
13. What are *gemeinschaft* and *gesellschaft*?
14. According to Lenski, how have changes in productive technology affected human societal organization?

THE CONCEPT OF SOCIAL STRUCTURE

As we observed in Chapter 1, just as the behaviors of individuals are stable rather than random over time, human social life in general is organized rather than chaotic. In every population, daily events seem to follow some pattern that is logical and makes sense to the members of the particular society. This patterning makes it possible for people to predict and anticipate what others are likely to do or say in a given situation. Using these predictions, individuals can plan their own actions accordingly.

What makes possibile an organized social life in which the behaviors of millions of individuals coordinate smoothly is a shared way of looking at the world. As we discussed in the last chapter, over a period of time the members of all human populations develop sets of values, beliefs, and norms—that is, a culture—that reflects their common, shared experiences with the surrounding world. These cultural systems give people a framework for observing and interpreting reality and a foundation for successfully dealing with one another. Within a given population, the formation of groups of different kinds, as well as the various patterned relationships that take place within and among these groups—what we term **social structure**—reflects the presence of an underlying, unifying culture.

Social structure represents the attempts of a given population to translate its particular view of the world into concrete terms. For example, in a culture whose beliefs define ordinary citizens as being capable of making intelligent decisions regarding the running of their own lives, some sort of democratic political system is likely to be the result. In this form of government, the decisions of political leaders reflect the will of the people, who maintain ultimate power and have the final say in deciding who does or does not serve in office. However, in a culture in which prevailing beliefs define ordinary citizens as being too stupid or otherwise incapable of making intelligent decisions, a more totalitarian political regime most likely will prevail. In this type of political structure, ultimate governing power is concentrated in the hands of a single person or a small group of rulers, with the overwhelming majority of population members effectively excluded from any real say in the running of their own individual and collective lives.

Whereas culture provides the members of a population with a blueprint for reality, social structure represents the rendering of that blueprint into some sort of inhabitable residence. The linkage between culture and social structure is much more complex than a simple one-way cause-and-effect relationship. Culture supplies the important backdrop against which organized social life is constructed. It lays out the pattern for assembling the different groups that will form the building blocks of social structure.

GROUPS AND OTHER COLLECTIVITIES

In ordinary language usage, the word *group* conjures up an image of numbers. We talk about such things as a group of people standing in line outside a shopping mall multiplex cinema to buy movie tickets, a group of people who share the same birth date, the group of friends with whom we study and party in college. In each case, what we have in mind is a situation involving more than one person. The specific numbers can vary anywhere from two (a couple in love) to more than 6 billion (the estimated population of the earth at the end of the twentieth century). No matter how else these groups may differ from one another, what they have in common is the fact that they all include more than one individual.

As we have already seen, the study of human groups is the central focus of sociology. But when sociologists talk of groups, they use the word in a much more restrictive way than other people. The term that properly applies to the three examples just described, as well as to any general situation featuring more than one person, is **social collectivity.** From the sociological perspective, all social groups are examples of collectivities, but not all collectivities are groups.

For example, the collection of people waiting to purchase tickets to a Friday night movie represents a **social aggregate.** Members of aggregates share the same physical space at a particular time but not necessarily anything else. As in the case of ticket buyers waiting in line, the individuals who make up an aggregate may be very different from one another in terms of race, gender, social class, personality, and many other characteristics. They may have little or nothing in common besides their physical proximity. They form a social collectivity only for as long as they remain standing together in that line. When the cinema doors open and the ticket holders disperse into the various theaters that form the multiplex, that particular aggregate will cease to exist.

In a similar way, people who were born on the same date do not constitute a group in the sociological sense of that term. Rather, they make up what is called a **social category,** a number of people who share some common characteristic(s). In this particular example, they share an identical age. By itself, the fact that these people are of the same chronological age tells us nothing at all about whether they ever did or ever will occupy the same physical space at the same time. They exist as a collectivity on paper only, as a statistical cluster based on one particular attribute. If we were to focus our attention on some other attribute, such as income level or participation in organized sports, the category would dissolve as its members were sorted into new and different statistical clusters.

Of the three examples just given, only the third—the collection of college friends—represents a true group in the sociological sense. The term **social group** refers to a number of people who possess a feeling of common identity and who interact in a regular, patterned way. To the extent that these friends think of themselves as a group and do things together (take classes, study for exams, hang out, party), they form an authentic social group. Social groups display the characteristics of both aggregates and categories. Their members often share space and time and usually share attributes and interests as well. As their members continue to interact with one another, groups develop additional traits that distinguish them from either aggregates or categories. Over time, these relationships come to form an organization or structure involving statuses and roles.

Status and Role

Status is another term that sociologists employ in a different way than nonsociologists. In ordinary usage, status implies some sort of social ranking or level of prestige. For example, we speak of certain sections of the city as being high-status neighborhoods, or of certain people we know as being very status conscious. In making these statements, what we really are saying is that such and such a neighborhood is associated with wealth and power. The

people who reside in this area are important and "classy." Someone who is known to be status conscious is perceived as being very concerned with money, fame, or other trappings of social rank. (Social class and rank are discussed in Chapter 5.)

In sociological usage, however, **status** simply means any defined or recognized position within a group or society. For example, one individual's status in the corporation that employs her may be that of municipal marketing officer, whereas a second person's status may be that of customer finance specialist. When used in this way, the term does not carry any connotations that one position is higher or better than the other. All that really is being implied is that one position is different from the other.

Ascribed Status and Achieved Status Individuals within a given society may come to occupy a particular status in any number of ways—by being something in particular (ascription), by doing something in particular (achievement), or perhaps by a combination of the two. The term **ascribed status** refers to a position assigned to individuals on the basis of their possession of some specific quality or attribute. For example, in many societies including the United States, people often are steered into certain occupations on the basis of their sex and the presumed characteristics that accompany being a member of that particular sex. Because females are believed to be naturally more nurturing than males, it is women and not men who usually perform various "mothering" jobs such as nurse, daycare worker, elementary school teacher, and other positions entailing the provision of emotional support. Because males are believed to be naturally more aggressive than females, it is most often men and not women who head corporations, law firms, governments, and other organizations in which competitiveness and even a certain amount of ruthlessness may be deemed necessary for success. The term **achieved status,** as the name might suggest, describes a position that individuals have attained on the basis of demonstrated performance or ability. In this instance, the selection criterion is not what one *is* but, rather, what one *does.* In modern societies such as the United States, achievement is at least the theoretical basis on which occupational, educational, and other important positions are filled. We attain a four-year scholarship to State University or an accounting job with the International Widgit Corporation by demonstrating that we are the best qualified candidate for the position. As we will discuss in Chapter 13, the change from ascription to achievement as the primary basis for filling social positions has been a hallmark of the societal modernization process. But even in the most modern of societies, ascribed traits in the form of race,

For most adults, occupation serves as a master status, defining their place in the social structure. These Chinese businessmen in Tianamen Square, Beijing, are easily identified as such by their trench coat "uniforms."

ethnicity, sex, and age (among others) continue to restrict the free movement of many population members into valued social positions.

Master Status   Individuals in every society normally occupy any number of statuses at a given time. But it often turns out that one such position—what sociologists call a master status—becomes the primary basis for forming the individual's social identity and general social standing. For people in premodern or traditional societies in which family and kin were the most significant groupings, location within a recognized kinship network—first-born son, for example—served as the master status from which many important social consequences flowed. According to the patriarchal practice of *primogeniture,* it was the first-born son who assumed the title (and property) of head of the family upon the death of his father. Regardless of whether or not he was the most qualified surviving family member, the first-born son automatically inherited the task of making decisions for all family members, including his mother and older sisters. For people in modern societies, occupation typically functions as a master status, shaping a host of other social experiences such as where one will live, who one will marry, what kind of overall life one is likely to lead, and perhaps even one's final resting place once that life has been concluded. (One of the authors had the experience of visiting a cemetery to pay his respects to a deceased relative, only to observe, on top of a small hill looking down on the burial ground, a large and ornate tombstone engraved with the occupation of the person being commemorated: "Here lies John Smith, M.D.") However, in those societies in which prevailing beliefs define some groups as inferior and ascription continues to play a significant part in filling social positions, one's sex or race or ethnicity or age or other devalued attribute may become one's master status, shaping the individual's access to educational, occupational, income, and other opportunities.

Formal Role and Role Performance   As noted above, the general use of the term *status* is to denote recognized positions that are different from one another. What makes these statuses different from one another is the role—the set of expected behaviors and attitudes—associated with them. The **role** or **formal role** defines what it is that someone who occupies a particular position is supposed to do. For example, because you are a student, you are expected to register for some specified number of classes, actually attend those classes, complete all assignments on time, take examinations, and do the other things that make up student life. Your instructor, on the other hand, is expected to perform the duties of a professor: to offer interesting and informative lectures, construct equitable examinations, grade students objectively and fairly, be available to students during office hours, and so on. Whereas status indicates the different recognized positions within a group or larger social body, role defines how and why these positions are different from one another.

Of course, the fact that people are supposed to think and behave in a certain way doesn't necessarily guarantee that they will or can perform exactly as expected. Sociologists recognize that formal roles define a utopian world with respect to what the holders of individual statuses should be like, whereas we live in an imperfect world in which not everyone can be the perfect student or the perfect professor. We use the concept of **role performance** to indicate an individual's actual behaviors and attitudes in response to formal role expectations. For a number of reasons, some of which are discussed in detail in Chapter 8, these everyday behaviors of real people may not always resemble the idealized actions specified by their social roles.

Role Strain and Role Conflict   Formal role expectations often are complex and difficult enough that carrying them out frequently becomes problematic. For example, despite changing gender roles in American culture, widespread beliefs continue to define adult males as the breadwinners in their families, even if their spouses are also working full time. For any number of reasons, however, some men can't find the kind of employment that would allow them to provide a comfortable life for their families. To the extent that they have accepted and internalized the assumption that they should be the ones to take care of their wives and children, these men likely will experience what sociologists call **role strain**—the inability to meet successfully all the expectations attached to a particular social role. Even if their unemployment or underemployment is the result of factors beyond their personal control (for example, a factory shutdown or job discrimination against their particular racial or ethnic group), the men may feel ashamed that they are letting their families down.

Individuals can also experience difficulty in meeting role requirements by virtue of the fact that they occupy several different statuses at the same time and may be expected to perform behaviors that are incompatible. For example, one of the things that you are at this point in your life is a student, but it is not the only thing you are. You may also be a spouse, a parent, and a full-time employee. Your professor expects you to be a good student and show up for next Wednesday night's final examination, and your husband and kids expect you to be a good wife and mother and attend the opening of your son's school play that same evening. Just to make life even more interesting, you may find that your employer expects you to be a good worker and be available next Wednesday evening for the start of a big holiday sale.

Congratulations! You have just experienced **role conflict,** the situation of being caught in the middle of the clashing role expectations that often accompany the multiple group memberships and statuses we hold in our social world. Unless you have yourself cloned or have mastered the trick of being in several different places at the same time, you will have to violate one or more of these role expectations in order to satisfy the other. Deciding which role takes top priority in your life at a particular time can be a very difficult process, but you may take some comfort in the knowledge that you are not alone in this regard. In a complex, modern society like the United States, millions of other people also find themselves between this proverbial rock and a hard place.

The moral of this story is that organized social life is much more than merely a case of individuals being plugged into statuses and then carrying out the directives of those position's associated roles. People's actual behaviors represent their attempts to negotiate a working relationship with the demands of the larger society of which they are a part. Statuses and roles may outline the structure of our social world, but they do not absolutely determine it. Groups envelop individuals but normally do not smother them. As we will see, many groups both allow and encourage the free expression of individuality by their members. Even in the most highly structured and depersonalized groups, the possibilities for human individuality are not altogether stifled.

TYPES OF SOCIAL GROUPS

Modern societies are characterized by highly differentiated social structures and populations numbering in the hundreds of millions. They also display an astonishingly large variety of social groups. Trying to understand the nature and workings of these groups on a case-by-case basis would be impossible. Consequently, sociologists have attempted to simplify the task by simplifying our conceptions of the social world.

Rather than treating each social group as a unique entity, we employ analytic devices that allow us to focus our attention on different kinds of groups. These **typologies** are ordering systems that sort and classify individual cases of some phenomenon (in this instance, social groups) on the basis of distinguishing characteristics. In effect, they create categories of groups, allowing us to examine both the common and the uncommon unique denominators of group life. Several of these typologies are of particular significance in the analysis of social groups.

Membership Groups and Reference Groups

One way of distinguishing among the various groups that make up our social environment is the nature of our involvement with them. The term **membership group** or **ingroup** (Sumner, 1960/1906) refers to a specific group to which given individuals belong and in which they participate as members. For example, if you happen to play point-guard on a basketball team, that team is, for you, a membership group. The members of your team meet on a regular basis for practice and, of course, for games against other basketball teams in the same league. Over the course of the season, you and the other team members will likely come to develop a sense of group identity and a feeling of belonging, based on your shared experiences on and off the basketball court. You may begin to think of yourselves as "we" and the rest of the world—what Sumner (1960/1906) called **outgroups**—as "they."

Sociologists regard these membership groups as important because they help us understand and perhaps predict people's behaviors and attitudes. All groups establish some pattern of norms, values, beliefs, and behaviors, and they expect and demand that their members will follow that pattern. Individuals' membership group affiliations thus provide us with a great deal of information about what they will be like. Within limits, people will do and be what the important membership groups in their life specify. For example, knowing that a particular man is a corporate executive with a $100,000 yearly salary, a registered and avid supporter of the Republican Party, and a member of several exclusive country clubs tells us something. It gives us the ability to construct a behavioral and attitudinal profile that will capture the spirit of who and what this individual is, even though we might not know him individually and personally. In this particular case, the experienced sociologist could safely discount the possibility that this man would be found marching on a picket line in support of higher wages and better working conditions for coal miners in Appalachia.

Sometimes, however, even experienced sociologists get fooled. People can and do often act in ways that are unexpected, given their membership group affiliations. For instance, despite his otherwise conservative credentials, the upper-middle-class man in our example could well have a very liberal attitude regarding the plight of mine workers in rural areas. On closer examination, we might discover that he is an amazingly sucessful son whose father and uncles had labored as unskilled workers in the anthracite mines of northeastern Pennsylvania. Even though he has traveled a great distance, both geographically and socially from his humble origins, he has never forgotten the harshness of family life in a coal company town. Though now leading an extremely comfortable existence, he remains much more sensitive than most of his current peers to the hardships and distress experienced by people in other walks of life.

Our hypothetical executives's surprising actions and attitude could not be explained in terms of his membership group linkages alone. On the contrary—if anything, knowing his objective group ties would lead to the opposite conclusion. His feelings about coal miners could be understood only by recognizing his subjective identification with a group in which he does not really participate as a member. Although not himself a member of any workers' advocacy group such as the United Mine Workers or the AFL-CIO, he is perhaps using one of these organizations as a **reference group,** a group whose values, beliefs, norms, and behaviors come to serve as the basis for one's own daily life.

For the most part, individuals' membership groups and reference groups are one and the same. As we have already stated, all groups exert pressure on their members to conform to group norms and values. As we will see in the next chapter, most individuals internalize their membership groups' perspectives, incorporating them into their own developing world views. However, on many occasions, membership groups and reference groups are not the same entities. For example, people who are in the process of preparing for some future social status often adopt

the perspective and behaviors of this sought-after group before they actually gain admission to it, a phenomenon known as **anticipatory socialization.** In the law school parking lot at a certain local university, for instance, sits a car with personalized license plates adorning the front and rear bumpers. The plates' message—"SUE THEM"—suggests that at least one aspiring lawyer has started to think the part. In a similar vein, some undergraduate pre-med students have been observed arriving for classes dressed in hospital "greens," even though they have just begun their long journey toward an M.D. degree.

At any given moment, then, individuals' behaviors and attitudes reflect the perspectives of both the groups in which they participate objectively as members and the reference groups with which they identify subjectively, perhaps as would-be members. As we will see, the nature of these objective and subjective groups has a great deal to do with the resulting orientations and actions of their respective members.

Primary Groups and Secondary Groups

Although it may be true, as the Declaration of Independence states, that all people are created equal, the same thing cannot be said of social groups. From your own experiences, you may realize that some groups (the friends whom you hang out on the weekend) are occasions for unwinding and just being yourself. Others (your community's town or city council) are no-nonsense vehicles for getting some specific job done. Some groups (the people who show up on Saturday morning for a game of pickup soccer) just seem to develop or happen over time. Others (the board of directors of the International Widgit Corporation) are deliberately and carefully created. Some groups (the regular Monday night football and pizza crew) are enjoyable and fun to be part of. Others (a sequestered jury in a prolonged criminal trial) may represent nobody's idea of a good time.

One of the first sociologists to draw these kinds of distinctions was Charles Horton Cooley, an important figure at the University of Chicago during the first few decades of this century. As we saw in Chapter 1, Cooley was interested in the process of human social interaction and its effects on individuals' perceptions of reality. He regarded involvement in group relations as a crucial mechanism for the social learning that gives humans a sense of their world and of their own humanity.

In looking at the connection between group involvement and human social learning, Cooley (1909) focused on the impact of what he called **primary groups.** These are groups such as the family in which individuals typically have their first social experiences and receive their first important lessons about social reality. Primary groups are essential in the formation of individual self-identity. It is through continuous and close interaction with primary groups that individuals begin to develop a self-concept, a notion of who and what they are in relation to the world.

Cooley determined that primary groups have such an important and lasting impact on their members because of the nature of the relationships that occur within them (see Table 3.1). The members, like families, are bound together in warm emotional relations. They interact as total or complete personalities, bringing with them to the relationship everything that is significant about them. Families and other primary group members (e.g., close friends) know and care about each other as individuals, and identify strongly with one another. Their interactions often tend to be spontaneous and usually involve face-to-face contact. Because of their emotionally supportive and satisfying atmosphere, these groups become valued by their members as ends in themselves. Families and friends seek each other out for the intrinsic or internal reward of being together. *business*

In contrast, **secondary groups** (a term implied but not actually used by Cooley himself) are less inclusive, less emotional, more formalized groupings created and organized for some specific purpose. A mortgage loan officer and her clients provide a good *working* example of this type of group.

In this particular relationship, the members of the group are directed to some defined goals—the securing of a real estate loan for a new home purchase, for example. Their interactions are limited to the issue at hand and typically follow established routines. The loan officer has a series of standard questions to ask the applicants concerning financial assets and liabilities and the nature of the property for which a loan is being sought. The applicants have sets of financial documents and receipts to give the loan officer. Some appropriate pleasantries ("Nice to see you, how are you doing?") may be exchanged, but the real focus of the group meeting is the preparation and completion of all the many forms typically necessary to obtain a mortgage loan. The complicated process of navigating through all the steps required to complete a real estate loan may generate any number of emotional responses from people, but the exchange of information between the loan officer and the loan applicants will be done impersonally and factually, as will the eventual signing of the final legal documents.

To a large extent, members of secondary groups are interchangeable. They are not so much individuals as they are role players. Within limits, all properly trained real estate loan officers are capable of completing the same types of mortgage transactions. Within limits, all individual loan applicants fall into recognizable categories, based on income level, credit history, and other relevant factors. Mortgage loan applicants may choose from among any number of loan companies and loan officers simply by paging through a telephone directory or their local newspaper's real estate section. Mortgage loan officers will deal with any number of clients during a given time period, especially when loan interest rates are low or have fallen.

Although the members of secondary groups may come to value their shared group experiences, the value lies in the group's utilitarian function, not in the relationship itself; that is, people find the group to be an important means to some other goal. Neither the mortgage loan officer nor the loan applicants may like one another personally or care to be in one another's company for any length of time, but will do so if it is to their mutual advantage. The applicants receive a loan that makes the purchase of their dream home possible; the loan officer receives a healthy commission for her professional services. These external or extrinsic rewards may be enough

TABLE 3.1	

Characteristics of Primary and Secondary Group Relationships

Primary Group (families, close friends)	Secondary Group (loan officer, clients)
Total personality involvement	Segmented personality involvement
Emotional warmth	Emotional coolness
Spontaneity, informality	Patterning, formality
Direct (fact-to-face) contact	Indirect (not face-to-face) contact
Smaller size	Larger size
Valued as end (intrinsic rewards)	Valued as means to end (extrinsic rewards)

to bring the group members together in the future for mortgage loan refinancing.

Such formulations of primary and secondary groups represent what sociologists call **ideal types**—logical constructions that present, in exaggerated and idealized form, the distinguishing features of some phenomenon. In the real social world, groups exist as combinations of both primary and secondary group characteristics. Even in such primary groups as friends and lovers, relationships can take a more formalized, depersonalized turn (perhaps an indication that the relationship is cooling), and relationships in such secondary groups as large-scale formal organizations often become highly personal. In this context, the terms *primary* and *secondary* should be thought of as representing the end points on a range of possibilities for social group relations, rather than as valid empirical descriptions of specific groups.

Thus, we could envision a continuum or array, with different groups located along the continuum in terms of how primary-like or secondary-like their atmosphere and members' interactions appeared to be (see Figure 3.1). At one extreme, we might list groups such as parent and child, or lover and lover, that come very close to approximating the ideal formulation of primary groups. Here, individual identities and complete, emotion-based interactions reach their maximum level.

Moving over a bit, we might list groups such as first- or second-grade school classes. These groups manage to retain much of their personal, emotional atmosphere while introducing specifically defined goals and more formalized, secondary relationships.

Continuing, we might recognize larger groupings created for a specific purpose and exhibiting clearly defined status and role structures but retaining something of a scaled-down, homey atmosphere. Small, "mom-and-pop" businesses that pride themselves on their friendly and personalized service might be located here.

The larger, single-unit business firm might be our next stopping point, as we begin to move well into secondary group territory. With staff and employees numbering into the hundreds, workers can become interchangeable units—names rather than faces and numbers rather than names.

Finally, at the other extreme, we might identify bodies such as modern multiple-unit corporations that seem to exhibit nothing but secondary group characteristics. These entities clearly exist for specific and defined objectives that are impersonal (economic profits). Interaction patterns are established through a set of corporate policies and directives, and individuals become and remain members on the basis of measurable skills, rather than personal identities or qualities. Participation is instrumental ("It's a job") and will end under clearly defined conditions (a better job offer, retirement, dismissal for a specified cause). However, as we will see shortly, even these gigantic groupings are not entirely devoid of primary-group undercurrents.

The Effects of Group Size Although the relationship is far from perfect, sociologists have long noted a significant association between group size and the likelihood of primary-like or secondary-like relations.

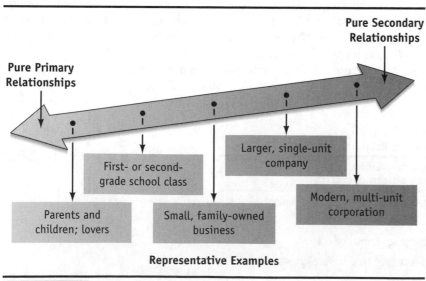

Pure Secondary Relationships

Pure Primary Relationships

Larger, single-unit company

First- or second-grade school class

Small, family-owned business

Parents and children; lovers

Modern, multi-unit corporation

Representative Examples

FIGURE 3.1

The Primary–Secondary Group Continuum

The classic work in this area is that of Georg Simmel (1858–1918), a German sociologist whose analysis of two- and three-person social groups (1950/1908) triggered interest in what is now called group dynamics or the sociology of small groups. Simmel was particularly interested in the effects of group size on the nature and the strength of the social bonds that formed between members.

According to Simmel, the **dyad,** or two-person group, is the most basic and intimate of all possible human groupings. It is in the social dyad (for example, that formed by married couples, two siblings, or two best friends) that personal identities and emotional relations are maximized, since only one linkage is possible between the members. The dyad is also special in the sense that it is the most fragile of social groups. Since it depends so heavily on the particular characteristics of its two members, the character of a given social dyad will be destroyed if either one leaves the relationship. Replacing one member with another creates an entirely new dyadic group, rather than a continuation of the old group. The dyad is thus the most mortal type of social group, existing only as long as its original members.

The addition of a third person to a dyadic relationship creates what Simmel termed a **triad.** The social triad marks the beginning of more-complex social interaction patterns and the development of an identifiable group structure. Three relationships now are possible, and the addition of the newcomer qualitatively alters the previous direct bond that may have existed between the original pair. Think, for instance, of the effect that a developing love interest between one of two siblings or best friends and a third person would have on the original relationship. Very often, it seems, one of the parties begins to feel like the proverbial third wheel, experiencing a distinct change in the previous relation. Simmel in fact noted a strong tendency for triads to re-form into a coalition of two members against the third, an observation that was confirmed by Theodore Caplow (1968). However, Simmel also examined other possible roles of the third person in a triad, including that of mediator when relations between the other two became strained.

The addition of other members dramatically increases the number of interaction linkages within the group. In turn, the rapidly expanding linkages create strong pressures to decrease personal relations and a movement toward more formal, role-defined, secondary involvement patterns. Larger group size makes it increasingly difficult to form primary-like relations with all the other members. A likely consequence is thus the creation of smaller, more intimate groups within groups. As we will see in the remaining sections of this chapter, the increase in size and complexity of societal populations has been linked historically to the qualitative change from primary to secondary relations at all levels of group life.

Formal Organizations

In our everyday lives, we routinely deal with a variety of special-purpose groups created to provide us with essential products and services. Our breakfast food probably came from the neighborhood branch of a regional or national supermarket chain. We prepare it using conventional, microwave, or toaster ovens manufactured by an electrical appliances company, as we watch the morning news on network television. Hopping into a vehicle mass-produced by one of the major domestic or foreign automobile companies, we head to our job in one of the large downtown firms that make up the local business sector. After work, we may rush to our classes at the community college where we are completing our general education courses before transferring to State University. As we drive along a freeway built and maintained by our state's transportation department, we are careful to keep an eye peeled for highway patrol or local police radar checks. No sense ending up in traffic court or traffic safety school again because of another speeding ticket!

These **formal organizations** are large, deliberately planned groups with established personnel, procedures, and rules for carrying out some particular objective or set of objectives (Scott, 1992). Producing reliable consumer goods, communicating important information, educating young adults, and developing mass transit systems are only a few such possible goals. In modern societies such as the United States, formal organizations have come to dominate the social landscape. They absorb the time, energy, and resources of countless millions of individuals who interact with them as employees, clients, regulators, or competitors. Formal organizations are both indicators and consequences of the increasing rationalization and elaboration of contemporary social life.

Types of Formal Organizations

In an attempt to make their analytic tasks more feasible, students of formal organizations have constructed typologies of the various kinds found in modern societies. One of the best known of these classification systems was developed by sociologist Amitai Etzioni (1975), who distinguished among normative, coercive, and utilitarian organizations on the basis of their members' motives for participation.

Normative Organizations   Sometimes also referred to as *voluntary associations,* **normative organizations** include charitable and community service groups as well as other public interest associations (for example, United Way, CHAD, Rotary Club, Girl Scouts or Boy Scouts, and youth sports leagues). People join them because they perceive the organizations' goals as being socially or morally worthwhile. The satisfaction members receive from participation is a sense of contributing to a good cause, rather than financial or other material payoffs. In this society, churches, schools, hospitals, and a host of other important social groupings historically have depended on the volunteer activities of their members.

Coercive Organizations   By way of contrast, this type of organization might be termed an *involuntary association.* **Coercive organizations** are formal organizations that force people to join and typically remove them from normal contact with the larger society for the duration of their membership. They also were described by Erving Goffman (1961) under the term "total institutions." Prisons and military boot camps are examples of this type of formal organization. As we will see in the next chapter, coercive organizations often are settings for a dramatic kind of adult social learning called resocialization.

Utilitarian Organizations   Etzioni's third type of formal organization, the **utilitarian organization,** attracts members who are seeking some sort of tangible, material benefit from their participation. People go to work for businesses, banks, or other corporations in order to make a living. Students en-

better yourself benefits

The separation of complex activities into more specialized individual tasks is a hallmark of bureaucratic organization. Specific functions are assigned to designated bureaus or offices whose members are selected on the basis of technical expertise. Sometimes, however, the resulting compartmentalization can lead to a sense of isolation and a decrease in organizational efficiency.

roll in universities to earn the degrees that will allow them to make a better living for themselves. Factory workers join labor unions to protect their rights and to give them better bargaining positions in their negotiations with management. Strictly speaking, membership in utilitarian organizations is voluntary rather than coerced. However, in modern societies in which most major societal activities have become specialized and elaborated, these organizations may be the only game in town. People who want or need a job, an education, or protection of their interests may have little choice but to join one of the many economic, educational, political, or other utilitarian organizations that, for better or worse, have come to define and dominate the social structure.

Bureaucratic Organization

The German sociologist Max Weber (1864–1920) was one of the first social scientists to offer a detailed analysis of formal organizations. He argued that the increasing complexity and division of labor in modern societies stimulates the development of patterned, formalized administrative procedures. These structures are necessary to coordinate the activities of the large groups that constitute the personnel in specialized units such as governments and businesses. Weber's systematic presentation of the principles and practices of administration (1946/1919) became a classic in the field of formal organizational research not only in sociology, but in business management, education, and other related fields as well.

According to Weber, bureaucratic organization is the tool that promotes successful administration in modern society. He saw **bureaucracy** as a device for maximizing human efficiency through the logical, orderly structuring of individual behaviors within a particular setting. Reduced to its essentials, bureaucratic organization is a set of principles for matching people, procedures, and circumstances to produce the highest level of productivity possible. In its pure or ideal form, bureaucracy involves several elements.

1. The different jobs necessary to fulfill organizational goals are identified, and objective, standard procedures are established for each. Specific jobs are assigned to designated positions, which are grouped in offices or "bureaus." Each bureau is responsible for completing the set of tasks assigned to it.
2. Each bureau is provided with the authority, personnel, and other resources required to meet its assigned jobs. Positions are filled on the basis of talent and ability rather than subjective, personal characteristics, and individuals are promoted on the basis of performance.

3. Individual bureaus are linked to one another through an established hierarchy of communications and decision-making channels. Each bureau is under the authority of, and reports to, the next higher bureau in the structure. The hierarchy defines the areas of responsibility and authority of each position in the organization.

4. Organizational norms govern interactions among members of the bureaucracy, as well as those between bureaucrats and the organization's clients and customers. All such interactions involve objective and impartial secondary relationships in which all members of a given category are treated alike.

5. A clear distinction is made between organizational life and personal life. Bureaucrats do not "own" their positions or the resources associated with them, nor do officials have authority over their subordinates in matters not related to organizational activities. Great care is taken to divorce objective, rational, goal-directed organizational concerns from the subjective, personal, and often emotional concerns of individuals.

In modern societies whose large populations are linked together in a variety of complex networks, many activities are too important to be left to chance. They require intelligent planning and coordination, and this is what bureaucracy is all about. It is hardly a coincidence that the overwhelming majority of our government, military, business, and most other private and public sector organizations are established and run according to the principles of bureaucratic organization. In a society that values and requires rational efficiency, bureaucracy can fill the bill.

Bureaucratic Shortcomings

If you have been reading this description of bureaucracy with a growing amount of skepticism, you are not alone. In the experience of many people, bureaucratic organization is associated with anything but smooth, efficient activity. Very often, it seems that little or nothing of substance actually is accomplished in bureaucracies. Wheels spin, people move, memos fly, but nothing seems to come out the other end. Somewhere along the way, the theory of bureaucratic organization seems to have lost something in translation as it moved from the logical realm of the ideal-type formulation to the less-than-ideal realm of the empirical world.

Bureaucracies often seem slow and unable to respond to novel situations demanding rapid social action. Because they view the world in terms of well-defined categories with clear-cut boundaries, they appear to grind to a halt when faced with peo-

ple, things, or situations that don't fit recognized patterns. When certain phenomena do not clearly fall into any one office's area of responsibility, they often become no one's responsibility. They can get lost, and stay lost, in the bureaucratic cracks. Bureaucrats seem unable or unwilling to interpret events and assume responsibility on their own (Silver and Geller, 1978). Things must be clarified and authorized by some higher-ranking office, and while this process is taking place, matters are left in a state of limbo. "No action is better than the wrong action" seems to sum up the operating philosophy of many career bureaucrats.

Government bureaucracies, in particular, seem to reflect and magnify the worst, rather than the best, potentials of bureaucratic organization. Whether democratic, socialist, or something in between, government agencies in many societies have become sources of constant frustration to the hapless citizens who must deal with them. In Venezuela, for example, citizens who attempt to follow proper channels and procedures rather than pay a bribe to one of the 1.35 million workers who make up the government bureaucracy can find themselves forced to make two dozen or more visits to the immigration office simply to acquire a travel visa. Venezuela's bloated bureaucracy, which employs one out of every six workers in the country and consumes a disproportionate share of the annual national budget, has been described as "a thousand-headed monster" by one of its own cabinet officers (Supelano, in Jones, 1997). The People's Republic of China once provided an "iron rice bowl" of lifetime employment to the 8 million civil servants who comprise the world's largest government bureaucracy. Reformist premier Zhu Rongji has vowed to cut the increasingly expensive and inefficient public workforce in half by the end of the year 2001, but faces extremely strong opposition from entrenched bureaucrats (Platt, 1998).

Bureaucratic Ritualism

Bureaucracies frequently give the impression of being more concerned with following rules to the letter than with doing a job or solving a problem. This phenomenon has been described as **bureaucratic ritualism** or **goal displacement** and is widely recognized both in the sociological literature (Blau and Meyer, 1987; Merton, 1968) and in popular literature. Anyone who has read Ken Kesey's powerful novel *One Flew Over the Cuckoo's Nest* (1962) will not easily forget "the Big Nurse," the perfect bureaucrat who was so consumed with maintaining order in her mental hospital ward that none of her patients ever received any genuine rehabilitative care. The activities that would have helped them therapeutically might have threatened the carefully created routine that she had worked so hard to establish. It was only after the hero, McMurphy, had completely disrupted Miss Ratched's mind-numbing ward pattern that any effective therapy occurred. But McMurphy's eventual fate at the hands of the enraged Big Nurse demonstrated chillingly what can happen to those who dare to challenge the bureaucratic machinery. In the entrenched ritualistic worlds of bureaucracies, messengers of change are not normally welcomed with open minds or open arms.

If these widespread perceptions of bureaucratic inefficiency are even partially accurate, how is it that bureaucracies are able to accomplish as much as they seem to? After all, U.S. political, military, and corporate organizations could not have been nearly as successful as they have been if they were subject only to the sorts of pathologies just described. Somehow, someone must be doing something right.

The Informal Organization

One answer lies in the existence of what often is called the informal organization that develops in the shadow of, and in response to, the formal bureaucratic structure. The **informal organization** can be thought of as the actual set of relationships developed by the real people who are the nameless, faceless officeholders plotted on organizational charts. If the formal structure exists in the diagrams that hang on corporate executives' walls or that appear in the company's annual stockholder report, the informal structure exists in the minds and the actions of the company's staff. In their daily activities, these flesh-and-blood people translate the generic procedures defined by bureaucratic principles into specific behaviors designed to fit immediate needs. Their friendships (and antagonisms) for one another fill in the emotional vacuum created by impersonal organizational rules and may help close gaps or loopholes in the formal structure that otherwise could cause severe difficulties for the organization.

For example, secretaries in universities or corporations and company clerks in military units typically establish primary group relations with other secretaries or clerks. They take coffee breaks together, have lunch together, swap war stories together (figuratively or literally), and do things for each other. These personal networks often can transmit information and supply or acquire necessary resources much faster than established bureaucratic channels. Information or materials that are required in a hurry can be received in a hurry. Activities that may be impeded by bureaucratic policies and channels can be facilitated by stepping outside the established structure. In an ironic way, ignoring the formal structure

can help preserve it. Since the members of bureaucracies spend a significant portion of their daily lives within these structures, they invariably attempt to make their organizational "homes" as comfortable as possible. In the process of so doing, they may strengthen and stabilize the structures.

Of course, it would be incorrect and rash to assume that these informal structures always work to the formal organization's advantage. In cases in which the organizational members perceive their best interests being threatened by the imposed official pattern, they may use informal, primary-group networks to resist or sabotage bureaucratic goals (Gouldner, 1954a, 1954b). When formal and informal organizational demands or expectations conflict, those of the informal structure may prevail for many individuals. They arise from primary-group relations that may be more satisfying and meaningful to participants than the depersonalized, secondary-formal structure.

Alternatives to Bureaucracy

At any given moment, the harmony between formal and informal structures is contingent on a number of factors whose fluctuations could generate deep antagonisms between the official and the unofficial faces of organizational life. If formal organizations are to be successful over the long run, they must satisfy human, as well as organizational, needs and goals. Many critics, including sociologist George Ritzer, argue that, by their very nature, bureacracies are unable to accomplish a compatible alliance of this sort. Ritzer views the increasing implementation of the bureaucratic method into many sectors of modern life, which he refers to as "the McDonaldization of society" (Ritzer, 1996), as antithetical to the human spirit. He and other critics claim that there must be a better way of organizing modern societal activities without doing serious harm to those who perform them.

One alternative that briefly stirred a great deal of interest and attention in the U.S. and other Western societies was the Japanese corporate model, Japan's answer to Western-style bureaucracy. For nearly fifty years, from the ruins of World War II until the beginning of the 1990s, Japanese business firms were amazingly successful in establishing that country as perhaps the world's greatest economic power.

Compared to the bureaucratic organization as described by Max Weber, the Japanese formal organization is an interesting mixture of more-authoritarian and more-democratic elements, of rational, goal-directed, and emotional, people-directed relations. The structure of the Japanese corporation was first described by William Ouchi (1981) in his analysis of "Theory Z."

According to Ouchi, the large Japanese business firm differs from the U.S. corporation in several major respects. First, in Japan, employees' relationships with the organization are much longer lasting. Japanese workers are not nearly as prone to changing jobs as their U.S. counterparts. For many Japanese, occupational careers unfold within a single organization.

Second, Japanese hiring, promotion, and pay practices emphasize groups, rather than individuals. The cohorts of employees who were initially hired together move through the ranks of the organization together. In the United States, by way of contrast, individual workers compete against one another for advancement in what amounts to a zero-sum game.

Third, unlike U.S. organizations, which demand a high level of specialized expertise from their employees, the Japanese corporation stresses a more generalized sphere of knowledge. Employees often are rotated through a series of different positions to give them a more complete picture of the various facets of the organization. This practice gives workers a greater understanding of the company's overall operations and objectives.

Fourth, the Japanese corporation is much more involved in the personal lives of its workers; that is, in their activities outside the company and many of their behaviors within the organization that Americans might regard as private matters. For example, a number of Japanese companies begin the work day with mandatory group calisthenics for all workers. As a result of this holistic orientation, primary-like social ties form between companies and workers. Thus, the company assumes the status of a second family.

Finally, decision making in the Japanese corporation is far less centralized and less "top-down" than in the typical U.S. bureaucracy. Workers are given opportunities to participate in a far wider and more significant range of work-related decisions. Through the medium of quality control (QC) circles that meet on a weekly or more frequent basis, Japanese employees can exercise meaningful input into the conditions of their jobs. Such participation gives them a sense of compatibility and harmony between their personal interests and goals of those of the company.

Despite its seeming potential compared to the traditional bureaucratic model, the Japanese organizational system has not been widely embraced by the Western industrial nations. During the 1980s and early 1990s, a number of companies in the United States and in Great Britain experimented with the Japanese corporate model, but with no real success. The model is, after all, the product of a very group-centered social and cultural philosophy that emphasizes belonging, duty, and obligation to a collectivity outside oneself. In much more individual-centered cultures with strong values on personal autonomy and democracy, the Japanese system was perceived as authoritarian and heavy-handed ("Japanese Owned Factories," 1992; Murray, 1992). Additionally, the collapse of the Japanese economy and the resulting widespread recessions of the 1990s led that country to reconsider its mode of doing business and to begin to adopt a more Western-style bureaucratic format, including individualized merit pay, dismissal of underperforming workers, and the "downsizing" of large numbers of employees in response to declining business revenues (Schmit, 1999).

It may be impossible to transplant an organizational structure developed in a radically different cultural setting to our own place and time, but there is no reason to assume that the traditional bureaucratic organization is the only viable way of doing things. In recent years, many U.S. companies (for example, Apple Computers, and Ben & Jerry's Ice Cream) have begun to experiment with more human-oriented, flexible administrative structures, particularly as more women have entered the full-time workforce and have risen to higher levels within that workforce (CNN Special reports, 1992). These arrangements attempt to capture some of the family atmosphere of the Japanese system while recognizing domestic cultural beliefs and priorities for individual expression. Research by sociologist Rosabeth Moss Kanter (1983, 1985) indicates that companies that are able to humanize their administrative structures are more profitable than those adhering to more traditional, rigid, bureaucratic procedures. In the context of an increasingly competitive global economy, success in finding a newer and better way of organizing and encouraging the productive efforts of the workforce may well become a matter of survival.

SOCIETIES AND SOCIETAL DEVELOPMENT

As discussed in Chapter 1, human societies were the focal point for the earliest sociologists and still are the basic unit of analysis for functionalists and other macro-level theorists. **Societies** can be defined as self-perpetuating groups of people who occupy a given territory and interact with one another on the basis of a shared culture. Having said that, we now can backtrack a bit to add on the limiting and qualifying phrases for which sociological definitions have become famous.

Like other groups (e.g., families, friends, neighbors, work associates), societies consist of some number of people whose patterned social interactions are based on a common definition of reality. In this instance, however, a society can be envisioned as the largest group of individuals within a specified territory who share the same world view. A group of friends share common beliefs and values, but those same beliefs and values may be held by people who are not part of that particular friendship; in fact, even people who are enemies may have much the same world view. Thus, societies are more encompassing than other types of human groups in the sense that they include many more individuals than any other group in the same geographical area.

Societies also differ from other social groups by virtue of the fact that they are self-perpetuating; that is, unlike the smaller groups contained within them, societies provide all the necessary resources and services to sustain their members over time and to replace the members who die or otherwise leave over the course of time. City councils and Girl Scout troops normally do not reproduce themselves biologically. New members for these groups must be recruited from the outside society. A family group may (and usually does) perpetuate itself through biological reproduction, but even that process requires other families to provide appropriate reproductive partners. Neither city councils, Girl Scout troops, nor families normally are capable of fulfilling all the economic, recreational, medical, nutritional, and other life-sustaining needs of their respective members. To accomplish this, they have to interact with other groups within the larger society.

Sociologists have made the study of human societies the central focus of their discipline. In fact, the literal (i.e., dictionary) definition of sociology is "the science of society." It was the massive changes sweeping through eighteenth-century European societies that triggered the creation of this field. Since that time, sociologists have continued their efforts to describe, explain, and predict how and why societies change over time. Their analyses have led to the development of a variety of typologies and models of societal structures. Some of these models are discussed below and later, in more detail, in Chapter 13.

Durkheim and Tönnies

The French sociologist Emile Durkheim saw the development of human societies as tied up with twin processes he called the *division of labor* and the *specialization of function*. Over the passage of centuries, human societies have grown progressively larger. As populations increased, what had been a simple but workable arrangement in which everyone participated in all necessary jobs became too inefficient to meet growing needs. It was refined into a more elaborate system in which specific individuals and groups began to specialize in particular tasks. As occupational structures became more complex, the members of societies became more and more unlike one another by virtue of their specialized roles and social functions. The **mechanical solidarity** or social cohesiveness of a community tied together by the common values and beliefs of its members began to be replaced by **organic solidarity;** that is, cohesiveness grounded in the interdependency and interlocking of functionally differentiated social statuses. Societies that had been anchored by the sameness of their people now began to be united by their members' differences (Durkheim, 1966/1895).

A similar theme had been developed a few years earlier by the German sociologist Ferdinand Tönnies (1855–1936). Tönnies (1963/1887) saw traditional human societies as organized along the lines of what he called **gemeinschaft** ("communal") relations among population members. In these societies, people interacted with one another on the basis of longstanding customs and personal emotions. Kinship and friendship groupings were of great importance, and people were known for who they were. In short, this type of society was premised on what we would call primary-group relations.

As societies increased in population size and became more highly differentiated, however, the quality of social relations changed dramatically. Interactions among individuals became more formal, impersonal, calculated, and directed to particular goals. For example, whereas people in traditional societies might exchange or barter goods and services with their neighbors, members of modern societies shop at food, clothing, hardware, and other specialized stores. They are not known as individuals, but rather are customers, paying a predetermined sum of money to an unknown clerk in exchange for items that were mass-produced by still other strangers in a factory located perhaps hundreds of miles away. Tönnies argued that, in this type of **gesellschaft** ("association") society, secondary-group relations dominate people's daily lives, just as large-scale formal organizations dominate all spheres of societal activity. Everyday life is more rational, efficient, and, perhaps, alienating. People who once had been oriented and integrated into emotional, cohesive groupings now are self-oriented and individualistic. For many members of societies that are in passage from gemeinschaft to gesellschaft forms of organization, the change can be troublesome.

For example, as a developing nation, Brazil is now going through the same kinds of structural and relational changes described a century ago by Durkheim and Tönnies. Rural peasants and many members of the urban lower and working classes in that country display apparent deep feelings of distrust, alienation, and hostility toward the large bureaucracies that now define Brazilian politics and business. The "popular classes" perceive these governmental and economic bodies as increasingly uninterested in and removed from the concerns and needs of a large majority of the people. In many cases, they have responded by retreating into the relative security of family relations.

But past experience indicates that the massive changes associated with societal modernization do not bypass the family. As we will see in Chapters 9 and 13, family units and kinship structures in developing nations are profoundly affected by these wholesale social and cultural changes. As buffers between individuals and societies, primary groups such as the family must absorb a great deal of pressure coming from both directions. Their ability (or inability) to do so is a matter of utmost significance for the individual population members who are forced to go along for the ride as their society jumps—or is pushed—into the modern world.

Lenski's Evolutionary Theory of Societal Development

A more recent attempt to catalogue the developmental changes that have characterized human societies from the past to the present has been offered by U.S. sociologist Gerhard E. Lenski. Over the past three decades, Lenski (Lenski, 1966; Lenski, Nolan, and Lenski, 1995) has refined an evolutionary model of human development that links societal change to changes in economic technology. In his view, economic surpluses created through improvements in productive technology have been the catalyst for changes ranging from population size to the number and content of organized religions.

According to Lenski, for well over 90 percent of our history as a species, humans existed in scattered nomadic groups that survived on the hunting and gathering skills of their members. Small in size and simple in organization, these early societies embodied the essence of primary-group relations. Family and kinship groups were about the only recognized social units, and group ties were close and personal. Showing little social differentiation, these hunter-gatherer bands practiced a primitive egalitarianism in which hierarchical property, power, and prestige differences among individuals were minimal. The need to be able to follow food supplies, as well as the absence of any real economic surplus, prevented the development of any significant or permanent social differences.

As our ancestors learned the rudiments of simple farming, things began to change significantly. With the advent of settled horticultural villages and the creation of food surpluses, populations began to grow and a division of labor began. The presence of surplus goods permitted some members of the village to be freed from actual participation in food growing or hunting. Full-time noneconomic statuses and roles were established (most notably, political and religious leaders), and these functions came to be performed by designated kinship groups. These leaders were able to acquire larger-than-average shares of social resources and to pass these advantages along to their descendants. Simple equality began to give way to simple inequalities.

The development of metal tools and other farming technologies led to the creation of agrarian societies with populations numbering into the tens of thousands, true urban settlements, complex divisions of labor, and large political, economic, and military bureaucracies. The needs of these bureaucracies and of the empires they sometimes served stimulated increasing specialization and rational planning of many societal activities. Objective, impersonal relations began to compete with more subjective and emotional primary relations in everyday life. As productive surpluses grew, so did the differential distribution of these resources to various segments of the population. Simple social inequalities began to develop into complex and significant inequalities.

Finally, within the past 300 years, the era of agrarian empires was eclipsed and replaced by the age of industrial (and, now, postindustrial) societies. The development and harnessing of mechanical power sources led to a dramatic shift from agriculture to manufacturing (and, now, to administrative and service work) as the major productive sources of economic wealth, power, and prestige. Societal populations grew extremely large and became thoroughly urbanized, rationalized, educated, differentiated, and stratified. Most areas of societal activity came under the influence of the large, specialized formal organizations that made up the framework of governmental, economic, educational, and other major institutions. In response to the increasing rationalization of human efforts, deliberate and impersonal secondary relationships began to characterize most spheres of social life. The modern age had arrived.

Durkheim, Tönnies, and Lenski differed in their terminology and specific focus, but all were in agreement about the general course of societal development. Over time, we have gone from from passive responders to active planners of events. In the process, much has been gained, but perhaps something has been lost as well. In the chapters that follow, we address some of the benefits and costs of the different forms of social organizations that characterize human life in the contemporary world.

Germany

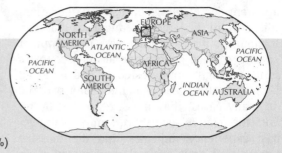

Population: 82,087,361
Life Expectancy at Birth (years): Male—74.01; Female—
    80.5
Form of Government: Federal Republic (Democracy)
Major Religions: Protestant (38%); Roman Catholic (34%)
Major Racial and Ethnic Groups: German (92%); Turkish (2%)
Population Doubling Time: No Growth
Per Capita GNP (1997 U.S. dollars): $28,280
Principal Economic Activities: Heavy Industries; Agriculture; Mining
Colonial Experience: Former Colonial Power
Adult Literacy Rate: 100% Male—100%; Female 100%

E Pluribus Einum? Reuniting a Divided Society

In April 1945, as the European theater of World War II wound down, Allied forces closed in on the German capital of Berlin, seat of the Nazi government and its leader, Adolph Hitler. As American, British, and French troops advanced on the last German stronghold from the west, they stopped to allow Soviet armies approaching from the east to enter the city first—in recognition, perhaps, of the horrendous losses suffered by the Russian people at the hands of the Nazis (an estimated 20 million Russians—including 7 million civilian men, women, and children—were killed during the Second World War). As the Soviets closed in on his bunker, Hitler, aware of his fate should he be taken alive by the Red Army, committed suicide on April 30, after ordering that his body be completely destroyed so that it could not fall into the possession of the vengeance-minded Russians. On May 8, 1945, Germany formally and unconditionally surrendered, ending the war in Europe.

However well intended the Allies' gesture of allowing the Soviets to capture Berlin may have been, it was to generate a series of unintended consequences that would shape the history of postwar Germany for the next forty-five years. Following the end of the war, the expansion of Soviet-

style communism throughout eastern Europe created an "Iron Curtain" that divided Berlin, Germany, and Europe itself in half, pitting socialism against capitalism, totalitarianism against democracy ("Berlin Airlift," 1998). Germany had been partitioned into four military zones—British, French, Soviet, and U.S. American—in the aftermath of agreements reached by those countries' leaders at the Yalta Conference in February, 1945, and the Potsdam Conference in July–August, 1945. And, although situated over 100 miles within the Soviet military zone, the city of Berlin was likewise divided into four military zones, with the eastern sector controlled by the Soviets and the western sector split among Britain, France, and the United States. This arrangement lasted less than five years as, in 1949, the Western powers–sponsored Federal Republic of Germany (FRG) and the Soviet-spearheaded German Democratic Republic (GDR) were formed as separate states, institutionalizing the division of the German nation. East Berlin was incorporated into communist-controlled East Germany, while West Berlin became part of West Germany ("Germany," 1999).

On June 24, 1948, in what has been described as "the formal declaration of the Cold War," the So-

viets blocked all ground access to West Berlin, hoping to starve the city into submission and force the Western powers to surrender it to East Germany. In response, the allies instituted "Operation Vittles," a massive airlift of food and other basic supplies that averaged 600 flights a day through the winter and into the next spring. In May, 1949, the Soviets ended their blockade, but continued to pressure for a solution to the Berlin question ("Berlin Airlift," 1998). In 1958 and, again, in 1961, Soviet Premier Nikita Khrushchev threatened to sign an agreement with East Germany that would end existing four-power agreements and effectively cede all of Berlin to East Germany unless the Western powers withdrew from West Berlin. In the meantime, between 1949 and 1961, an estimated 2.5 million East Germans fled to the West through West Berlin, threatening to destroy the fragile East German economy by draining it of skilled workers, professionals, and intellectuals. On the night of August 12–13, 1961, the Soviets suddenly began to erect a wall between the east and west sectors of the city, forcibly sealing off the residents of East Germany from their former pipeline to the West. Eventually reaching a length of nearly 30 miles through the city and another 75 miles around it, the Berlin Wall (*Berliner Mauer*) was to become the most enduring and most infamous symbol of the Cold War and the division of both Germany and Europe into East and West ("1961 Berlin Wall," 1999). But even this intimidating

15-foot-high concrete and barbed-wire-topped structure with its land mines and gun towers did not stop the flow of refugees entirely. Between 1961 and 1989, about 5,000 East Germans somehow managed to cross the Wall into the West. Another 5,000 were captured by the East German guards, and an estimated 200 to 400 more were killed in the attempt to escape to freedom ("1989 Berlin Wall," 1999).

In 1989, stimulated by the new "open" policies of Soviet Communist Party head Mikhail Gorbachev, social and economic reforms spread throughout communist Eastern Europe. In October, the hard-line East German communist government of Erich Honecker resigned, paving the way for a new, more flexible government. On November 9, 1989, that new government announced that travel restrictions for East Germans had been suspended. The next day, nearly 2 million East Germans crossed into the West. After 28 years, the hated Berlin Wall had come down, touching off celebrations around the world ("The Berlin Wall," 1999). By the end of the month, West German Chancellor Helmut Kohl announced plans for the reunification of East and West Germany.

On October 3, 1990, following free elections held in East Germany the previous March and approval by the West German parliament, Germany was re-united for the first time in over four decades ("Germany," 1999). In December, 1990, the first all-German election since the end of World War II was held, with Kohl's conservative Christian Democratic Union emerging to lead the new, unified government. German structural reunification had been formally attained, but the real work of uniting the two Germanies was just about to begin ("German Reunification," 1997; "1989 Berlin Wall," 1999).

You may recall, from our earlier discussion of societal develop-

The dismantling of the Berlin Wall opened up East Germany to the West—as well as a host of economic and social problems for the new "unified" Germany. Successful reunification of the country remains an ongoing goal and dilemma for the German government and the German people.

ment, that the French sociologist Emile Durkheim argued that societies are brought and held together by one or the other of two forces. In smaller, more simple societies, it is *mechanical solidarity*, the essential similarities of population members, that helps form the cohesive bonds necessary to maintain social order. Individuals can create and maintain viable social structures because they view and respond to the world in fundamentally similar terms. The result, in the words of one of Durkheim's contemporaries, the German sociologist Ferdinand Tönnies, is the *gemeinschaft* or "communal" society, characterized by primary-like groups and relationships. In larger, more complex societies, it is the *organic solidarity* brought about by the functional interdependence of the individual members of what are now larger, more heterogeneous populations that holds the system together. Even though individuals may be increasingly unlike or dissimilar to one another in many important respects, they depend on one another to survive, and it is that need that creates cohesion

and cooperation—what Tönnies called the *gesellschaft* or "associational" society dominated by large, secondary groups and rational, impersonal relationships. In the case of the 1990 reunification of East and West Germany, however, it seemed that neither of these two forces was present—at least not in the short run. For the first few years following reunification, the new Federal German Republic faced enormous integration problems that brought it worldwide attention and notoriety.

Although the population members of the prewar Weimar Republic and the wartime Third Reich may have shared a set of values and beliefs that translated into a common world view and a sense of peoplehood (and this assertion, itself, is a matter of some debate), that certainly was no longer the situation in the Germany that emerged on October 3, 1990. After almost half a century of living under radically different social, economic, and political conditions, the members of the former East Germany and West Germany were, in many basic respects, "foreigners" to one another.

In East Germany, life in the immediate post-war years was not appreciably different from what it had been during the war. As was the case during Hitler's reign, political democracy existed more as a slogan than as a reality. The country remained a totalitarian, single-party state, albeit communist rather than fascist. That communist government systematically suppressed institutions that fostered a civil society and imposed on the people a rigid social conformity maintained, in large part, by the despised and feared *Stasi,* the East German secret police (Kim, 1998b). And, much like the Third Reich in the final years of the war, the industrial economy of East Germany was largely non-operative. It had been weakened to the point of collapse by heavy reparations paid to the Soviet Union and by the steady flight of millions of skilled workers and professionals to the West. Increasing economic hardships led to a widespread workers' revolt and subsequent Soviet army intervention in 1953. In 1954, in an effort to bolster East Germany's faltering economy, the U.S.S.R. ended its collecting of war reparation payments. But the Soviets were unable to supply the immense capital needed to modernize the country's obsolete industrial infrastructure, leaving East Germany with a chemical- and manufacturing-based economy that was capable only of producing low-grade products in the "command market" system of the eastern bloc countries ("Germany," 1999).

In contrast to the East German experience, West Germany, much like Japan, was almost completely transformed following the war. Thanks to massive financial assistance for the rebuilding of the country provided by the United States' Marshall Plan, the West German industrial system was modernized and upgraded. By 1990, West Germany had become the world's third largest economy,

trailing only the United States and Japan. Thanks, also, to the Western powers' policy of granting the FRG government the autonomy to make most of its own domestic policy decisions, the West German people were able to gain real experience in democratic participation as the various political parties in West Germany's parliamentary system vied for their votes. This experience seemingly imbued them with what political sociologists call *personal and political efficacy,* a sense of individual and social confidence that comes from the perception of having some control over the conditions of one's life. Finally, the West German Chancellor, Helmut Kohl, had made it West Germany's policy to attempt to atone for past German sins "by reconciling Germany with its former enemies through unquestioned allegiance to the European Union and the Atlantic partnership . . . his determination [was] to create 'a European Germany, not a Germanized Europe' " (Drozdiak, 1998). This open and outward-looking stance stood in sharp contrast to the inward-looking, fortress-like orientation of East Germany under communist rule.

The reunification problems inherent in the different experiences and different world views of the two Germanies' populations were compounded by the fact that East Germany and West Germany approached this new union from very unequal economic positions that did not readily complement one another or translate into functional interdependency. Within a year of formal reunification the East German economy, unable to compete in the global marketplace, suffered a total collapse, with industrial production dropping by half from 1990 to 1991 ("Germany," 1999). According to some estimates, Germany (meaning West Germany) would have to invest $500 billion to restructure the East German economy in

order to turn it into a viable enterprise, an amount that would overtax the nation, which already was funding an extensive—and expensive—social welfare program ("Germany," 1994). That program was being stretched to the breaking point by the large number of people added to the welfare rolls following the economic collapse in the east and a slowdown of the previously-booming economy in the west. According to German Federal Labor Office figures, at one point, the nation's overall unemployment rate stood at nearly 13 percent, with the rate topping an astounding 20 percent in the eastern states. As of 1998, the national unemployment rate had dropped to 10.7 percent, but remained at a staggering 17.4 percent in eastern Germany (Sacirbey, 1998b).

The combination of high unemployment, disillusionment over the failure to achieve the economic prosperity they had believed would accompany reunification, and the perception that the 7.7 million resident "foreigners" in Germany—in particular, Turks—were stealing jobs from deserving Germans led to a rash of race-based hate crimes and a growth of neo-Nazi groups in the first few years following reunification. Much of this activity was centered in eastern Germany, where, according to some observers, "the people . . . live in a values system that is very vulnerable to right-wing extremism because it connects with their previous experiences" (Wagner, in Kim, 1998a). Though brought under control by the concerted effort of the FGR government, these problems surfaced again in the late 1990s, as xenophobic right-wing organizations were able to successfully exploit "the frustrations of older people who have known nothing but authoritarian rule and now have neither work nor prospects, and of school dropouts who find no job openings in a lagging economy" ("Neo-Nazis Numbers Growing," 1999). A significant amount of this resurgence of racist-based nationalism was apparently triggered by incoming Chancellor Gerhard Schroder's plan to liberalize Germany's citizenship rules, which have been in place since 1913. Germany is one of the few remaining major European nations in which citizenship is determined by "blood" (that is, by race) rather than by birthplace. Unlike, for example, the United States, in which anyone born on U.S. soil is automatically granted citizenship, native-born non-Germans are treated as foreigners, subject to a 15-year-long process before they can become citizens (Berger, 1999). Alarmed by the prospect of the nation's racial and religious heritage (Germany is a predominantly Christian country, with affiliation more or less evenly split between Roman Catholicism and Protestantism) being diluted, the Christian Democratic Union, Christian Socialist Party, and other conservative parties have taken decidedly anti-foreigner positions. Their "Germans first" stance has raised fears of the old racial politics of the National Socialist (Nazi) Party that culminated in the division of Germany nearly fifty years ago (Berger, 1998). And those fears may be well founded.

A decade after its formal structural reunification, Germany remains less than fully reunited socially and culturally. According to the most recent in a series of annual polls conducted by the Social Science Research Center of Berlin-Brandenburg and the Hans Boeckler Foundation, about two-thirds (65 percent) of east Germans do not yet feel like real German citizens, though they have no desire to return to the former communist state, and only 17 percent can identify with their new country ("Germans from east," 1998). A country not yet united can be more easily divided, and the consequences of another German division could be devastating for the prospects of a true European Union (Frank, 1998).

SUMMARY AND REVIEW

The Concept of Social Structure

1. *What makes organized human social life possible?*
Human beings typically spend most of their lives doing things and being with other humans. Their social lives are structured, showing order and predictability rather than randomness and chaos. This social structuring is made possible through a shared culture that gives the members of a population a common world view. (P. 54)

Groups and Other Collectivities

2. *What features distinguish aggregates, categories, and groups from one another?*
In describing populations and their activities, sociologists distinguish among several different types of collectivities or situations involving more than one person. Aggregates are made up of people who occupy the same physical space at the same particular time. Categories are distinguished by common or shared characteristics of their members. The people who constitute a given category may or may not ever be physically present with one another. Social groups are made up of people who interact with one another in a regular, patterned way and who come to form a sense of common identity. (Pp. 54–55)

3. *What is the difference between a status and a role?*
Group patterns are established by the statuses or recognized positions within the group and the formal roles or expected attitudes and behaviors associated with them. Ascribed statuses are assigned to individuals on the basis of their possession of some specific quality or attribute such as race. Achieved statuses are positions earned by individuals. In modern societies such as the United States, occupation may serve as a master status, forming people's self-identity and general social standing. People's role performances or actual behaviors in response to expectations may depart significantly from formal requirements, resulting in role strain. Individuals may also experience role conflict as they find themselves caught between the contradictory demands of two or more statuses occupied at the same time. (Pp. 55–56)

Types of Social Groups

4. *How do membership groups differ from reference groups?*
There are many different types of social groups in modern societies. Membership groups are those in which a given individual objectively belongs and participates. Reference groups are those with whom a given individual affiliates subjectively and whose beliefs, norms, values, and behaviors become the frame of reference for his or her personal life. People's membership groups and reference groups ordinarily coincide, but individuals who are going through a process of anticipatory socialization may identify with and imitate groups to which they do not yet belong. (Pp. 57–58)

5. *What is the difference between primary groups and secondary groups?*

Primary groups such as families and close friends display total personality involvement, warm personal relations, and informal interactions among their members. Because they are satisfying to their members, primary groups are valued as intrinsic ends in themselves. Secondary groups such as customers and clerks are characterized by more formal, less emotional, more deliberate social interactions. Their value lies in being a means to some important end for their members. (Pp. 58–59)

6. *How does group size affect relations among group members?*

Group size appears to be an important factor in shaping the likelihood of primary or secondary relations among members. The two-member social dyad is the most basic and intimate type of group. Its continued existence rests entirely on both members' participation in the relationship. Triads or three-person groups mark the beginning of groups having identifiable structure. They often re-form into a coalition of two against one. Increasing population size in societies historically has been associated with the movement from primary to secondary relations at all levels of group life. (Pp. 60–61)

7. *What is the connection between formal organization and bureaucracy?*

Formal organizations—large, deliberately planned groups designed to carry out some specific objectives—have come to characterize most important activities in modern societies. Etzioni's typology distinguishes among normative, coercive, and utilitarian organizations on the basis of their members' motivations for participation. Max Weber's description of bureaucracy as the logical, rationally planned administration of people and activities within a particular setting showed the bureaucratic organization to be a device for maximizing human productivity and efficiency. But observations of bureaucracies in action suggest that ritualism and rigidity often make these organizations less than ideal vehicles for accomplishing complex objectives. (Pp. 61–64)

8. *How does informal organization affect bureaucracies?*

The informal organization of social relations and practices that invariably develops among the people within bureaucratic organizations often can enhance the formal organization's effectiveness by complementing and supplementing official rules and procedures. But if employees perceive the formal organization's goals or activities as being opposed to their own personal best interests, they may use the informal organization against the bureaucracy. In the long run, the best solution may be the development of a very different type of formal organizational structure. (P. 64)

9. *How does formal organizational structure in Japan differ from that found in the United States?*

Much of modern Japan's economic success from the 1950s through the early 1990s has been attributed to the family style of Japanese formal organization. The Japanese company represents a near-lifelong commitment for many workers, whose personal lives merged with and were often regulated by the corporation. Such organizations are far less centralized in decision making than their counterparts in the United States, and their workers are able to participate more extensively in policy and procedure formation through quality control circles and other mechanisms. It is doubtful that the Japanese style of organization could be fully implemented in the United States, whose culture is far less group oriented and much more individualistic. Research by Kanter and others seems to indicate that a more flexible, humanized administrative structure may prove to be more efficient and more profitable than the traditional bureaucratic model. (Pp. 64–65)

Societies and Societal Development

10. *What are societies and, according to Durkheim, how do human societies develop over time?*

Societies are self-perpetuating groups of people who occupy a given territory and share a common culture. The study of societies was a major focus of early sociologists and remains so for macro-level researchers. Emile Durkheim, Ferdinand Tönnies, and Gerhard Lenski developed typologies of human societies in order to examine important developmental changes and trends over time. Durkheim argued that increasing population size, division of labor, and specialization of function led to the end of mechanical solidarity structures whose members formed cohesive bonds because of their shared social attributes and cultural world view and to the development of organic solidarity systems whose cohesiveness relied on the functional interdependency created as a consequence of increasing dissimilarities among members. (Pp. 65–66)

11. *How do the models of societal development offered by Tönnies and by Lenski differ from that of Durkheim?*

German sociologist Tönnies viewed societal change as a movement away from traditional *gemeinschaft* organization based on personal, primary-group relations toward *gesellschaft* organization—formal, impersonal, and rational interaction typical of secondary groups. For Lenski, changes in productive technology created larger economic surpluses as societies developed from hunting and gathering bands through settled horticultural and then agrarian groups and finally into modern industrial systems. These increasing surpluses permitted larger population sizes, which in turn fostered increasingly specialized social roles and greater societal complexity. Like Durkheim and Tönnies, Lenski saw human social history as the increasing movement from primary- to secondary-group relations. (Pp. 66–67)

Socialization

Beginning in the fifth century A.D., the city of Rome, the center of the civilized world, came under a series of attacks by barbarian invaders. In the years 410, 433, and 455, successive waves of Goths, Visigoths, and Vandals (from whose unparalleled acts of wanton destruction the modern term *vandalism* was derived) pillaged the city, putting to an end what had been the seat of one of the world's most powerful empires. Some observers at that time (and since that time) saw the overthrow of Rome by invading armies as a triumph of barbarism over civilization, a descent of humanity into a lower, more brutish form of existence.

Whereas the barbarian conquest of the Roman Empire stands as one of the major events of recorded history, history ordinarily does not record the fact that all contemporary human societies also face "barbarian invasions" of their own, though of a somewhat different kind. Every year, every human society must deal with an invasion of new population members who enter the ongoing social structure from the inside or from the outside. Whether infants born to current societal members, immigrants fleeing economic, political, religious, environmental, or other problems in their home countries, or involuntary spoils of military conquests, these newcomers pose a very real threat to the continued well-being of their adopted society, even though they may intend that society no harm.

As we saw in the two immediately preceding chapters, what makes organized social life as we know it possible both in the short run and over the long run is the existence of a shared set of beliefs, values, and norms—a common culture—and a complex set of groups and group relationships—a social structure—derived from that culture. In the final analysis, both the cultural system and the social structure to which it gives birth depend upon the population members' knowledge and acceptance of what might be termed "the basic rules of the game" of their society; that is, a set of ideas and actions that are so taken for granted that they are followed without question. It is exactly in this regard that newcomers to any ongoing society, however they may have arrived in that society, constitute what amounts to a barbarian invasion. They just don't know the basic rules of the game and, under the wrong set of circumstances, their ignorance could destroy the existing orderly way of life.

For example, in a fast-paced, highly mobile society in which motor vehicles play a central role in moving people and goods, it is essential that all vehicle operators understand and follow established traffic procedures and rules. At a bare minimum, it is imperative that all drivers keep to the proper side of the road when operating their vehicles, whether that happens to be the right-hand side (as in the United States, Germany, and Canada) or the left-hand side (as in Jamaica, England, and Japan). Without such a shared understanding, even the most routine drive could become extremely problematic and potentially lethal.

In recent years, Texas, California, and some other areas of the United States have experienced large and sudden influxes of immigrants from rural areas of developing nations. These newcomers, who hail from backgrounds where high-speed freeways, sports utility vehicles, and other trappings of modern living are in short supply, suddenly found themselves in radically different settings in which daily driving is almost a mandatory fact of life. Tempers often flared and fenders often crumpled as brand-new drivers unfamiliar with formal traffic rules, much less the informal nuances of driving in a postmodern society, collided (literally, as well as figuratively) with seasoned local drivers who simply assumed that everyone sitting behind the steering wheel of a car or truck was born with an instinctive knowledge of how to handle four-way-stop-sign and no-way-stop-sign traffic intersections.

As far as we currently can tell, human beings do not enter this world with anything resembling an established body of behaviors, values, beliefs, ideas, hopes, and fears. Indeed, as we discussed in Chapter 2, we do not arrive with even the ability to express ourselves in a coherent language. Rather, if all goes well, humans are born with a set of potentials for developing language, beliefs, values, information, and other skills and resources necessary for their survival. But these potentials do not automatically activate themselves. They must be developed and actualized through the intervention of other humans, in the lifelong experience of social learning known as **socialization.** Through the socialization process, parents and other family members, teachers of various kinds, employers, and a host of other people and groups attempt to pass on to these new arrivals a body of established knowledge, behaviors, and other tools intended to maximize their chances for survival. At the same time, they also try to instill in these individuals those collective cultural and social elements necessary for the continued survival of the society-at-large.

But socialization is not a simple "learn it once and it's yours forever" experience reserved exclusively for societal newcomers. Even long-term members of any given society must continuously alter their personal knowledge, values, beliefs, and behaviors as physical, cultural, societal, and other environments surrounding them undergo constant—and often unexpected—change. For example, during the two decades immediately following the end of World War II, the United States was very much a consumption-oriented society, as the nation's vast industrial machine returned to peacetime production and people by the millions tried to make up for the resource scarcity and mandatory rationing they had endured during the war years. In an age of unparalleled economic prosperity that seemed to be expanding infinitely, the nation as a whole adopted a "use it and toss it" ethos. Consumer goods of all sorts were in unlimited supply, it was more often cheaper to purchase a new item than to repair and reuse an old one, and, besides, it was good for the economy to keep on buying new things. Everyone benefited from the nonstop, materialistic way of life.

Not everyone really did benefit from the post-war lifestyle enjoyed in the United States and elsewhere, as people found out during a series of environmental crises beginning in the early 1970s with an oil embargo imposed on the industrial nations of the world by the Oil Producing and Exporting Countries (OPEC) cartel. Stung by the realization that their lifestyles had been exacting a high toll on the environment (a topic we discuss in Chapter 12) and this toll was rapidly becoming due, many people in the United States and in other industrial nations were forced to unlearn old beliefs and behaviors concerning humans' relationships to the environment and to other humans (a process known as **desocialization**) and to learn a new set of beliefs and behaviors more environmentally and people-friendly (a process known as **resocialization**). "Reduce, Reuse, and Recycle" became the core elements of a new ethos adopted by tens of millions of people across the planet as they began to confront the fact that things just weren't the same as they once had been.

In this chapter, we examine socialization, the social learning process through which individuals become functioning human beings and functioning members of their respective sociocultural systems. Contrary to the titles of several best-selling books, it is highly unlikely that we could ever learn everything we really needed to know in kindergarten, in first grade, in high school, in college, or from any one source at any one time during our lives. The conditions of human cultural, social, and physical life are always subject to change, and we must be prepared to change with them. We begin the socialization experience on the day of our birth, and we do not end that experience until the day of our death.

Questions to Consider

1. How are human social behaviors different from the behaviors of nonhuman beings?
2. Why is early contact with other humans so important for the social development of children?
3. How does increasing involvement in social group life affect individual personality development?
4. Why is successful socialization an important objective in all human societies?
5. Why is the family such a crucial socialization agent in most societies?
6. What is the role of formal education in the socialization process of modern societies like the United States and Japan?
7. Why do peer groups have such a significant influence on their members, especially among adolescents?
8. Why have mass media such as television become crucial agents of social learning in modern societies?
9. What has led to the increasing amount of adult socialization that occurs in contemporary societies?
10. How does the process of resocialization differ from other forms of socialization?

ON BEING HUMAN: BIOLOGY AND HUMAN NATURE

As we saw in Chapter 2, although human beings may be biological creatures, we do not show evidence of being biologically *determined*. Scientists' long search for a set of specific instincts that form the core of human nature has failed to demonstrate the existence of any such biologically grounded patterns. What this research does indicate is that biological factors form an important set of resources and limitations for humans. They significantly affect, but do not absolutely determine, the behaviors of human beings as a species and as individuals. For example, the fact that all the readers of this book are humans means that every so often they have to eat food to satisfy their biological need for nourishment. The fact that I am a large, tall person also means that typically I will have to eat more food than will a smaller, shorter individual. But the biological drive for nourishment that we all experience as hunger does not tell us what to eat or how to eat it. Samoans may favor a repast of fish and breadfruit, and the Ngatatjara aborigines of western Australia may prefer to dine on fruit and lizard meat (Ember and Ember, 1988), whereas many Americans' idea of the perfect meal may be a well-done cheeseburger and an order of crispy french fries. But many other Americans—strict vegetarians—may be physically sickened by the thought of consuming animal flesh. The question of how hunger is to be satisfied is primarily a matter of cultural preferences as well as the availability of different food resources rather than of human instinct. Biological drives may compel us to engage in certain common types of behaviors such as eating, drinking, and sleeping; but social and cultural considerations specify how, when, what, and where we should eat, drink, or sleep.

If there is such a thing as human nature, it defines only general behavioral possibilities and impossibilities rather than specific behaviors. Instead, culture provides the set of specific behavioral responses to the world that instincts supply for nonhumans. Since culture represents a human creation rather than an inherited biological program, it must be learned by the individuals who live under its influence. This learning normally occurs as a by-product of the close and sustained contact with other human beings that all individual humans require, and most will experience, by virtue of their biological makeup.

ON BEING HUMAN: SOCIAL LEARNING AND HUMAN NATURE

Human beings are vastly superior to most other living creatures in a variety of important ways, but biological superiority does not appear to be one of them. Many mammals (for example, horses) are able to walk, feed, and otherwise fend for themselves within a short time after their birth. Human infants, however, are so biologically helpless that they must depend entirely on other humans for their physical survival. Newborn humans cannot open bottles or cans of baby formula, change their soiled diapers, find shelter against wind and snow, or even roll out of the way of approaching danger. They require the physical assistance of others of their kind if they are to have their basic biological needs met. This physical dependency not only is complete, but also lasts for an extended period of time.

Sociologists argue that the resulting prolonged physical contact between human infants and their caretakers creates an environment of close social interaction that is essential to the development of attributes we normally think of as human. These traits include verbal and written language, rational thought, and the formation of a self-concept. The basic premise is that biological inheritance provides all humans with a pool of behavioral potentials. It is the quality and quantity of individuals' social and cultural experiences that largely decide which of these potentials will be actualized. Biology supplies the necessary raw materials that go into the creation of the finished human product. Through the socialization process, society and culture provide the necessary machinery through which the transformation of those raw materials takes place.

The Effects of Isolation: The Cases of Anna, Isabelle, and Genie

Compelling evidence to support this assertion has been provided by several documented cases of children who were raised in apparent isolation from other humans (Curtiss, 1977; Davis, 1940, 1947; Pines, 1981). The experiences of Anna, Isabelle, and Genie were remarkably similar in many respects. All were relatively young girls (ages 5, 6, and 13, respectively, when discovered by authorities) who had been subjected to extreme social deprivation from the first year or two of their lives. Anna and Genie had been shut away in closet-like rooms and had almost no interaction with other human beings outside of the occasional physical contact required to provide for their minimal physical needs. Isabelle was somewhat more fortunate in the sense that she had at least been hidden away with her mother, a deaf-mute. When discovered, none of these girls could talk, feed, or dress herself, or otherwise demonstrate an ability to interact with other human beings in a normal manner. Each gave the physical and behavioral impression of being in an arrested infantile stage, unable to maintain appropriate and expected standards of cleanliness or self-control.

After being removed from her captivity and receiving a great deal of attention from psychologists and social welfare workers, Isabelle was able to make extraordinary social and intellectual progress. Within a few years, she had acquired written and verbal language skills typical for other children her age and seemed to be well on her way to a normal life. The intensive remedial efforts of the concerned authorities apparently were sufficient to offset the effects of her prolonged social deprivation. The fact that she had remained in contact with her mother may also have played a crucial part in her successful entry into the social community, even though the two had not been able to communicate verbally (Davis, 1947).

Anna and Genie did not fare nearly as well. From the time of her discovery until she died some four years later, Anna did not make any substantial progress toward becoming a full-fledged human being. Although finally able to take care of her own physical needs and to follow simple instructions, she never really developed more than the simple rudiments of verbal language. At the time of her death, she remained intellectually and socially far behind other children of the same chronological age (Davis, 1947).

Like Anna, Genie never was completely able to develop normal human language skills or social behaviors appropriate for a person her age during the time of her attempted rehabilitation (Curtiss, 1977; Pines, 1981). Inasmuch as her mother later acquired custody of Genie and removed her from the therapy program, we cannot determine just how much developmental progress she would eventually have been able to make. However, her general lack of improvement, despite the intensive attention she received, suggested that she had suffered irreversible damage as a result of being isolated during a critical period of her life. Apparently, involvement in human social interaction must occur early in our lives if we are ever to become fully human. Unlike other animals, our biology represents possibility rather than destiny. As the unusual and tragic cases of Anna and Genie demonstrate, that possibility can become actuality only through the teaching of other human beings. This social learning comes in the course of sustained interaction with family, friends, and those others who make up our surrounding social world.

THEORIES OF SOCIALIZATION AS HUMAN DEVELOPMENT

Most social scientists agree that social learning experiences are crucial to creating beings who are truly human. Their specific visions of how this process occurs have been influenced greatly by their respective intellectual and academic backgrounds. Psychologists, for example, typically have stressed the interplay between internal conscious or unconscious personality forces and external social factors. The work of Freud is illustrative of this perspective.

Socialization as Conflict Management: Freud

The psychiatrist and psychoanalyst Sigmund Freud (1856–1939) developed what amounts to a conflict interpretation of the human socialization process. In the Freudian view, the objective of important **socialization agents**—parents, teachers, and other impor-

tant groups involved in the socialization of individual societal members—is to create within individuals a sense of moral right and wrong as these matters are defined by cultural values, beliefs, and norms. Freud (1930) maintained that such a social conscience or **superego** was necessary to counteract the antisocial impulses of the **id,** the bundle of unconscious aggressive and sexual drives inherited by all individuals from their prehuman ancestors. The imposition of such societal restraints on the individual and pleasure-directed id creates a series of conflicts within the developing personality structure. These conflicts ultimately will be negotiated by the **ego,** the conscious mechanism by which individuals are able to engage in deliberate decision making and other behaviors. The socialization process consists of the progressive development of the superego and the increasing submission of individual impulses to societal wishes and requirements.

Socialization as Cognitive Development: Piaget

Freud's model of human development spawned a number of similar efforts from other psychologists who were influenced by his writings. Although they differed among themselves individually in terms of specific emphases, collectively these theories focused on the dynamic interplay of unconscious and conscious personality components. For example, Erik Erikson (1950, 1982) envisioned the process as a series of identity crises that individuals must resolve at each given stage of life if they are to proceed successfully into the next developmental stage. One of the most famous and influential psychological interpretations of socialization, however, did not rely so heavily on biological drives and unconscious personality dynamics in explaining the process of becoming human.

Jean Piaget (1896–1980) believed that people's capacity for developing a true human personality through interactions with their surrounding world depends on their cognitive ability level. To benefit developmentally from contact with their social and physical environments, individuals must be able to organize and interpret impressions from those settings in a meaningful way. According to Piaget (1929, 1932), this level of cognition in turn depends on individuals' **maturation;** that is, on their level of neurological and physiological development.

Piaget saw such maturation as related to the chronological aging process, though by no means identical to it. He proposed a model that charted a sequence of progressively more-complex levels of cognitive ability ordinarily, but not invariably, found in individuals of a given age group. Each stage of cognition shapes the type of understanding the individual is capable of attaining at that particular point.

Specific levels and kinds of understanding then define the person's potential for deriving important information from socialization experiences during that period.

From birth to about age 2, children operate at what Piaget called the **sensorimotor stage.** Their knowledge of the world comes entirely from direct sensory contact; that is, by sight, smell, hearing, taste, and touch. Because children this age have not yet developed an ability to use language or otherwise employ symbols, their understanding of reality is limited to their immediate encounters with it. People, objects, and events outside young children's range of perception literally don't exist in their minds, since these children are not yet capable of forming and holding ideas.

As children begin to acquire language, they move into the **preoperational stage,** which lasts until about age 7. During this period, their cognitive skills expand to include the use of symbols, the formation of mental images, and the ability to differentiate between ideas and reality. At this developmental stage, children's images and ideas are restricted to specific objects or people. They have not yet acquired the cognitive tools required to manipulate concepts in the abstract.

During the **concrete operational stage,** which roughly spans ages 7 through 11, children develop a facility for logical thought processes. As they begin to understand cause-and-effect and other types of relationships, children become more able to manipulate symbols and ideas. They also exhibit the ability to envision things from different perspectives, to see concrete situations as other specific people (their parents, for instance) might see them.

Finally, during what Piaget termed the **formal operational stage,** children begin to display much more sophisticated levels of thought. They become able to conceptualize the world and themselves in abstract, rather than concrete, terms. They can evaluate general classes of phenomena from a wide variety of perspectives simultaneously. Individuals who reach this developmental stage can imagine themselves in any number of situations and then employ high-order systems of logic to assess and interpret these hypothetical scenarios.

According to Piaget, not all children ultimately reach the formal operational stage of development. The likelihood that they will do so is a function of variations in individual mental abilities, as well as differences in social institutions and cultural settings. These factors work in combination to create different environments that support or inhibit cognitive development. By acknowledging the role of such social and cultural factors in shaping developmental

opportunities and experiences, Piaget's theory paralleled those interpretations of human development more squarely in the realm of sociological thought.

Socialization as Self-Development: Cooley and Mead

In contrast to the biological focus of most psychological theories of human development, sociological approaches emphasize the social contexts within which this phenomenon occurs. The classic interpretations were offered by two men who taught at the University of Chicago in the early decades of this century. Both models stress the creative interplay between the developing person and the **significant others**—people who are important in establishing an individual's self-concept—who make up his or her immediate social world. These people play a primary role in creating the sense of **self** (one's awareness and concept of personal identity) that is a characteristic of true human beings.

Charles Horton Cooley (1864–1929) argued against the then-prevailing belief that humans are creatures whose basic nature is determined by genetic heritage and activated through biological maturation. Taking the opposite view, Cooley (1902) proposed that human development, including the critical ability to experience oneself objectively as well as subjectively, is a product of interaction with other humans in social groups. It is our close involvement with others that provides us with what he termed a **looking-glass self**—an impression of who and what we are that mirrors others' images of us. As he envisioned it, the formation of the looking-glass self is a three-step process.

In the first step, the reaction of these other people to us leads us to imagine how we must appear to them. Suppose, for example (in what is obviously a hypothetical illustration), after ten minutes of lecturing to an introductory sociology class one morning, I notice that many students are yawning and sitting slumped over with their eyes closed. I might interpret their responses to my presentation as a sign that I am boring them.

In the second step, we imagine what sort of judgment these other people are making about us. To continue with the example, the fact that I have been around college students for about twenty years and was once a college student myself leads me to recognize that boring professors are not regarded highly. I can anticipate some hard times on my course evaluations at the end of the semester. If student comments are sufficiently negative, I may even get some raised eyebrows from my departmental colleagues and my academic dean.

Finally, in the third step of the process, we experience some sort of self-feeling reflecting our perception of how these other people have seen and judged us. Having always thought of myself as a charismatic, dynamic lecturer, I am now more than a little embarrassed by the fact that I have just sent a room full of freshmen into a deep coma. I may begin to question or doubt my competency as an instructor and, as a result, may experience a reduction in self-esteem. Perhaps I should have become an anesthetist after all—at least in that line of work, successfully putting people to sleep is regarded as a job well done.

Silly examples aside, Cooley's basic assertion that the development of human attributes is contingent on social experiences remains profound and important. His seminal analysis of the relationship between group interaction and personal development reshaped social scientists' thinking on this crucial phenomenon. It remained for one of Cooley's colleagues to clarify and expand on his initial description of this vital aspect of the human socialization process.

George Herbert Mead (1863–1931) was a social philosopher who made a number of important contributions to the discipline we now call social psychology. In particular, he was interested in the process by which the human mind and sense of self developed. His own observations, as well as the work of his colleagues in the fields of psychology and sociology, led him to conclude that both mind and self are social products. They represent the outcomes of the individual's interactions with others in social situations rather than the outcomes of biological inheritance (Mead, 1934). Mead also argued that language, involving the use of significant symbols, is fundamental to the entire developmental sequence. In the absence of language skills, individuals cannot interact with others in such a way as to fashion a human personality. The cases of Anna and Genie seem to provide tragic support for this thesis.

Mead interpreted the socialization process that humanizes children as a series of increasingly complex interactions with a variety of significant others, including parents, siblings, peers, and teachers. Initially, the child's contact with parents and other people in her environment is primarily a physical and one-way process. As a helpless and dependent organism, the newborn infant requires and receives a great deal of physical attention from those responsible for her care. Children at this age act on the basis of physical stimuli (they cry when they are hungry, wet, or in pain) and react to the actions of other people (they calm down after they have been fed, changed, and had their diaper rash treated with soothing ointment). But they cannot yet initiate deliberate, meaningful interaction.

As physiological and neurological maturation proceeds, the growing child becomes able to move under her own power and to explore her world. With time, she is able to distinguish herself as a physical being distinct from other beings and objects in the environment. The child also begins to engage in an important type of nonverbal communication with others through gestures, sounds, and facial expressions. In the process, she begins to associate certain physical stimuli (a smile) with specific meanings (happiness) and to experiment with such stimuli to express herself to others.

As the child continues to mature, she becomes capable of exercising verbal language skills requiring an understanding and manipulation of symbols. Direct verbal communication with those other people who form the child's social world opens the door to a wide variety of learning experiences. It also makes possible a form of activity with significant consequences for the child's developing awareness of herself in relation to the world: play.

As Mead described the concept, **play** refers to that type of behavior in which the child pretends to be some specific person (typically, Mommy or Daddy) going about some specific task (preparing for a sales presentation to a client or shopping for tonight's dinner). In this way, the child acts as she has seen that person act (perhaps in previous trips to the office with Mommy or to the supermarket with Daddy). The actions of these people whom the child is pretending to be are in fact role behaviors defined by those people's statuses—Mommy is getting ready for the big meeting because she is the sales manager for her company; Daddy is going shopping because he is a house husband. Thus, without any real awareness by the child of what is taking place, play becomes an exercise in **role playing** and **role taking.** In the course of replicating the behaviors of Mommy and Daddy (role playing), the child begins to view and to evaluate the world, and herself as an element of that world, from that other person's frame of reference (role taking).

Increasing maturation and exposure to the organized social world expand the child's play activities. More people become the objects of pretend behavior, and more details of their roles become incorporated into play. The child's frame of reference for seeing and assessing things (including herself) also expands. The child is now ready to participate in more-complex game activities.

As employed by Mead, the word **game** applied to any organized group behavior. Although he happened to use the example of a genuine game (baseball) in his analysis, he could just as easily have talked about a Cub Scout den meeting or a Brownie troop overnight campout. Whatever the particular setting, participation in the game demands new abilities of understanding not required for successful play behavior.

The teams (groups) involved in game activities consist of a number of individuals linked together as a set of interdependent positions governed by rules. Each position has its own associated role, and to participate successfully in the game, the child must be aware of what is expected of her as an individual team member. Would-be pitchers must understand what it is that pitchers do, and would-be catchers must know what it is that catchers do. In addition, pitchers and catchers must understand each other's roles and those of the other seven team members on the field if either is to perform successfully.

Continued experience with the game brings the child a growing awareness of the concept of group structure and a group perspective. As this understanding develops, the child begins to use the group's frame of reference as her own in analyzing the world and herself. Little League baseball players adopt a sports view of the world and define themselves in terms of their athletic prowess. Members of scout troops begin to see the world in terms of woodcraft and public service activities and to define themselves in terms of merit badges.

Mead asserted that as children begin to participate in a growing number of game situations, they discover that the individual games and teams in which they are involved are linked through common beliefs, values, and norms as parts in a larger structure. This larger structure, or **generalized other,** as Mead called it, is the surrounding cultural and social community of which the child is a member. With increased exposure to this larger entity, the child comes to adopt the perspective of the generalized other—the entire sociocultural system—as her own. Society's interpretation of the world and of the child becomes the child's interpretation of the world and of herself.

The result of this lengthy, complex interaction process is a human personality structure (what Mead called the **social self**) that incorporates both a collective group dimension and an individual personal dimension. The "me" component of the social self is the objective, status-holding, role-playing aspect of the person. It reflects internalized cultural views and social practices. The me represents the aspect of the self that the individual can step outside of and evaluate from an outsider's perspective.

In contrast, the "I" component of the social self is the subjective, creative, individual aspect of the person. It is that part of each of us that is not so immediately observable or predictable to others who do not know us well. Although Mead was not entirely clear on this point, it seems that the I represents a personal assessment of our own social statuses and social roles and the resulting relationship we develop with ourselves as a result of that assessment.

Because one's social statuses and their associated roles are subject to change throughout the entire life cycle, the social self is never a final, completed product. Rather, the sense of self-identity, the concept of who and what one is, always remains in process, a continuing dynamic interplay between the individual and the larger society. In a very real sense, as long as the individual remains alive, the process of human self-development remains alive. It does not cease until the individual ceases to exist.

SOCIALIZATION AS SOCIAL LEARNING

Although socialization itself is a lifelong experience, we do not generally experience it in the same way across our entire lifetime. Depending on prevailing cultural beliefs and social practices within a given population, people of various age groups may be exposed to different kinds of messages from an assortment of socialization agents. Many important groups and organizations are involved in the social learning process. Collectively, they help to ensure the continuity of established social patterns by converting newborn organisms into functioning societal members whose daily lives reflect and reinforce current cultural and social arrangements.

The Family

For most individuals in traditional or premodern societies, the family was the single most important source of information about the surrounding world. This largely remains the case in developing nations today. It was from an extended family group, which typically included a variety of relatives in addition to parents and siblings, that new members received their introduction to social realities. This **primary socialization** entailed the establishment of one's initial societal position, the internalization of proper cultural values and beliefs, and the learning of appropriate communication and social interaction patterns. It even included preparation for later adult marital and occupational roles. As the all-encompassing, multipurpose group that formed the central axis of social organization, the family enjoyed a near monopoly as *the* agent of socialization for members of these traditional societies.

In modern societies, the differentiation and elaboration of more-specialized organizational units has eroded much of the family's traditional role as the exclusive source of social learning—a trend that has been decried both in the United States and Japan as contributing to increases in social problems among their youth. One Japanese Ministry of Education report (discussed in Gaouette, 1998) cites the degeneration of the traditional family as creating "a crisis of confidence in raising the next generation," and has called for the family to take back its traditional role in raising its children. But that is much easier said than done. Young children in modern societies now spend a considerable amount of time outside the family. At the same time, the family itself has changed considerably. The extended kin structure of the past has given way to the **nuclear family** composed of two spouses and their children. Changing gender roles (discussed more fully in Chapter 7) and increasing financial demands have also led to the rapid expansion of two-career families and a resulting child-rearing vacuum (Tobin, Wu, and Davidson, 1989). In a growing number of cases, this streamlined modern family structure has shrunk even further, as increasing numbers of divorces create more and more single-parent households.

Despite these significant changes, the family remains a critically important agent of socialization for most people. It still constitutes the initial setting of social interaction for newborn individuals and is likely to be the major source of the child's contact with the world over an extended period of time. The family also provides the first experience most of us have with primary group relations. As a result, in most cases, its impact on the child's developing self-concept (in Cooley's terminology, the child's looking-glass self) is enormous. By acting as the first medium for the introduction of accepted cultural and social wisdom, the family becomes a vehicle for their incorporation into the child's developing world view. For example, it is in the family that children begin to acquire a gender identity and a sense of what a girl or boy generally is like. This knowledge, of course, is a translation of cultural beliefs and values as mediated through the family unit. (The process of socialization into a gender identity is discussed in more detail in Chapter 7.)

Finally, the family continues to function as the initial and continuing determinant of the individual's social class position. Its beliefs, values, and behaviors reflect its own position within the societal hierarchy. In teaching these patterns to its members, the family thus operates as the continuing mechanism for socializing them into the existing stratification system of the larger society.

The School

Formal education was virtually unknown to most individuals in traditional societies, but it has become a fact of life for most members of modern social systems. The sophisticated economic, political, and social structures that distinguish modern societies are dependent on individuals who possess a body of technical knowledge and the ability to think. A basic formal education for the masses through some sort of public (state-run) school system now is the norm in modern societies such as the United States. Advanced education, provided through either public or private colleges and universities, is pursued by most members of the middle and upper classes in these societies.

For many individuals, entering school marks the beginning of sustained social interaction outside the sphere of the immediate family. During the process of being exposed to factual knowledge in the classroom, students must adjust their individual needs and whims to fit the requirements of the teacher and the school. They must also accept the fact that they are now being defined as members of some larger category and evaluated according to criteria that apply equally to all members of that category. Final spelling grades are determined by scores on tests and quizzes, not by virtue of being Mommy and Daddy's cute little Billy or Mary. This experience may come as a real shock to children who are used to being the centers of their family's universe. It represents the beginning of the individual's socialization into a large-scale, depersonalized structure that evaluates and places its members on the basis of universalistic performance criteria rather than personal identities. In this respect, the school may be viewed as an important instrument of anticipatory socialization. The everyday routine allows and requires students to develop attitudes and practice behaviors they will be expected to display later, as full-fledged adults.

Peer Groups

The term **peer group** or **peers** refers to people of approximately the same social position and age as oneself. Our peers typically form what we described in Chapter 3 as reference groups—people whose beliefs and behaviors serve as guidelines for our own personal orientation to the world. By definition, we might expect peers to be important agents of socialization for individuals. By observation and experience, this expectation has been validated, especially for adolescents in modern societies such as the United States.

For someone still in the fairly early stages of socialization, peers are buffers between the individual and the larger society (Berndt and Ladd, 1989). Adolescents are being introduced to the confusing

For these students in Kenya, as well as students in most other contemporary societies, peers are one of the most powerful and significant agents of socialization. Such peer groups often serve as a buffer between adolescents and the outside adult world.

expectations and demands of an age-stratified world in which their own status has not been defined clearly. Peer groups provide them at least temporary breathing space and a measure of freedom from adult control. They also give adolescents an opportunity to explore aspects of life (for example, smoking, drinking, sexual activity) normally discouraged and punished by parents or other authority figures. To individuals who experience the larger society as formalized and depersonalized, peers may represent genuine communities whose members are bound together in personalized, primary-group relations. It is no wonder that these groups exert profound social learning effects on adolescents—effects that at least one observer argues are much more significant and longer-lasting than those of parents. According to Judith Rich Harris (1998), the relationships children develop and share with their peers determine the sort of people they will be when they grow up. Adolescent peer groups can demand—and get—conformity to their values and standards of behavior.

Adolescents are by no means the only age group subject to important peer group influences, though pressures to conform to peer group norms may not be felt as intensely or responded to as fully by older, more established individuals. Adult workers in this society, for example, typically structure their own labor pace and productivity levels to conform to the informal expectations of their co-workers, a phenomenon first documented decades ago in the now-classic Hawthorne studies (Roethlisberger and Dickson, 1964/1939). The original research dealt with industrial blue-collar workers, but any college or university instructor can attest readily to the fact that informal collegial pressures operate just as effectively in academic departments as on factory assembly lines.

As we progress through the life cycle, we move into and out of a succession of age, occupational, marital, class, and other socially defined groups. At every step along the way, we form important social relationships with others like ourselves. These peer groups serve as our immediate connecting links to the larger world. We never really outgrow our peer group affiliations, and our peer groups never really stop educating us about the social world and our places in it. They provide us with the standards we use to measure our success or failure, our happiness or discontent. We tend to think of peer groups as being significant elements only in the lives of children and adolescents, but they remain important forces in all our lives, throughout our lives.

The Mass Media

Few of the many changes associated with the modernization process have had the same kind of far-reaching impact on social and cultural organization as those in the area of communications. The transformation of communication patterns from traditional to modern societies could well be called revolutionary. Mass communications systems make possible the rapid transformation of information, attitudes, and ideas over great distances to enormous audiences. They form a taken-for-granted but crucial component of modern life. In a very real sense, mass communication creates and sustains societal life as we know it.

Modern societies depend on the smooth, continuous flow of information. In the absence of accurate, up-to-the-minute data, for instance, government leaders could not possibly make effective, intelligent decisions relating to events halfway around the world (whether or not to intervene in the ethnic bloodshed taking place in the Yugoslavian province of Kosovo in 1999, for example). Economic planning by multinational corporations requires reliable financial statistics from many different areas of the world. In the case of both political and economic policymakers, even this morning's news is old, and old news is worse than useless. The mass media make such an instantaneous communications flow possible.

It is difficult to visualize life without television and radio programs, films, newspapers, magazines, books, and, now, the Internet. Without these avenues of information and entertainment, we would remain disconnected and fragmented, unable to comprehend or respond appropriately to the world around us. For example, think of the various kinds of reports—traffic, weather, stock market—that reach us over television, radio, and the Internet each day. They allow us to plan our commute to work or school, our activities for the weekend, and perhaps our investment futures from the comfort of our homes.

In modern societies, the mass media play a multifaceted and profound role in the human social learning process. Employed as tools by recognized socialization agents such as the school, their obvious contribution lies in being the backdrop through (or on) which important information is presented to students. Your reading of this textbook is a perfect illustration. In this context, the primary significance of the printed, visual, audio, and electronic media may lie in the sheer number of individuals who can be reached and affected by their messages at the same moment. Simply stated, the mass media make mass formal education possible.

But the socialization role extends well beyond the media's utility as audiovisual resources in public and private schools. As conduits of information and entertainment between individuals and the larger society, the mass media—television in particular—are important agents of social learning in their own right.

Our involvement with the media is staggering. On average, American adults spend more than half their waking lives with some form of media. They watch over four hours of television and listen to three hours of radio each day and read nine magazines each month. Two-thirds read at least one newspaper each day. In 1998, they spent an average of $48.55 per month on various forms of media (U.S. Bureau of the Census, 1998c). These media serve as important windows on the world, providing people with significant information. In turn, this information can become a major basis for the formation of an individual's orientation to the world. In all mass media–based societies, then, control over the content of media programming—and, consequently, over what societal audiences are likely to learn about their world—is a

matter of great concern to established and would-be power groups. In the modern world, the old adage that "The hand that rocks the cradle rules the world" might well be amended to read "The hand that produces the programming shapes the world." A crucial question, then, concerns the validity and reliability of media-provided information.

Adults who can distinguish between programs meant to entertain and those meant to inform understand that the former may take liberties with the facts in order to create a more interesting show. They expect that the latter will present a truthful portrayal of reality, but their expectations often do not reflect what actually occurs. Studies of newspapers and television news reporting (Gans, 1980; Tuchman, 1978) indicate that, contrary to popular belief, news facts usually do not speak for themselves. Like other aspects of perceived reality, the news is a social construct. In deciding such questions as how much air time or column space will be allocated to a particular story or what angle the story will receive, reporters and editors bend and shape events to fit their own priorities or requirements (Rosenberg, 1991). Even when this recasting of facts is done without any deliberate attempt to deceive or mislead, it nonetheless can have exactly that effect. Mass media news is not so much an act of reporting events as it is an act of filtering and interpreting those events for the audience (Tuchman, 1978).

During the past several U.S. presidential elections, charges of media bias from a so-called cultural elite were leveled by top members of the Republican Party. These officials claimed that a hidden liberal agenda on the part of major television, radio, and newspaper networks had led to distorted, unfavorable portrayals of Republican presidential and vice-presidential candidates over the airways and in the press. Campaign rhetoric aside, detailed analyses of the largest media networks and the people who control them (as discussed by Dye, 1995), suggest that there is some degree of truth to the assertion that these media are infused with an underlying liberal ideology—and perhaps a resulting liberal slant in their reporting of political events. But the contrived or inadvertent use of mass media channels for political purposes is hardly unique to the United States. Like other major social institutions, the mass media are seldom neutral players in the daily lives of their surrounding societies.

Children and the Media　If adults have a difficult time sorting out media facts from media fiction, children can find the task impossible. Since young children ordinarily do not read, their contact with mass media largely comes through watching television. However, they have no systematic interaction experience with

Some critics have blamed the Columbine High School shootings and other similar tragedies on the widespread availability of violent television shows and violent video games such as those evidenced in this Denver area arcade. Commenting on early (and inaccurate) reports that the Columbine shooters were members of a "Goth" group on campus, Goth, Jason Dickey (right) 19, a Centauris High School graduate said, "I felt the same way in Junior High. I had a 'hit list' . . . but these guys (the perpetrators of the Columbine shooting) are the people most Goths laugh at . . . Gothic is just about . . . what you look like, not the Nazi stuff."

the larger social world to serve as a reality check on what they see. Consequently, they are susceptible to accepting everything that is portrayed as the truth (Dorr, 1986). This vulnerability and the potential consequences of extensive, uncritical viewing have served as the basis of heated controversies concerning the effects of television watching on children. One study, for example, linked the arrival of American-style television programs in the Pacific Islands nation of Fiji to a 500 percent increase in eating disorders among adolescent Fijian girls. Nearly three-quarters of Harvard researcher Anne Becker's female respondents reported feeling "too big or fat," with 62 percent claiming to have been dieting during the previous month. According to Becker, these girls "look to television characters as role models . . . While it's an everyday concept to Americans, reshaping the body is a new concept to Fijians (reported in Chiu, 1999). One study respondent said that teenagers on television are "slim and very tall. We want our bodies to become like that . . . so we try to lose a lot of weight." Prior to the advent of television, traditional Fijian beliefs had placed a high value on eating well and looking robust, and female eating disorders were practically unknown.

One major area of criticism revolves around the effects of televised violence on children's developing personalities and social behaviors. At issue is the question of whether acts of aggression on the screen generate similar acts in reality. A large body of studies conducted through the 1960s and 1970s indicated that such an association does exist and may constitute a cause-and-effect relationship (National Institute of Mental Health, 1982). However, the issue is far from settled, as later studies (Josephson, 1987) suggested that the relationship may be weaker and more complex than first believed.

In the late 1990s, the question of TV-induced violence surfaced again with renewed passion, largely in the aftermath of a series of school shootings in which students armed with pistols, rifles, shotguns, and other weapons opened fire on fellow students and teachers. In a number of these cases, the shooters had been described as fans of violent television shows and video games. A few years earlier, new research studies had linked exposure to TV violence with subsequent tendencies toward violence. In 1993, for example, the American Psychological Association's Commission on Violence and Youth had concluded that there was "absolutely no doubt that higher levels of viewing violence on television are correlated with increased acceptance of aggressive attitudes and increased aggressive behavior" (Institute for Social Research, 1994, p. 6).

Whether or not television viewing is directly responsible for acts of aggression, it is clear that the medium itself is laced with violence. One study conducted by *TV Guide* magazine found over 1,800 acts of violence portrayed in a single day's programming in the Washington, DC, viewing area. The average child graduating from elementary school will have watched a cumulative total of 8,000 murders and more than 100,000 acts of violence on television (Disney, 1992). Responding to growing public concern and anger about TV violence, major networks agreed to scale down the number of such episodes, but critics assert that networks continue to ignore existing laws requiring improvements in children's TV programming to better serve the educational and informational needs of this audience.

For better or worse, television is an important element of children's social learning experience. Many children spend as much time with TV as they do in school or interacting with parents and other traditional socialization agents. They incorporate what they see on television into their growing understanding of the world and, to some extent, interpret the world in light of it. Later, as they become exposed to other media such as films, music, the Internet, and books, these factors are added to children's developing world view.

In a mass society whose members share in a mass culture, mass media add an important element to childhood and adolescence social learning already being shaped by family, school, and peers. But socialization does not end with adulthood, and no single group or organization is likely to have the only word or the last word in determining the final outcome of the individual's socialization. The interplay of diverse and sometimes conflicting forces may help people to retain their individuality throughout the learning process. It keeps them from becoming clonelike beings stamped out in their society's image.

Adult Socialization and Resocialization

Freud claimed that the essential details of the human personality are established through experiences occurring within the first five or six years of life. Perhaps influenced by this view, for a long period of time social scientists and lay people alike regarded socialization as primarily a childhood phenomenon. As children, we are taught the important facts of life we will need to know as adults. As adults, we behave according to the accepted patterns we learned as children.

Such an image of socialization may have been remotely true for slow-changing traditional societies, but it is not an accurate portrayal of the process that occurs in most societies of the contemporary world. In both modern and developing societies, a great deal of socialization takes place after individuals have passed through childhood and adolescence and have entered the adult world. Such **secondary socialization,** as it is sometimes called, is especially likely in the face of the rapid, significant changes that characterize contemporary life. In many instances, traditional values, beliefs, and practices taught to children bear little resemblance or relevance to the realities confronting them as adults. As we saw in the introduction to this chapter, in such instances the survival of both the individual and the society demands that people remain flexible enough to learn new life patterns as well as to unlearn old ones.

For most people, adult socialization occurs in the context of marriage and work. As we will discuss in greater detail in Chapter 9, traditional conceptions of marriage and family life have changed drastically. Dramatic increases in both the number of divorces and the number of women entering the workforce as full-time employees have created new marital and familial arrangements (dual-career couples, single parenthood) as well as new problems (finding day care services for young children, structuring so-called quality time into parent-child interactions) that often were not anticipated or covered during childhood. Adults who find themselves in family circumstances outside established cultural frames of reference have to rethink their roles as spouses and parents. Since they may have little or nothing in the way of existing knowledge to fall back on, this often takes the

form of on-the-job training. The proliferation of self-help counseling groups for single parents, spouses of workaholics, and other nontraditional role players may be indicative of this trend.

Like marriage and family, occupational roles also have changed considerably. Unlike "the old days" when parents taught children the occupational skills they would require, most children now do not learn specific occupation-related behaviors from their parents. Children of attorneys or physicians or accountants may follow those occupational footsteps, but they learn the tricks of their respective trades in graduate or professional schools. However, even these training centers do not prepare their students for the specifics of the jobs they will be performing after graduation. Newly minted tax law specialists or surgeons or certified public accountants must still learn how things are done in the particular organizations that employ them. In addition, to the extent that people change employers or occupations over the course of their working lives, they will encounter new socialization experiences throughout their adult lives.

Sometimes adult socialization involves rapid and dramatic social learning in which old, established attitudes or behaviors are removed and new patterns are implanted—a process known as resocialization. Resocialization often entails the construction of new personal and social identities for individuals and occurs within the confines of what sociologist Erving Goffman (1922–1982) called total institutions.

Goffman (1961) described **total institutions** as places where large numbers of people who are cut off from the larger society live and work for an extended period of time in a carefully controlled atmosphere.

As described by Erving Goffman, total institutions are organizations dedicated to the remaking or remolding of adults through a combined process of desocialization and resocialization. If things go as planned, these inmates at the Swan Lake, Montana, prison boot camp will be transformed into productive, law-abiding citizens.

Socialization as Social Learning

Focus on
Canada

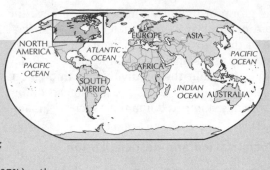

Population: 31,006,347

Life Expectancy at Birth (years): Male—76.12; Female—82.79

Form of Government: Confederation with parliamentary democracy

Major Religions: Roman Catholic (45%); United Church (12%); Anglican (8%)

Major Racial and Ethnic Groups: British Isles (40%); French (27%); other European (20%); Amerindian (1.5%); other—mostly Asian (11.5%)

Population Doubling Time: 162 years

Per Capita GNP (1997 U.S. dollars): $19,640

Principal Economic Activities: Industry; Agriculture; Mining

Colonial Experience: French Colony (17th cent.); British Colony (18th and 19th cent.)

Adult Literacy Rate: 97% Male—97%; Female—97%

Canadians Mount Policing of Mass Media

The plot of the wildly offbeat and highly scatological "adult" animated movie, *South Park: Bigger, Longer and Uncut* (1999) revolves around a brutal war between the United States and Canada. The war—which turns out to be Armageddon, the battle opening the gates of hell for satanic conquest of the world—has begun over an obscenity-ridden Canadian film that seemingly has corrupted and warped the "fragile little minds" of *South Park's* four 9-year-old heroes and their third-grade peers. Shocked and outraged by the vile language spewing from the mouths of their children, the parents of South Park, Colorado, reach the only possible logical conclusion: blame Canada. They kidnap the offending film's stars, Terrance and Phillip, and prepare them for execution. In retaliation, the Canadian Air Force bombs the United States' most precious resource—its Hollywood superstar actors—and the carnage is on.

Those who may be familiar with the ongoing "media wars" between Canada and the United States will recognize and appreciate the depth of the satire and irony at work in *South Park*. For, in the real world, it is Canada that has been subjected to an in-

vasion of offensive films, television shows, video games, magazines, and other mass media products from its southern neighbor. And it is Canadians who have been shocked and outraged by evidence of the damaging impact of that programming on the minds of their children, as well as on the continued viability of the Canadian way of life itself. The response to this invasion has not been armed conflict with the United States (at least, not so far) but, rather, a series of defensive measures designed to keep the most objectionable materials out of Canadian media airspace. The result, according to one U.S. observer (DePalma, 1999) is that Canada has become "the Death Star of cultural fortifications, bristling with regulatory armaments to preserve what little is left of its own cultural territory."

The primary defenders of Canadian media culture are the Canadian Radio-Television and Telecommunications Commission (CRTC), founded in 1968, and the Canadian Heritage Ministry, currently under the direction of Heritage Minister Sheila Copps. These two groups are responsible for a series of Canadian Content or "CanCon" Laws which first took

effect in 1970 and have been revised over the past three decades. Using a complex and sometimes confusing scoring system that assigns points to mass media products on the basis of such factors as the nationalities of the involved creative personnel; production location; thematic and substantive content; and source of production funding, these regulations specify the minimum mandated level of "Canadian content" programming for public and private television and radio stations throughout the country (Ricklefs, 1998). For example, as of 1998, Canadian radio stations were required to make sure that at least 35 percent of all music played on air all day, every day, was "Canadian" as defined by the formula ("CRTC Pushes for More CanCon," 1998). Similarly, 60 percent of television programming had to be Canadian, and the rules for meeting the criterion were even more stringent. Shows hoping to be subsidized by the Canadian Television Fund had to be set in Canada; written, directed, and acted by Canadians; and have at least 20 percent of their production costs covered by Canadian broadcasters ("Funding Rules Tightened," 1998). Stung by a poll indicating that 25 percent of Canadians mistakenly identified "life, liberty and the pursuit of happiness" as a Canadian Constitution slogan, Heritage Minister Copps has argued that "A kid in Canada watches television 23 hours a week, so we better make sure that some of what he watches reflects his own existence, and not just another country" (quoted in Ricklefs, 1998).

Radio and television are not the only media venues subject to Canadian Content standards. According to Heritage Ministry estimates, 95 percent of all movies screened in Canada and 83 percent of all magazines sold on newsstands are from foreign sources, primarily the United States (Ricklefs, 1998). In 1998, Heritage Minister Copps proposed a plan that would require the country's movie theaters to show a minimum percentage of Canadian movies (Tamburri, 1998a). In 1999, after an earlier effort to impose an 80 percent customs duty and excise tax on U.S. magazines was declared illegal by the World Trade Organization, Canada proposed a new bill (Bill C-55) that would make it illegal for Canadian companies or businesses to advertise in Canadian editions of U.S. magazines—so-called "split-run" editions (Bourrie, 1999). The intent was to protect the Canadian magazine industry from being swallowed up by its more powerful and wealthier U.S. competition. However, after vehement protests by the United States, the regulation was amended to allow split-run Canadian editions of U.S. magazines to contain a maximum of 18 percent advertising by Canadian firms. Canada has also joined France, Australia, Belgium, Greece, Italy, and Portugal in support of exempting books, magazines, films, television and radio programs, and other cultural products from provisions of the Multilateral Agreement on Investment, which would eliminate current and future ownership restrictions and other barriers to foreign investment among OECD (Organization for Economic Cooperation and Development) countries. Viewing the MAI as "the largest threat to Canadian culture ever" (Barrow, in Tamburri, 1998a), Canada claims that the agreement would threaten Canadian rules limiting foreign ownership in its book publishing, telecommunications, and broadcasting companies, thus giving foreign media an indirect entry into Canada and placing the nation's cultural identity at risk. In joining his colleagues in pressing for the MAI exemption, Ivan Fecan, president of CTV, one of Canada's largest commercial television networks, asserts that "I don't think anyone would confuse this with being anti-American. It's not. Canada is not another state, and we don't want to be one" (in DePalma, 1999). Nonetheless, the United States, the world's largest exporter of films, television programming, books, and other popular culture products, has led the opposition to granting this exemption. According to former U.S. trade negotiator William Merkin, "The U.S. is not in a position either politically or from a commercial perspective to grant any nation carte blanche to restrict our access in . . . the entertainment sector, which is an important export earner for the U.S." (in Tamburri, 1998a).

But Canada's legislative attempts to restrict the flow of culturally corrupting mass media from outside its borders represent just one element of the country's two-pronged effort to control the undesirable socialization impacts of the media on its children. By far, Canada's greatest efforts—and greatest successes—to date have been in the area of curbing the gratuitous portrayal of violence on television, whether from imported or domestic programming sources. In this respect, Canada currently leads the growing group of nations around the world that have become increasingly concerned about combating the negative effects of media-conveyed mayhem on their populations, especially their children. The country's position as leader of that pack came about largely as a result of two events that mobilized the Canadian people and their government into action.

In December, 1989, in what came to be called "the Montreal Massacre," 14 female engineering students at Montreal's École Polytechnique were killed in a shooting rampage by a lone gunman carrying out a vendetta against both women and universities. Stunned by the brutality of the shootings, nearly 200,000 citizens across Canada signed petitions asking the CRTC to investigate the link between TV violence and subsequent violence in the real world ("CRTC Announces Public Hearing," 1995; "The Media Violence Story," 1997). Not quite three years later, in November, 1992, after the rape and murder of her younger sister, 13-year-old Virginie Larivière presented then-Prime Minister Brian Mulroney with a petition bearing the names of 1.3 million Canadians (the total population of Canada at the time was 27 million) who, like her, were convinced that media violence had played a role in her sister's death. The petition demanded legislation prohibiting gratuitous violence on television ("The Media Violence Story," 1997).

In response to these public outcries and to the results of two newly commissioned studies reaffirming previous research findings of a negative impact of prolonged viewing of television violence on children, the CRTC began to take action. In 1992, it established a long-term goal of "making violence on television socially unacceptable, in much the same way as has already been done in Canada with other social issues such as drinking and driving, pollution, and cigarette smoking" ("Canada & TV Violence," 1996, p. 2). Drawing on the largely unsuccessful experiences of other societies in grappling with this problem, the CRTC structured its own efforts in a manner designed to move from discussion to action in as short a time as possible. To this end: (a) TV violence was defined as a major mental-health problem for Canadian children; (b) the issue was confined to violence in television programming;

(c) ideological rhetoric of "freedom of speech versus censorship" was avoided in favor of questions of "how can we best protect our children?"; (d) specific, concrete objectives were set; and (e) all concerned parties—government, parents, industry groups, and educators, among others—participated in the discussions from the very start. Utilizing these strategies, the CRTC was able to achieve a high level of success in a remarkably short time ("Canada & TV Violence," 1996). Canada now possesses a national rating system for television programming, an extensive public education program (funded both by private and public sources) concerning the effects of TV violence and ways to institute healthy television use in the home; and a broadcasting review board that has already been successful in removing several objectionable, overly violent programs from Canadian airways.

In essence, the Canadian approach to television violence, as summarized by CRTC chairman Keith Spicer (1995) is a program designed to get rid of unhealthy children's TV programming and encourage more intelligent, creative and healthy children's television through implementation of an "80-10-10 package": 80 percent public education to inform parents of the effects of televised violence viewing on their children and to help them develop plans for dealing with TV programming issues in their own families; 10 percent technological, utilizing parental control devices such as the "V-chip," a device installed in television controls to monitor the content of programming and automatically block any programs exceeding pre-set violence levels specified by parents; and the remaining 10 percent, voluntary codes adopted by the TV media. These codes were developed by the major industry groups themselves, through their participation in AGVOT, the Action Group on Violence on Television.

Although Canada possesses a formidable array of federal, provincial, and local laws concerning children and the audiovisual industry (summarized by Caron and Jolicoeur, 1996), the core of the Canadian approach to dealing with violent TV programming, according to one of its chief architects, CRTC chairman Keith Spicer, is

cooperation and consensus, not confrontation. That is the heart of the matter, that is how Canadians came together on this tough, potentially divisive issue. We're not naive. This cooperative approach is backed up by the always real, if undesirable, possibility of regulations, as well as by the vigilance of the public, the media, and politicians. When you recall how unsubtle, coercive approaches have so often led to futile confrontation, I think we're just being realistic. (in "Canada & TV Violence," 1996, p. 9)

Naive or realistic, this nonviolent approach to policing television violence seems to work in the context of Canadian culture and society. Whether the same approach could work—or would even be considered—in a more aggressive, competitive culture such as that found in the United States remains to be seen.

Examples include army barracks, convents, orphanages, mental hospitals, and prisons. Individually, total institutions serve a variety of social purposes; collectively, they involve attempts to remake individuals in a new mold. Personal identities and differences, as symbolized by such things as individual clothing and hair styles, are stripped away and replaced with a new, categorical identity—common uniforms and numbers rather than names. The objective is to break down individual resistance to the important learning of new, mandated behaviors and attitudes. Given the almost complete control such organizations exert over their inmates' lives, such resocialization efforts frequently are highly successful. People leave these centers prepared and knowing how to lead more moral lives (in the case of convents and monasteries) or how to put an end to those who lead less moral lives (in the case of military boot camps).

SOCIALIZATION, OVERSOCIALIZATION, AND SOCIAL CONTROL

We began this chapter with an examination of the argument that humans are biologically determined creatures whose basic nature has been shaped by forces outside their control. Rejecting that claim, we attempted to construct a case for the opposite assertion. We are social creatures whose human thoughts and actions represent the consequences of lifelong socialization. As far as we can establish, humans do not enter the world programmed by instincts or other inherited factors to develop in any sort of automatic fashion. Rather, the traits we normally associate with being human must be acquired from others through intensive and extensive social interaction. In the absence of such interaction (as in the cases of Anna and Genie), individuals may remain prehuman—biologically equipped to become human but unable to complete the process on their own.

The critical importance of social learning becomes even more evident as we examine the manner in which the members of a given population develop a sense of their surrounding social and cultural world. As we saw in the two preceding chapters, cultural and social structures are human creations that vary significantly over time and space. A quick look at any standard cultural anthropology textbook will confirm the fact that humans have an amazing ability to interpret their world and then to build on that interpretation in an almost endless variety of ways. That same textbook could also verify the fact that the members of those different sociocultural systems invariably come to view their own particular arrangement as being right and natural. Ethnocentrism, as we discussed in Chapter 2, appears to be a near-universal human phenomenon.

The fact that one has been born into a particular society in a given historical period might be interpreted as either blind chance or individual karma. The fact that the individual ordinarily comes to accept that society's basic cultural premises and to follow its basic rules should be interpreted as a matter of deliberate design. Every society has a fundamental interest in ensuring that its members internalize its established patterns. Its continued survival depends on the successful transmission of those patterns to each new generation. Important primary and secondary groups such as families, schools, peers, and the mass media cooperate (or conspire) to carry out this objective. So also (as we will see in Chapter 8 on crime and deviance) do larger organizations and institutions such as law and government. Fitting individuals into the surrounding sociocultural order is a crucial task, one on which socialization agents expend a great deal of time and effort.

Social systems have a need to direct and control the actions of their members, and most succeed in doing so to a large extent. Incidents of crime and deviance in modern societies often appear to be numerous, but the ratio of such acts to the entire body of social interactions that occur in a given day, week, month, or year is small. Every day of our lives, each of us has the opportunity to violate our society's established laws or formal norms hundreds of times. However, most of us do not do so, and the fact that

we do not has little or nothing to do with being monitored by police or other agents of social control threatening us with severe punishments if we step out of line. For the most part, we act as our own agents of control: We choose not to break the rules because to do so would be "wrong." For example, the feeling that taking another student's sociology textbook would be morally wrong illustrates the fact that we have accepted and internalized our society's view regarding theft of someone else's property. In Mead's terminology, we have taken the perspective of the generalized other and made it our own. As Mead suggested, this phenomenon is both normal and, from the standpoint of societal continuity, necessary.

But we should not rush to the conclusion that the social learning of accepted values, beliefs, and behaviors is equivalent to social programming. Most people accept and follow their society's rules most of the time. However, as any student who has ever left a textbook sitting unattended too long has learned the hard way, many do not. And most people break some rules at least some of the time. Even when we follow the established norms, we often do so only after a painful internal struggle between our individual desire and our social conscience.

In a famous and often-cited article, sociologist Dennis H. Wrong (1961) cautioned social scientists against accepting what he termed an **oversocialized conception of human beings.** By "oversocialized," Wrong meant a portrayal of people as puppets who have been manipulated by their society to believe everything they have been taught and to act blindly on the basis of those beliefs. In any given society, he stated, attempts to socialize individual members into complete knowledge and acceptance of the system invariably will fall short of perfection. The fact that modern societies are heterogeneous structures with racial, ethnic, class, religious, and other subcultural groups means that, in fact, no single integrated world view will be shared by all their members. The picture of the world that one is likely to receive will be a function of the values, beliefs, and experiences of one's subculture. Even if the social learning process worked exactly as intended, individuals still would exhibit different attitudes and social behaviors to the extent that their particular subculture differed from that of other individuals. Societies may control their members, but they do not own them.

SUMMARY AND REVIEW

On Being Human: Biology and Human Nature

1. *How do "instincts" affect human behavior?*

Unlike other creatures whose behaviors are shaped largely by instincts, humans learn most behaviors

through a process called socialization. This learning occurs as a by-product of the close social interaction young children have with parents and other important socialization agents. (P. 76)

On Being Human: Social Learning and Human Nature

2. *How does contact with other humans affect the social development of children?*

Several case studies of young children who were isolated from normal social contact shortly after birth suggest that early socialization is critical for the development of language skills and other human characteristics. (Pp. 76–77)

3. *How did Piaget view the process of socialization?*

Whereas psychological interpretations of socialization such as Sigmund Freud's focus largely on the interplay of conscious and unconscious personality forces, Jean Piaget's developmental model examined the interaction of individual, social, and cultural factors in shaping human cognitive ability levels. Piaget described socialization as a series of stages—sensorimotor, preoperational, concrete operational, and, for some individuals, formal operational—through which children pass in a movement toward increasing understanding of their surrounding world. (Pp. 77–78)

4. *What is the focus of sociological models of socialization?*

Sociological approaches to socialization examine the impact of group experiences on individual personality development. Two important theorists in this tradition are Charles Horton Cooley and George Herbert Mead. (P. 78)

5. *What was Cooley's notion of "the looking-glass self"?*

Cooley argued that humans are able to form a self-concept, a sense of individual identity, only through contact with other humans. He described a looking-glass self process in which the responses of other people to a particular individual give that person crucial information for forming a set of beliefs and feelings about his or her personal attributes. (Pp. 78–79)

6. *How did Mead view the socialization process?*

Mead portrayed socialization as a process in which increasing social contact between the individual and others creates role-playing and role-taking activities. In the play stage, young children pretend to be specific other people such as mother or father, learning something about the roles of parents in the process. In the game stage, the child interacts with others in group activities, developing a sense of social structures and the relationships among different statuses and roles. In the generalized other stage, the child comes to form a sense of self based on the whole system of social groups of which he or she is an acting part. (Pp. 79–80)

7. *According to Mead, what is the difference between "me" and "I" as components of the social self?*

Mead claimed the sense of self-identity, or what he termed the social self, is composed of two related elements. The "me" is the objective, predictable part, reflecting the individual's involvement in social roles and role playing. The "I" is the subjective, creative, unpredictable part, reflecting the person's individual attrib-

utes. Mead argued that the self is never fully finished. Rather, it is subject to significant modifications throughout one's lifetime, as one's social statuses and relationships change over time. (P. 80)

Socialization as Social Learning

8. *What roles do the family and education play in socialization?*

In modern societies, large numbers of groups and agents are involved in the socialization process. For most individuals, the family remains the single most important social learning influence. For a growing number of people, an educational system that takes students at earlier stages and keeps them for a longer time than ever before also has become a crucial source of social learning. (Pp. 80–81)

9. *How do peer groups affect the socialization process?*

For adolescents in particular, peer groups made up of people of the same age and social status are significant agents of socialization. Peers are buffers between the individual and the larger society. They create communities in which adolescents can experiment with behaviors forbidden by parents and other adult authorities. (Pp. 81–82)

10. *How do mass media such as television influence socialization?*

In contemporary societies, mass media such as television have become major sources of knowledge and social learning. A large amount of controversy exists over charges of distortion of factual news by the media, as well as the alleged effects of televised violence on young viewers. However, a simple one-to-one relationship between such programs and acts of violence by children has yet to be confirmed empirically. (Pp. 82–85)

11. *What is adult socialization?*

A great deal of the socialization that occurs in contemporary societies involves adult learning of marital and occupational roles in a changing social and cultural world. In some cases, this learning includes rapid and dramatic attempts to replace existing attitudes and behaviors with new patterns, a process known as resocialization. Resocialization often occurs within total institutions such as prisons, convents, and monasteries, where all aspects of people's lives are controlled and directed by agents of the organization. (Pp. 85, 88)

Socialization, Oversocialization, and Social Control

12. *Does socialization turn people into mindless conformists?*

Although socialization agents in all societies greatly shape the lives of their members, they never control them completely. Compliance with norms and values may be widespread, but such conformity is never automatic or achieved without difficulty. Sociologists must be careful not to develop an oversocialized concept of human beings. (P. 89)

Inequality and Stratification

5

Adopted on July 4, 1776, the Declaration of Independence signaled not only the rejection of British political rule by the thirteen American colonies, but a rejection of centuries of European social and cultural traditions as well. Asserting that it is a self-evident truth that all men are created equal, this document established the break-away colonies as a new, independent nation and formed the basis for the formal Constitution that would be ratified some twelve years later—the Constitution that continues to provide the framework for life as we know it in the contemporary United States.

As the one statement that, more than any other, defines the essence of the United States of America, the Declaration of Independence occupies a revered place in the hearts and minds of the American people. However, it would seem that even a casual glance at the conditions of life in the United States and across the world would raise serious doubts about its assertion that all men are created equal, for it is self-evident that humans are anything but equal. Some people are born into great wealth and power, spending their lives in positions of privilege. Other people are born into great poverty and hopelessness, spending their lives in futile attempts to escape their fate. Thomas Jefferson, the primary author of the Declaration of Independence, was a wealthy Virginia gentleman-farmer who later became President of the United States. He was also a slave-owner, employing the forced, unpaid labor of other humans defined as legal property to support his estate at Monticello. In more recent times, the wealthiest individual among *Forbes* magazine's 1999 listing of the "world's working rich," Bill Gates of Microsoft fame, possessed a fortune estimated at approximately $90 billion—an amount that would allow him to give each of the 6 billion inhabitants of the planet a ten-dollar bill and still retain a comfortable $30 billion for his own personal use (Weston, 1999). For many of the lucky recipients in this hypothetical scenario, that ten-dollar bill would represent several months' income; for still others, an amount they would never otherwise possess in their entire lifetime. Mexico, a country in which widespread, grinding poverty sends tens of thousands of people streaming across the U.S. border each month in search of work, boasts no fewer than 24 billionaires. And, at the global level, the world's richest 225 people possess as much combined wealth (over $1 trillion) as the world's poorest 2.5 *billion* people (United Nations Development Program, 1998).

But, as dramatic as these figures may be, it could be argued that they are not directly relevant to the claim that all men are created equal. After all, the intent of the Declaration of Independence was to assert that all men are equal in some basic "human" sense, not that they are (or should be) equal in terms of economic or other material conditions. Starting from a position of shared human equality and enjoying certain inalienable rights including life, liberty, and the pursuit of happiness, individuals are then free, within a society that provides the same or similar chances for all men, to strive to become as wealthy or powerful or otherwise successful as their talents and efforts can take them. In the language of modern sociology, so long as **equality of opportunity** prevails, the fact that individuals may end up with significantly different amounts of income, wealth, power, and other resources (what is called **inequality of outcome** or **inequality of condition**) does not invalidate the assertion that all men are created equal in some fundamental sense.

As we will see in Chapters 5–7, however, even this argument of a basic "human" equality is subject to empirical challenge. At different times and different places throughout human social history, including the present time in the United States, various groups of people—lower classes as compared to upper classes, people of color as compared to whites, non-Anglos as compared to Anglo Saxons, and women as compared to men, for example—have been the targets of philosophical ideologies and social policies that have defined and treated them as intrinsically inferior. Thomas Jefferson's own slaves certainly did not enjoy the "life, liberty, and pursuit of happiness" of which he had written so eloquently. The fact remains that, although formal documents such as the Declaration of Independence may claim the basic equality of all men, that claim has yet to be translated fully into social practices. True equality for all humans, including all men, is a goal whose time has yet to come.

In this and the next two chapters, we examine the general topic of inequality in its different guises. We begin, in this chapter, with socioeconomic inequality and stratification, perhaps the most obvious manifestation of the unequal lives led by most people in this society and throughout the modern world. In Chapter 6, we turn to matters of race and ethnicity, two often-confused (and confusing) phenomena representing major human efforts to group other humans on the basis of real or imagined traits and then to treat them according to the presumed differences in those group-based traits. Finally, in Chapter 7, we explore issues of sex and gender, especially with regard to their impact on making some people more equal than others.

1. Why do so many societal and global studies of stratification focus on economic measures of inequality?
2. Some theorists argue that social stratification is natural in human societies. In what way is such inequality thought to be natural?
3. Functionalists such as Davis and Moore argued that if all social inequalities were eliminated, the survival of societies would be jeopardized. Why did they feel this way?
4. How do conflict theorists such as Marx explain the existence of stratification in most human societies?
5. Why was Max Weber so critical of Marx's class conflict theory of stratification?
6. What major features distinguish open-class stratification systems from closed-caste structures?
7. How does structural mobility differ from voluntary social mobility?
8. What is the relationship between position in the inequality hierarchy and physical or mental health?
9. What are the connections among social class, crime, and the criminal justice system?

ASSESSING INEQUALITY AND STRATIFICATION

Although many people (including many sociologists) use the terms *social inequality* and *social stratification* interchangeably, there is an important distinction between the two phenomena. **Social inequality** refers to the unequal distribution of valued goods and services among the members of a given group or population at a particular point in time. **Social stratification** refers to such a distribution of goods and services that has become permanent over time; that is, to social inequalities that have become structured or patterned, are supported and justified by prevailing norms, beliefs, and values, and are transmitted from one generation to another (Kerbo, 2000). Confirming the existence of widespread social inequalities in the contemporary world is not a very difficult task, even for nonsociologists. However, accurately measuring the extent to which these observed inequalities are indicative of a full-scale system of social stratification is a challenge to the abilities of even the most sophisticated social scientists.

Both social inequality and social stratification are multifaceted phenomena that include intangible, as well as material, elements. Some of these components, such as income and education, can be quantified and measured fairly easily. But others, such as power, prestige, and a sense of personal well-being, are much less tangible—though no less important or less sought after—and, thus, much more difficult to measure (recall our discussion of research and measurement problems in Chapter 1). For this reason, studies of social inequality and social stratification at both societal and global levels typically include only those aspects of inequality that can be quantified and compared empirically. Consequently, they are more approximate than complete statements that in all likelihood understate the true scope of contemporary social inequalities.

Economic Dimensions of Inequality

To a large extent, existing societal and cross-societal studies of inequality have focused on economic resources such as income and wealth. These economic factors are not the only important dimensions of social inequality. However, they do play a crucial role in shaping an individual's (or a society's) chances for obtaining other resources necessary for maintaining a high-quality level of existence. In addition, different economic factors can be translated into a common denominator (U.S. dollars, for example) that allows meaningful cross-societal comparisons. In assessing the amount of inequality within a given society, then, sociologists typically examine income and wealth distributions within the given population. In examining international or global inequality, sociologists compare various countries in terms of their per capita gross national product (GNP), gross domestic product (GDP), or some similar indicator of their overall level of economic development.

Global Inequality

Just as contemporary societies are stratified into unequal segments whose constituent members are individual people, the contemporary world is likewise stratified into unequal segments whose component members are individual societies. *Developed* or *northern* and *developing* or *southern* are terms often used to describe a particular society's relative position on this global stratification ladder with regard to economic, educational, health care, nutritional, and other resources vital to human existence.

Developed or **northern countries** are composed of the more economically developed and politically democratic nations. These countries feature free-market economies dominated by advanced-technology industrial and administrative occupations, and display generally high levels of collective and per capita income. Many population members occupy what could be called "middle-class" socioeconomic positions and enjoy relatively comfortable lives. The United States and Japan are examples of this type of society.

Developing or **southern countries** currently are undergoing societal modernization (we discuss the modernization process more fully in Chapter 13). Their economies are a mixture of a large percentage of traditional agricultural activities and a growing proportion of industrial-oriented, factory-based manufacturing and processing occupations. In contrast to their counterparts in the developed world, these developing societies generally are characterized by much lower levels of overall and per capita incomes. Many, perhaps most, population members occupy very low positions in the socioeconomic hierarchy. They often lead lives at or near the basic survival level, and experience many economic and physical hardships. Often, though not always, developing societies are characterized by political systems that are nondemocratic and "less free."

Although all developing societies share this modernizing status, they differ significantly from one another in many other ways. Both the Republic of Korea (South Korea) and the African nation of Ethiopia are developing countries, but they are located at opposite poles of the modernization continuum with regard to economic and political development and the quality-of-life levels of their respective populations. South Korea is in many regards poised on the edge of "developed nation" status, whereas, in a number of respects, Ethiopia may well be the least developed society in the world. It is difficult to find truly typical examples of developing societies, since the category includes such a wide array of individual countries at different levels of societal and economic development.

Global Economic Inequality

Each year, international agencies such as the United Nations Development Program (UNDP) and the World Bank collect economic and other quality-of-life data from contemporary societies around the world. This information is then analyzed and presented in publications such as the UNDP's *Human Development Report* and the World Bank's *World Development Report* and *World Development Indicators*. Table 5.1 and Figure 5.1, which are based on data from this last source, show the extreme variations in per capita economic resources that existed across the world in 1997. At that time, more than 44 percent (93) of the 210 different countries examined had per capita GNPs under $2,000, and 30 percent (64) were under $1,000. In contrast, only about 13 percent of these societies (27) had per capita GNPs of $15,000 or more. For the world at large, per capita GNP averaged a little over $5,200. For industrialized nations as a whole, that figured soared to over $26,000, whereas for developing nations, it plunged to $1,250. On average, then, the populations of the developed nations enjoyed about twenty-one times the level of economic resources of their counterparts in developing countries. And some developing nations were far worse off than others. Per capita GNP in the least developed countries averaged only $350 in 1997, nearly seventy-five times less than that of people living in industrialized societies. At the two extreme ends of this continuum, the per capita GNP of both Ethiopia and the Democratic Republic of the Congo ($110) was four hundred and fifty-four times less than that of Liechtenstein ($50,000) (World Bank, 1999a).

Global Poverty The World Bank (1999b) estimates that over 1.3 billion people throughout the world live in abject poverty. Most of these people live in developing nations, where widespread poverty is significantly related to population growth. (We examine population dynamics in Chapter 12.) For

> **TABLE 5.1**
>
> **Variations in Annual per Capita Gross National Product, 1997**

Average per Capita GNP (in U.S. dollars)	Number of Countries
Less than $1,000	64
$1,000–$3,999	57
$4,000–$7,999	13
$8,000–$11,999	6
$12,000–$19,999	5
$20,000 and over	23

Source: Compiled from data in World Bank, *1999 World Development Indicators* (New York: Oxford University Press, 1999).

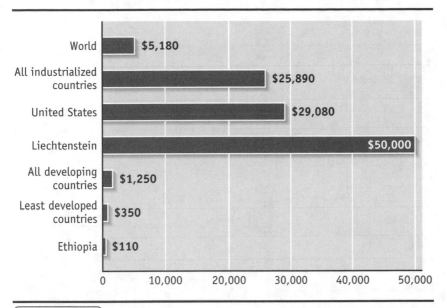

Average per Capita Gross National Product for Industrialized and Developing Countries, 1997

example, almost half of the entire population of Kenya—an estimated 13.2 million individuals–fall below that country's poverty line of 30 Kenyan shillings (about 50 cents) per day (Mwangi, 1999). In its annual survey of human development around the world, the United Nations Development Program has attempted to operationalize the concept of human poverty by translating it into a more tangible form. This group's *Human Poverty Index-1* (HPI-1) is a composite measure of living conditions in developing countries. The index includes data on the percentage of people not expected to survive to age 40, the percentage of adults who are illiterate, the percentage of people without access to health services and safe water, and the percentage of underweight children under age five. According to the most recent HPI-1 figures (United Nations Development Program, 1998, p. 2),

> Of the 4.4 billion people in developing countries, nearly three-fifths lack basic sanitation. Almost a third have no access to clean water. A quarter do not have adequate housing. A fifth have no access to modern health services. A fifth of children do not attend school to grade 5. About a fifth do not have enough dietary energy and protein . . . Worldwide, 2 billion people are anemic.

The UNDP estimates that the cost of rectifying the desperate situation of the world's poor would amount to about $40 billion a year, a figure that is less than 4 percent of the combined wealth of the 225 richest people in the world. According to the UNDP (1998, p. 30), the three wealthiest individuals in the

world have assets that exceeded the combined gross domestic product of the 48 least developed countries.

EXPLANATIONS AND INTERPRETATIONS OF STRATIFICATION

The continuing and apparently universal presence of such stark inequalities has made the study of social stratification a basic part of sociological concern since the field began. Given the existence of a number of competing theoretical paradigms in the discipline, social stratification has been subject to a variety of competing and often conflicting explanations. Several important interpretations have guided not only sociological research, but often social and political policies as well, over the past two hundred years.

Natural Superiority Theory

The beliefs embodied in natural superiority theory were found in popular thought long before the advent of the discipline of sociology. But they found early sociological expression in the writings of Herbert Spencer and William Graham Sumner. Both men were important figures in the history of **social Darwinism,** a social and political philosophy that believed in the existence of natural laws of social evolution and argued for a hands-off approach to human social affairs.

Although never really fully developed and stated as a formal theory, the natural superiority perspective

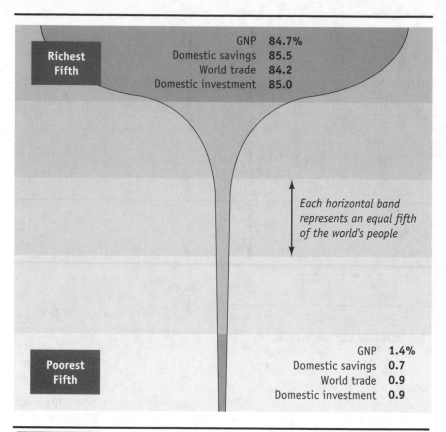

Richest Fifth

GNP	84.7%
Domestic savings	85.5
World trade	84.2
Domestic investment	85.0

Each horizontal band represents an equal fifth of the world's people

Poorest Fifth

GNP	1.4%
Domestic savings	0.7
World trade	0.9
Domestic investment	0.9

FIGURE 5.2

Disparity of Global Wealth

The wealthiest fifth of the world's population control about 85 percent of total economic activity as measured by four key indicators. The bottom fifth control about 1 percent.

Source: Herring in *The Christian Science Monitor.* © 1994 TCSPS. Original date from U.N. Development Program, 1991.

was an influential part of European and U.S. social thought in the late nineteenth and early twentieth centuries. It maintained that the social inequalities found in all human societies reflect underlying and fundamental natural inequalities among population members. For example, differences in people's wealth and privilege are the result of individual differences in physical strength, mental agility, intellectual capacity, or some other natural human trait.

Proponents of the approach viewed social life as a competitive struggle for existence among individual human beings. In this game of life, it was only natural that some people would win and some would lose. Individuals who were better equipped mentally or physically would emerge as winners, and those who were more poorly equipped would end up as the losers. "Survival of the fittest" (a phrase coined by Herbert Spencer, not Charles Darwin) was the harsh but very real fact of life. It might seem unfortunate that some people would experience great misery and distress while others around them prospered, but it would be even more unfortunate to intervene artificially on be-

half of the losers. To do so would be to interfere with the natural cleansing process that strengthened societies by purging them of their unfit members.

By the same token, it would be an equally serious mistake to restrict in any way the activities or lives of the prosperous. They, too, were part of the larger natural plan for the improvement of human societies. Since inequalities were grounded in natural human differences, any action taken to eliminate them through social means (for example, welfare programs for the poor funded through taxation of the rich) was doomed to failure. The best and only viable policy was a laissez-faire approach to social activities. (For what is probably the classic statement of the natural superiority-based, social Darwinist approach, see Sumner, 1883.)

The natural superiority argument was originally intended as an explanation of social differences among individuals. However, it was adapted rather easily to be an explanation—and justification—as to why certain kinds of people might be expected to occupy superior or inferior positions in a given society. Given

According to the Functionalist or Davis-Moore theory of stratification, these corporate executives have earned such privileges as limousine service and private jet travel because of their occupation's high level of importance to societal survival. Critics of the Davis-Moore interpretation might question why other socially important roles, such as that of mother, do not command equally lavish rewards.

the assumed superior natural abilities of males as compared to females, of whites as compared to nonwhites, and of Anglo-Saxons as compared to non-Anglos, it was only "natural" that United States society would be dominated by white Anglo-Saxon males over the past two centuries. Given their assumed inferior natural abilities, it was only "natural" that females, nonwhites, and certain white ethnic people would be relegated to the lower social positions. Historically, such arguments, as advanced by early sociologists such as Edward Alsworth Ross (1922), became a basis for a series of immigration quota laws first enacted during the 1920s. These laws were designed to halt or limit the flow of "inferior," undesirable people into the United States and thus prevent the ultimate catastrophe of (in Ross's words) "race suicide."

Empirical studies of human populations have failed to support the basic assumption that any specific racial, ethic, gender, class, or age group is natu-

rally superior or naturally inferior to any other such groups. Thus this approach has largely been discredited as a valid *scientific* explanation of social inequality. However, natural superiority interpretations of social stratification continue to exert significant influences over cultural beliefs, social actions, and political policies in many societies. As we will see in the next two chapters, hundreds of millions of people throughout the world are denied full access to social opportunities because of their presumed "natural" deficiencies. Unfortunately, natural superiority theory remains alive and well in the modern world.

Functionalist Theory

As discussed in Chapter 1, structural-functional theory represents an attempt to explain certain patterns of organized social action (social structures) by examining their contributions to the survival of the social system (their social functions) over time. The classic functionalist statement concerning the question of social inequality was made by Kingsley Davis and Wilbert E. Moore (1945). It has been a source of great debate and controversy within the field of sociology for over fifty years.

The functionalist theory of stratification, or, as it is often called, the **Davis-Moore theory,** seems to share some of the basic assumptions of the natural superiority approach. It asserts that social stratification is a natural and inevitable part of the human condition, a part of life that in fact may be necessary for the continued survival of society.

Davis and Moore began with the observation that virtually all human societies in the past and in the present have been characterized by differentiated social positions that receive unequal amounts of property, power, and prestige rewards. They then sought to explain these systems in terms of a basic survival problem (a "functional requisite") common to all societies.

In every society, they claimed, people with unequal kinds and amounts of talent somehow must be encouraged to assume and to perform various social tasks. These tasks differ in a number of significant respects, including required skills and impact on societal well-being. For example, Supreme Court justices have a much more important effect on U.S. life than do hair stylists. Although hair stylists may perform a positive function, its importance pales in comparison with that of the justices, who define the laws that govern our social relations. A successful career in hair styling does not require advanced formal educational credentials or an exhaustive knowledge of legal precedents; a successful court career requires both.

Davis and Moore argued that, to meet the challenge of matching talented people to crucial social roles, all societies have developed reward systems that offer individuals property, power, and prestige incentives proportional to the skill requirements and the functional importance of the positions they fill. The more important the task and the smaller the number of people with the abilities to perform it, the higher the reward level. The less important the task and the larger the number of people with the abilities to perform it, the lower the reward level.

Davis and Moore's underlying assumption appears to be that humans can be motivated best—or perhaps only—by appealing to their individual desires for fame, fortune, and power. At the same time, the collective actions of individuals who pursue their own self-interests create effects that promote the well-being of the larger society. For example, some people may enter the medical profession to acquire the finer things in life this line of work typically offers. If some of these physicians turn out to be inspiring healers, the fact that they were working just for the material rewards becomes irrelevant. What is important is that, without the tangible incentives that attracted these individuals to medical careers, society would have been deprived of activities important for the continuity of the system. Presumably, if talented individuals were not offered these reward incentives, they would not undertake such difficult, demanding, but important roles, since it would not be in their best self-interest to do so. Because crucial social positions would then go unfilled or would be filled by less-qualified, less-competent people, tasks necessary for social survival would remain undone. The preservation of the system then would be jeopardized.

Davis and Moore and other adherents of the functionalist approach recognized that some of the effects of social stratification might be dysfunctional for particular individuals or groups whose rewards did not permit them any level of material comfort. But stratification itself was functional and necessary for the continued well-being of the society at large. Like that of the natural superiority approach, the functionalist argument could be translated into a hands-off, non-intervention social policy (although Davis and Moore themselves never suggested such a practice).

Critics of the functionalist model such as Melvin Tumin (1953a, 1953b) claimed it is impossible to assess validly the exact levels of difficulty various types of work entail as well as the actual functional importance of specific social statuses. These critics also argued that stratified reward systems do not work in practice the way they are claimed to work in theory.

In what he termed the *strangulation of talent* effect, Tumin argued that any system of stratification created to promote the search for individual ability and talent ultimately will have the opposite effect. Offering different levels of rewards to different statuses may initially encourage open competition in which the most qualified people will win the most desirable (and important) social positions. But over time, the competition will become less and less open. Children born to successful parents will have an advantage over children born to less successful parents, even when ability levels are identical. For example, the likelihood that the talents of a gifted ghetto child will be discovered and developed by teachers is far less than that for a gifted child from the affluent suburbs. Individual social identity and background, rather than personal talents, eventually become the primary criteria for filling social positions. Over the span of several generations, Tumin stated, what began as a mechanism for identifying and promoting talented people becomes a device for ignoring and stifling them. In the long run, therefore, stratification systems are dysfunctional for societal preservation.

Perhaps the most serious charge against the Davis-Moore interpretation of stratification is that it ignores the role of power in creating and maintaining social inequality systems. Critics (Dahrendorf, 1959; Lenski, 1966; Tumin, 1985) claimed that Davis and Moore treated power solely as a type of reward attached to individual social statuses, failing to recognize its potential as a resource employed to establish which specific positions will be defined as most important for societal survival. In addition, Davis and Moore did not investigate the use of power by individuals or groups to restrict access to highly valued, highly rewarded statuses (Tumin, 1953a). For example, in the United States, powerful professional organizations such as the American Bar Association and the American Medical Association have been able to set limits or quotas for openings in law schools and medical schools. Some critics of these associations have interpreted such actions as an attempt to keep the supply of professionals artificially low, thus increasing the demand (and the fees) for their services.

Davis and Moore apparently viewed the structure of unequally rewarded positions as forming a free-market system in which people competed for specific statuses on the basis of their individual talents and abilities. Conflict theorists, in contrast, take a dramatically different approach. They see a social world in which individuals and groups use their power to manipulate economic, social, and political markets to their own best advantage. Although it predated the Davis-Moore statement by decades, Karl Marx's work in many ways represents the antithesis of the functionalist approach.

Marxist Class Conflict Theory

Karl Marx (1818–1883) focused on the phenomenon of social power. For him, the system of stratification in any society was rooted in people's relationship to the economic process, a relationship that was central to all societies. Marx regarded the power struggles that inevitably ensued between the stratified groups in all societies, that is, **class conflicts**, as the driving force of human social history (Marx and Engels, 1955/1848).

Marx's theory represents an example of *materialistic determinism*, the claim that all aspects of human social life are determined by the material or physical conditions of the given time and place. For Marx, the single most important fact of life for every human population was its **mode of production**, the mechanism by which wealth was produced in the given society. This economic **substructure** shaped all other significant material and nonmaterial aspects of societal life. Politics, law, religion, and even cultural forms were **superstructures** derived from and reflective of this economic foundation.

For individuals, the single most important fact of life was their relation to the *means of production;* that is, whether they were owners whose living was derived from the control of their property resources, or nonowners whose living had to come from the sale of their labor to others. Ultimately, Marx argued, societies would polarize into two distinct **objective classes** (in modern industrial societies, bourgeoisie and proletariat) along the lines of this basic economic distinction. This division of societal populations into rich and poor segments is very evident throughout the contemporary world. Many modern societies, including the United States, are showing signs of shrinking or deteriorating middle classes as their populations are reshuffled into higher and lower class groups (Kerbo, 2000).

According to Marx, the fundamental interests of these two classes—maximum profit for owners, maximum wages for workers—are inherently incompatible. This conflict of interests puts the two classes into continuing opposition with one another. The owners possess great economic, political, social, and other power resources. They also exist as a **subjective class,** conscious and aware of their own collective position and interests within the mode of production. Together, these factors give this class an overwhelming advantage in its relations with workers.

Workers generally lack effective economic, political, and social power, as well as the ability to recognize their historical role in the economic productive process. Consequently, they are dominated and exploited by the superior powers of the owners. They will remain so until their objective living conditions deteriorate to the point at which they are unable to maintain even minimum survival standards. Only then will they begin to recognize their plight as a collective problem and identify the source of the problem as the self-seeking policies of the ownership class. At this point, they will finally begin to take collective, conscious, revolutionary action to end their exploitation once and for all.

Marx claimed that human social history is a series of such revolutionary conflicts, and it is exactly as a result of these class upheavals that social and cultural change occurs. Past class revolutions succeeded only in replacing one ruling class with another. However, in industrial society, the proletarian revolution that was to come would end this "changing of the palace guard" history for good. Modern workers would recognize private property as the ultimate source of class divisions and antagonisms and would act to abolish it. With the elimination of private property, the basis for human social inequalities would be removed, and social stratification itself would become a thing of the past.

Marx believed that social stratification was neither natural nor inevitable, nor did it serve the best interests of societal survival. The interests of human populations were far better served by systems of social equality. He argued strongly for interventionist, indeed, revolutionary, action to create and maintain such egalitarian systems.

Thus far, history has failed to verify Marx's predictions. A worldwide proletarian revolution resulting in the destruction of private property–based economic systems and the elimination of social stratifications as a basic component of social life has yet to materialize. If anything, the demise of the Soviet Union and the collapse of many other socialist societies around the world would seem to signal the final blow to Marxist class conflict theory. In many of these societies, including the People's Republic of China, capitalist-flavored free-market economics and democratic forms of government have emerged in response to popular cries for greater individual freedom.

Conflict interpretations since the time of Marx (Collins, 1975; Dahrendorf, 1959; Wright, 1985) have modified and broadened his original formulations to reflect the complexities of modern stratification structures. Marx's image of a society fundamentally divided along economic property lines may have been rendered obsolete. But a model depicting societies stratified into opposing groups whose memberships change with shifting interests and issues remains a powerful analytic tool for the study of stratification in the contemporary world. Sociologists owe a large debt to Marx for his outlining the basic concepts and premises of the conflict interpretation of social stratification. They owe a similar debt to one of Marx's critics, Max Weber. Weber's **multidimensional model** of modern stratified societies became the basis for a great deal of stratification research in the United States and in other contemporary societies.

Weberian Multiple-Hierarchies Model

Perhaps the most widely known and frequently applied model of stratification in modern societies is that of the great German sociologist Max Weber (1864–1920). His explanation of social inequality systems was developed as a rebuttal of Marx's economic-based class conflict theory. Weber believed that Marx's analysis of social stratification was dangerously simplistic. He also regarded Marx's call for a proletarian revolution as an essential violation of the principle of "value free" inquiry in the search for sociological truths.

Although he himself was a conflict theorist, Weber rejected Marx's materialistic determinism and exclusive focus on economic stratification. He argued, instead, that in modern, complex societies, individuals and groups are ranked in hierarchies across a number of important dimensions. These inequality hierarchies might overlap, but they are at least partially independent in their effects on both individuals and the social structure (Weber, 1946).

Weber acknowledged that economics were an important part of the system of inequality in any society, but rejected the claim that economic-based inequalities were the only significant component. It was not ownership of private property, but the level of **life chances**—access to basic opportunities and resources in the marketplace—that defined the individual's **class** position within the larger society. Further distancing himself from Marx on this issue, Weber asserted that economic classes were not responsible for significant social or cultural changes in human societies. Instead, the important societal changes that Marx had incorrectly interpreted as the result of class dynamics were brought about by the actions of groups stratified socially or politically.

For Weber, two other dimensions of inequality were crucial for understanding modern stratification structures and processes. In the **social hierarchy,** individuals were ranked according to the level of prestige or honor accorded them by others. People came to occupy a particular level, or **stratum,** in this hierarchy by virtue of a certain **lifestyle,** a distinctive orientation or relationship to the social world. Various lifestyles (whether of the rich and famous or the poor and obscure) were reflected in artistic tastes, leisure pursuits, fashion styles, and—significantly—the company one kept. Unlike economic classes, the members of specific social strata were self-conscious communal groups. Their relationships with one another and with members of other strata were grounded in considerations of prestige and reputation.

In the **political hierarchy,** individuals were ranked as **parties** by virtue of their different abilities to mobilize and employ power. Such power was a function of the degree and type of organization developed by individuals in groups. For example, in most societies, bureaucracies have come to dominate government and business sectors because of their success in organizing and coordinating the activities of large numbers of people. Weber claimed that power was sought deliberately as a means to influence and structure societal activities on behalf of the particular party. Like strata but unlike classes, parties were self-conscious, organized groups.

Power-seeking groups might be drawn from a particular class or stratum, from a set of classes and strata, or from sources completely unrelated to the economic and social hierarchies. In the United States, for example, economic and social position typically is a major shaper of political party affiliation. Generally speaking, Democrats draw their strength from the lower and working classes, and Republicans appeal primarily to middle-, upper-middle-, and upper-class groups. However, on occasion, specific issues relating to race, gender, age, and morality (abortion, gay rights, etc.) create coalitions that have little or nothing to do with socioeconomic position (this may be the origin of the old notion that "Politics makes strange bedfellows"). For Weber, Marx's assertion that economic position and political power were one and the same was false.

Weber saw the connections among economic, social, and political hierarchies as flexible and changing over time. For example, whereas prestige and power generally are associated with economic wealth, the relationship does not always hold. In Ireland and in many Latin American countries, Roman Catholic priests have little in the way of personal wealth but exercise considerable power over their congregations and are highly respected by the faithful. To comprehend the realities of social stratification in the modern world, one must understand the workings of the multiple inequality systems within each society.

As already noted, Weber's interpretation has become the fundamental model for much of the enormous body of stratification research generated during the past half-century. Individual sociologists might disagree on such matters as the relative importance of economic, social, or political inequality factors in a given society at a given time. Others might question the appropriateness of a specific empirical measure of these inequalities. Nevertheless, a majority of contemporary sociologists are committed solidly to Weber's model of a complexly stratified world as providing the most accurate and productive portrait of human social inequality.

OPEN AND CLOSED STRATIFICATION SYSTEMS: CLASS, CASTE, AND SOCIAL MOBILITY

In attempting to study social stratification across different societies and different time periods, sociologists have had to deal with hundreds of individual inequality systems. To help make sense out of what might otherwise be an impossibly complex task, these researchers have employed a number of devices to simplify and organize their observations. One such device is the construction of ideal types of stratified societies.

As you may remember from our discussion of ideal types in Chapter 3, the word *ideal* as used here does not mean "best." Rather, it refers to logically extreme forms of social inequalities that may be thought of as the end points in a continuum of such inequalities. By elaborating the structural features that characterize such polar opposite types, the researcher can locate a specific society along the continuum in terms of its amount and kind of inequality (see Figure 5.3).

At one end of this hypothetical inequality continuum is the minimally stratified society, an attempt to approximate social equality. At the other end is the maximally stratified society, an embodiment of extreme inequality.

In the first hypothetical system, minimal inequalities of condition (differences in Weber's *life chances*) are combined with maximum equality of opportunity. All members of society have about the same possibility of attaining any given level of life conditions. In the second system, profound inequalities in condition are present. They are reinforced and preserved by great disparities in opportunities for different individuals and groups within society. For some members of society, wealth and power are almost certainties. For others, poverty is inevitable.

The first case describes what sociologists call an **open-class society,** and the second a **closed-caste society.** Although many significant discrepancies exist between the actual society and the model (discussed in Chapters 6 and 7), the contemporary United States is often cited as the working example of an open-class society in action. Traditional (pre-twentieth-century) India, with its thousands of caste and subcaste groups, most often provides the working illustration of the closed-caste society.

The Open-Class System: (Nearly) All Things Are Possible

As used to describe societies such as the United States, "open" means that the stratification system allows for the possibility of individuals' **vertical social mobility**—movement from one level or rank to a different level or rank within the social hierarchy—in this case, from a lower level to a higher one. No formal organizational arrangements, laws, customs, or cultural traditions deliberately bar or significantly

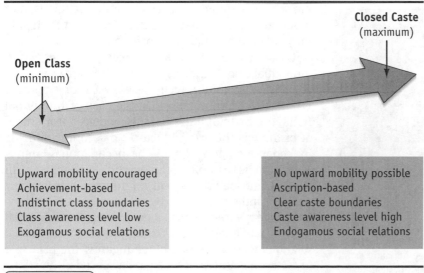

Closed Caste
(maximum)

Open Class
(minimum)

Upward mobility encouraged
Achievement-based
Indistinct class boundaries
Class awareness level low
Exogamous social relations

No upward mobility possible
Ascription-based
Clear caste boundaries
Caste awareness level high
Endogamous social relations

FIGURE 5.3

Ideal-Type Formulation of Stratification Systems (amount of social inequality; inequalities of condition and of opportunity)

restrict the free circulation of people up (or down) the social ladder. Such movements are in fact common and widespread.

What makes such social movements possible is the fact that, in the open-class system, positions at all levels are filled on the basis of achievement. Abilities and performances—what people can do—are the keys to location. A number of alternative routes to social success are present, so that individuals who may somehow be deficient in one particular area can compensate through accomplishments in another. Social mobility is also assisted by the overlapping and vague nature of class boundaries, as well as the relatively low levels of class awareness among people in most levels in the hierarchy. In combination, these factors make the transition from one social level to another relatively free of culture shock and permit socialization to new class behaviors and attitudes to proceed smoothly. Finally, relations among people are characterized by **exogamy,** the freedom to engage in secondary and primary relationships outside one's own group. Thus social interactions across class and status boundary lines are not formally restricted or limited in any way. (Tumin, 1985, provides a more detailed description of the characteristics of the open-class system.)

In the United States, most people occupy a specific rung on the social ladder by virtue of income, prestige, and power derived from their occupation. In turn, occupation is most often a function of one's level of formal education. Since people presumably attain education on the basis of academic abilities and performances, anyone with talent is capable of

earning advanced university degrees. In theory, at least, race, sex, and social class do not aid or interfere with one's educational accomplishments.

Armed with the proper credentials, individuals can acquire good jobs that will give them access to a better life. They can purchase a dream house in the suburbs, join the local country club, and send their children to quality private schools. Perhaps a son or daughter will meet, fall in love with, and marry someone from an affluent family. This pattern obviously is not likely for everyone, but it is at least possible for some, and that is the whole point of the open-class system: Such things are possible.

The Closed-Caste System: Stay Where You Were

The systems of contemporary class-stratified societies such as the United States, Canada, and Japan presumably promote the open and free movement of individuals through the various ranks. In contrast, the closed-caste structures of traditional societies such as nineteenth-century India captured individuals and froze them in social space.

What little vertical social movement between ranks existed was of the downward variety. An individual might lose caste but could not gain it. For all practical purposes, upward mobility into a higher caste was impossible within a given lifetime. (In the context of the Hindu religious belief in reincarnation and multiple existences, people thought it was possible to attain upward mobility across different lifetimes.) Socialization practices operated in such a way as to discourage the very thought of upward movement, as individuals were taught to accept their positions and to carry out assigned roles with diligence and dignity. An imposing array of established social, cultural, religious, and other institutional barriers effectively thwarted any misguided individual attempts at upward movement.

Caste positions in these societies were assigned to individuals on the basis of ascription; that is, personal characteristics such as sex, race, or age, over which one has no control. In the case of traditional India, the caste of one's parents, acquired from them at birth, was the critical factor. No accomplishments in economic, educational, or occupational arenas were sufficient to offset the overriding effect of birth caste. Caste behaviors and boundaries were clearly defined and understood by all members of society, and caste awareness was a central part of individual and collective identities. Virtually all important social relations were governed by **endogamy,** the principle of restricting and limiting everyday social interactions to other people in one's own membership group.

In short, one's life was spent within the physical and social confines of a particular inherited position,

In closed-caste stratification systems, virtually all important aspects of people's lives are shaped by the social positions into which they are born and from which they normally cannot escape. Although she may share the same physical space as the pavement dwellers she is stepping around, this Indian woman inhabits a very different social world. (Photo: Delip Mehta/Woodfin Camp & Associates)

carried as a burden (or privilege) throughout life and bequeathed to one's children. Caste identity was the paramount fact of life in a society that was minutely and rigidly structured to emphasize the disparities and inequalities of human social life (Tumin, 1985).

Social Mobility Principles and Patterns

The term *social mobility* refers to the movement of individuals and groups through social space within stratification systems. Historically, great differences in social mobility patterns helped distinguish open-class systems from closed-caste societies. Such differences also serve as important indicators of various amounts of inequality within given types of societies. For example, comparative studies of contemporary class-stratified societies invariably use social mobility data to draw some conclusion about whether one particular is "more equal" or "less equal" than another.

Some of these studies focus on what sociologists call **horizontal mobility,** the movement of people within a given level of the hierarchy. Most, however, focus on vertical mobility, both upward and downward. In the United States, upward mobility (*social climbing*) is the American dream. Downward mobility (*skidding*) is the American nightmare.

Although sociologists talk of social class mobility in their studies, often what they are actually examining is occupational mobility. Ambiguities in the conceptualization and measurement of social class make its use in mobility research problematic. If we don't know exactly how many different social classes there really are in a given society or what their precise boundaries are, we are not in a very good position to examine the movements of people from one of these classes to another.

Occupations can be defined more clearly and measured more easily. In addition, they show fairly significant and consistent linkages to education and income, as well as to prestige and power factors. Thus, they can serve as an (imperfect) operational measure of social class without doing serious injustice to the spirit of the concept.

Studies of social mobility rates and patterns typically examine one or both of two different types of occupational movement. **Intergenerational mobility** studies chart the movement of people within the social structure across several different generations. The social positions of individuals at a particular point in their careers (for example, age 45) are compared to the corresponding positions of the individuals' fathers and grandfathers—or, in the more recent cases of female intergenerational mobility studies, individuals'

mothers and grandmothers—at the same point in their respective careers.

The term **intragenerational mobility** refers to the extent of social movement experienced by individuals within their own occupational careers. People are examined at a number of significant points for evidence of upward or downward (or no) movement. For example, we might track a graduating college class, beginning with the new graduates' first full-time jobs. Later, we would return to see how our graduates, now preparing for their fifteenth college reunion, are doing. Then we might look in on them, now pushing age 50, to see how things are going. Finally, we might attend their retirement ceremonies to see exactly what positions they are retiring from. In a related vein, studies of what has been termed the *status attainment process* have focused on factors that, singly and in combination, influence and shape people's occupational careers (Blau and Duncan, 1967; Featherman and Hauser, 1978; Kerbo, 2000).

Several major studies of social mobility in the United States have indicated that both intergenerational and intragenerational mobility are widespread in this society. However, in most cases, the movement is rather modest—short steps rather than system-spanning rags-to-riches leaps. In addition, research suggests that this pattern may be slowing down or even reversing itself. As accumulating data point to the growth of the bottom layers of the social hierarchy and a growing distance between top and bottom segments, researchers have begun to raise questions about the erosion and possible eventual disappearance of the middle class (Barlett and Steele, 1991; Duncan, Smeeding, and Rodgers, 1992).

In attempting to understand and interpret mobility patterns, analysts make a further distinction between what is called *voluntary* or *exchange* or *individual mobility* and *structural* or *demand mobility.* **Voluntary mobility** represents the effects of individual efforts in propelling people up the social structure. The ambitious person who holds two jobs, takes courses in night school, and sees her hard work rewarded with a vice presidency in the corporation that once employed her as a secretary is an example of this type of social movement.

Structural mobility represents the effects of significant changes in one or more components of the social system (for example, a society's economy) on the social movement of large numbers of people. The experience of Irish immigrants to the United States illustrates this type of mobility. Many of these people arrived in the country at a time when the rapid change from a small-town, agrarian system to an urban-based, industrial economy created a need for huge numbers of laborers to fill mills and factories

Upward social mobility remains the dream in the United States and in many other societies. However, it is extremely unlikely that these children scavenging for recyclable materials at the Payatas Dumpsite in the Philippines will ever experience significant opportunities to improve their impoverished condition.

and to build railroads and canals. It even created a need for a smaller number of supervisors to direct and oversee these laborers. Thus, many immigrants who might otherwise have remained locked in place at the bottom of an agrarian class hierarchy were pulled up into higher-level and higher-paying jobs by the needs of the new industrial order.

Historically, it appears that the relatively high rates of mobility experienced by various immigrants to this society during the nineteenth century and by their descendants during the twentieth century were related primarily to such structural or demand mobility factors (Levy, 1988). Comparable patterns and rates of upward mobility observed in many other modern societies may also stem from the same structural sources; that is, by systemic changes associated with the modernization process itself.

These observations are not meant to downplay the role of individual effort in achieving social mobility. In expanding, receptive economies in which many people are moving up the social ladders, hardworking, committed individuals will move up farther and faster. In shrinking, nonreceptive economies in which few people are moving up, perhaps only hardworking, committed individuals will experience upward mobility.

INEQUALITY AND STRATIFICATION IN THE UNITED STATES

Economic Inequality

To a large extent, income and wealth distributions in the United States reflect the same patterns currently found between developed and developing countries. The United States is one of the world's most affluent societies, but this general affluence is not shared equally by all population segments. U.S. Bureau of the Census data (1999a) indicate that, in 1998, the mean yearly income of all households in the country was $51,855. However, for those households making up the lowest quintile (fifth) of the income-receiving population that year, the average was only $9,223. In contrast, the mean income of $127,529 for households in the highest quintile was almost 14 times greater. And, for those households in the top 5 percent of all income-receiving units, the average was more than $220,000—over 24 times as high as the lowest quintile's. Table 5.2 shows not only that the shares of total U.S. yearly income received by the different household quintiles are very unequal, but also that this inequality has been growing more pronounced since 1967. One analysis of Congressional Budget Office data conducted by the Center on Budget and Policy Priorities indicated that, after adjusting for inflation, between 1977 and 1994, the average after-tax income of the top 1 percent of Americans rose 72 percent and that of the highest-earning quintile rose 25 percent, whereas the average incomes of the poorest quintile of American families actually shrank 16 percent (Chandler, 1998). According to the Census Bureau, the annual income of the typical U.S. household fell 7 percent (a drop of $2,344) between 1989 and 1993. Even though some of this loss was later offset by four straight years of real-income gain for all household, the Census Bureau (1998a, pp. xii–xiii) nonetheless concludes that "the long term trend indicates increasing income inequality . . . over the past three decades." Comparing income and

TABLE 5.2

Share of Aggregate Income Received by Each Fifth and Top 5 Percent of U.S. Households, 1967–1998

Year	Distribution of Aggregate Income (Percent)					
	Lowest Fifth	Second Fifth	Third Fifth	Fourth Fifth	Highest Fifth	Top 5 Percent
1967	4.0	10.8	17.3	24.2	43.8	17.5
1972	4.1	10.5	17.1	24.5	43.9	17.0
1977	4.2	10.2	16.9	24.7	44.0	16.1
1982	4.0	10.0	16.5	24.5	45.0	17.0
1987	3.8	9.8	16.1	24.3	46.2	18.2
1992	3.8	9.4	15.8	24.2	46.9	18.6
1998	3.6	9.2	14.9	23.3	49.0	21.4

Source: U.S. Bureau of the Census, *Current Population Reports,* P60-206 (Washington, DC: U.S. Government Printing Office, 1999).

human development levels in the industrialized societies of the world, the United Nations Development Program concluded (1998, p.2): "The United States, with the highest average income of the countries ranked, has the highest population share experiencing human poverty." And, with regard to the distribution of wealth, this pattern is even more extreme.

Wealth   Whereas income is a measure of all monies obtained from different sources within a specified time period, wealth is a measure of the economic value of all of one's financial assets, including stocks, bonds, savings and checking accounts, and real estate holdings. Because reliable data concerning wealth are much harder to obtain than reliable income data, estimates of how wealth is distributed in the United States sometimes amount to little more than educated guesses based on information provided to government agencies by individuals and families.

According to Federal Reserve and Internal Revenue Service data, by the end of 1989, the 834,000 households that constituted the top 1 percent of the U.S. population had more wealth than the 84,000,000 households that made up the bottom 90 percent. This group's net worth of $5.7 trillion (compared to the $4.8 trillion net worth of the bottom 90 percent) was based on its holding of 78 percent of all bonds and trusts, 62 percent of all business assets, 49 percent of all publicly held stocks, and 45 percent of nonresidential real estate in the United States. The top 1 percent group's share of the country's net wealth increased from 31 percent to 37 percent between 1983 and 1989, the first significant rise in wealth concentration since the 1920s. At the start of the 1990s, the richest 10 percent of the population claimed an esti-

mated 68 percent of all the nation's wealth (Nasar, 1992), and the richest 20 percent held more than 80 percent of all wealth. By the end of 1995, the richest 1 percent of Americans held 21.4 percent of the country's wealth (Schlesinger, 1998). These figures are larger than those found in any other industrial nation.

This growing concentration of immense wealth in the hands of a small segment of the population has been fostered to a large extent by the "wealthfare" system that allows the rich to avoid federal and state income taxes designed to promote the greater equalization of wealth in this society. For example, IRS figures show that, despite the existence of an alternative minimum tax intended to ensure that high-income people are subject to at least some tax liability, 1,137 individuals with reported annual incomes of $200,000 paid no federal income taxes at all in 1994 (Schlesinger, 1998). According to a *Wall Street Journal*/NBC News poll conducted in 1998, 56 percent of all Americans, including 43 percent of those Americans with annual incomes above $100,000, believe that the wealthy in this country are undertaxed and are not paying their fair share (Wessel, 1998a).

Wealthy businesses have also benefited from what amounts to a government policy of "corporate welfare." One comprehensive study (Barlett and Steele, 1998, p. 39) reported a staggering $125 billion a year in tax breaks and subsidies to private industry from local, state, and federal governments, a situation decried by former Labor Secretary Robert Reich (in Murdock, 1995) as "aid to dependent corporations." However, in spite of growing public sentiment against such taxpayer-funded subsidies, these welfare benefits for the rich did not end or decrease

---

appreciably under the first Clinton administration, nor under the Republican-controlled Congress during the second Clinton administration. Like all other contemporary societies, the United States continues to be marked by significant income and wealth inequalities. Indeed, in many respects, this society has now become "the most economically stratified industrial nation" (Bradsher, 1995, p. A1).

Social Class

So far, decades of efforts to describe *the* social class structure of the United States have not been very successful. To a large extent, this situation may reflect the fact that this society's open-class stratification is characterized by vaguely defined, overlapping class boundaries and generally low levels of class awareness. These conditions may make social mobility easier for members of the population, but they also make research more difficult for sociologists who seek a complete description and understanding of the system.

Further difficulties encountered in the pursuit of a precise description of the U.S. social class system reflect the fact that sociologists have conceptualized and measured "class" in a wide variety of ways. Many studies of social class have focused on the distribution of objective resources such as income, education, and occupation among population members. They assume that these socioeconomic status factors define people's class positions and shape personal and social behaviors. However, voting and other forms of political participation, child-rearing practices, crime and deviance, leisure activities, and a host of other behaviors associated with socioeconomic status do not show any clear natural breaking points with respect to income, education, or occupational level. For example, no single yearly income figure marks the precise boundary line between those who vote and those who don't. In general, higher-income groups have higher rates of voting and lower-income groups have lower rates. But not all high- and middle-income people vote, and not all lower-income people fail to vote. Because of the overlapping of these behavior patterns, the number and location of objective class boundaries always represent a decision made and imposed by the researcher.

Studies of stratification that use the objective method often present their findings in the form of a composite portrait of the U.S. social class structure (see Table 5.3 for some examples). In these composites, the researchers have tried to simplify a complex reality for the sake of clarity. Like other such simplifications, they should be taken as useful analytic devices rather than true-to-life portraits of social reality.

Subjective Social Class   Other studies of the U.S. social class system have focused on the subjective aspects of stratification. Based on the premise that a wide array of attitudes and behaviors are the result of individuals' perceptions of their own class memberships, these studies let respondents "speak for themselves" on the question of social class. Respondents are given the opportunity to locate themselves on the stratification ladder either by choosing their appropriate class designation from a list provided by the researcher or by creating and selecting their own class categories.

Studies of the U.S. social class system that use the subjective approach consistently find that most people think of themselves as being "middle class." One 1994 survey conducted by the Roper Research Organization discovered that, in spite of enormous differences in their individual incomes, 93 percent of all study respondents saw themselves as members of some segment of the middle class. By way of contrast, only 1 percent called themselves "upper class," and 5 percent answered "lower class." Commenting on these findings, noted economist Lester Thurow (in Chandler, 1994–1995) remarked that, with so many people identifying themselves as middle class, the only criterion for inclusion in this group might as well be "everybody who isn't richer than Ross Perot." Other observers have argued these responses are perfectly logical and predictable, in that " 'middle class' may be more of a state of mind—a set of values and aspirations—than an economic statistic" (Zaldivar, 1995).

Proponents of the subjective class perspective would agree with this assessment. However, it is nonetheless true that the inability to distinguish, on the basis of subjective class identification, among individuals who otherwise display significant differences in socioeconomic situation, poses a significant—if not fatal—research problem. If the goal of social-class analysis is to delineate and understand class-based differences in attitudes, values, behaviors, and other lifestyle elements, that goal is doomed to failure if one particular social class becomes an all-encompassing category. Economist Stephen J. Rose (1992, p. 15) has argued that "middle class" has become a category "so broad that it not only blurs real distinctions in income, lifestyle, and well-being but often clouds public discussions as well."

THE CONSEQUENCES OF SOCIAL STRATIFICATION

As Max Weber noted many years ago, people's positions within the social stratification system generate

TABLE 5.3

Composite Portraits of the U.S. Class Structure

Class According to Gilbert and Kahl	Class Features	Class According to Rossides
Capitalist (1%)	Very high income (over $500,000) Elite/prestige university degree Executive/professional occupations	Upper (1–3%)
Upper middle (14%)	High income ($50,000 plus) Elite college/graduate training Upper manager/professional occupations	Upper middle (10–15%)
Middle (60%— combined middle and working)	Modest income (about $30,000) High school/some college training Lower manager/semiprofessional/sales occupations	Lower middle (30–35%)
Working	Low income (about $20,000) High school/ Grade school/some high school Skilled/unskilled/service labor	Working (40–50%)
Working poor (25%—combined working poor and underclass)	Low income (below $15,000) Some high school Service work/laborers	
Underclass	Poverty income (below $10,000) Illiteracy/primary school Unemployed/surplus labor	Lower (20–25%)

Source: Adapted from Dennis Gilbert and Joseph A. Kahl, *The American Class Structure: A New Synthesis,* 3rd ed. (Chicago: Dorsey Press, 1987), p. 332; and Daniel W. Rossides, *Social Stratification: The American Class System in Comparative Perspective* (Englewood Cliffs, NJ: Prentice Hall, 1990), pp. 406–408.

both life chances and lifestyle consequences that affect nearly every aspect of their lives. We will be examining many of the significant linkages between social inequality systems and other fundamental facets of human life—marriage and family, religion, and education, for example—in later chapters. However, it is appropriate, at this point, to offer a brief sampling of some of the many ways in which social stratification can shape life in ways that often go unrecognized by those whose lives are so being shaped.

Physical and Mental Health

Economic affluence does not necessarily guarantee happiness, but it does seem to foster levels of physical and psychological well-being that may make happiness more likely. At the global level, people in wealthy developed nations such as Japan and the United States live longer and become ill less often and less seriously than individuals in poorer, developing nations such as Rwanda and Sierra Leone. For example, in 1996, the life expectancy at birth in Japan was 80 years (83 years for females and 77 years for males) compared to 36.5 years (38 years for females and 35 years for males) in Sierra Leone. In that same year, the infant mortality rate in the United States was 7 per 1,000 live births; in Rwanda, the comparable figure was 129 per 1,000 live births (World Bank, 1999b, Table 2 and Table 7). This pattern of better physical health for the more affluent and worse physical heath for the poor is replicated among individuals at the societal level. In the United States, for example, members of higher socioeconomic groups can seek treatment from some of the finest medical and health care facilities in the world. But these resources are beyond the reach of people in the lower social classes, who cannot afford the high financial costs of getting treatment and who are much less likely to have adequate medical insurance. By the end of 1997, an estimated 43.4 million Americans—including 10.7 million children under the age of 18—lacked health insurance coverage and, therefore, had no access to medical care at all. In spite of the

Brazil

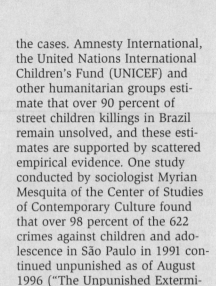

Population: 171,853,126

Life Expectancy at Birth (years): Male—59.35; Female—
69.01

Form of Government: Federal Republic (Democracy)

Major Religions: Roman Catholic (70%); Umbanda and other
Vodoun (28%)

Major Racial and Ethnic Groups: White (55%); Mixed Black and White
(38%); Black (6%)

Population Doubling Time: 45 years

Per Capita GNP (1997 U.S. dollars): $4,790

Principal Economic Activities: Agriculture; Heavy Industries; Mining

Colonial Experience: Former Portuguese Colony

Adult Literacy Rate: 85% Male—85%; Female—85%

Brazil's Children Face Dead End Street

On July 24, 1993, television, radio, and newspaper audiences around the world were shocked to learn of a horrible shooting that had occurred the previous evening. On the fateful night of July 23, a group of 50 to 70 *meniños de rua* ("street children") were fired on by members of a death squad as they lay sleeping on the steps of the Candelaria Cathedral in the heart of Rio de Janeiro, Brazil. Shot through the head, five children died on the spot. After remaining in a coma for several days, a sixth died in the hospital. Two other children were forced into the gunmen's vehicle and driven off into the night. Their bodies were found the next day. Like their peers, they had been shot execution-style, through the head. The "Candelaria Massacre," as the killings came to be called, outraged the international community and generated tremendous pressures on the Brazilian government to take swift action in finding and punishing those responsible for the atrocity.

In an almost unprecedented turn of events, six men—including five local and state police officers—subsequently were arrested for the shootings. Three years later, as their cases came to trial in April 1996, three of the five policemen confessed to the crime. One later died, but the other two were sentenced to lengthy prison terms. However, in December 1996, following a trial described as a "clown show" and boycotted by the prosecution, the remaining two policemen and a civilian were acquitted of all charges in the murders. In that trial, the presiding judge refused to allow testimony from any of the shooting survivors, completely undercutting the state's case and forcing the jury to acquit the defendants for lack of evidence. Commenting on the trial's disheartening outcome, an attorney for the victims claimed that "What we gained with the earlier convictions, we are losing in credibility now" (Leonardo, in "3 Acquitted of Killing," 1996).

Credibility has been and continues to be a significant problem for the Brazilian government in their handling of the street children problem, both prior to and since the 1993 massacre. The Candelaria killings ultimately led to the arrests and convictions of at least some of the murderers but that was an extremely rare outcome. Most crimes against street children go unpunished, largely because of the reluctance of government officials at any level—local, state, or federal—to pursue the cases. Amnesty International, the United Nations International Children's Fund (UNICEF) and other humanitarian groups estimate that over 90 percent of street children killings in Brazil remain unsolved, and these estimates are supported by scattered empirical evidence. One study conducted by sociologist Myrian Mesquita of the Center of Studies of Contemporary Culture found that over 98 percent of the 622 crimes against children and adolescence in São Paulo in 1991 continued unpunished as of August 1996 ("The Unpunished Extermination," 1998).

According to critics, perhaps the most significant factor responsible for government officials' failure to take action against those responsible for murders, assaults, and other crimes against Brazil's street children is the fact that many of these offenses are committed by current or former police officials, as was the case in the Candelaria killings. Speaking at the United Nations Social Summit in Copenhagen, Tania de Almeida, head judge of Duque de Caxias Court (a municipal court in the Rio area) described a "vicious circle of impunity" in which killings of street children are carried out by private security agencies hired by shopkeepers and members of Rio's elite to "clean up the streets" of children viewed as both a nuisance and a menace. Headed by state police officers or chiefs of the Military Police and staffed by rank-and-file police officers who are little more than "professional killers," these security agencies are protected by several Rio city officials who themselves were once professional killers working private security (in Brandao, 1995). But the problem of impunity is not confined to this one city. Like Rio, other Brazilian cities have done little or nothing to apprehend and prosecute killers of street children. In Belem, where no policemen accused of crimes against children and adolescents are arrested, the number of murders actually increased 72 percent from 1996 to 1997, according to the Center of Defense of the Child and the Adolescent, one of many private and NGO (non-governmental organization) groups in Brazil devoted to protecting the life and well-being of the country's young people ("The Unpunished Extermination," 1998).

What may be even more incredible than the fact that lethal violence against street children is so widespread and so officially ignored is the fact that—on paper, at least—Brazil is among the most progressive countries in the world in terms of its formal recognition of the human rights of children and adolescents. For decades, government responses to problems of child and adolescent homelessness had consisted largely of rounding up and incarcerating young people in "vocational training" schools that were little more than juvenile prisons. But, as the country's era of military rule came to an end and democratic government returned in the mid-1980s, Brazil began to reshape its official policies dramatically (Pfister, 1995). On January 26, 1990, Brazil signed the United Nations' *Convention on the Rights of the Child,* an internationally binding agreement setting out specific rights of children under the age of 18 and mandating governments to honor and protect those rights (International Bureau for Children's Rights, 1998). And, in July of that same year, the Brazilian Congress ratified the *Child and Adolescent Statute*

(ECA), one of the most radical children's rights statutes in the world: "The 267 articles of the document grant full human rights to children and youth and form a legal and institutional structure for issues relating to children and youth. The rights are spelled out in extensive detail: right to use public space; free expression; freedom of religion; ability to practice sports and engage in leisure activities; participation in family, community, and political life; access to refuge and assistance; and freedom from violence" (Pfister, 1995, p. 2). More specifically, article 5 of the ECA states that "No child or adolescent will be subject to any form of negligence, discrimination, exploitation, violence, cruelty, or oppression, and any violation of their fundamental rights, either by act or omission, will be punished according to the terms of the law" (in International Child Resource Institute, 1995).

The problem, then, is not that children's rights are an unknown or foreign legal concept in Brazil. Rather, the real problem is that government leaders have chosen not to make that legal concept an ongoing part of the country's day-to-day social practices: "The lack of political will to effectively tackle the wide-spread violence against the children of the poor in Brazil and to prosecute their assailants is one of the key reasons for the four daily murders of children and adolescents in that country" (International Child Resource Institute, 1995). To understand why that has been the case, it is first necessary to understand the forces at work creating and increasing the street children population, as well as public perception of that population—forces intimately intertwined with the nature of socioeconomic inequality and stratification in Brazil.

Geographically and demographically the largest country in Latin America, Brazil is also the region's wealthiest nation and the

world's eighth-largest economy (U.S. Department of State, 1999). In spite of the country's overall wealth, however, Brazil ranks 62nd on the United Nations Development Program's "Human Development Indicators" list, largely because of the way in which that wealth is distributed. In Brazil, the wealthiest 10 percent of the population own over half (51.3 percent) of the nation's wealth, while the poorest 20 percent of the population own just 2.1 percent of the wealth. According to some estimates, at least one-half of all Brazilian children live in families having a monthly income less than half the legal minimum wage level, and another 25 percent live in families where the monthly income is less than one-quarter the legal minimum wage level (International Bureau for Children's Rights, 1998). Over 43 percent of Brazil's 168 million inhabitants must try to survive on the equivalent of less than $2 per day (Novartis Foundation for Sustainable Development, 1999). Summarizing these patterns, the International Bureau for Children's Rights (1998, p. 2) argues that "All social indicators point to the existence of two separate 'countries' sharing this same geographic space; the rich one, where people have access to the same goods and technology available in the first world, and the other, where individuals' most basic needs, are not met." It is from this "other country," the impoverished rural northern and northeastern states, that Brazil's estimated 8 to 10 million street children and their families have been drawn to the nation's largest cities in the more prosperous southern and southeastern regions. There, they take up residence in the many *favelas* or shanty towns that have become familiar features of the urban landscape (Rich, 1999).

Contrary to popular belief, the majority of Brazil's street children are not orphans. Most have at least one parent (usually their mother) at home, but have chosen—or been forced into— life on the street for reasons associated with their families' abject poverty. The largest number of street children represent what have been called "children *in* the streets"; that is, children who spend the greater part of the day working or begging in the streets but who normally return home at night to sleep ("Brazil's At-Risk Children," 1999). Often sent into the streets by their families, their activities are centered around earning money that eventually becomes indispensable for the family's well-being. A São Paulo State Department of Children's study of families who sent one or more children out to beg in the streets found that these families earned, on average, more than $700 a month—almost 10 times the minimum wage and enough to provide not just food and clothes, but luxury items such as TVs and tape players as well. But the cost is heavy: "These kids have become the bread-winners in the family, at the expense of their childhood and their education" (Rich, 1999, p. 3). The cost can become even heavier, as these children are subject to the same attacks as their peers who actually live in the streets.

This second group, "children *of* the streets," are the "true" street children; that is, children and adolescents who not only spend their days working or begging in the streets, but who sleep in the streets at night, as well ("Brazil's At-Risk Children," 1999). For the most part, this group is comprised of children who have fled their homes to escape hunger, neglect, physical or sexual abuse, or other ravages of profound poverty (Rich, 1999). Forced to fend for themselves, these children of the streets often turn to prostitution and crime as their best—or only—chance for survival. It is

People look at the body of one of eight street children shot to death in Rio de Janeiro, Brazil, July 23, 1993. Six children were killed while sleeping in the square outside Candelaria Cathedral; two more were reportedly taken to the waterfront and executed. Five police officers were among the six men charged in the shootings, which sparked both international and national outrage.

their involvement in petty thefts and burglaries, drugs, and (occasionally) assaults and other violent crimes that has led them to be perceived by merchants and other members of Brazil's urban middle and upper classes as a threat to the social fabric. Viewed in this light, street children then become part of a "refuse" problem that must be swept from the streets by whatever means necessary. In the extreme case, members of the general public and of some government agencies have come to define all street children as real or potential criminals who, if left unchecked, will cause serious or fatal harm to decent society. Though most often left unspoken, this belief was articulated by one city official, who re-

putedly stated that "We have to kill when they are still young, so they do not bother us after they grow up" (de Lima, in International Child Resource Institute, 1995, p. 2).

According to some observers, this stereotyping of street children as dangerous criminals and the resulting willingness to take any and all steps to defuse their threat is inherently connected to the system of socioeconomic and racial stratification in Brazil (Sanchez, 1994/1995; Scheper-Hughes and Hoffman, 1994a, 1994b). From this perspective, it is not at all coincidental that the overwhelming majority (over 90 percent) of all street children—and of the street children whose bodies turn up in alleyways and on the side of roads—are of African or Afro-Brazilian descent. Nor is it coincidental that the middle and upper classes who allegedly are the prime movers behind the extermination of street children are largely of European descent. This is merely the latest reflection of a long-standing historical pattern in which Africans originally were brought to Brazil to work as slaves in the plantation-like *latifundios* that dominated the agricultural economy and in which the descendants of those slaves are still largely excluded from any real land ownership by a legal system that continues to favor a few privileged population segments (Inter-American Development Bank, 1999; McKaugiran, 1997; Novartis Foundation for Sustainable Development, 1999). Displaced from the land, Afro-Brazilian families joined the mass migration of jobless people to the large cities, transforming rural poverty into urban poverty and setting the stage for increased class antagonisms (Tavares, 1995).

Anthropologists Nancy Scheper-Hughes and Daniel Hoffman (1994a, 1994b) argue that the end of military rule and the former police state in Brazil has resulted in the disintegration of the structures that had kept the social classes safely apart. Coupled with an increase in public violence that seems to have accompanied recent economic crises in the country, the sudden arrival of so many poor people—and their children—into the cities has resulted in a perception, by the middle and upper classes, that something is "wrong" with the society:

> What is rarely articulated but nonetheless quite clear is that street kids are poor children in the wrong place. A street child is, like our definition of dirt, soil that is out of place. Soil in the ground is clean, a potential garden; soil under the fingernails is filth. Likewise, a poor, ragged kid running along an unpaved road in a *favela* or playing in a field of sugar cane is just a kid. That same child, trans-ported to the main streets and plazas of town, is a threat, a potentially dangerous "street kid." (1994a, p. 2)

"Fixing" the street children problem is not and cannot be simply a matter of an increasingly fearful middle class periodically "cleaning up the streets" of unwanted children or instituting a kind of "street children apartheid" (Castilho, 1995, p. 2). Nor does the answer lie in remedial measures that attempt to "fix" the life situations of individual street children, though that may be a necessary component of the solution. The real solution, according to many observers, lies in attacking the structural sources of the profound socioeconomic inequality that continues to subject so many Brazilians to impossible living conditions: "Alcohol- and drug-free parents must have access to unskilled jobs or training programs. Families need to be pro-vided with incentives to keep their children in school instead of begging. And the children themselves must have access to after-school programs and activities to keep them from being drawn back to the street" (Rich, 1999, pp. 4–5).

Structural changes of the magnitude necessary to break the cycle that puts and keeps so many children on Brazil's mean streets require a great deal of both economic and political capital, both of which are currently in short supply in the country. But, "Until the chaotic economic and social conditions that cause desperately poor parents to 'lose' their children to the streets are reversed, childhood for the vast majority in Brazil will continue to signify a period of adversity to be survived and gotten over as quickly as possible, rather than a time of nurturance to be extended and savored" (Scheper-Hughes and Hoffman, 1994b, p. 2).

Medicaid program for the poor, almost one-third of all poor people (11.2 million) had no health insurance of any kind. An additional 31 percent of the "near poor" (3.8 million people) also were left without health insurance in 1997 (Benefield, 1998). According to "an explosion of research" summarized by Erica Goode (1999, p. E-1), "social class—as measured not just by income but also by education and other markers of relative status—is one of the most powerful predictors of health, more powerful than genetics, exposure to carcinogens, even smoking."

These well-documented findings are now being supported by a large and growing body of research pointing to the fact that the overall pattern of socioeconomic inequality found in a given society has a profound effect on the physical health of all of its members. Societies that are more highly stratified are also more unhealthy for the bulk of their population members, regardless of the overall level of societal wealth. As Lardner (1998) notes, "if you live in a place where differences in income and wealth are unusually large (the United States, for example), your chances of escaping chronic illness and reaching a ripe old age are significantly worse than if you live in a place where differences are not as large (Sweden, for example)."

Like physical health, psychological well-being or mental health is also distributed unequally among the various socioeconomic classes in this and other societies. Individuals from higher-class backgrounds are far less likely than those from the lowest social classes to experience serious psychological disturbances or impairments (Gallagher and Rita, 1995). When they are in need of psychological care, they have access to individual therapists or private psychiatric care. When psychiatric care is available at all to members of the lower classes, it most often takes the form of state mental hospitals in which less-effective treatments such as chemotherapy are widely employed. However, serious psychological problems among members of the lower classes more often go untreated, and many of these individuals end up living on the streets. Some observers claim that as many as 30 percent of homeless people in the United States suffer severe mental problems, especially manic depression and schizophrenia (Jencks, 1994).

Political Involvement

In democratic political systems, participation in the electoral process represents perhaps the most significant way for average people to influence their society.

This is especially true if that society does not seem to be operating in their best interests. To the extent that government decisions and policies set the course of economic, social, and even cultural patterns, individuals can help shape these patterns by selecting those who will serve in the government.

However, data from a wide variety of studies (Conway, 1991; U.S. Bureau of the Census, 1998c) clearly indicate that members of the lower classes in this and other democratic societies have opted out of the electoral process. Compared to members of the higher strata, lower-class and working-class people display much less interest in and knowledge of political issues and political actors. They have significantly lower rates of voter registration and correspondingly lower rates of actual voting among those who are registered. Participation beyond the act of casting a vote, such as becoming involved in campaign activities or running for elected office, is even more uncommon among these individuals.

In the absence of widespread participation from lower-class and working-class levels, upper-middle-class and upper-class groups can maintain control of the political structure. Once in command, they can set policies and make decisions in accordance with their own best interests and their own view of the world. Given the generally more conservative, status quo social and economic orientations of these higher-strata groups, both domestic and foreign societal policies typically end up supporting and maintaining the existing social system (Dye, 1995). For example, under a ten-year, $792 billion tax plan proposed by the Republican-controlled Congress in 1999, nearly 80 percent of tax cuts (an average of $4,592 in the first year) would go to families making over $81,966 a year, whereas families making under $30,964 a year would receive only 2 percent (an average of $55 in the first year) of the tax benefits. The net effect of these tax proposals thus would be to increase existing inequities in the U.S. income and wealth structure (Greenwald, 1999).

Crime and Criminal Justice

People from all classes face the possibility of some contact with crime, whether as victims or as perpetrators. But individuals on the lower rungs of the social ladder have a much higher probability of both types of contacts than do those situated above them. Lower-class people are more frequently the victims of various street crimes, especially those involving violence, such as aggravated assault and homicide. According to data reported by the Justice Department, for example, people from households with less than $7,500 in annual income are victims of all crimes of violence more than twice as often (65.3 per 1,000 compared to 30.5 per 1,000 persons) as individuals from households with annual incomes of $75,000 or more (U.S. Bureau of the Census, 1998c, Table 347).

There seems to be a widespread pattern of family violence among lower-class groups, especially within the underclass of racial minorities at the very bottom of the income structure (W. J. Wilson, 1987, 1989). At the present time, for example, murder is the single most frequent cause of death among young African-American males in the lower classes of U.S. society. The enormous financial pressures and the general lack of economic resources to deal successfully with these pressures that are characteristic of lower-class conditions may be important factors in the origin of homicidal and other violence. For example, one New Orleans study found that poverty, not race, accounted for the sixfold difference in black and white rates of domestic homicides in that city. Focusing on "household crowding" as its measure of socioeconomic standing, the study concluded that "New Orleans blacks were no more likely to murder a relative or acquaintance than were whites in similar socioeconomic circumstances" (Centerwall, in Evans, 1995).

Compared to members of higher social classes, lower-class individuals also are perpetrators of crime more often, at least according to official crime statistics and with respect to conventional or so-called street crimes. Although members of the middle and upper classes also are involved in significant and socially costly amounts of criminal activities, these white-collar, corporate, and elite offenses often go unrecognized and unpunished. Crimes committed by lower-class people receive more attention from police and court agencies, and lower-class people receive more frequent and more serious punishment for their offenses (Rossides, 1990). The complex relationship between social class, crime, and criminal justice is examined in more detail in Chapter 8.

SUMMARY AND REVIEW

Assessing Inequality and Stratification

1. *What is the difference between social inequality and social stratification?*

Social inequality refers to the unequal distribution of valued goods and services among the members of a given group or population at a particular point in time.

Social stratification refers to social inequalities that have become permanent over time: they are patterned or structured, are supported and justified by prevailing norms, beliefs, and values, and are transmitted from one generation to another. (P. 93)

2. *What is the connection between economic inequality and social stratification?*

Stratification is often measured in terms of economic inequality. At the global level, the world's societies form an international stratification system with a wealthy upper class of developed northern societies and a poorer lower class of developing southern societies. (Pp. 93–94)

Explanations and Interpretations of Stratification

3. *How do natural superiority and functionalist theories explain social stratification?*

Different theories have offered a variety of explanations for social stratification. Natural superiority approaches interpret social inequalities in wealth, power, and prestige as reflections of natural inequalities in mental and physical abilities among individuals. Functionalist theorists such as Davis and Moore view systems of unequally rewarded positions as incentives motivating talented people to perform important social tasks. (Pp. 95–98)

4. *How do Marxist conflict theorists explain stratification?*

Critics of functionalism claim that this theory ignores the role of power in the creation and preservation of stratification systems. Conflict theorists such as Karl Marx focused on power factors to explain inequality structures. For Marx, differences in property ownership created objective classes whose opposed interests put them into conflict with one another. As these classes (owners and nonowners) became subjectively aware of their respective circumstances, the class struggle would lead to a revolution by the workers and the violent overthrow of the property-based capitalist system. (Pp. 98–99)

5. *What is Max Weber's multiple-hierarchies model of social stratification?*

Max Weber criticized Marx's theory for its oversimplicity and for ignoring important noneconomic inequality dimensions. According to Weber, modern stratification systems rank people socially and politically as well as economically. Strata and parties are often more significant than classes in bringing about social and cultural changes. Weber's multiple-hierarchy approach has guided a great deal of stratification research over the past fifty years. (P. 100)

Open and Closed Stratification Systems: Class, Caste, and Social Mobility

6. *What features distinguish open-class stratification systems from closed-caste systems?*

Sociologists often distinguish between two logically extreme, ideal types of stratified systems in order to locate specific societies on a continuum of social in-

equality. The open-class system represents minimal social inequality. It is marked by free movement among social ranks, achievement-based criteria for filling positions, indistinct class boundaries and low levels of class consciousness, and exogamous social relations across class boundaries. The closed-caste system represents maximum social inequality. People are born into groups that are characterized by great differences in life conditions, and they remain there throughout their lives. Boundaries between the stratified groups are distinct, and awareness of caste membership is high. All important relationships are confined within individuals' caste. (Pp. 101–103)

7. *What is social mobility?*

Social mobility refers to movements of people through social space within stratification systems. Most mobility research has focused on movements within the occupational structures of societies. Intergenerational studies analyze patterns of mobility across several generations, and intragenerational studies focus on mobility patterns within a given generation. Both indicate that a great deal of social mobility in modern societies is the result of significant structural changes brought about by the modernization process. Successful mobility also reflects the result of individual or voluntary efforts. (Pp. 103–104)

Inequality and Stratification in the United States

8. *How are income and wealth distributed in the United States?*

Economic resources are distributed very unequally in the United States. The top fifth of U.S. income earners receive almost 14 times the income of the lowest fifth, and the top 1 percent of households possess more wealth than the bottom 90 percent. The United States has become the most economically stratified industrialized society in the world. (Pp. 104–106)

The Consequences of Social Stratification

9. *How does stratification affect people's daily lives?*

Social stratification generates many significant consequences for members of human societies. People who occupy the higher rungs in the social hierarchy enjoy better physical and mental health. They are more likely than the members of lower-ranked groups to be involved in political activities and less likely to be victims of violent crimes. If accused of criminal acts, members of higher-ranking groups are less likely to be convicted and punished for their actions. (Pp. 107, 111–112)

6

Race and Ethnicity

The final few years of the twentieth century were not an especially good period for race and ethnic relations in the United States. In New York City, one white veteran police officer pleaded guilty to avoid a jury trial, and a second was found guilty following a jury trial, for a brutal attack in which a Haitian immigrant was beaten and then sodomized with a broomstick while in custody at a police station house (Hayes, 1999). At about the same time, in February 1999, New York City police again were the focus of public outcries following the shooting of an unarmed West African immigrant. Amadou Diallo died after being hit by 19 of the 41 bullets fired at him by four white undercover police officers. Sparking numerous demonstrations and the arrests of several "high-profile" protestors, these two episodes became the catalyst for a nationwide review of police department enforcement policies and practices regarding racial and ethnic minorities (Pugh, 1999). In Jasper, Texas, James Byrd Jr., a 49-year-old African American, was chained to a pickup truck and dragged to his death by three white supremacists as part of an initiation rite to the Klan-like hate group they were forming. Sentenced to execution by lethal injection for his leading role in Byrd's murder, John William King hurled an obscenity at the victim's family as he was led off to death row. Showing no apparent remorse for his crime, King also reputedly wrote a supporter that "Regardless of the outcome of this, we have made history" (Bai and Smith, 1999, p. 22). In Riverside, California, hundreds of marchers led by the Revs. Jesse Jackson and Al Sharpton took to the streets to protest what they charged was the "firing-squad" death of a 19-year-old African American woman shot 12 times by white police officers who allegedly shared "high fives" following the episode (Deutsch, 1999). The fatal shooting of Tyisha Miller came only two years after an equally notorious incident in which white Riverside sheriff's deputies were videotaped beating two unarmed illegal Mexican immigrants. The tape was subsequently broadcast on national television, generating outrage from both Hispanics and supporters of immigrants' rights (Morgan, 1999). In New Jersey, three black men and one Hispanic were shot after their van was pulled over on the turnpike by white New Jersey State Police Troopers. The four men filed a massive lawsuit, claiming that they were victims of a long-standing police practice of racial profiling, in which blacks and other people of color are routinely stopped and questioned for no apparent reason other than being nonwhite. Their claim echoed an earlier finding by a New Jersey state judge that such racial profiling was, indeed, systematic (Hosenball, 1999). So widespread is racial profiling by police in a number of different eastern and southeastern states that members of minority communities have come to refer to the practice as "being stopped for driving while being black or brown."

At the same time that the United States is becoming an increasingly racially and ethnically diverse society, the sheer number of hate groups and hate crimes has been steadily growing, fed by a variety of conservative white rights and neo-Nazi white supremacist organizations. According to the Southern Poverty Law Center's (SPLC) *Intelligence Report,* the number of active hate groups across the country increased by over one-third (from 395 to 537) between 1996 and 1998. This growth was paralleled by the proliferation of white supremacist propaganda on the Internet. As of 1998, the SPLC had identified 254 Internet hate sites, up from 163 in 1997 (Southern Poverty Law Center, 1999b).

But blacks and Hispanics are not always the victims, nor whites always the perpetrators, of racial and ethnic violence in U.S. society. In May 1998, a 35-year-old white Colorado man was savagely beaten to death with a shovel by four African American men following a racial altercation in a local bar. Later that same year, white men in St. Louis and in Buffalo were beaten or stomped to death by groups of black men following racially charged confrontations (Southern Poverty Law Center, 1999a). The Southern Poverty Law Center's annual "The year in hate" survey (1999b) counted 29 black separatist groups among the 537 hate groups and group chapters actively engaged in racist behaviors during 1998. In describing 1998, the SPLC concluded that "Men and women of all races were attacked and sometimes murdered in a year that underscored the pervasive nature of hate crimes in America."

Racial and ethnic tensions are hardly limited to the United States. Indeed, when compared to the wholesale violence unfolding in many other parts of the world, the domestic situation can seem to pale by comparison. In the Yugoslavian province of Kosovo, thousands of ethnic Albanians were killed, and hundreds of thousands of others displaced, during a Serbian "ethnic cleansing" campaign ordered by Yugoslav President Slobodan Milosevic (the crisis in Kosovo is discussed in this chapter's *Focus on* section). In Indonesia, the sharp economic decline that pushed nearly half the population below the poverty level and led to the removal of long-term president Suharto in 1998 also triggered mass rioting directed largely at the country's ethnic Chinese population. Though comprising under 4 percent of Indonesia's population of 202 million, ethnic Chinese hold most of the nation's private wealth and are widely resented across the country: "The Chinese are snobby about their wealth. They control the economy. We don't like them" (Daulay, in Landler, 1998). According to survivors, the riots targeted ethnic Chinese businesses for destruction and ethnic Chinese people for killing and assault, including the gang raping of hundreds of women (Mydans, 1998). In the African nation of Rwanda, a half-dozen years after a genocidal civil war that left as many as 1 million people dead, Hutu rebels "solely motivated by ethnic hatred" and with the support of the country's largely Hutu population continued their campaign of assaults and killings of minority group Tutsi (Santoro, 1998). Meanwhile, in the neighboring country of Congo, growing anti-Tutsi sentiment erupted into the killing of hundreds of Congolese Tutsi women and children, under the assumption that Tutsi leaders were behind an ongoing rebellion against Congolese President Laurent Kabila (Santoro, 1999).

In this chapter, we explore the phenomena of race and ethnicity, two concepts widely used across the world to classify individuals into various social categories. These assignments are made on the basis of presumed differences in physical, intellectual, temperamental, and other attributes believed to be critical in determining our possibilities and limitations as human beings. Race and ethnicity also are two concepts that are frequently misunderstood in popular thought and misapplied in social policy, often with tragic results.

Questions to Consider

1. Why do members of minority groups occupy subordinate positions in the larger society?
2. What is the difference between a racial group and an ethnic group?
3. In what ways does prejudice differ from discrimination?
4. Why do functionalists regard assimilation as a desirable form of racial and ethnic intergroup relations?
5. What were the major differences between *melting pot* and *Anglo conformity* immigration policies in the United States?
6. From a Marxist conflict perspective, why have racial and ethnic minorities been the objects of continued subjugation in societies such as the United States?
7. In what ways does de jure racism differ from de facto racist practices?
8. How has the historical fact of slavery affected relations between whites and African Americans in the contemporary United States?
9. What factors account for the high levels of poverty and low levels of education among many Hispanic groups in the United States?
10. What is meant by the term *model minority*?
11. How does relative poverty differ from absolute poverty?
12. What is the relationship between minority group status and absolute poverty in the modern United States?
13. What is meant by the term *ethnic cleansing*?

RACE AND ETHNIC RELATIONS: AN OVERVIEW

The history of racial and ethnic groups in many human societies, including the United States, is largely a history of majority-minority group relations. It is this fact as much as any other that has made these intergroup encounters so problematic. As long as these groups remain in majority-minority social patterns, tension and conflict are likely to follow.

The term **minority group** refers to a recognizable group occupying a subordinate position in the social structure. Lacking important power resources, minorities are subject to unequal treatment at the hands of powerful **majority groups**—those in dominant positions within the society. Denied equal access to educational, occupational, and other opportunity structures, minorities are relegated to the lowest rungs of the stratification ladders in their respective societies. This holds true even when pure achievement criteria presumably serve as the formal mechanism for filling social roles. (Recall our discussion of ascription and achievement in the previous chapter.)

Minorities are groups of people who possess (or are thought to possess) physical, cultural, mental, lifestyle, or other characteristics that are valued negatively in a given society. Because of these negative or stigmatizing traits, members of minority groups are believed to be inferior to the dominant societal group and, thus, somehow deserving of unequal treatment. The fact that the term itself invariably carries such connotations of inferiority has led some people to challenge the continued use of the term *minority* as a viable concept in sociological research. According to this argument, although the word may be intended merely as a descriptive term, it may have the unintended effect of further stigmatizing the people so described. From this perspective, some other term that is not infused with the same negative symbolism—"historically underrepresented group," for example—should be used in future research to designate such groups. To date, however, *minority group* remains the commonly employed term.

As we saw in Chapter 5, minority group stratification represents a prime example of the continued existence of natural superiority thinking, with its emphasis on ascribed personal qualities as the basis for social placement. In the particular case of minorities, these personal qualities typically are presented as stereotypes. Differences in attributes among individual members of the group are discounted or ignored altogether, and real or imagined traits common to all members of the group are emphasized as the basis for social relations with the societal majority. For example, all members of one ethnic or racial group may be pictured as lazy and sneaky, and the members of another group as industrious and honest.

Such stereotyping of minorities appears to be a basic and recurring theme in intergroup relations. These portrayals ignore the actual differences that exist among people and, in doing so, greatly oversimplify and distort reality. The social world is defined (in this case, perhaps literally) in terms of black and white.

Stereotypes foster a climate that encourages the development of **prejudice**—irrational, negative beliefs and feelings about members of certain groups based on generalizations about the characteristics of those groups. Such prejudicial beliefs are rigid and inflexible, not easily changed once fully formed. And, while prejudice does not absolutely guarantee that **discrimination**—unequal and unfair treatment of a given group—will follow automatically, it nonetheless makes such behaviors toward minority group members highly likely (Vander Zanden, 1983).

Race

From a purely scientific standpoint, the term *race* denotes a classification of human beings based on the relative frequency of some gene or genes. **Races** are groups of people defined by specific genetic characteristics (what are termed *genotypical differences*). These characteristics develop over time, are hereditary, and often—but don't always—manifest themselves as *phenotypical differences* in such visible physical features as skin color, hair texture, and body build (Schaefer, 1990).

Although this definition seems straightforward, attempts to translate the concept into valid empirical terms have not been successful. Important questions of which particular biological characteristics are of most importance in defining the various races, and of how many different races there really are, have yet to be answered.

Decades of genetics research have demonstrated the futility of conventional racial categories and the existence of important human traits that cut across these categories. Based on these findings, in 1993, the executive council of the American Association of Physical Anthropologists called for the abolition of race as a scientifically meaningful way of classifying humans. According to their statement, "The idea of discrete races made up chiefly of typical representatives is untenable" (quoted in Wheeler, 1995). Rejecting the idea that overt distinctions such as skin color are significantly related to fundamental biological human differences, a growing number of scientists argue that "Race is a social construct derived mainly from perceptions conditioned by events of recorded history, and it has no basic biological reality" (Brace, in Hotz, 1995). This sentiment was reiterated by President Clinton's Council of Economic Advisors in their 1998 report on the state of racial and ethnic groups in the United States (*Council of Economic Advisors*, 1998, p. 3). "The classification of individuals by race and ethnicity is a complex and controversial undertaking. The concepts of race and ethnicity lack precise and universally accepted definitions. Their economic and social significance depend on a variety of factors, including how individuals identify themselves racially or ethnically and how others identify and treat them."

In practice, the notion of "race" has been widely misapplied, with a host of significant consequences. In different times and places, people have believed that race is the single most important determinant of individual mental, physical, emotional, and moral capacities, and have developed drastic policies toward their fellow human beings solely on that basis. For example, prevailing beliefs in Nazi Germany during the 1930s and 1940s claimed that members of "the Jewish race" were inherently sneaky, conniving, and driven by a lust for money: their greed was responsible for the economic ruin of Germany. Since, in the Nazis' view, these behaviors were an inborn racial trait, nothing could be done to change them short of wiping out the race itself. The fact that Jews are not a race at all and do not exhibit the attributes ascribed to them proved irrelevant. In the ensuing program of genocide carried out against the Jews as Adolph Hitler's "final solution" to the Jewish problem, more than 6 million people were put to death. This widespread tendency to attribute particular characteristics to members of a supposed race, and then to conclude falsely that these traits somehow are natural to that race, represents a sinister example of symbolic interactionist theorists' arguments that situations defined as real can have consequences that are all too real.

Ethnicity

Whereas race represents a way of classifying individuals on the basis of biological differences, ethnicity represents a way of grouping individuals on the basis of cultural differences. An **ethnic group** consists of people who possess a distinctive, shared culture (such as ancestry, language, folklore, traditions, food, music, and residential patterns) and a sense of common identity or "peoplehood." Ethnic groups are seen by themselves and others as being culturally distinctive (Alba, 1992).

Ethnicity itself does not necessarily have anything to do with race, but common physical characteristics do constitute an important shared attribute for many ethnic groups. For example, many Mexican Americans have a number of "racial" features, including

Seen here relaxing on the steps of their *barrio* homes, these Latinos are part of the United States' fastest growing ethnic minority group. According to U.S. Census Bureau projections, people of Hispanic origin will comprise approximately 25 percent of the country's total population within the next fifty years, and will form the numerically dominant population group in southern California and in south Florida. However, in spite of their large and growing numbers, Latinos have yet to emerge as a significant political force in most parts of the country.

skin tone and hair color, that distinguish them as much physically from their Anglo neighbors as their ethnic heritage does culturally. On many occasions, their physical resemblance to undocumented immigrants from Mexico has led to embarrassing episodes with U.S. Border Patrol agents in California, Texas, and other southwestern states.

In contrast, members of a given ethnic group may belong to any number of different racial groups. For example, the U.S. Bureau of the Census uses the umbrella term "Hispanic origin" to describe individuals of Spanish origin or culture, regardless of their race. In the 1990 census, a total of 57 percent of Hispanic respondents identified themselves as being members of one of the four "minimum race categories" ("White," "Black," "American Indian or Alaskan Native," and "Asian or Pacific Islander") used by the Census Bureau that year, but 43 percent placed themselves in the residual "Other Race" category. Of all people in the "Other Race" category, 95 percent were of Hispanic origin (O'Hare, 1992).

As the case of U.S. Hispanics shows, common ancestry or an ancestral homeland forms an important component of ethnic-group identity (Alba, 1992). But nationality and ethnicity are not always the same thing. *Nationality* refers to individuals' geographic and political backgrounds—that is, their country of origin. For example, "Latvian" describes a U.S. population group based on common national origin—in this case, all those people born in Latvia. However, not all those individuals born and living in Latvia are members of the same ethnic group. In that Baltic nation of 2.6 million, which has existed as a sovereign state for only 30 years over the past seven centuries, about 661,000 are ethnic Russians who form the country's most recognizable minority group (Matloff, 1998).

Switzerland is a recognized political unit whose citizens claim Swiss nationality, but there is no "Swiss" ethnic group to speak of. The country's population is divided into French, German, and Italian subgroups that occupy different geographic regions and maintain their own languages and sense of peoplehood. The German Swiss make up over two-thirds of the population and live primarily in the northern and eastern parts of the country. At 18 percent of the total population, the French Swiss live primarily in the western cantons. Forming 10 percent of the population, the Italian Swiss reside principally in the south (J. W. Wright, 1992).

The distinction between race and ethnicity is one that has not always been consistently maintained by sociologists, much less by the general public. Some observers prefer to use *ethnic group* as the more inclusive term and to treat *race* as a special case of ethnicity. In this view, a race is "an ethnic group whose members are believed, by others if not also by themselves, to be physiologically distinctive" (Alba, 1992, p. 576). To a large extent, these classification problems may reflect the reality of a world in which social definitions of race and ethnicity are imprecise and subject to constant change. The important considerations are the consequences that flow from people's tendency to categorize one another on the basis of assumed physical or cultural differences and to act on the basis of those categorizations.

PATTERNS OF RACIAL AND ETHNIC GROUP RELATIONS

As discussed in Chapter 3, virtually all human societies have developed over time in the direction of larger, more heterogeneous (differentiated) populations. Compared to societies that existed 10,000, 1,000, or as recently as 300 years ago, contemporary societies are much larger in population size. Many now number into the hundreds of millions of inhabitants. Most are also composed of people who in many ways, including biological and cultural features, have become more and more unlike one another.

Although most societies may have followed the same general developmental pattern, not all have been alike with respect to relations among their constituent racial and ethnic subgroups. Racial and ethnic intergroup relations have taken many different forms from one place and time to another. Sociologists George Simpson and J. Milton Yinger (1985) described six distinct patterns of majority-minority racial and ethnic group relations. These patterns— assimilation, pluralism, legal protection of minorities, population transfer, continued subjugation, and extermination—are not mutually exclusive, nor do they necessarily follow any invariable or natural sequence. They represent dominant or majority group policies toward minorities in the given society.

Assimilation

Assimilation is the process in which minority groups become absorbed or incorporated into the majority's sociocultural system, eventually losing their distinct cultural and physical identities. Milton Gordon (1964) identified several different types or stages of assimilation, indicative of progressive entry into the mainstream of societal life.

Cultural assimilation (acculturation) involves changes in behaviors, beliefs, values, and attitudes among minority group members to approximate more closely the patterns of the dominant societal group. In the language of symbolic interaction theory, incoming ethnic groups are resocialized into a new set of symbols—a cultural world view—necessary for successful everyday interaction in their adopted society. For example, in the United States, non-English-speaking immigrants are expected to surrender their native tongues in favor of the English language.

Structural assimilation involves the gradual acceptance and admittance of minority group members into secondary- and, later, primary-group relationships with members of the dominant societal group. As foreign-born immigrants to the United States during the nineteenth and early twentieth centuries became more Americanized and less culturally distinct, they were more acceptable as friends and neighbors to majority group members and were gradually drawn into more intimate interaction networks. This was especially true as the immigrants' income, educational, and occupational statuses began to improve toward middle-class level.

Finally, **marital or physical assimilation** (amalgamation) involves large-scale intermarriage and biological reproduction across majority-minority group lines, resulting in the gradual decline of distinctive physical features that may have been associated with particular minority groups. In the continuing illustration of foreign-born immigrants to the United States, marital assimilation occurred between, for example, Polish Americans and WASPs (white Anglo-Saxon Protestants, generally regarded as the dominant or majority group in U.S. society) or between Swedish Americans and Italian Americans.

The Melting Pot For almost two centuries, one of the most enduring images of American (that is, United States) society has been that of the melting pot. According to this metaphorical portrayal of the immigration experience, the great social experiment that attracted so many diverse groups of people to the New World in search of a better way of life had also created a new breed of person. The "American" was a distinctive physical and cultural type born of a hundred Old World heritages and representing the very best that each had to contribute. Melting pot theory envisioned the assimilation of individual immigrant groups into American society as an amalgamation of cultural and physical traits. It offered a model of intergroup relations that emphasized each group's surrendering of individual ethnic and national identities on behalf of an end product that was unique unto itself. "Americans" might be of English and German and French and Dutch and Italian and Greek and Polish and other origins (Figure 6.1), but they were much more than any or all of these individual strains. They were, in effect, the

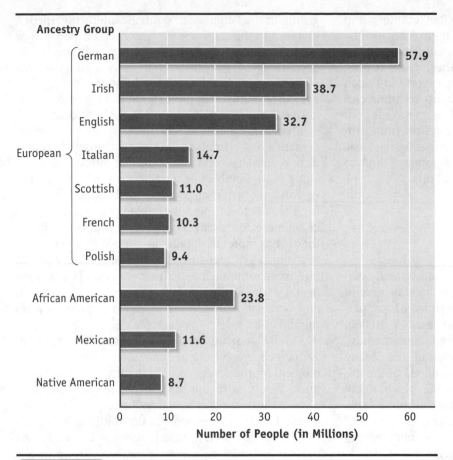

Ancestry Group

German	57.9
Irish	38.7
English	32.7
Italian	14.7
Scottish	11.0
French	10.3
Polish	9.4
African American	23.8
Mexican	11.6
Native American	8.7

European

Number of People (in Millions)

FIGURE 6.1

U.S. Population by Selected Ancestry Group, 1990 (in millions)

Note: Numbers to the right of the bars indicate actual numbers of people in each ancestry group.

Source: U.S. Bureau of the Census, *1990 Census of the Population, Supplementary Report* (Washington, DC: U.S. Government Printing Office, 1990).

best of all possible cultural and physical blends (Parrillo, 2000).

Anglo-conformity　The reality of the U.S. immigrant experience was quite different from the highly idealized portrait of the melting pot. White ethnics of both the Old Wave (northern and western European) and the New Wave (central, southern, and eastern European and Asian) immigrations were expected to assimilate into their new society, but it was to be a one-way process. From the early days of this society, the United States has been characterized by a high degree of ethnocentrism. For the dominant host group, the established Anglo-Saxon (British) cultural pattern already represented the best of all worlds and was a pattern to which arriving ethnic immigrants must learn to adapt. *Anglo-conformity,* as this belief was known, became the operating policy throughout the nineteenth and early twentieth centuries. In practice, becoming an American meant becoming as much like

the dominant Anglo-Saxon group as was possible. Immigrant groups were to give up their existing values, beliefs, and behaviors (that is, their cultural world views) and replace them with the "correct" (majority group's) frame of reference. And, although white ethnic immigrants might hope to become fully Americanized in this sense, nonwhites could not. The combination of their overt physical differences from the majority group and prevailing racist notions of the innate inferiority of people of color branded them as foreign. As an ideological symbol, the melting pot was a tremendous success. As a statement of historical reality, it is an abject failure.

Sociologists operating within the structural-functional theoretical perspective have tended to regard assimilation as the most desirable form of intergroup relations. In their view, successful assimilation of population subgroups promotes social and cultural unity and thus is functional for the social system as a whole. At the same time, complete assimilation is functional for the subgroups themselves. It provides them with the means for economic advancement and success, as well as other group goals. For these reasons, functionalists view assimilation as the preferred and ideal pattern for ethnic and racial groups.

Pluralism

The term **pluralism** refers to the retention of minority group identities and diversities, with individual racial and ethnic groups (majority and minorities) accommodating themselves to one another's individual differences. It entails the acceptance of different symbolic world views within the same social structure. Modern Switzerland is perhaps the best example of successful pluralism in action. As was discussed earlier, the nation is composed of German, Italian, and French subpopulations who maintain their individual languages and cultural traditions while cooperating with one another on matters or issues of mutual importance. However, such cooperation is not automatically guaranteed in pluralistic societies, where diverse group views and interests may place great strains on social and political cohesion. For example, as a society composed of population segments from both English and French origins, immigrants from many other parts of the world, and a variety of indigenous peoples, modern Canada has been faced with a growing number of serious challenges to national unity. In Quebec, Bill 101, intended to protect and preserve Quebec's French culture from the influences of surrounding English-speaking provinces, was fully implemented in 1978. Bill 101 mandates education in French for most of the province's children, excluding only those whose parents or siblings had been taught in English elsewhere in Canada (Walker, 1998). A 1995 Parti Quebecois–led referendum to secede from the Canadian federation failed to pass by the most narrow of margins, prompting Canada's Supreme Court in 1998 to rule that Quebec cannot separate unilaterally from the rest of the country. In the event of a Quebec vote for independence, the rest of the country must negotiate a secession with the break-away province (Urquhart and Chipello, 1998). Faced with rapidly mounting costs for language training for new immigrants and mounting problems with newly arrived immigrants integrating into Canadian life, in 1998 a government-commissioned report recommended restricting immigration to English and French speakers—a proposal promptly and widely criticized as pandering to a growing anti-immigrant sentiment and as being "not what Canada is about" (Thom, in Tamburri, 1998b).

According to evidence summarized by anthropologist Conrad Kottak (1994), pluralist societies have the greatest chance of success when their constituent ethnic and racial groups do not interact in a zero-sum game setting. (Recall the discussion of the zero-sum game in Chapter 1.) In those societies, ecological interdependence resulting from the different activities of each ethnic and racial group within the same region, or from the settlement of different regions within the same nation-state by different groups, allows noncompetitive group relations. If and when those intergroup relations become competitive, as the different groups pursue the same resources or the same goals, pluralist societies can easily be transformed into systems marked by ethnic and racial group conflict. Such conflicts have already erupted in many areas of the former Soviet Union, making the concept of pluralism in the new Commonwealth of Independent States an empty dream. In the Transcaucasus region, for example, bloody ethnic wars have kept the oil-rich republics of Armenia, Azerbaijan, and Georgia from translating that resource wealth into real wealth for their populations (Sneider, 1995).

Legal Protection of Minorities

In some societies, the civil rights of various racial and ethnic groups that otherwise might be jeopardized by local prejudices and discriminatory practices are safeguarded by political and judicial actions. This legal protection of minorities may be accomplished through laws, constitutional amendments, court directives, or other means. For example, in the United States, the Thirteenth, Fourteenth, and Fifteenth Amendments to the Constitution; various civil rights laws passed during the past three decades; and a number of affirmative action directives have helped establish and maintain the legal rights of African Americans, women, and other minority groups. In Australia, the senate in 1993 passed the Native Title Bill guaranteeing a number of territorial rights to the continent's indigenous peoples some two hundred years after they had been driven from their ancestral lands by European settlers. These lands had been claimed by Europeans under the doctrine of *terra nullius* ("the land was unoccupied"), despite the fact that aboriginal groups had occupied the area long before the arrival of the first Europeans. Government leaders saw the bill as a necessary step in their attempted reconciliation with Aborigines. However, the Native Title Bill, welfare, and other measures to protect the country's indigenous people have sparked a backlash on the part of many European Australians, particularly in economically hard-hit rural areas. Formed in 1996, the One Nation Party has gained significant

Focus on
Yugoslavia

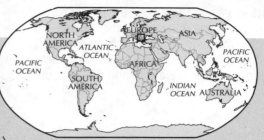

Population: 11,206,847
Life Expectancy at Birth (years): Male–71.8; Female—77.9
Form of Government: Republic
Major Religions: Orthodox (65%); Muslim (19%);
  Roman Catholic (4%)
Major Racial and Ethnic Groups: Serbian (63%); Albanian (14%)
Population Doubling Time: 365 years
Per Capita GNP (1997 U.S. dollars): N.A.
Principal Economic Activities: Heavy Industries; Mining; Agriculture
Colonial Experience: Under control of Ottoman Turks for 500 years
Adult Literacy Rate: 98% Male—N.A.; Female—N.A.

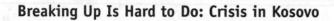

Breaking Up Is Hard to Do: Crisis in Kosovo

On June 28, 1389, Serbian forces under the command of Prince Lazar fought a heroic but disastrous battle against the Ottoman Turks on the Field of Blackbirds at Kosovo Polje. The seemingly unstoppable Turkish armies were sweeping northward through the Balkan peninsula, conquering everyone in their path. This famous Serbian "last stand" at Kosovo Polje was to have significant and long-lasting consequences for the subsequent history of the entire region. Prince Lazar died that day—and so, also, did the medieval Serbian Empire, whose aristocracy were slaughtered in the battle. For the next 500 years, the Serbs and their land remained under the rule of the Ottoman Empire. And, over the course of that half-millennium, the long-dead Prince Lazar and the ground on which he died defending his homeland came to assume a sacred, mythical stature among the Serbian people.

According to legend, on the eve of battle the Ottoman leader, Sultan Murat, gave Prince Lazar a choice of surrendering his armies or fighting to the death. Visited that night by the prophet Elijah, an emissary of the Virgin Mary, Lazar chose "a kingdom in heaven"—death—rather than "a kingdom on earth"—surrender with dishonor ("Why Do Serbs Care?" 1999). For the next 600 years, Prince Lazar's name (and, on occasion, his earthly remains) would periodically be resurrected by leaders and would-be leaders as *the* symbol of the heart and soul of Serbian nationhood, the core element of "a quasi-religious national creed . . . that has been abused to inculcate a sense of victimisation in Serbs which has blinded them to the plight of other peoples in the Balkans" (Bennett, 1999). It was in Prince Lazar's name and on the anniversary of his death that, on June 28, 1914, Serbian nationalists in Sarajevo assassinated Archduke Franz Ferdinand of Austria-Hungary, plunging the world into its First World War. It was also in his memory and to protect Kosovo, a territory "of exceptional importance for the Serbian history and for the cultural-civilizational identity of Serbia . . . the centre of the Serbian statehood" ("Kosovo and Metohija: History," 1999) that, in 1999, Serbian nationalists came close to plunging the region, if not the world, into another major war.

On March 24, 1999, armed forces from NATO—the North Atlantic Treaty Organization—took the historically unprecedented step of launching military attacks against a sovereign European country without first obtaining the approval of the United Nations. Their target was Yugoslavia and the attacks, which featured 78 days of aerial bombings, came after seemingly irrefutable evidence that the Yugoslav Serbian government, under the direction of President Slobodan Milosevic, was pursuing a policy of *ethnic cleansing* against ethnic Albanians in the southern Yugoslavian province of Kosovo. The world had first been introduced to the term "ethnic cleansing" seven years earlier, in 1992, following the collapse of the Soviet Union and the resulting disintegration of the Socialist Federal Republic of Yugoslavia. At that time, Serbian forces under Milosevic's direction had undertaken genocidal attacks on Croats and Muslims in the break-away provinces of Croatia and Bosnia-Herzegovina. Later, in 1995, Croatian army forces responded with their own ethnic cleansing of tens of thousands of Serbs in Croatia. The final toll of the Croatia and Bosnia-Herzegovina bloodbaths was hundreds of thousands of people dead, and tens of thousands of others wounded, raped, and displaced from their homes (Bonner, 1999; Watson et al., 1992). But the practice of ethnic warfare and ethnic cleansing, if not the name, has been a part of the history of the Balkans for centuries.

Balkan is the Turkish word for "mountain," an apt description of the mountainous south-central European peninsula that includes Albania, Bulgaria, Croatia, Greece, the eastern part of Turkey, and Yugoslavia, among other countries. The Balkans have also been called "the powder keg of central Europe" because of the historic propensity for major wars to start in this region; and that, too, is an apt description. In the space of the last 120 years, the political map of this area has been drawn and redrawn and then drawn and redrawn again in the aftermath of warfare between the major European powers and among the lesser nations. And, as a result of the settling of each prior war with the establishment of new state boundaries largely on the basis of political power considerations, the way has been paved for each succeeding war. Time after time, captive ethnic and national groups have attempted to break away from their imposed status as territories within states and form their own nation-states, typically with ferocious conflicts against other such groups with similar objectives. So legendary have these regional ethnic and nationalistic wars become that the term *balkanize* has come to mean "to break up into small, mutually hostile political units" (*Webster's*, 1983, p. 142). And, throughout the twentieth century, the history of balkanization has largely been the history of the once and former state of Yugoslavia.

Yugoslavia means "land of the southern Slavs" and there have been three Yugoslavias over the course of the past century, each of which was born (and two of which thus far have died) of ethnic nationalist struggles. Originally called "the Kingdom of Serbs, Croats, and Slovenes" until being renamed by King Alexander I in 1929, the first or original Yugoslavia was created by the Treaty of Versailles at the end of World War 1. It incorporated lands formerly under the control of the Ottoman Empire, including Serbia (with Kosovo, which had been reconquered from the decaying Ottoman Empire in 1912), Croatia, Montenegro, and territories to the north of them. Nominally a kingdom of co-equal powers, Yugoslavia at this time in fact was dominated by the autocratic rule of the Serbs ("Yugoslavia and the Balkans," 1999). Though strained by ethnic tensions and periodic internal conflicts between Serbs (who wanted to continue their domination of the state) and Croats (who wanted to break away and form their own separate nation-state), this first Yugoslavia lasted until the outbreak of World War II.

In 1941, following German occupation of Serbia and Italian occupation of Montenegro, Adolph Hitler established a new puppet state with Croats as nominal leaders. The next four years were a series of overlapping civil wars among the various ethnic group constituents of the old Yugoslavia (especially between Serbs and Croats) featuring numerous killings and atrocities committed by parties on all sides of the conflicts. For Croats, it was "payback" time for previous hardships endured under Serbian domination, and they took their revenge on Serbian Jews in particular (Bennett, 1999). During this period, the sacred (to the Serbs) province of Kosovo, whose population by this time was primarily ethnic Albanians, was occupied by Albanian troops. Resistance to the Germans and other Axis invaders was conducted by rival partisan groups under the command of Josip Broz Tito, an avowed communist, and Dragoljub Mihailovic, a Serbian nationalist ("Yugoslavia and the Balkans," 1999).

Following the end of World War II, Tito emerged as the strongman, and communism as the dominant ideology, in the region. In 1945, Tito declared a new (second) Yugoslavian state, the Socialist Federal Republic of Yugoslavia. This new state was composed of the nominally equal republics of Croatia, Montenegro, Serbia, Slovenia, and Bosnia-Herzegovina, each of which was viewed as constituting a nation based on its population's common ethnicity. Within the Republic of Serbia, the provinces of Kosovo and Vojvodina were given autonomous status, based, again, on the common ethnicity of their respective populations ("Yugoslavia and the Balkans," 1999). From almost the first day of its inception, however, this new Yugoslavian state was plagued by problems stemming from the conflicting aspirations of its constituent ethnic and national groups. As Balkan scholar Vesna Pesic (1996, p. 6) has noted,

The very existence of Yugoslavia seemed to defy the history of relations among its different nations, which had already waged one ethnic and religious war among themselves with the collapse of the first Yugoslavia . . . Yugoslavia's national groups all share a common history of struggling to save their distinct identities and renew their lost medieval states—a history of repressive domination that fostered disloyal and militant minorities and arrogant and repressive majorities. Almost every one of these peoples has been perceived as a threat to another national group and has felt threatened itself.

Tito's solution to the problem, through the League of Communists of Yugoslavia, was to suppress (at times, brutally) individual ethnic and nationalist aspirations in the name of the universalistic principles and ideology of communism. However, this policy of repressing individual interests in favor of the presumed common good laid the groundwork for future nationalist-based horrors, for "In the process of maintaining a balance of power among national groups, every nation/republic had reason to believe that it had been unjustly treated in the Yugoslav state" (Pesic, 1996, p. 6).

Tito's death in 1980 and the death of the Soviet Union a decade later removed both the local apparatus of nationalist suppression in Yugoslavia and the ideological principles in whose

This group of ethnic Albanians is fleeing their native village in war-torn Kosovo, having been driven out by Serbian military and paramilitary forces. The fear of a genocidal "ethnic cleansing" program similar to that carried out some years earlier in Bosnia-Herzegovina led to unprecedented bombings of Serbian strongholds by NATO forces and the patrolling of this former Yugoslavian province by international peace-keeping troops.

name that suppression had been conducted. Under these circumstances, the gates were opened to new nationalist tensions and pretensions, especially on the part of the Serbs, Yugoslavia's dominant group (Pesic, 1996, p. 9). As Balkan scholar Veljko Vujacic (1995, p. 5) has argued, "As long as the central state (whether unitary or federal) remains the ultimate locus of sovereignty, the dominant group is likely to be satisfied with its role of 'people of state.' When the larger state comes under threat, however, it is highly likely that dominant national groups will begin to reassert particularist claims." In the case of the Serbs in Yugoslavia, that claim meant consolidating political control over other ethnicnationalist groups and establishing a "Greater Serbia" similar to the long-lost medieval Serbian Empire. This goal has primarily been attempted under the leadership of Yugoslavia's president, Slobodan Milosevic.

The son of a Serbian Orthodox priest, Milosevic rose through the ranks of the Serbian Communist Party, becoming party president in 1986. Sent to Kosovo Polje on April 24, 1987, to hear the grievances of local Serbs and Montenegrins who felt they were being mistreated by the majority Albanian ethnic group in the province, he made an impromptu speech that "almost instantly turned him into a charismatic leader in the classic, Weberian sense of the term (Vujacic, 1995, pp. 7–8)." After witnessing the predominantly Albanian police force using batons and riot sticks to break up the Serbian crowd that had assembled to see him, Milosovic suddenly shouted a sentence "which ensured him a place in the national mythology for years to come: 'From now on, no one has the right to beat you!' " Riding a wave of "extreme nationalism, populist adoration for the leader, frustrated aspirations for social justice and reform, and a nostalgia

for the glorious days of Yugoslavism," Milosevic was elected President of Serbia in November 1989.

Following his election, Milosevic revoked the autonomy previously granted to Kosovo and Vojvodina by a 1974 constitutional amendment and began a process that has been called the "serbianization" of Kosovo (Society For Threatened Peoples, 1998). This attempt to reclaim the province from the numerical majority Albanians (who made up about 90 percent of the population) included the closing down of schools and universities using the Albanian language, the banning of all media broadcasts in the Albanian language, and a campaign to change the ethnic composition of Kosovo by offering free land and interest-free loans to Serbs to live in the province. In defiance, in 1991, the Assembly of the Republic of Kosovo officially declared Kosovo to be a sovereign and independent republic. The following year, in elections declared illegal by the Serbian government, the Democratic League of Kosovo won an overwhelming majority of seats—96 out of 130—in the Kosovo parliament. Milosevic responded with increasing acts of physical violence against ethnic Albanians by Serbian police and military forces ("Kosova," 1999).

Following the bloody but ultimately successful secessions of Slovenia, Croatia, and Bosnia-Herzegovina from the Federal Republic of Yugoslavia, in 1995, the Yugoslav Federation—the third Yugoslavia—emerged. It consists of just two republics, Montenegro and Serbia (including the two formerly autonomous provinces of Kosovo and Vojvodina). In 1996, when a new Kosovan independence group—the Kosovo Liberation Army (KLA)—began to make increasing demands for the establishment of Kosovo as an autonomous nation-state, the Serbian-dominated Yugoslavian government sent in military and paramilitary forces to quash the movement. Wholesale violence began to escalate as ethnic Albanians were systematically driven from their villages and homes, and KLA forces retaliated with attacks on the Serbs.

In October 1998, a cease-fire was negotiated to give time to the Serb and the Albanian factions to try to find a peaceful resolution to the situation. But that cease-fire was short-lived. On January 15, 1999, 45 ethnic Albanian civilians were massacred by Serbs in the village of Racak; two weeks later, another 24 were killed during a Serbian raid on a suspected rebel hideout ("Chronology to a Crisis," 1999). Following the expulsion of peace monitors from Kosovo and government refusal to allow entry to a United Nations prosecutor sent to investigate war-crime allegations, NATO issued an ultimatum to Milosevic: withdraw Serbian military and paramilitary troops from the province and negotiate with the Kosovo Liberation Army, or be bombed. In the absence of compliance by the Yugoslav government, bombing began on March 24.

The Serbian government responded to the NATO bombings by intensifying their attacks on the ethnic Albanian Kosovars before finally ceasing fire. By the end of the three-month Serbian campaign, an estimated 10,000 ethnic Albanians had been killed—many, the victims of executions and massacres—and at least 350,000 more forcibly driven out of Kosovo and into neighboring countries (Kifner, 1999). Additional evidence indicated that, as had happened in Bosnia-Herzegovina in 1992, Serbian forces had used rape as a weapon of terror and shame against Albanian Kosovar women (Montgomery, 1999).

As of August 1999, an uneasy peace had returned to Kosovo. Following the withdrawal of Serbian forces, ethnic Albanian Kosovars took over local and provincial governance, though with internal dissention and bickering among various factions (Qena, 1999; Wakin, 1999). In the Yugoslavian capital of Belgrade, hundreds of thousands of people took to the streets to demand the ouster of Slobodan Milosevic as President, but these opposition groups, too, were split by internal dissention and fighting for position ("150,000 Besiege Belgrade," 1999). In the meantime, the ultimate fate of Kosovo remains undecided. Members of the Kosovo Liberation Army continue to press for full sovereignty as an independent state. But that alternative is not favored by the United States and other powerful members of the international community, who fear that changing Yugoslavia's borders would trigger a larger, more ferocious Balkan war ("Key Facts About Kosovo," 1999). They also are concerned that a precedent would then be established for other ethnic or national populations around the globe to seek their own statehood by seceding from existing states—a possible balkanization of the world-at-large. They would prefer to see Kosovo remain within the Yugoslavian Federation, though as an independent republic. Given the strong and continuing nationalism of Serbia and the hallowed place of Kosovo in Serbian history and mythology, it is highly unlikely that the Yugoslav government will quietly allow Kosovo to go its own separate way, especially under the direction of an Albanian government. It is equally unlikely that President Milosevic will remain passive in the face of the widespread reprisal killings of Kosovan Serbs by Albanians that have begun in the province (Rozen, 1999). Given the history of past Balkan ethnic and national conflicts, it may well be the case that the worst is yet to come in Kosovo.

and rapid success on the strength of its platform of ending welfare and other forms of "special treatment" to Aborigines, freezing immigration from Asia, and raising trade barriers to protect local agricultural interests. Claiming that her party is not a racist group, One Nation's leader Pauline Hanson has argued that Australia's national identity is "in danger of being swamped by Asians," just as many Australians' economic well-being is in danger from unfair advantages provided to Aborigines and unfair competititon in the global marketplace (Stohr, 1998).

Population Transfer

One way racial or ethnic groups who find themselves in competition and conflict with other such groups have attempted to resolve the situation is by voluntary or involuntary population transfer, or movement of minority group members from one geographic region to another to avoid contact with majority group members. In the United States, for example, Native American tribes were forcibly removed from the eastern states to lands west of the Mississippi River in the nineteenth century. Similarly, Japanese-American citizens were relocated to internment camps by order of the federal government during World War II.

More recently, in the Yugoslavian province of Kosovo (as discussed more fully in *Focus on Yugoslavia*), the overwhelming bulk of the surviving ethnic Albanian population fled the region after being brutalized by Serbian forces as part of the Milosevic government's effort to build a Serbian nation-state. Such mass exoduses are not uncommon in the Balkan region: Following Croatia's 1991 break from the Federal Republic of Yugoslavia, some 350,000 ethnic Serbs fled or were expelled from the region; as of 1999, fewer than one-fifth of these displaced people had returned to their former homes (Pearl, 1999).

Continued Subjugation

The term **continued subjugation** refers to a variety of formal or informal practices that are undertaken by the dominant group to maintain the powerless and subservient position of some particular minority group(s) in a given society. Perhaps the most obvious example of this pattern is the former South African system of apartheid. Under this imposed arrangement, strict racial separation and severe restrictions on the lives of millions of South African blacks in social, economic, and political spheres were, for many years, the law of the land (**de jure racism**). Even after many of these laws were formally rescinded, racism remained the prevailing pattern in everyday social practices (**de facto racism**). Full political and social equality for black South Africans was not achieved until the election of a democratic government and the creation of a "new" South Africa in 1994. In Turkey, the political and economic lives of the approximately 13 million ethnic Kurds who comprise one-fifth the country's population continue to be constrained significantly by repressive government policies. Fueled by the capture of Abdullah Ocalan, leader of a 14-year-long Kurdish rebellion, racial tension between Turks and Kurds has been steadily growing (Pope, 1999).

Just as functionalist sociologists find the assimilation model compatible with their view of the social world, so do conflict sociologists with the subjugation model. As discussed in Chapter 5, the conflict theory of social inequality focuses on the different power resources of various groups and the use of power by some societal groups to exploit and subordinate others. According to sociologists such as Edna Bonacich (1992), the subjugation and exploitation of racial and ethnic minorities by powerful majority groups remain a continuing part of the history of the United States and other modern societies. Although assimilation may be the stated or formal goal in these societies, the actual social and political policies have been to dominate minorities, to keep them in their proper place.

For many years, social scientists interested in the dynamics of racial and ethnic intergroup behaviors have examined the role of economic factors in what have so often been conflict relations. Marxist conflict theorists, in particular, advanced the argument that majority-minority conflicts ultimately are a subset of class conflicts. Prejudice and discrimination against some specific racial or ethnic group are motivated by the economic exploitation of that group and the need to legitimize its subordination. A racist ideology that defines the subjugated group as somehow inferior to the majority and, thus, undeserving or incapable of equal treatment, serves this purpose well. It takes the burden of responsibility for the minority group's subordinate social position off the shoulders of the dominant group and transfers it to the minority. The subordinate group then is seen as the cause of its own inferior status. Thus, the position of African Americans in the United States was explained (Cox, 1948) as a continuing consequence of a white belief in the inherent inferiority of black people. This doctrine was developed over 200 years ago to support and justify the plantation system of the South, which required a large, cheap workforce for the labor-intensive agrarian economy. Similarly, the current positions of Native Americans and Mexican Americans have been interpreted as consequences of the internal colonial policies of the dominant Anglo group in U.S. society (Bonacich, 1992; Russell, 1994).

The race-as-class hypothesis is far from being universally accepted among sociologists. But there is ample empirical evidence to support the argument that economic factors are an important contributing element to the development of prejudice and discrimination against racial and ethnic minorities. One version of this line of reasoning argues that direct competition between members of the majority group and a specific minority for such rewards as jobs, education, and housing creates hostilities. These hostilities are expressed through prejudicial attitudes and acts of discrimination against the threatening minority group. This would explain, for instance, white lower-class and working-class racism, as well as similar attitudes and behaviors often displayed by minorities toward other minorities. These groups are in direct competition with one another for the meager rewards to be found in their segment of what Bonacich (1992) termed a "split labor market" created and maintained by the dominant group to further its own advantaged social position.

A second version of this economics-based argument views the economic decline of the majority group (or some segment of the majority group) as the underlying source of prejudice and discrimination against minority group members. Here, minorities are made into **scapegoats,** innocent targets for the majority group's frustrations and aggression, even though they may be blameless for the dominant group's perceived deprivation. In this instance, the minority group's primary failing is its lack of power and its high visibility. Minority people are powerless and therefore a safe target. They are made to bear the brunt of dominant group members' frustrations with a larger and perhaps not fully understood world (Allport, 1958).

From the standpoint of symbolic interaction theory, the power struggles that are so characteristic of majority-minority interaction might be interpreted as an outgrowth of the different world views of these groups. To the extent that people who share the same societal space do not share a common symbolic (cultural) perspective, divergent values and meanings might set them on a collision course that finds expression in economic and political conflicts. In this interpretation, conflict resolution involves the development of a new world view acceptable to all parties (as in the melting pot model) or the triumph of one world view over its competitors (the Anglo conformity model).

Extermination

The term **extermination** refers to attempts to destroy physically or annihilate members of particular minority groups. For members of the majority group, intergroup relations problems are solved by eliminating the offending minority group(s). *Genocide,* as this practice often is called, has had a long history in human intergroup relations. Adolph Hitler's mass murder of some 6 million Jews during World War II and the systematic killing of 1.5 million Cambodians by the Khmer Rouge in Southeast Asia are two twentieth-century examples of this extreme policy. More recently, in the east-central African country of Rwanda, long-standing ethnic hatreds culminated in the annihilation of upwards of 1 million Tutsi people by extremist Hutu militias in what has been described as a "wave of mass killings . . . [that] . . . built up faster than during any other such episode in the last half century" (Masland, 1994). United Nations inves-

tigators have termed the wholesale slaughter of the Tutsi not merely an act of passion but, rather, "preplanned genocide" (Press, 1994). In 1999, fearing the likelihood of a similar genocidal attack by Serbians against ethnic Albanians in the Yugoslavian province of Kosovo, NATO (North Atlantic Treaty Organization) military forces began a systematic air warfare campaign against the Yugoslavian government. Although universally condemned, extermination continues to be employed by groups throughout the world as an instrument of gaining or maintaining political power.

RACIAL AND ETHNIC INTERGROUP RELATIONS IN THE UNITED STATES

Throughout the history of racial and ethnic majority-minority group relations in the United States, virtually all the policies just discussed have been attempted by dominant societal groups. A complete discussion of the many racial and ethnic groups that make up the contemporary U.S. population would be well beyond the scope of this text. But even a brief overview of some of the more visible or more important minority groups will illustrate the point. (For a more comprehensive review, see Parrillo, 2000.)

African Americans

Nearly thirty years after the National Advisory Commission on Civil Disorders issued its now-famous indictment of the United States as "two societies, one black, one white—separate and unequal" (1968, p. 1), that description remains largely true. This nation's largest racial or ethnic group (African Americans constitute about 13 percent of the population) is still very much a minority group whose members experience significantly poorer living conditions than their white counterparts. As Table 6.1 shows, African

TABLE 6.1

Selected Quality-of-Life Indicators for Whites and African Americans, 1998

Indicator	Whites	African Americans
Life expectancy at birth (years)	76.8	70.2
Percent below poverty level	10.5	26.1
Percent of children below poverty level	15.1	36.7
Percent female-headed households	13.1	44.7
Percent over age 25 without high school diploma	17.0	25.1
Median family yearly income	$49,023	$29,404
Per capita yearly income	$21,394	$12,957

Source: U.S. Bureau of the Census, *Current Population Reports,* P60-206; P60-207 (Washington, DC: U.S. Government Printing Office, 1999).

Americans continue to trail whites in such fundamental areas as life expectancy as well. Black infants are more likely than white infants to be born underweight and are less likely to survive their first year. As adults, blacks are nearly twice as likely as whites to die from strokes, and have rates of heart disease 40 percent higher than those of whites. Compared to white men, black men have cancer death rates that are 50 percent higher (Meckler, 1998). According to the United Nations' HDI or Human Development Index (a composite of life expectancy at birth, educational attainment, and income), as of the early 1990s, the United States as a whole trailed only Canada in terms of human development scores among 174 contemporary societies. However, if separate HDI scores were calculated for whites and for African Americans, "whites would rank number 1 in the world . . . [and] . . . blacks would rank number 27 . . . full equality still is a distant prospect in the United States" (U.N. Development Program, 1995, p. 22).

To understand both the creation and the persistence of these conditions, it is necessary to remember one crucial fact. African Americans were originally brought to this society involuntarily, to work as slaves in the southern plantation economy. During nearly 250 years of slavery, they endured incredibly demeaning and dehumanizing conditions. At the same time, many whites developed a set of attitudes and beliefs justifying the buying and selling of human beings as property. These beliefs involved the basic and deep-rooted feeling that black-skinned people are somehow naturally and profoundly inferior to whites.

The system of slavery was formally destroyed by the Civil War. However, the reconstruction of the South after the war led to the development of a set of segregation laws—the so-called Jim Crow laws—that effectively barred the newly freed slaves from any real participation in the social, political, and economic order on a par with whites. In effect, these laws locked them into a subservient social position.

The U.S. Supreme Court's historic 1954 *Brown v. Board of Education* decision declared racially segregated school facilities unconstitutional and opened the assault on the Southern Jim Crow system. The often heroic efforts of civil rights leaders such as Dr. Martin Luther King, Jr., during the 1950s and 1960s led to the passage of sweeping legislation during the 1960s and 1970s that dismantled the formal, de jure segregation system. However, this legislation did not really eliminate prejudice and discrimination against African Americans in U.S. society.

What had been formal and legally supported mechanisms of repression now became informal, de facto practices. These were often embedded within established institutional structures (e.g., the neighborhood school system), a pattern sociologists call **institutionalized racism,** and seemed immune to attempts to correct them through legislative action. If anything, attempts to legislate racial equality through measures designed to deal with the subtle but persistent consequences of such institutionalized practices seem to have had an opposite effect. In some instances, these efforts increased feelings of antagonism against African Americans and other minorities, who were seen as undeserving beneficiaries of government intrusion at the expense of innocent majority group members. Many whites have come to see affirmative action and preferential treatment directives as reverse discrimination against their own group.

This interpretation was reflected in a series of U.S. Supreme Court rulings begun during the Reagan and Bush presidential administrations. The net effect of these rulings was to narrow substantially the scope of previous minority rights legislation. More recently, state and federal court rulings during the Clinton era have effectively dismantled many of the core principles and directives of the affirmative action program. These decisions have largely been supported by whites and opposed by African Americans. Their responses reflect fundamental differences in the two groups' beliefs about both the basic responsibilities of government in addressing continuing racial inequalities (Morin, 1995) and the need for preserving the traditional role of affirmative action (Merida, 1995). Whether or not affirmative action survives in some limited form or other, the fact remains that, after a nearly 400-year history in this country, African Americans remain second-class citizens. Assessing the current state of racial and ethnic groups in the United States, the Council of Economic Advisors for the President's Initiative on Race found that "Over the second half of the 20th century, black Americans have made substantial progress relative to whites in many areas. But this progress has greatly slowed, or even reversed, between the mid-1970s and the early 1990s. In many cases large discrepancies persist" (Council of Economic Advisers, 1998, p. 2).

Hispanic Americans

Sociologist James W. Russell has noted in his study of race and class in North America (1994, pp. 8–9), "the naming of Latin American–origin people is a problem in the United States and Canada. A wide number of terms are in use, some of which are considered objectionable, but by different people." For example, the term *Hispanic origin* or *Hispanic* is used by the U.S. Bureau of the Census and is widely employed in the eastern part of the United States. But it is opposed by some groups because it implies a complete Spanish background as well as a unitary cultural identity among Spanish-speaking peoples that in fact does not exist. The term *Latino* is more widely used in the U.S. West and Southwest. However, it, too, implies a single cultural identity, which is at odds with the multitude of racial, ethnic, and national origin backgrounds of Spanish speakers. As one commentator (Booth, 1998) has observed, "It is a particularly American phenomenon, many say, to label citizens by their ethnicity. People living in El Salvador, for example, see themselves as a nationality. When they arrive in the United States, they become Hispanic or Latino." Recognizing the impossibility of selecting a blanket term to try to describe such a diverse group of people, we have nonetheless chosen to follow the lead of the U.S. Census Bureau and employ the term *Hispanic American* or *Hispanic* to designate those people of Latin American origin currently residing as citizens in the United States. Among others, this category includes Mexicans, Puerto Ricans, Cubans, Argentines, Salvadorians, and a number of other specific nationality groups.

By whatever name they may be called, Hispanics form a large, rapidly growing segment of the U.S. population. Making up an estimated 10 percent of the total U.S. population in 1998 and showing a 34 percent growth rate during the previous decade, Hispanics are projected to surpass blacks and become the nation's largest minority group by as early as the year 2005 and to account for about 25 percent of the overall U.S. population by the year 2050 (Booth, 1998).

To date, sheer numbers have not translated into economic and social equality for Hispanic Americans any more than they have for African Americans. If anything, the overall educational, income, and other life conditions of U.S. Hispanics compared to those of non-Hispanic whites may be worse than those of African Americans (see Table 6.2). The same U.N. Development Program report that ranked U.S. blacks 27th on the HDI index ranked U.S. Hispanics in 32nd place, a position shared with the South American country of Uruguay (U.N. Development Program, 1995). Of course, not all Hispanic Americans share this fate. For example, descendants of the old Spanish elite in New Mexico continue to enjoy high social and economic status, and many middle-class Cubans who fled Castro's regime during the 1960s have socioeconomic profiles that match or exceed those of most Anglos (non-Hispanic whites).

The overall lower levels of income, education, and other quality-of-life indicators for Hispanics are significantly related to the high rates of immigration

among this group. In 1997, 38 percent of the Hispanic population was foreign-born, compared to only 8 percent of Anglos and 6 percent of African Americans (Council of Economic Advisors, 1998, p. 7). These immigrants most often arrive with little or no formal education or technical training, forcing them into low-wage, dead-end jobs that perpetuate their situation. It is also this fact of large-scale immigration, especially illegal immigration, that has put Hispanics on a collision course with the dominant Anglo group.

Many Anglos view Hispanics as a threat to the economic well-being of the United States because they often will accept substantially lower wages than Anglo workers, thus displacing deserving citizens from the labor force (Graham and Beck, 1992). Hispanic immigrants also are seen as a massive drain on legal, educational, health care, and other social services funded by taxpayers. For example, one 1997 study conducted by the National Academy of Sciences concluded that, in New Jersey, households headed by native-born citizens paid an average of $232 a year more in state and local taxes because of the presence of immigrants. The comparable figure for households in California, one of the nation's top destinations for immigrants, was $1,178 (Dugger, 1998). However, other reports argue that immigrants are an overall economic plus for the nation, primarily through tax payments that exceed the cost of their use of social services by as much as $30 billion each year (Cleeland, 1994). Whatever the actual net economic impact of Hispanic immigrants may be, it was public perception of, and frustration with, a Hispanic-led charge on taxpayer funds that sparked the passage of California's Proposition 187 in November 1994. Hailed as immigration reform by its proponents and damned as Mexican bashing by its opponents,

TABLE 6.2

Selected Quality-of-Life Indicators for Whites and Hispanics, 1998

Indicator	Whites	Hispanics
Percent below poverty level	10.5	25.6
Percent of children below poverty level	15.1	34.4
Percent female-headed households	13.1	21.6
Percent over age 25 without high school diploma	17.0	45.3
Median family yearly income	$49,023	$29,608
Per capita yearly income	$21,394	$11,434

Source: U.S. Bureau of the Census, *Current Population Reports,* P60-206; P60-207 (Washington, DC: U.S. Government Printing Office, 1999).

Proposition 187, which severely restricts or eliminates altogether a variety of social services for illegal immigrants, became the inspiration for similar proposals in other U.S.-Mexico border states. However, nearly six years after its passage, Proposition 187 remained unimplemented as a result of a series of suits challenging its constitutionality.

Hispanic immigrants are also perceived as a threat to the cultural well-being of the United States because of their refusal to abandon the Spanish language in favor of English and to become Americanized. Consequently, the continuing influx of Hispanics has become a social problem for many members of the dominant Anglo group. Twenty-five states currently have laws making English their official state language. Nationally, the U.S. English movement is a similar attempt to have English become the official language of the United States. According to their supporters, these efforts represent an attempt to preserve U.S. culture by preserving a critical source of cultural cohesiveness—its grounding in a common language. Supporters also promote fluency in the English language as an important vehicle for increasing employment and income opportunities, and thus upward mobility, for Hispanics themselves. In this regard, one study conducted by the Federal Reserve Bank of Atlanta found that men with weak English skills earn almost 10 percent less in states that designate English as the official language than do workers with weak English skills in states without such laws. With or without such state laws, fluent-English speakers earned from 91 percent to 113 percent more than poor-English speakers (reported in Bodipo-Memba, 1999). In spite of these findings—or perhaps because of them—some critics have called official-English laws "a new form of Jim Crowism," claiming that "It's more difficult to discriminate on the basis of the color of your skin, so they are using language to discriminate against people and threaten their livelihoods" (Rijos, in Bopido-Memba, 1999). In many cases, the factual merits and demerits of establishing English as the nation's official language have been lost in the emotionality generated by the proposal. As with so many other aspects of Anglo-Hispanic relations, this issue remains extremely volatile.

Asian Americans

The umbrella term *Asian American* refers to a number of individual ethnic minority groups, including Japanese, Chinese, Koreans, and various Indochinese peoples (Vietnamese, Laotians, Cambodians, Thais, Hmong). In all, Asian Americans comprise about 3.7 percent of the total U.S. population (about 10.1 million people). Since the late 1980s, social scientific and public attention has been drawn to the economic, educational, and occupational accomplishments of these groups. Their often startling successes rival the best examples in the rags-to-riches tradition, earning them praise as "American success stories" (Suro, 1994). Asian Americans have the highest median family incomes of all ethnic groups in the United States. They also show the highest level of formal education of any group in this society, including non-Hispanic whites. Fifteen percent of Asian Americans held master's, professional, or doctoral degrees in 1997, compared with 9 percent of Anglos (Council of Economic Advisors, 1998, p. 20) However, these impressive profiles are deceptive. For example, despite their higher median incomes, Asian Americans have a poverty rate more than 50 percent higher than that of non-Hispanic whites (p. 33). Members of the Asian American community claim that their popular image as a "model minority" is "more a curse than a blessing for Asian Americans," (Chen, in Tyson, 1994) inasmuch as it is a greatly oversimplified and misleading portrayal damaging to their efforts to gain equal treatment in U.S. society.

Asian Americans have very high proportional representation among high-status, highly compensated managerial and professional occupations. They also have very high proportional representation among low-status, poorly compensated service occupations (N. R. Brooks, 1994). Large numbers of Asian Americans have, in fact, been able to fulfill the American dream of upward mobility and success. But many of the recently arrived immigrants who have contributed to the explosive growth of the Asian American community in the past several years (in 1997, 61 percent of the U.S. Asian population were foreign-born) have sunk to the very bottom of the occupation and income ladder. In one especially notorious case that gained national attention in August 1995, seventy-two Thai workers were found working seventeen-hour days for as little as 60 cents an hour in a Los Angeles garment industry sweatshop described by authorities as "a virtual slave labor camp" (Branigin, 1995). Unfortunately, the persistence of the model minority stereotype often blinds the government and the larger majority group community to the plight of many such refugees. Episodes such as that in Los Angeles are seen more as extraordinary aberrations rather than as all-too-frequent facts of life for many new Asian immigrants.

Native Americans

Much as the poverty of some Asian Americans remains hidden from the larger society, low visibility remains a source of continuing problems for Native Americans in the United States. Hidden out of sight (and, thus, out of mind) on isolated reservations, many members of this oldest American group lead lives of true desperation. Like most other indigenous peoples in the Americas, "Indians" in what is now the United States have fared poorly during the more than 500 years since the beginning of contact with Europeans. The early period of that contact was characterized by cultural and physical conflicts, a pattern that was repeated throughout much of the history of the United States following the country's break from Britain. Viewed as foreign nations by the U.S. government, Native American tribes became the opponents of that government in a series of "foreign wars" that almost invariably resulted in defeat for Native Americans. By the mid-1800s, nearly all tribes living in the eastern half of the nation had been forcibly relocated west of the Mississippi River. Estimated to have once been as large as 8 million, their numbers had been reduced by this time to about 250,000 as a result of dwindling food resources and the effects of previously unknown diseases transmitted by European settlers (Parrillo, 2000).

The opening of the western frontier following the Civil War led to further conflicts with white settlers who, in their search for land, gold, and other fortune, simply swept native tribes aside. Because they were unable to assimilate to Anglo culture and posed a physical threat to settlers, Native Americans once again were forcibly relocated, this time to lands that typically were so resource poor as to be of no interest to whites. Tribal members languished for many years in "benign neglect" on these reservations as wards of the federal government, their lives controlled and structured by the Bureau of Indian Affairs (BIA).

For the most part, BIA policies seemed to be directed to forcing the assimilation of Native Americans to white cultural patterns and to breaking up traditional tribal groupings. For example, children often were taken from the tribes to be educated in distant "Indian schools" that used Anglo curricula and taught traditional Anglo subjects rather than the knowledge and customs of their particular tribe. The result was large groups of people who were unable to cling to old ways of life that had been virtually destroyed and who were unable to adapt to a new way of life that was both culturally foreign and unwilling to accept them.

Tired of their steady decline under the BIA, in the 1960s and 1970s, Native American groups undertook a series of dramatic acts of protest to focus public attention on their plight. These actions included the seizure of Wounded Knee, South Dakota, the site of the massacre of 300 Sioux by U.S. Army troops in 1890, and the occupation of Alcatraz Island, California. Native Americans also organized a pan-Indian movement, a coalition of various tribal groups united in common cause to pursue common interests against a common enemy—the federal government. This was an extraordinarily difficult undertaking, inasmuch as it required groups whose world views in some respects were poles apart to bridge that cultural chasm.

Although the pan-Indian movement achieved some positive results in securing tribal land rights and in pursuing several court cases against the government and private corporations, its overall success has been mixed (Parrillo, 2000). Whether measured in terms of economic, educational, or physical health, most of the estimated 2 million Native Americans today remain near the bottom of the U.S. socioeconomic hierarchy. For example, Native Americans in the 15- to 24-year-old age bracket have the nation's highest death rate, largely as a consequence of their extremely high incidence of alcoholism. For Native Americans, rates of cirrhosis of the liver and diabetes are three times higher than the national average, and their accident rate is two-and-a-half times higher than the national average. As a group, Native Americans also have the highest suicide rate of any racial or ethnic group in U.S. society (Council of Economic Advisors, 1998, p. 47).

Unemployment and poverty rates among some individual tribal groups are exceptionally high. For example, according to data presented before a U.S. congressional committee in 1990, 87 percent of the 10,300 Lakota Sioux who inhabited the Standing Rock Reservation in North and South Dakota were unemployed and 90 percent were living in poverty in 1988–1989 (Kennedy, 1991). Their situation has not changed appreciably: in July 1999, when President Bill Clinton visited Standing Rock on his tour of high-poverty areas across the country, it remained the poorest census tract in the entire United States.

Beginning in the mid-1980s, many tribes turned to "gaming" (casino-style gambling) as a means of climbing out of poverty. Although reservation-based gambling has become a $7 billion industry and has reversed the economic fortunes of some tribal groups, its success has been limited. Only about one-third of tribes receive any incomes from gaming, and 8 of the 184 tribal casinos operating in 1998 generated 40 percent of all Native American gaming revenues that year (Baldauf, 1998a). Additionally, tribal gaming has been challenged by a growing number of states, including California and Texas, which view tribal casinos as illegal and claim the right to regulate them under the provisions of the federal Indian Gaming Regulatory Act of 1988. In California, following attempts by then-governor Wilson to impose a gaming agreement regarded as unacceptable by many of the state's tribes,

The lavish Foxwoods Resort Casino on the Mashantucket Pequot Indian Reservation in Ledyard, Connecticut, is a far cry from the decrepit buildings more commonly found on other reservations across the United States. Awash in cash from the vast casino, the Pequots are thriving in the world of high finance, snapping up scores of properties in Connecticut and Rhode Island, opening their own shipbuilding business, and hob-nobbing with politicians, including President Clinton.

Native Americans spearheaded the passage of Proposition 5, allowing tribal self-determination with respect to such issues as the number of casinos and the number and types of gaming devices in those casinos (Wood, 1998b). Reflecting the magnitude and intensity of the issue, Proposition 5 supporters (largely, Native American tribes) and opponents (largely, Nevada and other established gaming industries) spent a record $110 million during the heated campaign, which resulted in a victory for the tribes. However, in August 1999, Proposition 5 was voided by the California Supreme Court on the grounds that it violated the state's constitution. Tribes were then forced to negotiate a working compromise with Governor Davis pending the gathering of enough signatures to put on the ballot another proposition that would amend the California State Constitution to allow full-scale gaming with Las Vegas–style electronic machines. It remains to be seen if tribal gaming will prove to be the salvation for Native Americans, who remain at the bottom of the social heap.

MINORITIES AND POVERTY IN THE UNITED STATES: A DECLINING SIGNIFICANCE OF RACE?

With few exceptions, the pattern of racial and ethnic minority group linkages to the social stratification system in the United States has remained remarkably stable over time. Nearly sixty years ago, pioneer social class researcher W. Lloyd Warner and his associates (Davis, Gardner, and Gardner, 1941; Warner and Srole, 1945) noted that two separate paths were followed by or available to minorities in this society.

For white ethnics (European-born immigrants who physically resembled the dominant WASPs), the pattern was one of initial rejection by and subjugation to the majority group. Dominant group prejudices and discriminatory acts were reflected in restricted economic, educational, occupational, and other opportunities for the white ethnics. However, as their cultural assimilation progressed, these groups were able to take advantage of rapidly expanding social, economic, and political structures to move up in the social class structure. Improved status in turn led to the ethnics' increased acceptance by the dominant societal group. The resulting structural and marital assimilation finally created a condition in which the distinctive cultural and physical traits of the ethnics all but vanished. Original ethnic group membership then ceased to be an important factor in the shaping of social opportunities and social class membership.

For racial minority groups, the path has been quite different. Unlike white ethnics, who could physically blend in with the majority group after reaching a certain level of cultural assimilation, people of color remain physically distinctive even after they have attained full cultural assimilation. Prevailing racist ideologies of the dominant societal group continue to associate skin color and other physical characteristics with intellectual and moral inferiority. Thus, racial minorities' physical visibility has meant that they are the objects of continued prejudice and discrimination. For them, race has remained a crucial determinant of position in the stratification hierarchy, and that position has been on the bottom rungs of the ladder. Caste rather than class factors characterize relations between the racial majority and minority groups.

Poverty

Data relating to income distribution and patterns of economic poverty in the United States during the past three decades certainly seem to verify the validity of this argument. As has already been discussed, median yearly incomes for African Americans, Native Americans, and many Hispanic and Asian groups are substantially below those of non-Hispanic whites. So, also, are educational and occupational profiles. This pattern is even more pronounced when the issue being considered is poverty.

Poverty, or economic deprivation, is a politically and socially sensitive issue. It is also a concept that lends itself to a variety of interpretations. Relative poverty definitions compare various groups in order to draw conclusions about the economic circumstances of one group relative to others. From this perspective, **relative poverty** is the situation of being economically deprived compared to some other particular group. For example, in comparison to the upper-middle class, the lives of the working class may be described as involving relative poverty or deprivation. Typical working-class incomes do not permit the same types and levels of material goods as do upper-middle-class incomes. Working-class people may have all the material necessities of life, but they do not possess the same level of material comfort as do upper-middle-class people. In this sense, they are poor.

In contrast, absolute poverty definitions measure economic deprivation in terms of an objective, fixed standard. From this perspective, **absolute poverty** refers to the inability to maintain physical survival on a long-term basis. Conceptualized in this manner, poverty can be measured as incomes that fall below the amount of money needed for a minimally adequate supply of material resources such as food, clothing, and shelter. It must be recognized, however, that "There is no scientifically adequate method for determining the minimally acceptable living standard: this will vary from society to society and over time as living standards and social norms change" (Council of Economic Advisors, 1998, p. 33).

In spite of the inherent difficulties in constructing a valid objective measure of poverty, for over forty years the federal government has employed just such a measurement to define poverty and to examine its prevalence in this society (see Figure 6.2). The *poverty line*, as this index is called, represents the yearly income required to provide a nutritionally adequate diet for a typical family of a given size (most commonly, a family of four). For 1998, the poverty line was set at $16,660. In that year, approximately 12.7 percent of the U.S. population, or 34.5 million people, were officially defined as poor. This figure represents a decrease of some 4.8 million individuals

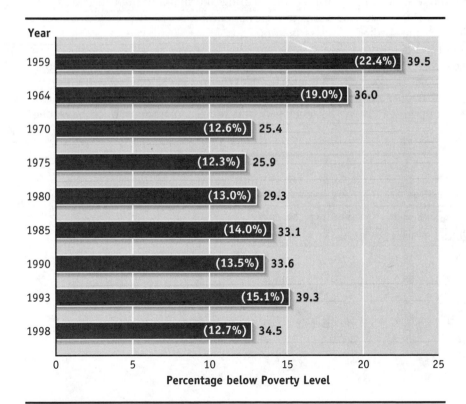

FIGURE 6.2

Persons below Poverty Line, 1959–1998

Note: Numbers to the right of the bars indicate actual numbers of persons below the poverty level (in millions); numbers within bars indicate the actual percentage of the population they represent.

Source: U.S. Bureau of the Census, *Current Population Reports,* P60–207 (Washington, DC: U.S. Government Printing Office, 1999).

Minorities and Poverty in the United States: A Declining Significance of Race?   **133**

from 1993's ten-year-high 15.1 percent poverty rate (U.S. Bureau of the Census, 1999b). Whether or not these figures are an accurate assessment of the real extent of poverty in the United States is controversial. It is widely recognized that the calculation of "official" poverty is a flawed process subject to as much political distortion as mathematical manipulation (Milbank, 1995). Many observers are convinced that the current method of measuring poverty on the basis of pretax income greatly underestimates the extent of poverty, and have called for the creation of a more realistic measure (Pear, 1995). However, other observers claim that current procedures greatly overestimate the true extent of poverty, arguing that the Census Bureau misses an annual $2 trillion in income expenditures (Rector, in Francis, 1998).

Who are the poor in the United States, and how does being a member of an ethnic or racial minority group affect one's likelihood of being poor? At first glance, government figures might appear to refute the hypothesis that minority group status is a significant factor in the experience of poverty. Contrary to prevailing stereotypes, white people form the bulk—over 68 percent—of the poverty population. But this figure is misleading, since whites are the overwhelming numerical majority within the United States. A more accurate measurement is the proportional representation of each racial or ethnic group that falls below the poverty line.

Table 6.3, which is based on 1998 data, shows that being a member of a minority group greatly increases one's likelihood of poverty. Whereas most poor people are white, most whites aren't poor—only 10.5 percent of all white people were living below poverty in 1998. However, African Americans, who constituted about 13 percent of the total U.S. population in 1998, had a poverty rate of 26.1 percent. And people of Hispanic origin, who made up 10 percent of the population in 1998, had a poverty rate of 25.6 percent. This pattern of significantly higher rates of poverty for African Americans and Hispanic Americans holds across age, sex, and family composition categories.

Race and ethnicity are major factors in the phenomenon of poverty in the United States, just as they are in other societies that have identifiable minority groups. In the U.S., this is especially evident when we direct our attention to what has been called "the American underclass" (Wilson, 1987, 1989). This group consists of the hardcore poor for whom poverty has become a permanent way of life and who are becoming increasingly separated and isolated from mainstream American life. What is not entirely clear is exactly how much race per se contributes to creating and maintaining this truly disadvantaged group compared to the effects of social class factors.

Wilson on Race, Class, and Poverty Sociologist William Julius Wilson (1978) offered a highly controversial hypothesis with respect to this issue. He acknowledged that racial factors may once have been

---

TABLE 6.3

Poverty Status of Persons by Family Composition, Sex, Age, and Race: 1998

Characteristic	Below Poverty Level (percent)			
	White	Black	Hispanic	All Races
All Ages	10.5	26.1	25.6	12.7
Male	9.2	23.0	23.2	11.4
Female	11.8	28.7	28.0	14.3
Under 18 Years	15.1	36.7	34.4	18.9
Male	14.7	36.0	33.7	18.4
Female	15.5	37.3	35.2	19.4
Family Composition				
Married couple	5.8	8.6	17.8	6.2
Female head, no spouse present	27.6	42.8	46.7	33.1
Female head, no spouse present, children under 18	40.0	54.7	59.6	46.1

Source: U.S. Bureau of the Census, *Current Population Reports,* P60–207 (Washington, DC: U.S. Government Printing Office, 1999).

Chapter 6 • Race and Ethnicity

important in originally pushing many minority people into poverty. However, it is class-related factors of occupational skills and educational levels, not racial group status, that now keep some people trapped in poverty over the long run. To make his point, Wilson cited the growing number of African Americans who have moved into middle-class and upper-middle-class occupations and income levels. He argued that such upward mobility patterns demonstrate the fact that white prejudices and discriminatory actions no longer operate in such a way as to suppress all African Americans uniformly on the basis of race.

What these data show, according to Wilson, is that race per se has declined as an important determinant of socioeconomic status. What has caught and trapped some African Americans in underclass life is a series of occupational and other structural changes in the United States. These changes include a decline in the types of unskilled, semiskilled, and service jobs that in the past provided employment opportunities for people with lower levels of education and fewer occupational skills. They also include the geographical relocation of many industries and businesses that, in the past, provided local employment opportunities for residents of inner-city areas. Wilson concluded that, if racism were still a paramount factor in the determination of socioeconomic situation, no—or only a very few—African Americans would have achieved middle-class and upper-middle-class status.

Wilson's hypothesis was criticized sharply by a number of analysts (for example, Willie, 1978, 1979), who challenged his assertion that race and racism are no longer significant factors in the structuring of African Americans' stratification. These critics claim that blacks and other people of color still face daily instances of prejudice and discrimination regardless of their socioeconomic status. Firsthand accounts of otherwise successful African-American professionals and managers who have experienced subtle but devastating forms of racial indignities (for example, Barrett, 1999) would seem to lend support to Wilson's critics.

Although overt racist patterns may have declined and majority-minority relations may appear to have improved over the past several decades, race- and ethnicity-related problems in this society are far from over. Recent studies indicate that, in a more "civilized" racial climate of less fist waving and name calling, a growing number of whites simply are physically abandoning schools, cities, and regions as increasing numbers of minorities (especially immigrant minorities) start to move in (Belsie, 1999; El Nasser, 1998).

SUMMARY AND REVIEW

Race and Ethnic Relations: An Overview

1. *What are the distinguishing features of minority groups?*

Minority groups are composed of people who possess traits that make them distinctively different from dominant majority societal groups and that are negatively valued in the larger population. These minorities are often relegated to subordinate positions at the bottom of the stratification hierarchies of their societies. (P. 116)

2. *What is the difference between race and ethnicity?*

Race and ethnicity are concepts that give rise to much confusion and misunderstanding. Racial minorities consist of people who are (or who are thought to be) genetically and physically different from the majority group. Ethnic minorities are composed of people who are culturally different from the dominant societal group. Both racial and ethnic minority groups face stereotyping, prejudice, and discrimination by the majority. (Pp. 117–118)

3. *How do stereotyping, prejudice, and discrimination differ from one another?*

Stereotyping is the tendency to ignore individual differences among members of a given group and to define all its members as alike. Prejudice is an irrational, negative feeling or belief about members of some particular group. Discrimination is unfair, unequal treatment of members of a particular group. (P. 117)

Patterns of Racial and Ethnic Group Relations

4. *What is assimilation, and what has been the U.S. experience with this form of intergroup relations?*

In different times and different societies, members of majority and minority groups have interacted in a variety of ways. Assimilation is the incorporation of various minorities into the mainstream of their surrounding society culturally, socially, or biologically. Although the United States has often been described as a melting pot of diverse racial and ethnic groups, the actual pattern was more often one of Anglo-conformity, in which immigrants were expected to become Americanized in the prevailing Anglo-Saxon cultural pattern. Functionalists regard assimilation as the most desirable form of racial and ethnic intergroup relations. (Pp. 119–120)

5. *What is pluralism?*

Pluralism is the retention of individual racial and ethnic group differences in a given society and the accomodation or mutual adjustment of these groups to one another. In some societies, the rights of minorities are maintained through legal protection. In other societies, population transfers may keep minorities separated from majority group members. (P. 121)

6. *How do conflict theorists interpret the subjugation of racial and ethnic minorities that continues in many societies today?*

Economic, political, and social subordination of minorities is a fact of life in many societies. Conflict theorists in the Marxist tradition claim that it is based on economic exploitation by powerful social classes. (P. 126)

7. *What is extermination?*

Extermination or genocide is the attempt to annihilate or physically destroy a given racial or ethnic group. Hitler's treatment of the Jews during World War II is the best-known modern example. (P. 127)

Racial and Ethnic Intergroup Relations in the United States

8. *What is the largest racial or ethnic minority group in the United States today?*

African Americans constitute the largest racial or ethnic minority in the United States and are the only group in this society to have been held in slavery. Although legal segregation and other forms of racial discrimination have been abolished, institutionalized racist practices continue to restrict income and educational and occupational opportunities for this group. African Americans remain significantly below whites in most quality-of-life indicators. (Pp. 127–128)

9. *Who are Hispanic Americans?*

Hispanic Americans or Hispanics are people from Spanish or Latin American origins. This group includes Mexicans, Cubans, and Puerto Ricans, among others. Their economic and social circumstances differ by subgroup, and many experience economic, educational, and occupational deprivation. A rising tide of illegal immigrants, especially in the Southwest, has led to growing resentment of many Anglos (non-Hispanic Whites) against this group. (Pp. 128–130)

10. *What is a "model" minority?*

Because of their educational and economic successes, Asian Americans have been portrayed as a model minority. However, many recently arrived immigrants from Southeast Asia have not been able to share in these successes; nor have all Chinese Americans or Japanese Americans done well. (P. 130)

11. *What is the most severely disadvantaged minority group in the United States today?*

Native Americans preceded white European settlers in the United States, but they lacked the newcomers' military technology and were overwhelmed by the colonists. Both physically and culturally distinct from the Anglos, Native Americans have been relegated to reservations managed by the Bureau of Indian Affairs. They remain the most severely disadvantaged minority group in terms of income, education, occupation, and other quality-of-life factors. (P. 131)

Minorities and Poverty in the United States: A Declining Significance of Race?

12. *What is the relationship between poverty and minority group status in the United States?*

Poverty is the experience of economic deprivation. Relative poverty is the deprived condition of a specific group compared to that of another group. Absolute poverty is the inability to meet minimum requirements for physical survival. Racial and ethnic minorities are overrepresented among those living in poverty in the United States, but the specific factors responsible for this observed pattern remain the subject of much dispute. (Pp. 132–135)

Gender and Gender Issues

I n Jordan, a 16-year-old girl is shot and killed by her older brother for bringing such disgrace to her family that the family's honor or *scharaf* can be restored only by her death. Her "crime" was to have reported to the police the fact that she had been raped. "She committed a mistake, even if it was against her will," said her executioner. "Anyway, it's better to have one person die than to have the whole family die from shame" (Sirhan, in Beyer, 1999). For shooting his sister four times in the head, the 35-year-old murderer will receive a jail sentence of six months. In a second, eerily similar case, another 16-year-old girl is tied in a chair and stabbed to death, again by an older brother, again for being raped—by her younger brother. This time, the executioner will be sentenced to a seven-year prison term, though it is highly unlikely that he will serve the full sentence. Judges often reduce "honor killing" sentences by half or more, and one or two years in jail is the average penalty in cases involving the murder of a woman who has been suspected of illicit sex. In those cases in which a man kills his wife or other close female relative after having caught her in an act of adultery, the typical punishment is no punishment at all (Beyer, 1999; Prusher, 1998c).

Of the approximately 100 murders committed in Jordan each year, an estimated one-fourth to one-third are "crimes of honor" in which girls or women have been killed by their own relatives to "cleanse" the family name from the effects of some real or imagined sexual offense. Jordanian men place an extremely high cultural value on female purity, and even the merest hint of a sexual scandal can be a woman's death sentence. The director of Jordan's National Institute of Forensic Medicine reports that, in 80 percent of the cases in which he conducts a hymenal exam of a girl who has been reported missing—a routine procedure in Jordan—the same girl will be returned to him soon after as a corpse, even if she proved to be a virgin (Hadidi, in Beyer, 1999).

With the support of Jordan's royal family, especially Queen Noor, local human rights activists are attempting to change this long-standing tradition, but the going has been slow, at best. Some reformers claim that one of the biggest hurdles in the battle against honor killings is the court system's seeming legitimization of the crime. In addition to slap-on-the-wrist punishments for men found guilty of honor killings, no action whatsoever is taken against the men who threaten women until those threats have been carried out to their lethal conclusion. When such threats do occur, it is more often the women who are jailed, for protective custody. In the women's prison at Amman, for example, more than 50 of the 190 inmates are girls and women who have been incarcerated to keep them out of the reach of fathers, brothers, and uncles who have threatened to kill them (Prusher, 1998b).

Jordan is by no means the only Arab country in which women face life-threatening or life-restricting inequalities. Though the Islamic religion itself supports women's rights at home and at work, including property rights and control of their inheritances, local traditions often run counter to religious precepts. In Saudi Arabia, for example, women are barred from driving, do not have identity cards in their own names (they must use family identity cards for all their official and banking transactions), and must have written permission from a male relative in order to travel (Abdallah, 1999). In the ongoing war being carried out by militant Islamic fundamentalists in Algeria, women in particular have been targeted for death, with more than 400 girls and women killed as "object lessons" between mid-1992 and the end of 1994 (Bowers, 1995). And, as we will discuss in detail in this chapter's "*Focus on* Afghanistan," the governing Taliban in that society have attempted to completely roll back the clock as far as women's rights are concerned, reducing women to the status of little more than slaves.

But discrimination against women is hardly unique to Islamic nations. According to Joan Ruddock, Britain's minister for women, "That women and men should enjoy all human rights equally is beyond doubt, but almost nowhere in the world is this the case. To be born female is, in many parts of the world, an automatic barrier to equality" (in Prince, 1998). For example, in the African country of Zimbabwe, the nation's Supreme Court declared that "the nature of African society" dictates that women are not equal to men, especially in family relationships, stating that centuries-old African cultural norms say that women should never be considered adults within the family, but only as a "junior male" (Tucker, 1999). Observers claim that this legal ruling, from which there is no appeal, effectively eliminates virtually all rights gained by women since the country's independence in 1980. In South Korea, India, and China, the highly disproportionate ratio of men to women has been interpreted as the consequence of preferential treatment given to boys and men in such fundamental areas as food and health care allocation, and the resultant deaths of millions of girls and women from their denial of these basic resources (Prince, 1998).

In 1979, during its "decade of women," the United Nations adopted the *Convention on the Elimination of All Forms of Discrimination Against Women*, an international agreement intended to ensure women's rights in employment, education, voting, nationality, marriage and divorce, health care, and equality before the law. As of 1999, that convention had been ratified by 163 member countries (the United States remains one of the 22 member nations that has not ratified the agreement). However, after concluding that it was still the case that "no country treats its women as well as it treats its men" (United Nations Development Program, 1996, p. 32), in 1999, the U.N. adopted a protocol allowing women suffering any form of discrimination banned by the 1979 convention to appeal directly to a committee of the U.N.'s Commission on the Status of Women once they had exhausted all means of redress in their own country. The committee has no power to compel a government to change its discriminatory behavior, but can make recommendations for correcting women's rights abuses (Lewis, 1999). Though hailing the protocol as an important step in promoting the rights of all women in all nations of the world, human rights activists nonethe-

less are dismayed that such a mechanism is needed at all and that it took twenty years to be established. As one observer has noted, "Governments talk a lot about women's rights but don't do anything concrete to enforce them" (Brown, in Lewis, 1999).

In this chapter, we examine the social consequences of biological differences in sex and gender. Whether one has been born female or male, as we will see, is sufficient to create separate and unequal futures for new human beings who in all other respects—race, ethnicity, social class, religion, and even physical size—may be virtually identical. Quite apart from considerations of individual abilities and limitations, people's likely social paths will be steered in different directions by virtue of their sex and gender. In nearly all human societies, anatomical and other biological differences among individuals have become the basis for a host of social, political, economic, and other differences that drastically affect the quality of people's lives.

Questions to Consider

1. What is the difference between sex and gender as social categories for classifying human beings?
2. What does existing research from the biological and social sciences tell us about natural physical, intellectual, and emotional differences between women and men?
3. What is *gender assignment,* and why is this phenomenon such an important factor in the lives of individuals?
4. How does chronological aging affect people's gender identities and behaviors?
5. According to classical functionalist theorists such as Talcott Parsons, in what ways are traditional gender roles and a sex-based division of labor functional or beneficial for society?
6. From the standpoint of conflict theory, what is the major function of a sex-based division of labor in a modern society such as the United States?
7. What is the *pink-collar ghetto?*
8. How do human capital interpretations explain observed male-female occupational income differences in modern societies?
9. What is the *feminization of poverty,* and what factors have contributed to the development of this phenomenon?
10. What difference does it make that relatively few women hold political office at the higher levels of government in most contemporary societies?
11. What is *Roe v. Wade?* Why was this such an important event for proponents of greater gender quality?

UNDERSTANDING SEX AND GENDER

Like race and ethnicity, sex and gender are concepts that are subject to misunderstanding and confusion in popular usage. They have often been thought of

as alternative names for the same phenomenon and frequently have been employed interchangeably. They certainly are related in the sense that both are ways of classifying people on physical grounds; however, they are by no means equivalent terms.

Biological Considerations

From a purely scientific standpoint, **sex** represents a classification system based on anatomical differences among individuals. In addition, sex differences include chromosomal and hormonal factors that distinguish females from males. Thus, members of the female sex have different physical organs from males (ovaries and a vagina rather than testicles and a penis). They display a particular chromosomal pattern (XX) that differs from that of males (XY), and their bodies produce hormones in different proportions from those of males (primarily estrogen rather than androgens).

Psychological and Sociocultural Considerations

In contrast to sex, which classifies people entirely on the basis of anatomical and biological features, **gender** classifies people on the basis of physiological, psychological, and sociocultural characteristics. An individual's gender is a function of his or her identification with a given sex and adoption of a lifestyle deemed appropriate for that sex. If I define myself as a man, think and feel like a man, and behave in a "masculine" way, my gender is that of man.

One's identification as either female or male is based on anatomical characteristics that are presumably objective and obvious. But the whole process is infused with nonobjective and nonphysical considerations as well. In most societies, cultural beliefs have established the basic "truth" that differences in human physical anatomy are linked inherently to important differences in intellect, emotions, and other dimensions. By virtue of their physiology and its connection to the childbearing process, for example, women are "known" (that is, believed) to be naturally gentle and nurturing. Lacking such a basic and intimate connection to childbearing, men are thought to be naturally less gentle and less nurturing. By virtue of their hormonal cycles, women are considered to be more emotional and more subject to mood swings than men. Lacking these monthly cycles and the hormonal changes that accompany pregnancy and childbirth, men are believed to be emotionally stable, more rational and logical. By virtue of their smaller physical size, women are thought to be weaker and more frail than men and thus dependent on men for continued survival. Being physically larger and temperamentally more aggressive, men are believed to be best suited and responsible for the continued survival of women.

These **gender stereotypes** or categorical portrayals of women and men are common throughout the world. In all societies in which they have been found, stereotyped beliefs and assumptions about the basic natures of women and of men have served as the bases for the formation of gender roles. These **gender roles** assign individuals to particular and different social tasks specifically because of their sex and its assumed characteristics. Typically, they involve the assignment of individuals to positions that categorically lead to unequal rewards for women and men. The result is that **gender stratification**—the formation of inequality hierarchies based on sex—has been an enduring feature of most human societies.

Our gender identity represents much more than simply a realization that we are anatomically female or male. It involves the recognition of what it means to be a woman or a man as those meanings have been established within a specific social and cultural context. Gender also involves an acceptance and internalization of this cultural definition and an attempt to structure our lives by it. Thus, sex—being female or male—is thus a matter of biology, whereas gender—being woman or man—is a matter of cultural orientation and social practices as well as biology. Gender is our individual interpretation of our society's interpretation of anatomical differences among its population members.

TRADITIONAL GENDER STEREOTYPING AND GENDER ROLES

Sexual Morphology and Gender Differences

The assertion that women and men are intellectually, emotionally, and in other ways profoundly dissimilar is based on the premise that differences in sexual morphology (anatomical features) generate inherent differences in rationality and temperament—in other words, the premise that anatomy is destiny. For centuries, people throughout the world have believed that women are the way they are because they are female, and that men are the way they are because they are male (Basow, 1986).

Empirical evidence from a growing inventory of biological, psychological and anthropological research has challenged these long-standing beliefs. This research has involved detailed examinations of female-male differences within given societies, as well as comparisons of women and men across different societies. Although the final word on this subject has yet to be written, existing evidence strongly suggests that many traditional beliefs concerning "natural" differences between the sexes lack empirical support.

Biological Findings

One common element of gender stereotyping is related to physical size. Because men generally are larger and stronger, they are assumed to be physically superior.

The fact that most men in a given society may be physically larger than most women in that same society does not necessarily imply that they are physically superior. Cultural values notwithstanding, bigger does not always mean better. The larger frame and heavier musculature of men do give them the advantage in terms of sheer physical strength. However, women have the advantage in terms of long-term physical endurance. The question of which of these two traits, short-term strength or long-term endurance, is superior is typically answered by cultural preferences rather than purely biological considerations.

Evidence that women are not biologically inferior to men can be found in birth and death patterns. Male embryos are more likely to abort spontaneously than female embryos, and males are more likely than females to die during infancy (United Nations Development Program, 1995). Furthermore, females outlive males in all but two societies for which life expectancy data are available. In the United States, for example, female life expectancy in 1995 was 79.7 years, compared to 73 years for males. For industrial societies, females averaged 7.5 years more than males (77.9 versus 70.4) that same year. For the world as a whole, female life expectancy was 2.4 years more (65.3 versus 61.9) in 1995 (United Nations Development Program, 1998, Table 2). Contemporary data thus fail to validate the assumption of male physical superiority (Figure 7.1).

Psychological Findings

A second component of gender stereotyping relates to intellectual and emotional traits. According to common belief, women and men view and respond to the world in ways that are inherently different. Women are thought to be more emotional and artistic, whereas men are seen as much more rational and

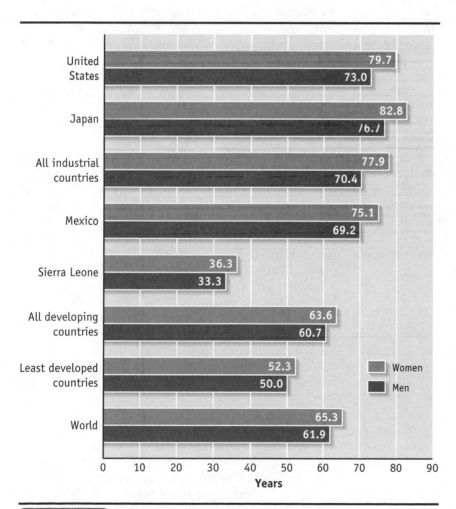

FIGURE 7.1

Female and Male Life Expectancy at Birth, Selected Countries, 1995

Source: United Nations Development Program, *Human Development Report 1998* (New York: Oxford University Press, 1998) Compiled from Data in Table 2.

Traditional Gender Stereotyping and Gender Roles

pragmatic. These presumed differences in thought and temperament, it is believed, will continue as long as women and men remain physically different. They represent the effects of the different ratios of estrogen and androgen hormones that distinguish the two sexes and that play such a major role in shaping their respective personality structures and behavioral patterns. To quote the catch-phrase from one best-selling series of books in the 1990s, "Men are from Mars, Women are from Venus" (Gray, 1992).

These may be widespread beliefs about the psyches of women and men, but what are the facts? The existence of female hormonal changes associated with menstruation, childbirth, and menopause is a matter of established record. However, the exact consequences of such changes insofar as female psychology and temperament are concerned are matters of continuing dispute. So, too, are questions concerning the relation between sex-linked hormones and intellectual, emotional, and behavioral patterns of women and men.

What do we know about such patterns? Several reviews of the existing research literature (Deaux, 1992; Jacklin, 1989; Shapiro, 1990) suggest that the actual range of consistent female-male differences may be much smaller than is commonly believed. Evidence indicates that females show somewhat higher levels of verbal ability than men and that men demonstrate somewhat higher mathematical and visual-spatial abilities as well as higher levels of physical aggression. But, though these differences appear to be linked to body chemistry differences between the sexes, they are not always large or stastically significant (Blum, 1999). Collectively, research findings do not support the conclusion that women and men are significantly different in intellect or in temperament (Deaux, 1992; Shapiro, 1990).

Anthropological Findings

For many years, anthropologists have made the study of cross-cultural differences in sex and gender an important part of their ethnological research. As a result of their efforts, we now possess a great deal of information about how people in different parts of the world conceptualize and treat anatomical differences among their respective population members. Collectively, these ethnological data point to the variability and elasticity of what we otherwise might take to be natural biological differences.

The most famous work in this tradition is Margaret Mead's classic study of three tribal groups in New Guinea (Mead, 1963/1935). In two of these groups, Mead found very few differences between women and men in terms of psychological patterns or social behaviors. Among the Arapesh, both women and men displayed what we might think of as essentially feminine traits: sensitivity, cooperation, and overall absence of aggression. In contrast, among the Mundugumor, both women and men typically were insensitive, uncooperative, and very aggressive—traits our culture might define as essentially masculine.

The third group studied by Mead, the Tchambuli, made clear and significant distinctions between women and men. Surprisingly (at least from the standpoint of our culture), these distinctions were quite the opposite of what we might have expected. The Tchambuli defined women as the aggressive, rational, capable sex and men as the emotional, flighty sex. Women were socially dominant, assuming primary economic and political roles within the tribe. Men were socially passive, assuming artistic and leisure roles.

The lesson to be drawn from the work of Mead and other anthropologists is clear. Like race and age, sex may be a biological phenomenon, but it is not merely biological. Sex may provide certain resources and impose certain limitations on members of specific groups, but these resources and limitations form only broad outlines of what may or may not be possible for people. The specific detailing of these outlines—what people will actually do and what will actually be done to them—is more likely to be the result of social and cultural factors than of biological determinism (Gould, 1976).

Sex and gender research has grown increasingly sophisticated in recent years. However, we may never be able to resolve the question of innate differences between women and men completely. Biological differences are surrounded and confounded by cultural beliefs and social practices that especially manifest themselves in the ways in which members of the two sexes are socialized, making the task of splitting apart biology and culture "analogous to splitting hairs" (Breedlove, in Blum, 1999, p. 50). As another researcher (Deckard, 1983, p. 26) has observed, "So long as boys and girls are brought up to behave differently, it will be impossible to disentangle the innate from the learned." And, in most societies, boys and girls *are* brought up to behave and think very differently.

BECOMING WOMEN AND MEN: GENDER SOCIALIZATION

As we saw in Chapter 4, human beings are not born with any preexisting knowledge of, or particular orientation to, their surrounding world. What we come to know and think and feel about life (and about ourselves) we learn through socialization. So it is with gender identities and behaviors. We are born female or male; we become girl or boy, then woman or man. The social mechanism through which this transformation occurs is that of **gender socialization.** Like other aspects of socialization, it is a lifelong process, beginning at birth and continuing to death.

Infancy and Childhood

The presentation of the newborn infant to its parents as girl or boy is just the first in a long line of social classifications to which the typical person will be subjected throughout life. This **gender assignment,** or categorization of the individual as female or as male, is of enormous significance in structuring the infant's relationships to its immediate world, both inside and outside of the family.

The use of gender assignment and stereotyping to define appropriate relationships toward and by children is widespread and effective. By the time children are 3 to 4 years old, they have already formed an image of themselves as girl or boy and are gaining growing knowledge of what being girl or boy means in terms of their own behavior (LaFranchíe, Stryer, and Gauthier, 1984). With relatively little actual social experience behind them, they are well on their way to absorbing and accepting society's definition of what they, as individuals, should be like by virtue of their anatomy. "She" and "he" are becoming important considerations in the development of "I" and "me."

Adolescence and Early Adulthood

Adolescence represents a critical period for gender socialization. It is during these difficult years of transition between childhood and adulthood that gender identities and roles are consolidated and solidified (Eccles, 1987). For the majority of adolescents, this means accepting the patterns to which they were exposed during childhood. A good deal of the socialization efforts of parents, teachers, counselors, and others during this time period seems to be directed to this end. Preparation for future adult roles often entails learning about activities deemed appropriate for members of one's sex. Learning to be an adult thus translates into learning to be a proper adult woman or adult man.

By the time most individuals cross the threshold from adolescence into adulthood, they have accepted the gender information offered them by the major agents of socialization in their society. Young adult females leave the world of formal schooling and step into the occupational, marital, and parental roles that await them. In many instances, these roles embody prevailing cultural definitions of what is natural and normal for women. Their primary emphasis is on nurturing activities, whether for one's own family or for others.

Young adult males also complete their formal education and begin to assume adult occupational, marital, and familial roles. These, too, often reflect stereotyped assumptions and beliefs about the nature of men. Successful careers and occupational achievements come first. Successful family life, that is, earning a good living for one's family, represents the fruits of one's labors.

Middle and Late Adulthood

For the average person, advancing age brings increasing participation in traditional adult social roles. Careers must be constructed, daily living needs attended to, and children looked after. Prevailing beliefs in most societies typically define certain of these activities as being the primary responsibility of one sex rather than the other. The time and energy commitments required by these stereotyped roles lock individuals into a set of structured behaviors and relationships that reiterate and reaffirm their sense of femininity or masculinity.

Movement into later adulthood precipitates a number of gender role changes. For women who have defined themselves primarily as mother and wife, the loss of children through their own passage into adulthood or the loss of husband through death represents a potential crisis of self-identity and self-worth (Williamson, Munley, and Evans, 1980). For many other women and most men, significant role changes associated with advancing age arrive in the form of retirement from an occupational career.

In this culture and many others, the adult role is defined as one involving active mastery of some occupational task and productive contribution to society. Jobs provide people with positive social identities and, as we saw in Chapter 5, also serve as a major indicator of their position in the socioeconomic hierarchy. Perhaps even more fundamentally, occupation is the primary vehicle for acquiring the material resources that make life possible and comfortable. Retirement therefore may symbolically tell the world—and the retirees—that their days of productive contribution to society have come to an end. This realization, coupled with the financial decline that often accompanies retirement, may generate a severe identity crisis for some individuals.

Another major role change for many people occurs with the decline of health and physical abilities that is associated with advancing chronological age. Such physical decline may be forestalled for a time, but it cannot be held off forever. In a culture in which adult status is defined in significant part by physical vigor, the loss of such capacities may be read by the individual and by others as loss of adulthood.

Thus, with advanced age, both women and men face the prospect of having to redefine their conceptions of who and what they are. This process of un-learning an old social identity and learning a new one necessarily involves a reassessment of one's femininity or masculinity. This may consist of the realization that one can no longer measure up to pre-vailing cultural ideals of gender appearance and ac-tivities. In a society in which youth is valued and old people are subject to negative stereotyping, the new self-identity of many older people may be that of someone who is a lesser person than before.

Alternatively, the changes experienced with age could lead people to reassess the nature of gender roles and gender stereotypes. Conceivably, they could recognize that these cultural portraits no longer apply to them or to many others like them. They could begin to challenge the validity of gender ideals that appear so far removed from the real world. But this second alternative is likely to remain more of a theo-retical possibility than an actual occurrence.

THEORETICAL INTERPRETATIONS AND EXPLANATIONS OF GENDER ROLES

The presence of distinctive gender roles in virtually every human society has been subjected to a number of differing theoretical explanations. This sex-based division of labor has been interpreted as a mecha-nism for creating and maintaining a successful social system. It also has been seen as a mechanism for the systematic and deliberate exploitation of more than half of the world's population.

Gender Roles as Salvation: Classical Functionalism

Structural-functional theorists have attempted to ex-plain gender roles in terms of their contributions to societal survival. They argue that there must be some good and compelling reason for the fact that separate social roles for the sexes have been found throughout human history. The classic statement of this position was offered by the foremost functionalist theorist of the twentieth century, Talcott Parsons (1954), and his associate Robert Bales (Parsons and Bales, 1955).

Parsons and Bales assumed the critical importance of the family as a basic unit of human social organi-zation. It is the family, after all, that has ultimate re-sponsibility for producing and raising new members of society. In addition, it is important for consump-tion in the modern economy. Consequently, the con-

Classical functionalist theory posited that the gender-based division of labor found in most contemporary societies is the result of innate differences in temperament between the sexes. According to this perspective, this Japanese woman's natural nurturing abilities make her better suited to be helper and assistant to her male manager, whose natural competitiveness makes him better suited to lead in the world of high-powered business.

tinued viability of the family is a matter of great sig-nificance for the survival of the society itself.

Like other units, the family must deal with two kinds of relationship problems if it is to persist over time. The first involves **instrumental tasks**—goal-directed activities that link the family to the surround-ing society in order to acquire necessary material resources. A family member must take on a full-time occupation as a source of income and must assume responsibility for deciding how this income will be spent on different types of needed goods, such as food, housing, and medical care.

The second problem involves **expressive tasks**—the creation and maintenance of a set of positive, supportive, emotional relationships within the fam-ily unit. Family members have to feel loved and cared for so that they can develop their full poten-tials as individuals. Therefore, someone within the family must take on the responsibility for these ex-pressive tasks. The expressive role creates the kind of atmosphere that will nurture the growth of all family members, allowing them to deal successfully with the challenges and disappointments they will face in the larger society.

Parsons and Bales maintained that these two dif-ferent but complementary roles could be performed most efficiently if they were undertaken by different individuals. Traditional patterns of socialization that prepared women and men for separate roles also cre-ated different personality profiles in the two sexes. According to Parsons and Bales (recall that they wrote in the generally conservative atmosphere of the 1950s), women were better suited to perform tasks oriented toward people and relationship. Compared to men, they were more emotional and empathetic. Most men were more interested and skilled in performing activities that were oriented to tasks and production. Compared to women, they were more competent and more confident in these areas.

The net result is that a division of labor by gender is functional for the continued survival of the family. The assignment of the expressive role to the wife/mother and of the instrumental role to the husband/father ensures that both types of tasks will be performed at the highest level of effectiveness. Thus, the family will prosper and, with it, the larger society. By implication, any significant change in this beneficial arrangement will lead only to decreasing efficiency in the performance of these vital roles. The family will then suffer and, with it, the larger society.

Critique of the Functionalist Perspective   Like other functionalist interpretations of social phenomena in the contemporary world, this explanation for the existence and persistence of sex-based divisions of labor has been criticized severely. For one thing, it failed to take into account the fact that throughout history, women in many societies frequently played important roles in economic and other productive activities. In fact, their instrumental actions often have been crucial for maintaining the viability of the entire society (Layng, 1990). As Chinese leader Mao Zedong once observed, "Women hold up half the sky."

Second, in their efforts to describe the positive or beneficial aspects of the sex-based division of labor, the classical functionalists ignored its dysfunctional consequences. Gender identities and roles are based on assumptions about differences in female-male abilities and interests that often simply aren't true. Prevailing cultural beliefs and social practices define certain types of behaviors as natural for one sex or the other, and other types of behaviors as unnatural. In so doing, they may misallocate and waste a great deal of individual talent and potential contributions to societal well-being.

For example, women who might otherwise make world-class engineers or corporate chief executive officers are prevented from even considering these career options by cultural beliefs and prohibitions that limit their role to the domestic sphere. Men who might otherwise make superb childcare providers are kept from pursuing this possibility by prevailing beliefs that emphasize the association of members of their sex with economic, political, and other instrumental roles. In both cases, much like the "strangulation of talent" effect discussed in Chapter 5, the larger society suffers when well-qualified people are removed from serious consideration for important social roles. The potential loss and misapplication of talent are enormous and represent a decreased capacity of society to deal successfully with survival problems.

Finally, the functionalist interpretation fails to explain why social roles differentiated on the basis of gender should be stratified. If both instrumental and expressive tasks are equally important for societal survival, they should receive equal rewards for successful performance. But expressive roles seldom command the levels of property and prestige awarded to instrumental roles. For example, in the United States, the services of mothers and of elementary school teachers (most of whom are women) receive a great deal of verbal praise and support. But their yearly incomes from these roles—nothing in the case of mothers, slightly more than nothing in the case of most elementary teachers—do not at all reflect the importance of their work with children. Some critics (Collins, 1988a) argue that what these unequal rewards reflect significant power differences built into the structure of society. By ignoring the power differentials that exist between instrumental and expressive roles (and between the people who perform them), classical functionalists have missed a crucial element in the gendered work arrangements of most societies.

Gender Roles as Suppression: The Conflict Model

The portrait of gender roles offered by conflict theorists stands in stark contrast to that of the functionalists. Conflict theorists view traditional gender definitions and gender roles as instruments of oppression in society. Their only real function is to preserve patriarchal systems in which cultural patterns and social practices are structured to ensure the individual and collective advantages of males over females in most aspects of social life (Basow, 1986; Collins, 1971, 1975).

According to this interpretation, gender role differences in human societies have never been based solely on biological considerations. Rather, they are a consequence of advances in productive technologies that created economic surpluses, inheritable private property, social class hierarchies, and a structure of patriarchy (Engels, 1902/1884). Women were defined as a form of property and came under the possession and control of men, who were able to dominate women by virtue of the men's superior physical strength. Males increasingly became involved in economic, political, and military roles, and females increasingly were restricted to domestic, nurturing roles (Collins, 1975).

As male dominance and the role separation of the sexes increased, cultural ideologies were established to explain and to justify this arrangement. Typically, these ideologies stressed the supposed natural physical and intellectual superiority of males over females and the natural mothering and nurturing instincts of females. However, these arguments were merely a convenient fabrication. The real basis for gender stratification was that patriarchal systems clearly were beneficial for males, who had the physical power to impose their will on females. Economic, political, and social dominance allowed men a disproportionate share of all the good things that life had to offer, and they were not about to let such a system slip through their hands (Layng, 1990).

Conflict theorists agree that significant changes in this long-standing patriarchal pattern are not likely to occur unless women make them happen. Just as an aggressive, politically active civil rights movement was necessary before conditions for racial minorities in the United States improved, a comparable women's rights movement is necessary if their case is to advance. As an oppressed class, women must come to recognize their own collective exploitation and organize effectively to end it.

Critique of the Conflict Perspective Like functionalism, the conflict explanation of gender roles and gender inequality represents a selective, simplified view of a more complex reality. It can be criticized for its overemphasis on the inherent conflicts between women and men and on the destructive consequences of all existing gender relations. If at least some radical feminist versions of the conflict model (for example, Barry, 1979) were taken at face value, we would have to rule out entirely the possibility that women and men ever do things together in a cooperative spirit of sharing or love. Rather,we would have to conclude that the appearance of such harmony is always just an appearance—a hidden agenda maintaining the oppression of one sex by the other lies somewhere under the surface.

A second criticism of some (Marxist) versions of conflict theory relates to the assertion that gender oppression is associated exclusively with capitalism. Both Marx and Engels viewed the social position of women in modern industrial (and, now, post-industrial) societies as an extension of the system of class exploitation and conflict. Women's oppressed condition could be improved only as the oppressed conditions of all laboring people could be improved; namely, by the destruction and elimination of the private property systems on which class distinctions were founded. From this perspective, economic stratification is the spring from which all other forms

of social inequality flow. But an examination of gender relations in noncapitalist societies shows that this argument is without merit.

Before its demise and subsequent breakup into the Commonwealth of Independent States, the Soviet Union was a society founded on a revolution driven by socialist ideas and structured on socialist principles. It was also a society in which occupational, economic, and other forms of gender inequalities were significant and widespread. Like many women in capitalist societies, women in the Soviet Union were concentrated in lower-paying occupations and largely excluded from important political leadership roles (Daniloff, 1982; Rossides, 1990).

Spanning a wide range of societal types, then, gender stratification is not a consequence of any one particular economic or political system. Gender inequalities may be similar to class inequalities in some important respects, but they are not identical to them. As Max Weber pointed out, modern stratified societies are multidimensional systems whose individual hierarchies are at least partially independent of one another. An understanding of socioeconomic class arrangements in a given society may promote a better understanding of gender dynamics and arrangements in that society, but it cannot be a substitute for an examination of gender inequality phenomena (Crompton and Mann, 1986). It is to an examination of such phenomena that we now turn.

PATTERNS OF GENDER STRATIFICATION

All of us at one time or another encounter firsthand evidence of social inequalities in our society. This evidence may come in the form of a sleek new BMW convertible racing past our Ford sedan on the freeway or of a homeless person scouring the dumpster behind our favorite restaurant for leftover food. It may even present itself as the college degrees that allowed a fortunate few from our home town to escape a life of manual labor in the local factory or mill.

For the most part, our experiences with these inequalities are likely to be personal. We encounter and deal with them as individuals. But as we have attempted to show in this chapter and the two preceding ones, social inequalities are more often categorical than individual, more often patterned than random. The inequities faced by women are no exception.

Although they may be encountered individually by women or men, different kinds of inequalities confront individuals exactly because they happen to be women or men. Many of the most important experiences that we are likely to have in our lives—occupational, economic, political, and legal—are shaped by sex and gender considerations. In the majority of such cases, the pattern is the same: Men dominate and women are subordinate. These widespread institutionalized inequities are indicative of the fact that the United States, like almost every other society in the modern world, is a gender-stratified system.

Gender and Work

Although some women in our society have always worked outside the home, female participation in the U.S. labor force increased steadily and dramatically in the last half of the twentieth century. A large number of women who would otherwise have remained out of the workforce were pressed into service by the acute shortage of men during World War II. Most of them returned to their households and their families after the war, but many remained gainfully employed.

Between 1960 and 1997, the number of working women in the United States nearly tripled, reaching 63 million. In 1960, 37.7 percent of all women who were eligible to work were in the civilian labor force; by 1997, that figure had increased to 59.8 percent (see Table 7.1). Many of these women were married and living with their husbands. Although fewer than one-third of all married women (31.9 percent) were working in 1960, well over one-half of all married women (61.6 percent) were in the labor force by 1997 (U.S. Bureau of the Census, 1998c). Many women may work because they want to, but most do so because they have to. Frequently, they help to provide their families with basic resources such as housing and education. Far from being a luxury or an indulgence, their contribution has become a necessity for family sur-

TABLE 7.2

Pink-Collar Occupations in the United States, 1997

Occupation	Total Employed (in thousands)	Females as Percentage of Total Employed
Dental hygienists	103	98.2
Secretaries	3,033	98.6
Receptionists	1,005	96.5
Childcare Workers	260	96.8
Cleaners and servants	512	94.9
Dental assistants	231	96.7
Family childcare providers	513	98.2
Early childhood teachers assistants	432	95.6

Source: U.S. Bureau of the Census, *Statistical Abstract of the United States: 1998* (Washington, DC: U.S. Government Printing Office, 1998). Table 672

vival. This is especially true for divorced or separated women with children and for single mothers.

Many women entering the workforce find their employment prospects limited in ways that those of men are not. Depending on their educational backgrounds, both women and men might opt for a variety of blue-collar, white-collar, or professional and managerial occupations. But within these categories, women often are steered into a much narrow range of choices that are largely segregated by sex. Thus, they come to occupy what sociologist Jesse Bernard (1981) first termed "pink-collar jobs." Collectively, these occupations comprise what is sometimes called the *pink-collar ghetto*.

The kinds of occupations that make up the pink-collar ghetto tend to be in some way or other extensions of the traditional female nurturing role. They include such positions as licensed and practical nurses, prekindergarten and kindergarten teachers, childcare workers, dental assistants, receptionists, and secretaries (see Table 7.2). In each case, 95 percent of all people who are employed in these occupations are women. Even outside of their own households, many women end up performing what amount to domestic roles. More than 95 percent of all people employed in child care or as servants in private households in the United States are women.

But things have begun to change. As Table 7.3 indicates, the number of women completing specialized postgraduate training in the United States has increased dramatically since 1960. Once only a

TABLE 7.1

U.S. Female Labor Force as Percentage of U.S. Female Population, 1960–1997

Year	Percentage of All Females	Percentage of Married Females
1960	37.7	31.9
1965	39.3	34.9
1970	43.3	40.5
1975	46.3	44.3
1980	51.5	49.9
1985	54.5	53.8
1990	57.5	58.4
1997	59.8	61.6

Source: U.S. Bureau of the Census, *Statistical Abstract of the United States: 1998* (Washington, DC: U.S. Government Printing Office, 1998). Table 653.

Patterns of Gender Stratification

TABLE 7.3

Females as Percentage of Degrees Conferred in Selected Professions, 1960–1995

Year	Medicine (M.D.)	Law (L.L.B. or J.D.)	Dentistry (D.D.S. or D.M.D.)	Theology (B.D., M. Div., M.H.L.)
1960	5.5	2.5	0.8	(Not Available)
1970	8.4	5.4	0.9	2.3
1975	13.1	15.1	3.1	6.8
1980	23.4	30.2	13.3	13.8
1985	30.4	38.5	20.7	18.5
1990	34.2	42.2	30.9	24.8
1995	34.8	42.6	36.4	25.7

Source: U.S. Bureau of the Census, *Statistical Abstract of the United States: 1998* (Washington, DC: U.S. Government Printing Office, 1998). Table 327.

negligible minority in law, medicine, and dentistry, women now constitute a significant and growing proportion in these prestigious occupations. In 1997, the proportion of women in the labor force employed in executive, managerial, or professional positions (34.2 percent) actually exceeded the comparable figure (30.3 percent) for men (U.S. Bureau of the Census, 1998c). Thus, for many women, advanced education has become a ticket out of the pink-collar ghetto.

Gender and Income

In 1998, women working full time in the United States had a median annual income of $25,862, or 73.2 percent of men's median of $35,345 (U.S. Bureau of the Census, 1999a), a proportion which holds across all major job categories (see Table 7.4). These figures reflect a pattern found throughout the contemporary world. Comparing data on nonagricultural employment from a set of 55 countries, the United Nations

Development Program (1995, p. 4) discovered that females average only 75 percent of males' wages in these societies. Women may now be full participants in the labor market, but most have yet to receive a full share of the economic rewards for their labor.

These income discrepancies have been interpreted by economists and sociologists in a number of different ways. One explanation centers on what are called **human capital factors,** the resources that individuals bring with them to the labor market. Such resources include interests and aptitudes, formal education, occupational training, and previous work experience. They represent "investments" made by job seekers to enhance their employment prospects, making some individuals more attractive and desirable to employers, who will pay a premium for their services. These higher-paying jobs represent the occupational "return" on the human capital investments made by successful applicants (Bianchi and Spain, 1996).

TABLE 7.4

Median Annual Earnings by Type of Occupation and Sex, 1998

Type of Occupation	Male	Female
All workers	$35,345	$25,862
Managerial and professional	51,351	34,755
Technical, sales, and administrative support	40,546	27,849
Service	22,515	15,647
Precision Production	31,631	23,907
Operators, fabricators, and laborers	27,890	19,015
Farming, forestry, and fishing	18,885	15,865

Source: U.S. Bureau of the Census, *Current Population Reports,* P60–206 (Washington, DC: U.S. Government Printing Office, 1999). Table B.

According to the human capital argument, the salary discrepancies reflect the fact that men typically possess more resources than women. They generally have more interest, training, and previous work experience in occupations (for example, law, medicine, business, science, engineering) that command the highest salaries. Because men have more human capital to offer, they are able to negotiate better positions and higher salaries for their services.

Many women, on the other hand, have chosen to invest their time and energy in having and raising children rather than in pursuing a career. The demands of child rearing keep them out of the labor force for an extended period of time, during which years their male counterparts gain job experience and seniority. Child raising might also require women to take jobs that are close to home or that offer flexible hours so they can be with their children when necessary. For example, as of 1997, 63.6 percent of all U.S. married women with children under 6 years of age were in the employed labor force. Because the obligations associated with their role as mothers put these women at a human capital disadvantage in the job market, they must settle for whatever positions and salaries they are offered. They are no longer in a position to bargain with employers as effectively as men who are not encumbered by domestic considerations.

Several studies of female-male income differentials in the United States and other industrial societies conducted during the mid-1980s (England and Farkas, 1986; Roos, 1985) found some support for the human capital interpretation. But these same studies observed that human capital resources are not the only, or even the most significant, contributing elements in the income gap between the genders. Two additional factors may be of equal or greater importance.

First, the United States and many other industrial societies have a **dual-labor** or **segmented-labor market** structure containing two distinct tiers of jobs. The top tier consists of professional, administrative, and technical occupations offering high income and prestige rewards but requiring high levels of skills and training. The bottom tier is comprised of service, domestic, and other unskilled jobs that do not require much formal education or training, but do not offer many income or prestige rewards. According to some analysts (Bielby and Baron, 1986; Roos, 1985; Roos and Reskin, 1984), the sex-segregated, pink-collar jobs filled primarily by women are, not coincidentally, those at the lower tier of the dual-labor market structure. A good deal of women's work is largely supportive, nurturing, and at least symbolically domestic in nature. This type of work is neither desirable nor financially rewarding in modern economic systems. Because far greater income and prestige rewards are to be found among the occupations that make up the top tier in the dual-labor market, these lesser-rewarded jobs will be relegated to less powerful, less valued groups. In this respect, women may be considered a minority group who must compete against racial and ethnic minorties for low-echelon, low-paying jobs (Hacker, 1951, 1974).

The second factor that must be considered in understanding the female-male income differentials is gender discrimination. Simply stated, the large and widespread gaps between women's and men's incomes can be explained by the fact that women continue to be treated unequally and unfairly in the labor market (Beeghley, 1996). This pattern holds true even when women's educational qualifications match or exceed those of men (see Table 7.5).

Gender discrimination occurs in any number of different forms. Women may be excluded systematically from certain types of occupations on direct grounds ("this is no job for a woman"). That is, they are denied the right to hold the position just because they are female. In the U.S. armed forces, women are currently prohibited from serving in direct combat roles. Presumably, their nurturing instincts would make it very difficult or impossible for them to take the lives of other human beings. Not being burdened by such instincts, men are supposedly able to meet the requirements of the job without undue stress.

Women also face systematic exclusion from certain occupations on indirect grounds. Here, job requirements are structured to eliminate all (or most) women from consideration, even though sex itself may not be a formal criterion for the position. For example, police and fire departments in many U.S. cities may impose minimum height and weight requirements that

---

TABLE 7.5

Median Annual Earnings by Education Attainment and Sex, 1998

Education Level	Male	Female
Less than 9 years	$18,553	$14,132
9–12 years (no diploma)	23,438	15,847
12 years (high school diploma)	30,868	21,963
Some college, no degree	35,949	26,024
Associate's degree	38,483	28,337
Bachelor's degree	49,982	35,408
Master's degree	60,168	42,002
Professional degree	90,653	55,460
Doctoral degree	69,188	52,167

Note: Figures are for year-round, full-time workers, 25 years old and older.
Source: U.S. Bureau of the Census, *Current Population Reports,* P60-206 (Washington, DC: U.S. Government Printing Office, 1999). Table B.

effectively eliminate virtually all women candidates. Even after court rulings that these physical standards often have little or nothing to do with intrinsic requirements of the job, they continue to be used until they are challenged on a case-by-case basis.

Discrimination is also reflected in promotions. Even when women are hired in substantial numbers for a given occupation, men are much more likely to be on the fast track, receiving larger and more rapid promotions than women. This may be especially true in organizations and work settings that traditionally have been dominated by men (Blum and Smith, 1988). Women executives at middle and higher levels in some of this country's largest corporations have testified to the federal government about a "glass ceiling" of entrenched male discrimination that keeps them from moving successfully into the companies' upper echelons (CNN Special Reports 1992). Even though no formal or visible barriers keep women out of these elite positions, the beliefs and values that make up the male subculture of the corporate upper class effectively exclude women from real consideration (Superville, 1995). Mounting evidence also points to the presence of what have been called "glass walls" that prevent corporate women from moving laterally from managerial support staff positions (in human resources and public relations, for example) into managerial line positions (in sales, production, and marketing, for instance). Unable to make the horizontal moves necessary to acquire the kinds of hands-on experiences required for top executive positions, many women are removed from the vertical mobility process before they ever encounter a glass ceiling (Lublin, 1996). These glass walls apparently are related to the fact that women are "less frequently perceived as equal to men in areas such as career commitment, risk taking and initiative" (Lewis, 1992).

The Feminization of Poverty   A further indication of women's subordinate economic status relative to men is an alarming trend that has been termed the **feminization of poverty** (Pearce, 1990; Peterson, 1987). Throughout the last thirty years, growing numbers of women of all ages have been descending into the ranks of poverty. Of the approximately 1.3 billion people currently making up the world's poor, 70 percent are female (U.N. Development Program, 1995).

By the mid-1990s, close to two-thirds of all adult poor in the United States were women, many of them members of racial and ethnic minority groups. Much of this growth in female poverty since the 1960s is related to major changes in the composition of the family; most significantly, the dramatic increase in single-parent families headed by women. Between 1970 and 1997, the proportion of all white families maintained by women rose from 9 percent to 14.1 percent. For African-American families, the increase was from 28 percent to 44.7 percent; for Hispanic families, from 21 percent (in 1976) to 21.6 percent (U.S. Bureau of the Census, 1999a).

Whereas female-headed families made up 17.1 percent of all families in the United States in 1998, they constituted over half (53 percent) of all poor families that year: 78.7 percent for African Americans, 44.5 percent for Hispanics, and 48.1 percent for whites. A great deal of the poverty found in these families is related to the presence of dependent children. The number of children under the age of 18 living with one parent has doubled since 1970, and nearly 90 percent of these children live with their mothers rather than with their fathers. Their average family income is substantially less than that of children living with both parents or with their fathers alone. For children under 18 years of age, the overall poverty rate in 1998 was 18.9 percent: 15.1 percent for whites, 34.4 percent for Hispanics, and 36.7 percent for African Americans (U.S. Bureau of the Census, 1999b).

A number of factors have made it difficult for single mothers to avoid falling into poverty or, once in poverty, to escape from it. As we have seen, women face the likelihood of lower-paying, less-prestigious jobs in a labor market that is segmented on the basis of gender. Many are unable to find adequate childcare arrangements and must restrict their employment to meet the needs of their dependent children. Still others receive little or no child support under a legal system that often seems unable or unwilling to ensure adequate financial assistance from absentee fathers.

Women are also at a decided disadvantage in terms of social and political power. They are likely to remain in that position until they can mobilize effectively to gain a measure of control more in proportion to their population numbers and their many contributions to society.

Gender and Politics

In a democratic political system, election to government office represents one major avenue for individuals or groups to improve their social situations. The political structure (that is, the state) serves as the primary mechanism for distributing the various rewards that society has to offer its members. The people who control the offices of the state can shape this distribution system to meet their own specific needs and interests. It is perhaps not surprising, then, to learn that those who control the offices of the state throughout the world are males. According to the United Nations Development Program's annual survey of human development patterns and trends in the world's societies, "Despite the wave of democracy, women everywhere do not enjoy the same opportunities for participating in public life as men. They occupy only 12% of parliamentary seats and 7% of cabinet positions" (1998, p. 24). With the exception of the Scandinavian countries, whose female representation in parliament ranges from a high 40.4 percent in Sweden to a low of 33 percent in Denmark, "all countries conduct politics in a way that excludes nearly half of their human resources and talents" ("Women Gaining Few Seats," 1997). In some of these countries, as this chapter's *Focus on Afghanistan* chronicles, this exclusion of women from the societal mainstream is both systematic and profound, extending into nearly every aspect of their lives.

This domination of formal politics by men has been accomplished in any number of ways. For example, in the United States, women were denied any measure of real involvement in the political process during the eighteenth and nineteenth centuries by the fact that they were prohibited from voting. It was not until 1920 and the ratification of the Nineteenth Amendment that women's constitutional rights to full participation in national, state, and local elections were formally guaranteed. The passage of this constitutional amendment came only after intense and sustained efforts by members of the women's suffrage movement. At the time, it was bitterly opposed by many men (and some women), who felt that giving women the right to vote would destroy an effective and orderly way of life. After all, voting requires a certain degree of rationality and calculation, and women were believed to be deficient in this department. The prevailing sentiment was that women might be able to vote with their hearts but not with their heads.

Predications of doom notwithstanding, the voting rights of women in the United States have been in place for eighty years with no apparent ill effect on the country. Women register to vote in slightly larger numbers than men and have a voting turnout record virtually identical to that of men. They have provided the difference for victory in numerous Senate and gubernatorial elections during the 1990s, and also played a significant role in the 1996 presidential election. In that election, women helped secure President Clinton's reelection by voting for him over Senator Bob Dole by a 54 to 43 percent margin (Center For The American Woman And Politics, 1997). However, in spite of their record participation, women remain grossly underrepresented in political office at the higher levels of government. In 1999, only 65 women served in the 106th Congress—56 representatives out of a total of 435, and 9 senators out of a total of 100. Another 2 women served as Delegates to the House from the Virgin Islands and Washington, DC. Al-

though small in absolute number terms, these figures represent the largest number of women in the United States Congress in the history of that body. Only three states (Arizona, New Hampshire, and New Jersey) had female governors, and women constituted only a little over 22 percent of all state legislators across the country in 1999 (Center For The American Woman And Politics, 1999). The crucial question is, Exactly what does this political underrepresentation mean in terms of women's societal position?

The mere presence of some specific number or proportion of women in federal, state, and local governmental offices does not guarantee that "the women's view" will automatically be considered and promoted. Indeed, to assume that there is such a thing as a unitary "women's view" is to ignore the fact that women have as many different beliefs and viewpoints on various issues as do men. But it would be a mistake to assume that the presence of female political officeholders makes no difference at all. An absence of women from important decision-making positions promotes the likelihood that women's perspectives and interests will not be taken into account at all in the creation and implementation of social and political policies. A case in point is the fate of the Equal Rights Amendment (ERA).

Approved by both houses of Congress in 1972, the ERA was designed to eliminate discrimination on the basis of sex. Although it enjoyed widespread support among the U.S. public, the ERA expired in June 1982, lacking ratification by the necessary minimum number of state legislatures (it fell three short).

Pictured here is one of the few female heads-of-state during the last half of the twentieth century. Cory Aquino assumed the office of President of the Philippines following the removal of longtime dictator Fernando Marcos and led that island nation until 1992. On a global basis, only 11 percent of executive and cabinet-level political offices are held by women, a proportion far below their presence among the societal populations of the world.

Focus on
Afghanistan

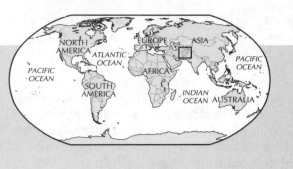

Population: 25,824,882
Life Expectancy at Birth (years): Male—47.82;
   Female—46.82
Form of Government: In transition
Major Religions: Sunni Muslim (84%); Shi'a Muslim (15%)
Major Racial and Ethnic Group: Pashtun (38%); Tajik (25%);
   Hazara (19%); Uzbek (6%)
Population Doubling Time: 28 years
Per Capita GNP (1997 U.S. dollars): N.A.
Principal Economic Activities: Agriculture; Industry
Colonial Experience: Former colony of various European and Asian powers
Adult Literacy Rates: 31.5% Male—N.A.; Female—N.A.

Taliban Imposes Total Ban on Women's Rights

Perhaps more than those of many other contemporary societies, the history of Afghanistan is largely a history of war. The modern state of Afghanistan itself was created by the British following the end of the Second Anglo-Afghan War in 1880 to serve as a buffer between the British and the Russian Empires. It became fully independent of British political influence in 1919 after the conclusion of the First World War (Rubin, 1996). But long before its modern incarnation, Afghanistan's position in "the crossroads of Central Asia" had subjected the country to constant invasion and conquest, starting with the Persian armies of Darius I in the sixth century B.C. and continuing through the Soviet invasion of 1979 ("Afghanistan: The Facts," 1999). Over the millennia-long course of these wars, millions of Afghans have been killed and many more millions have been forced to flee for their lives. During the height of the most recently attempted outside conquest, the 1979–1989 Soviet occupation, an estimated one-third of the entire population left the country, making Afghanistan "the world's leading producer of refugees and displaced persons" (Rubin, 1996, p. 1). Over 6 million Afghan refugees fled to Pakistan and Iran, and thousands of others to India, Europe, and the United States (*CIA World Fact-*

book, 1998). As is so often the case in times of war, life during the Soviet occupation was hard for nearly all members of the population. An estimated 1.5 million Afghan people—many of them, civilians— were killed and countless others maimed by the more than nine million land mines planted during the war ("Afghanistan: The Facts," 1999).

Following ten years of Soviet occupation of their country, a coalition of *mujahedeen* (Islamic resistance groups) who had declared a *jihad* or holy war against the communists succeeded in forcing a Red Army withdrawal in February 1989. But the departure of the hated Soviet troops did not signal an end to warfare or to human rights abuses. Within three years, the Soviet-supported government of President Mohammad Najibullah had been overthrown and fighting broke out among the various militant factions, plunging Afghanistan into a bitter civil war. To date, that civil war has resulted in the deaths of over 500,000 people and the virtual enslavement of half the Afghan population—its women.

In 1994, a new and powerful Islamic faction—the Taliban— began to emerge as the dominant group in the fierce in-fighting to take control of the country. The Taliban or "Religious Students Movement" consists largely of

young, often illiterate, Sunni Muslims of the dominant Pashtun ethnic group who had studied in religious schools while refugees in neighboring Pakistan (Amanpour, 1997). In those same refugee camps, according to many experts, members of the Taliban also were schooled in military tactics by Pakistan's military intelligence units. Fierce, honest, and devoutly Islamic, the Taliban initially were perceived as a reformist group that promised to restore peace and order to a war-weary Afghanistan (Pratap, 1996). But that first impression quickly changed as the religious zealots gained power, as reflected in the words of one middle-aged woman: "On the first day, the people were happy. Now the Taliban are trying to kill the mind of the Afghan people" (in Spaeth, 1996).

On September 27, 1996, Taliban forces captured the capital city of Kabul, consolidating their control over about three-fourths of the country. On that same date, their leader, Mullah Mohammad Omar, announced the first of a series of assaults on the freedoms and needs of Afghan women that has been described by Physicians for Human Rights as "unparalleled in recent history" ("The Taliban's War on Women," 1998). On September 26, 1996, women had comprised 70 percent of the schoolteachers, 50 percent of the university students, 50 percent of government workers, and 40 percent of the doctors in Kabul (Johnson, 1998). But, effective the next day with the Taliban takeover, women and girls were forbidden to work or to go to public schools. At the same time that most female

      Chapter 7 • Gender and Gender Issues

doctors and nurses were forced out of their jobs, women and girls were denied admittance to most hospitals and were prohibited from being examined or treated by male physicians. Women who defied the edict were publicly beaten or otherwise humiliated and forced to return home ("Stop Gender Apartheid," 1999). Nearly two years later, in June 1998, the Taliban suddenly closed down more than 100 private schools that had continued educating girls, including home-based vocational training programs run by international aid groups. Under the new rules imposed at this time, girls could be educated only until the age of 8, and their education was to be limited to lessons about the *Qu'ran* (Koran), the Muslim holy book (Abdullah, 1998).

In what has been described by Amnesty International ("Women in Afghanistan," 1997) as repression solely on the basis of gender, subsequent edicts by the ultraconservative Taliban have restricted women's rights even further. According to these directives, no woman may appear in public unless accompanied by a close male relative. Women who dare travel unescorted risk imprisonment and beating, and women caught traveling with an unrelated male are sentenced to death by stoning for their presumed adultery. When they do travel outdoors, women must wear a *burqa,* a head-to-toe robe that covers the body entirely and leaves only a small mesh opening over the eyes. Vision and movement are so restricted in the *burqa* that scores of women have been injured while wearing it (Johnson, 1998). Even when properly attired in *burqas,* women are prohibited from wearing white socks, white shoes, or "noisy shoes" (high heels), items viewed by the Taliban as sexually provocative (Amanpour, 1997). In March 1997, the residents of Kabul were ordered to screen or paint ground-floor and first-floor windows in their homes to ensure that women could not be seen

A young girl peers out from a group of Afghan women wearing the required Burqa covering at a Red Cross distribution center in Kabul, November 13, 1996. The Red Cross were distributing flour, coal, stoves, soap, candles, and matches to needy people as winter approached and temperatures dropped in the Afghan capital. Under the Taliban regime, the social rights of Afghan women have dropped faster and farther than the winter temperature.

from the street since, according to Taliban officials, "The face of a woman is a source of corruption for men who are not related to them." Apparently wishing to further spare male pedestrians from the risk of such corruption, in December 1998, the Taliban ordered that buses carrying women be shrouded in curtains. Female passengers must also be hidden from bus drivers by a curtain, and only young boys below age 15 are allowed to collect bus fares from women ("Taliban Impose New Rules," 1998). Compliance with these laws is enforced by the Department for the Promotion of Virtue and Prevention of Vice (DPVPV), the Taliban's religious police force. According to one report, in a single month, 225 women in Kabul were lashed on the back and legs for violating Taliban rules on clothing. Another woman reportedly had the end of her thumb cut off by the DPVPV after being caught wearing nail varnish ("Women in Afghanistan," 1997). In addition to being victimized by institutionalized discrimination in the form of Taliban law, women in Afghanistan have also been treated as "the spoils of war," becoming the victims of wide-

spread informal acts of terrorism such as rape and forced work as *kaniz* (servants) to be married off to Taliban militia deployed at war fronts ("AI Report 1999: Afghanistan," 1999; "Human Rights Abuses Against Women," 1999).

The combination of systematic hardships imposed by the Taliban and brutalities inflicted by both the Taliban and other military factions in the continuing civil war has had a devastating impact on the physical and mental health of Afghan women, as evidenced by the country's vital statistics. As of 1998, Afghanistan was one of less than a handful of countries worldwide in which female life expectancy at birth—46.29 years—was less than that of males—47.35 years—and in which the sex ratio (the number of males per hundred females) actually increased rather than decreased with advancing age. According to one 1998 estimate, for the under-15-year-old group, there were 105 males per 100 females; for the 15–64-year-old cohort, 107 males for each 100 females; for the 65-years-and-over-group, 112 males per 100 females (*CIA World Factbook,* 1998). These unusual trends were confirmed when, in 1998, a U. S.-based humanitarian group, Physicians for Social Responsibility, conducted an unprecedented study of the health and human rights conditions and concerns of Afghan women ("The Taliban's War on Women," 1998). The study included a survey of 160 women from Kabul, 40 case testimonies of other Afghan women, and interviews with 12 humanitarian assistance providers, health personnel and other experts—all of whom had firsthand experience of life under Taliban rule. Concluding that the Taliban's claim to be restoring peace in Afghanistan is "one of the cruelest ironies of our time, as they have virtually imprisoned Afghan women in their homes and threatened their very survival" (Rubenstein, in "Physician Group's Unprecedented Study," 1998), the report documents in chilling detail the genocidal-like consequences of the regime's deliberate and systematic assault on women's basic rights. Among other things, the study found the following:

- 71 percent of the 160 survey respondents had experienced a decline in their physical health over the past two years.
- 87 percent of the 40 women interviewed in depth reported a decrease in their access to health services; 53 percent described occasions in which they were seriously ill and unable to seek medical care.
- 81 percent of the 160 survey respondents reported a decline in their mental condition over the past two years.
- 97 percent of the survey respondents exhibited major depression; 86 percent showed significant signs of anxiety, and 42 percent met the diagnostic criteria for post-traumatic stress disorder.
- 21 percent of the survey respondents stated that they had suicidal thoughts "extremely often" or "quite often."
- 69 percent of the respondents had been detained at least once by Taliban religious police or security forces. In 72 percent of these cases, the detention followed violations of the Taliban's dress code for women.
- More than 95 percent of survey respondents disagreed with the Taliban dress codes and did not believe that the teachings of Islam mandated such restrictions; the same percentage stated that women should have equal access to education, equal work, and freedom of movement and expression.

This latter sentiment is shared by many observers throughout the world, including a large number of Islamic scholars. These critics view the Taliban's treatment of women as based more on archaic local tribal traditions rather than on Islamic religious principles. Some have condemned the Taliban for attempting to sanction their barbaric actions in the guise of religion. Citing a growing trend in which " 'Islamic movements' are turning Islam, a religion, into a political 'ism,' " one observer (Bassouni, 1998), has argued that "there are sufficient egalitarian arguments in the holy texts of Islam to back women's rights in civil participation . . . Women in Islam have been victims of deliberate distortion, gross misconceptions and misinterpretations of their position in Islam by groups such as the Taliban in Afghanistan." Echoing this argument, Fatiha Allab, a political scientist at the Institute of Political Science and International Relations in Algiers, has stated that the increasing politicization of Islam "is a dangerous deviation. My Muslim brothers vulgarize the religion. I have no problem with Islam; it's with Islamismo" (in Bowers, 1995). Commenting on the state of women in Afghanistan under Taliban "Islamismo," Eleanor Smeal, President of the Feminist Majority Foundation, claims that "If this was happening to any other class of people around the world, there would be a tremendous outcry. We must make sure these same standards are applied when it is women and girls who are brutally treated (in "Stop Gender Apartheid," 1999).

So far, Taliban leaders have remained remarkably unaffected by these criticisms and by condemnations from such groups as Amnesty International and the United Nations. Dismissing critics as "infidels who want to see women shed their veils and bring humiliation to our traditions and our religion," they claim that "The Taliban has respect for March 8, which is being called International Women's Day. Islam gives full rights to women and we, too, uphold women's dignity" (Ottaqi, in "Taliban Defends Its Policies," 1998). According to Taliban leaders, schools will be reopened for girls and women will be allowed to return to work, "as soon as we can restore peace and security." However, critics note that restrictions on women remain in place even in those areas of the country, such as Kabul, in which the Taliban have enjoyed complete control for over three years.

In the final analysis, according to some observers, it may be economic realities, not moral persuasion, that will bring about significant changes in the Taliban's treatment of Afghan women. The country's economy was largely destroyed by the fighting during and since the Soviet occupation, and remains in disarray. Half of the nation's workforce has been eliminated by religious edict, and poverty has skyrocketed across the population, especially among tens of thousands of war widows and their children. International economic and humanitarian aid agencies have scaled back or withdrawn their efforts altogether as a result of assaults against their own female staff and, without official recognition as a legitimate government by other nations, the Taliban thus far has not been able to secure needed rebuilding loans from the International Monetary Fund or other sources. Only three countries—Pakistan, Saudi Arabia, and the United Arab Emirates—have granted recognition to the ruling Taliban group, and none is in a real position to supply the massive funds needed to restart the Afghan economy (*CIA World Factbook,* 1998). It may well be the case, as humanitarian groups have argued, that "Lasting peace and stability will not be achieved unless the fundamental human rights of all Afghanistan's tribal, ethnic and social groups, including women, are respected by those who wield power" ("Women in Afghanistan," 1997). It remains to be seen if Taliban leaders are able or willing to learn this lesson.

Had there been more women in governors' offices and in state assemblies to lobby for the ERA and to push its passage, the ERA might now be part of the Constitution. If organized politics represents the voice of the people, the fact remains that women in this society have spoken most often in a whisper.

But things are improving. In 1999, Elizabeth Dole, spouse of the Republican Party's unsuccessful 1996 presidential candidate, was able to conduct her own campaign to become the next Republican presidential candidate and be treated as a serious contender by her party and by the American public. Additionally, women have begun to move more heavily into political offices at the local (that is, municipal and county) levels. They also have established and sharpened important leadership skills through significant involvement in grass-roots political movements. As they become increasingly experienced and as growing public attention has been directed to pay equity, day care, sexual harassment, and other related issues, women's political voice has grown louder and been heard more often than in the past.

Gender and Law

In contemporary societies like the United States, individuals are likely to interact with the legal system in a variety of ways. At the most general level, we all experience the law on a daily basis as a set of rules to be followed for the common good. At a more specific level, some individuals may experience the legal system in a more immediate way. They may interact with the criminal justice system either as accused perpetrators of some crime or as wronged victims seeking justice. In such dealings, women are quite likely to be treated significantly differently from men.

Like politics, the law has historically been dominated by males, who overwhelmingly make up legislative, judicial, and police bodies in this society and most others. From the perspective of conflict theory, this might illustrate the use of societal superstructures by one group to develop and employ power over other groups. In this interpretation, as advanced by a number of socialist feminists (for example, Jaggar, 1983), men recognize law as a critical power resource and have deliberately seized control over the legal structure to further their own ends. They have created, interpreted, applied, and enforced the law to maintain their own advantaged position in the economic hierarchy. Law is employed as an instrument of patriarchy.

But one does not have to be a conflict theorist to recognize the potential for social domination that exists when most members of a given institution as powerful and important as law are drawn from a single social group. From a symbolic interactionist perspective, for example, such effective domination is a consequence of a unified world view. The law reflects men's belief in the natural physical and intellectual inferiority of women. It defines women as helpless and in need of protection by and from men. That is, women are logically impaired and therefore not capable of such intellectually demanding activities as property ownership and voting. The overall effect has been to preserve gender inequalities that are already in place and to create new ones (Kirp, Yodof, and Franks, 1986). Noting the fact that "90 countries have not yet accepted all the tenets of legal equality for men and women," the United Nations Development Program's *Human Development Report* (1995, p. 7) has referred to such gender-based legal discrimination as "the starkest reflection of the low status accorded to women" around the contemporary world.

In the United States, existing laws concerning rape and abortion illustrate this phenomenon. These laws typify what has been called a "double standard of morality based on biological deterministic thought" that is built into the legal process (Richardson, 1988, p. 104).

Rape Historically, rape was regarded legally as a crime that could be committed only against women. Laws were designed specifically to protect the chastity of women, especially girls (Richardson, 1988). Girls who were under a specified legal age (typically 16 or 18, depending on the individual state) were defined as being incapable of consenting to sexual intercourse, although no similar assumption was made regarding boys of the same age. On the other hand, women over the specified legal age often were implicitly perceived as inciting or tempting men to commit rape. They were regarded as somehow being responsible for the crime in ways that victims of other crimes were not. Whereas past sexual histories of accused rapists, including previous rape accusations or convictions, were not admissible as evidence in trial, past sexual histories of the victims were examined in detail. For many women, the trials were often as much of an ordeal as the crime itself. In effect, they were being raped twice—once by the perpetrator and once by the criminal justice system. For this reason, a high percentage of rapes are never reported to authorities.

Feminists argue that rape is an act of power and violence, not of sex (Brownmiller, 1975; Richardson, 1988). From their perspective, rape is an act of terrorism, a tangible and a symbolic method for men to keep women in their supposed proper place. At the same time, it is an act of symbolic violence against another male, a husband or boyfriend who possesses exclusive sexual access to the woman. According to this interpretation, rape is a form of property crime, the property in question being a woman.

Thus, the "owner" (husband or boyfriend), as Griffin (1973) ironically noted, is as much a victim as the woman herself.

Regardless of how one wishes to interpret rape, the fact remains that the high frequency of this crime in the United States and the fear of it restrict the lives of women in ways foreign to men (Salholz et al., 1990). Prudence requires that women limit their choices of jobs, travel, education, recreation, and residence to safe areas and safe times. In effect, women are subject to what might be thought of as self-imposed barriers to full social opportunity.

Abortion A second significant and controversial area of sex-related law concerns abortion, which many observers regard as *the* crucial gender issue of the past (and perhaps next) several decades. Abortion is a complex and explosive question that has divided the public as few other issues have in recent years. For many people it has come to symbolize the continued viability of gender equality and the feminist movement.

In 1973, the U.S. Supreme Court issued its landmark *Roe v. Wade* decision affirming the constitutional right of women to decide for themselves whether or not to terminate a pregnancy during the first trimester. This decision was hailed by various feminist and other change-oriented groups as a major step in granting women control over their own bodies and freedom from male domination of their reproductive activities. It was also condemned by many conservative and antifeminist groups as legalized murder of unborn human beings. These two interpretations of abortion—reproductive rights versus homicide—defined the boundaries of the dispute and made any sort of real compromise impossible.

Supporters of the *Roe* ruling describe themselves as "pro-choice." Individually, they may or may not be advocates of abortion itself. But collectively, they affirm a women's right to choose the course of action for her own pregnancy that she deems appropriate. In addition, pro-choice advocates hold an implicit or explicit belief that, in its earliest stages of development, the fetus cannot be considered a human being.

Opponents of the *Roe* decision describe themselves as "pro-life." Both individually and collectively, they affirm the humanity of the fetus from the moment of conception. For them, the termination of a fetus at any stage of development represents the unjust taking of a human life. As such, abortion is legally and morally wrong under any circumstances. Their efforts are geared toward establishing the right of the states to intervene in the lives of individual women in the name of the higher common good by regulating (that is, virtually eliminating) abortion.

In the twenty-plus years since *Roe v. Wade*, pro-life groups have mounted a series of challenges to the principle of individual decision making established by that ruling. Reflecting the growing political and religious conservatism of mainstream America during the 1980s and 1990s, individual state legislatures (for example, Louisiana, Pennsylvania, Utah) passed bills that significantly restrict women's autonomy in the question of abortion. Pro-choice groups responded by appealing these legislative actions to state and federal courts or by lobbying sympathetic state governors to veto the bills.

Amid great speculation that *Roe v. Wade* would be overturned by an increasingly conservative Supreme Court, the fundamental provisions of the *Roe* decision were upheld by the Court by a narrow 5–4 margin in June 1992. But at the same time, in a 7–2 vote, the justices affirmed the rights of individual states to impose broad restrictions on women's access to abortions (Hearn, 1992). Though technically a victory for pro-choice advocates, the Court's ruling did not really satisfy either side of the abortion controversy.

As each side continues to redefine and enlarge the scope of the question, abortion promises to become perhaps the watershed issue for both proponents and opponents of gender equality. Pro-choice groups such as the National Organization for Women argue that an overturning of the *Roe* decision would be the first step in sustained attempts to limit or ban altogether contraceptive freedom for women. Women's reproduction would once again be in the hands of men, who would use this power and control for their own collective advantage. Pro-life groups argue that any continuation of the *Roe* decision would be the first step in a society-wide attempt to enlarge the population of expendable human beings. They claim that if the lives of unborn infants are sacrificed in the name of greater freedom for women, perhaps in the near future the lives of the aged and the severely disabled might also be jeopardized for the sake of social convenience.

Gender Equality and Social Theory

As might be anticipated, functionalist, symbolic interactionist, and conflict analyses of the gender equality movement differ substantially in their reading of this phenomenon.

Functionalism For functionalists, the greatest challenge may be the one posed to society if that movement succeeds. Functionalists, it may be recalled, maintain that traditional gender roles promote societal survival and stability. These definitions maximize effective social relations within families and between family units and the larger society. The performance of expressive roles by women and instrumental roles by men complement one another on behalf of greater social productivity. Deeply embedded in cultural definitions of the nature of reality, these gender-based role assignments also serve as anchors for a host of other social relationships and social structures. Any challenge to their basic premises of traditional gender roles thus represents a genuine threat to crucial social and cultural patterns that have made human survival and comfort possible.

Functionalists believe that, because the gender-equality movement raises just this type of fundamental challenge, it will encounter strong natural resistance—and this resistance is in the best interest of the social system. If the movement succeeded too well and too quickly, it could generate catastrophic changes that might destroy society. Certainly, not all functionalists would oppose all the goals of the gender equality movement, but most might be opposed to a rapid and wholesale implementation of those that would shatter the equilibrium of the established order so completely that it could not be restored. As in the case of other movements seeking radical social transformations, the pace of gender equality must be maintained at a tolerable level if the system is to avoid being fatally disrupted.

Symbolic Interactionism   For symbolic interactionists, the gender equality movement is essentially a question of the meanings attached to the concepts "women" and "men" and the significance of these cultural meanings for societal relations. Existing gender stereotypes and roles are embedded deeply within a web of cultural beliefs and social patterns. They are supported by a host of daily individual and institutional practices that have the very real—if not always intended—effect of perpetuating them over time. These gender conceptions form an intrinsic part of the social definition of reality into which members of a given population are born and often are accepted as a given element of the natural world by that population. Any serious attempt to question their validity would thus require a symbolic deconstruction and reconstruction of the world that people have come to take for granted as real and natural. Such an action could pose a serious threat of culture shock to those attempting it.

Seen in this light, for symbolic interactionists the real objective of and challenge to the gender equality movement is the reconceptualization of sex and gender, an acceptance of the new premise that anatomy is *not* destiny. The success of the movement ultimately will hinge on its ability to promote this new portrait of women and men as fundamental equals, distinguished but not determined by physiological differences. For these theorists, socialization practices of such important agents as parents, schools, the mass media, and peers are of crucial significance. It is through their efforts that individuals first come to form an impression of the world, and it will be through their efforts that this world-taken-for-granted will be changed. Unless and until the symbolic significance attached to sex and gender is altered, social roles and opportunities will continue to be based on the assumption of natural, intrinsic inequalities of males and females. In this particular struggle, the first battle must be waged and won inside people's minds.

Conflict Theory   For conflict theorists, the greatest challenges to the gender equality movement lie in the area of generating enough effective power to overcome the massive resources and deliberate resistance of entrenched ruling groups. Such power will be created only if the differences that currently divide gender and other minority groups can be overcome.

Subgroup Differences   Women as a group may have in common their sex and the gender stereotypes that have developed around that sex, but they nonetheless are characterized by a number of important subgroup differences. Their membership includes individuals of various racial and ethnic backgrounds, class levels, religions, and sexual orientations—differences that are likely to generate different kinds of social realities. For example, African-American women may find that in many important ways they have less in common with white women than they do with African-American men. Upper-class women may find they have less in common with lower-class women than they do with upper-class men. Lesbians may find they have less in common with gay men than they do with heterosexual women.

The net effect of these subgroup differences is to make it difficult for the larger group to achieve a high level of overall unity and cohesion. Women speak with many different voices reflecting their diversity, rather than in a single voice. Being divided in social objectives and political agendas, they find themselves politically weakened.

Equality Strategies   To have any reasonable chance of success, gender equality movement leaders must convince members of racial, ethnic, age, and sexual orientation minorities that their interests are compatible with those of all women. Such a "pan-minority" movement, as this might be termed, is not an easy or likely prospect. Moving beyond the real differences in social experiences and subcultural perspectives that separate these minorities has been problematic in the past and will continue to be so in the future.

It is in the best interests of established dominant groups to keep potential coalitions of minority groups from forming. They will pursue this strategy by using available social resources to play minorities off against one another. For example, in the dual or segmented labor market, minorities are put into direct competition for low-paying, low-prestige jobs that are becoming increasingly scarce. Elite-controlled media may emphasize the divisive aspects of affirmative action directives that again place various minority group members in direct competition for established quotas of more desirable jobs. The net effect in both cases is that minority gains are portrayed as a zero-sum game in which one group's advancement comes at the expense of other minority groups. Under such perceived conditions, it may be nearly impossible to develop cohesive coalitions of the socially disadvantaged. As long as such coalitions can be blocked, real equality for any minority group will remain only a dream.

The focal points of conflict analyses of the gender equality movement, then, are the strategies and resources employed by movement leaders, by leaders of the status quo, and perhaps even by counter-movement leaders (Richardson, 1988) to generate power. Like money, power talks, and ultimately, the loudest voice will have the final word on the topic of full equality for women and men.

SUMMARY AND REVIEW

Understanding Sex and Gender

1. What is sex, and what is its significance as a method for classifying individual humans?

All human societies distinguish among their members on the basis of sex or differences in physical anatomy, chromosomes, and hormones. In most societies, sex also is believed to be responsible for important differences in physical and intellectual abilities, as well as psychological temperament. (P. 140)

2. What is gender, and what is the impact of gender stereotyping on human beings?

Gender is the sense of being either woman or man and of possessing the attributes characteristic of one's sex. In a large number of societies, gender stereotypes categorically portray the two sexes as possessing different essential attributes. This has led to the creation of gender roles that assign individuals to social positions based on their sex, and to gender stratification systems in which sex differences become the basis for social inequality hierarchies. (P. 140)

Traditional Gender Stereotyping and Gender Roles

3. Are females and males naturally and fundamentally different from one another?

A large body of biological, psychological, and anthropological research findings indicates a general absence of significant and consistent intellectual or emotional differences between females and males. These same data suggest that assumptions about what is natural for the sexes depend more on cultural beliefs and values than on empirical realities. (Pp. 141–142)

Becoming Women and Men: Gender Socialization

4. How do individuals acquire a sense of gender identity?

People acquire their gender identities and behaviors through the lifelong process of socialization. From the time they are first introduced to their society as girls or boys, individuals are subjected to powerful influences of parents, teachers, peers, the mass media, and other important agents of socialization. Throughout childhood and adolescence, they learn and practice attitudes and behaviors deemed appropriate for someone of their particular sex, establishing a self-image based on sexual identity in the process. (Pp. 142–143)

5. In what ways do adult experiences affect gender identity?

As adults involved in a web of occupational, marital, and parental roles that often reflect traditional gender beliefs, individuals have their sense of femininity or masculinity reinforced. However, these identifies may later be threatened by retirement from occupational careers, declining health and physical abilities, and other age-related changes. (Pp. 143–144)

Theoretical Interpretations and Explanations of Gender Roles

6. How do classical functionalist theorists view gender roles?

Classical functionalist theorist Talcott Parsons attempted to explain the nearly universal existence of gender roles in terms of their contribution to societal survival. He argued that it was much more efficient and productive for men to specialize in the instrumental family tasks and for women to perform the expressive family tasks for which they were best suited on the basis of their sex. This sex-based division of labor thus promoted the well-being of the larger society. (Pp. 144–145)

7. Why are conflict theorists opposed to the continuation of traditional gender roles?

Conflict theorists interpret gender roles as mechanisms for the exploitation of women. Building on the work of Marx and Engels, they view traditional cultural beliefs and social practices as devices for preserving power structures that clearly favor the interests of men over those of women. These patriarchal arrangements will end only when women and other suppressed minorities can acquire enough power to force basic social changes. (Pp. 145–146)

Patterns of Gender Stratification

8. *How does gender discrimination affect the occupational, income, and other experiences of women in the United States?*

Like many other modern societies, the United States perpetuates significant inequalities between the sexes in the areas of work, income, politics, and law, among others. Despite the fact that most women now work full time, many remain in low-paying, sex-segregated, pink-collar jobs. Whereas female-male occupational and income differences have been treated to a number of explanations including differences in human capital resources, gender discrimination seems to be a significant contributing factor. Women whose educational credentials are equivalent to men's nonetheless are paid less and often encounter obstacles to promotion to the highest ranks of corporations or other organizations. Within the past thirty years, the feminization of poverty has become a significant problem in the United States. Increasing numbers of females and female-headed families are experiencing severe economic deprivation. (Pp. 147–150)

9. *Why have the governments of the United States and many other societies been slow to institute policies that might promote greater gender equality?*

Women register and vote in numbers equal to or greater than those of men, but they remain underrepresented in political office at federal and state levels. This lack of representation may be at least partially responsible for the absence or slowness of government policies that might promote gender equality. At the local level, women have gained numbers in city and county offices and also have gained important political leadership experiences through involvement in grassroots movements. (Pp. 151, 155)

10. *How does the existing structure of law affect gender inequality?*

Laws concerning rape, abortion, and other sex-related issues also contribute to gender inequality. Both the frequency and the fear of rape restrict women's lives in many ways. The handling of this crime by the criminal justice system often puts the victim on trial and implies that women somehow are at least partially responsible for their own attack. As both pro-life and pro-choice forces mobilize for action, abortion promises to become the major gender issue of the decade. The Supreme Court's 1973 *Roe v. Wade* decision is being challenged by state laws that limit or deny women's access to abortion. Both sides view abortion laws in terms of larger ideological issues. (Pp. 155–156)

11. *In what ways do functionalist, symbolic interactionist, and conflict perspectives differ from one another in their view of the gender equality movement?*

The three major sociological theoretical perspectives view the gender equality movement in very different ways. For functionalists, a major question revolves around the scope and speed of social and cultural changes brought about by the movement. Changes that are too rapid and too far-reaching could threaten the foundations of the social order and thus the survival of society. For symbolic interactionists, the main considerations are the meanings attached to "male" and "female" and the social significance of prevailing cultural views of gender. From this perspective, socialization agents and the socialization process itself are critical variables, since the most important battle to be won lies inside the heads of the population members. For conflict theorists, the key issue concerns strategies for acquiring effective power to overcome the resistance of established elites and bring about necessary fundamental social changes. In this view, gender equality is essentially a political question whose answer will be based on power considerations rather than on moral or philosophical merit. (Pp. 156–158)

8

Crime, Deviance, and Social Control

The United States is a dangerous place to be a child. Children under 15 years of age in this country are 16 times more likely to be killed by a gun than are children in 25 other industrial nations. When the murder rate includes all manner of weapons, American children are still five times more likely to be victims of a criminal homicide than their counterparts in other developed countries (Klein, 1997).

While some victims die at the hands of adults and other care givers, the majority of young casualties in the U.S. are killed by other children. Kids kill other kids via robberies for basketball shoes, a jacket with a coveted sports logo, or for a few dollars in change. In some cases an adolescent is gunned down for no other reason than to enhance the "bad-ass" reputation of the killer. What particularly worries some criminal justice practitioners is that a significant number of these young "stone killers" (as in "hearts of stone") will take a life with no more remorse than if they had squashed an insect. As attorney Adam Walinsky (1995, p. 39) has noted, "Too many have learned to kill without remorse, for a drug territory or for an insult, because of a bump or look on the sidewalk or just to do it. Why not?" Asked why he shot three people and stabbed another in a convenience store robbery, a young criminal replied "I had a boring day" (Minerbrook, 1994 p. 35).

Beginning in the fall of 1997, another type of "stone killer" captured the public's attention. Within the span of a few months 11 children and 1 teacher were gunned down in and around schools. All of the young victims were killed by one of their classmates, and psychologists coined a new term for this kind of schoolyard violence, "intermittent explosive disorder" (Fritz, 1998). A U.S. Education Department report stated that more than 6,000 students across the country were expelled in 1997 for bringing guns to school. Whereas during the height of the Cold War years (1950s and 1960s) students regularly practiced drills (going to bomb shelters or taking cover under their desks) to survive a nuclear attack, in some schools today children "sit quietly in locked classrooms while a hypothetical psycho stalks the halls" (Fritz, 1998).

One national survey of gun owners discovered that 14 percent of these individuals with a child under 18 years of age reported having a gun in the home that was loaded and unlocked (Hemenway and Solnick, 1995). In many households children are encouraged to become proficient with firearms, and even play gun games that include rapid fire shooting at targets shaped like human beings. Attorney Alan Dershowitz (1998) argues that just as parents "do not have the right" to teach their children to gamble, watch pornographic films, or consume alcoholic beverages, "there can be no constitutional argument supporting the right of children to use deadly weapons" (p. B5).

Because the majority of young killers use guns as their weapon of choice, efforts to reduce this kind of violence have focused on keeping firearms out of their hands. Between 1989 and 1997, 14 states passed "child access prevention" or CAP laws that make gun owners criminally liable if someone is injured or killed (by accident, suicide, or homicide) because of a child's unsupervised access to firearms. Comparing data from 12 states with CAP laws (1990 thru 1994) to the remaining states and the District of Columbia, Peter Cummings (1997) and his colleagues found that accidental shootings declined 23 percent among children under 15 years of age in CAP law states. There was a "modest decrease" in suicides and homicides on the part of young children in these states. The overall reduction in childhood/gun-related deaths was greatest in Florida, California, and Connecticut, the three states that allowed for more severe felony—as opposed to misdemeanor—prosecutions. In Florida, for example, an adult convicted under that states CAP law can be sentenced to five years in prison and fined up to $5,000 (Faltermayer, 1998).

In this chapter we examine street and corporate crimes committed by individuals of all ages as well as a variety of other deviant and criminal acts. Theories that attempt to explain why people commit unlawful and/or deviant acts are examined in some detail. Finally, attention is given to some of the techniques and strategies used to control these acts. However, before launching into these topics we must take a closer look at the phenomenon of deviance from a sociological perspective.

Questions to Consider

1. What is deviance? Do all societies have deviant behavior? Why?
2. What are the differences among the absolutist, normative, and reactive perspectives of deviance?
3. What is the difference between deviant behavior and criminal behavior?
4. According to Emile Durkheim, in what sense is criminal behavior "normal"?
5. How is crime "functional," or good for society?

Continued

6. According to Robert Merton, what is anomie? What types of deviant behaviors does anomie produce?
7. Is differential association simply a "bad apple" theory?
8. According to Marxist theorists, why are prisons in the United States filled with poor people?
9. What is the difference between white-collar crime and occupational crime?
10. What are some of the arguments for decriminalizing drugs?

DEVIANCE: A SOCIOLOGICAL VIEW

All societies, from the most primitive to the most advanced, have a system of norms designating acceptable and unacceptable types of behavior. These norms regulate all facets of human conduct such as sexual activity, marriage, the ownership of property, and the division of labor. **Deviance** is behavior contrary to norms of conduct and social expectations. Some rules of conduct thought to be especially important to a society's well-being are codified, or put into a legal code. Violation of this code (criminal laws) constitutes a crime and is subject to formal punishment by the state.

Just as rules of conduct are found in all human societies, so too are people who violate these rules. Erich Goode (1990) theorized that deviance exists because human beings are "evaluative creatures" who continually make judgments about their own behavior and that of others. In other words, people in every society divide much of the social world into two broad categories: the good and desirable, and the bad and undesirable. Behavior falling into the latter category is considered deviant and is usually subject to some form of social control.

One can define deviance from the absolutist, normative, and reactive perspectives (Clinard and Meier, 1992). From the **absolutist perspective**, "deviance resides in the very nature of the act itself" (Goode, 1990, p. 13) and is wrong at all times (past, present, and future) and in all places. A deviant act may be thought of as an "offense against the order of the universe" (p. 13) or a transgression against God. The absolutist perspective is characteristic of people who have strong (and often unyielding) religious views. For example, some right-to-life adherents believe that abortion is "absolutely" wrong under any and all circumstances. They argue that abortion can never be justified, regardless of the circumstances surrounding the pregnancy, including rape and incest. From this perspective, even if the laws of society permit abortion, the laws of God are supreme, and the act of terminating a pregnancy is murder. The absolutist position is also embraced by those psychologists and psychiatrists who use a "medical model" of deviance. Just as people suffering from cancer or tuberculosis are physically sick, drug addicts, alcoholics, and people who engage in aberrant sexual behavior have psychological diseases that are "universal expressions of individual maladjustment" (Clinard and Meier, 1992, p. 7).

The **normative perspective** sees deviance as the violation of a specific group's or society's rules at a particular time in history. Deviance, therefore, is a relative phenomenon, not inherent in the act or behavior itself. As stated by Goode (1990), "We can tell when an action is deviant by consulting the customs of society" (p. 14). Throughout most of human history, abortion has been an acceptable and widely practiced form of birth control. It was so common in post–World War II Japan that by 1950 the number of terminated pregnancies exceeded that of live births (Warshaw, 1988b). In the United States, the 1973 *Roe v. Wade* Supreme Court decision ruled that states do not have the right to restrict women from having abortions. Nevertheless, millions of Americans oppose the practice (some violently) for religious and moral reasons. Although the laws of the country as well as the norms of some people condone a woman's right to terminate a pregnancy, the values and norms of other people strongly condemn such action. If the laws are eventually overturned, antiabortionists will have the law on their side, so to speak.

To take another example, opium was used in virtually all segments and classes of U.S. society before and during the Civil War. Rambunctious children were routinely calmed with opium derivatives, and the drug was a principal ingredient in many patent medicines. After the war, however, opium was redefined as troublesome and dangerous, and laws were eventually passed prohibiting its distribution and use. In both of these illustrations, the prevailing normative order of different groups at different moments in history determined the extent to which the behavior in question was considered deviant.

From the **reactive perspective**, behavior is not deviant until it has been recognized and condemned. In other words, deviance lies in the sanction or disapproval of behavior, not in the behavior itself. Keeping with the abortion example, the practice would be considered deviant *only* when it was discovered and prosecuted by the criminal justice system. If an abortion did not come to the attention of the authorities, it would not be considered deviant. From the reactive perspective, then, it is the *negative sanction* and not the behavior that constitutes deviance. Pollner (in Goode, 1990) summarized it in a simple, straightforward manner: "No reactions, no deviance" (p. 15). Those who adhere to this position would argue that the tens of thousands of people who commit crimes in the United States each year but are not caught and punished, are not deviant.

Figure 8.1 shows the relationship between deviant behavior and criminal behavior. When a person is following group standards and by doing so is also obeying the law, he or she is engaging in **conforming behavior.** Virtually everyone engages in conforming behavior most of the time. **Deviant behavior** is a violation of reference group or subcultural group norms but is not in violation of the legal code of the larger society. It may include the violation of religious laws and customs, severe ideological differences between group members, homosexuality where not illegal, divorce, alcoholism, mental illness, and spouse swapping. **Criminal behavior** occurs when the laws of the larger society are not supported by the norms of an individual's subculture. A good deal of criminal behavior is not considered deviant according to the values and norms of the subculture. Examples include gambling, prostitution, incest, fighting, taking drugs, stealing, and cheating on one's income tax. **Deviant and criminal behavior** violates both subcultural norms and society's laws. Examples are murder, rape, treason, arson, and child molestation.

As we saw in Chapter 4, individuals become committed to the values and norms of their group and the larger society to such an extent that they engage in conforming behavior most of the time. (Even criminals marry and have families, buy presents for their children, etc.) If this were not the case, societies would crumble under the weight of widespread deviance and crime, or turn into totalitarian states that ruthlessly control every aspect of human conduct. Socialization is never completely effective, however, and rule violation does occur. When people violate rules and laws and their transgressions are discovered, they typically are subject to the disciplinary action of some agent of social control. As Table 8.1 indicates, this control can take place within a formal or an informal setting. Young children caught smoking generally are punished by their parents (informal social control). If they are discovered smoking at school, they will also be disciplined by teachers and administrators in an organizational setting (formal social control). The state, through the criminal justice system, is the one agent of social control empowered to place people on probation, imprison them, and even take their lives by execution.

Approaches to both explaining and controlling deviance have varied and "competed for ascendancy throughout Western history" (Little, 1989, p. 337). Under the influence of Christianity in medieval Europe, deviance was thought of as sinful and evil—a fall from grace. Mechanisms of social control emphasized atoning for one's sins through penance or corporal punishment. However, over the past hundred years, with the decline in the influence of religion and the corresponding rise of modern medicine, more and more deviance is being both explained and "cured" from a medical perspective. In other words, the origin of deviance has shifted from the spiritual soul and mind to the physical body and brain. The deviant is thought of as physically or mentally ill and in need of treatment, increasingly some form of drug therapy. The disease model of deviance took a significant step forward with the formation in 1935 of Alcoholics Anonymous, the first "12-step" program. Since the mid-1960s, this perspective has gained in popularity and resulted in the creation of groups such as Narcotics Anonymous, Cocaine Anonymous, Overeaters

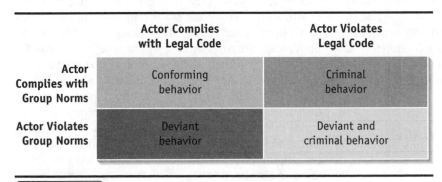

	Actor Complies with Legal Code	Actor Violates Legal Code
Actor Complies with Group Norms	Conforming behavior	Criminal behavior
Actor Violates Group Norms	Deviant behavior	Deviant and criminal behavior

FIGURE 8.1

Deviant and Criminal Behavior

TABLE 8.1

Institutions, Rule-Violating Behaviors, and Sanctions

Institution	Agent	Rule-Violating Behavior	Sanction
Family	Parents	Youth disobedience	Spanking, "grounding," withholding privileges
Clubs, social organizations	Officers	Violations of club rules	Fines, suspension of privileges, expulsion
Religion	Minister, priest, rabbi	Sin	Penance, withholding rites, excommunication
Business	Employer	Absence, laziness, violation of work rules	Fine, suspension, dismissal
Professional group	Officer	Ethical violations	Fine, license revocation, expulsion from group
Political state	Police, prosecutor, judge	Violation of civil and criminal laws	Fine, probation, imprisonment, damage suit, execution
Military	Superiors	Disobeying orders	Fine, imprisonment, loss of rank and privileges
Schools	Teachers, administrators	Disobeying rules, failure to maintain appropriate grade point average	Probation, expulsion

Source: Adapted from *Sociology of Deviant Behavior,* 10th edition, by M. Clinard and R. Meier, copyright © 1997 by Harcourt Brace & Jovanovich, reprinted by permission of the publisher.

Anonymous, Sex and Love Addicts Anonymous, Gamblers Anonymous, Workaholics Anonymous, Swearers Anonymous, and Fundamentalists Anonymous (for those who join fundamentalist religions).

In his book *Diseasing of America*—a scathing critique of the "addiction as disease" model and 12-step programs—psychologist Stanton Peele (1999) argued that the disease theory of addiction is based on the following assumptions: (1) the addiction exists *independent* of the rest of the person's life and *drives* all of his or her choices; (2) the disease is progressive and irreversible, so the addiction *inevitably worsens* unless the persons seeks medical treatment or joins an AA-type support group; and (3) addiction means the person is incapable of controlling his or her actions. The person engaging in deviant behavior is considered a victim rather than an abuser, as in the phrase "alcohol-abuse victim." The exercise of free will has been removed to a great extent regarding the behavior in question, and people are viewed as being pushed or driven into deviance by physiological or psychological factors beyond their control.

THEORIES OF CRIME AND DEVIANCE

Biological Explanations

Biologically grounded explanations of behavior in general, and criminal behavior in particular, go back

hundreds if not thousands of years and are all based on the same fundamental assumption: Structure determines function. In other words, human behavior is directly related to, and somehow a result of, an individual's physical makeup. It logically follows, therefore, that if our actions are a function of our physiology, those who are structurally different should engage in different forms of behavior. Criminals, according to this argument, should be physiologically distinct from the noncriminal population and similar to one another.

In the aftermath of Charles Darwin's groundbreaking work in biology, some researchers attempted to ascertain anatomical differences between criminals and noncriminals. One of the pioneers in this area was the Italian physician and criminologist Cesare Lombroso (1835–1909). According to Lombroso, some people are born criminals and destined to a life of crime. These individuals are atavistic, or biological throwbacks to a "past race" of mankind. The born criminal is physiologically distinct from noncriminals, and these differences are measurable and predictable (Savitz, 1972). It is important to understand that these physical distinctions do not cause criminal behavior but are indicators of biological deficiency; they are outward manifestations of underlying physiological and mental inferiority (Bryjak and Soroka, 1985).

Lombroso and his disciples found numerous similarities between the anatomy of criminals and that

Although O.J. Simpson was acquitted of murder charges, millions of people believe he killed his wife Nicole and Ronald Goldman. Whereas the Hall of Fame football player once earned a substantial amount of money endorsing products, his deviant identity now precludes him from such activity. Whether or not he committed the crimes, the label of "killer" is likely to stay with Simpson for the rest of his life.

of animals, especially primates. Criminals, for example, often have a "chin receding or excessively long, or short and flat, as in apes" (Lombroso-Ferrero, 1972, p. 16) and "ears of unusual size, or occasionally very small, or standing out from the head as those of chimpanzees" (p. 19). Implicit in Lombroso's criminology is a belief in the stratification or inequality of the human races. This racial hierarchy is the result of various courses and speeds of human evolution. Working in a period of European expansion and colonialism, Lombroso put Caucasians at the top of his hierarchy, followed by the numerous "other races" and peoples to which he often referred. Although he made a valuable contribution in attempting to find the root causes of crime, his work was not very scientific. For example, his physical measurement of criminals was limited to individuals incarcerated for crimes, hardly a representative sample of the criminal population. Although he claimed

that criminal tendencies were inherited, Lombroso never gathered evidence to support this assertion (Sanders, 1983).

Contemporary researchers in the biological tradition have focused on at least three major areas of inquiry: (1) criminal behavior as a consequence of innate predispositions that are transmitted genetically from one generation to another; (2) criminal behavior as an outcome of chemical changes in the body caused by exposure to environmental pollutants; and (3) crime as a result of particular foods, food additives, and other substances (especially drugs) that individuals ingest. Vitamin deficiencies are also included in this latter category.

The following is a brief look at a study in each of these areas. Regarding the innate predisposition to commit crimes perspective, if "biology is destiny," then individuals who are biologically identical should have approximately the same levels of criminal behavior even if they are raised in different environments. To test this proposition, a number of studies have examined identical twins separated shortly after birth and raised in different households. One study of 2,692 twin pairs in the U.S. and Australia found a "substantial genetic influence on risk for conduct disorder," a term that included lying, stealing, truancy, fighting, and cruelty to animals among a long list of antisocial and illegal behavior (Slutske et al., 1997). Roger Masters (1997) found that toxicity is one of many risk factors associated with crime, and countries with high levels of environmental pollution (lead and manganese) "have two to three times higher rates of violent crime than those without pollution . . . " (p. 2). After controlling for a number of relevant variables (birth weight, socioeconomic class, maternal age at childbirth), Dutch researchers (Orlebeke, Knol, and Verhulst, 1997) concluded that three-year-old children whose mothers smoked when they were pregnant were more aggressive than children of the same age whose mothers did not smoke at this time.

Although biological explanations of crime derived from studies in the post–World War II era are much more sophisticated than the early theories (and research) of Lombroso and others, this perspective continues to have major shortcomings (Barkan, 1997). For example, whereas the findings of twin research have been "mixed," most of the twins in these studies, although raised in different households, were brought up by parents who were themselves related or lived in the same neighborhood. In some cases the twins even spent considerable time with each other. This calls into question the major objective of the study, that is, to remove the common elements of socialization and shared experience that could account for criminal behavior.

Another major problem with biological interpretations is that they do not explain why an individual with an innate predisposition to violence turns to armed robbery, for example, as opposed to playing football or becoming involved in other aggressive activities such as boxing, football, or karate. To paraphrase McGaghy and Capron (1994), habitual street fighting will lead to arrest and incarceration while a season of fighting in the National Hockey League is likely to result in the adulation of hundreds of thousands of fans and a significant pay raise.

Whereas biological explanations may help us understand why a certain individual commits a particular crime, they are all but useless in our attempt to make sense of differing rates of crime both within and across societies. For example, the robbery rate (the number of robberies per 100,000 population) in cities of over 1 million in the U.S. is typically 10 times higher than the rate in smaller cities, and over 50 times as high as robbery rates in rural areas. Similarly, crime rates can increase or decrease dramatically in a relatively short period of time. In one recent seven-year period, the rate of violent crime in this country went up over 40 percent. Is it possible that human physiology (at least in the United States) changed so much in a mere seven years to account for this difference, and then changed again as the rate of violent crime began to decrease? Looking at cross-cultural statistics, we find that rates of violent crime in the United States are significantly higher than violent crime rates in Canada. Are Americans and Canadians biologically distinct regarding criminal tendencies and behavior, or are there other factors (social, cultural, political, economic) at work here?

Although many biologists (and some criminologists) "are enthusiastic about the potential of biological theories to explain crime," the majority of social scientists are more skeptical (Barkan, 1997, p. 135). While this latter group of researchers may entertain the notion that biological interpretations are helpful in explaining why some individuals commit certain crimes in particular situations, there are too many crime-related questions that biological theories simply cannot answer. For example, why and under what conditions do certain aspects of human behavior become illegal in the first place? In other words, under what circumstance does the criminal law emerge and whose interests are served by the enforcement of these laws? Finally, an especially important question in a heterogeneous society like the U.S.; historically, why have criminal laws and sanctions been applied to some groups of people (racial and ethnic minorities) more than to others?

Sociological Perspectives

Functionalist Theory The first ten minutes of the local television newscast in any big city is usually a chronicle of the day's criminal events. We see tearful individuals recount stories of assault, robbery, and rape and police officers working around the clock to fight the rising tide of crime. At election time, politicians routinely tell us they will get tough with criminals and make the streets safe for law-abiding citizens. Is it possible to rid society of crime once and for all, or is the loss of life and property, as well as the incalculable human suffering that results from criminal behavior, something we have to accept?

According to the great French sociologist Emile Durkheim (1938/1895), crime is "normal" because it is impossible to imagine (or find) a society that does not have criminal behavior. Durkheim did not mean crime is normal in the sense that it is good. Rather, he used the term in the sense of statistical normalcy; crime is everywhere. Therefore, Durkheim reasoned, if it is present in all societies at all times, it cannot be abnormal. He gave three reasons for the normalcy of criminal behavior.

First, crime and deviance persist because it is impossible to reach complete agreement on what the rules and norms of society are or should be. Without absolute agreement and acceptance of the rules, the behavior of one group of people will be considered deviant by the standards of another group.

Second, crime is normal because no society can enforce total conformity to its rules and laws (Coser, 1971). Even under the most repressive regimes and totalitarian governments, officials find it impossible to gain complete obedience to the laws of the land. For example, robbery, murder, prostitution, and black market activity existed even in the darkest days of the Stalinist era in the former Soviet Union.

Third, crime is inevitable because "man is a normative creature" (Nisbet, 1974, p. 216), continually dividing the social world into what is acceptable and unacceptable. That which is deemed unacceptable becomes criminal.

Although Durkheim believed that crime was normal and inevitable, he did not mean that all societies would have identical rates of crime, nor would the same acts be considered criminal in every social group. Depending on the forces in society contributing to criminal behavior and the mechanisms of social control, rates could be high or low. Also, behavior considered criminal will vary across social groups. In one of his most famous passages, Durkheim (1938/1895) asked us to "Imagine a society of saints, a perfect cloister of exemplary individuals. Crimes, properly so-called will be there unknown; but faults which appear venial to the layman will create the same scandal that the ordinary offense does in ordinary consciousness" (p. 53). He was saying that even in a society of perfect human beings, there will be deviance, although not the types of deviance we are used to seeing in the modern world. Rather, it will consist of rule-violating behavior of that specific group. In Durkheim's society of saints, it might be praying six hours a day instead of eight and failing to meditate in a strict, erect posture.

Durkheim argued further that if crime is present in all societies, it must be functional, or necessary. In other words, the continuous violation of rules and laws must result in some social good. Remember that functionalist sociologists consider the consequences of behavior at the group, institutional, and societal levels of analysis. Therefore, the impact of crime may be harmful (dysfunctional) for individual victims and their families, while this same behavior is functional (desirable and necessary) for the larger society. According to Durkheim, crime is functional for society in four ways (Martin, Mutshnick, and Austin, 1990).

There is a "vital relation between deviance and progress" in society (Nisbet, 1974, p. 219). The same tolerance that permits the healthy flow of originality, resulting in positive social change in society, also opens the door for a good deal of undesirable deviant behavior. One seemingly obvious solution to this problem would be to permit and encourage positive deviance and discourage negative deviance. In hindsight, this is relatively simple, but at the moment of occurrence, it is not always easy to tell what forms of behavior will transform society for the better. Labor leaders, suffragettes, abolitionists (those who opposed slavery), Jesus Christ, Mohandas Gandhi, and Martin Luther King, Jr., were all treated as radicals and/or criminals whose ideas would contribute to the destruction of the established social order.

The second function of deviance is that of a warning light, a visible signal that something is wrong in society and in need of immediate attention. The high rate of drug use in this country should result in probing questions on the part of citizens and politicians as to why this behavior is so widespread. What is happening (or not happening) politically, socially, and economically in the United States at this moment in history that so many people from every social stratum are using and dealing drugs? In this warning light function, Durkheim compared crime to physical pain: It is normal and necessary, as it tells us something is wrong with the body social (Martin, Mutshnick, and Austin, 1990).

Crime also helps to clarify boundaries. Every time a rule or law is violated and society reacts to it, it sends a message stating this sanction is important and the law must be obeyed. Conversely, if the violation of a norm is ignored or results in only a minor sanction, the message is that this norm at this particular time is not considered as important as others. For example, with few exceptions, prostitution is illegal throughout the United States; however, prostitutes can be seen walking the streets and working out of bars with little if any fear of being arrested. They know police are using their limited resources to fight the "war on drugs." They also realize that neither the police nor society in general considers prostitution as dangerous (and "dysfunctional") as the drug problem.

Finally, criminal behavior facilitates social solidarity. Violation of the law can draw members of a community together in their revulsion toward the criminal act and the criminal. Speaking of a murder in his district, a Wyoming police chief states, "It was a crime against everyone. It's drawn the whole community together" (Magnuson, 1981, p. 18). Functionalist sociologists do not advocate mass murders to enhance social cohesion. Nevertheless, crimes can bind a community together like few other events.

Anomie Theory Durkheim used the word **anomie** to describe the breakdown of societal rules and norms that regulate human behavior. Examining France and other European countries in the years after the Industrial Revolution, he argued that the rapid economic, political, and social transformation of these societies produced anomie, or normlessness. This condition resulted in disruptive patterns of social interaction and high rates of suicide (Williams and McShane, 1988).

In 1938, Robert Merton used the concept of anomie to characterize a feature more firmly rooted in the social structure of society and responsible for a variety of criminal and deviant behaviors. For Merton, all societies socialize their members to aspire to a number of culturally defined and acceptable goals and teach people to attain these goals by a variety of available and legitimate means of behavior. In other words, societies provide a set of culturally acceptable goals, as well as the means for achieving them. However, in societies of the "American type," the emphasis is much more on being successful (goals) than on how success is attained (means). This overemphasis on achieving one's goals, and the corresponding underemphasis on how they are realized, is at the heart of Merton's theory and is responsible for a significant amount of deviant behavior in U.S. society.

Merton (1968) used monetary success as an example of a goal actively pursued by individuals in every stratum of society in the United States. The "goal—means dysjunction" (or gap) results in five different types of behavior, or adaptations, depending on whether individuals accept or reject both the goals and the means of achieving them. Note that these adaptations do not represent personality types. People can move from one adaptation to another at different points in their lives (Table 8.2).

1. *Conformity* This adaptation is followed by most of the people most of the time. Individuals accept both the culturally prescribed goals and means, which include working in an automobile factory, striving for a professional career by way of a college degree, and starting one's own business.
2. *Innovation* This adaptation is the most common of the four deviant types and usually takes one of two forms. In the first instance, an individual ac-

---

TABLE 8.2

A Typology of Modes of Individual Adaptation

Modes of Adaptation	Culture Goals	Institutionalized Means
I. Conformity	+	+
II. Innovation	+	–
III. Ritualism	–	+
IV. Retreatism	–	–
V. Rebellion[1]	±	±

\+ signifies "acceptance"

– signifies "rejection"

± signifies "rejection of prevailing values and substitution of new values"

[1]Merton notes that the "fifth alternative"—rebellion—"is on a plane clearly different from that of the others. It represents a transitional response seeking to *institutionalize* new goals and new procedures to be shared by other members of the society. It thus refers to efforts to *change* the existing cultural and social structure rather than to accommodate efforts *within* this structure."

Source: Social Structure and Anomie by Robert K. Merton, New York: Free Press, p. 194, 1968.

---

cepts the societal goal of financial success. However, the "opportunity structure," or means of achieving this goal, is blocked. Merton argued that this lack of opportunity is most evident in the lower classes and places tremendous pressure on these people to engage in deviant behavior. Because of high rates of unemployment, inadequate school systems, and racial and ethnic discrimination, people in the lower classes resort to "innovative" or criminal means of attaining financial success. In the second instance, the legitimate means for achieving one's goals are available but rejected because they are not expedient or take too much effort. Students who cheat on examinations are innovators inasmuch as they have accepted the goal of doing well in school but reject the legitimate means of studying and working hard for grades. Many white-collar and corporate criminals are also innovators. Although they may be quite wealthy, they want even more money and material possessions and are willing to circumvent the law to satisfy their desires.

3. *Ritualism* A strong desire for financial gain may result in a life of luxury, but for everyone who becomes a multimillionaire, tens of thousands fail. Because it is often associated with a significant loss of self-esteem, failure can be difficult for people to accept. One way to avoid personal defeat is to scale down or reject ambitious goals while continuing to work hard and to meet one's economic

and social obligations. Although this adaptation is not deviant behavior of the same magnitude as crime, Merton considered it deviance because ritualists reject a fundamental value in the United States of continually striving for monetary success and upward mobility.

4. *Retreatism* Retreatists take ritualism one step further and reject culturally prescribed means as well as goals. Some homeless people, chronic alcoholics, and drug addicts are retreatists. Merton (1968) noted that these individuals have turned their backs on the social world and are, strictly speaking, "*in* the society but not *of* it" (p. 207). Retreatists are a twofold social liability. Not only are they nonproductive members of society, but many use social services in the form of the criminal justice system, mental institutions, and rehabilitation programs. William Sanders (1983) described some retreatists as "double losers," as they fail both to achieve their goals by legitimate means and to become successful criminals or innovators.

5. *Rebellion* This revolutionary adaptation comes about when people reject both the culturally prescribed goals and means and substitute an alternative set grounded in different values. Rebels want to change society in fundamental ways, not reform it. Many of those involved in the radical and abrupt transformation of eastern European nations in 1989 and 1990 were rebels.

Merton's perspective of deviance is important for at least two reasons. Written when biological and psychological theories of deviant behavior were popular and readily accepted, his view of deviance offered a purely sociological interpretation of rule-violating behavior. Instead of innate biological impulses or psychological maladies, the social structure exerted "a definite pressure upon certain persons in the society to engage in nonconforming rather than conforming conduct" (Merton, 1968, p. 186). Second, the same pressure in society that produces conformity (striving for success) also produces nonconformity: "a cardinal American virtue, 'ambition,' underlies a cardinal American vice, 'deviant behavior'" (Merton, 1957, p. 146).

Differential Association According to Edwin Sutherland, a noted U.S. criminologist, criminal behavior is not the product of inborn biological abnormality or the result of low intelligence or personality defects. People are not predisposed to commit crimes, and criminal behavior does not occur spontaneously; instead, such behavior is learned. Sutherland advanced these ideas as part of his **differential association** theory. He argued that criminal behavior is not learned

from the mass media but "is learned in interaction with other persons in a process of communication" (Sutherland and Cressey, 1970, p. 75). People learn techniques for committing crimes as well as "the specific direction of motives, drives, rationalizations, and attitudes" (p. 75). In other words, people learn much more than the mechanics of how to commit a crime. They also internalize a series of attitudes that permit them to rationalize this behavior to themselves and others.

Sutherland stated, "A person becomes delinquent because of an excess of definitions favorable to violation of law over definitions unfavorable to violation of law. This is the principle of differential association" (in Sutherland and Cressey, 1970, p. 75). Criminologist William Sanders (1983) offered a simple formula to illustrate this crucial aspect of the theory:

$$\frac{\text{Definitions favorable to violations of the law (DFVL)}}{\text{Definitions unfavorable to violations of the law (DUVL)}}$$

If an individual receives more definitions favorable to the violations of the law (DFVL) than definitions *unfavorable* to the violation of the law (DUVL), he or she is likely to engage in criminal behavior. However, the number of favorable or unfavorable definitions regarding law violations is not the only factor involved in producing criminality. Sutherland (in Sutherland and Cressey, 1970) also stressed the "duration," "priority," and "intensity" of relationships in determining whether or not a person would perform criminal acts. Duration is the amount of time we have known people who are giving us these definitions. Individuals we have just met will not have as much influence on our behavior as people we have known for many years. Priority is how early in life we have been exposed to DFVL and DUVL. Patterns of criminality observed or learned early in life will have a greater impact on our behavior than those learned later in life. Intensity is a measure of the strength of the relationship. People with whom we have a strong emotional bond ("primary relations") will influence us more than people with whom we have a more "secondary" relationship. Putting these three components together, if an individual learns definitions *favorable* to the violation of the law early in life (priority), from influential people (intensity), and over a long period of time (duration), he or she is very likely to engage in criminal conduct.

Differential association has been dismissed as nothing more than a "bad apple" theory; someone who hangs around with criminals will naturally become a criminal. However, the theory does not focus on the person making DFVL or DUVL, but on the definitions themselves. For example, if children see their parents steal ("borrow") things from work on a regular basis and hear them brag about these activities, the children are receiving powerful DFVL even though the parents are not criminals (i.e., they have never been caught and punished) and do not think of themselves as criminals. Similarly, a new insurance agent may learn from co-workers the best ways to cheat customers ("aggressive sales techniques") and how to rationalize this behavior ("everybody does it"). Even though DFVL are not coming from "criminals," they have the effect of facilitating criminal behavior. Differential association goes beyond the commonsense notion that law-violating behavior is learned only from juvenile delinquents, gang members, and hardened criminals.

Labeling Theory Most theories of deviant and criminal behavior attempt to explain why people engage in rule-violating acts by identifying factors that cause people to transgress social norms or to break the law. The **labeling theory** shifted the focus, concentrating instead on the social creation of, and reaction to, deviant behavior. Howard Becker (1963) noted that "*social groups create deviance by making the rules whose infraction constitutes deviance*, and by applying those rules to particular people and labeling them deviant" (p. 9). From this perspective, "deviant behavior is behavior that people so label" (p. 9).

Labeling theorists argue that since so many laws and rules govern human conduct, almost everyone engages in deviant or criminal behavior. The important question, therefore, is not why they do so, but rather why only certain people are labeled deviants and criminals. But do most people routinely violate rules and laws? According to the results of one study, an estimated 90 percent of all youths commit delinquent and criminal acts. Other research suggested that little difference exists between the behavior of incarcerated youths and that of typical high school students (Siegel, 1998).

The labeling perspective of deviance can be divided into two parts: (1) an explanation of how and why some people are labeled and (2) what effect the label has on a person's future behavior (Orcutt, 1973). Regarding the first aspect, people with low social status and little power are most likely to have the acts they engage in defined as deviant and are also more likely to be labeled as deviants by formal agents of social control—the criminal justice system and mental health professionals. For example, tens of thousands of people have been convicted and sentenced to prison by criminal courts for committing burglary, whereas the relatively few individuals and corporations convicted of cheating the public (often out of enormous sums of money) typically serve lit-

tle if any jail time. Inasmuch as labeling theorists view laws whose infraction constitutes deviance as created by the powerful to control the lower classes, the labeling perspective of deviance is quite compatible with conflict theory.

Individuals and organizations who actively campaign to discredit an activity or lifestyle of another group of people are called *moral entrepreneurs* (Becker, 1963). In the 1970s, a number of Christian fundamentalist groups and their spokespeople attempted to stigmatize further (and, if possible, to criminalize) homosexual behavior in the United States. These individuals tried to convince the nation their views of sexuality were correct and should be regarded as the standard for evaluating everyone's sexual orientation. Politically active antiabortionists who vociferously denounce pro-choice supporters as "murderers" and "baby killers" would also be considered moral entrepreneurs.

The process by which people become labeled and recognized as deviants is called a *status degradation ceremony* (Garfinkel, 1956). When an individual is convicted and sentenced in criminal court, the state is making a public declaration that this person has violated the public trust (laws) and is "not one of us." The problem with this aspect of social control is there is no "status reintegration ceremony" (Garfinkel, 1956, p. 423) whereby a person can be given back his or her status as a citizen in good standing on completing a prison term. As a result of degradation ceremonies, individuals may be forced to live with a master status for an extended period of time (if not the rest of their lives). A *master status* is a central identifying characteristic of an individual and takes precedence over any other role the person plays. For example, an individual who has served time in prison may be viewed by others first and foremost as an "ex-con." It is as if this person were walking around with a neon sign proclaiming, "I spent time in prison," in much the same way as Hester Prynne was forced to wear a crimson *A* for her adulterous behavior in Nathaniel Hawthorne's *The Scarlet Letter*.

The concept of master status is also an important component of the social control aspect of labeling theory. According to this argument, people who are labeled criminals in degradation ceremonies often end up committing additional crimes because they have so much trouble finding jobs. Once the label becomes a master status, individuals may find that criminal activity is the only way they can survive in a society in which people think in terms of "once a deviant, always a deviant" (Goode, 1990, p. 66).

A person can also internalize the given label until he "becomes the thing he is described as being" (Tannenbaum, 1938, pp. 19–20). In other words, the label may become an important part of the self-concept. It makes little difference if the label is applied by those who are trying to punish or by those who are trying to help the individual. For example, some drug treatment programs believe the first step to recovery is admission that one has a serious illness in the form of a drug problem, to admit that one is an addict. From the labeling perspective, individuals can easily become trapped in this negative definition of self. If they accept the label of drug addict (internalization of a master status), they may also accept the corresponding idea that addicts are never really cured.

Speaking of labels applied by the "addiction treatment industry" and internalized by their members, Peele (1989) noted, "The person is now convinced that a single slip will mean a complete return to the addiction or to alcoholism—a fate that befalls many 'successful' graduates" (p. 112). In other words, the label of alcoholic may become a self-fulfilling prophecy, helping to ensure that a person continues to drink and is dependent on alcohol for the remainder of his or her life. Deviant behavior that occurs as a result of being labeled is called **secondary deviance** (Lemert, 1951). The initial act, or first few episodes of nonconforming behavior, is **primary deviance**. Labeling theorists are much more concerned with secondary deviance, the deviant behavior an individual engages in after he or she has been labeled by control agents.

Although sociologists have been critical of self-help organizations that encourage members to label themselves and others, they generally agree that many one-time alcoholics have abstained from drinking for considerable periods of time thanks to the Alcoholics Anonymous program. Shur (1979) commented that "contrary to the central labeling thesis, the application of 'negative labels' in this context appears to have predominantly deviance-reducing effects rather than deviance-amplifying ones" (p. 388). Similarly, members of a weight-reducing self-help organization were continually reminded they were *fat* and that the word *fat* was an essential and permanent component of their identity, no matter how much weight they lost. According to this program, a change in identity would remove the best safeguard a person has against future weight gains. Researchers concluded that the internalization of a negative label—fat—helped bring about the desired nondeviant behavior: reduction in food intake and slimness (Laslett and Warren, 1975). However, a successful behavior change may require a lifetime commitment to the organization.

Marxist Theory Power, profit, and class struggle are concepts at the heart of the **Marxist theory of crime.**

In a capitalist society, the bourgeoisie (capitalist class) own and control the "modes of production" (factories, machinery, technology) and, in so doing, systematically exploit the working class (proletariat). Their superior political power and economic holdings permit the bourgeoisie to accumulate vast amounts of wealth at the expense of the proletariat, who lead lives of poverty and despair. Because their economic interests are different and incompatible, these two groups are locked in a continuing antagonistic relationship, or class struggle. This struggle between the capitalist and proletarian classes produces crime.

Marxist criminologist Richard Quinney (1977) asserted that class conflict even determines what types of crimes the two groups will commit. Members of the capitalist class commit crimes of "domination and repression." These are motivated by the desire (1) to extract as much money as possible from the lower classes and (2) to prevent the proletariat from disrupting society and challenging the position and power of the bourgeoisie. The proletariat, meanwhile, engage in crimes of "accommodation and resistance." These are primarily motivated by a desire to survive in a repressive society and the frustration, rage, and anguish resulting from this repression.

For Quinney (1977) and other Marxist criminologists, crime in a capitalist society like the United States is not a disease, but a symptom. The real disease is the unequal distribution of wealth and power that results in poverty, unemployment, and the economic crisis of the capitalist state. The economic crisis inherent in capitalism is the real cause of crime. This is why Marxist sociologists do not focus on criminal behavior per se, but rather on how criminal laws come into being, whose interest they serve, and how they are applied. Quinney (1970) called crime a "social reality" in that it is created by people in society. That is, criminal definitions (laws) are made by the capitalist class and enforced by their agents (police, judges, prison personnel).

It follows from Quinney's analysis that the behavior of rich and powerful people (those who directly or indirectly make the laws) is less likely to be defined as criminal than the behavior of relatively powerless numbers of the lower classes. That is why U.S. prisons are disproportionately filled with African Americans and Latinos who commit street crimes, rather than affluent Caucasian males who engage in various forms of corporate and white-collar crime.

For Marxist sociologists, there is only one solution to the crime problem: the end of capitalism. Since the unequal distribution of wealth and the resulting class struggle are inherent in capitalism, the system cannot be salvaged. Capitalism generates racism, sexism, and myriad social injustices, all of which directly or indirectly cause crime. The answer to the crime problem is a society established along socialist principles of criminal justice, a system that satisfies the needs of all members of society.

DEVIANT AND CRIMINAL BEHAVIOR

Counting Crime

Published annually by the Federal Bureau of Investigation, the *Uniform Crime Report* (UCR) is the best known and most widely used source of criminal statistics. Approximately 17,000 law enforcement agencies throughout the United States voluntarily send the FBI crime reports on a quarterly basis. These statistics are not a measure of all the crime that occurs in the United States annually, but rather of all crimes known to police. The UCR gives detailed information on four violent crimes (murder, robbery, rape, and aggravated assault) and three property crimes (burglary, larceny-theft, and motor vehicle theft). Usually referred to as the *index crimes*, these seven offenses are expressed in terms of the total number of crimes committed in a particular area (city, state, region, nation) and a crime rate. For example, in 1998, 12,475,634 index crimes in the United States were known to police. The *crime rate* is the number of crimes committed per 100,000 population. Table 8.3 indicates that in 1998, 4,615.5 index crimes were committed for every 100,000 people.

Crime rates allow us to compare rates of criminal activity in cities and states of various size. For example, common sense would tell us that Los Angeles had more index crimes than a city one-tenth its size. However, by computing a rate of criminal activity, we might find that the smaller city had a much higher crime rate (the number of crimes per 100,000) than Los Angeles did. Using crime rates, we can also compare the rate of criminal activity across time as the population of cities, states, and the nation changes. Table 8.3 shows that the rate of violent crime in the United States declined from 758.1 in 1991, to 566.4 in 1998, a decrease of 25.3 percent.

The UCR has been criticized (especially by Marxist sociologists) because it is primarily a count of street crimes committed by the lower classes and excludes white-collar offenses, which are more likely to be committed by middle- and upper-class individuals. As a result, the crime problem in the United States is typically reported and viewed by the public as a series of offenses committed by the poor. The UCR also undercounts the frequency of crime. Hundreds of thousands of people do not call the police when they are victimized, for a variety of reasons, including fear and hatred of the police, fear of the reprisal from the offender, and a belief that the police can do little if anything to rectify the problem (apprehend the offender, retrieve their stolen property).

To learn more about crime victims (who they are, what happened to them, why they do not always contact the police) the National Crime Victimization Survey (NCVS) was begun in 1973. This *victimization survey* is a survey of 49,000 households containing approximately 101,000 people. Household members over 12 years of age are interviewed twice a year and asked how many times in the past six months they have been victims of specific crimes. On the basis of these findings, projections are made regarding the total number of victimizations for a select number of crimes every year. Over the years NCVS data have consistently revealed that different subgroups of the population have different rates of victimization. For example, victimization rates for crimes of violence are relatively high for males, African Americans, poor people, and both young and single individuals.

The final mechanism for gathering information about crime in society is the *self-report study*. People are asked to reveal their involvement in certain types of criminal and deviant activities, for example, the number of times they used illegal drugs, cheated on their income tax, were engaged in domestic violence, and were driving while intoxicated. Self-report studies are especially important in addressing questions concerning the relationship between social status and crime. Do people in the lower classes really commit more crimes (as indicated by arrest rates and the prison population) than individuals in the middle and upper classes? What offenses do people in the middle and upper classes commit? What types of offenses are class linked and which are not?

After peaking in 1991, crime began dropping with rates (combined violent and property offence) decreasing from 5899.8 per 100,000 in that year to 4615.5 in 1998. Declines in both the actual number and rates of violent crime were especially significant in cities of over 250,000 people. For example, murders in New York City fell from 1,946 (5.3 a day) to 633 (1.73 a day) in 1998. The following is an overview of the most salient reasons usually given for this reduction in crime (Witkin, 1998; Lardner, 1998; Cohen, 1998; and "Defeating the Bad Guys," 1998):

1. *The Police* In 1994 President Clinton stated that he wanted to put 100,000 more police on the streets of America, and by 1997 money had been allocated for about 70,000 new officers. More police means an increase in criminal arrests, prosecutions, and

TABLE 8.3

Index of Crimes, United States, 1989–1998

Population	Crime Index Total	Violent Crime	Property Crime
Total Number of Reported Crimes, 1989–1998			
Population by year			
1989—248,239,000	14,251,400	1,646,040	12,605,400
1990—248,709,873	14,475,600	1,820,130	12,655,500
1991—252,177,000	14,872,900	1,911,770	12,961,100
1992—255,082,000	14,438,200	1,932,270	12,505,900
1993—257,908,000	14,144,800	1,926,020	12,218,800
1994—260,341,000	13,989,500	1,857,670	12,131,900
1995—262,755,000	13,862,700	1,798,790	12,063,900
1996—265,284,000	13,493,900	1,688,540	11,805,300
1997—267,637,000[5]	13,194,600	1,636,100	11,558,500
1998—270,296,000	12,475,600	1,531,040	10,944,600
Percentage change, number of offenses:			
1998/1997	−5.4	−6.4	−5.3
1998/1994	−10.8	−17.6	−9.8
1994/1989	−12.5	−7.0	−13.2
Number of Crimes per 100,000 Inhabitants, 1989–1998			
1989	5,741.0	663.1	5,077.9
1990	5,820.3	731.8	5,088.5
1991	5,897.8	758.1	5,139.7
1992	5,660.2	757.5	4,902.7
1993	5,484.4	746.8	4,737.6
1994	5,373.5	713.6	4,660.0
1995	5,275.9	684.6	4,591.3
1996	5,086.6	636.5	4,450.1
1997[5]	4,930.0	611.3	4,318.7
1998	4,615.5	566.4	4,049.1
Percentage change, rate per 100,000 inhabitants:			
1998/1997	−6.4	−7.3	−6.2
1998/1994	−14.1	−20.6	−13.1
1998/1989	−19.6	−14.6	−20.3

Source: Federal Bureau of Investigation, U.S. Department of Justice, *Uniform Crime Reports* (Washington, DC: U.S. Government Printing Office, 1999).

a corresponding escalation in the number of people incarcerated.

2. *The Prisons* In 1998, 461 (1 of every 113 men and 1 of every 1,754 women) of every 100,000 people in this country were in prison, a figure that is over twice the incarceration rate of 1985. This tremendous increase in the prison population is thought to reduce crime in two ways. First, criminals behind bars cannot victimize the general public (although they can brutalize each other), and second, successfully prosecuting and imprisoning felons deters some would-be offenders.

3. *Zero Tolerance*   Some cities have attempted to arrest individuals for even relatively minor infractions (vandalism and petty theft, for example) with the intent of sending a message that no criminal behavior will be tolerated. The rationale for this crime explanation/intervention strategy has been called the "broken windows" approach. If a broken window is left in disrepair it becomes a signal that no one cares what happens in this neighborhood. It also serves as an invitation to perpetrators that it is relatively safe to engage in additional (and possibly even more serious) transgressions.

4. *The Economy*   To the extent that criminal acts such as burglary, robbery (especially muggings), and shoplifting are poverty driven, economic prosperity in recent years has resulted in more jobs and a reduction in "deviant motivation" that manifests itself in street crime. Census data indicate that between 1993 and 1995, poverty rates declined in all but three states and Washington, DC.

5. *Crack Cocaine*   The popularity of crack (most notably in inner-city America) ushered in a wave of violence that lasted from the mid-1980s to the early 1990s. Thousands of small-time crack dealers across the country had two things many people wanted: drugs and money. To protect themselves from assailants, these criminal entrepreneurs bought guns, a move that touched off an arms race among young males. It soon became a status symbol to have a gun, and fights usually settled with fists or knives now turned into shootouts as the number of aggravated assaults and homicides escalated. In the past few years inner-city violence has subsided as a result of what Richard Curtis (in Lardner, 1998, p. 38) calls the "younger-brother syndromes." From this perspective younger children became disillusioned with crack cocaine as a consequence of watching older siblings suffer the pains of addiction, arrest and incarceration, and/or become victims of crack-related violence.

6. *Marriage and Divorce*   Criminologist Alfred Blumstein (in "Defeating the Bad Guys," 1998) has argued that in an age of easy divorce and casual relationships, people are more likely to leave a troubled romance before the marriage deteriorates to a homicide-producing situation. Between 1976 and 1996, homicides wherein one person in a love relation took the life of his or her partner declined 40 percent.

7. *Change in Routine Activities*   According to the routine activities approach of Lawrence Cohen and Marcus Felson (1979), three things are necessary for a crime to occur: first, the presence of an attractive target in the form of property or a person; second, the absence of "guardianship"—some person or thing (an alarm system, for example) that can prevent the crime from taking place; finally, a motivated offender. The widespread use of computers means that an ever-increasing segment of the population can work at home either full or part time. Likewise, the proliferation of cable television, VCRs, and video games has resulted in a growing number of people spending more evenings at home. As the routine activities of millions of Americans changes, it has become increasingly difficult for motivated offenders who spot an attractive target to find that target unguarded.

8. *Changing Demographics*   Declining crime rates have coincided with a drop in the number of males between the ages of 15 and 21, the years of greatest risk for many forms of deviant and criminal behavior. Inasmuch as street crime is overwhelmingly a young man's game, the amount of this form of criminal activity a society will experience is directly related to the number and percentage of young high-risk males in that society. As the number of males in this age category will soon begin increasing before leveling off in the year 2010 (the children of the last of the baby boomers), crime rates should begin rising again.

While crime is (partially) amenable to factors that can be controlled by governments (the number of police, prosecutors, judges, and prisons), criminal behavior is also a function of factors that are difficult if not impossible to anticipate or regulate. For example, will another crack-like epidemic spread throughout big-city America with similar consequences? Will the use of computers to store information regarding almost every facet of our lives bring about crimes such as "identity theft" and "cyberterrrorism" (the unauthorized use or destruction of data sets, from bank accounts to medical and mental health records)? As the population grows older and wealthier in a service-oriented economy, will white-collar crimes (committed by middle-age men *and* women) ranging from embezzlement to insider trading become more prevalent?

The Offenders

Information regarding the composition of the criminal population in the United States is incomplete and limited primarily to individuals arrested and incarcerated for index or "street" crimes. Since the criminal justice system (police, courts, and prisons) spends such a small portion of its time and resources investigating and prosecuting white-collar crime, we know relatively little about the people who commit these offenses.

The following is a profile of criminal offenders in the United States. Keep in mind that these observations are based primarily on street criminals and on only a fraction of that population. In any given year no more than one of every five index crimes known to police results in an arrest.

Gender Men commit more crimes than women. This is true not only in the United States but in "all nations, all communities within a nation, at all age groups, and all periods of history for which data are available" (Sutherland and Cressey, 1970, p. 126). In 1998, 78 percent of people arrested in this country were males, and men are much more likely to be arrested for serious crimes such as murder, robbery, assault, and burglary. Arrest records as well as data from jails and prisons indicate that women who commit crimes are typically involved in minor property offenses (larceny and fraud), forgery, drug offenses, and prostitution. Males also have a "virtual monopoly" on the commission of organized, corporate, and political crime in the United States (Beirne and Messerschmidt, 1998). Although male criminality is always higher than female criminality, the two rates move in concert. That is, as the rate of male criminality increases or declines the rate of female criminality does the same. This suggests, as sociologists Darrell Steffensmeier and Emilie Allan (1995, p. 87) note, "that the rates of both sexes are influenced by similar social and legal forces, independent of any condition unique to women."

Age Crime is overwhelmingly a youthful (male) activity. In 1998, approximately 59 percent of the people arrested for all crimes (not just the index offenses) were 29 years of age or under, and 18 percent were under age 18. However, victimization studies indicate that youths under 18 commit fewer serious crimes than adults. After age 29, arrest rates begin to decline and continue to drop sharply until they are negligible for people 60 and over.

The decline in the crime rate as people age is called *aging out* or the *desistance phenomenon* (Siegel, 1998). Wilson and Herrnstein (1985) noted that after the transition from adolescence to adulthood "one would expect crime to subside" (p. 147). Whereas as young people often commit crimes for money, sex, alcohol, and status, they have access to these things as adults. At the same time, social and psychological reinforcers for not committing crime increase as people marry, start a family, and are integrated into the larger community. Sociologists Hirshi and Gottfredson (1983) rejected the "life course" explanation, however, stating that as plausible as this interpretation may sound, rates of crime decrease as people grow older regardless of whether or not these events occur.

Criminologist Larry J. Siegel (1998) notes that aging out or desistance may be a function of an individual's criminal specialization. For example, the commission of street crimes may peak at a relatively young age and then decline while crimes such as embezzlement, fraud, and insider trading are mostly committed by people in their late 30s to mid-50s. Therefore, the criminal population may be comprised of three subgroups: one set of offenders whose criminality declines with age, a second set of individuals (career street criminals) whose rate of law violating remains relatively constant as they grow older (Siegel, 1998), and a third group that engages in occupational and corporate crime during their middle years.

Race and Ethnicity The racial-ethnic breakdown of the people arrested in 1998 for all crimes is as follows: 71.3 percent white, 26.0 percent African American, 1.1 percent American Indian or Native Alaskan, and 1.6 percent Asian or Pacific Islander. An analysis of data in the late 1990s found that almost one in three African-American men between 20 and 29 years of age was behind bars, on probation, or on parole. In 1985 that number was one in four. Just under 5 percent of young black women were serving criminal sentences in the mid-1990s as compared to 1.4 percent of white females (Cass, 1995). Nationwide, African Americans comprised almost 50 percent of all jail and prison inmates in the late 1990s. The percentages of blacks arrested and incarcerated are disproportionately high inasmuch as African Americans account for only 12.5 percent of the population.

The obvious question after considering these statistics is why do African Americans have such disproportionately high rates of arrest and incarceration? There are at least two explanations for this phenomenon. Traditionally in the United States, crime has been conceptualized, counted, and dealt with (by the criminal justice system) in terms of violations committed by poor people; and since approximately one-third of blacks are members of the lower class, their law-breaking activity is much more likely (than individuals of other races and classes) to result in arrest and incarceration. Sociologists Anthony Harris and Lisa Meidlinger (1995, p. 118) note that it is not just that the crime index (UCR) "is biased *against* lower class black street crime per se, but, rather it is biased *away from* middle class and elite whites' 'suite' crime." In other words, people commit the types of crime that are available to them. White business executives in office suites commit corporate crimes, and unemployed, inner-city black youths commit index crimes such as robbery and burglary. It is highly unlikely that a Fortune 500 business executive is going to sell crack cocaine in an urban ghetto, or that a 19-year-old from an inner-city neighborhood will be involved in an antitrust conspiracy to fix the price of airline tickets. However, the criminal justice system does not measure crime (the UCR) in terms of corporate offenses, nor does it seek out and prosecute white-collar offenders with the same intensity that it does street criminals. Inasmuch as the police and courts are primarily interested in controlling street crime, it is hardly surprising that such a disproportionate number of Black Americans are in prison.

High rates of black crime, arrest, and incarceration have also been linked to poverty. That is, African-American crime has much more to do with unemployment, low wages, and few prospects for upward mobility than it does with skin color (Gibbons, 1997). Speaking of the growing concentrations of wealth and poverty in the U.S., demographer Douglas Massey (1996, p. 2) stated that "no consequence of concentrated poverty is as destructive as the proliferation of crime and violence."

Social Class As the previous discussion clearly indicates, race, class, and crime are intertwined. Harris and Meidlinger (1995) are correct when they note that the relation between race and crime may be nothing more than a "cloaked" relation between social class and crime. One of the oldest, most perplexing, and certainly controversial topics in criminology concerns the relation between social class and crime. Official statistics (UCR) have reported consistently that rates of crime and arrest are highest in urban ghettos and lower-class neighborhoods. But do these statistics accurately reflect the true picture of law-violating behavior? Is there really more crime in lower-class America?

Charles Tittle and his colleagues (Tittle, Villamez, and Smith, 1978), in what has been called the "definitive work" on this subject (Siegel, 1998), reviewed 35 studies that estimated the relation between social class and crime. The authors found a very weak association between the two variables and concluded that it was time for researchers to "shift away from class-based theories" (Tittle, p. 64). In 1990, Tittle and Meier examined the class/delinquency relation and found this same weak relation. John Braithwaite (1981) looked at over 200 studies of social class and crime and concluded that lower-class youths did have higher rates of criminal activity. He also noted that whereas a criminal justice system biased against the lower class may be a problem in some jurisdic-

tions, "for many courts and police departments this bias may be minimal or nonexistent" (p. 40). Therefore, it would be a mistake for sociologists to move away from class-based theories of criminality. The contradictory findings of these studies can be at least partially explained by taking into account methodological problems of social research including the measurement of social class and some forms of criminal behavior. Nonetheless, the class-crime question is far from being resolved.

Sexual Deviance

Prostitution In its earliest form, prostitution—the sale of sex for money—was associated with temple orgies and fertility rites (Miller, 1991). At the time of Christ, the city of Rome had 36,000 *registered* and taxed prostitutes. This activity increased rapidly in money-based urban economies, and by the Middle Ages, prostitution was firmly entrenched in European societies. Attempts to eliminate what is often referred to as "the world's oldest profession" were abandoned (Little, 1989). Today, prostitution flourishes in rich and poor countries throughout the world. As is the case with numerous types of deviant behavior, it is difficult to determine the number of people who make all or part of their living via prostitution. According to some estimates there are between 100,000 and 500,000 prostitutes in this country (Clinard and Meier, 1992), and from 100,000 to 300,000 child prostitutes in the United States and Canada (Clayton, 1996). Data from the Uniform Crime Report indicate that approximately 100,000 individuals are arrested annually for engaging in prostitution, with two of five of these arrestees being male (Seigel, 1998). This latter figure indicates that prostitution also occurs among the homosexual population.

The majority of prostitutes live in a dangerous world. They are at risk of being physically abused by customers and pimps, arrested by the police, and infected with sexually transmitted diseases including acquired immunodeficiency syndrome (AIDS). Streetwalkers are especially vulnerable when they get into a car with an unknown "John" or "trick" (customer). *Mission-oriented* serial killers who believe it is their job to rid society of some undesirable category of people have often targeted prostitutes as their primary victims (Holmes and De Burger, 1988). *Streetwalkers* are often poor women of color who become prostitutes to finance their drug habit (Lesieur and Welch, 1995).

The role of the *pimp*—an individual who derives some or all of his income from the earnings of prostitutes (Siegel, 1998)—has figured prominently in the literature on this form of deviance. Larry Siegel

(1998) characterizes the pimp as a man who steers customers toward women in his "stable," protects his girls from Johns who would abuse them, and posts bail when they are arrested. The pimp is the most important person in the life of many prostitutes (especially "streetwalkers" and "bar girls") as he serves as a surrogate father as well as a husband and lover. Pimps may pick up women with previous experience in "the life," or "turn out" girls who have never worked the streets or bars (Siegel, 1998).

David A. Ward and his colleagues (Ward, Carter, and Perrin, 1994) have a somewhat different interpretation of the pimp/prostitute relation. For these sociologists, since the pimp is seldom with his girls on the street, he cannot effectively protect them from abusive customers or police harassment. Rather than "turn out" prostitutes, working girls train themselves by way of trial and error. Also, prostitutes choose their pimp ("the man") rather than the other way around, and often move from one pimp to another in the hopes of improving their status (and income) in the prostitution subculture. In responses to the question concerning the role of the pimp, Ward and colleagues (1994, p. 253) offer the following response:

> First, and foremost, the pimp takes 100 percent of the prostitute's earnings. He also manages the money, provides her with clothing, jewelry, food, an allowance; and he often keeps her children and gives her a home. His relationship with his women involves a complex of roles. He is her "businessman," her "father," her "brother," her "therapist," and her "lover."

Whereas macro-level theorists in the functionalism and conflict tradition have attempted to explain "the origin and persistence" of the sex for money trade (Ward, Carter, and Perrin, 1994), other researchers (including psychologists) have focused on the personality characteristics and life circumstances of females who become prostitutes. The literature clearly indicates that adolescent prostitutes are often runaways from "dysfunctional" families with a history of parental alcoholism and violence. As young girls, these females were frequently victims of physical and sexual abuse and had problems with drugs and alcohol. In a study of 45 adolescent prostitutes and 37 adolescents who were not prostitutes, the researchers found that although the above-mentioned characteristics and family situations were frequent among teenage prostitutes, they were just as common in the backgrounds of the girls who did not trade sex for money. On the basis of their research the authors concluded that being raised in a dysfunctional family "might not be critical for entry into prostitution" (Nadon, Kaverola, and Schludermann, 1998).

These "hostesses" at a nightclub in Thailand are waiting for patrons. In some establishments, prostitutes wear official looking badges that say "AIDS Free" to help entice customers. Clearances by local health officials notwithstanding, are they really free of this disease and how many will eventually succumb to the AIDS virus?

In many developing countries prostitution is a major growth industry. A United Nations report of commercial sex in Indonesia, Malaysia, the Philippines, and Thailand concluded that although it is not recorded in official statistics, the money generated by prostitution is "crucial to the livelihoods and earning potential of millions of workers beyond the prostitutes themselves" (Olson, 1998, p. A11). The authors of the report estimated that Thailand's annual income from prostitution is between $22 and $27 billion, a substantial sum of money for a nation whose gross national product in the mid-1990s was approximately $355 billion.

In nations with high rates of population growth where hundreds of millions of people (especially females) have little education and almost no chance of finding decent-paying jobs, prostitution may be an occupation of last resort. In Shenyang, a city in northern China with a high rate of unemployment, an estimated 100,000 women (a significant number of whom are prostitutes) are employed in some 3,000 hotels, dance halls, coffee houses, and bars. Women who trade sex for money can earn up to $12,000 a year, 10 times as much as the typical factory worker. To gain a share of this lucrative business, the local government is taxing "san pei" ladies (bar hostesses) at the rate of $35 a month. The sex trade is also a dangerous business in China as 90 san pei were murdered in a recent three-year period (Lin, 1998).

Homosexuality Sexual activity between same-sexed individuals has existed in the majority of cultures throughout history (Little, 1989). In some societies, this behavior is tolerated, but in others it has been repressed, sometimes violently. Homosexuality is considered deviant behavior in the United States because most people do not approve of it, and their disapproval takes the form of condemnation, stigmatization, and punishment (Goode, 1990).

People typically consider (and react to) an individual's sexual orientation as either heterosexual or homosexual, but this is not always the case. In their famous report on sexuality in the United States, Kinsey and his associates (Kinsey, Pomeroy, and Martin, 1948) revealed that almost one-half of American men fell between the group who were exclusively heterosexual and those who were exclusively homosexual. Approximately 37 percent of white American males had at least one homosexual experience between their teenage years and old age.

The prevalence of homosexuality can be especially high in institutions like the military and prisons where individuals are segregated by sex for extended periods of time. Sometimes referred to as *situational homosexuality*, this behavior is more a function of available alternatives than of sexual preference. In prison, one has only three choices regarding sexuality: abstinence, masturbation, and homosexuality (Little, 1989). One study found prison homosexuality especially prevalent for females, with over 50 percent of inmates sexually active with other women (Ward and Kassebaum, 1965). Only 5 percent were homosexually active before entering prison.

Efforts to discover the cause(s) of homosexuality, especially one specific reason, have not been successful. *Biological explanations* have focused on chemical or hormonal unbalances in the body as well as genetically determined difference between "straight" and gay people. Results of studies that examined hormonal levels of homosexuals and heterosexuals have been described as inconclusive, contradictory, and methodologically suspect (Nass and Fisher, 1988). However, biological interpretations were bolstered with the publication of two studies in 1991. In the first study, a team of researchers found that a tiny section (the size of a grain of sand) of the hypothalamus (located in the brain) that controls sexual behavior was only half as large in homosexual men as it was in heterosexual males, resulting in speculation that the brains of gay men had become "feminized." One neurologist stated that this discovery "would begin to suggest why male homosexuality is present in most human populations despite cultural constraints" (in Maugh and Zamichow, 1991, p. A12).

The second study (reported in Maugh, 1991) examined fifty-six pairs of *identical* twin males in which at least one member of the pair was gay. Inasmuch as identical twins have the exact genetic makeup, one would expect the majority (if not all) of brothers also to be homosexual. This is what researchers found in 52 percent of the cases. A second group (fifty-four pairs in which at least one brother was gay) of *fraternal* twins was also examined. In this group, in which brothers share only some of their genes, 22 percent of the brothers were gay. In a third group of fifty-seven pairs of *adoptive* brothers, only 11 percent of the time were both men homosexual. A similar study of female homosexuals found that when one of a set of identical twins was a lesbian, in 48 percent of the cases the second twin was also a lesbian. However, only 16 percent of nonidentical twin sisters were also homosexual (Maugh, 1993).

According to one of the authors of this study on male homosexuality, "The research strongly suggests a genetic contribution to sexual orientation" (Maugh, 1991, p. A43). The key word in that summary statement is "contribution." If genetic factors were solely responsible for sexual orientation, why were both identical twins homosexual in only 52 percent of the cases for males and 48 percent of the cases for females? Why didn't both twins have the same sexual proclivity in each and every case?

A study by George Ebers of the University of Western Ontario of 52 pairs of gay brothers failed to produce a linkage of homosexuality on the X chromosome or anywhere else (Horgan, 1995). A twin study in Minnesota concluded that there was "no significant genetic effects" for same-sex sexual encounters or sexual orientation for men or women (Hershberger, 1995). According to neurobiologist Evan Balaban (Horgan, 1995, p. 26), despite the claims of various researchers and the media on the genetic link to alcoholism, mental illness, and homosexuality, there is no solid evidence to support this position.

Violence

The recent decline in crimes against persons notwithstanding, the United States is still a very violent society. A 1991 Senate Judiciary Committee report noted that the United States is "the most violent and self-destructive nation on earth" ("U.S. Leads World," 1991). Although the statement that "Violence is as American as apple pie" may be an exaggeration, few people would doubt the magnitude and seriousness of this problem. Of the 12,475,634 index crimes known to police in 1998, 12.2 percent (1,531,044) were crimes of violence (murder, robbery, rape, and aggravated assault). Of particular concern to many observers is the amount of violence experienced by children both as perpetrators and victims. For example, over the past few years the U.S. has accounted for almost 75 percent of all the murders of children among the world's 26 industrialized countries. In addition, the rate of juvenile crime (including violent juvenile crime) has escalated faster than that of adult crimes (Havemann, 1997). In this section we will examine some crimes of violence as well as the relation between guns and violent crime.

Murder Criminal homicide is the unlawful killing of one human being by another. Homicide rates in the U.S., which have fluctuated between 6.3 and 10 (per 100,000 population) over the past decade, are three to ten times higher than in other comparable modern industrial states such as Japan, Austria, France, Canada, and New Zealand. As is the case in other crimes of violence (with the exception of rape), criminal homicide is overwhelmingly a crime committed by males against other males. From the most to least frequent, gender relations in criminal homicide are as follows: males killing males, males killing females, females killing males, and females killing females. The average age of people arrested for murder has declined from 32.5 years in 1965, to 27 in the mid-1990s. This drop is largely a function of the number of juveniles (12 to 17 years of age) arrested for murder, which increased from 1,860 in 1980 to 3,790 in 1993 before beginning to decline in 1994.

Comprising just under 13 percent of the overall U.S. population, African Americans in any given year account for roughly 50 percent of the nation's killers and 50 percent of the victims. From these latter statistics one might accurately surmise that homicide is overwhelmingly an intraracial crime. For example, based on one victim/one offender incidents in 1998, 94 percent of black victims were slain by black offenders, and 86 percent of white victims were killed by white assailants. The geography of criminal homicide reveals that this behavior is disproportionately a big-city crime with homicide rates in the nation's largest urban areas nearly twice as high as rates in smaller cities and rural districts. While homicide rates are lowest in the Midwest, traditionally they have been highest in the South with the Western United States a close second.

Sociologists David Luckenbill and Daniel Doyle (1989) posed the question, "What is there about residing in an urban or southern area that generates a high rate of violence?" They noted that a significant number of people in these areas (young, male, lower-income) have a lifestyle characterized by "disputatiousness." That is, these individuals share a culturally transmitted willingness to settle disputes (especially ones perceived to be a threat to their masculinity or status) by using physical force. In an earlier, related work Luckenbill (1977) stated that homicide is the product of a "character contest." During the course of an argument, insults and threats are traded until escalating tension brings the matter to a point of no return, with participants and bystanders agreeing that the "contest" can be resolved only by violence. Obviously the more people settle their disputes by physical force, the greater the likelihood that someone will be killed, even if the intent to do so is absent. Many homicides take this form and can be characterized as overly successful aggravated assaults: A wants to hurt B (not to kill him), but in the heat of battle and with use of weapons, B ends up dead.

Robbery This crime involves the taking of something of value from an individual either by force, the threat of force, or by placing the victim in a state of fear. Robberies can be divided into two categories; personal ("muggings," for example), and commercial (banks, convenience stores, liquor stores, etc.). According to UCR data (crimes known to police), robbery rates reached a high of 272.7 incidents per 100,000 population in 1991, and declined to a rate of 165.2 in 1998. Approximately two-thirds of robberies are personal with overall robbery rates being especially high in cities of over one million population.

A significant number of robberies are committed by *addict robbers,* individuals supporting their drug habits via this form of crime (Conklin, 1972). Eric Baumer and his colleagues (Baumer, Lauritsen, and Wright, 1998) noted that robbery and burglary rates move in tandem (that is, they were both increasing or decreasing at the same time) for decades. However, this pattern changed radically in the late 1980s. According to the researchers, with the proliferation of crack cocaine in urban America, there was an *increase* in violent crime (including robbery) and a concomitant *decrease* in property crime. Because crack cocaine produces a short, intense "high" (typically no more than 10 minutes), and an almost immediate (ongoing) craving for mind-altering experience, crack users are always in need of drug money. Inasmuch as crack addicts find it virtually impossible to work, these individuals support their habit via crime. As the crack "epidemic" spread, burglary became less of a viable crime option because (1) people are typically home during late night and early morning hours when crack use is the heaviest; (2) users had little if any skills in overcoming sophisticated alarm systems that protect commercial establishments and homes; and (3) neighborhoods where crack use is most prevalent had already been saturated with relatively inexpensive "hot" merchandise. The demand for stolen guns, jewelry, and electronic goods had decreased significantly, and translating merchandise into drug money takes both time and effort. Whereas burglary was becoming less attractive for crack users, robbery "usually nets cash directly and is easily perpetuated during the hours of darkness when the streets are less crowded" (Baumer, Lauritzen, and Wright, 1998, p. 318).

These findings are in line with what has been referred to as the "de-skilling" of crime. As the result of ever-increasing technology, many crime targets are more difficult to penetrate. For example, a burglar attempting to steal precious stones from a jewelry store would have to make a double entry, successfully bypassing a sophisticated burglar alarm and then opening ("cracking") an equally sophisticated safe. While *target hardening* may deter people from attempting to burglarize commercial establishments, it does not necessarily reduce their deviant motivation, that is, they still intend to enrich themselves by way of illegal activity. Therefore, a latent or unintended consequence of technological change is that a certain (and unknown) amount of nonconfrontational property crimes are being replaced by a crime of violence—robbery.

Rape A recent National Crime Victimization Survey (NCVS) study of almost 400,000 women is the most comprehensive source of data regarding violent crimes against females ever collected in the United States. Entitled *Violence Against Women* (Bachman, 1994), the report defined rape as "forced sexual intercourse" and includes both psychological coercion as well as physical force. Forced sexual intercourse means vaginal, anal, and/or oral penetration by the offender(s). This category also includes incidents where the penetration is from a foreign object such as a bottle" (p. 14). The data indicated that annually between 1987 and 1991, approximately 58,600 females 12 years of age and older were victims of a completed rape, and another 73,500 females were targets of an attempted rape. The following are some of the major findings presented in the *Violence Against Women* report:

- Rape victims were more likely to be assaulted by someone they knew (55 percent) than by a stranger (44 percent).
- Women raped by a stranger were more likely to be physically harmed (and suffer serious injuries) than women raped by someone they knew.
- Women in the lowest annual family income level of under $10,000 had the highest rates of rape victimization. Rates of rape victimization *increased* as income levels *decreased*.
- Females between 12 and 34 years of age were much more likely to be rape victims than females in the 35 and older category. Never married and di-

vorced/separated women had significantly higher rates of rape victimization than married or widowed women.
- Less than 10 percent of all rapes involved more than one offender.

Criminologist Jay Livingston (1996) notes that a category of rape likely to be "missed" by both the UCR and NCVS are those crimes committed by men with whom the victim has a close relationship such as a husband or lover. Victims may be quite reluctant to inform either the police or an NCVS interviewer of such a crime. Livingston states that the offender may even be in the house when the interview is being conducted. A study of college women found that 15.4 percent of the respondents stated they had experienced a situation that met the legal definition of rape during a one-year period, while an additional 12.1 percent of these females reported at least one or more incidents of attempted rape (Lanier et al., 1998). Other researchers found that one in 12 male students interviewed reported having committed an act that met the legal definition of rape or attempted rape (Koss and Harvey, 1991).

Prior to the late 1970s in the United States, a man having forced sex with his wife was not guilty of committing a crime. This "marital exemption" meant that women had no legal recourse to the unwanted sexual advances/acts of their husbands. Whereas only three states had laws against marital rape in 1980, today almost every state has such statutes in place. Marital rape is often accompanied by wife beating and may be more a mechanism of control and dominance than a manifestation of sexual interest (Allison and Wrightsman, 1993). Marital rapes can be especially traumatic to the victim because they have to live with the offender (Finkelhor and Yllo, 1983).

Stalking A relatively new *crime*, stalking is "a course of conduct directed at a specific person that involves repeated visual or physical proximity, nonconsensual communication, or verbal, written or implied threats, or a combination thereof, that would cause a reasonable person fear" (Tjaden and Thoennes, 1998 p. 2). California passed the first antistalking law in 1950, and by 1995 all 50 states and the District of Columbia had enacted similar legislation. Although much has been written about this phenomenon over the past 15 years (especially "celebrity" stalking), a 1998 nationally representative telephone survey of 8,000 men and 8,000 women 18 years of age and older was the first comprehensive study of stalking.

Analysis of survey data indicated that stalking is considerably more prevalent than previously thought. Just over 8 percent of women and 2.2 percent of men

TABLE 8.4

Percentage and Estimated Number of Men and Women Stalked in Lifetime

Group	Persons Stalked in Lifetime	
	Percentage[a]	Estimated Number[b]
Men (N = 8,000)	2.2	2,040,460
Women (N = 8,000)	8.1	8,156,460

[a]Differences between men and women are significant at ≤ .001.

[b]Based on estimates of men and women aged 18 years and older, U.S. Bureau of the Census, Current Population Survey, 1995.

Source: *Stalking in America: Findings from the National Violence Against Women Survey,* by Patricia Tjaden and Nancy Thoennes, National Institute of Justice Centers for Disease Control and Prevention—Research Brief, p. 3, April 1998.

reported being stalked sometime in their lives (See Tables 8.4 and 8.5). Seventy-eight percent of stalking victims are female and 87 percent of stalking offenders are male. Women are most likely to be stalked (62 percent of female victims) by a spouse/ex-spouse, cohabiting partner/ex-partner, or a date/ex-date, while men are typically stalked (70 percent of male victims) by an acquaintance or stranger. Regarding females, 52 percent of victims are between 18 and 29 years of age. Just over 4 of 5 women stalked by a current/former husband or cohabiting partner were also physically assaulted by that same individual at some point in their relationship. Thirty-one percent of females stalked by a husband/ex-husband or cohabiting partner had been sexually assaulted by that same partner. The data indicate that American Indian/Alaskan Native women are *more* likely to be stalked than females in other racial/ethnic groups, while Pacific Islander and Asian women are *less* likely to be so

victimized. However, because of the number of minority women in the sample, these findings have to be viewed with caution (Tjaden and Thoennes, 1998).

Although stalking can produce a high level of fear and lead to a violent confrontation, less than 50 percent of victims in the survey (male and female) were directly threatened by offenders. When asked why they were stalked the three most prevalent responses were that the stalker wanted to control the victim (21 percent of responses), the offender wanted to keep the victim in a current relationship (20 percent of responses), and the offender wanted to scare the victim (16 percent of responses). Approximately two-thirds of stalking cases last a year or less with the average case continuing for 1.8 years (Tjaden and Thoennes, 1998).

Street Gangs and Violence   While virtually all academic researchers and criminal justice practitioners agree that the number of gangs and gang members have increased over the past 25 years, there is no consensus on the scope of this escalation. Consider the following recent estimates on the prevalence of gangs and gang members in the United States: 4,881 and 249,324 (Wilson, 1994), 8,625 and 249,324 (Curry and Decker, 1998), 16,000 and 500,000 ("Gangs in the Heartland," 1996), and 23,000 and 625,000 (Lozada, 1996). A major reason for the tremendous disparity in these figures is that there is no one definition of a gang that is accepted and utilized by the police, the courts, researchers, community activists, or anyone else that is interested in and attempts to monitor gangs and gang activity.

While there is little chance a definition that proves acceptable to all parties will emerge, the following conceptualization of "What is a gang?"

TABLE 8.5

Percentage and Estimated Number of Men and Women Stalked in Previous 12 Months

Group	Persons Stalked in Previous 12 Months	
	Percentage[a]	Estimated Number[b]
Men (N = 8,000)	0.4	370,990
Women (N = 8,000)	1.0	1,006,970

[a]Differences between men and women are significant at ≤ .001.

[b]Based on estimates of men and women aged 18 years and older, U.S. Bureau of the Census, Current Population Survey, 1995.

Source: *Stalking in America: Findings from the National Violence Against Women Survey,* by Patricia Tjaden and Nancy Thoennes, National Institute of Justice Centers for Disease Control and Prevention—Research Brief, p. 3, April 1998.

With the flair of actors, these young gang members display hand signs that identify their group. "Throwing hand signs" also increases in-group solidarity and helps distinguish "gang bangers" from outsiders and rival groups.

Deviant and Criminal Behavior

offered by G. David Curry and Scott Decker (1998, pp. 3–6) appears to be especially useful from a sociological perspective.

1. A gang is a *group* of minimally two members that is typically larger (and in some case significantly larger) than this number.
2. *Symbols* and *communication* are defining aspects of gangs. Clothing (color, style, the manner in which apparel is worn) and symbols (hand signs, for example) identify gang membership with the latter also a form of nonverbal communication. Graffiti is also a mechanism of conversing commonly used by gang members.
3. Gangs must have *permanence,* that is, they must exist for a prolonged period of time, at least one year.
4. Gangs have a *turf,* or some physical territory that the group claims as its own. (Curry and Decker note that this component of the definition becomes problematic with Asian "gangs" that do not declare or stake out a turf, but otherwise meet the remaining gang criteria.)
5. What distinguishes a gang from other groups is involvement in *crime,* and in some cases violent crime.

Street gangs are especially numerous in large cities, especially New York City, Chicago, Los Angeles, and Philadelphia. Chicago alone is reputed to have as many as 100,000 gang members (Painter and Weisel, 1997). Malcolm Klein (in "Gangs in the Heartland," 1997) estimates that whereas 100 cities and towns had active gangs in 1970, that number had climbed to almost 800 locales in the mid-1990s. The rapid proliferation of gangs is a function of family members of gangs relocating, the emergence of local gangs, and members of "supergangs" attempting to extend their territory. Records of the Illinois State Police indicate that Chicago-based gang members have been spotted in every county in the state ("Gangs in the Heartland," 1997), while members of the Los Angeles "Crips" and "Bloods," have migrated to 45 western and midwestern cities (Wilson, 1994). Some observers are of the opinion that the semi-permanent if not permanent movement of gang members for criminal purposes has been overstated and undersubstantiated.

Prior to the late 1950s most gang members were white males of European heritage. However, beginning in the 1960s the racial/ethnic composition of these groups began to change, and by the 1970s approximately 80 percent of gang members were African American and Hispanic. In a heterogeneous city like Los Angeles, gang members come from a variety of backgrounds including Chinese, Vietnamese, Filipino, Korean, El Salvadoran, Guatemalan, Samoan, and Jamaican.

Youth gangs have become increasingly violent over the years (killing each other as well as people who are not gang members) regardless of whether this behavior is motivated by long-standing turf wars with rival gangs, or is an effort to protect and expand one's territory primarily to enhance the business of drug dealing. In Los Angeles County, the gang-related homicide rate for African-American teenage males (ages 15 to 19) jumped from 60.5 per 100,000 county residents in 1979–1981, to 192 per 100,000 in 1989–1991. Almost 7,300 gang-related homicides were recorded in that California county between 1979 and 1994 ("Gang Related Homicides," 1995). In some cities as of late, one in four homicide victims was a gang member (Curry and Decker, 1998).

Curry and Decker (1998) note that gang members are often both perpetrators as well as victims of violence. This is especially true of females. As part of the initiation ceremony (into the gang), some females interviewed by Molidor (1996) commented on having to "pull a train," that is, engaging in sex with as many as 11 male gang members in one night. While this sexual initiation may be voluntary, at times "it resembles rape" (p. 255). As is the case with gangs and gang members in general, guesstimates of the number of female gang members range from 3.7 to 10 percent (in 1975) of the total population of this subculture. However, no recent data support the 10 percent figure which most authorities believe is too high.

Guns, Violence, and Politics The controversy regarding the relationship between guns and violence (especially criminal violence) has been one of the most contentious disputes in recent American history. From the National Rifle Association (NRA) perspective, the private ownership of firearms is an American birthright guaranteed in the U.S. Constitution. Responsible gun owners not only enjoy activities such as target shooting and hunting, but law-abiding armed citizens can actually deter crime. After analyzing crime data from all 3,054 counties in the United States from 1974 to 1994, John R. Lott Jr. (1998) concluded that an increase in the number of people with concealed-gun permits was associated with a decrease in the incidence of violent crime. Five years after concealed-gun permits went into effect, murder rates declined by "at least" 15 percent, rape by 9 percent, and robbery by 11 percent. Lott gives examples of armed criminals being stopped from shooting people by gun-toting, law-abiding citizens.

Gun control advocates argue that if the United States was not awash with more than 225 *million* firearms (including approximately 75 million hand-guns) a significant number of the 881,000 violent crimes committed with handguns in 1993 would not have been committed in the first place. While some NRA opponents would like to see a legal ban on all privately owned firearms, most gun control advocates have a less ambitious objective, that is, to rid the nation of handguns (including inexpensive "Saturday Night Specials") and military-style assault weapons. Handguns are increasingly the weapons of choice of killers in this country. Although they comprise about one-third of all firearms, these easily concealable weapons are used in almost two-thirds of all homicides (Shapiro et al., 1998). It is with these statistics in mind that gun control advocates take issue with the slogan that "Guns don't kill people, people kill people." They argue that while this now popular piece of folk wisdom is true in a literal sense, it is also quite meaningless. UCR statistics clearly indicate that people with guns kill more individuals than people without guns.

Whereas the NRA claims that gun control laws do not effectively keep guns out of the hands of criminals ("When guns are outlawed only outlaws will have guns"), supporters of much more stringent gun laws counter that firearms enthusiasts have worked hard (and successfully) to make sure that no comprehensive gun control legislation is passed. Before they ever become law, prospective gun control bills are watered down to the point where they are all but useless. According to gun control advocates one gun control law that has saved lives is the Brady Bill, legislation that is reputed to have kept weapons out of the hands of approximately 242,000 felons, fugitives, and drug addicts between 1994 and 1998 (Alter, 1998). While many of these individuals undoubtedly purchased guns illegally and/or stole firearms, it is just as likely to assume that many (perhaps many more) did not.

In one sense the gun/gun-control battle has already been fought and won by the NRA and its allies. Even if the manufacture and sale of handguns would come to an immediate halt, and the possession of such weapons was deemed illegal, only a small percentage of the 75 million handguns owned by private citizens would ever be turned over to the law enforcement officials. Although about 2 million firearms are added to the U.S. arsenal each year, the annual production of these weapons has decreased from 4.4 million in 1989 to 3.8 million in 1996 (Walsh, 1998). In an attempt to boost sales, gun manufacturers have been targeting women (to date unsuccessfully) as prospective gun enthusiasts and owners (Walsh, 1998). At least one gun maker offers handguns with pink grips and advertises three small weapons under the caption "3 Little Ladies That Get the Job Done" (Levin, 1997). With the blessing of gun manufacturers, the NRA's "Eddie Eagle" program ostensibly teaches gun etiquette and safety to children. Critics contend that this cartoon-like character is the gun makers' equivalent of Joe Camel, and that the real agenda is to turn children into adolescent and then adult firearms consumers.

In a new twist to the gun rights/gun control controversy, New Orleans and Chicago (among other cities) recently filed lawsuits against gun manufacturers arguing that these companies are liable for the medical bills incurred by people wounded in gun-related crimes. In February, 1999, a federal jury in New York City found that 15 of 25 gun manufacturers named in a civil law suit (regarding three area shootings) were responsible for permitting these weapons to fall into the hands of criminals. The jury concluded that the makers of handguns oversupply gun-friendly markets (mostly in the southern states) with the full knowledge that excess firearms eventually make their way into states with stricter handgun laws (Hays, 1999). One economist testified that 90 percent of the handguns used in New York City crimes came from southern states.

Just as tobacco companies have been sued for contributing to the death of smokers, some gun control advocates are of the opinion that verdicts against gun manufacturers will bring some regulation and accountability to an industry that has until recently had little to fear from either lawmakers or the courts. It remains to be seen what consequences lawsuits will have on the sale and distribution of handguns as well as their use in violent crimes, suicides, and accidents.

White-Collar Crime

The two forms of *white-collar* crime are occupational and organizational (Clinard, 1983). **Occupational crime** is committed by individuals in the course of their work against organizations for personal gain (Glasberg and Skidmore, 1998). These offenses are not limited to business people and high-status professionals (physicians, attorney, politicians, etc.) but can be committed in one form or another by almost anyone who is employed. Individuals working as waiters, truck drivers, supermarket clerks, taxi drivers, fishermen, garbage collectors, even prison guards, to name but a few blue-collar occupations, engage in a wide variety of work-related crimes (Barlow, 1990). For example, a bartender can charge a customer $20 for a round of drinks, ring up a $15 sale on the register and pocket the $5 difference. People stealing tools, supplies, and/or the products they help make from the workplace is a common form of occupational crime.

Like other law violators, individuals who commit occupational crime engage in a form of mental gymnastics or rationalizations whereby they convince themselves (and others) that their behavior is "noncriminal," even "necessary" (Cressey, 1953; Clinard, 1974). These people "neutralize" the laws they violate (that is, they convince themselves these statutes do not apply to them) by using a number of rationalizations (Sykes and Matza, 1957). Justifications in the form of "the company can afford it," "they owe me that much and more," and "everybody does it" allow them to maintain a positive self-image in spite of their criminal activity.

Organizational crimes are offenses committed by individuals or groups to further the goals of a particular organization. **Corporate crime** is a type of organizational crime behavior committed by representatives of institutions (typically managers and executives) on behalf of those institutions (Glasberg and Skidmore, 1998). These illegal acts also include the crimes of the organization itself (Clinard, 1974). According to Clinard and Yeager (1980), two of the foremost authorities in the area of corporate crime, three industries seem to violate government regulations and laws more than any others. The oil industry has been involved in the restriction of independent dealers, excessive profits, contrived shortages, misleading advertising, and interlocking directorates. The auto industry has engaged in deceptive advertising, unreliable warranties, unfair dealer relations, and violations of safety standards. The pharmaceutical industry has been guilty of false advertising, inferior product quality, and excessive markups.

The following is a list of recent corporate crimes that came to the attention of authorities and were successfully prosecuted (Sherrill, 1997; Holmstrom, 1997):

- The Archer Daniels Midland Corporation pleaded guilty to conspiring to fix prices of a feed supplement for livestock as well as an ingredient used in making soft drinks and detergents. The company was fined $100 million, the single largest monetary penalty in a criminal antitrust case.
- For their part in engaging in a practice called "churning," the Prudential insurance company was fined $35 million and agreed to pay restitution to clients of more than $1 billion. Affecting as many as 10 million customers, churning was the name for talking people into using the cash value of their *old* policies to pay the premiums on *new*, more expensive policies. However, these individuals were not told that upgrading policies would "eat up" their equity (the cash value of the

old policy) leaving them with insurance they could not afford, and, eventually, no coverage.
- A cruise ship line was fined $500,000 for illegally dumping garbage into the sea. Another cruise ship company was convicted of releasing waste oil in bilge water near Puerto Rico. The company also falsified records stating that the oil had been removed from the water.
- Economist Alan Krueger (Sherrill, 1997) stated that as many as 3 million American workers are paid less than the legal minimum wage. Among the worst offenders are the garment industry, trucking companies, construction firms, and restaurants. In addition, not being paid the overtime wages they are entitled to may cost employees up to $19 billion a year.

While the fines levied against corporate offenders may appear to be substantial, they are often inconsequential when compared to a company's annual profits and overall net worth. Robert Sherrill (1997) noted that the $100 million the Archer Daniels Midland company was fined is relatively small change as the company had $13.6 *billion* in revenues from its agricultural products in a recent fiscal year. The way some statutes are currently written, it makes economic sense to violate (at least occasionally) these laws. "Violating the minimum-wage law has a certain economic logic to it because the employer, if caught, usually has to pay only the back wages that were due. Penalties are generally levied only on repeat offenders" (Krueger in Sherrill, 1997, p. 16).

Both the certainty and severity of punishment for engaging in occupational crime and (especially) corporate crime are relatively low. As one observer noted, the only corporate price fixers likely to be apprehended for their transgressions are those that are extremely greedy or extremely careless ("Catch Us if You Can," 1996). The number of investigators and prosecutors working this category of offenses as compared to street crimes is exceedingly small. Also, without "hard evidence" it is almost impossible to gain a conviction for price rigging, and corporate boardrooms (where these crimes often occur) are hardly accessible to the general public or law enforcement officials.

Finally, the punishment for corporate offenses in the U.S. has traditionally been no more than the proverbial slap on the wrist. Note that in the examples of corporate crime given, no company officials were imprisoned, even in cases where the public was victimized to the amount of tens of millions of dollars. Judges continue to treat occupational and corporate criminals with considerable leniency (see Figure 8.2).

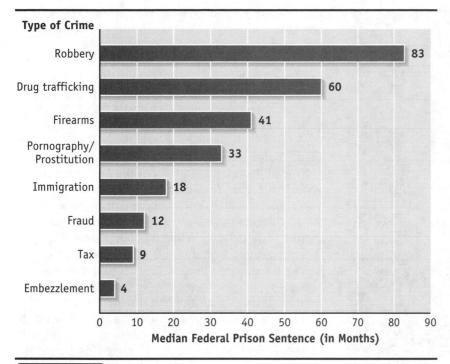

Type of Crime

Robbery	83
Drug trafficking	60
Firearms	41
Pornography/Prostitution	33
Immigration	18
Fraud	12
Tax	9
Embezzlement	4

Median Federal Prison Sentence (in Months)

FIGURE 8.2

Crime and Punishment

Drug and Alcohol Abuse

The crack-cocaine epidemic that began in the mid-1980s and started to wane in the early to mid-1990s is but the latest drug crisis to occur in the United States. These epidemics follow a cycle of predictable events that play themselves out over a number of years (Musto in Kagan, 1989). The recent "crack crisis," therefore, is similar to an earlier cocaine era that began in the 1880s and the marijuana-hallucinogen years of the 1960s.

In the initial phase of the cycle, one or more drugs are "discovered" and considered harmless (if not beneficial) by responsible people. In the absence of proof to the contrary from medical experts, the drugs are generally accepted and used by a significant portion of the population. As a result of deaths and a rising crime rate, health officials re-evaluate the harmful effects of drugs. The weight of changing public opinion and accumulated scientific evidence begins to stem the use of drugs. At this point in the cycle, people start to associate drug use with the lower classes as well as racial and ethnic minorities, regardless of the truth of this association. Drug use becomes a powerful symbol of evil and increasingly differentiates middle-class America from the hated and feared lower-class minorities (Kagan, 1989).

Some have argued that drug use is an inevitable consequence of human nature. Psychopharmacologist Ronald K. Siegel stated, "I have come to the view

that humans have a need—perhaps even a drive—to alter their state of consciousness from time to time" (Beaty, 1989, p. 58). Donald X. Freeman, an expert on substance abuse policy, thinks that drugs have such a powerful allure simply because they make people feel so good (Parachini, 1986). Even if this practice does have a biological basis, it does not negate the fact that people learn how to use and abuse drugs; they do not instinctively smoke crack or know how to freebase cocaine. In addition, a biological explanation in and of itself does not tell us why the rate of drug use varies so dramatically both between and within cultures and from one historical period to the next. Any biological drive toward mind-altering substances would have to be extremely malleable and susceptible to social pressures, values, and norms to account for the fundamental observation that tens of millions of people do not use drugs.

The long use and transitory acceptance of drugs as outlined by Musto (in Kagan, 1989) have led to hundreds of studies conducted in an effort to discover why people use and abuse mind-altering substances. Although the results have been varied and at times contradictory, one general and important finding has emerged: Drug use, at least initially, is learned behavior. Even if there is such a thing as an addictive personality, individuals must learn where to buy drugs and how to use them, as well as how to rationalize such use to themselves and others. We

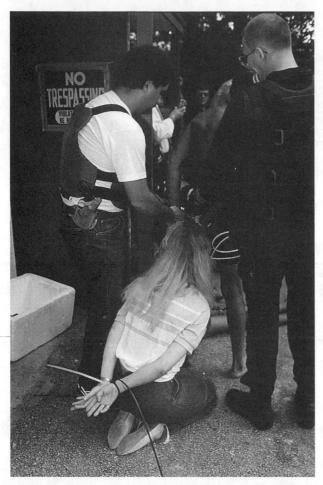

Each year in the United States well over a million people are arrested for illegal drug offenses (possession or trafficking). In 1980, about six percent of inmates in state prisons were serving time for drug crimes, a figure that increased to almost 25 percent by the mid 1990s. Proponents of drug legalization argue that substance abuse offenses needlessly waste vast amounts of criminal justice system resources that could be directed at more serious crimes.

know that some of these attitudes and patterns of behavior are learned in ghettos, in middle-class neighborhoods, and in corporate boardrooms. With users from all social classes and every racial and ethnic background and occupation, it is evident that people use, abuse, and deal drugs for a number of reasons: because they do not have enough money or have too much, because they are attempting to escape painful situations or seek adventure, because they are depressed or overjoyed, bored or have too much to do. Regardless of whether people are pushed by emotional problems or pulled by the allure of money and excitement, drug use is learned and reinforced in a social context (Bryjak, 1990).

Data from the government's annual National Household Survey on Drug Abuse (NHSDA) indicate that the use of most drugs increased from the early to late 1970s; peaked in 1985 when some 37 million people acknowledged using an illegal substance, and then declined. By 1988, that number had plummeted to 28 million and remained low until 1992 when slight increases in marijuana and LSD use were reported by eighth graders and college students. A 1993 nationwide survey of 50,000 junior and senior high school students revealed a marked increase in marijuana use (and smaller rises in the use of other drugs) among high school students. Data from the 1997 NHSDA revealed that drug abuse among individuals 12 to 17 years of age was up as 11.4 percent of those surveyed stated they had used an illicit drug within the past month. Although marijuana was the preferred drug in this age group, a total of 3.9 million teenagers used heroin for the first time in 1996; this latter number being a significant increase over the 2.2 million who used that narcotic for the first time in 1995.

The use of inhalants (especially aerosol cans of cleaning products and spray paints as well as glue) in the 12-to-17-year-old age category has also increased in the first half of the 1990s (Neumark, Delva, and Anthony, 1998). Users spray the contents of these products into plastic bags and then inhale the fumes, a process called "huffing" or "sniffing." Because of the toxicity of these chemicals, huffing is estimated to result in more brain damage than the effects of all other drugs combined. In spite of the health risks that inhalants pose, only 40 percent of high school students view these substances as dangerous. As a result of its high toxicity, relatively easy access (inhalants are not illegal), and the scant attention paid to this form of drug abuse when compared to other mind-altering substances, huffing has been referred to as the "Silent Epidemic" (Neumark, Delva, and Anthony, 1998).

High rates of drug use on the part of young people coupled with a forthcoming "demographic explosion" of this age group does not bode well for the overall substance abuse problem in this country. Speaking of this age/drug-use-rate relationship, Richard Clayton (Kolata, 1996, p. B10) stated that "By 2010 we will have more teenagers than at any time in history. We are at the front end of what could be a disaster for the whole society."

Another form of drug use and abuse prevalent among young people involves the consumption of alcohol. A Harvard University study of the drinking habits of 17,000 college students revealed that 84 percent of the respondents reported drinking alcohol on a regular basis during the academic year. Almost 44 percent of students said they engaged in "binge drinking," that is, downing five or more drinks for a male and four or more for a female in a short period

Focus on
South Africa

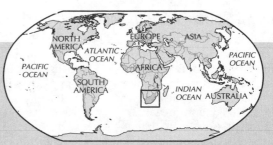

Population: 43,426,386
Life Expectancy at Birth (years): Male—52.68;
Female—56.90
Form of Government: Republic
Major Religions: Christian (68%); Traditional, Animistic (29%)
Major Racial and Ethnic Groups: Black (75%); White (14%);
Colored (9%)
Population Doubling Time: 43 years
Per Capita GNP (1997 U.S. dollars): $3,210
Principal Economic Activities: Industry; Agriculture; Mining
Colonial Experience: Former Dutch, later British, colony
Adult Literacy Rate: 82% Male—82%; Female—82%

The Demise of Apartheid and Death in the Streets

One significant, latent (unintended and unanticipated) consequence of the political/social transition that began in South Africa in 1991 has been the tremendous increase in crime, especially crimes of violence. With the government's recognition of the previously banned African National Congress (ANC), and the release of Nelson Mandela from prison after serving more than 27 years of a life sentence, 1991 was a pivotal year in South African history.

In 1994, the year Mandela was elected president and the legal system of racial segregation or "apartheid" was dismantled, South Africa had a criminal homicide rate of 53.5 (per 100,000), prompting the World Health Organization to note that it was the most murderous country in the world (Ransdell, 1995). In the city of Cape Town that figure was 67.7, and in some designated "homicide areas" the rate was even higher. By way of comparison, murder rates in Russia (the second most murderous nation), the United States, and the United Kingdom were 30.4, 9.8, and 1, respectively, with an international average of 5.5. The risk of being a criminal homicide victim was 20 time greater for a black South African than for a white citizen of that country (Louw, 1997). A

study of murder and assault rates in 72 nations found that these offenses accounted for, on average, 3 percent of all crimes known to police, whereas they comprised 16 percent of all such crimes in South Africa (Matloff, 1995). One observer noted that "While violence and lawlessness are nothing new in South Africa, people of all classes and colours are being battered by the intensity of and increase in crime in the post-apartheid era" (in Gilbert, 1996, p. 876).

Carjacking increased from under 1,900 incidents in the first six months of 1993 to over 4,200 cases in the first half of 1998, with dozens of people being killed during the commission of these crimes. Robbers as young as 12 years old armed with AK-47s (military assault rifles) order drivers out of cars at gunpoint and shoot their victims if they do not comply. A South African motorist is 10 times more likely to be a carjacking victim than is a driver in the United States (Wilkerson, 1994). Some stolen vehicles end up in "chop shops" to be disassembled for parts while others are shipped to neighboring countries. Organized gangs of carjackers routinely take orders for specific cars to steal. Insurance rates have increased by more than 50 percent

resulting in 70 percent of South African cars having no coverage at all. Taxi drivers are hijacked at the end of their shifts (when they are carrying the most money) and trucks are commandeered for their cargo (Wilkerson, 1994).

The number of rapes known to police increased from 20,000 in 1990 to 37,000 in 1995. If only one of 35 rapes is reported to authorities as the group Rape Crisis estimates, then over 1.25 million females—on average 3,500 a day—were raped in that latter year (Louw, 1997). This is a staggering figure in a nation of 40 million people.

A unique form of South African crime dubbed "taxi violence" stems from the fierce competition among taxi and minibus companies for customers who reside in mostly impoverished communities. Often resulting in death of innocent bystanders, these crimes are considered a major contributing factor to the nation's high level of criminal violence (Gilbert, 1996; Richburg, 1997).

Heavily armed gangs of between 15 and 30 members have taken to robbing banks and armored cars. There are so many bank robberies that some financial institutions provide regular counseling sessions for their employees (Richburg, 1997). With the lifting of trade sanctions in the post-apartheid era, South Africa has become a much more "open" society. For example, there has been a significant increase in the number of incoming and outgoing international flights, as well as an influx of people from Nigeria and Zaire, some of whom are drug couriers (Charney, 1996). South Africa appears to be the latest destination for international drug dealers who are always looking for new markets. Authorities estimate that approximately 500 well-financed and armed gangs/syndicates, many of which are extremely violent, operate throughout the country. Along with distributing a variety of drugs these gangs are engaged in vehicle theft, commercial crime, and the smuggling of gold and diamonds (in Lyman, 1996; Louw, 1997).

Explanations for South Africa's recent upsurge in criminal violence are numerous and diverse. Many observers believe this problem is rooted in the apartheid era when political demonstrations by blacks toward the end of dismantling a system of enforced racial segregation triggered brutal responses on the part of the police and military. In addition, the government engaged in a deliberate policy of making the black townships ungovernable. From this essentially "culture of violence" perspective, people became habituated to a life of violence. The ever-increasing frustration and rage that mounted as a consequence of living in abject poverty also contributed to violent crime. Guns smuggled into South Africa during the years of political struggle meant that much of this violence would lead to serious bodily injury and death.

As Nelson Mandela noted, the police in apartheid South Africa were neither organized nor deployed to control crime. The "official historian" of the South African police conceded that during this period only 10 percent of the force was engaged in crime detection and investigation. There was also a significant maldistribution of police resources, with approximately 80 percent of the force concentrated in white residential areas while only 8 percent of the officers patrolled black townships (Louw, 1997). In non-

white communities the primary responsibility of the police was to suppress (usually with considerable force) political activity while street crime in these locales was typically ignored. Residents of white neighborhoods were afforded police protection from protesting blacks (Lyman, 1996).

No longer a tool of political repression, police in the new South Africa are, on the whole, barely literate, poorly trained, poorly equipped, corrupt, and ineffective. *New York Times* reporter Suzanne Daley (1997) found that 33 percent of the police force the outgoing National Party left behind does not have a high school diploma, 27 percent of the detectives had never been trained in crime-solving procedures, and 40 percent of officers in Johannesburg did not have driver's licenses.

At a 6:00 A.M. roll call in a Soweto police station, Daley observed that less than half of the officers assigned to the morning shift were present, and of those that reported to work only about 50 percent were wearing uniforms. Officers not properly attired stated they had never been issued uniforms, or that their uniform was in the laundry. In another station 5 of 80 officers were facing criminal charges, one for carjacking. The commander of this precinct stated that 30 of his charges were never enrolled in the six-month police training course (Daley, 1997).

Poverty, the unequal distribution of wealth, and lack of opportunity are considered to be at the root of South Africa's crime problem. The most affluent 20 percent of the population (mostly white) account for 65 percent of all income, while the poorest 20 percent (mostly black) earn only 3 percent (Dunn, 1998). Comparable numbers in the United States are 46.3 percent and 3.6 percent. Whereas unemployment in this country is consistently between 6

and 12 percent, in South Africa people without work comprise between 40 and 50 percent of the labor force. Unemployment in some black townships is estimated to be as high as 65 percent (Ransdell, 1995).

Journalist Des Wilson (1997, p. 15) argues that crime in South Africa is a product of the "un people," those individuals who are "unemployed, uneducated, unskilled, unhoused, unfed, unwell . . . and unsatisfied." The fact that shantytowns exist but a short distance from wealthy suburbs is a constant reminder to the poor that some people are living very well. While this gross disparity in wealth may lead to a sense of hopelessness and withdrawal on the part of many poor individuals, it can trigger resentment and intense anger in others. Wilson (1997) is of the opinion that this anger is the reason why so many robberies in South Africa result in injuries and death.

As a consequence of these "pathologically high rates of violent crime," the populace has become increasingly worried and armed, with gun sales up throughout the country. In 1992, one in ten people regarded crime as the nation's most pressing problem, a figure that jumped to almost one in two by 1995 (Louw, 1997). Many suburban white South Africans live in jail-like compounds surrounded by barbed or razor wire and/or high fences. Homes are equipped with sophisticated warning systems and some individuals carry guard-summoning "panic buttons" everywhere they go. Attack dogs are a routine part of the suburban landscape and executives ride to and from work with armed guards. To combat carjackers, a local company is marketing the "Blaster," an under-the-car flamethrower that at the flip of a switch will send a stream of liquified gas (ignited by a spark) from the nozzles beneath the front doors. "If an attacker is lucky, he will be singed, possibly blinded. If he isn't, he will be flambeed by a seven-foot fireball" (Block, 1999, p. 1). To keep themselves safe from attackers, some households spend up to 25 percent of their annual incomes for safety services and equipment (Matloff, 1995; Chenault, 1997; Wilson, 1997).

While more affluent individuals were hiring private security officers to protect them (in the mid-1990s there were 150,000 police officers and 130,000 private security personnel), poor people were taking justice into their own hands via vigilante groups. However, not all such groups are comprised of impoverished citizens. Members of one of Cape Town's richest and most conservative Islamic mosques have formed a group known as PAGAD, People Against Gangsterism and Drugs (Daley, 1996). These individuals meet regularly to do what they believe the government cannot or will not do: rid their neighborhoods of drug dealers and street criminals. In one highly publicized incident, PAGAD members shot and killed a high-profile drug dealer, set his body on fire, and continued to riddle the dead man with bullets while police and journalists looked on. Not to be outdone by PAGAD, well-armed, crack-smoking drug dealers have taken to the streets demanding police protection. Inasmuch as drug dealers often give money to the poor they have some enthusiastic supporters. Recipients of these gifts note that while the government has done little if anything to improve their lives, local gangsters funnel a portion of their profits back into the community (Daley, 1996).

Bomb disposal unit of the South African Police search for evidence after a bomb exploded at Planet Hollywood in Cape Town. One person was killed and at least 25 injured. A previously unknown Islamic militant group "Muslims against oppression in the world" claimed responsibility for the attack.

The irony of widespread criminal activity is that it has cost South Africa the one thing many observers believe it so badly needs to reduce violent crime: jobs. Overseas firms are less likely to invest money and personnel in such a dangerous and unpredictable environment. In 1996, the South African Reserve Bank reported a "substantial decline" in net capital entering the country. This in turn pushed down the value of the rand and changed (for the worse), "foreign investors'" assessment of the country (Chenault, 1996).

Evidence from the former Soviet Union, Eastern Europe, and the African nation of Namibia indicates that crime escalates significantly during periods of political transition, instability, and uncertainty. This cause-and-effect relation between major political change and crime has occurred yet again in South

Africa. Rates of property crime also go up in part as a nation modernizes because there are more things to steal and more opportunities to steal them. The increasing discrepancy between the haves and haves nots (especially in the cities) generates deviance in the latter. Antoinette Louw (1997) of the Centre for Social and Developmental Studies, University of Natal, South Africa, is of the opinion that rates of property crime in her "developing" country can be expected to increase "well into the future."

While the actual rates of violent crime begin to decrease "over the medium term," official statistics are likely to indicate an increase in criminal violence as improved relations with and trust in the police by poor people leads to more reporting of serious crimes. This in turn will lead to more crimes being officially recorded.

of time (Sanchez, 1998; Thompson, 1998). The study also found that 23 percent of male students and 17 percent of female students are frequent binge drinkers, chugging alcoholic drinks in rapid succession on three or more occasions in a two-week period (Thompson, 1998).

While abusing drugs and alcohol poses numerous health hazards including the risk of death (an estimated 50 college students die as a result of binge drinking each year), the consumption of mind-altering drugs is linked to an assortment of nonproductive, deviant, and illegal acts. Drug use on the part of adolescents is associated with increased dropout rates and a higher incidence of sexually transmitted diseases including HIV (Kirchner, 1998). One study found that "A" students (at the college level) averaged three alcoholic drinks a week while those earning Ds and Fs averaged 11 drinks a week. Student binge drinkers were 2 to 5 times more likely than other drinkers (or abstainers) to have unplanned and/or unprotected sex, damage property, engage in fights, or have trouble with the police (Thompson, 1998).

A Bureau of Justice Statistics random sample of inmates from 45 states found that almost 33 percent of the prisoners surveyed had used drugs at the time of their most recent offense with a significant number of these individuals committing crimes to buy drugs (Chong, 1998). The substance abuse problem is costly to the nation in a number of ways (for example, physical and psychological injury to abusers, time lost from work, and providing treatment programs) including the cost of imprisoning 400,000 individuals (eight times the number in 1980) convicted of violating drug laws ("A Social Profile," 1998).

Based on a review of the pertinent literature and her own research, Jenny Chong (1998) concluded that alcohol use and abuse is associated with violence, disorderly conduct, neglect of responsibility, and drunk driving. Of the 102,000 adults 18 years of age or older interviewed in a national telephone survey, 2.5 percent acknowledged driving a motor vehicle "after having had perhaps too much to drink" on at least one occasion within the previous month. Based on these findings the researchers estimated that there are approximately 123 million incidents of drunk driving annually in the U.S., or 14,000 an hour (Coleman, 1997).

SUMMARY AND REVIEW

Deviance: A Sociological View

1. *What are the major perspectives or explanations of deviance?*

There are three basic perspectives of deviance. From the absolutist perspective, deviance resides in the nature of the act itself and is wrong at all times and in all places. The normative position sees deviance as a violation of a group's or society's rules at a particular moment in history. According to the reactive position, behavior is not deviant until it has been recognized and condemned. (Pp. 162–163)

2. *What is the medical model of deviant behavior?*

Over the past one hundred years, an increasing amount of deviance has been explained and "cured" from a medical perspective. Deviants are thought of as sick and in need of treatment. (Pp. 163–164)

Theories of Crime and Deviance

3. *What is the underlying logic of biological theories of deviant behavior?*

Biological explanations go back hundreds of years. The basic logic of all these theories is that "structure determines function"; that is, human action is in some manner the result of an individual's physical makeup. (P. 164)

4. *According to Durkheim, in what sense is crime "normal?"*

According to functionalist sociologists like Emile Durkheim, crime is "normal" because all societies have criminal behavior. Crime and deviance persist in human societies because it is impossible for all members of society to agree on what the rules and norms should be. Crime is also inevitable because human beings are moral animals who continually divide the social world into the good and the bad. Behavior that is bad or undesirable is deviant. (Pp. 166–167)

5. *In what sense do functionalists see crime as good or functional for society?*

Functionalists also believe that a certain amount of crime is functional or "good" for society for a number of reasons: (a) Tolerance permitting the existence of crime and deviance results in tolerance for the creativity and originality that produce social change; (b) crime serves as a warning light that something is wrong in society and requires remedial action; (c) crime clarifies the social boundaries of society; and (d) crime facilitates group solidarity. (Pp. 167–168)

6. *What is Merton's theory of deviance?*

In his theory of anomie, Robert Merton noted that a significant amount of crime and deviance in societies of "the American type" is caused by the pressure put on people as a result of the gap between the institutionalized goal of monetary success and the means available for achieving this goal. Deviant adaptations to this pressure are innovation, ritualism, retreatism, and rebellion. (Pp. 168–169)

7. *According to Sutherland, how is criminal behavior learned?*

Criminologist Edwin Sutherland stated that criminal behavior is learned in interaction with other people. If individuals have an excess of definitions favorable to the violation of the law over definitions favorable to obeying the law, they are likely to be involved in criminal activities. (Pp. 169–170)

8. *How do labeling theorists explain crime and deviance in society?*

Labeling theorists argue that social groups create deviance by making laws whose infraction results in deviance. They are interested in how these laws are applied to particular people who are then labeled as deviants. "Moral entrepreneurs" campaign to have their values translated into laws designating some behavior as criminal. Primary deviance is the initial act, or first few episodes of deviant behavior, and secondary deviance is the behavior that results from being labeled. (Pp. 170–171)

9. *How do Marxist criminologists account for crime in capitalist societies?*

According to Marxist criminologists, the struggle between the capitalist class and the proletariat produces crime. Members of the capitalist class commit crimes of domination and repression, and the working class engages in crimes of accommodation and resistance. Crime is symptomatic of the real problem in a capitalist society—the unequal distribution of wealth and power. (P. 171)

Deviant and Criminal Behavior

10. *How is crime measured in the United States?*

Crime is measured by the *Uniform Crime Report* (UCR), victimization surveys, and self-report studies. The UCR is primarily a measure of street crimes (murder, robbery, rape, aggravated assault, burglary, auto theft, larceny, arson). Victimization surveys indicate significantly more crime is committed than reported by the UCR. (P. 172)

11. *Who commits crimes in this country?*

Data on offenders indicate that (a) men commit more crimes than women, (b) crime is primarily a youthful activity, and (c) a disproportionate number of people arrested for street crimes are minority group members. A controversy exists among sociologists regarding the class origin of offenders in the United States. Some researchers maintain that criminals come disproportionately from the lower classes. Others argue against any class-linked explanations. (Pp. 175–176)

12. *How many prostitutes are there in the United States and in what sense do they live in a dangerous world?*

There are between 100,000 and 500,000 prostitutes in this country. These girls/women are at risk of being physically abused by customers and pimps, becoming addicted to drugs, acquiring a variety of sexually transmitted diseases (including AIDS), and in some instances are targets of "mission-oriented" serial killers. (P. 176)

13. *What do we know about crimes of violence in this country?*

Although rates of criminal violence have declined in the past 10 years, the United States is still a very violent society with homicide rates in this country significantly higher than in other comparable modern industrial democratic societies. Although they account for just under 13 percent of the population, African Americans comprise approximately 50 percent of the nation's killers and murder victims. Rape victims are more likely to be assaulted by someone they know as opposed to a stranger. Recent studies have concluded that stalking is much more common than previously thought. (Pp. 178–181)

14. *What are occupational crime and corporate crime?*

Occupational crime is committed by people in connection with their work. Corporate crime is committed by officials for their organizations, and includes crimes of the organization itself. Corporate crime costs the American public much more than street crime, and can also be violent. (Pp. 183–184)

15. *What is the cycle of a drug epidemic?*

Drug epidemics occur in the United States in predictable cycles. Drugs are "discovered," widely used, and then condemned. In this final stage they are typically associated with racial-ethnic minorities, whether this association is true or not. (P. 185)

16. *In what sense is drug use learned behavior?*

Drug use (at least initially) is learned behavior. People may eventually become addicted to drugs, but they had to learn where to buy and how to use them. They also had to learn how to rationalize this behavior to themselves and others. (P. 185)

9

Marriage and the Family

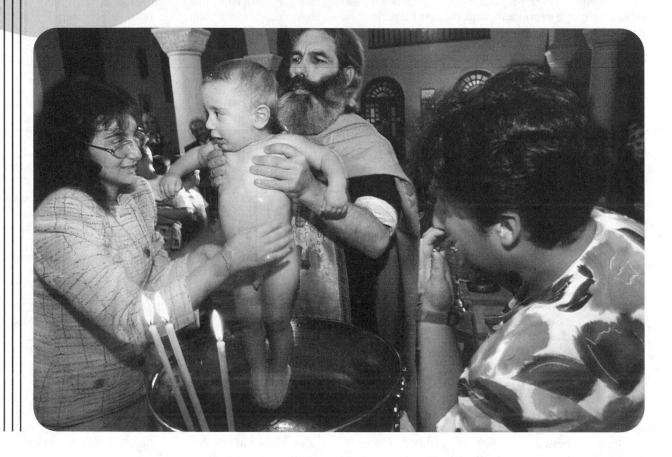

Family portraits often include smiling grandparents looking lovingly at their children and grandchildren. Three generations of family members—the young, the middle aged, and the elderly—nurturing each other in a harmonious relationship has long been viewed as the American ideal. However, with life expectancy now at 75 years (and increasing), the question of what to do with grandma and grandpa when they can no longer fend for themselves is creating significant problems for all concerned.

Local officials have discovered that just as people often leave their children in libraries while they work or run errands, many individuals are doing the same thing with their aging parents (Kamm, Anderson, and Leek, 1994). Hospitals report that elderly individuals are regularly brought to emergency rooms by relatives under the pretext of illness, or that the person is confused or tends to wander from home. When hospital staff attempt to contact the family after tests have been run they discover the telephone number is incorrect and the address fictitious. In a less-serious variant of this behavior, a family member will return a few days later for the elderly patient (Becker and Gordon, 1991).

Hospitals refer to the short- and long-term abandonment of the elderly as "granny dumping." A Senate Aging Committee discovered that 38 percent of hospitals surveyed reported incidents of "elderly abandonment," with some physicians noting that as many as eight older people a week are "dumped" in their emergency rooms. While hospitals may file abandonment charges against offenders, they are typically sympathetic to the problem. One individual noted that "To blame the families . . . is sort of blaming the victim" (in Becker and Gordon, 1991, p. 64). Health care practitioners realize that caring for someone 24 hours a day is a major responsibility, and that people can eventually be overwhelmed. A buildup of stress in these situations in almost inevitable, and stress often leads to violence, with family members taking out their frustrations on one another. Susan Steinmetz (in *Domestic Violence*, 1991, p. 133), one of the foremost experts on domestic violence, stated, "The bottom line is that if you increase the stress on family members without adding supports to help them cope with it, you increase the likelihood because a person and family can only handle so much."

At least one solution to this problem would appear to be affordable nursing home care for the elderly. However, families that can afford to pay for these services outright, or those that are reimbursed (in whole or part) by their insurance or Medicaid, may unknowingly be putting their loved ones in an uncomfortable, dangerous, even life-threatening situation. In a recent study, nearly 10,000 of the 15,000 nursing homes inspected by state officials across the country were found to be operating in violation of one or more statutes.

One researcher examined the death certificates of people who died in California nursing homes between 1986 and 1993. In nearly 22,000 (7.3 percent) of the more than 300,000 cases looked at, the cause of death (at least in part) was lack of food or water, untreated bedsores that became infected, or internal obstruction. In other words, these people died in large measure as a result of neglect (in Thompson, Graff, and Gwynne, 1997). When asked if conditions and staff behavior at a home for the elderly where she worked had contributed the death of patients a nurse stated "I'm 100 percent sure. People would come in, they'd get depressed, stop eating and start falling. They they'd get tied down to a chair, and they rapidly decline and die" (p. 37).

In 2011, the first of approximately 75 million "baby boomers" (those individuals born between 1946 and 1964) will turn 65. If questions such as who will care for the elderly, who will pay for these services, and what organization(s) will be responsible for seeing that this giant health care system is running without abuses are not addressed presently, the nation will be facing a problem of catastrophic proportions in the near future. As a society we have not done a very good job in determining where the obligations of the family end and those of other institutions begin.

This brief look at one of the problems associated with the elderly illustrates the interplay of three of society's most important institutions: the family, the government, and the economy. From a sociological perspective, **social institutions** are orderly, enduring, and established ways of arranging human behavior and doing things. Social relationships in institutions are structured for the purpose of performing some task(s) and accomplishing some specific goal. In this and the following two chapters we discuss five social institutions: the family, education, religion, the polity (or politics), and the economy. Obviously, all the aforementioned institutions have a significant impact on our daily lives, beginning with childhood socialization (the family); our understanding of how the world works and our preparation for a lifetime of employment (education); our belief in the hereafter and how these belief affect our actions in this life (religion); the distribution of income, income, wealth, and the opportunities for upward mobility (the economy); and finally how much freedom or power we have in determining how our society will be governed (politics). Keep in mind that although these institutions are analytically separate and for the most part will be discussed individually, they are interdependent and continually affect each other. We will draw attention to these interconnections whenever possible.

Questions to Consider

1. What are social institutions?
2. How do functionalist sociologists see the role of the family in society?
3. How do conflict sociologists view the family in society?
4. What factors are associated with a successful marriage in the United States?
5. What psychological and social factors are associated with divorce in this country?
6. What effects does divorce have on children?
7. Why has the number of single-parent families increased so dramatically in the United States over the past thirty years?
8. What effects does being raised in a single-parent family have on children?
9. What are the major impediments to gay families being accepted in a predominantly heterosexual society?
10. What impact does being raised in a gay family have on the sexual orientation of children?
11. How many children in the United States are abused each year? What are the principal causes of child abuse?
12. What is the connection between social class and spouse abuse?
13. Why do many women physically abuse their husbands?
14. What is the relationship between modernization and the family?

THE FAMILY IN AMERICA: A BRIEF HISTORY

Family life in late seventeenth-century Plymouth Colony, Massachusetts, was probably quite similar to family arrangements and patterns of living in other frontier communities of that era. Although a nuclear family with parents and children living together in rather tightly knit, religious communities was the norm, divorces were not unknown, and marriages could be dissolved for bigamy, desertion, and adultery. As the population increased and settlements expanded westward, husbands often left their wives and children behind in search of better farmland and a more prosperous life. Family members followed a year or two later, once the husband/father was established in a new location. In these mostly agricultural communities, the home was the center of both outdoor farm work and indoor housework. Because so few manufactured goods were available, household activities (often associated with female labor) such as preserving food and making clothes, candles, soap, and other necessities were vitally important to the family (Mallinger, 1990).

With few exceptions, there has never been a strong tradition in the United States of "extended" families in which several generations of relatives are obligated to live in the same household. In the latter half of the nineteenth century, immigrants from southern and eastern Europe who lived with family members because of economic necessity typically abandoned this living arrangement when they could afford to leave (Blumenstein and Schwartz, 1983). In an era of geographical expansion and a growing economy, parents encouraged their children to strike out on their own. Blumenstein and Schwartz note that young people were eager to head for the cities, the Midwest, and the West Coast. In doing so, they revised the commandment "Honor thy father and mother" to "Honor thy father and mother—but get away from them" (p. 26).

Even during slavery, when husbands and wives were separated by force, the slave trade, and death, African-American families were characterized by strong kin relations. Pregnancies out of wedlock were encouraged by plantation owners, who viewed these births as a return on their investment. In the post–Civil War era, an extended network of relatives helped blacks in both their migration and adaptation to northern cities. Newly emancipated blacks were often subject to deep-seated prejudice and widespread discrimination. As a consequence of racist attitudes and behavior, African-American women could often find employment as domestics and provide a small but reliable income while their husbands were being turned away from jobs (Blumenstein and Schwartz, 1983).

In the past 150 years, the family has been significantly affected by demographic changes (increased ethnic diversity, generally lower fertility, and mortality), the urbanization and suburbanization of society, and most especially, the consequences of industrialization and the economy. One of the most profound effects of the Industrial Revolution was the separation of the workplace and the home—a shift in activity that affected the family in at least three ways: (1) Removal of the father/husband from the home for at least eight hours a day and minimally five days a week meant that much more of the responsibility for raising and socializing children was left to mothers and older siblings. (2) Industrialization began a pattern of geographical mobility as families moved from rural to urban areas in pursuit of work. Extended family ties were altered as people left the farms for opportunities in the cities. (3) Whereas the family had previously provided a significant amount of what it consumed, commodities used on a daily basis were increasingly purchased in stores that carried a growing array of products. In addition, the proliferation of specialized institutions meant the family no longer had to serve as reformatory, asylum, hospital, church, and school. As a result of these changes, "housework" lost many of its productive functions and was devalued. Since most of this household labor was done by females, the role of the housewife lost a good deal of status, which it never recovered (Mallinger, 1990).

As we saw on the chapter on gender, economic and social changes in the post–World War II period resulted in significantly more American women in the paid labor force. Whereas 30 percent of married women worked outside of the home in 1960, that figure had increased to 58 percent in 1998. Women's increased participation in the labor force has created additional work-family conflicts. In addition to childcare dilemmas, dual-career families are less available for work-related relocation (Hendershott, 1995). Women are particularly resistant to moving for their own careers. Nearly every survey of the demogrpahics of moving for work indicate that compared to men, women—especially married women—are much less likely to move for work. Given the choice between career or relationships, they tend to limit their own career mobility rather than inconvenience family harmony and well-being (Hendershott, 1995).

At least partially the result of higher expectations for marriage, an increased social and religious tolerance for dissolving marital unions, and the growing financial independence of women (Mallinger, 1990),

the number of people divorced in the United States increased almost four-and-a-half-fold, from 4.3 million in 1970 to 19.3 million in 1997. During that same period, couples living together both before marriage and after divorce became much more common. The number of unmarried (opposite sex) couples sharing the same residence (nonmarital cohabitation) reached approximately 4.1 million in 1997, with children under 15 years of age present in just over one-third of these households. Both the number and percentage of unmarried adults has also increased dramatically as of late. Whereas 38 million Americans over age 18 (28 percent of the adult population) were single in 1970, 77 million individuals in this same age category (40 percent of the adult population) were not married in 1997.

Another (and many would argue, disturbing) trend over the past thirty years is the unparalleled rise in single-parent families. In 1970, 3.8 million family groups were headed by single parents; by 1996, that number had jumped to 11.7 million, 84 percent of which were headed by women. As we will see later in the chapter, this more than tripling of such families in little more than a generation has significantly affected the lives of millions of adults and children.

THEORETICAL PERSPECTIVES

Because the family is such a basic and important social institution, sociologists have attempted to explain not only how it works, but also how it relates to other institutions from different perspectives.

Functionalist Theory

Functionalists are concerned primarily with how the family contributes to the overall functioning of, and therefore the good of, society. From this perspective, the family performs six major functions in all societies to one degree or another, although the way they are performed varies significantly (Queen, Habenstein, and Quadagno, 1985, pp. 5–6).

1. The family meets its members' biological and economic needs for food, clothing, and shelter as well as providing for other material necessities.
2. The family legitimizes some sexual relationships while at the same time prohibiting others. For example, in Western societies, it is believed that the exclusive sexual bond between husband and wife strengthens their commitment to each other, which in turn helps them meet familial duties and responsibilities. In every known society, incest taboos regulate the sexual behavior of people related within certain degrees of kinship.

3. Every society must reproduce to survive and ensure the continuity of the group. Reproduction typically occurs within the family unit.
4. A significant portion of childhood socialization takes place in the family. Children learn standards of behavior appropriate to their age and gender, as well as internalizing ever-increasing aspects of their material and nonmaterial cultural heritage.
5. As a social hierarchy, the family provides membership within a societal structure that gives individuals an ascribed status.
6. Finally, the family provides members with emotional support and companionship. It also acts as a buffer between the individual and other institutions such as the workplace that can be competitive, tiring, stressful, and even degrading. It is this final function that makes the family an especially important institution in modern, industrial states.

Conflict Theory

Conflict theorists who view the family as an institution of "power, dominance, and conflict" have been highly critical of the hidden conservative view they see built into the functionalist interpretation (Collins, 1985, p. 18). Friedrich Engels wrote about the link between exploitation in the larger society and the exploitation of women and children in the family. According to Engels, men who are paid subsistence wages by powerful corporate owners in a capitalist society that cares nothing about their well-being soon become demoralized, frustrated, and callous. Misery breeds misery as workers beaten down by the capitalist system in turn exploit and brutalize their families. It is not as if men enjoy terrifying loved ones; rather, they take their frustrations and hostilities out on the most readily available individuals.

From a Marxist perspective, women are victimized twice in a capitalist society. Fulfilling their roles as wives and mothers, they are unpaid for their work in the home, and they toil for less than what men earn if they do enter the workforce. Having women work at home without pay allows men to leave their families and be turned into what Marxists call "wage slaves" by the capitalist class. In other words, exploitation of women at home is necessary for capitalism to exist. Joan Landes (1979) described how the family socializes children to be obedient wage slaves as they are prepared for a life of dutiful exploitation: "Within the family, patterns of hierarchy (of men over women and parents over children) serve to introduce workers to the hierarchical labor patterns of the workplace. The ideology of the workplace helps to teach workers that these patterns are 'natural' as well as legitimate" (p. 224).

From a conflict perspective, the family is hardly a sanctuary full of love, companionship, and emotional support. Instead, in a capitalist society it is a microcosm of the tension, conflict, and exploitation existing in the larger society. Marxist sociologists use the family as an example of how the evils of capitalism pervade our most "sacred institution" and negatively affect the lives of men, women, and children at the most personal and intimate level.

Sociologist Randall Collins (1975) observed that conflict within the family goes well beyond capitalist societies. Stable family organization is the result of sexual conquest and dominance. Males, who are on average bigger and stronger than females, physically overpower women, who become "sexual prizes." The men who take permanent possession of particular females create biological families. Collins notes that men now own these women and the children they bear. The fundamental motive for subordinating women is the sexual gratification of men, but females (and later their children) can be used for their labor value as well.

Another conflict interpretation was offered by sociologist Jetse Sprey (1966, 1969), who contended that the impartiality of the world of work, casual associations, and friendships may counteract the conflict and hostilities that are built into the family bond. In a complete reversal of the functionalist position, Sprey saw conflict anchored in the family as members compete with each other for real and symbolic resources such as money, attention, and power. Marital problems leading to separation and divorce are not due to personality differences between partners (these are natural and inevitable), but occur because husbands and wives have not learned to live with and successfully negotiate each other's differences.

LOVE, MARRIAGE, AND DIVORCE AMERICAN STYLE

Anthropologists Serena Nanda and Richard Warms (1998, p. 158) maintain that whenever and wherever human beings live collectively they must solve a number of fundamental problems: "Every society must regulate sexual access between males and females, find satisfactory ways to organize labor between males and females, assign responsibility for childcare . . . and provide for the transfer of property and social position between generations." The universal practice of marriage is the way societies typically regulate relationships between men and women and resolve these basic problems. Marriage can be defined as the socially approved sexual union between a man and a woman that is presumed to be permanent and

TABLE 9.1

Marriage and Family Terminology

Term	Definition
Family Structure	
Nuclear family	Family group consisting of a mother, a father, and their children. This is the family of procreation.
Extended family	A family group that extends beyond the immediate relationship of husband, wife, and their children and includes several generations.
Blended family	The family created by remarriage. It includes stepchildren and half-brothers and -sisters.
Mate Selection	
Endogamy	Custom that requires individuals to choose marriage mates from within their own tribe, community, social class, nationality, or other grouping.
Exogamy	Custom that requires individuals to choose marriage mates from outside certain groups.
Residence	
Matrilocal residence	Residence of married partners near or in the wife's family's home.
Patrilocal residence	Residence of a married couple near or with the husband's family.
Neolocal residence	System in which both marriage partners reside apart from their family of orientation.
Forms of Marriage	
Monogamy	Marriage form permitting each person to have only one spouse.
Polygamy	Marital system that permits the taking of several spouses. It includes both polygyny and polyandry.
Polygyny	Marital system that permits the taking of several wives.
Polyandry	Marital system that permits the taking of several husbands.
Authority	
Matriarchy	A system in which power and authority are vested primarily in females.
Patriarchy	A system in which power and authority are vested primarily in males.
Egalitarian	A system in which power and authority are shared equally by husbands and wives.
Descent and Inheritance	
Matrilineal descent	Family membership and inheritance traced through the female line, from mother to her children.
Patrilineal descent	Family membership and inheritance traced through the male line, from father to his children.
Bilineal descent	Family membership and inheritance traced through the lines of both parents to their children.

Source: Adapted from Randall Collins, *Sociology of Marriage and the Family—Gender, Love, and Property* (Chicago: Nelson-Hall, 1985), pp. 477–483; and Gerald R. Leslie and Sheila K. Korman, *The Family in Social Context* (New York: Oxford University Press, 1989), pp. 581–592.

is recognized as such both by the couple and others. Although marriage and the family are common to all human societies, family structure, customs of mate selection and residence, marriage forms, and patterns of authority and descent vary considerably across cultures. In the United States, most people live in nuclear families, practice endogamy in the selection of a spouse, have a neolocal residence, are monogamous, are moving toward or are in an egalitarian marriage, and have a bilineal descent system (See Table 9.1 for a definition of these terms.)

One of the most significant changes in the structure of the American family has been the reduction in the size and importance of kinship networks. Extended families and large kinship groups, once common among New England upper classes, southern plantations, and *haciendas* (ranches or farms) in the Southwest, have given way to smaller nuclear families. Personal ties and patterns of interaction that once united three or four generations and a host of cousins are much less evident today than in the past (Queen, Habenstein, and Quadagno, 1985). Today, Americans live in nuclear families that have significantly diminished in size since the first census was taken in 1790. Almost 99 percent of married couples maintain a household of their own, and approximately 60 percent of married women have jobs outside the home. The number of working married women will continue to increase because women are becoming better educated, having fewer children, and living longer (Queen, Habenstein, and Quadango, 1985). Women have demonstrated they can work as well as men in hundreds of occupations and currently have the protection of laws (albeit incomplete) against gender discrimination in the workplace that did not previously exist. With women bringing home a paycheck in over half of the marriages, power relationships in the family are shifting to a more equal or egalitarian form.

In the majority of American families, children are preceded by marriage, which in turn is preceded by dating and romantic love. Although there are no laws in the United States requiring people to date and marry within a specific group (endogamy), most people select mates with backgrounds much like their own. The tendency to marry individuals whom one resembles physically, psychologically, and/or socially is called **homogamy.** In the United States, most marriages occur between two people of the same social class, within the same racial group, of the same religious faith, with similar levels of education, with the same physical and psychological characteristics, and who live within a few miles of each other (Collins, 1985).

Homogamy occurs because people are attracted to one another in a system of exchange that could be characterized as a marriage market. Just as goods and services are exchanged in the economic marketplace, human resources are negotiated and traded in the social world. According to Collins (1985, pp. 121–124), everybody has a market value and typically dates and marries someone of approximately the same worth: "Your own resources include your social status (class, race, ethnicity; your family background; your current occupation), your wealth and your prospect for making more in the future, your personal attractiveness and health, your culture. Even personality traits such as your 'magnetism' or charisma are social resources. . . . The people in your 'opportunity pool' of course have their own degrees of attractiveness depending on their resources." Although people may not be consciously making comparisons in the dating—marriage marketplace, we have all been socialized to play "Let's Make a Deal" on the basis of our current and potential value.

Marriage

After people sort themselves out in the dating marketplace, they eventually marry (see Figure 9.1). The success or failure of their marriages is linked to a number of social, psychological, and economic variable. Jeanette Lauer and Robert Lauer (1985) interviewed 351 couples who had been married for at least 15 years in an effort to discover why these marriage lasted. The top four reasons given by both husbands and wives for what keeps are marriage going were: (1) My spouse is my best friend; (2) I like my spouse as a person; (3) Marriage is a long term commitment; and (4) Marriage is sacred. While the first two (basically psychological) reasons have to do with compatibility, the latter two reveal people's commitment to the institution of marriage and belief that marriage is something sacred. Lauer and Lauer's research indicates that although we tend to think of marriage and divorce almost exclusively in terms of psychological variables (love, compatibility, trust, etc.) and interpersonal dynamics, we should not overlook factors that bind people to the institution of marriage itself.

The aforementioned perspective is in sharp contrast to what Louis Russel (in Goode, 1993) believes is characteristic of the way millions of people in many nations (including modern industrial states) view marriage today. For these individuals marriage is no longer a primary institution "but simply an emotional relationship" (p. 10). When the emotional enjoyment derived from the marital union has diminished and/or a more satisfying relationship is encountered, the likelihood of separation and divorce is increased. Similarly, the high rate of divorce in middle-class America has been called "expressive divorce" in that reasonably affluent people are terminating their marriages as a step toward what they perceive to be a new life of self-renewal and fulfillment (Whitehead, in Kirn, 1997).

People who divorce (and do not remarry) in search of a more satisfying life may be doing so at a significant cost to their physical and psychological health. Being single can have a more detrimental effect on life expectancy than being poor, overweight, or having heart disease. David Larson (in Mattox, 1997, p. B7) of the National Institute for Healthcare Research stated that "Being divorced and a nonsmoker is only slightly less dangerous than smoking a pack or more and staying married." Compared to married men, divorced males are twice as likely to die prematurely of hypertension, twice as likely to die prematurely from cardiovascular disease, and seven times more likely to die prematurely of pneumonia. One reason why married men outlive their single counterparts is that having a wife and children engenders a sense of obligation (emotional and financial) that discourages high-risk behavior like driving too fast and drinking too much. Marriage also encourages the making and saving of money that

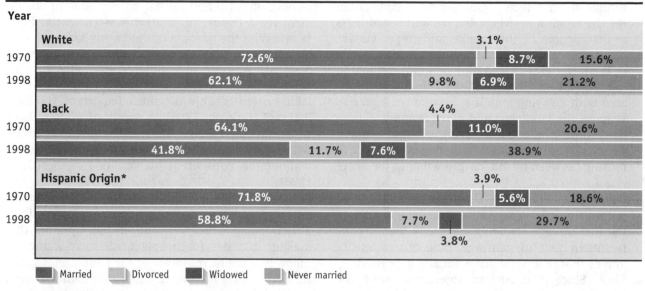

Year

	Married	Divorced	Widowed	Never married

White
- 1970: 72.6% | 3.1% | 8.7% | 15.6%
- 1998: 62.1% | 9.8% | 6.9% | 21.2%

Black
- 1970: 64.1% | 4.4% | 11.0% | 20.6%
- 1998: 41.8% | 11.7% | 7.6% | 38.9%

Hispanic Origin*
- 1970: 71.8% | 3.9% | 5.6% | 18.6%
- 1998: 58.8% | 7.7% | 3.8% | 29.7%

*Persons of Hispanic origin may be of any race.

FIGURE 9.1

Marital Status by Race and Hispanic Origin: 1970 and 1998 (persons 18 years and over)

Source: U.S. Bureau of the Census, *Marital Status and Living Arrangements, March 1998* (Washington, DC: U.S. Government Printing Office, 1998)

can be used for buying better health care and affording to live in safer surroundings (Mattox, 1997).

Although part of the reason for the difference in mental and physical health between married and unmarried individuals is that well-adjusted individuals are more likely to marry than less well-adjusted people (and stay married), approximately 50 percent of the difference between these two groups can be attributed to the beneficial impact marriage has on personal well-being (Glenn, 1998). A long-time researcher on various aspects of marriage and the family, sociologist Norvall Glenn (1998, p. 11) has noted that one of the best predictors we have of personal happiness in adults "is whether or not they are in a satisfactory marriage."

Divorce

In his book *World Changes in Divorce Patterns*, eminent sociologist William J. Goode (1993, p. 336) stated, "almost all of the highly developed societies are, or are becoming, high divorce societies." With recent legal changes in Ireland, every Catholic country in Europe now permits people to divorce, the governments of these nations having recognized that this was a necessary step inasmuch as "hundreds of thousands of couples had already made some formal adjustment to their marital conflict" (p. 325). The high rate of divorce in the United States (one of the highest in the world) is likely to continue, with "perhaps two-thirds of all recent marriages" ending in separation and/or divorce (Bumpass and Martin, in Goode, 1993, p. 154).

In this country the probability of marital breakup is not randomly distributed throughout the population; rather, it is associated with a number of factors (Thornton, 1985; Raschke, 1988; Leslie and Korman, 1989; Eshleman, 1996; Collins and Coltrane, 1995; Hutter, 1998):

1. *Age* Couples who marry prior to age 18 have an especially high rate of divorce, often due to emotional immaturity. Young people may also be pressured to divorce by parents and relatives who oppose the marriage. Collins and Coltrane (1995, p. 308) speak of "spur-of-the-moment marriages, quickly put together, quickly torn apart." Lower-class individuals tend to marry at a younger age than people from other classes, so that the age-divorce relation may be more a function of social class than of age.

2. *Socioeconomic Class* Although divorce has been increasing in every stratum of society, there is an inverse relation between socioeconomic class and marital dissolution in the United States. The lower the income the higher the divorce rate. This is especially true if desertion is factored into the equation. In the poorest segment of society people frequently abandon a spouse in lieu of filing a

formal divorce decree. One possible explanation for the relation between divorce and social class is that people in the middle and upper classes have more years of formal education than people in the lower classes and may be more inclined to pursue careers. Both of these factors are associated with delaying marriage beyond the high-risk years of the late teens and early twenties. Financial problems due to low-paying jobs and frequent periods of unemployment can also be a source of tension between husbands and wives in the lower classes.

3. *Duration of Marriage* Divorce generally occurs within the first seven years of marriage, rates in the first three years being especially high. By the twentieth year of marriage, nine out of ten divorces that will occur have already happened.

4. *Race* Since 1960, African Americans have had a divorce rate higher than that of whites, Asian Americans, and Hispanics. Higher rates of divorce among African Americans exist at all income, educational, and occupational levels. These findings have been explained in part by higher rates of black teenage and premarital pregnancies. Another explanation points to the disproportionate number of African Americans who are poor. A particularly "independent style" of living among African-American women less willing to accept male-dominated marriages has also been offered as a reason for the high rate of marital failure in this racial group (Collins and Coltrane, 1995,p. 509).

5. *Religious Affiliation and Attendance* Marital dissolution is slightly higher for Protestants than for Catholics, with Jews having a lower divorce rate than either of the aforementioned groups. The divorce rate for white males who never attend religious services is three times higher than for those who go to services at least once a month. A similar, although not as significant, difference was found for white female religious-service attenders and nonattenders. People who participate in religious services and hold religious beliefs may have a stronger commitment to the institution of marriage (and a disdain for divorce) as a result of their faith. As sociologist Mark Hutter (1998,p. 512) noted, there may well be some truth to the adage that "the family that prays together, stays together."

Divorce and the Law

Prior the late 1960s, divorce laws in the United States were based on the notion of "fault." That is, either the husband or wife was considered responsible for the problems leading to the divorce. The problem-causing spouse was typically guilty of adultery, de-

sertion, physical and mental cruelty, long imprisonment for a felony, or drunkenness (Fine and Fine, 1994). With the passage of the Family Law Act, California became the first state to permit divorce on the basis of "irreconcilable differences" between husband and wife. By 1985, every state had replaced the fault system entirely or added important "no-fault options" (Galston, 1996). A subset of no-fault laws widely adopted were "unilateral" provisions under which either spouse could terminate the marriage without the consent of his or her partner (Gray, 1998).

Because divorce rates across the country rose significantly in the years since divorce laws were liberalized, some observers are of the opinion that making it easier for people to dissolve a marital union is a major reason why the United States has so many failed marriages. From this point of view, "no-fault" (and especially "unilateral") laws have contributed to the view that marriage is just another contractual agreement that can be terminated by one or both parties at any time of their choosing (Fine and Fine, 1994).

Opponents of this position note that it is much too simplistic to attribute the nation's high marital failure rate to a change in divorce laws. They note that the divorce rate was on the upswing *before* more liberal divorce laws were enacted. In addition, people are living longer today than in past generations, which affords them more time and opportunities for marital conflict and divorce (Fine and Fine, 1994). William J. Goode (1993) argued that "Both the rise in divorce rates and the laws come from the same sources, changing values and norms in the larger society, alterations in economic opportunities, political ideologies, even models presented by the mass media" (p. 322).

Striking a middle ground, social commentator William A. Galston (1996) is of the opinion that while economic and cultural changes certainly pushed divorce rates upward, no-fault laws had a measurable impact on accelerating this process. More liberal divorce laws contributed to what he refers to as the "destigmatization effect" wherein divorce is now viewed as "no particular moral problem" (p. 18). That is, there is nothing particularly wrong, bad, or evil with divorce or the people who terminate their marriages.

Why Marriages Fail

After interviewing 52 married couples, a trio of psychologists was able to predict with a high degree of accuracy (94 percent) which couples (who all stated that they were happily married at the time of the interview) would divorce in the following three years (Buechlman, Gottman, and Katz, 1992). Although husbands and wives did not always have similar responses, couples who eventually divorced scored *low* on the following dimensions: (1) fondness and affection, or how much a couple appeared to be in love with and fond of each other; (2) weness versus separateness, the degree to which marriage partners see themselves as part of a couple as opposed to emphasizing their independence; and (3) glorifying the struggle, the sense that hard times have actually brought them closer together and their marriage is the most important thing in the world. Couples who stayed married were likely to say such things as "Marriage is the hardest job in the world, but it's well worth it" (p. 312). In addition, divorcing couples scored *high* on these characteristics: (1) negativity toward a spouse, vagueness about why they were attracted to each other in the first place as well as having disagreements during the interview; (2) chaos, or how much control a couple felt they had over problems and hardships that affect their relationship—couples who eventually divorced encountered problems they were not prepared to deal with; and (3) marital disappointment and disillusionment, the degree to which both husband and wife had given up on or felt defeated by their marriage. This variable was the single most powerful predictor of divorce.

Just as psychological variables and interpersonal dynamics do not completely explain why some marriages endure, these same factors give an incomplete picture of why other marriages fail. Divorce in the United States is associated with general economic trends, something that affects everyone in the country to a certain extent. For example, the divorce rate in the United States rose slightly during the prosperous Roaring Twenties and began to decline with the stock market crash of 1929, reaching a low in the depths of the Great Depression in 1933. With the sluggish economy of the mid-1970s, the rates peaked at 5.3 per 1,000 population in 1981 and then declined to 4.3 in the late-1990s (see Figure 9.2). Higher rates of unemployment and an uncertain financial future preceding the economic boom of the late 1990s kept families together even if internal factors were pulling them apart.

Unfortunately, economic factors such as high unemployment and high inflation cannot be controlled at the family level. This is yet another link between institutional variables and individual behavior. Economic slowdowns and inflation, which hit people in the lower classes the hardest (including the disproportionate number of African Americans in this category), partially explain why divorce is inversely related to social class and is higher among blacks than whites.

Given the connection between society's major institutions (especially the economy and polity) and divorce, what, if anything, can be done to lower the rate of marital breakups? William A. Galston (1996) had devised a three-point plan of intervention that he believes could reduce the incidence of divorce in the United States. Note that his program depends almost entirely on institutional support/change, underscoring once again that the success or failure of marriages is largely contingent upon social forces outside of and independent of the family.

1. The first intervention occurs prior to people marrying. Just as sex education is taught in schools across the country, courses should be added to school curriculums that instruct children on the "social institution" of marriage. Also, since most people associate marriage with religion (they marry in churches, temples, and synagogues), religious organizations have a responsibility for preparing young people for marriage. Educational programs such as these should be mandated by state law. Completion of a church-sponsored counseling program (or a secular equivalent for those who are not religious) would be required before a marriage license is issued.

2. The second intervention occurs during marriage. Economic (tax codes) and social policies should be instituted that promote a "marriage-friendly environment." Both the private and public employment sectors can contribute to marital stability by offering flex-time, job-sharing, and part-time work with better benefits, and creating more generous leave policies for family emergencies.

3. The final intervention comes at the point of divorce. To date we have gone from one extreme to another, that is, from fault-based divorces that were difficult to obtain, to unilateral no-fault decrees that leave the decision to remain married or to divorce up to either the husband or the wife. For Galston (1996) the reasonable alternative is a no-fault system wherein divorces are granted only by the mutual consent of both husband and wife. While some states have already adopted mutual consent laws, this must be taken a step further by way of returning to an "updated fault system" (updated in the sense of taking into account what we know about spousal abuse) for couples with minor children. Even when both parties agree to a divorce, Galston sees the need for a one-year ("at least") waiting period, a time for "reflection, counseling, and mediation" before the marriage is legally terminated.

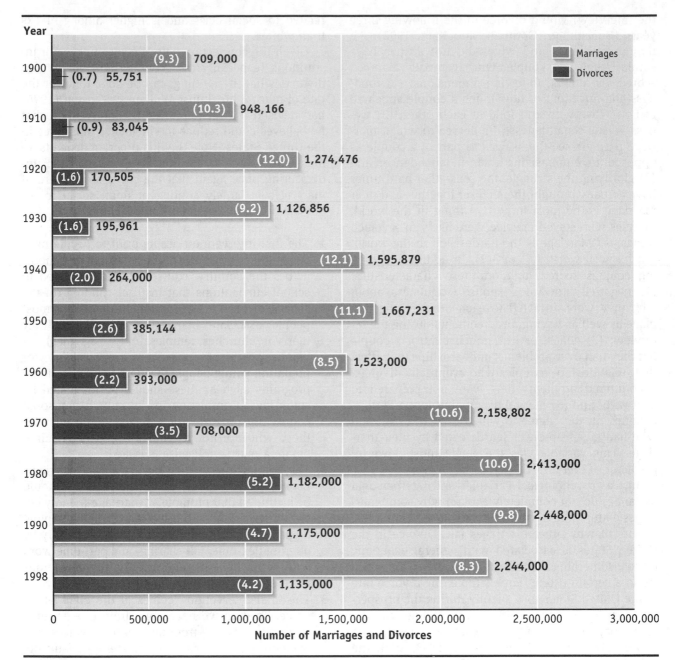

FIGURE 9.2

Marriages, Divorces, and Rates in the United States (per 1,000) 1900–1997

Source: National Center for Health Statistics, U.S. Departments of Health and Human Services. Adapted from
The World Almanac and Book of Facts (New York: Pharos Books, 1992). U.S. Bureau of the Census, *Monthly Vital
Statistics Report* (Washington, DC: U.S. Government Printing Office, May 1998)

Divorce and Children

Divorce affects not only the men and women who terminate their marriages, but hundreds of thousands of children as well. Since 1900, approximately 25 to 30 percent of all children in the United States have experienced divorce, and by the 1980s, 40 to 50 percent were so affected. Of the almost one million children who have witnessed their parents divorce annually over the past few years, almost 50 percent are between 2 ½ and 6 years of age (Galston, 1996; Wallerstein and Lewis, 1998). The manner in which children are affected by a marital dissolution is contingent to a great extent on their age (Furstenberg and Cherlin, 1991). Because of their inability to

This non-custodial father picks up his son from his former wife's home. Half of all American children will see their parents divorce, and as many as one in ten will experience three marital breakups. What impact will these marital failures have on children not only when they are young, but as they mature, marry and have children of their own?

comprehend the situation, preschool youngsters are typically frightened and bewildered when they learn one of their parents will no longer be living with them. Children at this age are often terrified that the remaining parent will eventually abandon them, and suffer with "fears of starvation, of waking up in the morning to a deserted house, of returning from nursery school to find no one at home" (Wallerstein and Lewis, 1998, p. 369). Older children are better able to understand what is happening, although they may become very anxious regarding how the divorce will affect them. Teenagers are more likely to get angry at one or both parents for breaking up the family.

Psychological studies suggest that the consequences of a divorce are different for boys and girls, with the former having more difficulty coping with a changed life situation than the latter (Furstenberg and Cherlin, 1991). Boys are more likely to engage in "externalizing disorders"—outwardly directed problem behavior such as aggression, disobedience, and lying. While the findings for girls are less conclusive, females appear to be more prone to "internalizing disorders" such as depression and lowered self-esteem. For boys the negative effects of the marital breakup tend to occur rather quickly, whereas for girls, divorce-related problems may not emerge until they are adults (Galston, 1996).

As a result of "hundreds of hours of face-to-face" interviews with 130 children (now adults) and their divorced parents over a 30-year period, psychologist Judith Wallerstein (Wallerstein and Lewis, 1998) and her colleagues have come to the conclusion that a child's suffering does not peak when the marriage is terminated and then level off. Rather, the effects of the divorce are "played and replayed throughout the first three decades of the children's lives" (p. 382).

Children of divorced parents are more likely than children raised in intact families to have emotional problems and to abuse alcohol as well as other drugs. In addition, they have lower levels of marital satisfaction, and, not surprisingly, a high rate of divorce. Sociologist Nicholas Wolfinger (in Morin, 1998b) reported that prior to 1974, a child who lived with a divorced single mother at age 16 was three times as likely to be divorced later in life than a child who lived with both biological parents at age 16. However, by 1994 this divorce rate was down to slightly more than one-and-a-half times that of children from intact families. Wolfinger (in Morin, 1998) speculates that a declining stigma against single mothers may partially explain his findings. Because these women are more likely to get better jobs and earn higher salaries, they can provide a more stable, financially secure home for their children. Also, with an elevated standard of living, single mothers may be less inclined to marry again, a marriage that may also turn sour and be detrimental to their children. Finally, recent no-fault divorce laws may have some impact on the reduced divorce rates of the children of broken marriages. Under a fault-based system, when marriages were much more difficult to terminate, many couples did not divorce until parental conflict was at its worst. Children suffered accordingly and their often-severe emotional difficulties carried over into marriages which failed at a very high rate.

While our presentation of material on this subject may lead one to believe that ending a marriage always has negative consequences for children, this is not necessarily the case. After reviewing the work of leading researchers in this field, William Galston (1996) concluded that there is a "critical distinction"

Population: 8,911,296
Life Expectancy at Birth (years): Male—76.6;
  Female—82.1
Form of Government: Constitutional Monarchy
Major Religions: Evangelical Lutheran (94%)
Major Racial and Ethnic Groups: Swedish (89%); Finnish (2%)
Population Doubling Time: No Growth
Per Capita GNP (1997 U.S. Dollars): $26,210
Principal Economic Activities: Industries; mining
Colonial Experience: Major power in seventeenth century
Adult Literacy Rate: 100%   Male—100%; Female—100%

The Future of the Family, or a Future without Families?

With a history of government-assisted family-support programs that began in the 1930s, no other nation has attempted to provide more benefits for its citizens than has Sweden. Mothers and fathers can take up to a year off work when a child is born and receive 90 percent of their normal salary. Individuals are also guaranteed that when they return from parental leave their jobs will be waiting for them (Willen and Montgomery, 1996). Parents also have the right to cut their work hours up to 25 percent until their children reach school age. By way of comparison, the 1993 Family and Medical Leave Act in the United States requires companies with more than 50 employees to offer up to 12 weeks of *unpaid* leave when a child is born or becomes seriously ill (Hass and Hwang, 1995). This legislation covers approximately half of the nation's workers. The Swedish government provides childcare benefits for children up to six years of age whose parents are working. Children between the ages of 7 and 12 are cared for in after-school "leisure centers." In addition to subsidized child-care, the state provides free education from kindergarten through the university level (Adams and Winston, 1980; Popenoe, 1988; "Progress," 1989).

Child welfare services match "contact families" with "client families" that are experiencing difficulty. Client families are usually single-parent families headed by women with a high school education (or less), who are unemployed or hold low-paying jobs with few opportunities for advancement. These women usually experience one or more of the following problems: loneliness, lack of contact with other adults, depression, substance abuse, and lack of parenting skills (Barth, 1991). The children of some of these women often have psychological problems. Contact families receive a "modest" amount of training and are matched with clients (with input from the latter in the selection process) and provide childcare ranging from a few hours to an overnight stay one or two weekends a month. For this they receive approximately $160 from the government with an additional reimbursement of $10 for each overnight visit (Barth, 1991). Handicapped adults receive a guaranteed income of approximately $1200 a month that is taxed at the lowest rate (De Bernardi, 1995).

One might well expect that such an extensive, well-funded support system would result in a nation of vibrant families with few social problems. However, sociologist David Popenoe (1991 p. 68), who has closely examined Swedish society, believes the traditional family in this nation is a "waning social institution." According to Popenoe, society's most fundamental institution has declined faster in Sweden than in any other Western industrialized country. "The family is smallest in size, least stable, and has the shortest lifespan. People are, therefore, family members for the smallest amount of time" (Popenoe, 1992, p. 117).

Marriage rates decreased sharply beginning in the mid-1960s, registering a 40 percent drop in 8 years. Swedish sociologist Jan Trost (in Popenoe, 1988, p. 169) notes that a decline of this magnitude and duration has not occurred "anywhere else or at any other time." By the late 1980s, this unprecedented 25-year period of declining marriage rates began to level off ("Stork's Return," 1991). Not only are Swedish marriage rates lower than those in any other industrialized country, but the average age at matrimony may well be the highest. Although a significant number of people have decided against making legal commitments to each other, they are still living together. Rather than marry, many Swedes have opted for nonmarital cohabitation, with some individuals moving routinely from one relationship to another (*serial monogamy*). Both cohabitation and marriage are now considered social institutions in Sweden; and while many people who live together plan to eventually marry, in the long run their wedding day never arrives. Many will terminate the relationship while others die before they are married (Trost, 1996).

As a consequence of these consensual unions, half of all Swedish children are born out of wedlock (the comparable number in the U.S. is 22 percent), and 65 percent of all first births are to unwed mothers (Trost, 1996). However, only 3 percent of births in Sweden are to mothers without partners either by way of cohabitation or marriage. Trost (1996) states that in his country marriage is no longer necessary for a "respectable" woman to have a baby.

While almost all children in Sweden are born into families with a mother and father (even if they are not married), children born out of wedlock are approximately three times more likely to see their parents separate as are individuals whose parents are married. Only two of five Swedish children will live continuously to the age of eighteen with both biological parents (Popenoe, 1992). People living together outside the institution of marriage appears to be a major factor in the dissolution of parental relationships. One need only walk out the door to end a nonlegal partnership (cohabitation), and there are no legal/financial consequences that must be faced once the relationship is over.

The decline of the traditional family must also be considered when examining the nation's growth rate. With the average woman having only 1.6 children during her childbearing years (15 to 49), this Scandinavian country of 8.9 million is experiencing negative population growth as there are 10 births and 11 deaths annually per 100,000 people. The current "mini" baby boom in Sweden has been viewed as merely a short-run compensation for previously delayed childbearing. Another explanation is that many women have decided to give birth to their second child closer to the birth of their first. These changes are not likely to result in a significant or long-lasting increase in the nation's overall fertility rate (Willen and Montgomery, 1996).

Not only are there fewer marriages in Sweden, but both marriages and consensual unions are dissolving at a rate that may be higher than in any other Western nation. Under the 1973 Swedish Marriage Code, "no-fault" divorces have a maximum six-month waiting period, although most divorces were to be granted immediately. Swedish law advocates a "clean break" philosophy, of divorce, meaning that each spouse should be responsible for his or her own financial support after the marriage has been terminated. As a consequence, alimony is almost nonexistent, and pensions are considered "special property" that cannot be divided upon divorce (Fine and Fine, 1994). Economic considerations that keep people form divorcing such as a lowered standard of living via alimony payments or loss of a portion of one's pension to a former spouse, are irrelevant in Sweden.

Staying in a relationship solely for the financial well-being of the children is not a concern for Swedish women (who are typically awarded custody of the children). If an ex-husband fails to make court-ordered child payments, the government meets his financial obligation and assumes responsibility for collecting money from the "deadbeat dad." These laws are an outgrowth of the Swedish philosophy that marriages should not remain intact simply for "external" reasons, in this case, financial security. Regardless of the intent of their framers, Swedish divorce laws, as well as much of the country's social welfare system, have been criticized for undermining the economic dependence of children on their parents and husbands and wives on each other.

From a sociological perspective, the destruction of traditional family relationships and values are latent consequences of government social policies. By meeting so many of their economic needs, the state has cut fundamental bonds that hold families together. As a result, family cohesion has been reduced to the emotional attachments members have for each other. And as any family therapist can attest, bonds of love and affection are all too easily broken by the pressures of daily life in modern societies.

Popenoe (1991) also argues that *familism* as a cultural value has diminished in Sweden. "Familism refers to the belief in a strong sense of family identification and loyalty, mutual assistance among family members, and a concern for the perpetuation of the family unit: the subordination of the interests and personality of individual family members to the interests and welfare of the family group" (p. 68). The well-being of individuals, therefore, and not the well-being of families is of primary importance in Swedish society. While sociologist Jan Trost (1996) of Sweden's Uppsala University might take issue with Popenoe's overall critique of the family, he would agree that the importance of *familism* in his country has declined. Trost notes that both politicians and "the rest of us" tend "to look at the individual *or* the household as a unit, *not* the family" (p. 724).

Another important factor in the transformation of the Swedish family has been the changing role of women who now earn approximately 90 percent of what Swedish men do (in the United States the comparable number is 76 percent). Approximately 80 percent of Swedish women are employed (one of the highest levels in the world), and half of these women work full time (Olin and Tandon, 1994). This means that hundreds of thousands of children are substantially raised by staff members in day-care centers. A government study revealed that at least half of the children in day-care facilities spent nine or more hours a day away from their parents, while 20 percent of those cared for by state employees were separated from family members for 10 hours or more each working day (Adams and Winston, 1980). No matter how professional and well-meaning, care given by employees may lack the "human touch" that can only be given by parents, siblings, and relatives. Although psychologists, social workers, and home helpers are proficient at attending to the specialized needs of children, who is to look out for the "whole person" (Popenoe, 1988, p. 206)?

While David Popenoe has been critical of the impact that Swedish welfare policies have had on the family, he is quick to point out the "benevolent" aspects of these policies. Along with parental leave and child allowances he ap-

plauds "the freedom of women in Sweden today, the nation's very low rate of teenage pregnancy and birth" as well as "the remarkable degree to which Sweden has minimized the economic luck of the draw in determining the material quality of people's lives" (Popenoe, 1992, p. 118). Social programs in Sweden have all but eliminated poverty and many of the problems associated with this condition such as hopelessness, substandard housing, hunger, malnutrition, and untreated health problems (Rosenthal, 1994). Because single women are provided with a minimum standard of living, poor females and children are better off in this Scandinavian nation than they are in most other countries (Spakes, 1992).

If too much of a good thing (the welfare state) has threatened

the traditional family in Sweden, one could argue that a lack of governmental support in this country has been just as detrimental (if not more so) to society's most fundamental institution. A lack of financial support and family services has contributed directly or indirectly to high rates of poverty (especially among minority children), juvenile crime, lack of education, meager health care, latchkey children, and hopelessness in the United States.

Perhaps some as yet unidentified middle ground between the indulgence of the family on the part of the Swedish government, and the comparative neglect of the family by the U.S. government will prove to be the most beneficial course of action for both the family and the larger society.

---

between divorces involving physical abuse or extensive emotional cruelty and those divorces that result from less serious problems. Minor children living in high-conflict families are usually better off when their parents divorce, while children residing in "lower-intensity" conflict homes are not. It is important to note (especially in high-conflict families), that a significant portion of what is typically considered the negative impact of divorce on children is caused by the marital discord (arguing and fighting) that precedes the breakup of the family (Cherlin et al., 1991). These are the *preseparation* problems associated with growing up in a "dysfunctional" family. Frank Furstenberg and Andrew Cherlin (in Galston, 1996, p. 15) have summarized their findings regarding marital conflict, divorce, and children:

> It is probably true that most children who live in a household filled with continual conflict between angry, embittered spouses would be better off if their parents split up—assuming that the level of conflict is lowered by the separation. . . . We think there are more cases in which there is little open conflict, but one or both parents finds the marriage personally unsatisfying . . . divorce may well make one or both spouses happier, but we strongly doubt that it improves the psychological well-being of the children.

SINGLE-PARENT FAMILIES

Although the number of single-parent families has increased dramatically in the post–World War II era, children living with either their mothers or fathers is not a recent phenomenon. For most of the history of this country (when life expectancy was less than 50 years), single-parent families were the result of the death of a spouse, typically the husband. However, as longevity has increased to approximately 75 years, one-parent families are overwhelmingly the product of both a high divorce rate and a significant number of children born out of wedlock. Between 1970 and 1984, the number of infants born to never-married mothers *increased* 500 percent, and although the number of teenagers (a significant percentage of whom are not married) having babies declined 12 percent from 1991 to 1997 (Havemann, 1998), the annual number of births to unmarried females remains high. Not surprisingly, the number of children living with both parents *decreased* from 85.2 percent in 1970 to 68.1 percent in 1998. Although 74.0 percent of white children resided with both parents in 1998 (see Table 9.2), only 36.2 percent of black youngsters lived with their fathers and mothers. Almost one half of all children born in

TABLE 9.2

Living Arrangements of Children Under 18 Years of Age by Race and Hispanic Origin (Percent Distribution): 1970, 1980, 1993

	Two Parents	Mother Only	Father Only	Neither Parent
All Races				
1970	85.2%	10.8%	1.1%	2.9%
1980	76.7	18.0	1.7	3.6
1998	68.1	23.3	4.4	4.2
White				
1970	89.5	7.8	0.9	1.8
1980	82.7	13.5	1.6	2.2
1998	74.0	18.2	4.6	3.2
Black				
1970	58.5	29.5	2.3	9.7
1980	42.2	43.9	1.9	12.0
1998	36.2	51.0	3.7	9.1
Hispanic Origin[a]				
1970	77.7	NA	NA	NA
1980	75.4	19.6	1.5	3.5
1998	63.6	26.8	5.0	4.0

Note: Does not include children living with other relatives or nonrelatives. NA = not available.

[a]Persons of Hispanic origin may be of any race.

Source: U.S. Bureau of the Census, *Marital Status and Living Arrangements: March 1998* (Washington, DC: U.S. Government Printing Office, 1998).

recent years will spend (or have already spent) some portion of their lives living with a single mother or father (McLanahan and Sandefur, 1998).

The following is a brief summary of the major characteristics associated with single-parent families in the United States having at least one child under 18 years of age (Norton and Glick, 1986; Dornbusch and Gray, 1988; Eggebeen and Lichter, 1991; Eggebeen, Snyder, and Manning, 1996). Approximately nine out of ten single-parent families are headed by women. However, while single-mother families increased by 160 percent from 1960 to 1990, the number of single-father families escalated by 245 percent during that same period. One reason for the rapid increase of the latter is that more fathers are now being awarded custody of their children as a consequence of divorce than in the past. Although divorced or never married, a significant number of single mothers and fathers live with a cohabitating partner. African Americans comprise just under 13 percent of the population, yet about one-third of all mother-child families are headed by black women. Single parents have less education than married couples;

approximately 30 percent of lone mothers and fathers have less than a high school education. In 1995, the median income of single-mother households was $21,348, less than two-thirds the $33,534 earned by single-father families.

In their highly acclaimed work *Growing Up with a Single Parent—What Hurts, What Helps,* sociologists Sara McLanahan and Gary Sandefur (1994) state that after ten years of research the evidence is "quite clear." Children who grow up in a household with only one biological parent are worse off, on average, than children who grow up in a household with both of their biological parents . . . " (p. 1). Children raised in single-parent families are less likely to graduate from high school and college, more likely to become pregnant teenagers, and more likely to be idle (unemployed and out of school) as young adults than their counterparts raised in intact two-parent families. However, McLanahan and Sandefur (1994) are quick to point out that while growing up in single-parent family increases the risk of "negative outcomes," it is not the singular nor necessarily major cause of these consequences.

"Deadbeat dads" who contribute little or no money toward support of their offspring are another major reason why hundreds of thousands of single mothers and their children are mired in poverty. For every million births to unmarried mothers, only 20 to 30 percent of fathers are identified. Of those women who do receive court-ordered child support payments, only 51 percent obtain the full amount (Lynch, 1995). As much as $27 billion in child-support payments go unpaid each year (LaRocco, 1994). The situation is especially difficult for poor single mothers. A study examining the support extended by the fathers of just over 6,000 children from inner-city neighborhoods in three cities concluded that these males "provide little social and economic support to their children" (Rangarajan and Gleason, 1998, p. 175). These fathers provided less support over time as their offspring grew and their relationships with the mothers became even more distant.

In an effort to help women collect child support payments, as of October 1996, the federal government requires employers to send the names, addresses, and social security numbers of all employees to child-support agencies. This same law mandates every state to set up a system matching that state's list of deadbeat dads against a list of people who have bank accounts in that state (Doherty, 1997).

The two most common explanations for the rise in single-parent families (the majority of which are in the lower class) are as follows: First, beginning in the 1970s the number of well-paying (manufacturing) jobs significantly fell, especially in the cities. From 1972 to 1994 the median income of men between 25 and 34 years of age declined by 26 percent after adjustment for inflation. In a recent sixteen-year period the wages of African-American males who did not finish high school dropped 50 percent. A report by the Annie C. Casey Foundation stated, "the simple truth is that disadvantaged young men who do not have the examples, education or opportunity to succeed in today's economy are not prepared to contribute as providers, protectors and mentors to their children" (in Vobejda, 1995, p. 34).

From this perspective both the cause *and* the solution to this problem are rooted in the opportunity structure for lower-class males. Regarding the latter, sociologist Christopher Jencks (in Ingwerson, 1994) notes that the earning potential of the poorest American men will have to be enhanced if children are to be raised by both their mothers and fathers. He states, "It seems likely that if you can raise employment and wage prospects for the bottom quarter of men, then more of them would be able to start a family" (p. A1).

Second, starting in the 1970s a loss of stigma associated with premarital sex developed together with a decline in "family values." This position appeals to political conservatives who very often downplay or reject structural explanations for a given phenomenon in favor of one that sees changes in human behavior as a function (almost exclusively) of changing values.

POLYGAMOUS FAMILIES

A marital system involving multiple spouses—husbands or wives—is called polygamy (see Table, 9.1), whereas an institutionalized pattern of marriage limited to multiple wives only is known as polygyny. The most well-known practice of polygyny in the United States is associated with the Church of Jesus Christ of Latter Day Saints, also known as the Mormons. Polygamy (we will employ this commonly used although technically incorrect term) was practiced by Mormons in the (then) Utah Territory as early as the 1830s and 1840s, and became an official part of Church doctrine in 1852 (Weisberger, 1996; Biele, 1998).

One of the misconceptions about polygamy is that all Mormons engaged in this marital practice. However, since there are approximately an equal number of males and females in any human society, there would hardly be enough women for every man who wanted more than one wife. Sociologists William Kephart and William Zellner (1994) estimate that at the height of Mormon polygamy in 1860, no more than 10 to 15 percent of the population of this religious group lived in families with multiple wives. Although there are instances of men having as many as 18 spouses and 65 children, in the "clear majority" of cases, husbands "had but one additional wife" (p. 245).

In his book *Isn't One Wife Enough?* Kimball Young (a grandson of Brigham Young) commented on the living arrangements of nineteenth-century polygamous Mormons. Concerning the case of a man who lived with six wives in a house he had specially built for his family Young wrote (1954, p. 218):

Each wife had her own bedroom but there was a common kitchen and dining room. There was a living room which was used by the husband as his office. He also had his own bedroom. The duties of the wives were systematically organized by the husband. Some were assigned to the laundry or to cleaning the house; others to the sewing room, or the kitchen. Each one's task was a duty performed for the whole family.

Chapter titles in Young's book—"Plural Wives in Competition and Conflict," "Cooperation Among Wives," and "Some Couldn't Take It: Desertion and Divorce"—reflect the positive and negative aspects of polygamous relationships. Since no systematic investigation of these unions was conducted in the last century, and, as Young (1954, p. 227) states, separation, divorce, and remarriage was a "hit and miss affair," it is impossible to know how many of these marriages were harmonious, and how many resulted in misery for some, if not all, family members.

From its inception, polygamy was severely criticized by non-Mormons, and in 1856 the national platform of the newly formed Republican Party linked polygamy with slavery, referring to both as instances of "barbarism" (Weisberger, 1996). The U.S. Congress prohibited polygamy in 1862 with the Mormon Church outlawing this practice in 1890, most observers agree, as a precondition for statehood. (Utah became the forty-fifth state in 1896.) While the Church of Jesus Christ of Latter Day Saints has become part of (conservative) mainstream America, splinter groups that broke away from the main church continue in the polygamous tradition. Today, an estimated 20,000 to 90,000 individuals are currently thought to be living in polygamous families (Biele, 1998; Cart, 1998).

Living arrangements of contemporary multiple-wife families vary. As it was in the last century, in numerous instances, everyone resides under one roof with each woman having her own bedroom. A "visiting" schedule is determined by the husband and may be posted conspicuously so that all of his wives are aware of the sleeping arrangements. In more affluent families women and their biological children may live in separate homes with the husband making the rounds on a regular basis (Udall, 1998).

In recent years a group called "Tapestry of Polygamy" (comprised of women formerly part of polygamous marriages) has been highly critical of this marital arrangement. They claim that polygamy victimizes women and "puts children in harms way" (Biele, 1998, p. 3). Although polygamy as it is currently practiced in Utah and neighboring states is technically legal (marriages beyond the first are solely religious and not state-sanctioned ceremonies), because of the stigma attached to this practice, pregnant women rarely if ever receive prenatal care and many children have no health or dental coverage. Critics contend that child abuse and incest are rampant, and that girls as young as 10 years old are forced into arranged marriages. An additional criticism is that polygamy has produced an untold number of invisible "nonpeople," that is, individuals with no birth certificates or drivers licenses who neither pay taxes nor vote (Cart, 1998). Although polygamy has been defended on the grounds of religious freedom, Utah's Attorney General (Graham in Murr, 1998, p. 37) stated that "The claim of religious freedom is no defense to the crimes of statutory rape, incest, unlawful sexual conduct with a minor, child abuse or cohabitant abuse."

Individuals much more sympathetic to polygamy contend that the problems associated with this lifestyle exist in the same proportion as would be found in any other segment of society. Psychologist Irwin Altman (in Biele, 1998) is of the opinion that polygamy is a "form of enormous social security" as family members are part of a larger, mutually supportive group. Utah attorney and journalist Elizabeth Joseph (1998) would agree.

> I know that if I have to work late my daughter will be at home surrounded by loving adults with whom she is comfortable and who know her schedule without my telling them. . . . And I know that when I get home from work, if I'm dog-tired and stressed out, I can be alone and guilt free. It's a rare day when all eight of my husband's wives are tired and stressed out at the same time. (p. 27)

Joseph views polygamy in terms of a "free-market" approach to marriage inasmuch as under this system a women can wed the best man available, regardless if he is married or not. For her, the only sensible marital alternative for women is polygamy, "the ultimate feminist lifestyle" (p. 28).

GAY FAMILIES

According to some estimates, as many as 25 million people—approximately 10 percent of the population—are predominantly or exclusively homosexual. As a result of gay activism, favorable court rulings, gay rights legislation, and a more tolerant (heterosexual) public over the past twenty-five years, homosexuals have made great strides toward the overall acceptance of their lifestyle. In what has been referred to as the "last great civil rights revolution" (Harris, 1991), many gay men and women have been fighting for and have achieved some (albeit limited) victories. While a number of cities allow "domestic partnerships" that give gay couples benefits such as health coverage and sick leave, many people in the gay community want the right to marry legally. Legislation recognizing gay marriage not only would be an important symbolic victory, but would also give homosexual couples access to tax breaks, Social Security

This lesbian couple share a playful moment with their child. A number of homosexual women have given birth after being artificially inseminated; other lesbian couples have adopted children. Are these same-sex unions an alternative lifestyle, or another example of the demise of the American family?

Advocates of same-sex marriages have argued that society has a good deal to gain from committed, lasting relationships, be they heterosexual or homosexual, and that "Gay marriages wouldn't weaken the family; it would strengthen it" (Hartinger, 1991, p. 683). Permitting homosexuals to marry would reduce the promiscuity in the gay community and reduce the spread of sexually transmitted diseases (including AIDS) that also affect heterosexuals. Children raised in loving, intact gay families would not be subject to the problems faced by children in single-parent households. Homosexual marriages would also reduce the number of secret ("closet") gays who marry heterosexuals in an effort to be part of a family or conform to a straight world. According to some estimates, 20 percent of all gays eventually adopt this strategy. Economically, many industries such as insurance companies and toy manufacturers would benefit as gay families and their children adopt the same patterns of spending as heterosexual families.

Opponents of same-sex marriages believe that by definition marriage is the union of individuals of different sexes. By definition, therefore, homosexuals do not meet the fundamental requirements of marriage, and "same-sex marriage" is an oxymoron (Bolte, 1998). They argue that these marriages are ungodly, and constitute a further attack on the already weakened "traditional" American family. Finally, many adherents of this position are convinced that children raised in gay households are at risk of becoming homosexuals themselves.

Brent Hartinger (1991) dismisses this latter contention stating that a review of thirty-five studies of homosexual parents found that parents' sexual preference had no effect on children's sexual orientation. In other words, children raised by gay parents are no more likely to become homosexuals than children brought up in heterosexual households (Bolte, 1998). Children raised by gay parents may also be more sensitive to the suffering and struggles that minority groups (racial, ethnic, and gender as well as sexual-preference groups) have endured for so long in this country. These individuals may well reach adulthood with a more defined sense of social justice (Clay, 1991).

The issue of same-sex marriage has been a contentious one in state legislatures across the country and will continue to be so in the foreseeable future. Bills banning these marriages have been introduced in 32 states; seven have failed and five have passed (Gallagher, 1997). In December 1999, the Vermont Supreme Court ruled that although same-sex couples cannot be legally married, they are entitled to all of the same benefits (state income tax breaks, for example) that heterosexual couples enjoy (Cloud, 1999). If

benefits for surviving spouses and dependents, comprehensive family health plans, and financial discounts that are now available exclusively to married heterosexuals (Rebeck, 1990). In short, the legal recognition of same-sex marriages would provide gay couples the rights and economic advantages currently reserved for "straight couples."

According to one estimate there are three to four million homosexual parents raising between six and fourteen million children in the United States. These children are the product of adoptions, artificial insemination, and prior heterosexual unions (Bolte, 1998). Regarding artificial insemination, while most doctors will not perform this procedure on a single woman, some lesbian health centers cater to the desires of lesbian women to become mothers. The growing number of children being raised by homosexual couples in the past 20 years has been referred to as a "gay baby boom" (Bolte, 1998).

openly gay marriages become a reality in the United States, demonstrations against homosexuals could turn violent and result in an escalation of physical attacks against gays. Also, if same-sex marriages are legalized in some but not all states (which is the most likely scenario) there might well be a migration of homosexuals into these states from other more conservative parts of the nation where similar laws have little chance of being passed.

VIOLENCE IN THE FAMILY

As we noted in the section on theory, conflict sociologists view the family as a microcosm of the tension and conflict that exist in a larger capitalist state. Other social scientists would argue that this turmoil, which often results in domestic violence, is hardly limited to capitalist societies in the modern world. The history of Western civilization is rife with examples of children subjected to "unspeakable cruelties" (Gelles and Pedrick-Cornell, 1990, p. 27). Much the same could be said for women. In ancient Rome, men had almost unlimited power over the lives of their wives and children. Husbands could chastise, divorce, even kill their wives for adultery, public drunkenness, or attending public games (Gelles and Pedrick-Cornell, 1990). During the Middle Ages, women were burned alive for talking back to a priest, for stealing, for scolding and nagging, for masturbating, and for homosexual behavior (Strauss and Gelles, 1986).

Survey research reveals that domestic violence is pervasive in the United States, with one nationwide study concluding that approximately 16 percent of married couples engage in at least one act of violence annually (Straus and Gelles, 1990). In 1976 almost 3,000 people were killed by an intimate (spouse, ex-spouse, common-law spouse, same-sex partner, boyfriend, girlfriend), a number that dropped to just under 2,000 in 1996. These figures represent 13.6 and 8.8 percent of all homicides in those years respectively. About one in four violent offenders in local jails and 7 percent of violent offenders in state prisons committed their crime against an intimate (*Violence by Intimates,* 1998).

Child Abuse

Violence has been defined as an "act carried out with the intention or perceived intention of causing physical pain or injury to another person" (Gelles and Pedrick-Cornell, 1990, p. 2). Regarding this behavior as it exists in the family, a distinction is often made between *normal violence* and *abusive violence.* The former consists of the slaps, pushes, shoves, and spankings people generally consider part of raising children or interacting with one's husband or wife. Abusive violence is significantly more serious and consists of punches, kicks, bites, choking, beatings, stabbings, shooting, or attempted stabbings and shootings (Gelles and Pedrick-Cornell, 1990). Because so much domestic violence never comes to the attention of the police, school officials, or child protection services, estimates of the extent of child abuse in this country vary from a low of several thousand cases a year to a high of 3 million incidents annually. It should be kept in mind that most of our estimates and projections concerning the incidence of child abuse are "educated guesses" (Gelles, 1978, p. 582).

In contemporary American society a child is more likely to be killed by a parent than by a stranger. A national survey of two-parent households concluded that an estimated 6.9 million children are physically abused each year by their parents (Rudo and Powell, 1998). Approximately one million cases of abuse (physical and sexual and including neglect) come to the attention of officials (school, police, and child protection services) annually. Many children are abused repeatedly, even after their cases have been brought to the attention of local authorities (DePanfilis and Zuravin, 1998). The U.S. Advisory Board on Child Abuse and Neglect states that each year in this country an estimated 2,000 children (the majority under 4 years of age) die at the hands of their parents and primary care givers ("Parents Who Kill Their Children," 1995; "Child Abuse and Neglect," 1997).

Research indicates that mothers are somewhat more likely to physically abuse their children than are fathers. The explanation usually given for this finding is that mothers typically spend considerably more time than fathers in the day-to-day socialization of their offspring. They are more likely than fathers to witness the transgressions of their children and punish that behavior. It also appears that boys are more likely to be physically aggressive than girls. Some investigators argue that being more aggressive, boys commit more punishable offenses than girls and that our society tolerates more physical punishment for boys as a method of toughening them up (Gelles, 1978). Abusers believe (or rationalize) that this behavior prepares boys for their roles as adult males in an aggressive, competitive, often violent society.

In addition to the gender of the adult care giver, his or her biological relationship to the child is of importance. Looking at data from their country, Canadian psychologists Martin Daly and Margo Wilson (in Tudge, 1997) discovered that children under 3 years of age are at least seven times more likely to be abused by stepparents than by biological mothers and fathers, and that children under age 2 are more than 100 times more likely to be killed by a stepparent (especially a stepfather) than by biological parents. It appears that the biological relationship offers protection from some forms of child abuse.

Although research examining the relationship between age and abuse is somewhat contradictory, younger children appear more likely to be abused than their older siblings. The period between 3 months and 3 years of age is a particularly dangerous time in a child's life. Younger children cry more and therefore interfere with the activities of adults to a greater degree. Lacking sophisticated cognitive skills, these children are less likely to respond appropriately when their parents attempt to talk and reason with them. Infants under 2 years of age are vulnerable to the "shaken baby syndrome," brain injuries incurred when a crying baby is shaken vigorously by an angry adult.

Approximately 13 percent of abuse cases known to authorities involve sexual abuse, with girls at least three times more likely to be (official) victims of this crime than boys ("Young and Abused," 1996). Although children as young as 2 and 3 have been abused in this manner, the typical child sexual assault victim is between 8 and 12 years of age. Whereas girls in single-parent families headed by women are especially vulnerable to their mothers' boyfriends (and if they should marry, stepfathers), boys are more often taken advantage of by neighbors or an authority figure such as a coach. While some social scientists have found that sexually abused girls were much more likely to become pregnant before age 18 than girls who were not abused in this manner (Zierler et al. 1991), other researchers failed to find a causal relationship between sexual abuse and teenage pregnancy (Herman-Giddens, et al., 1998).

The sight of a badly beaten 2-year-old inevitably raises the question "How could anybody possibly do that to a helpless child?" To the general public, the answer typically focuses on the mental health of the perpetrator—a "sick individual." However, the psychopathological explanation does not apply to the majority of parents (Emery, 1989). In other words, no "abusive personality" type of victimizer has been identified. Rather, factors such as situational stress, lack of child-rearing knowledge and skills, and misunderstanding children's motives for misbehaving are related to child abuse. Parental stress resulting from unemployment, problems at work, serious illness, and the death of a loved one contributes to higher rates of violence for both mothers and fathers. Work-related causes of abuse means that the welfare of the nation's children is contingent to some extent on economic factors such as rates of employ-

ment, job satisfaction, job turnover, and the number of people living below the poverty line as well as political decisions concerning the amount and duration of unemployment compensation, and job training.

Parents battling each other on a regular basis can be considered an indirect form of child abuse inasmuch as witnessing this behavior can result in a number of difficulties for children (McNeal and Amato, 1998).

1. Research indicates that both boys and girls react to parental conflict with feelings of fear, anger, and depression suggesting that "marital violence is inherently stressful for children" (p. 125).
2. Because they are egocentric, children often blame themselves for their parents behavior, resulting in a feeling of guilt and a decline in self-worth.
3. Parental conflict can produce emotional insecurity in children which may lead to an inability to trust other people and form close, stable relationships.
4. Interparental hostility can teach children that it is acceptable to resolve disagreements via physical force, thereby increasing the chances that they (the children) will turn to violence as a means of settling conflict in their relationships.

It is "highly probable" that children living in homes where parental violence occurs regularly are well aware of the situation. Guesstimates on the number of children who witness their mothers and fathers fighting range from 3.3 to 10 million a year (Rudo and Powell, 1998).

Battered Women

Domestic violence is the leading cause of death and injury to women in this country, resulting in more physical (and probably emotional) harm than the combined number of motor vehicle accidents, rapes, and muggings. Estimates regarding the number of females abused by their boyfriends and husbands each year range from just over a million to as many as 18 million. This wide discrepancy is explained in part by the "type and purpose of the survey, the definition of abuse used, and the political context" of the research ("Violent Relationships—Battering and Abuse Among Adults," 1997, p. 12). Like physically mistreated children, abused women are slapped, punched, kicked, burned, stabbed, and occasionally shot. They often require medical attention and overnight hospitalization. Battered women have higher levels of headaches, nervousness, and depression and lower self-esteem than other women.

Numerous studies have found that the majority of husbands who beat their wives use and abuse alcohol and other drugs. This association has given rise

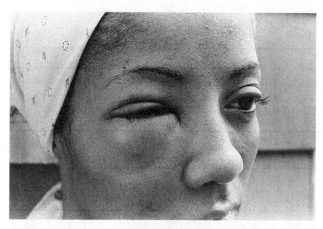

This woman has been severely beaten by her husband. Domestic violence is the leading cause of death and injury to women in the United States, resulting in more physical (and probably) emotional harm than the number of motor vehicle deaths, rapes, and female muggings combined.

to the "demon rum" explanation of domestic violence (Gelles and Pedrick-Cornell, 1990). Alcohol and drugs serve as "disinhibitors"; that is, they reduce men's inhibitions and unleash their violent tendencies. From this perspective, the solution to the battered female syndrome is simple and straightforward. Keep husbands and boyfriends away from drugs, and they won't abuse their partners. However, there is little evidence to support this purported cause-and-effect relationship. Rather, the use of alcohol and other drugs is used as an excuse by men who want to physically harm their wives and girlfriends. The ingestion of these substances provides a handy, and too often accepted, rationalization for their crimes. "It wasn't me beating my wife, it was the drug." "I was drunk and didn't know what I was doing." As Gelles and Pedrick-Cornell (1990,p. 16) point out, "Violent spouses and parents learn that, if they do not want to be held responsible for their violence, they should drink before they hit or at least say they were drunk."

Data from numerous studies indicate that spousal abuse, like other forms of family violence, is most prevalent in the lower classes. Experts in this field tend to agree that the employment status of males is a major contributing factor to this problem. "Being unemployed is devastating to men in our society" (Gelles and Pedrick-Cornell, 1990, p. 75). A significant component of being a man (especially a husband and father) is to provide for the financial well-being of one's family. This is very important in a status-conscious, consumer-oriented society like ours in which self-worth is linked to material success and the esteem (or lack of esteem) derived from one's occupation and economic status.

Whereas people usually look to the police and courts for help (and justice) when they become victims of a violent crime, for most of the history of this country battered women found that law enforcement officials and district attorneys were less than enthusiastic both in arresting and prosecuting male offenders. There are a number of reasons for this apathy on the part of the criminal justice system (Hirschel and Hutchinson, 1992): (1) Violence within the family has traditionally been considered a private matter that should be settled by those involved in the dispute, (2) Victims have been characterized as uncooperative, that is, although they want the violence to stop, women are often unwilling to press charges or testify against their husbands. As such, police officers and prosecuting attorneys have viewed intervention in family disputes as a waste of time. (3) Officials are often of the opinion that arresting the husband would cause additional problems inasmuch as the offender was typically the family's only financial provider. (4) Officers who responded to these calls were usually male. Siding with the abuser they failed to intervene formally (make an arrest).

In recent years the attitudes and policies of police officers, prosecutors, and judges has changed considerably regarding domestic violence. For example, in California, an individual convicted of misdemeanor (a less serious offense than a felony) domestic violence is likely to be ordered by the judge to complete a year of group counseling in addition to going to jail and doing community work (Brooks, 1994b). In a growing number of states police are required to make arrests in all domestic violence cases even if the abused spouse does not want to press charges. However, the deterrent effect of mandatory arrests as opposed to other interventions (mediation, imposed separation for a specified number of hours or days) has been called into question (Hirschel and Hutchinson, 1992).

The first shelter for battered women in this country was established in 1965 by an Al-Anon group (wives of alcoholics) in Pasadena, California. As of 1980 there were approximately 190 such havens across the United States with that number increasing to about 1,400 in 1997 (Johnson, 1997). The individuals who administer and staff these shelters have played an important role in protecting battered women.

Abused Males

In a male-dominated society like the United States that has produced a long line of cowboy, military, and police officer/private eye tough guys, as well as the actors who have portrayed these individuals, many people are surprised to learn that males are somewhat more likely to be abused in a domestic situation than are females (Straus, Gelles, and Steinmetz, 1980; Saunders, 1986; Straus and Gelles, 1986; Voelker, 1997). However, while victimization rates of husbands/boyfriends and wives/girlfriends are approximately the same, the circumstances surrounding violent incidents of this nature and the consequences of these acts are very different.

Kevin Hamberger and his colleagues (1997) have summarized the research regarding these differences: The motivation that propels this violence is gender specific. Males abuse females to punish and control them (often for challenging their authority) as well as to gain their partner's attention. As a result of her cross-cultural research, Rebecca Morley (1994) argues that although the specific stresses that lead to wife battering are "local and various," the fundamental motivation for this behavior is the same: "the husband's assertion of his perceived right to make claims on and control his wife, and his corresponding denial of this right to his wife" (p. 46).

Females engage in violence for self-defense, to escape an abusive male, in retaliation for abuse, and out of anger toward an abusive partner. A significant amount of violence on the part of women is retaliatory, that is, women fighting back after prolonged abuse at the hands of their mates. In many instances women are protecting their children (who are also being abused) as well as themselves. Men tend to engage in violence more frequently than women, and male violence is more severe than female violence, leading to greater injuries on the part of the women.

Although men generally deliver the last and most damaging blow in a domestic confrontation (Eshleman, 1996), this is not always the case. Hundreds of men are killed by their wives and girlfriends each year (*Violence by Intimates,* 1998). Approximately two-thirds of these women are convicted of murder and spend considerable time (for some, life) in prison. One reason for this high rate of conviction is that in the majority of states judges are not required to hear evidence of spousal abuse during the trial. From a conflict perspective, this is the final act of violence against women in a male-dominated society.

THE FAMILY AND MODERNIZATION

In countries like the United States, the family has changed significantly in the past 200 years. Since these changes paralleled the industrialization of society, it is not difficult to reach the conclusion that industrialization has been the principal, if not sole, factor responsible for them. Sociologist William J.

Goode (1963) argued persuasively, however, that the relation between Western industrialization and the family is much more complex than simply cause (industrialization) and effect (family). To begin with, families in Europe were already changing from an extended to a nuclear structure in the seventeenth century, long before the Industrial Revolution (approximately 1800) began to spread. This certainly calls into question the commonly held assumption that the nuclear family "emerges when a culture is invaded by industrialization and urbanization (Goode, 1963, p. 10).

According to Goode, the link between the nuclear family and industrialization is one in which the former met the "demands" of the latter. For example, an achievement-based, open-class, industrial society requires both geographical and social mobility. Neolocal nuclear families facilitate this mobility, allowing people to break kinship ties and sell their labor in the open market. Freed from the intense social control of nearby relatives, individuals can more easily change their speech, dress, and overall lifestyle while conforming to the demands of new jobs in an urban environment. Goode contended that Western industrialization would have been much more difficult (and certainly slower) if "family systems had perhaps been patriarchal and polygamous, with a full development of arranged marriages and a harem system" (p. 22).

In a similar line of thinking, sociologist Brigitte Berger (1992, p. 28) has argued convincingly that the nuclear family "is the precondition rather than the consequence of modernization and economic development." She states that in the "protoindustrial" households that were spreading throughout Europe in the seventeenth and eighteenth century, households where rural people were engaged in cottage work associated with the textile industry, a system of values was emerging that emphasized hard work, frugality, habits of saving money, personal drive, and self-regulation. These values ushered in a heretofore unknown way of life that was absolutely essential to the new capitalist industrial system (Berger, 1992).

The fit between the nuclear family and "certain industrial demands" was enhanced by the ideologies of economic progress and upward mobility and of the conjugal family itself. These are powerful assertions that destroy hundreds of years of tradition. They emphasize the worth of the individual rather than the inherited aspects of wealth and social position. In other words, individuals are to be evaluated on the basis not of lineage (an ascribed status), but of ability (an achieved status). Goode noted that a "strong theme of democracy runs through this ideology" (1963, p. 19) and encouraged people not to submit to the tyranny of the group, including the family. If an individual is not satisfied with family life, then he or she has the right to change it.

Inasmuch as the nuclear family is bilineal and does not pass on its wealth to the eldest son (or give it exclusively to males), the difference in life chances for sons and daughters is much less unequal than in other inheritance systems. Therefore, significantly more young people are able to develop their talents and take their place in an industrializing society. The nuclear family ideology enters society before industrialization has begun and prepares individuals for the demands of the new economic order that is to follow (Goode, 1963).

THE DEVELOPING WORLD

Goode's work sheds light on the relation between industrialization and the family in developed countries such as the United States, but how can we apply these insights to the relation between the family and modernization now occurring in the developing world? To begin with, the ideologies of economic progress and the nuclear family are known in the developing world, at least among the educated classes. We can also assume that, with the spread of information by movies, radio, and television in the so-called global village, these ideologies are common knowledge to tens of millions of less-educated people as well. Given that knowledge, any further movement from traditional family structures to nuclear families is likely to depend on economic conditions and political philosophies. As a country industrializes, the demands of progress will affect family structures as people change their patterns of behavior, including the organization of the family to meet those demands. One does not have to be a Marxist to see how the economic and material conditions of a society affect its patterns of behavior.

According to the modernization perspective, agricultural societies are characterized by early marriages, a high birth rate, and people living with extended families in rural areas. While marrying at a young age and having large families is advanta-

geous in a farm setting that requires a significant amount of labor, this situation is disadvantageous to females as it keeps them continuously dependent on males, initially on fathers in their family or origin, and then on (usually older) husbands in their family of procreation (Oropesa, 1997). However, as countries develop and females have greater access to an expanding infrastructure (education, health care, the economy, transportation, and communication) their status within the family increases. As a nation modernizes, rural-to-urban migration (see Chapter 13) increases dramatically as people move to cities in search of greater economic opportunities. Kemper (in Oropesa, 1997, p. 1295) noted that this geographical transition can lead to more egalitarian marriages as nearly all of these families "demonstrate a low level of male authoritarianism and a high degree of 'democratic' conflict resolution between spouses." The marginalization perspective predicts that development will make the already very difficult lives of women in poor countries even worse. Adherents of this position begin with the assumption that economic development leads to increased mechanization in both agriculture and fledgling industries. However, because women are likely to be excluded from these "core economic activities," their status is lowered. Economic development can work against women in another, more physically dangerous manner. When men become unemployed as a result of economic changes, or women obtain a job for the same reason, husbands may attempt to maintain their position of dominance within the family by beating their wives (Oropesa, 1997).

Although it is impossible to predict how family structures and relationships will change as a result of modernization, we can be certain of at least two things: Change will come much faster than it did in the past as many poor nations attempt to develop as soon as possible; and governments both democratic and totalitarian will have a growing impact on the family as they attempt to control population growth, limit migration from rural to urban areas, and maintain control over specific segments of the population (e.g., women).

SUMMARY AND REVIEW

Theoretical Perspectives

1. *According to functionalist sociologists, what are the major functions of the family in society?*

From the functionalist perspective, the family performs six major functions in all societies to one degree or another. It meets the biological and economic needs of its members; it legitimizes some sexual relation-

ships and prohibits others; biological reproduction within the family ensures the group's continuity over time; it is where a major portion of childhood socialization takes place; it provides individuals membership within a larger social structure; and it provides people with emotional support and companionship. (Pp. 195–196)

2. *How do conflict theorists view the family in capitalist societies?*

Conflict theorists are more likely to see the family as an institution of domination and exploitation. According to this perspective, males exploited by the bourgeoisie in a capitalist society become frustrated and abuse their wives and children. The family is considered a microcosm of the tension, conflict, and oppression that exist in the larger society. (P. 196)

3. *What do we know about the social and psychological background of the vast majority of married couples in this society?*

In the United States, most marriages occur between two people (a) of the same social class, (b) within the same racial group, (c) of the same religion, (d) with similar levels of education, (e) with the same physical and psychological characteristics, and (f) who live within a few miles of each other. (P. 198)

Love, Marriage, Divorce, and Nontraditional Families

4. *What variables are associated with divorce in the United States?*

In the United States, the chances that a marriage will end in divorce are associated with the following: age at marriage, length of marriage, social class of the couple, race, religion, and whether their parents have been divorced. (Pp. 199–200)

5. *What effect does divorce have on children?*

Research on the effect of divorce on children is inconclusive and sometimes contradictory. Some investigators report that children adjust to a divorce and their new family setup within two years of the breakup. Others have found that the negative consequences of divorce can affect children for many years, even after they have become adults. (Pp. 202–203)

6. *Why has the number of single-parent families increased dramatically over the past thirty years?*

The number of single-parent families in this country has increased dramatically in recent years primarily because of (a) the high divorce rate and (b) a large number of children born to never-married mothers since 1970. Approximately nine out of ten single parents are female, and many of these women are poor as a result of low levels of education and husbands who pay little if any child support. In 1998, 51 percent of all African-American children lived only with their mothers, compared to only 18 percent of white children. When compared to their married counterparts, single mothers suffer greater job-family role strain and are more prone to depression and decreased life satisfaction. One study found that young adults raised in single-parent families had lower levels of educational, occupational, and economic achievement than young adults from two-parent families. (Pp. 206–208)

7. *What are the major arguments of the advocates and opponents of homosexual marriages?*

Over the past twenty-five years, there has been a growing acceptance in the country as a whole of ho-

mosexuals and a homosexual lifestyle. Many individuals in the gay community are striving for the right to marry legally (same-sex marriages) and enjoy the advantages (Social Security benefits, family health insurance) currently reserved for heterosexual couples. Advocates of homosexual marriages argue that such unions would reduce promiscuity in the gay community and diminish the spread of sexually transmitted diseases that also affect heterosexuals. It appears that being raised by homosexual parents has no effect on children's sexual orientation. Some school districts are informing students about same-sex relationships, marriages, and families. If legally sanctioned same-sex marriages are to become a reality in one or more states, the gay community will have to overcome the verbal (and possibly physical) attacks of conservative religious and political groups. (Pp. 209–211)

Violence in the Family

8. *What are some of the major findings regarding domestic violence in the United States?*

Family violence has a long history in the Western world. In male-dominated societies in which physical punishment was the prevailing method for maintaining law, order, and respect for authority, it is hardly surprising that men would resort to violence for the purpose of disciplining their wives and children. As many as 3 million children may be abused in the United States each year. Mothers are somewhat more likely than fathers to abuse their children, probably because mothers spend more time in the day-to-day socialization of their offspring. Children are more likely to be abused by their stepparents than by their biological parents. Domestic violence is the leading cause of death and injury to women in the United States. Not only do these women suffer from the physical consequences of their abuse, they also endure the psychological ramifications of being battered. One aspect of domestic violence against women that is often overlooked is marital rape. Husbands are physically abused by their wives in large numbers, although the circumstances surrounding this abuse are often very different from those of husbands beating their wives. In many instances, women who are being abused by their husbands retaliate to protect themselves and their children. (Pp. 211–214)

The Family and Modernization

9. *When and why did families change from an extended form to a nuclear structure?*

According to William J. Goode, families in Europe were changing from an extended to a nuclear structure before the beginning of the Industrial Revolution. The nuclear family met the needs of an achievement-based, open-class industrializing society that also required both geographical and social mobility. Freed from traditional patterns of behavior and the intense social control of nearby relatives, individuals could adapt to the demands of an emerging industrial, urban society. (P. 214)

Education and Religion

On April 20, 1999, two teenaged boys, embarking on what was later described by authorities as "a suicide mission," walked into Columbine High School in Littleton, Colorado, and opened fire with an assortment of weapons, including homemade bombs. The two members of a loosely knit group of student outcasts known informally as "the Trench Coat Mafia" shot and killed twelve fellow students and a teacher before taking their own lives.

Occurring as they did in an affluent suburban neighborhood and involving middle-class and upper-middle-class students both as perpetrators and victims, these shootings seemed to especially shock and horrify the nation. But, though the most deadly incident of its type, the Columbine episode was by no means the first multiple-victim school shooting in recent U.S. history. Beginning some three years earlier, in February 1996, a series of attacks by teenaged students had left at least 15 people dead and dozens of others wounded at rural and suburban high schools and middle schools across the country. Nor was Columbine the last episode in this tragic series: Exactly one month after the Colorado killings, a 15 year-old Georgia student shot and wounded six fellow students at his suburban high school (Schmidt, 1999). Something was going terribly wrong.

That "something" has been the subject of a heated and continuing debate among members of the media, educators, social scientists, politicians, members of the clergy, concerned parents, and a host of other groups. Just about everyone and everything—the easy availability of deadly weapons; the proliferation of violence on television, in films, and in video and computer games; the decaying family structure; liberal politicians and judges; widespread abortion and birth control; the general lack of "morality" in American society—has been cited by some party at some point as being the single most significant cause of tragedies such as Columbine. As might be expected, suggestions for policies to deal with escalating school violence have varied widely, depending on the particular factor or factors defined as responsible. These proposals have ranged from very specific gun-control measures (called for by, among other people, President Clinton) to more general calls for reestablishing and strengthening both the traditional American family and traditional American values (an approach advocated by a number of religious leaders and groups).

Spurred by public outrage over the growing wave of violence in U.S. schools, the House of Representatives passed a resolution in June 1999, permitting the posting of the Ten Commandments in public schools throughout the country. The purpose of that resolution, according to its backers, was to provide a "moral compass" to young people who are growing up in difficult times and facing hard choices (Aderholt, in Arvidson and Leaming, 1999). However, the resolution—which generated immediate negative responses from a variety of groups across the nation—will likely trigger an eventual U.S. Supreme Court decision if also passed by the Senate. In 1980, the Supreme Court had declared unconstitutional a 1978 Kentucky state law "requiring the posting of a copy of the Ten Commandments, purchased with private contributions, on the wall of each public school classroom in the state" on the grounds that the law violated the constitutional mandate of separation of church and state (Thollander, 1997). But, in spite of that existing ruling and the strong likelihood of civil lawsuits, in August 1999 at least one school district in Kentucky began posting the Ten Commandments in school classrooms as part of "an effort to start having good morals in school . . . because of all the violent issues that have been showing up" (Bond, in "Kentucky School District," 1999). Both school district officials and the members of the House who voted in favor of the resolution argue that its intent is not to impose any one religion on students but, rather, to give them a sense of the moral principles on which the United States is premised. According to the resolution's sponsor, Rep. Robert Aderholt (in Arvidson and Leaming, 1999, p. 2), "Every one of the supporters of this amendment understands that Congress should not mandate that anyone should bow to one particular religion. But to completely divorce ourselves from the fact that our country was founded on the basis of the Ten Commandments is wrong."

Intentions notwithstanding, the possible posting of the Ten Commandments in the nation's public schools has reopened old conflicts and old wounds regarding the role of religion in public education. In the modern era, this battle began with the famous Scopes "Monkey Trial" of 1925, and accelerated following the U.S. Supreme Court's 1960s rulings that government-sponsored prayer and Bible readings in public schools are unconstitutional. It pits those who believe that religious doctrines of any kind have no place in public schools against those who believe that public schools have the right—if not the obligation—to teach their students religious beliefs and moral principles. The battle has continued, with varying intensity, over the past 75 years, and shows no signs of abating. Should students in public schools be taught important moral lessons? If so, *whose* morality should they learn? In modern societies such as the United States, diversity or heterogeneity in religious affiliation is a fact of life. Granting equal teaching time and emphasis to the many different religious beliefs and practices found among the population becomes extremely problematic—a task, according to critics, best not undertaken by an already hard-pressed public education system.

In this chapter, we examine religion—an institution dedicated to preparing its members for an after-life—and education—an institution charged with preparing its members for the present life—as important components of contemporary human societies. Although perhaps separated in theory, in practice they remain complexly intertwined, with significant consequences for each other and for a host of other groups and institutions as well.

Questions to Consider

1. What are the major functions of education in modern societies such as the United States?
2. In what ways does formal education serve as a political resource in modern societies?
3. What is the relationship between formal education and social stratification?
4. In what sense and to what extent is formal education in the United States a "democratic" institution?
5. What is the *school choice* or *voucher* program?
6. What is the *standards movement*?
7. Why is some form of religion found in every human society?
8. According to functionalists such as Durkheim, how does religion benefit society?
9. For conflict theorists such as Marx, what is the primary role or consequence of religion in modern societies?
10. What is the Protestant ethic?
11. What is the "electronic church"?
12. What is the relationship between religion and societal modernization?

EDUCATION AS A SOCIAL INSTITUTION

As we saw in Chapter 4, the modernization of societies has entailed what can truly be described as an explosion of human knowledge. It has also been accompanied by a comparable explosion of information-gathering and information-transmitting groups and organizations. Socialization in modernizing and modernized societies is passing out of the exclusive control of the family and into the hands of more formalized structures created expressly for that purpose. For better or worse, young people in many contemporary societies spend a large portion of their pre-adult and early adult lives in one or another segment of what have become large, complex educational systems. The systems through which they pass reflect the increasing rational organization and administration of the knowledge acquisition process. To the extent that the various activities associated with this process involve recognized, defined social statuses and roles and are carried out according to a set of accepted cultural values and norms, we can speak of education in contemporary societies as constituting a social institution.

Theoretical Interpretations of Education

The Functionalist Perspective   As is the case with their analyses of other social phenomena, sociologists operating within the functionalist framework examine the institution of education from the standpoint of its supposed contributions to societal survival. Jonathan H. Turner (1997) has identified five major functions or survival-related consequences of education in any society. The relative importance of these general functions varies from one society to another, depending on (among other things) the degree of development—the level of modernization—found in the particular society.

Social Reproduction   According to Turner (1997, pp. 229–230), education in modern societies has important effects on creating population members who can participate in, and fit into, the economic, political, cultural, and other institutional spheres of their surrounding world. Formal education exposes students to an accumulated body of knowledge that they come to absorb and accept. It also instills in students the motivations, perspectives, and interpersonal skills required for success in economic, familial, and other adult roles. In so doing, education helps ensure the continuity of these established patterns over time. This is especially the case with the polity (the political structure), which employs formal education to create a sense of citizenship and loyalty to the state.

Cultural Storage   Turner notes (1997, p. 230) that,"To reproduce culture, schools must first store this culture and then pass it on." In contemporary societies such as the United States, the sheer quantity and complexity of knowledge has grown beyond the memory capacities of any one individual or group. In such a societal setting, education has become an important "cultural warehouse" for storing knowledge and other cultural elements in such a way that they can easily be retrieved as needed for immediate usage or for passing on to new generations as part of the social reproduction process.

Social Placement   In both modernizing and modern societies, formal education serves as an important mechanism for placing individuals in the social structure. This placement takes two different, but increasingly related, forms: membership in status groups, and incumbency in occupational positions (Turner, 1997, pp. 231–232). With regard to membership in status groups, formal education as carried out in prestigious elementary, secondary, and tertiary schools gives selected students exposure to music, art, and other elite cultural forms and behaviors, thereby preparing them to assume a place in those upper-strata groups. With regard to incumbency in occupational positions, formal education imparts to students specific vocational knowledge and skills required by changing economic systems and typically beyond the ability of the family to teach its members. In modern societies, young people learn principles of business management, physics, and civil engineering not from parents but from professionals trained in those areas. As achievement principles begin to replace ascriptive criteria in filling occupational positions (recall our discussion of these concepts in Chapter 5), formal educational attainment becomes an increasingly important mechanism for placing people in the economic structure. What one knows replaces who or what one is in the shaping of individual occupational careers, and what one knows comes to depend on formal educational experience.

Conflict Management   In modern societies, conflicts arising from class, racial, ethnic, gender, and other basic inequalities can have system-destroying consequences. But, in these societies, formal education helps lessen the likelihood of such lethal conflicts by transforming them into debates over individuals' access to schools and the benefits offered by formal education. By defining the issue as a matter of making education more available to all population members rather than as one of making fundamental changes in existing economic and political arrangements, tension is deflected and potentially catastrophic conflicts can be avoided altogether or mitigated when they do arise. Furthermore, as Turner (1997, p. 233) observes, "If the schools can be expanded and if their incumbents can come to believe that access to an education is more equally distributed, then those who do not perform well in the system can be stigmatized for their personal failings or limitations, while the broader patterns of societal stratification can escape criticism."

Social Transformation and Change   In addition to minimizing unwanted, potentially threatening social change, education also plays a critical role in the creation of desired change. Formal education provides people with a more comprehensive, sophisticated view of the present, a vision of alternative possible futures, and a detailed knowledge of how social processes work. Thus, it can inspire attempts to create different and better social realities. This role is well recognized by the polity, which, according to Turner (1997, pp. 233–234), associates education with economic development and social progress, viewing it as an important vehicle for creating and implementing social change.

Custodial Care   These five areas comprise what might be thought of as the manifest functions of formal education. To them, we could add at least one more function, more latent in nature. In modern societies, the nuclear and single-parent families that now make up the majority of family units often have both parents (or the only parent) engaged in full-time employment in the outside labor force. With many parents thus not available to supervise children and outside day care facilities nonexistent or too expensive, schools in effect have become major providers of custodial day care. Children who otherwise might be left on their own (possibly to get into trouble) are kept out of harm's way by schools that frequently are given legal permission to act *in loco paretis*—literally, "in place of the parent." In addition to teaching students basic or more advanced principles of reading, writing, arithmetic, and other selected subjects, many schools also serve as their chaperones.

The Conflict Perspective   Conflict theorists offer an altogether different picture of formal education in modern societies. From this perspective, the institution of education exists to advance the interests of those who control the social structure, not the best interests of the population at large.

Education as Superstructure   Conflict theorists in the Marxist tradition argue that, in capitalist societies, the institution of education forms a societal superstructure, derived from and dependent on the underlying economic substructure. Like other superstructural elements, formal education in these societies exists to further the domination of the non-propertied classes by the propertied and powerful ruling class. Formal education involves a *hidden curriculum* that infuses the teaching of basic information and skills with values, norms, and myths supportive of capitalism and capitalists. The very selection of what constitutes basic information and skills is itself an artifact of the needs of the prevailing economic system. Thus, formal education acts as a powerful tool in the establishment and maintenance of a false consciousness among members of the working and middle classes. Schools bombard students with images of a benign economic system dedicated to the well-being of all its people and reward or punish them to the extent that they accept and internalize these images. Once they come to accept the basic premises of the system that oppresses them, these students become co-conspirators in their own oppression. From this viewpoint, if formal education has any so-called functions, its primary function is to preserve an exploitative status quo by shaping the minds of the exploited.

Political Education   According to conflict theorists, all political regimes have a vested interest in exercising control over the content of their society's formal educational process, and all will take steps to do so. To one degree or another, political socialization takes place in the schools of virtually every modern industrial society (Braungart and Braungart, 1994). A good deal of this activity is designed deliberately and overtly into the formal educational curriculum. It is reflected through such devices as civics classes, the pledge of allegiance to the flag, and the celebration of patriotic holidays—for example, Presidents' Day in the United States, the emperor's birthday in Japan, September 16 (the beginning of the War of Independence from Spain) in Mexico. But much of this political socialization occurs in more subtle ways.

Textbooks in history, literature, and other academic fields may be chosen by federal, state, or local boards of education as much on the basis of their political content (or, some critics contend, their political correctness) as their pedagogical merit. For example, for many years, most history texts used in elementary and secondary schools in the United States presented a whitewashed, Anglocentric picture of the U.S. westward expansion during the nineteenth century. The wholesale destruction of indigenous Native American cultures was seldom discussed. Most often, "Indians" were depicted as hostile, temporary problems encountered by heroic white settlers in the process of fulfilling their manifest destiny of taming the frontier and developing the continent from sea to shining sea.

Similarly, for more than forty years, until the early 1990s, the Japanese Ministry of Education continued to approve only history textbooks that offered a sanitized account of Japan's military aggression in Asia throughout this century, especially the invasion of China in the 1930s and World War II. Finally, under pressure from the courts, the ministry approved new social studies texts that are somewhat more detailed and less euphemistic in their discussion of past Japanese militarism.

During his six-year term (1988–1994) as Mexico's president, Carlos Salinas de Gortari was accused of ordering the rewriting of history textbooks used in elementary schools to suit his own political ends. Critics charged that the new texts deliberately distorted Mexico's revolutionary past in an attempt to justify Salinas's neoliberal economic programs, especially his promotion of the North American Free Trade Agreement. They also claimed that the new books greatly overstated Salinas's own role in late twentieth-century political and economic affairs. In effect, President Salinas literally rewrote his own place in Mexico's history books (Miller, 1992, Scott, 1992).

Education and Stratification   Conflict theorists of both Marxist and non-Marxist persuasions also view education as an important mechanism for the reinforcement and perpetuation of social stratification systems (Bowles and Gintis, 1976; Collins, 1979; Kerbo, 2000; Oakes, 1985; Weis, 1988). In contemporary societies, formal education is both an indicator of current social position and an important resource for attaining future higher positions. Modern societies are "credential" systems (Collins, 1979) featuring occupations that increasingly demand formal certification of competency. Higher education, especially at the college and university level, provides the certification necessary to gain entry to high-status, high-salary jobs (see Table 10.1). Historically, formal education has been an escape mechanism for many members of the lower classes who otherwise would have remained stuck at the bottom of the social hierarchy. At the same time, the historical experience

TABLE 10.1

Median Incomes of U.S. Households by Educational Attainment of Household Head, 1998

Head of Household's Educational Attainment	Number of Households (in thousands)	Median Income
Less than ninth grade	7,047	$16,154
Ninth to twelvth grade (no diploma)	9,407	$20,724
High school graduate	30,613	$34,373
Some college (no degree)	17,833	$41,658
Associate's degree	7,468	$48,604
Bachelor's degree	16,781	$62,188
Master's degree	5,961	$71,086
Professional degree	1,623	$95,309
Doctorate degree	1,373	$84,100

Source: U.S. Bureau of the Census, *Current Population Reports,* P60–206 (Washington, DC: U.S. Government Printing Office, 1999). Table 2.

is one of formal education playing an important role in preserving existing hierarchies.

In traditional societies, such formal education as existed was reserved solely for the use of the nobility and other privileged classes. There was no need for literacy among peasants or serfs, who were believed to be too intellectually inferior to qualify for or benefit from formal education. In developing societies in which only the established upper classes can appreciate it or afford it, education again is reserved for elites. Even in modern societies such as the United States, in which free public education exists as a reality as well as a concept, the system of higher education continues its close association with the socioeconomic class system.

In the United States, white upper-middle and upper-class children are far more likely to attend a college or university than their counterparts in the lower and working classes, especially more so than African-American and Hispanic children. This pattern

Historically, formal education has served as an important vehicle for upward social mobility for members of the lower socioeconomic classes in the United States. However, it is doubtful that students in schools such as the South Bronx's P.S. 37 will actually be exposed to the educational tools that make such mobility possible. The physical decay that too often marks inner-city schools is symptomatic of what many critics claim is an intrinsic decay in the structure and operation of America's public school system.

holds true even when children's individual ability levels are held constant (Farkas et al., 1990; Steele, 1992; Teachman, 1987). Upper-middle and upper-class children are also far more likely to attend an elite, prestigious university—one of the Ivy League schools, for example. The financial and other admissions requirements of these universities lie beyond the means of most lower- or working-class families, effectively putting the benefits of graduating from one of them out of their reach. The academic currency value of degrees from such schools tends to be much higher than that of degrees from lesser-known schools. In a society in which a college-level education is becoming more commonplace (by 1998, over 24 percent of all people age 25 and over had completed four or more years of college, compared to only 4.6 percent in 1940), the source of one's degree becomes increasingly important in shaping occupational and other career lines (Useem and Karabel, 1986).

Close linkages to the stratification system also exist at the primary-school level. Children from high-status families often attend private boarding or "country day" schools that serve as important agents of class socialization (Baltzell, 1958; Levine, 1980). In addition to the more standard educational components found in public schools, the curricula in these elite schools include cultural values and social behaviors appropriate for their particular social class.

Within the public school system, children from the middle- and upper-middle classes fare better academically than lower-class students, in part because they are much more likely to have had the benefit of one or more years of prior education in nursery school or prekindergarten. In 1996, for example, more than 60 percent of 3-year-olds and nearly 81 percent of 4-year-olds from households with annual incomes of over $50,000 were enrolled in preprimary schools, compared to 30.5 percent of 3-year-olds and not quite 59 percent of 4-year-olds from households with annual incomes of $10,000 or less (National Center for Education Statistics, 1999). Although children may not actually learn a great deal in the way of academic information in prekindergarten classes, they do learn the behaviors and attitudes appropriate for school. They also learn important lessons in student-teacher and student-student interactions. By the time they arrive in kindergarten, where it counts (they will be formally evaluated, graded, and either promoted or held back from the next formal grade level), middle-class children know the educational ropes (Gracey, 1977).

Having no such prior experience, lower-class children entering school for the first time in kindergarten have to start from scratch to learn the rules in what is basically a system structured along the lines of middle-class values and norms. They find themselves at an immediate and continuing disadvantage, in which their normal behaviors and beliefs from outside the classroom setting may be held and used against them inside the classroom. Most schools "track" students into separate academic and career paths ranging from college prep to vocational training. Not coincidentally, members of minority and lower socioeconomic status groups are overrepresented among vocational and other dead-end tracks, whereas white middle-, upper-middle-, and upper-class students form the overwhelming majority in college prep and other fast tracks (Navarrette, 1992; Turner, 1997).

Daily confrontations with the educational system, coupled with a less education-oriented home environment and real pressures from the economic environment (the need to get a job), create high dropout rates for these groups both before and during high school. As we saw in Chapter 6, African Americans and Hispanics have significantly lower rates of educational attainment than whites in the United States. In 1998, 24 percent of African-American adults and 44.5 percent of Hispanic adults lacked a high school diploma, compared to 16.3 percent of Anglos (Day and Curry, 1998). The resulting differences in educational diplomas and degrees among these groups then sort their members into different segments or tiers in the dual labor economy. (Recall our discussion of the dual labor market in Chapter 7.) The salary and other reward disparities that are characteristic of occupations in the different labor market segments guarantee a replication of the existing stratification hierarchy. Formal education is a crucial resource for securing jobs and money in contemporary societies, and like other important societal resources, it tends to be distributed unequally along established class lines.

The U.S. Educational System

Size and Scope Formal education in the United States is a sprawling system of approximately 117,000 public and private schools spanning the range from kindergarten to postgraduate levels (Wright, 1998, p. 359). According to data compiled by the National Center for Education Statistics (in Snyder, 1999), in the fall of 1998, 75.4 million people in this country—about 28 percent of the total population—were actively involved in education, whether as students, teachers, administrators, or support staff. In 1997–98, a total of about $584 billion was spent on public education. As impressive as this figure sounds (and is), U.S. funding of education is only "average" compared to that of similar societies. According to a study conducted by the Organization for Economic Cooperation

Focus on
Latin America

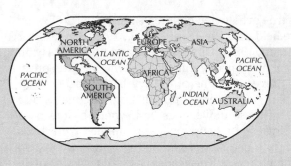

Population: 512,000,000

Life Expectancy at Birth (years): Male—66.0;
Females—73.0

Forms of Government: Republics; Parliamentary Democracies;
Constitutional Monarchies; Independent Commonwealths,
Communist State (Cuba)

Major Religions: Overwhelmingly Roman Catholic; Protestant;
Vodoun (voodoo) in some countries

Population Doubling Time: 38 years

Per Capita GNP (1997 U.S. dollars): $3,950

Principal Economic Activities: Agriculture; Industries; Mining

Colonial Experience: Many nations were once colonies of various
European powers

Adult Literacy Rate: Varies widely; typically near or below 90%

"ABC" Countries Must Rethink Educational ABCs

Argentina, Brazil, and Chile—the so-called "ABC Countries"—are part of one of the world's most socioeconomically diverse geographic areas. Collectively, the nearly three dozen nations that comprise the Latin America–Caribbean region (LAC) span a wide range of development levels, They include societies (such as Haiti) that are just beginning the long march toward modernization as well as others (such as Argentina) that are on the verge of taking their place among the select group of modern industrial societies. The United Nations Development Program (1998, p. 138) reports that, of the 174 nations of the world for which Human Development Index (HDI) scores—a composite of life expectancy, educational attainment, and income measures—are available, societies in this region rank from a high of 24 (Barbados, with an HDI value of 0.909) to a low of 159 (Haiti, with an HDI value of 0.340). By way of comparison, the world's top-ranked society, Canada, has an HDI value of 0.960; the world's lowest-ranked society, Sierra Leone, has an HDI value of 0.185.

According to the World Bank (1999b, p. 4), although the LAC has the highest per capita income of all the developing regions of the world, approximately 37 percent of its population lives below the poverty line and 16 percent live in extreme poverty, with "an income that does not afford an individual to provide him or herself the minimum of an adequate diet, even if all expenditures were devoted to the consumption of food." And, in Bolivia, Guatemala, and Haiti, more than 70 percent of all households live in poverty. This apparent incongruity between the size of the LAC's per capita income and the size of its poverty population is a function of the highly unequal distribution of income within the region. "On average, the lowest 20 percent of the population in a typical LAC country earns only about 4 percent of total national income, while the upper 10 percent receives about 45 percent of the total income" (World Bank, 1999b, p. 4).

After examining the forces at work in creating and maintaining this highly skewed economic pattern, the World Bank (1999b, p. 4) was led to conclude that "Inequalities in access to education, particularly quality education, constitute an important structural factor exacerbating poverty and inequality in the region"—a sentiment widely shared in other quarters as well. In ana-

lyzing the interplay between education and economic growth in the area, Marma de lbarrola observed (1996, p. 2) that "Latin American countries have consistently increased schooling between the sixties and the nineties but education still means in fact a scarce service and usually a poor one, unequally distributed." Data compiled by the United Nations Educational, Scientific, and Cultural Organization (UNESCO) lend strong support to these assertions. They indicate that, whereas 91 percent of all primary school–age children in LAC countries were enrolled in primary schools in 1995, that number dropped off dramatically in secondary schools. Enrollment among secondary school–age children that year ranged from a high of 64 percent in Jamaica to a low of only 19 percent in Brazil. The regional average for secondary-school enrollment was below 50 percent (cited in World Bank 1999c, Table 6, pp. 200–201). Utilizing data collected by the Inter-American Development Bank, Nelly P. Stromquist (1996, p. 3) notes that "Latin America turns out to have the lowest rates of success in the world, as only 54 percent of those who enter primary school reach grade four and only four Latin American countries have primary completion rates higher than 75 percent."

This tremendous decline in the percentage of children attending secondary schools is largely a function of economic need—that is, the need of the poor families from which many of these students come for their labor earnings. Poverty-stricken rural students, especially those from indigenous populations in countries such as Brazil and Mexico, typically begin to drop out in the third grade as they seek (or are forced to seek) full-time employment in order to help support their families. Both countries have recently instituted programs to help keep these at-risk students in schools by paying their families a monthly subsidy as long as the children remain enrolled. In Mexico, for example, families can earn as much as $65 a month if their children—especially their female children—continue with their schooling. To help overcome "the traditional prejudice that girls don't need as much education as boys, girls who stay in high school 'earn' more than boys—about $26 a month—for sticking to the books" (La Franchi, 1998c). A similar program in the federal district of Brasilia, Brazil, pays poor families the equivalent of the minimum wage ($80 a month) for each child kept in school, as well as a special year-end bonus which is accessible only after a minimum of four years of schooling. Brazilian government officials estimate that the program has so far helped about 50,000 poor children who otherwise would have dropped out of school before completing even a primary-level education (La Franchi, 1998c).

In addition to the need to leave school to find work, another factor contributing to the low levels of secondary education—and the even lower levels of tertiary education—in the LAC is the fact that many students simply are not learning information or skills necessary for better job opportunities and a higher quality of life. Consequently, for them, time spent in school is wasted and pointless. As Jeffrey M. Puryear has noted (1997, p. 2), "much of what is learned in school has only limited application in the modern workplace. These deficiencies have a

particularly negative impact on the poor, who depend heavily on education for social mobility, and have little choice but to attend public schools." According to Puryear (1997, p. 4), "many children do not achieve basic mastery of language and mathematics, secondary schools do not equip students to function effectively in modern societies, and many of the new universities are hardly more than secondary schools."

Educational experts assembled by the Council on Foreign Relations to examine educational problems and prospects in the LAC are in agreement that there is a "disjuncture between education supply and demand . . . [a] general dissociation between schools and the demands of a modern economy" (Puryear, 1997, p. 2). They are also in agreement that "there is no single model that can be used successfully in all cases of public education reform in Latin America. Each country must develop its own model, based on its unique historical, cultural, and social context" (de Cerreño and Pyle, 1996, pp. 1–2). However, individual societal differences notwithstanding, the group has identified several important similarities that cut across national boundaries and generate similar negative consequences as far as educational quality throughout the region is concerned. These common factors include inadequate educational models; educational inequalities along class, gender, and ethnic lines; and poorly trained teachers (de Cerreño and Pyle, 1996; de lbarrola, 1996; Puryear, 1997).

Inadequate Educational Models
During the 1970s and 1980s, much of the emphasis on (and funding for) education in LAC countries was directed toward eliminating illiteracy by expanding public access to formal education, especially at the primary level and particularly among formerly excluded population groups—most notably, the rural poor and members of indige-

nous peoples. The focus was on providing a basic body of information, largely through rote learning—that is, by memorization of "facts." Universal primary education and universal literacy were the stated educational goals and, during this time period, many LAC nations came close to achieving at least one of these two objectives: in a number of countries, enrollment in primary schools among the relevant age groups approached 100 percent. However, as Puryear notes (1997, p. 4), this emphasis on educational quantity rather than quality came at a high price: "Funds that might have been spent on laboratories, textbooks, or teacher training have been spent instead on additional classrooms, administrators, and inadequately paid teachers. Programs to assess and promote quality, such as reliable measures of student performance, teacher output, and institutional excellence, have not been established." The result, as noted above, was that although more students were enrolling in schools, they tended to learn very little and to drop out early. Consequently, "new generations of illiterates are still formed; the difference now is that many of them are illiterate despite having spent a few years in primary school—a reflection of the poor quality of schooling" (Stromquist, 1996, p. 3). Recognizing these problems, a number of LAC countries have already begun to take corrective measures. In El Salvador, for example, a seven-year reform effort known as the SABE Project (Strengthening Achievement in Basic Education) has resulted in significant improvements in that nation's 5,000 public elementary schools. New sets of K–6 (kindergarten through sixth grade) reading and mathematics textbooks that encourage critical reasoning over rote learning have been introduced, and a large cadre of teachers have been trained in the use of a revised set of K–6 curriculum guides. Based on the success of

The entire faculty and student bodies assemble for class at a rural school near Cochabamba, Bolivia. With underfunded, underequipped schools and high rates of school dropout the norm across the Latin America-Caribbean Basin, widespread illiteracy and widespread poverty remain serious problems throughout this vast region. The introduction of new educational technologies such as computer-assisted instruction and distance learning may provide some future relief in meeting the LAC's pressing needs.

this project, a similar program has been introduced in Nicaragua (Academy for Educational Development, 1999, pp. 2–3).

Educational Inequalities along Class, Gender, and Ethnic Lines

It is still the case, in the overwhelming majority of LAC countries, that gross inequalities distinguish the education received by the upper and upper-middle classes from that received by the masses; the educational experiences of men compared to women; and the education of people of European descent (who tend to make up the upper and upper-middle classes) from that of people of indigenous and African ancestry (who form the bulk of the lower classes and, especially, the poor). Virtually all observers are in agreement about the "remarkable inequities" of Latin American educational systems and the "increasing bifurcation" of the educational system into public and private schools. Students from among the poor and the lower classes almost always attend poorer quality public primary schools, and most do not continue beyond that level. Upper-middle and upper-class children attend

higher quality private primary and secondary schools, and typically advance to either public or private universities, where almost all students come from privileged social class backgrounds. Very few poor children ever make it all the way to the university level. The problem is compounded by the fact that in most LAC countries, public education funds have largely been directed toward the upper (university) levels, reflecting the greater political and social power of middle- and upper-income groups. Rather than using funds to reduce quality differentials at the primary level, governments have, instead, used funds to expand secondary and higher education (Puryear, 1997, p. 5). For example, in Chile, half of all private schools are financed with public funds (de Ibarrola, 1996, p. 3). These educational disparities not only reflect current socioeconomic class differences throughout the region but help perpetuate them as well.

Poorly Trained Teachers

A third major factor contributing to both the poor overall performance of LAC educational systems and the marked quality differentials between public and private schools is the generally low quality

of teaching found in public schools. Much like other current problems in the region's educational institutions, this situation has been traced to past governmental emphasis on growth and expansion of public education at the expense of quality education during the 1970s and 1980s. Among the strategies pursued at that time, according to de Ibarrola (1996, p. 3), were reducing teachers' salaries to what amounted to a subminimum wage level; recruiting teachers without professional qualifications; and doubling and tripling teachers' work shifts, "thus asphyxiating all possible improvement in the use of teaching and learning time." Poorly trained teachers are a problem that continues to plague most LAC countries at the close of the 1990s. In Brazil, for example, teacher quality varies tremendously from region to region within the country, reflecting prevailing urbanization and socioeconomic patterns: "In Rio, the norm [for teachers] is now a university education, but in the northeast, many teachers don't even have a complete elementary education themselves" (Faller, in La Franchi, 1998a). Brazil is attempting to deal with the problem through a 40-program series of TV broadcasts developed by teachers for teachers and beamed into remote areas of the country by satellite. Brazil and other LAC countries are also attempting to put their public schools online, linking them to the vast informational resources available on the World Wide Web. Drawing on the negative experiences of some European nations in this regard, Brazil is computerizing its teachers and its schools at a more deliberate pace, with the goal of training 25,000 teachers a year on the use of this promising educational technology (La Franchi, 1998b).

Nelly P. Stromquist argues (1996, p. 9) that teachers remain underpaid, and teaching itself remains undervalued, because the teaching profession is highly feminized: "The highest proportion of female teachers [in the world] is found in the Latin American and Caribbean region, with an average of 77 percent in primary schools and 47 percent in secondary schools." In countries such as Argentina, prevailing social views portray teachers as "apostles" engaged in the mission of nurturing young minds—an assumption that, according to Stromquist, "diminishes the nature of teachers as professionals." This is a problem that could very well remain so long as traditional gender stereotypes and a *machismo* mind set found throughout the region continue to define women as the nurturing, gentle, and subservient sex.

Given the present condition of education in the LAC, significant reforms will undoubtedly prove expensive financially, socially, and in a myriad of other ways. But it would seem that not reforming the state of schooling is not a viable option. If Latin American and Caribbean countries have any expectation of modernizing and competing successfully in the new global marketplace, they must bring their schools into the twenty-first century and provide a meaningful, quality education for all population groups, rich and poor alike. It remains to be seen if the ABC countries and other members of this region are prepared and able to make that move.

and Development, in 1994, the United States ranked behind 9 other industrialized democracies in public spending on education, measured as a proportion of each country's gross domestic product. The U.S. figure of 4.8 percent was almost the exact average of the 18 countries studied (National Center for Education Statistics, 1999). International comparisons notwithstanding, formal education is nonetheless an institution with enormous economic implications in the United States. Collectively, schools employ nearly 8 million people, or about 5.9 percent of the total U.S. civilian labor force (Snyder, 1999).

Of the approximately 67.3 million students currently in the educational system, about 86.5 percent are enrolled in public elementary, secondary, or postsecondary schools. The remaining 13.5 percent are enrolled in a variety of religious-affiliated or nonsectarian private schools. Sectarian or religious-affiliated schools account for approximately 80 percent of all private elementary and secondary schools. Roman Catholic schools—8,223 schools with combined enrollments of over 2.6 million students in 1998—comprise the single largest religious denomination (National Catholic Educational Association, 1999).

Democratization The sheer scale of the U.S. educational system is testimony to the fact that formal education in this society is democratic in nature. In theory, at least, education is open to virtually every citizen, regardless of social class, racial, ethnic, or other varying group affiliations; and many individuals avail themselves of this opportunity (see Table 10.2). Well over 90 percent of all 5- to 17-year-olds are enrolled in school (largely as a result of compulsory education laws), and nearly 83 percent of all Americans age 25 and over had completed high school as of 1998. But, as we have already seen, not all individuals from these different groups will do equally well once in the system, and their educational success or failure may have little or nothing to do with their individual ability levels.

Decentralization Although formal education in the United States spans the entire nation, education itself is not a centralized system. Unlike virtually all other modern industrial and post-industrial societies, the United States has no national agency to supervise the development of classroom materials and no national education curriculum (Kantrowitz and Wingert, 1992). Public education content and policies reside formally in the hands of the individual state governments, not the federal government. Local school districts generally have a great deal of latitude in setting specific educational policies and practices, as long as they meet legislative guidelines set by their particular state (Warren, 1991). Major funding for public schools comes from state and local sources with support from the federal government. For example, federal government expenditures accounted for about $73.1 billion of the $584 billion spent on education in 1997–98 (U.S. Bureau of the Census, 1998c, Table 253). The net result is a decentralized system in which significant variations in educational philosophy and practice can be found

TABLE 10.2

Educational Attainment of U.S. Population Age 25 Years and Over, 1940–1998

Year	Completed Four Years of High School or More		Completed Four Years of College or More	
	Male	Female	Male	Female
1940	22.7%	26.3%	5.5%	3.8%
1950	32.6	36.0	7.3	5.2
1959	42.2	45.2	10.3	6.0
1970	55.0	55.4	14.1	8.2
1980	69.1	68.1	20.8	13.5
1990	77.7	77.5	24.4	18.4
1998	82.8	82.9	26.5	22.4

Source: U.S. Bureau of the Census, *Current Population Reports,* P20–513. (Washington, DC: U.S. Government Printing Office, 1998).

from one region and state to another and, within states, from one local district to another. As observers have described the system: "Each of the nation's 15,367 school districts is a kingdom unto itself—with the power to decide what its students will be taught" (Kantrowitz and Wingert, 1992).

Bureaucratization The U.S. educational system as a whole may be decentralized, but state- and district-level components of that system, as well as individual units, are highly bureaucratized. This hierarchical bureaucratic structure may be necessary to coordinate the activities of the massive numbers of students, teachers, and other personnel found at any given time in the educational system. But many public school districts are top-heavy with administrative officials, and elaborate sets of bureaucratic procedures greatly restrict the flexibility and autonomy of individual teachers and the maximum development of individual students. As Turner (1997, p. 242) has noted, "once this organizational form is imposed on educational systems, grades, tests, required sequences, set time periods, and certification become prominent . . . With these as organizational tools, sorting and tracking [of students] are inevitable." The educational bureaucracy often seems to embody the worst, rather than the best, potentials of bureaucratic organization. (Recall our discussion of bureaucracy in Chapter 3.) It has been identified as a significant source of dissatisfaction among educators, students, parents, and almost everyone else involved in secondary school education (Sizer, 1984, 1992). Reform-oriented analyses of the U.S. educational system have termed this huge administrative infrastructure "one of the major obstacles to quality education" in the country today (Toch et al., 1993).

Problems and Proposals in U.S. Education

Problems Although the United States can boast of having one of the largest, wealthiest, and most democratic educational systems in the modern world, it is a system with serious (some might say fatal) flaws. In 1983, the National Commission on Excellence in Education, formed by then-President Ronald Reagan, issued a devastating analysis of the state of U.S. Education (National Commission of Excellence in Education, 1983). In this report, *A Nation at Risk,* the commission warned of a "rising tide of mediocrity that threatens our future as a nation and as a people." The report's subtitle, *The Imperative for Educational Reform,* made it clear that a significant restructuring of the U.S. educational system was an absolute necessity, not an option. However, nearly two decades later, that restructuring has yet to occur. In 1996, voters for the first time ranked education as their top priority (over such other pressing issues as crime, health care, and Social Security) in the upcoming presidential elections, with two-thirds of those surveyed in national polls citing it as a major concern (Walters, 1996). In his first State of the Union address following his victory in those elections, President Bill Clinton called for a "national crusade" to revitalize American education, and vowed to make educational reform the "Number 1 priority" of his second term in office (Clinton, in Haworth and Lederman, 1997). And education—"the problem everyone talks about, but no one ever wanted to deal with" (Kronholz, 1998b, p. B1)—also emerged as a decisive issue in gubernatorial races in Iowa, Alabama, South Carolina, California, and several other states in 1998. At the end of the twentieth century, the American public remained very concerned about the state of public education—and with good reason.

Student Performance Levels Beginning in 1980 and continuing periodically since then, standardized test performances of U.S. students from kindergarten through twelfth grade have been compared to those of their counterparts in a number of Asian and European nations. Although the results of these international comparisons have varied somewhat depending on the grade levels and subject areas being assessed, the results have been depressingly consistent. In almost every test area and at virtually all grade levels, U.S. students trail their peers in all but a very few countries. Math and science scores, in particular, indicate a wide performance gap. For example, in the Third International Mathematics and Science Study (TIMSS) tests given in 1995, American high school seniors scored lower in math than their counterparts in eighteen of the twenty-one participating countries, outperforming only Cyprus and South Africa. In science, U.S. student scores fell below those of fifteen other countries. And, among "the best and the brightest"—the top-performing 10 percent to 20 percent of each country's students—the U.S. scored second from the bottom in mathematics, and at the very bottom in science (Chaddock, 1998a; Kronholz, 1998a).

With respect to a third basic academic skill—reading—the picture is only a little less bleak. According to the 1998 National Assessment of Educational Progress (NAEP), reading scores for U.S. fourth-, eighth-, and twelfth-grade students were measurably higher than those reported in 1995. In spite of this progress, however, results indicated that 38 percent of fourth graders, 26 percent of eighth graders, and 23 percent of twelfth graders still read at below-minimum-achievement levels (Kronholz, 1999a). The NAEP also reported that three in five high school seniors don't read well enough to handle challenging subject matter, and 60 percent of African-American and Hispanic fourth graders can't read well enough to understand what's going on in class (Chaddock, 1999).

According to the National Center for Education Statistics (1999), approximately 30 percent of first-year college and university students in the U.S. are enrolled in remedial courses in reading, writing, or mathematics because they enter higher education lacking minimum skills in these areas. Concerned about the money and other resources that must be expended in these courses, a number of states, including California, Georgia, Massachusetts, and New York, have taken steps to drastically decrease or eliminate these courses altogether, putting the burden back on high schools to prepare their students for college work (Wessel, 1998b). Beginning in 1999, college-bound students in Massachusetts must pass not only entrance tests to get into the state's public colleges and universities, but also exit tests in order to receive their diplomas (Clayton, 1998).

Illiteracy As most commonly used, the term *illiteracy* is a concept related to reading and writing ability. More specifically, what is termed **functional illiteracy** refers to the lack of basic reading and writing skills necessary for everyday life. In theory, the near-universal rates of primary education and very high rates of secondary education in the United States should translate into near-universal literacy among its population. In practice, however, this hardly appears to be the case. Individual study results vary greatly but indicate that as many as over 40 million American adults are functionally illiterate, a fact that each year costs American businesses an estimated $60 billion in productivity because of employees' lack of basic skills (Chaddock, 1998c). According to an American Management Association report, 36 percent of job applicants tested by major U.S. companies in 1998 lacked sufficient reading and math skills to do the job they sought—an increase from 23 percent in 1997 and 19 percent in 1996 ("They're Not Writing Either," 1999). International comparisons of adult literacy conducted by the Organization for Economic Cooperation and Development (OECD) indicate that Americans are among the industrialized world's least literate populations (Bronner, 1998b).

The concept of illiteracy can also be extended to include a lack of basic understanding in specific subject areas of knowledge. In this respect, evidence also points to a widespread absence of what has been termed "cultural literacy" (Hirsch, 1987), especially in history and politics. For example, according to a 1998 survey reported by the National Constitution Center, only 41 percent of American teenagers could name the three branches of government, but 59 percent could name the Three Stooges. Seventy-four percent knew that cartoon character Bart Simpson lives in the fictional town of Springfield, but only 12 percent knew that Abraham Lincoln lived in Springfield, Illinois ("A Poll Jay Leno Would Love," 1998). Only 40 percent of adults surveyed during congressional proceedings on the issue of impeaching President Clinton knew that "impeachment" does not mean removal from office, whereas another 42 mistakenly believed it did (Morin, 1998c). The late singer Sam Cooke's 1960s rock-and-roll lament that he didn't know much about the subjects he took in school could apply equally well to many contemporary graduates of American public schools.

Proposals Many different strategies have been proposed for dealing with the deficiencies so apparent in the U.S. educational system. They run the entire gamut from ignoring the embarrassing international comparisons of American, Asian, and European students to dismantling and then rebuilding from the ground up the structure responsible for those embarrassing comparisons. In this section, we will briefly discuss several of the more controversial proposals for resolving this society's educational problems.

An Asian Model? The consistently superior performances of Japanese, Chinese, and South Korean students in mathematics and science have led some U.S. educators and other observers to propose a reshaping of this society's educational system in those other societies' images. Among the specific recommendations that stand out are a call for a longer school year featuring more hours of in-school and at-home assignments (Barret, 1990); the creation and implementation of a rigorous, comprehensive national curriculum (Kantrowitz and Wingert, 1992); and, in general, more of a "get tough" approach to discipline (Chaddock, 1998b).

Critics of these proposals argue that the profound cultural differences between the United States and these Asian societies make it impossible to transplant educational structures and practices with any real hope of success. In addition, they point to the fact that both the Japanese and Korean systems have been coming under a great deal of criticism from within their own ranks. The strict regimentation, fear of shaming failure, and emphasis on rote memorization have been cited for high levels of student stress and widespread student inability to cope in a rapidly changing world (Barr, 1995; Choe, 1999; Gaouette, 1998). According to one Korean parent, "Korean high schools are like factories. Only the

scores on your exams matter, and the only way to get into university is to pay for after-school tutoring, six days a week until 11 o'clock at night" (Jai-ok, in Woodard, 1998). In Japan, the excesses and "soullessness" of the school system have been viewed as significant factors in the recruitment of many highly educated young adults into the fringe Aum Shinri Kyo sect which, in 1995, launched a lethal poison-gas attack in Tokyo subways (Nishizawa, 1995).

In rebuttal, supporters of these proposals claim that, despite the obvious significant cultural differences that separate the United States from China, Japan, and Korea, there are nonetheless several crucial changes that can be implemented successfully in our system. Students can be given a clear picture of their own education's purpose and direction, and the content of that education can be made more interesting and meaningful. Parents and teachers can learn to see effort, rather than "ability," as the key to student accomplishment. Teachers can be given time to prepare their lessons at school, during the day, with their colleagues. Parents can raise their expectations for their children's education and not be so complacent (Mathews, 1992). None of these changes is drastic individually, but collectively, according to their supporters, they can effect dramatic improvements.

School Choice, Vouchers, and Charter Schools Widespread dissatisfaction with public school systems serving the poor, particularly in inner-city areas, has led to the growth of so-called *school choice* programs. Under these school choice plans, lower-income parents are given taxpayer-funded vouchers for tuition at their choice of schools for their children, whether that choice is a public school, a nonsectarian private

Looking much like trainees at a military boot camp, Japanese school children assemble for the start of another day's classes. With its seeming record of producing larger numbers of high-performing students, the Japanese educational system has been proposed as a model for school reforms in the United States. However, many observers have voiced strong concerns that the strict regimentation and emphasis on rote learning characteristic of Japanese schools would lead to more harm than good being done to students in a sociocultural system so profoundly different than that found in Japan.

Chapter 10 • Education and Religion

school, or some other alternative (Bronner, 1998a). One popular and growing alternative is *charter schools,* taxpayer-funded schools chartered or commissioned by the state but operated by parents, civic groups, entrepreneurs, or some other group independently of local school districts. By 1999, thirty-four states had passed legislation permitting charters, and over 1,100 charter schools were in place. With 274 charters, Arizona is the leading state in this movement (Kronholz, 1999). Able to operate without bureaucratic restrictions imposed by local school boards and teachers' unions, and more able to accommodate the particular needs of nontraditional students such as single mothers, charter schools have been called "the most vibrant force in American education today" (in Wood, 1998a).

As of 1999, two cities—Cleveland and Milwaukee—had citywide programs providing taxpayer money to parents sending children to private schools. Milwaukee's Parental Choice Program also allows parents to use vouchers for religious private schools, a practice initially ruled unconstitutional by a Wisconsin state court. That lower-court ruling, however, was overturned by the Wisconsin State Supreme Court and, in effect, upheld by the U.S. Supreme Court, which declined to hear an appeal of the state Supreme Court's decision, thus opening the possibility of greatly expanding other city and state school choice programs (Baldouf, 1998a; Lefkowitz, 1998). In 1999, Florida became the first state to enact a statewide school voucher plan, giving at least $4000 a year toward tuition at private or parochial (religious) schools to students in the worst public schools (Silva, 1999).

Proponents of the school choice/voucher plans and charter schools argue that these programs give poor children, who otherwise might not learn anything in overcrowded, underperforming public schools, a real chance at a decent education. By introducing competition into what had been a public school monopoly, school choice also forces public schools to make genuine improvements or risk losing their reason for being (Kronholz, 1999). According to the president of the Center for Education Reform in Washington, "It's great for kids. You have, first and foremost, a law that puts public schools on notice that they have to fish or cut bait, and you have a bill that helps children that are most in need" (Allen, in Kallestad, 1999).

Critics of school choice and voucher plans claim that these programs will further weaken and perhaps ultimately destroy public education in the United States. They argue that these programs rob public schools not only of desperately needed funding, but of the best students and most motivated, involved parents as well (Havemann, 1998). The net result,

according to critics, is that the quality of public education will continue to deteriorate as everyone who can afford to will abandon public schools, leaving behind those too poor to escape—largely, racial and ethnic minority students. Charter schools, in particular, "have triggered a reincarnation of the segregation issue that will create a class stratification and in the long term destroy public education as we know it" (Peterson, in Wood, 1998a).

Whatever the long-term effect of school choice, vouchers, and charter schools, it is clear that these programs enjoy a great deal of support from a cross-section of the U.S. public. Polls show that a majority of Americans are in favor of the government giving at least partial support to parents who send their children to private and parochial schools, with 56 percent of African Americans and 65 percent of Hispanics supporting the concept of school choice, whether public or private (Baldauf, 1998b).

The Standards Movement Despite statements by groups such as the American Federation of Teachers that the lack of a rigorous, standardized educational program is a major cause of U.S. students' poor academic performances in international student comparisons (Grier, 1995), such a standardized curriculum has been very slow in developing in this country. In 1994, President Clinton signed the *Goals 2000: Educate America Act,* a program designed to provide federal funds to states implementing a set of national educational goals intended to raise student competencies in core academic subjects. Viewed by its critics as an attempt by the federal government to take over control of education from state and local school districts, the Goals 2000 program quietly died as states refused the offered monies. In 1997, President Clinton proposed the development of a series of national assessment tests, to include standardized mathematics tests for all eighth graders and standardized reading tests for all fourth graders, beginning in 1999 on a voluntary basis. Though at first embraced by educators and legislators, the plan was shelved indefinitely by Congress after strong attacks by an unlikely mixture of very liberal and very conservative opponents (Morse, 1999).

The defeats of Goals 2000 and national assessment testing did not end growing pressure from parents and other concerned citizens to do something about dismally performing students and schools. Faced with increasing demands for action, twenty states have adopted sets of mathematics, reading, writing, and other educational standards as desired objectives or "outcomes," and some form of standardized tests designed to hold students and their schools to those standards. In some states, students, teachers, administrators, and schools themselves are subject to sanctions from the state if test scores indicate that the standards (as defined by the individual states) are not being met. For students, these sanctions include not being promoted to the next higher grade (or, in the case of twelfth graders, not being awarded a diploma); for teachers, withholding of pay bonuses; for administrators, termination of employment; for schools, loss of accreditation (Morse, 1999; McLaughlin, 1998).

Supporters of the standards movement argue that real school improvements will take place only when goals or standards are clearly defined and when specific people—whether students, teachers, administrators, or some combination of these groups—are held responsible and accountable for failing to meet those goals. Critics claim that holding students back for failing standardized tests has no educational value, citing research showing that students who repeat a year in school are as much as 20 to 30 percent more likely to drop out of school, and that students who repeat two grades "have a probability of dropping out of nearly 100 percent" (Shepard, in Wood, 1999). Additionally, critics charge, standardized tests discriminate against minority and low-income students, who are less likely to test as well as white middle-class students (McLaughlin, 1998).

Ironically, one of the most controversial aspects of the standards movement is that requiring would-be teachers to pass standardized competency tests in order to become certified, and current teachers to pass such tests in order to be recertified. Forty states currently have some form of teacher testing, but members of the National Educational Association (one of the nation's largest teacher's unions) passed a resolution that these tests should not be used as "a condition of employment, license, retention, evaluation, placement, ranking, or promotion" (in McLaughlin and Chaddock, 1998, p. 14). Teacher competency tests came to public attention in 1998, after nearly 60 percent of prospective teachers in Massachusetts failed a newly instituted "language and communications skills" examination. The Massachusetts Board of Education responded to this embarrassing situation by lowering the score required for a passing grade, on the grounds that it was a first-time test and teachers hadn't had enough chance to prepare for it. Following public outrage, however, the minimum passing grade was quickly returned to its original level ("Welcome to Teacher Testing," 1998).

Much as in the case of student testing, proponents of teacher testing argue that such examinations are necessary to improve the quality of public elementary and secondary education, by keeping incompetent teachers out of the classroom. Citing studies indicating that teachers are one of the most significant factors affecting student learning, they argue that, if schools "were going to have higher standards for students, we had to have higher standards for teachers" (Zipko, in McLaughlin and Chaddock, 1998, p. 14). Critics of teacher testing argue that these standardized tests are not valid or reliable devices for assessing true teaching ability, and that they discriminate against members of ethnic and racial minority groups, who are already in short supply in state public school systems. Maintaining an adequate supply of teachers is likely to become a critical problem throughout the country, as many current teachers rapidly approach retirement age. Estimates indicate that schools will need to hire about 200,000 teachers per year over the next decade, a number which greatly exceeds the number of students graduating from education schools and programs (Newcomb, 1999).

The need for serious educational reform in the United States is clearly at hand. Unfortunately, what has also been at hand is an array of reform proposals that have been inconsistent at best, and contradictory and mutually exclusive at worst. Many people view the cost of significant educational change as prohibitively high. What needs to be recognized is that the cost of making no changes may be even higher.

RELIGION AS A SOCIAL INSTITUTION

Throughout our history, we human beings have attempted to understand and explain the world in which we live. During all that time, religion has been an important part of social life. In one form or another, organized religious beliefs and practices have been present in all societies, from the earliest hunting and gathering bands to the most modern industrial and postindustrial systems. Such activity reflects our need to deal with what French sociologist Emile Durkheim (1965/1915) called the **sacred**—those extraordinary elements of life that inspire a sense of reverence, awe, and fear in people.

Our attempts to make sense out of the world invariably have fallen short of perfection, and it seems that some areas of existence will always remain outside the limits of science or other rational mechanisms of knowledge. It is exactly these areas, according to Durkheim, that make up the essence of human religion. Religious beliefs are matters of faith, which, unlike the **profane** (commonplace or ordinary elements of everyday life) cannot be proved or disproved through empirical means.

Religious statuses and roles were among the first noneconomic positions to be defined and differentiated in early societies in which a surplus of resources existed (Lenski, 1966; Lenski, Nolan, and Lenski, 1995). As the economic surplus grew and these societies became further differentiated and increasingly complex, religious activities became more elaborate. They were entrusted to a group of full-time specialists who exercised a great deal of influence over all or most group behaviors. Durkheim (1965/1915) claimed that religion was such an important and integral part of these early societies because it involved a symbolic recognition of the power of the society itself over its individual members. In worshipping supernatural deities, humans in effect were celebrating their own collective existence.

As societies developed and understanding became more sophisticated, philosophical and then scientific explanations of the world replaced supernatural interpretations, and the actual need for a body of sacred beliefs perhaps decreased. But, by that time, religion as an institutionalized social structure had become intertwined with other major institutions. It was a fundamental part of the world-taken-for-granted, Even in highly rational, highly secular societies (such as the contemporary United States) that rely heavily on science, religion continues to exert considerable influence on many areas of life.

Theoretical Perspectives on Religion

Functionalist Interpretations Durkheim's analysis of religion, which was one of the first attempts to understand this phenomenon in sociological terms, was also cast squarely in the functionalist theoretical mold. He sought to explain the universal presence of religion throughout human history in terms of its contributions to societal survival. In this regard, he was led to conclude that religion served several important functions, all related to the establishment and furthering of social solidarity.

Religion provides a basis for *social cohesion* by uniting the members of the population in shared beliefs and values, as well as in a common set of rituals. For example, for more than 350 years, roughly two-thirds of the people of Benin, West Africa, have followed the vodoun (voodoo) religion. Driven underground by that country's socialist regime of the 1970s and 1980s, in 1996, vodoun was given official recognition by Benin's Roman Catholic president, Nicephore Sogio ("Practice of Voodoo Gets Official Status," 1996). This renewed state tolerance for the vodoun religion has been seen by some skeptics as little more than an obvious bid for political support. Whatever the merits of that argument in this particular case, it is true that religion has played an important historical role in promoting *social stability* by

infusing cultural norms and political rules with sacred authority (remember, for example, Christ's message to "render unto Caesar the things that are Caesar's"), thus increasing the likelihood that people will follow them. Sociologist Peter Berger (1967) viewed this legitimizing effect as providing a "sacred canopy" that shields and protects political regimes.

Finally, Durkheim claimed that religion helps to maintain people's allegiance to societal goals and participation in social affairs by giving them a sense of *meaning and purpose*. It tells people why sometimes, in the words of one best-selling book, "bad things happen to good people" (and why good things sometimes happen to bad people). By providing people with a larger context—a divine plan—in which to understand specific events, religion keeps them from falling into despair and withdrawing from society. As we saw in Chapter 1, Durkheim also thought that religion often prevented people from withdrawing from life altogether through suicide.

Conflict Interpretations Conflict interpretations view religious beliefs and practices from an entirely different vein. For conflict theorists, religion is a means of exploitation rather than integration, of social damnation rather than heavenly salvation. As Karl Marx so eloquently put it, "Religion is the sigh of the oppressed creatures, the heart of a heartless world and the soul of soulless conditions. It is the opium of the people" (1970/1844, p. 131).

Marx claimed that organized religion, like other social and cultural patterns, is a reflection of the underlying mode of economic production whose basic structure is responsible for shaping all other facets of human social life. Like those other superstructural elements, religion's purpose is to preserve the economic substructure and the relations of production that allow one class to enslave all others. By focusing workers' attention on the sweet by-and-by of the afterlife with its promise of eternal bliss, religion deflects their attention from the not-so-sweet here and now and thus perpetuates their misery in the present life. Religion is a smokescreen, blinding the workers from recognizing the ruling class as the true source of that misery. As long as the proletariat remain focused on the afterlife, they will never be a revolutionary threat to the ruling class in this life. For this reason, religion, like the productive system it serves, is inherently detrimental to the survival of everyone but the ruling class. It is a powerful weapon used by capitalists in the class struggle.

Conflict theorists since Marx have also emphasized the dysfunctional elements of religion, especially in large heterogeneous societies such as the United States. Differences in beliefs and values often serve as the basis for the formation of subcultural groups with radically different moral views and policy agendas. Attempts by particular groups within the society to impose their own religious views and practices on all other groups result in power struggles and conflicts that divide these groups and the society at large. One need only think of the current religion-based controversy over abortion that has polarized the population of the United States to understand the dynamics at work here.

The Protestant Ethic and the Rise of Capitalism

These divisions, however, point to a significant role of religion overlooked by Marx—that of a catalyst for social change. Just as (according to Marx) changes in the organization of the proletariat would lead to class conflict and the eventual overthrow of the capitalist system, changes in the organization of the religious system could lead to fundamental and sweeping changes in the larger societal system. This argument, in fact, was the basis for one of the most famous sociological analyses of religion to date: Max Weber's examination of the role of the **Protestant ethic,** the world view and values associated with the new Protestant religions, in the rise of modern capitalism (1958/1904).

In this well-known, controversial thesis, Weber argued that the European system of capitalism that triggered Marx's critique of religion represents an outcome of the Protestant Reformation that swept through western Europe during the sixteenth and seventeenth centuries. Before that time, the Roman Catholic Church had dominated the European continent and supported the existing feudal system. Catholicism discouraged economic expansion or change through its doctrine that making money through lending money (what was called *usury*) was sinful. However, Martin Luther's break from the Catholic Church led to the development of several new religious systems—in particular, Calvinism—that created an ideological climate supportive of rational economic activity and the accumulation of wealth.

One significant component of this climate was the concept of **predestination,** the belief that one's fate in the afterlife was decided before (or at) one's birth and that no amount of prayer or good works could change that outcome. According to Weber, this belief created an uncertainty in people's minds as to their own particular fate. Although the question could never be answered fully, one likely indicator of success or failure in the afterlife was success or failure in this life. Economic prosperity, therefore, became a fundamental goal and a driving force in people's lives. Though not a cause of spiritual salvation, such prosperity was a sign that one was among the elect.

A second critical element in this new religious ideology was the doctrine of **worldly asceticism,** or denial of material self-indulgence. According to this belief, the simple, frugal life was morally superior to foolish concern for the things of this world. Like prosperity, thrift became a sign of virtue.

Weber concluded that, in combination, these two beliefs encouraged people to try to succeed in their work efforts and directed them to apply and reapply the proceeds of past efforts to future efforts. In short, the Protestant ethic led them to activities that translated into capital formation and capital expansion. The result was a revolutionary change in the structure of European social systems.

Weber recognized that the change from feudalism to capitalism was not the direct result of the Protestant ethic alone and that a reciprocal or two-way relationship existed between the new belief system and the new economic system. His point was that religion can serve and has served as an important medium for significant social change. It is a point well taken.

Religion in the United States: From Puritans to Televangelists

Since the first days of its existence as New World colonies, what is now the United States has been somewhat unique in terms of religious expression. Unlike the European societies from which the largest numbers of its population have come, this society has been one of religious pluralism and tolerance. Many of the early settlers were religious dissenters fleeing persecution in their homelands. They came seeking a new land in which they would be free to worship as they saw fit. This cultural value of freedom of religious expression and the rejection of a state-supported or state-imposed religion was incorporated into the U.S. Constitution. It has been the guideline for the social organization of religion in the country since that time.

From its founding, the United States has been a society whose members at least claim a set of religious beliefs and practices. Many of the original thirteen states were the successors of colonies (for example, Puritan settlements in Massachusetts Bay) that had been conceived as religious experiments. Their founders viewed these colonies as attempts to establish the heavenly society in an otherwise unheavenly world (Erikson, 1966). The social patterns of these communities were grounded in the religious beliefs of their people, who attempted to construct all aspects of daily life according to their particular reading of the Word of God. They were joined later by millions of ethnic immigrants from traditional societies for whom religion also was an important organizing social force. These immigrants brought their old religions with them, adding to the growing number of faiths in American society.

The number of specific religious groupings that have appeared in the United States at one time or another has been very large. But most people have affiliated historically with one of the three "great traditions" (Williams, 1989): Protestantism, Catholicism, and Judaism. These three form what sociologists refer to as **denominations,** or formal religious organizations that are well integrated into their society and recognize religious pluralism. Such denominations coexist with the larger society and with one another. According to a 1998 Gallup survey, 87 percent of all those claiming religious affiliation in the United States described themselves as Christians of one sort or another (in Alsop, 1998). With membership of 61.2 million people, the Roman Catholic Church is the single largest denomination in the U.S., followed by the various Baptist Churches at 35.4 million (Lindner, 1999). Of the approximately 14.8 million religiously affiliated Americans claiming membership in a non-Christian faith, 62 percent are Jews (5.5 million) or Muslims (3.8 million) (in Brunner, 1998). But some religious experts claim that the true number of Muslims in the United States is more on the order of 5 to 6 million and is increasing rapidly as a result of immigration from the Middle East and the conversion of many African Americans to Islam. They argue that "America's Muslim population is set to outstrip its Jewish one by 2010, making it the nation's second-largest faith after Christianity" (Power, 1998). The three great traditions may soon be joined by a fourth.

Although Protestantism, Catholicism, and Judaism have defined the general shape of the religious landscape in the United States, they have not accounted for all its specific features. Peter Williams (1989) chronicled the development of what he calls "little traditions" of folk and popular religions throughout U.S. social history. **Folk religions** represent particular interpretations and modifications of more formalized religious traditions to meet the needs of specific population groups—for example, the set of beliefs and practices of Italian Catholic or Polish Catholic immigrants, or the particular devotion of Mexican Catholics to the Virgin of Guadalupe. These little traditions can be thought of as translations or adaptations of mainstream denominational religions.

In contrast, what Williams terms **popular religions** represent sets of beliefs and practices that lie outside of, or perhaps span, the boundaries of recognized denominations. Their appeal is not to a specific group or groups but rather to large-scale or mass audiences drawn from a variety of backgrounds. These popular religions are generated by people's experiences of cultural and social disorganization and the inability of established denominations to resolve this confusion and chaos. As such, they generally stand in opposition to the established sociocultural order. They offer their members a different vision of what societal life could and should be like and a different path to achieve that vision. In this respect, they resemble what sociologists refer to as religious **sects.** Christian evangelical and Pentecostal movements and the various "televangelistic" ministries illustrate popular religions in the contemporary United States.

Religion in the Counterculture Movement During the 1960s and the decade of the counterculture movement, observers in the United States were proclaiming the death of God and of religion. The increasing rational planning and organization of nearly all societal activities, coupled with the increasing concern of people with material comfort and affluence, presumably had led to the **secularization** (the transformation from a religious to a civil and worldly basis) of society and a significant decline of religion in everyday life. Attacks on "the establishment" by the so-called hippies that occurred during this decade also seemed to involve a defection from established religious traditions as well as a rejection of the secular social order.

The members of the counterculture may have been seeking mystical experiences in their struggle against what they saw as a depersonalized, militaristic society, but they were not finding those experiences through traditional American religions. In their eyes, established denominations had themselves become bureaucratic and depersonalized, out of touch with the real world and its many social injustices. Traditional religious groups, especially Roman Catholicism and mainline Protestant denominations such as Presbyterians, Methodists, and Episcopalians, began to experience significant declines in membership and attendance.

Whereas some members of the counterculture in fact did reject religion altogether, many others began to experiment with new, nontraditional systems of religious expression. These new forms ranged from simple beliefs and rituals last practiced in hunting and gathering or horticultural societies to Hinduism, Buddhism, and other Eastern religions dating back thousands of years. Their common denominator seemed to be the strong sense of community that had been lost from the churches and synagogues of established American denominations. Religion itself was not dead in the United States, although some conventional religions were looking a little unhealthy.

To combat declining memberships, some of the traditional denominations began to become more involved with the surrounding world, addressing themselves to pressing social issues such as poverty and racial discrimination. At the same time, they developed a new ecumenical spirit that emphasized the underlying continuities among various established groups rather than doctrinal differences. Within the Catholic Church, the Second Vatical Council, held in Rome from 1962 to 1965, eased many of that religion's traditional authoritarian rules. It also introduced a number of liberal and local elements into U.S. Catholicism. Masses were now conducted in English (or other local languages) rather than Latin, and folk songs often replaced conventional organ music and church choirs. The regimented convent life of many Catholic nuns was replaced by more egalitarian communal living arrangements and a more active role in societal affairs.

The Rise of Fundamentalism Ironically, the changes introduced by these established denominations to attract and retain members during the 1960s seem to have helped spark the fundamentalist revival that began in the 1970s and is still prominent today. The groups that make up this "resurgence of conservative Christianity" (Dobson, Hindson, and Falwell, 1986, p. xiv) are appalled by what they see as the triumph of the secular over the sacred in everyday life, as well as the steady rise of **humanism,** the belief that humans, rather than God, are the center of their own destiny.

Fundamentalists see evidence of *secular humanism*, as they call it, in changing public attitudes and political policies toward homosexuality, abortion, and women's proper roles in society, among other things. They are convinced that this trend is one of the most dangerous threats of the modern age to decent Christians throughout the country. They are also convinced that many, if not all, of the established Catholic and Protestant denominations are not much better than secular institutions. In their view, in becoming more connected to the world of secular affairs, these churches have become too much like that world. The war against liberal Protestantism that spawned fundamentalism in the early twentieth century now has intensified into a war against the secular humanism that they believe is poisoning government, education, the family, and mainstream religious denominations in the United States. These contemporary fundamentalists are also militantly opposed to a number of other "isms"—liberalism, communism, and left-wing evangelicalism (Dobson, Hindson, and Falwell, 1986, p. 2)—that they see as antithetical to the goals of true Christianity.

In the 1980s, this militant opposition and anger took a decidedly political turn. Mobilizing their members in record numbers, conservative Christian action groups claimed to have played a decisive role in shaping the outcomes of the 1980, 1984, and 1988 presidential elections, as well as many state and local campaigns. But in 1992, widespread public perception that the Republican Party platform had been captured by an ultraconservative religious right helped sweep President George Bush out of office and Arkansas Governor Bill Clinton into the presidency. Large numbers of otherwise loyal Republicans (in particular, women) defected to Clinton and the more moderate Democratic Party platform. In 1994, however, the pendulum once more swung the other way. The religious right again asserted its considerable political influence, helping scores of conservative Christian candidates win legislative seats at both the state and federal levels (Broder, 1995; Roberts et al., 1995). In 1996, the Republican Party was once again perceived as catering to the Christian Coalition, the Family Research Council, and other groups that make up the so-called "religious right." Flushed with successes in the 1994 elections and record amounts of financial contributions, "At the 1996 [Republican] convention, Christian conservatives moved to make their intraparty advantage permanent and institutional, much as radical and social liberals had done before the 1972 Democratic

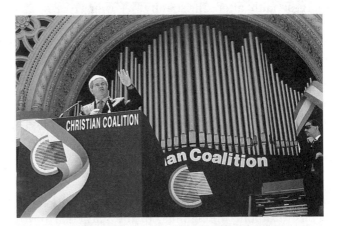

Then-Speaker of the House Newt Gingrich addresses the faithful at a Christian Coalition "God and Country" rally. The increasing infusion of conservative Christian religions into local, state, and national political affairs and political parties—especially the Republican Party—has become a matter of great controversy. Heated disputes over the role of religious beliefs in political decision making and public policy formation have created significant rifts across U.S. society. At times, political groups such as the Christian Coalition have played important roles in the selection and election of candidates for political offices at all levels.

convention" (Caldwell, in Hunt, 1998). However, in the subsequent presidential election, Republican Party candidate Senator Bob Dole was defeated by incumbent President Bill Clinton. Over the next two years, the Christian Coalition lost its leader, Ralph Reed, and went through a period of retrenchment and reorganization (Connolly and Balz, 1998) until galvanized into new life by events unfolding in the Clinton White House.

Clinton's second term as president was plagued by a series of finance and sex scandals, resulting in his impeachment by the House of Representatives following an extended investigation by Independent Counsel Kenneth Starr. (Though impeached by the House, Clinton was not convicted by the Senate and remained in office.) Many observers saw conservative Christians as the driving force behind Clinton's impeachment, with critics asserting that the enormous expenditure of time, money, and other resources by Starr's committee and certain members of Congress was motivated by the religious right's outrage over the President's alleged moral offenses, not by any criminal wrongdoings (Grier and Thurman, 1999). They claimed that what had begun as an inquiry into questionable actions by the Clintons in an Arkansas land deal had quickly deteriorated into a witch-hunt orchestrated by conservative Christians out to "get" the President. Concerned by what they perceive as "the manipulation of people of faith for the purposes of building support for a partisan political agenda" (Gaddy, in Hunt, 1998), moderate religious groups such as the Interfaith Alliance—a coalition of Christians, Jews, and Muslims— have begun to speak out about what they see as the religious right's monopolization of the religious voice in national and local politics. While acknowledging the right of conservative Christians to become involved in political discussion and policy making, religious moderates are attempting to make sure that more than one religious view will be heard in political debate. From their perspective, "Conservatives don't have a right to claim that theirs is the only viable expression of faith that should guide public policy. Yet their message seems to be that the only good Christians are Republicans, and that God has taken up residence in the Republican Party . . . [the religious right] does not speak for all Christians, nor does it speak for all people of faith" (Carrier, in Lloyd, 1998). For its part, the conservative Christian movement is not prepared to see its influence on the Republican Party weakened by moderate Republican candidates hoping to broaden their public appeal. According to the Rev. Jerry Falwell, an early force in the religious right, "That is not going to happen . . . The Republican Party could never win a na-

tional election again—never—without the support of social conservatives . . . You are not going to find anybody who hopes to be president one day to ever say a thing like that" (in Dolbee, 1999).

Like the "old" fundamentalism, the groups that make up this new Christian movement stress a back-to-basics approach that distinguishes them sharply from mainline Protestantism. But the new fundamentalism differs from the old in several important respects. In the first place, it is not identified with specific and well-defined denominations. Rather, it represents what Williams (1989, p. 3) called "extra-ecclesiastical" religion. The people who make up the new religious right come from a variety of established religious groups, or from none at all. They do not refer to themselves in terms of a specific denominational affiliation (for example, Methodist or Lutheran), preferring instead the more diffuse term *Christian* or, for those who have had a life-altering conversion experience, *born again Christian.*

Second, whereas the old fundamentalism was almost exclusively a lower-class, rural, and regional (southern) phenomenon, the new fundamentalism appeals to a much wider array of socioeconomic class, residential, and geographical backgrounds. At least one U.S. president, (Ronald Reagan) espoused what certainly appeared to be fundamentalist Christian beliefs.

Finally, a good deal of the new fundamentalism is conveyed through the medium of television, appealing to a dispersed mass audience that numbers in the millions. Conservative Christian ministers such as Jerry Falwell, Jimmy Swaggart, and Pat Robertson have become nationally known (and controversial) figures. But the message of this "electronic church," as it has been called, has been transformed significantly by its preaching medium.

The Electronic Church Television is a visual medium that relies on the pictorial image rather than the spoken word to make its primary impact. It also requires large sums of money to purchase broadcasting time or to maintain broadcasting facilities. The wholesale and, in some cases, exclusive use of television to convey religious beliefs has led to programming that is often more in the nature of entertainment than doctrinal enlightenment. A large portion of this "entertainment" is often devoted to appeals for financial offerings from faithful viewers. These appeals have been successful enough that the electronic church has taken in hundreds of millions of dollars to further its work and carry on its ministries. Obviously, these programs must be appealing to someone and something in U.S. living rooms.

The "someone," according to observers of the phenomenon, is generally older people of lower income and educational levels who are already involved in religion through church membership and participation in activities such as Bible reading. Women and nonwhites are more likely to be regular viewers of televangelists than are men and whites. For these people, the electronic church is an extension of, rather than a substitute for, more conventional religious expression (Hoover, 1988).

The "something" that religious television broadcasting appeals to can and does vary from viewer to viewer. According to Hoover (1988), personal crises of some sort—the sudden and tragic death of a loved one, serious illness, financial misfortune—initially attract many viewers. Other analysts (Williams, 1989) claim that these programs appeal to those segments of the population who are most likely to feel a sense of social and cultural dislocation. In a sense, these people are part of the human wreckage of the modernization process and are looking for some means to make sense out of a world that is puzzling and increasingly hostile to them. If this is the case, the future of the electronic church may be assured for some time to come.

Religion Today Recent studies suggest that, although significant changes have occurred over the past forty years and are occurring now, the place of religion itself in American society seems secure. For example, comparative surveys conducted in over 60 countries show that the United States is the most religious country in the developed world. Forty-four percent of the Americans responding to the World Values Survey claim to attend church once a week, and 53 percent say that religion is very important to them. By way of contrast, only 38 percent of Canadian, 27 percent of British, 21 percent of French, 4 percent of Swedish, and 2 percent of Russian respondents report attending religious services on a weekly basis. And only 16 percent of British, 13 percent of French, and 13 percent of Germans claim that religion is very important in their lives (reported in Morin, 1998a). Surveys of this type, as well as data from the 1990 United States Census, show that religion in the U.S. has not declined appreciably over the last several decades. Overall, they suggest a restructuring of existing religious affiliations rather than a decline of religious expression per se. The losers in this restructuring have been traditional Catholic and Protestant denominations. The winners have been the rapidly growing, branchline evangelical, Pentecostal, and charismatic Christian groups. About two-thirds of Americans claim membership in a church, but these churches are more often eclectic than traditional; that is, mixtures of several faiths rather than just one established set of beliefs and practices. In this regard, no less a person than the Dalai Lama has called the United States "the spiritual supermarket" (in Miller, 1999, p. B1). Young people, in particular, have taken to this religious eclecticism, although a significant minority are joining evangelical denominations emphasizing strict obedience to church doctrine (Belsie, 1999a).

Religion in this society is not likely to become extinct in the foreseeable future. Although no "official" religion is promoted by or required by our government, we nonetheless are a recognizably religious society. Our daily public lives are infused with the symbols of being a population steeped in a belief in a supreme being and dedicated to a moral course of action. Both U.S. presidents and witnesses in criminal court trials are sworn into office with their hand resting on a Bible. "In God We Trust" is engraved onto our paper currency, and we pledge allegiance to one nation under God. This *civil religion,* as Robert Bellah (1988) called it, reflects the fact that this country was founded, and still operates, on a Judeo-Christian moral and religious framework. The Scripture-spouting fundamentalist may be an object of people's ridicule and sometimes even anger, but the avowed atheist has an equally poor reputation. Most Americans may be only sporadic church or synagogue attendees, but many claim to be religious in their own way and acknowledge that faith is an important part of their lives.

In the final analysis, the same force that has led us to a greater knowledge and appreciation of our surrounding physical world—the rational development and application of the scientific perspective—may be responsible for the persistence of religious sentiments and practices. As one old saying puts it, the more we learn, the more we find we don't know. For many people in this society, religion will continue to offer an understanding of what we don't yet know. "Besides providing a sense of orientation and security in an insecure world, one of the functions of religion is to help satisfy the need to know where we come from and where we're going" (Inglehart, in Morin, 1998a).

Religion and Modernization

Approximately 80 percent of the world's population profess some religious belief, with two-thirds stating that they are active in their faith (see Table 10.3). Like other societal institutions, religion is a dynamic

TABLE 10.3

Religious Affiliation in the World, 1998

Religious Affiliation	Estimated Membership (in millions)
Christian	1,966
Muslim	1,179
Hindu	767
Buddhist	357
Tribal religions	244
New religions	99
Sikh	23
Judaism	15
Baha'i	6
Confucian	5
Shinto	3
No religion	767
Atheist	146

Sources: International Bulletin of Missionary Research, January 1998. (Religion News Service, 1998); Russell Ash, *The Top 10 of Everything, 1998.* (New York: DK Publishing, 1998).

entity. Some faiths are gaining adherents, while others are losing members. According to Samuel Huntington (1998, pp. 65–66):

> The percentage of Christians in the world peaked at about 30% in the 1980s, leveled off, is now declining, and will probably approximate to about 25% of the world's population by 2025. As a result of their extremely high rates of population growth, the proportion of Muslims in the world will continue to increase dramatically, amounting to 20 percent of the world's population about the turn of the century, surpassing the number of Christians some years later, and probably accounting for about 30 percent of the world's population by 2025.

As students of sociology, we are concerned with more than just the number of people who believe and worship in a particular manner. For sociologists, the more important issues are how religion affects the way people behave socially, economically, and politically, and how belief systems are related to social change—especially to modernization. The relationship between religion and modernization is complex, inasmuch as religion can influence the modernization process or, in turn, be changed by the forces of modernization. With regard to religion's effect on modernization, there are many examples of how religion has acted both to help and to hinder de-

velopment in the now-rich countries as well as the less-developed nations of the world.

A Force Promoting Modernization As societies develop, they require educated, literate groups of people who can fill the growing number of management, leadership, and technical positions in business, industry, and government. At the time of the Industrial Revolution in Europe, it was the Catholic Church, together with numerous Protestant denominations, that provided a system of formal learning from the primary to the university level. The free, universal, compulsory, state-sponsored education system typically associated with modern industrial and postindustrial nations did not begin to appear until much later in the nineteenth century. Similarly, in the United States, the earliest and most prestigious universities—Harvard, Yale, and Princeton, for example—were church affiliated. In fact, all three of these Ivy League schools were originally seminaries.

In addition to a literate population, modernization also requires an appropriate population world view or mind-set that prepares people for the many new behaviors required to support basic and massive societal changes, especially in economic organization. We have already discussed Max Weber's thesis that the Protestant ethic, with its associated emphasis on hard work and thrift, provided a moral climate that was particularly conducive to the rise of capitalism in western Europe and, later, in North America. A similar role has been played in Brazil by the Umbanda religion.

A mixture of Roman Catholic, African vodoun, and indigenous Indian religious beliefs that began as a small cult in the 1920s, Umbanda now numbers over 30 million members and is a powerful religious and political force in Brazilian society. It accompanied the economic and industrial expansion of Brazil as a whole and, more specifically, the development of the nation's two largest cities, São Paulo and Rio de Janeiro, where it is most deeply rooted. The earliest adherents of Umbanda were former slaves and newly arrived immigrants anxious for economic success and upward mobility, drawn to the religion's promise that individuals who were good in this life would see their social and economic positions improve in a future incarnation (de Queiroz, 1989). This view of the world was very compatible with the goals of the lower and middle classes in a growing urban, consumer-oriented society. By convincing people that their dreams would be fulfilled in the next life, Umbanda kept them working hard in this life. By integrating people of different races and classes in an extremely heterogeneous society, it aided political stability, an important component of the modernization process.

A Force Opposing Modernization   Religion has at times also acted as a powerful force against modernization. In 1863, Roman Catholic Pope Pius IX's papal decree declared that it was heresy for anyone to believe "that the Roman Pontiff can, and ought to, reconcile himself to, and agree with, progress, liberalism, and modern civilization" (in Bettenson, 1974, p. 273). In 1907, Pope Pius X wrote an encyclical thoroughly condemning "modernism." He noted that the basic error of this process was "twisting unalterable truth to suit modern thought" (Wilson and Clark, 1989, p. 171). Religious opposition to stabilizing population growth through various methods of birth control makes it more difficult for many developing nations to modernize successfully. Most, if not all, of their economic progress is consumed by a larger and younger population. In 1968, Pope Paul VI issued an encyclical reaffirming the Catholic Church's position against all artificial forms of contraception; a position reiterated in 1995 by the most recent Pope, John Paul II. In the Muslim world, some conservative religious leaders, especially in Pakistan, have denounced birth control as un-Islamic (Smith, 1971).

In India, liberal Hindus argue that the beliefs of more strict, orthodox Hindus have contributed to their nation's poverty, disease, hunger, and overpopulation. For example, orthodox Hindus who believe in *karma*—the idea that one's present condition in life has been earned by his or her own past deeds—adhere to a fatalistic world view whereby people passively accept their lot in life as unalterable. Orthodox Hindus are also likely to believe that the world is currently passing through a cycle in which conditions are naturally and increasingly growing worse (Converse, 1988). These beliefs are contrary to the view held by most people in modern societies that human beings control their own destiny and, within limits, can change the world to suit their needs and desires. Hinduism is a religion with hundreds of holidays at the individual, regional, and national levels that result in an annual loss of tens of millions of labor-hours of work and other productive activity. Millions more hours are lost to sometimes daily rituals concerning purity and pollution, as well as to pilgrimages to hundreds of holy cities and shrines. In addition, the many ascetic holy men who wander through the streets and countryside represent a double loss to society: they must be supported by others, while making no contribution themselves to the economic well-being of the nation (Converse, 1988).

Conservative Muslims in many countries have attempted to impede values and behaviors typically associated with modernization. Following a 1979 revolution that deposed Mohammed Reza as Shah and established the Islamic Republic of Iran under the leadership of the Ayatollah Khomeini, *mullahs* (holy men) created a kind of religious morals police that monitored the behavior of people in public places. Teenagers were chastised for listening to music from the Western world, and women were scrutinized to make sure they were properly veiled and their hair was not showing (Nordland, 1993). In 1999, tens of thousands of students in fifteen cities across Iran demonstrated against the government, demanding more jobs, an end to intrusive restrictions of individual rights, and greater freedom of expression (Zakaria, 1999). At about the same time, the Turkish military was cracking down on what it described as "the Islamic threat" in that nation (Kohen, 1998). And, in Pakistan, military leaders were voicing concern about the spread of fundamentalist Islam from the Taliban in neighboring Afghanistan, describing them as "medievals who would medievalize our society" (Masood, in Marquand, 1998, p. 6). Their fears are based on the experience that "Islamic societies do not seem able to make the transition to modern societies with individual rights, separation of church and state, and a prosperous economy" (Zakaria, 1999).

Of all the major world religions, Buddhism appears to have had the least effect (positive or negative) on the modernization process. In some nations, Buddhism is attempting to adapt to the changes brought about by economic development. Maraldo (1976, p. vi) has noted that present-day Buddhism is "prepared to encounter and learn from the secular world." As stated by one Zen scholar (in Maraido, 1976, p. 224), "The Buddhism of the future . . . will be grounded in the natural sciences and in a humanism which liberates and cultivates human nature; and it will be open to all the world."

These examples indicate that religion and modernization are involved in a complex web of cause-and-effect relationships that have both helped and hindered the societal development process. When we consider how important religious beliefs and behavior are to so many people, this intricate relationship—especially the relationship between religion and politics—is hardly surprising. Henry St. Simon, one of the founders of sociology, noted years ago that "the religious institution—under whatever spirit envisages it—is the principal political institution" (in Robertson, 1989, p. 20). Although St. Simon may have overstated the political significance of religion, there can be little doubt that religious beliefs and institutions will be a major factor in the modernization of the less developed countries of the world.

Education as a Social Institution

1. *What are the major functions of formal education in contemporary societies?*

Formal education has become a crucial institution in modern and modernizing societies, overtaking the family as the main agent of socialization. Functionalists claim that education serves as a device for social reproduction, cultural storage, social placement, conflict management, and social transformation and change. Schools have also become providers of custodial day care for many children. (Pp. 219–220)

2. *How do conflict theorists view formal education's role in modern societies?*

Conflict theorists interpret education as a means to advance the interests of the people who control society. Marxists view education as a societal superstructure that operates to create a false consciousness among powerless, nonpropertied groups. Conflict theorists claim that education has a hidden political curriculum designed to teach support for existing governments and government leaders. (P. 221)

3. *What is the relationship between formal education and social stratification in contemporary societies?*

Formal education can promote social mobility by providing minority and lower-class group members with proper credentials for higher-level, higher-salary occupations. Perhaps more often, education helps to preserve existing stratification systems through the tracking of different class groups into different academic and career paths. Lower-class and minority students have higher dropout rates and lower levels of academic success than white middle-, upper-middle-, and upper-class students. (Pp. 221–223)

4. *How is education as an institution structured in the United States?*

The U.S. educational system is a vast structure that lacks any central or national administration but is bureaucratized at state, local, and individual school levels. Education is democratic, and many people take advantage of the openness of the system. More than one-fourth of the American population are involved with education, whether as students, teachers, administrators, or support staff. (Pp. 223, 227–228)

5. *Why has formal education in the United States been subject to such severe criticism in recent years?*

Education in the United States has been criticized for its students' low performances on math, science, and other standardized tests in comparison to Asian and European students and for the high levels of functional and cultural illiteracy found among the graduated adult population. Some reformers have called for the adoption of an Asian education model in the United States, with longer school years, more in-class and homework assignments, and a rigorous standardized curriculum. Others claim that cultural differences make the implementation of an Asian-based model impossible. (Pp. 228–230)

6. *What is the school choice or voucher program?*

School choice or voucher programs have also been proposed as a means of educational reform. Government would give parents educational tuition vouchers, which could be cashed in at any school of the parents' choice, whether public or private (Charter schools, in which tax-funded schools are run by groups independently of local school boards, are also included in these programs. This free-market educational system would presumably motivate public schools to become more productive and efficient, and would give parents greater freedom in shaping their children's education. Opponents argue that school choice would merely add to the deterioration of public schools and cause a further education polarization along racial, ethnic, and class lines. (Pp. 230–231)

Religion as a Social Institution

7. *Why has religion been found, in one form or another, in human societies from ancient times to the present?*

As a long-standing social institution, religion reflects humans' need to deal with sacred aspects of life—those elements that inspire a sense of reverence, awe, and fear. Religious statuses and roles were among the first specialized positions to be differentiated in early human societies. (P. 232)

8. *How do conflict theorists' views of religion differ from those of functionalist theorists?*

Functionalists such as Durkheim contend that religion promotes societal solidarity, strengthens social control, and gives population members a sense of meaning and purpose in life. As a conflict theorist, Marx claimed that religion was a powerful tool employed by ruling classes in capitalist societies to maintain their position by deflecting the attention of oppressed classes from real-world concerns to those of an afterlife. For Marx, religion was the "opium of the people." (P. 233)

9. *According to Max Weber, how has religion affected social change?*

Max Weber disagreed with Marx, maintaining that religion could be an important factor in promoting societal change. His analysis of the Protestant beliefs in predestination and worldly asceticism indicated that this Protestant ethic created a climate that encouraged the development of capitalism in European societies. (P. 234)

10. *What is the state of religion in the United States today?*

For most of its history, the United States has been both a religious and a religiously tolerant society. Most Americans may identify as Protestant, Catholic, or Jewish, but many folk religions and popular religions cut across traditional religious denominational lines. Islam is perhaps the fastest-growing religion in the U.S. today, claiming as many as 6 million followers. In recent years, Christian fundamentalism, stressing a back-to-basics religious approach and a rejection of secularism and humanism, has become a growing and important social and political force. This fundamentalist revival has used television and other mass media as effective channels for reaching millions of people. (Pp. 234–238)

11. *What is the relationship between religion and societal modernization?*

The relationship between religion and modernization is complex, with religious beliefs both helping and hindering the development process. As noted, Protestant and Catholic churches in Europe and in the United States established systems of formal education long before any schools were funded and controlled by the state. Yet, religious opposition to artificial birth control as a method for, slowing rapid population growth has made modernization increasingly difficult for some poor nations. Large-scale, violent clashes between Muslims and Hindus, as well as recent events in the Middle East, clearly indicate that religion will be a significant factor in the economic and political development of many nations. (Pp. 238–240)

Economy and Politics

Shortly after the April 1995 blast that destroyed the federal building in Oklahoma City and killed 168 people, government officials, the media, and the general public began speculating on who was responsible for such a deadly assault. Virtually all initial suspects were foreign individuals and nations, including Saddam Hussein of Iraq, Libya's Colonel Qaddafi, and the governments of both Iran and North Korea. Largely as a result of the mass destruction and heavy loss of life in the bombing, few Americans were willing to believe that the perpetrators of this crime could be their own countrymen.

However, it soon became evident that the killers were, indeed, homegrown U.S. citizens engaged in **political terrorism,** "the use of violence by a group acting either on behalf of, or in opposition to, an established political authority" (Jary and Jary, 1991, p. 518). The Murrah Federal Building in Oklahoma City was no doubt selected because it was a highly visible symbol of the hated United States Government. Other favorite targets of domestic terrorist groups are organizations that represent the power of the federal government, such as the Federal Bureau of Investigation, the Internal Revenue Service, and the Bureau of Alcohol, Tobacco, and Firearms.

Although antigovernment groups are active in 40 states and count tens of thousands of people among their members, hard-core extremists comprise no more than a few hundred individuals (Kaplan et al., 1997). There is no single, coherent political philosophy that unites the "radical right," but a sizeable percentage of these people believe that, in its effort to form a one-world government, the United Nations plans to invade and conquer the United States. In 1997, FBI agents and local police confiscated weapons from an assault team set to attack the Fort Hood Army Base. The group believed that United Nations troops from China were training at the Texas military facility in preparation for their invasion and conquest of this country.

Racism and anti-semitism are common themes in many right-wing organizations, and dovetail with their antigovernment views. They think of Jews as the plotting masterminds behind grandiose schemes to dominate the world. The Modern Christian Identity group sees Jews as a "separate creation"; that is, as the illicit children of Eve and Satan. One of the "Sixteen Commandments" of another group reads, in part, "Do not employ niggers or coloreds. Have social contact only with members of your own racial family" (Kaplan, 1995, p. 65).

Yet another supposed federal government conspiracy embraced by many individuals in the radical right is that the U.S. military deliberately exposed American troops to biological and chemical agents during the Persian Gulf War of 1990–1991. The goal of this supposed operation was to weaken and reduce (by way of sickness and death) the U.S. population, making it that much easier for the survivors to be controlled by the "New World Order." A somewhat related belief is that HIV-1 (the virus that causes AIDS) was one of ten such biological agents developed by the military and field-tested in Haiti and Africa. When the experiment got out of control, the HIV-1 virus made its way into local populations and, from there, eventually spread throughout the world ("Crossing the Threshold," 1997).

The radical right also views man-made diseases as potential weapons in their struggle with the government. In *The Terrorist Trap: America's Experience With Terrorism,* Jeffrey Simon (1994) outlines a gruesome scenario wherein foreign or domestic terrorists release deadly agents into the air, creating a biological cloud of "suspended microscopic droplets of bacterial or virus particles." This could be accomplished via-low flying airplanes, trucks equipped with spray tanks positioned upwind of densely populated cities, aerosol canisters with timing devices left in subways, airports, and/or the air-conditioning systems of buildings, and by directly contaminating bulk food supplies destined for supermarkets and restaurants. Physician Laurie Garrett (1996) states that enough anthrax spores to kill as many as six million people could be loaded into a taxi and pumped out of its tailpipe as it cruised the streets of a major city.

The relative ease with which these weapons can be produced is a major concern to many who study terrorism. One expert in biological warfare noted that just $10,000 and slightly over 200 square feet of floor space are the only requirements for producing enough biological agents to satisfy the needs of an entire army. Most of the ingredients needed to manufacture these weapons can be purchased legally, and the information to assemble them can easily be obtained through books and articles available on the Internet. One knowledgeable observer (Reynolds, in "Crossing the Threshold," 1997, p. 9) has noted that "It is only a matter of time before some unknown zealots strike a government facility or civilian community with homegrown biological or chemical weapons."

Explaining the emergence of radical groups advocating, if not actually engaging in, politically motivated violence, is a much more difficult task than than simply counting them and describing their activities. One interpretation is that these groups grow in number and size during an economic downturn characterized by high unemployment, inflation, and reduced chances for upward mobility. Organizations such as the Ku Klux Klan can target racial and ethnic minorities, using them as scapegoats in coming to grips with their own low economic standing. As one might predict from this interpretation, the number of Klan-like "hate" groups has decreased from the early to late 1990s as the country has experienced a period of sustained economic growth.

But the state of the economy alone seemingly cannot adequately explain this phenomenon, inasmuch as the number of radical-right militias has increased dramatically during this same economic boom period. However, upon closer examination, it appears that many Klansmen have simply exchanged their white sheets and hoods for military uniforms ("Too Busy To Hate," 1997). To their racist philosophies, they have added a fierce hatred of the federal government and many of its constituent agencies.

The arrest of ten militia members in Arizona yielded a "mix of high school graduates and dropouts" mostly stuck in low-paying, low-prestige jobs (for example, janitor, used-furniture salesman, and doughnut baker, among others). Experts are of the opinion that the socioeconomic standing of these arrestees is typical of members of radical-right groups (Brooke, 1997, p. 66). From this perspective, even during those periods in which the nation's economy as a whole is robust, there always will be a significant number of people toiling for low wages in dead-end jobs. It is from this stratum of society that militia members are successfully recruited.

Political and economic institutions are so closely intertwined in modern societies, with the well-being of one contingent on the well-being of the other, that many social scientists speak of (and study) them in terms of an interdependant **political economy**. Although militant right-wing radicals are far from the mainstream of the American political system, they are worthy of our attention not only because of their capacity for violence against that mainstream, but also because they are, in part, a product of the existing political economy. In this chapter we explore the economic and political institutions that, together, make up the basic fabric of this and other contemporary societies.

Questions to Consider

1. What is the "adaptation" problem, and how does the economy help solve it?
2. From a conflict perspective, what is meant by the idea of the economy as the substructure of all societies?
3. What is the relationship between economic development and political democracy?
4. What is meant by *corporate capitalism*?
5. What is a *postindustrial* society?
6. What are the "four dragons," and why have their economies grown so rapidly since 1960?
7. Why has economic growth in sub-Saharan Africa been so slow?
8. What are the major obstacles facing economic development in Russia?
9. From a functionalist standpoint, what is the function of the state or polity in modern societies?
10. How do conflict theorists like Marx interpret the role of the state as the major political institution in modern societies?
11. Who (or what) is the *power elite*?
12. How does socioeconomic status affect political participation in the United States?
13. What is the difference between *power* and *authority* as forms of political rule?
14. What is *devolution*?

ECONOMY AS A SOCIAL INSTITUTION

In a now-classic **Saturday Night Live** TV sketch, comedian Don Novello as "Father Guido Sarducci" outlined his plan for a fifteen-minute college degree program. Most of the information students receive during their four years of higher education, he claimed, has absolutely no bearing on their subsequent occupational or social careers (a claim, incidentally, which contains a certain amount of truth).

The good father then offered his viewers a bare-bones undergraduate curriculum designed to give students a basic working knowledge of traditional academic fields yet still allow them to finish college before lunch. In this streamlined approach to the liberal arts, the field of economics was reduced to just three words: "Supply and Demand."

Although obviously meant as satire, this synopsis in fact does capture the essence of economics as the study of human economies. In any society, the economy consists of a system of units (individuals, groups, and organizations) and activities (hunting, gathering, farming, herding, or manufacturing, among other things) involved in the production, distribution, exchange or consumption of goods and services. In other words, economies consist of attempts to create or provide a supply of resources to meet the needs, wants, or demands of some societal population—supply and demand. When societal development progresses to the point at which these economic activities become assigned to a recognized set of statuses with specific, defined roles, and are directed by a set of widely accepted norms, we can speak of the economy as forming a social institution. Sociologists of all theoretical persuasions recognize the critical role of economic institutions in contemporary societies, although their interpretations and analyses of this role differ dramatically.

Theoretical Interpretations of the Economy

Functionalist Theory From a functionalist perspective, the economy is one of the most fundamental and essential of all human institutions. Economic structures and operations are intimately involved in the resolution of what functionalist theorists call *functional prerequisites,* the basic survival problems all human societies share in common (Tumin, 1985). More specifically, according to Talcott Parsons (1966; Parsons and Smelser, 1956), economies help deal with "adaptation" problems.

Before societies can become anything else, they first must become capable of providing their members with at least the minimal levels of essential materials necessary for physical survival—food, clothing, and shelter. Unless and until these subsistence needs are satisfied, humans cannot and will not engage in other types of individual or collective activities. In point of fact, there will be no one left alive to engage in any other kinds of activities—the population will have become extinct. Economies, then, are the means through which human populations adapt to the possibilities offered and the limitations imposed by their specific physical environments. Economies allow people to extract from their surrounding environments the raw materials necessary for human existence.

Once the minimal survival needs of a population have been met, any excess materials produced by the economy become surplus resources that can be applied toward other uses—supporting full-time political and religious leaders, maintaining a standing army for protection from enemies, exchanging for other supplies from neighboring populations, supporting a larger population at home, or any number of other objectives. In this interpretation, economic

success is a prerequisite for other types of societal activity. As the level of economic development and resulting supplies of resources increase, societies become larger in size and more complex in social organization, capable of sustaining larger numbers of people at higher levels of comfort. Gerhard Lenski's evolutionary theory of societal development, discussed in Chapter 3, represents an elaboration of this functionalist view of economy and society.

Conflict Theory Though acknowledging the critical importance of the economy in human societies, conflict theorists tend toward a far less benign interpretation of this fundamental institution. Marxists, in particular, view economic systems as the mechanism responsible for inequality and conflict in human societies, the single most important vehicle for the oppression of the many by the few. From our discussions of Marx in previous chapters, you may recall that, in his world view, the economy formed the basic substructure of all societies, the foundation on which all other social and cultural institutions were constructed. The specific "mode of production" determined how many and what kinds of resources would be created for a given population. The relative positions of different groups within the relations of production determined how these resources would be distributed within the population. Politics, law, education, and all other superstructural elements both reflected and protected the underlying productive and distributive economic substructure. Control of the economy was the most sought-after prize among different population subgroups, since that control translated into political, legal, social, and cultural power over other groups. Once controlled, economies became the means to promote group, rather than societal, interests and objectives.

Types of Economies

Throughout human social history, economic systems have assumed a wide variety of forms. To assist in individual and comparative analyses, social scientists often employ two criteria to help define and distinguish among different types of economies: the nature of property ownership and the extent of government market control. The phrase *property ownership* refers broadly to ownership of resources (such as land, animals, factories, and machinery) used to produce economic goods or services. The phrase *market control* refers broadly to government regulation of the exchange system through which economic goods and services are transferred from producers to consumers. The interplay of these two factors can be used to construct logically distinct ideal types of economies for analytic purposes. (Recall our discussion of ideal types in Chapter 5.)

Capitalism Marx's critique of economy was directed specifically at one particular type of economic organization—capitalism. **Pure capitalist** economies are distinguished by private ownership of the means of production and markets controlled by "the pure play of economic forces." In a pure capitalist system, economic actors (individuals or groups or organizations) use resources to produce goods or services for the purpose of private profit. What they produce, how much they produce, and how they dispose of what they produce are all determined by the goal of personal wealth. The economic market through which various goods and services are moved is shaped by a combination of the supply of particular goods and services offered to consumers and the demand by consumers for particular goods and services. The market is free from government regulation or interference, as well as from the undue influence of any specific economic actor. Production and price levels are shaped by the aggregated buying and selling activities of all the actors involved in the market. Nineteenth-century Great Britain and the United States are historical examples of societies that came close to capturing the essence of pure capitalism (Plotkin, 1991).

In the contemporary world, no individual society possesses all the features—and only the features—of a pure capitalist system. Although the United States is often cited as (or accused of being) the epitome of capitalism, its economy could more accurately be termed *welfare capitalism*. **Welfare capitalist** systems are characterized by private property ownership and a market that is partially regulated by government on behalf of specific public interests—minimum wage, social security, or welfare laws that promote social stability, for example. Most modern capitalist societies in fact represent some variation of welfare capitalism.

Socialism Socialist economies may be thought of as the polar opposite of capitalist systems. In **pure socialist** economies, all productive property resources are owned by the population at large, rather than by private actors, and are used for public, not private, interests. Profits or other benefits derived from that property go to the collectivity, not the individual. To ensure that the public or societal good is maximized, government plans and regulates the operation of the economic market system. Pure socialism is the type of economic system advocated by Marx, a structure in which each person would contribute to productivity according to individual ability

and benefit from the system according to individual need. The People's Republic of China and the late Soviet Union represent the two best-known illustrations of pure socialist economies in recent history.

Pure socialism, as the Soviet Union learned the hard way and the People's Republic of China is also discovering, is difficult to maintain in practice in the modern world. Many former and would-be socialist systems have tempered socialist principles with capitalist elements, resulting in what is termed *democratic socialism*. In **democratic socialist** economies, private ownership of productive property is largely regulated by government direction of markets in the interest of the collective or public good. All essential services are directed by government action and supported by taxation. Nonessential or surplus resources are left to private market forces. Denmark, Sweden, and a number of other western European societies represent this mixed type, and even the People's Republic of China has begun to move somewhat in this direction. Former Soviet president Mikhail Gorbachev's policy of *perestroika* was an attempt at a more democratic form of socialism that came too late to stave off the collapse of the Soviet state. Most contemporary socialist systems represent some variant of democratic socialism.

Economy and Democracy In theory, the structuring of a society's economic system and that of its political system are independent of one another. In practice, however, cross-societal observations indicate a strong, though not perfect, empirical association between "economic liberalization" (decreasing government involvement in economic activities) and "political democratization" (increasing public control over political structures and activities). Samuel P. Huntington (1992–1993) argues that these two events do not cause one another and stem from different (though related) sources. Yet each involves a limitation of government authority and the power of the state over society and may be thought of as interrelated elements of a larger, apparently global, trend. As either economic liberalization or political democratization grows, it creates pressures that favor the growth of the other.

What does seem to be very clear is that economic success, as measured in terms of **gross national product (GNP),** the market value of all final goods and services produced by the economy during a given year, is a necessary condition for the maintenance of political democracy. Some societies can prosper economically without democracy, but political democracies normally cannot survive without economic prosperity. According to Huntington (1992–1993), most of the countries that moved to democracy during the 1970s and 1980s were at the upper-middle levels of economic development. Of the forty-two countries classified by the World Bank as "poor" in 1989, only two were democracies; of the twenty-four classified as "high-income," only three were not democracies (R. Wright, 1992a). The poorest of the newly formed eastern European democracies that were brought into being in the early 1990s by the collapse of the Soviet Union may be especially vulnerable to political upheaval unless they can make significant progress in raising their citizens' living standards.

The U.S. Economic System

The economic structure whose misfortunes swept Bill Clinton into the White House in 1992 and whose good fortunes helped reelect him in 1996 and helped him survive impeachment in 1999, is a conglomeration of tens of millions of individual actors and an even larger number of individual exchanges of goods and services. In this section, we briefly examine some of the major characteristics of the system in which all members of this society participate, in some fashion, each day.

Corporate Capitalism One striking feature of the U.S. economy is the domination of economic activity by a relatively small number of large, powerful corporations. A **corporation** is an organization with large numbers of owners (in the form of stockholders) and unified management (in the form of a board of directors and senior corporate officers) that has the legal right to buy, sell, produce, consume, or otherwise engage in economic activities as though it was an individual person. Corporations and corporate activities represent an enormous concentration of power and influence in their respective markets (Dye, 1995), a trend that accelerated during a rash of mergers and takeovers during the 1980s. Alone or in combination, these economic behemoths have come to dominate market activities, rendering the concept of a free market governed by the pure play of economic forces a myth. Government agencies at all levels routinely intervene in economic markets, presumably to regulate corporations and promote public interests, but also to provide the stable setting necessary for corporate long-term planning (Domhoff, 1998; Galbraith, 1978). Government deregulation of many industries during the 1980s was intended to "get government off people's backs" and allow the free-market system to do what it did best—make money. However, in many cases, deregulation resulted in unsettled market conditions that drove many smaller corporations out of business (as in the airline industry), allowed for the takeover and dismantling of oth-

ers (in steel, food, and other manufacturing sectors), and resulted in business failures that left the public saddled with huge bailout costs (as in the savings and loan industry) (Gwynne, 1992).

Segmentation The term *segmented labor market* describes a system in which a society's economy is divided into "core" and "periphery" occupational segments or tiers. This distinction reflects the differences between economic activities deemed more important to the overall economy and carried out by large corporations, and those deemed less important to the overall economy and carried out by smaller corporations and companies. Core occupations (managerial, professional, white-collar, skilled blue-collar) demand higher levels of education and training but return higher levels of income, power, and prestige rewards. Peripheral occupations (unskilled blue-collar and service jobs) do not require much education and training but return lower levels of income, power, and prestige rewards. In the late 1980s and early 1990s, the U.S. economy was marked by an increasing loss of some core occupations, especially in the skilled blue-collar area, and a corresponding growth of some peripheral occupations. This shift was partially brought about by the loss of many manufacturing jobs overseas or to Mexico, the increasing automation of many other manufacturing jobs that remained in the United States, and the loss of jobs from the takeover and subsequent breaking up of many once-healthy companies. The result was increasing unemployment and underemployment for many people in the labor force, particularly minorities and women (Hearn, 1988). And, though the economy as a whole has picked up dramatically in the late 1990s, the economic fortunes of many of these displaced workers continue to lag behind those of the population-at-large.

Postindustrialization *Postindustrialization* describes the progressive movement of an advanced industrial economy dominated by machine-intensive, production-oriented "secondary" occupations (skilled manufacturing jobs) to an economy dominated by information-intensive, service-oriented "tertiary" occupations (managerial, professional, technical support, and service jobs). A highly educated workforce, highly automated and computerized production procedures, increased government planning and direction of the economy, and higher levels of affluence for members of the workforce all typify the postindustrial society (Bell, 1973, 1976). Presumably this is the direction in which the U.S. economy is moving.

The increasing levels and importance of formal education, computer literacy, and people-oriented skills in the contemporary U.S. labor force are very apparent. Similarly, no one could deny the decline in traditional manufacturing and other blue-collar occupations and the rise of technical support and service jobs. What is debatable, however, is the extent to which these changes or the increased involvement of government in economic planning and operations have translated into higher levels of economic and social well-being for the U.S. workforce. We have already noted the fact that many jobs in the booming technical and service sector are not of the high-salary, high-prestige variety. On the contrary, they more often resemble lower-tier peripheral occupations in this regard. In addition, a more active involvement by government in economic markets generally has not had the anticipated effect of increasing productivity and efficiency. On the contrary, the increasing inefficiency, lack of productivity, and mounting budget deficit that have accompanied government efforts at economic regulation have been a major factor in the growth of the "neoliberal" policies espoused by President Clinton and others inside and outside of government circles. This new liberal economic philosophy calls for decreased government activity in the economy and a return to a private enterprise-based system guided by public as well as private concerns but not hindered by public regulation (Huntington, 1992–1993). The postindustrial society may be a state whose time has yet to fully arrive.

Internationalization   Although perhaps slow to recognize and respond to the reality of the times, the U.S. economy nonetheless is fast becoming more international in character as it has become increasingly forced to participate in a global economic market. Intense competition from Japanese, German, Chinese, and other foreign producers as well as loss of jobs to developing countries with lower labor and other production costs has forced a closer look at increasing U.S. participation in international economic communities. Since 1994, the United States has been linked with Canada and Mexico in NAFTA, the North American Free Trade Agreement, a hemispheric economic community. NAFTA's trade, tariff, and quota easements are designed to promote the common economic interests of all three member societies and combat the economic clout of Japan, the European Union, and other major players in the global economy.

"Haves" and "Have Nots" in the International Marketplace

In the first decade of the new millennium, we will see the continuation of three significant trends regarding the international distribution of wealth as well as the structure and working of the global economy.

1. *The widening income gap*   In a world of over six billion people, the richest 1 billion individuals (or approximately 17.5 percent of the population) hold 83 percent of the global wealth, while the poorest 1 billion hold only 1.4 percent of the planet's riches. The wealth gap between the "haves" and the "have nots" has more than doubled since 1960, producing an international upper class and a lower class, with the latter living in abject poverty. The extremes in this international distribution can be seen in the 1997 per capita GNPs of Liechtenstein ($50,000) and Ethiopia ($110), a ratio of over 450 to 1 between the two countries (World Bank, 1999a). (How this tremendous economic disparity came into existence in the first place is discussed in Chapter 13.) At the same time that the populations of approximately fifty developing countries must try to survive on an annual income of $1000 or less, designer handbags costing considerably more than that amount of money are routinely sold in fashionable boutiques in cities such as New York, Paris, Berlin, and Tokyo.

   This monetary gap between the world's rich and poor is also pronounced within developing countries. In Brazil, for example, the poorest 50 percent of the population received just 11.6 percent of national income in 1995, while the richest 10 percent received 63 percent (United Nations Development Program, 1998, p. 29).

2. *Unemployment, underemployment, and poverty*   In a world where one out of every three workers is unemployed or underemployed, (not earning enough money for subsistence levels of food, clothing, and shelter), over 1 billion people are forced to exist on the equivalent of approximately $1 a day. Official unemployment rates in Africa range from 15 to 20 percent, with underemployment accounting for another 50 percent of the labor force. In some North African cities, the unemployment rate for teenagers and young adults runs as high as 70 percent. In Mexico and most Central American nations, unemployment rates are as high as 50 percent. And, because of high rates of population growth, the labor force in these countries is expected to triple in the next 50 to 60 years.

   People lacking enough money to support themselves and their families can easily become frustrated, and eventually resentful of the existing power structure. These attitudes can lead to criminal behavior (crimes of survival such as burglary

These women are assembling oil filters in a factory that is part of a joint Thai-China business venture. In developing countries, poor people (especially impoverished women) typically work for low wages because of high rates of population growth, unemployment, and underemployment. In Indonesia young women earn less than twenty cents an hour making running shoes that will sell in the United States for up to $150.

and robbery), large-scale protest and food riots, and revolutionary activity.

3. *Economic growth in the developing world* While some poor nations will see their economic situation improve in the coming years, the short-term (at least) forecast for the developing nations as a whole in not very optimistic. George Soros (1998) notes that in a global capitalist system that is "coming apart at the seams," approximately one-third of the world is in a depression. President Clinton (in Longman, Egan, and Garrett, 1998, p. 50) stated that widespread economic problems on four continents constitute "the biggest financial challenge facing the world in 50 years." Although there are numerous, often complex factors responsible for problems in the global economy, the following components appear to be especially relevant. Perhaps the most significant factor is a worldwide oversupply of basic industrial goods ranging from steel and cement to automobiles and computer memory chips. Overproduction and reduced demand result in lower profits and stock prices as well as less capital for investment (Samuelson, 1998). As one analyst noted regarding Asia, "Everyone was chasing too small a market without regard to what competitors were doing" (in Samuelson, 1998, p. B12). The production of light trucks declined by 63 percent in Thailand and 25 percent in South Korea between 1996 and 1998 as thousands of workers were laid off or had their salaries reduced.

An economic philosophy sometimes called the "Washington Consensus" called for the integration of developing countries into the world economy by way of encouraging the free flow of foreign investment, dropping trade barriers, reducing budget deficits, and promoting local investment over consumption. However, not only has this prescription for success failed, but in many instances the economic conditions of countries following this plan worsened (Longman, Egan, and Garrett, 1998).

Finally, there is increasing volatility in world markets because of the flow of enormous amounts of money that is "almost completely unregulated." The global transfer of capital every 48 hours in the form of currency exchanges, international bank loans and settlements, and direct investment is greater than the annual gross domestic product of the United States. While the movement of so much money can stimulate growth and "improve methods of production and other innovations" (Longman, Egan, and Garrett, 1998), it can also result in volatile swings in the global marketplace regarding currency values, the price of stocks, and investor confidence. The flow of capital does not necessarily go where it will benefit the largest number of people; rather, as George Soros (1998) noted, money moves to "where it is best rewarded" (p. 78).

In this section of the chapter, we present an overview of the world economy on a regional basis and consider recent changes and trends in economic development in these areas. Knowledge of the trends and summary statistics just presented will help us better understand the dynamics of the international marketplace.

East Asia: Land of Dragons, Big and Small The twenty-first century has been referred to as the "Asian century," meaning that this continent will become a major player in world affairs (especially economic), if not the preeminent region on the planet. The modernization of many Asian nations can be traced to the end of World War II when Japan lay in ruins, partially as a result of the destruction of Tokyo, Hiroshima, and Nagasaki (the latter two cities being leveled by atomic bombs). The country was in shambles and its economy was virtually nonexistent. In the late 1940s and early 1950s, the Japanese produced a variety of inexpensive items (plastic toys, cheap tools, kitchen utensils, etc.) of such poor quality that the phrase "Made in Japan" was synonymous with junk. However, the country's businessmen quickly realized that if they were to be successful in the global marketplace, they would have to improve the reliability and durability of their products dramatically. And improve they did. Optical equipment and cameras soon rivaled those made in Switzerland and Germany, and the "Japanese miracle" was under way. Automobiles and electronic equipment rolled off assembly lines and were shipped around the world as the government began to nurture designated industries with tax breaks and subsidies. Exports were priced low enough to make them as affordable as possible, while trade barriers were implemented to protect local manufacturers from foreign competition ("The Asian Flu," 1998). By 1990, Japan's economy was the second largest in the world and its GNP was two-thirds that of the United States (with approximately half the population of this country).

Japan was not the only East Asian country to flourish economically in the post–World War II era. In 1960, the combined gross domestic product of East Asia (including China and Japan) accounted for 4 percent of the world economy, and by the year 2010, that number is expected to be 33 percent (Wallace, 1994a). Without a doubt, South Korea, Taiwan, Singapore, and Hong Kong (the latter now a part of China) have been the most successful developing nations in this region over the past 40 years and have made a significant contribution to the economic boom currently underway in East Asia. Often referred to as the "little dragons" (Japan is the big one), the economies of these countries grew at an annual rate of 7.4 percent in the 1980s compared to those of African and Latin American nations, which grew by only 1.8 and 1.2 percent respectively during this same period. From 1960 to 1996, South Korea's per capita GNP increased from $675 to $10,610. Hong Kong's per capita GNP (1996) of $24,290 was only slightly lower than comparable figures for France, Belgium, and the Netherlands.

With few natural resources, little arable land, and some of the highest population densities in the world, how did the four dragons accomplish so much in so little time? Paul Kennedy (1993, pp. 34–45) argues that these countries share "certain basic characteristics that *taken together*, help to explain their decade-upon-decade growth." The first characteristic they have in common is an emphasis on education grounded in a Confucian tradition of respect for learning and competitive examinations. For example, not only do a significant number of young South Koreans attend college, but many (a higher percentage than in most nations) pursue degrees in the physical sciences and engineering, fields of study that lend themselves to modernization in an increasingly technical world.

A second common feature of these countries is a high level of national savings (much higher than the U.S.). As a result of encouraging personal savings, restricting the movement of capital out of the country,

and setting limits on foreign luxury goods coming into Korea during the first few decades of development, a large amount of low-interest investment capital was available to members of the business community. This readily available capital served as the fuel for the development of new industries and the expansion of existing ones. A third characteristic has been a strong political system providing a stable atmosphere within which fledgling economies could develop and thrive. (However, political stability in South Korea and Taiwan has come at the price of personal freedoms for many people. Rather than viewing these countries in the 1970s and 1980s as emerging economic powers, some have labeled them as nothing more than economically advancing "prison camps." Although the latter characterization may be too harsh, there have been many instances of torture and abuse over the past 40 years.)

A fourth common feature was a strong commitment to exports, a stark contrast to the economic policies of countries such as India that emphasized production primarily for domestic markets and strictly limited the amount of imported goods. In all of these countries, the value of the currency was kept low to facilitate exports. These nations also profited from the relatively low cost (when compared to the U.S., much of Europe, and Japan) of domestic labor. Finally, Kennedy argues, the four dragons benefited from a local, very successful role model: Japan. This nation's economic growth was proof that an Asian nation could compete (and win) in the international marketplace heretofore dominated by the United States and Europe. Like the little dragons, Japan is also a resource-poor, densely populated country. To date, the developing nations of Africa and Latin America have lacked a regional role model that has anything near the success of Japan.

Rapidly developing East Asian economies hit a roadblock in the 1990s, first in Japan and then in the rest of the region. The big dragon's GDP declined from 5 percent in 1990 to 0 percent in 1993 and, with the exception of 1996, has been around the 1 percent mark ever since. In the late 1980s, the economy was growing largely as a result of speculation; that is, money kept pouring in because investors remained confident they could continue to make a profit. However, when some people started to sell their real estate holdings and stocks because they believed these commodities were overvalued, thousands of other individuals followed suit. The Tokyo Stock Market lost 50 percent of its value in a relatively short period of time and the real estate market plummeted as well ("The Asian Flu," 1998). This crisis was compounded by banks that made hundreds of billions of dollars in bad loans as these institutions accepted

Focus on
South Korea

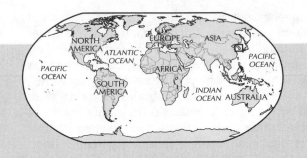

Population: 47,369,000
Life Expectancy at Birth (years): Male—70.4;
   Female—78.0
Form of Government: Republic
Major Religions: Christianity 49%; Buddhism 47%
Major Racial and Ethnic Groups: Korean
Population Doubling Time: 70 years
Per Capita GNP (1997 U.S. dollars): $10,550
Principle Economic Activities: Industry, mining, and agriculture
Colonial Experience: Colony of Japan from 1910 to 1945
Adult Literacy Rate: 98% Male—99%; Female—97%

A Wounded Dragon Meets the IMF

Much has been written about the "Japanese Miracle," that is, the transformation of Japan's ravaged (almost nonexistent) economy at the end of World War II (1945) to the "Japan Inc." of today, the world's second-wealthiest nation. However, the phenomenal growth of the South Korean economy over the past 40–45 years is no less a financial miracle. In 1960, South Korea's per capita gross national product (GNP) was $230, approximately the same as that of poor sub-Saharan countries. By 1996 per capita GNP in this far East Asian country was $9,700, while the comparable figure for sub-Saharan Africa was $510. South Korea's GNP increased from less than one billion dollars in 1945 to $455 billion in 1995 as the nation became the world's eleventh-largest industrial power. Social gains were also significant as life expectancy at birth increased from 47 years in 1955 to 73 years in 1998, the same as that of the United States.

Some of the reasons for this remarkable economic transformation can be attributed to a number of characteristics that South Korea shares with the other regional "dragons" (See "East Asia: Land of the Dragons, Big and Small," p. 250). In addition to these common traits, the South Korean success/economic collapse story is a product of a unique set of features and circumstances.

Chief among these reasons has been the federal government's role in planning, directing, and (indirectly) funding the industrial base toward the end of increasing the country's economic production and wealth in the shortest period of time (Hart-Landsberg, 1993). More specifically, the government decided which industries would receive bank loans (and the amount of these loans) thereby determining the course of economic development. Between 1961 and 1981, the federal government had almost total control over the country's financial network including all five commercial banks, all six special banks, and two of the three financial development services. South Korean businesses were not free to secure funds from overseas investors as all incoming capital (loans) had to be approved by the government. In addition, the outflow of capital was tightly controlled, with individuals who engaged in illegal transfers of $1 million or more subject to punishments ranging from 10 years in prison to death (Hart-Landsberg, 1993).

At the core of South Korea's economy are *chaebol*—large family-owned and -controlled conglomerates (Philo Kim, 1992). The four largest *chaebol*—Samsung, Hyundai, Lucky-Gold-Star, and Daewoo—collectively account for almost half of the nation's total GNP, with the top 50 of these organizations dominating the South Korean economy. Imagine General Motors owning 100 or more companies that made not only automobile-related equipment (tires and auto parts, for example) but products and services as diverse as food, insurance, oil, explosives, advertising, and clothing. This is exactly the situation with South Korean *chaebol* (Wittenborn, 1998), the top five of which own on average 140 different businesses each ("The End of the Miracle," 1997). While the subsidiary companies have their own presidents and managerial staffs, they are all under the direct control of the *chaebol's* owner and chairman. Although managers make decisions (often important ones) on a routine basis, the final say so always rests with the owning family. This system of control flows downward to highly skilled and low-level employees all of whom "are trained to follow strong leadership, not develop their own" (Kim Yong Son, in Baker, 1998, p. 9).

Because of this rigid structure of control and accountability, the government viewed *chaebol* as vehicles for "promoting the country's rapid expansion into new capital-intensive areas of production" that it (the government) considered crucial to the nation's development. The government directed banks to loan money to these organizations without screening companies to see if they were credit worthy or if their plans for expansion were sound (that is, competitive in the inter-

Protestors and riot police clash during a demonstration in Seoul, South Korea in 1999. About 20,000 workers and students gathered at a downtown plaza to demand more labor rights and a shorter work week. The rally came on the fifth day of joint protests by South Korea's two main umbrella labor groups against what they called government indifference to their demands. Many workers in South Korea believe that they are being forced to bear a disproportionate burden of the nation's recent economic trouble, financial problems that they did not create.

national marketplace). One consequence of pumping huge amounts of capital into these conglomerates is that *chaebol* typically have a debt-to-equity (the value of property beyond the total amount owed on it) ratio of three, four, or even five to one as opposed to the roughly one to one ratio in the rest of the industrialized world ("The End of the Miracle," 1997). When *chaebol* could not sell sufficient numbers of their products (domestically and in foreign markets), loan payments could not be made. The nation's major banks had billions of dollars of outstanding loans that were increasingly overdue, and because of the high debt-to-equity ratio, the physical assets of the *chaebol* (factories, machinery, material, etc) were worth little even if they could be sold by banks to repay the money owed them. By the spring of 1998, *chaebol* owed the nation's banks some $300 billion. The recent economic crisis in South Korea is also a striking example of the interconnectedness of the world economy inasmuch as approximately $100 billion of investment capital from Japanese, European, and Americans banks was funneled into this Asian nation (Chanda, 1998)—money that may never be paid back in full.

The system of government-directed loans to favored *chaebol* and industries resulted in a significant amount of corruption and personal enrichment of top government officials (Hart-Landsberg, 1993). "Corporate giving" was widely understood to be nothing more than a payoff to maintain good working relations with bureaucrats who determined what industries would receive bank loans (and the refinancing of these loans when necessary). One South Korean banker noted that "Anytime the government chooses to close a company or break it up, it can do so. All it has to do is call the so-called Korean commercial banks, which it controls, and tell them not to refinance a company's debt" (in Hart-Landsberg, 1993, p. 70). This is exactly what happened to a *chaebol* leader whose contribution was only $400,000 as opposed to the standard $1 million that other such organizations were making. Angered by this paltry contribution, then–South Korean President Chun ordered the banks to stop honoring the checks (to creditors) written by the *chaebol*. Within weeks, the offending conglomerate was forced to declare bankruptcy and its assets were sold off (under government direction) to

politically loyal *chaebol*. Martin Hart-Landsberg (1993) noted that during this entire procedure none of the factories in question were closed, nor did any workers lose their jobs.

"Crony capitalism" as the close relationship between the government, banks, and *chaebol* has been called, was a major contributing factor in South Korea's fall of 1997 economic crash. Government officials directed banks to finance conglomerates that had little knowledge or experience in the industries they were pursuing, and/or to fund ventures that were already oversaturated by the giant corporations of other industrialized nations. The South Korean automobile industry is a perfect example of the latter. In 1985 there were barely one million cars in all of South Korea, whereas that nation's capacity to produce motor vehicles is between 5 and 6 million in the year 2000. Domestic consumption cannot possibly absorb that many cars, and overseas markets are saturated with Japanese, American, and European vehicles. As the planning director of Daewoo Motor Company stated, "We have set a goal of being among the top ten global auto manufacturers by the year 2000. The problem is, that's the same goal of each of the Big Three Korean (auto) manufacturers" (Lee, in Einstein, 1996, p. 8).

Overborrowing, reckless expansion, and unrealistic production/sales goals knocked South Korea off the economic fast track and set the stage for an economic collapse that shook the nation, from high-ranking government officials on down. Within three months of the 1997 crash most of the country's banks were "insolvent," meaning that liabilities exceeded assets (Sender, 1998), and over 3,300 companies declared bankruptcy (Efron, 1998). Eight of the 50 largest *chaebol* were either bankrupt or facing severe economic problems. According to one estimate, unemployment jumped dramatically (from 3.1 to 11 percent), and the value of the South Korean won dropped 50 percent against the U.S. dollar. With local credit tapped out, *chaebol* found themselves in a precarious situation wherein they had no money to pay workers, or purchase raw materials from foreign suppliers that would only deal with them on a cash basis. Estimates of how much money it would take to recapitalize the nation's failed banking system, and jump-start the South Korean economy ranged from $60 to $100 billion.

To keep the South Korean economy from completely collapsing (and triggering financial problems around the world, especially in neighboring Japan), the International Monetary Fund (IMF) agreed to loan that nation's banks $57 billion. As was the case in previous bailouts (in other countries), IMF money flows in incrementally (a few billion dollars at a time) and only if the government agrees to reduce spending on social programs such as financial aid to schools and health care institutions, and to significantly increase bank interest rates to stop the cycle of reckless borrowing and default (Butler and Egan, 1997).

Breaking the cozy link between banks and the government "that will make business as usual for *chaebol* impossible" (Lee, 1998, p. 62) is not the only thing that has to be changed if a future economic disaster is to be averted. The prevailing strategy that whatever is produced can be exported, and that an export-oriented economy is the key to wealth will have to be changed, and changed immediately. Not only have the currencies of Asian nations with their own economic problems decreased in value, making it much more expensive to buy South Korean products, but all of these countries are attempting to "export their way out of economic trouble while slashing imports" (Lee, 1998, p. 60). Almost 50 percent of South Korean exports go to neighboring countries.

Another key factor in South Korea's recovery is the nation's powerful—and often militant—labor unions. After lengthy negotiations by representatives of the unions, the government, and corporations, union leaders agreed to layoffs (as opposed to guaranteed lifetime employment) as a mechanism to help the badly damaged and downsized economy. In return for this major concession, the government agreed to pay the cost of retraining dismissed workers as well as provide as provide them with financial assistance until they find jobs. In addition, labor unions will be allowed to form their own political parties and teachers will be permitted to unionize.

A dissenting voice in the widescale cry for fundamental changes in South Korea is economist Jeffery Sachs, director of Harvard's Institute for International Development. According to Sachs, "What we have experienced is massive inflows (of capital) based on high optimism about the region followed by massive outflows that one can only characterize as a panic" (in Chanda, 1998, p. 48). While Sachs does not completely dismiss the "crony capitalism" argument, he believes it has been overplayed and "cannot begin to account for the collapse."

If Sachs is correct, South Korea's economic turmoil is primarily a function of external investor confidence rather than some combination of internal problems. However, alleviating these latter shortcomings can only strengthen the nation's economy in the long run, and, therefore, bolster the confidence of foreign investors.

the inflated value of real estate as collateral. In late 1998, Japan's major cities announced that they were bankrupt, or very close to it. Tokyo, for example, had a debt of almost $60 billion. One way to cut expenses (and pay off the debt) is to halt public works projects, a strategy that would hurt the nation's construction companies, many of which owe banks substantial amounts of money (Bremmer and Tanikawa, 1998).

Some observers are of the opinion that Japan could be on the verge of a "great depression" (Dornbusch, 1998). This would not only be a disaster for Japan but would quickly turn into a financial calamity for the entire region, as Japan is considered the engine that pulls the economic train for much of Asia. To avert this situation, the government will have to bail out the nation's banks to the tune of $600 billion, and convince the public to spend, invest, and deposit (in banks) some portion of the $3 *trillion* that people keep tucked away at home.

As a result of corruption in government, poor leadership at the national level, "crony capitalism," and greed, the economic fortunes of the four dragons also suffered in the late 1990s (see *Focus on South Korea*"). As is the case in Japan, unregulated banks in these countries lost enormous amounts of money because of incredibly bad loans ("lending decisions governed by noncommercial criteria") that will never be repaid (Sender, 1998). When these institutions failed, it was only a matter of time before the rest of the economy was spiraling downward. One analyst noted that "Many banks in Asia are just large-scale pawnshop operations" (Sender, 1998, p. 29).

The Asian "economic flu" spread to Thailand, Malaysia, the Philippines, and Indonesia in the summer of 1998 with conditions becoming particularly severe in the latter nation. Whereas approximately 23 million people in a nation of 200 million were poor in 1996, almost 80 million individuals lived below the poverty line in 1998. A World Bank report stated that "No country in recent history, let alone one the size of Indonesia, has ever suffered such a dramatic reversal of fortune" (in Barr, 1998, p. 6). Three decades of economic growth collapsed quickly as the Jakarta Stock Market plummeted from a total worth of $100 billion to $15 billion in a matter of weeks (Barr, 1998). Once again, corruption and mismanagement were at the heart of this economic collapse that turned violent as widespread protest and rioting claimed the lives of 1,200 people (mostly ethnic Chinese) in a two-day period.

China and India: Struggling Giants On June 3 and 4, 1989, the world watched heavily armed troops of the People's Liberation Army march into Beijing's Tiananmen Square and open fire on the protesters who had occupied the square intermittently since the end of April. Estimates on the number of individuals killed in the assault ranged from 300 (a figure released by the Chinese government) to as many as 5,000 (based on firsthand accounts of observers). Although the government's brutal response has been explained primarily in terms of its refusal to acquiesce to student demands for democracy and freedom, existing economic conditions must also be considered. Still an integral part of the current economic scene in China, these conditions were not radically altered by the events of June 1989.

In its drive to transform Chinese society, the government targeted four areas (the "Four Modernizations") thought to be especially important to development: industry, defense, agriculture, and science. According to official statistics from the government

of China, the economy expanded rapidly during the 1980s, growing at an average annual rate of 9 percent ("China's Economy," 1992). The average net income of a farmer increased by 8.4 percent a year, while the average real income of urban dwellers rose by 4.5 percent per year. The income disparity between rural and urban workers resulted in frustration and resentment on the part of many residents of metropolitan areas.

Under the "responsibility system" instituted by Deng Xiaoping, rural communes and collective farms were effectively dismantled and replaced with a program whereby peasants used government land to produce whatever they desired as long as their contractual obligation to the state was fulfilled. Surplus fruits, vegetables, and other products could now be sold on the open market. As a consequence of this economic reform, millions of peasants were able to generate the extra funds needed to purchase "luxury" goods such as watches and cassette players, as well as "big-ticket" items like color television sets, stereos, refrigerators, and washing machines (Liu, 1999). Meanwhile, urban economic reforms were moving at a much slower pace. Under this new program, the policy of lifetime employment (the "iron rice bowl") was abolished, and state subsidies of essentials such as rice, cooking oil, and sugar were reduced (Liu, 1999). As a consequence of diminished subsidies, the price of some food items "officially" increased as much as 36.8 percent (unofficial estimates are higher), and inflation increased by almost 20 percent. Finding it increasingly difficult to purchase basic foodstuffs, million of urban workers were forced to take part-time jobs. The long period of "relative equality of income" that had been achieved as a result of both deliberate government policy and Maoist ideology had come to an end (Howe, 1992).

Since the early 1980s, the Chinese economy has averaged 9.8 percent annual growth and attracted billions of dollars in foreign investment at the rate of $100 million per day (Groombridge, 1998; Tong, 1998). Over the past 20 years, China's leaders utilized the same "pick winners" strategy that other Asian nations have employed. That is, rather than use a free market, supply-and-demand approach, the government selects companies in industries it believes will be successful (to date automobiles, steel, and chemicals, among others) and gives them preferential treatment in the form of tax breaks, protective tariffs, loans, and even cash payments. The problem with this "cozy relationship between governments, banks, and industry" (Groombridge, 1998, p.35) is that in many instances bureaucrats guess wrong (that is, they pick losers) and enormous amounts of money are wasted. As of 1998, approximately 40 percent of the state-run Commercial Bank of China's loans were unrecoverable, nonperforming, or more than two years past due.

In 1998, growth slowed to 7 percent (official figure) although some observers believe the true number is closer to 3 percent (Ramo, Beech, and Gibney, 1998) as China also caught the Asian economic flu. Fortunately, the world's most populous country did not become as financially ill as many of its neighbors. Another problem in the world's seventh-largest economy is that the "new socialism with Chinese characters" is falling victim to a malady most often associated with capitalism: a (rapidly) growing disparity in the distribution of income and wealth. In pre-reform days (prior to 1980), managers of state-run companies received salaries no more than three or four times that of the average worker. Now, the managerial class earns up to 300 times as much, and this does not include money received via corruption which is rampant in Chinese society (Pehrson, 1998). This economic inequality has some people longing for the days of the "iron rice bowl." Referring to the era of Chairman Mao, one woman whose husband and son lost their jobs in a state-owned firm noted, "Our lives were better then. We may not have had much, but we all suffered together. We at least had jobs and hope—now we have neither. We watch a few others get rich while we grow poorer."

How widespread the feelings of discontent expressed by this woman are, and, more important, what impact (if any) they might have on long-term political stability in China is, as yet, unknown. Another problem Chinese leaders will certainly encounter is rooted in the divergent paths that the government and the economy are travelling. While the ruling Communist Party is one of central planning and authoritarian control, the economy is increasingly decentralized and entrepreneurial, gaining its vitality from millions of people making their own financial decisions. How long will it be before individuals now used to having a say in their financial lives want more input in politics (from local to national issues) via a democratic, multiparty system? In *Political Order in Changing Societies,* written over 30 years ago, the esteemed political scientist Samuel Huntington argued that modernization was not necessarily compatible with political stability because industrialization, urbanization, and universal education created new forces (such as an urban middle class) that would challenge existing institutions (Lane, 1998).

According to a recent World Bank report, if all goes well in China over the next 20 years, the economy of this Asian nation will account for 10 percent of the world's exports (up from 3 percent in 1998), and trail only North America and the European Union in economic power. The problem of political stability—or more accurately, the collision between freewheeling capitalism and an authoritarian state—will come to a head sometime during this next period of economic growth.

As for India, when approaching any and almost every aspect of this society, the concept to keep uppermost in mind is diversity. If the 42 independent nations of Europe were to become one political state, this new political entity would not be as racially, ethnically, linguistically, religiously, or economically diverse as modern India. Indian states such as Maharashtra and Punjab have income levels much higher than the national average, while economic development in the extremely poor states (sometimes referred to by Indians as "backward states") of Bihar and Madhya Pradesh is almost nonexistent. Wealthy landowners using modern farm equipment, chemical fertilizers, and irrigation practice high-productivity commercial agriculture, while tens of millions of desperately poor farmers scratch out a living on small plots of land much as they have for hundreds of years. Similarly, modern factories in the world's tenth-largest industrial nation coexist with simple "backyard" technologies (Chaudhuri, 1992). Partially as a result of these economic disparities, as many as 400 million Indians (significantly more than in any other nation) live in poverty.

Upon independence in 1947, India's first prime minister, Jawaharlal Nehru (1889–1964), wanted his new nation to be part of the coming era of scientific socialism. For Nehru, capitalism was an outdated, immoral, and exploitative system that would only make India's already poor economic condition worse. As a result of opposition to his vision of the future, the new prime minister had to accept the Industrial Revolution of 1948, a compromise calling for a "mixed" economy—an economic system that is part socialist and part capitalist (Hardgrave and Kochanek, 1986). Although the government's declaration about "taking India into the twenty-first century" is a move toward the capitalist end of the economic spectrum, it does not represent a major shift in that direction.

Close to bankruptcy in 1991, with the federal government having no more than 20 days reserve to pay for imported food and fuel, the Indian economy rebounded and expanded at approximately 7 percent per year for most of the 1990s before growth trailed off to 5 percent in fiscal year 1997. This latter figure was the lowest since India introduced free-market economic reforms in 1991 and prompted some analysts to suggest that the nation was heading "for the slow old days of the so-called Hindu rate of growth" (Sidhvar, 1998, p. 67). In an effort to stimulate economic growth, the government increased spending for infrastructure projects (in energy, transportation, communications, education, and agriculture) 35 percent in 1998 (Sidhvar, 1998; Karp and Sharma, 1998).

Issues of foreign investment and the presence of multinational corporations have been controversial among Indians as of late (see the discussion of "World System Theory" in Chapter 13). While some individuals welcome both, others see international companies and overseas capital as a way of controlling ever-increasing components of the economy ("economic aggression") and maximizing profits at the expense of an already poor nation (Venkataraman, 1998). This latter sentiment was expressed by Finance Minister Yashwant Singa of the Hindu-Nationalist Bharatiya Janata Party (commonly referred to as the BJP) when he stated that "Foreign consumer-goods companies are coming to exploit the Indian market and consumer" (in Karp, 1998, p. A14).

As is the case in other developing nations, economic and population issues are interrelated. With over 1 billion inhabitants and an annual growth rate just under 2 percent, India adds approximately 20 million people to the earth each year, a number equal to the combined populations of Sweden, Finland, and Denmark. Consequently, any economic gains are nullified in large measure by the steady population growth (Venkataraman, 1998), which makes it all but impossible for hundreds of millions of people to lift themselves out of poverty. There can be little doubt that India will remain a poor country (per capita GNP $370 in 1997) as long as this rate of population increase continues.

Latin America: Riding the Economic Roller Coaster

In the three decades following World War II, Latin American countries participated in a global economic upswing and appeared to be well on the road to modernization. A recipient of considerable foreign investment, this region benefited from increased demand for coffee, timber, beef, and oil (Kennedy, 1993). Between 1960 and 1979, overall economic growth in Central and South America was even greater than economic expansion in the United States. However, this era of sustained growth and general progress came to a crashing halt in the 1980s (average annual growth rate for the region was only 1.2 percent), a period of Latin American history that has been called the "lost decade." The region's gross domestic product (GDP) declined by 8 percent, and real income in Peru and Argentina dropped by as much as 25 percent. By 1992, 44 percent of Latin Americans—some 183 million people—lived below the poverty line, 50 million more than in 1980. This rapid economic decline occurred at a time when other areas of the world (most notably East Asia and the dragons) were prospering.

Paul Kennedy (1993) has outlined the most salient reasons for this collapse. While governments of the most successful nations were encouraging industrialists to stimulate domestic growth by cultivating foreign markets and exporting as much as possible, Latin American leaders pursued a policy of import substitution. Homegrown industries were given tax breaks, subsidies, and the benefits of protective tariffs with the goal of cornering the local market and shielding domestic products from international competitors. As a result of these policies, Latin American countries lost the ability to sell their products (and generate capital) in the international marketplace.

In an effort to stimulate their economies and facilitate modernization, governments in Central and South America began to borrow money from major banks in the United States, Europe, and Japan. Officials began spending billions of dollars on a variety of projects (many of which were poorly planned and carried out) that helped drive inflation rates by 1989 to over 3,000 percent in a number of countries. The economically struggling nations of this region paid $296 billion just in interest on the debt in the 1980s and, as of 1998, still owed world banks a staggering $600 billion. Every dollar paid on the interest of these loans means one less dollar available for local development. In an effort to repay this debt, governments have drastically reduced domestic spending on everything from food and transportation subsidies (bus and subway fares as well as gasoline) to funds for education and health. These "austerity" measures have contributed significantly to the rise of both poverty and collective violence (protesting rising costs) in a number of Latin American countries.

Beginning in 1991, the economic fortunes of much of Latin America began to improve. Exports increased as a result of the newly formed South American Common Market (Mercosur), a trade pact that linked the economies of Brazil, Argentina, Paraguay, and Uruguay (the agreement has since expanded to include Chile and Bolivia, and as of 1999 negotiations were underway to include Venezuela and Peru). Governments also sold many state-run companies, a move that substantially increased foreign investment. Regional inflation that averaged 49 percent in 1991 was reduced to 19 percent in 1993.

Between 1990 and 1998, Chile's economy expanded by almost 8 percent a year while poverty was reduced approximately 50 percent ("All Good Things Must Slow Down," 1998). Currently the fifth largest food producer in the world, Argentina's economy increased by more than 5 percent annually during the

1990s (Menen, 1998) with a similar rate of growth forecast through 2003 (Chambers, 1998). Early in the next century, Argentina will surpass some European nations in both population and economic growth. As a result of Brazil's "Real Plan" (named for the adoption of a new currency that was part of a monetary reform plan implemented in 1994), inflation in that country declined from over 5,000 percent in 1994 to 6 percent at the end of 1997. During that same period annual GDP increased approximately 3 percent a year (Rezende, 1998).

By the end of the decade, this latest period of prosperity was in jeopardy as Latin American economies were affected by problems in other parts of the world. The price of copper (a resource that made up 42 percent of Chile's exports), dropped sharply, and East Asia, a region that became a major trading partner of some South American nations, suffered a major economic setback that sharply curtailed their imports. With almost 50 percent of South America's population, Brazil's economy was so weak in the fall of 1998 (the nation was $152 billion in debt) that it required $42 billion in loans from the International Monetary Fund, the World Bank, and the United States to keep it solvent (Lehman, 1999).

A major market for U.S. products, according to one estimate, Brazil supports over 200,000 highly skilled jobs in this country through imports of American goods (La Franchi, 1998a). To repay their most recently incurred debt, Brazilians were subject to higher taxes, a variety of spending cuts, and social security reforms, measures that angered both the rich and the poor ("Resentment Mounts in Brazil," 1998). The distribution of wealth in Brazil is one of the most unequal in the world and any new taxes will be a disaster for tens of millions of already destitute people. On the other side of the economic fence, the nation's privileged groups (including military and government officials and workers) are bitterly opposed to any reduction in social security payments, which allowed them to retire at just over age 50 with incomes 20 percent *above* their highest salary prior to retirement (Rezende, 1998).

One of the strongest economies in Latin America, Mexico's GDP grew 7.2 percent in 1997 (although it slowed to approximately 4.5 percent in 1998), the highest rate in 16 years. Because it has free access to the United States and Canada by way of the North American Free Trade Agreement (NAFTA), Mexico was not hurt as much as other Latin American countries by the "Asian meltdown" of 1998 (Sissell, 1998; Smith and Malkin, 1998a). Whereas Mexico once produced cheap, poorly made goods, the country now manufactures a variety of high-quality products such as automobiles (Volkswagen Beetles, for exam-

ple) and laptop computers. Unfortunately, Mexico continues to have problems with relatively high inflation and interest rates (the latter over 40 percent) as well as high unemployment. An estimated one million jobs will have to be added annually to keep up with the number of young people in a rapidly growing nation who enter the labor market each year (Smith and Malkin, 1998a, 1998b).

In October 1998, hurricane Mitch devastated much of Nicaragua and Honduras, the two poorest nations in Central America. Over 9,000 people were killed and more than one million were made homeless as the storm did an estimated $50 billion in damage (National Public Radio, 1999). A country with an agriculturally based economy, Honduras saw its $250 million banana crop almost completely wiped out. Companies like Chiquita and United Fruit laid off thousands of workers, so people who lost their homes and possessions to massive flooding also lost their jobs. A Honduran economist stated, "Our big problem is going to be unemployment and the multiplying effect of lost production" (Bueso, in La Franchi, 1998b, p. 1). By the "multiplying effect" he means that people without jobs can no longer purchase goods and services from individuals who are employed, which will eventually threaten the jobs of the latter group and compound the nation's problem. Nicaragua and Honduras were so financially troubled *before* the storm hit that 40 and 50 percent (respectively) of the income their exports generated was used to make payments on the money they borrowed from international banks. It could take these two countries as long as 50 years to recover financially from the effects of the 1998 storm. Flash floods and mudslides in Venezuela in December 1999, claimed the lives of as many as 50,000 people, destroyed 23,000 homes, and left an estimated 200,000 individuals without jobs. It will take approximately $2 billion to repair material damages as a result of the worst natural catastrophe to strike this South American nation in the past 200 years. Largely dependent on oil production for export revenues, Venezuela has a substantial foreign debt and is in the midst of a recession ("After Venezuela's Flood," 1999).

Sub-Saharan Africa: A Glimmer of Hope in a Sea of Despair With almost 660 million people in the year 2000 and a population doubling time of only *twenty-seven years,* sub-Saharan Africa is the fastest growing region in the world. This is also a very young land, with 45 percent of the population under 15 years of age. Because these individuals will come of reproductive age in the next generation, the population will continue to increase even if women started having only two children (see Chapter 12 for a more comprehensive discussion of population growth).

Almost all of the countries in sub-Saharan Africa are very poor and the region as a whole cannot feed itself. In 1962, sub-Saharan Africa changed from a net food *exporter* to a net food *importer* and the quantity of imported foodstuffs has been going up ever since. Major droughts in 1972–1974 and in the mid-1980s took a severe toll on the region's agricultural output. To make a critical situation even worse, an infestation of locusts devastated large areas of Africa's Sahel. Massive amounts of food were sent to sub-Saharan Africa to avert a famine in 1983. Nevertheless, hundreds of thousands of people died (Matthews, 1989; Population Reference Bureau, 1986). In a famine borne primarily of war, 2.6 millions Sudanese faced starvation in the late 1990s, with as many as 28 of every 10,000 dying every day in some parts of the country (Prusher, 1998b). If sub-Saharan African nations are to make any meaningful economic progress, they will have to become much more productive agriculturally. "The first step for African nations is the step back from the edge of famine" (McGeary and Michaels, 1998, p. 40).

This region of the world also fell victim to human-made disasters as contrived oil shortages and price increases in 1973 and 1979 meant more money had to be spent on this much-needed commodity. A global recession in the late 1970s and early 1980s meant fewer African goods being purchased worldwide and, therefore, less capital flowing into the region. During this period, African nations also spent billions of dollars on weapons "as the international arms industry had a field day" (Smith, 1992).

Over and above the self-inflicted wounds of inefficient and corrupt government, almost-never-ending warfare has been sub-Saharan Africa's greatest tragedy in the post-colonial era. For example, Sudan has been ripped apart by civil war intermittantly since gaining its independence from Britain in 1956. As a result of 15 years of fighting between the Muslim north and Christian south, an estimated 2 million people have lost their lives, from either the ongoing conflict or the largely man-made famine. Forced off their land by the fighting, farmers cannot plant crops, and foreign investors are loathe to put money in a country where turmoil never ends. In Angola, where an on-again, off-again war has dragged on for 30 years, the situation is much the same.

It is hardly surprising that a desperately poor continent, unable to feed itself, has a near monopoly of countries with low ratings of social well-being indicators. On virtually any "quality of life" index (for example, literacy rates, access to health care, and access to clean drinking water) sub-Saharan countries are at the bottom of the list. Perhaps the most telling statistic of the overall poverty of the region is the life expectancy, which at 49 years, is the lowest (by far) in the world. Even in a poor country like Bangladesh, an infant born today can expect to live to age 59 under current mortality rates. More than one individual has referred to sub-Saharan Africa as "the third world's third world."

In spite of the size and scope of the problems facing this region, there is cause for optimism. The newly independent (1993) nation of Eritrea has very little foreign debt and has rejected almost all outside aid. Crime rates are minuscule and, as one advisor to a local bank stated, "The corruption is the lowest of any government I've worked for, including in Santa Rosa, California" (O'Neil, in McGeary and Michaels, 1998, p. 42). In Mali, one of the world's poorest countries, literacy increased from 19 percent in 1991 to 32 percent in 1998.

President Clinton (among others) has spoken of an "African Renaissance," a social and economic rebirth taking place in countries such as Ghana, Uganda, Benin, Botswana, Ivory Coast, and Tanzania (McGeary and Michaels, 1998). However, if an African Renaissance is to be sustained, the inhabitants of this region will have to do a much better job of helping themselves as well as making the most of the aid they receive. The international community will also have to include sub-Saharan African nations as full-fledged trading partners, reversing a history that witnessed the continent's wealth and resources flowing primarily to rich nations while receiving little in return.

North Africa and the Middle East: Land of Princes and Paupers The popular, often stereotypical view of the Middle East (and to a lesser extent North Africa) is that of a people made fabulously wealthy (almost overnight) because of their good fortune to reside atop the world's most critical resource: oil. Although the per capita GNPs of some of these countries are among the highest in the world, the oil-produced wealth is not very evenly distributed. Countries like Saudi Arabia, Kuwait, and the United Emirates (with a combined population of 27 million in 2000) are three times as wealthy as Jordan, Iran, and Iraq (with a total population of 93 million in 2000). In addition, tremendous internal disparities of wealth exist in many of these nations.

As a result of this inequity, the hundreds of billions of petroleum-generated dollars in this region have been both a blessing and a curse. The disparity between the region's "superrich" and "dreadfully poor" is much greater than the wealth gap between the "haves" and "have nots" in Central America and sub-Saharan Africa. The resentment among the poor is further accentuated by the millions of poor Egyptians, Jordanians, and Palestinians who left their impoverished homelands to work for low wages in the region's oil-rich states. "Is it any wonder," as Paul Kennedy (1993, p. 38) notes, "that the badly housed urban masses . . . are attracted to religious leaders or 'strongmen'; appealing to Islamic pride, a sense of identity, and resistance to foreign powers and local lackeys?"

As a consequence of the Iran-Iraq War of 1980–1988 and the Gulf War of 1990–1991, Iraq's economy is in shambles. Per capita Gross Domestic Product (GDP) dropped from over $8,000 to less than $1,000 in 1998 (Peterson, 1998). An $80 billion debt incurred during the conflict with Iran, coupled with the economic sanctions Iraq has been forced to endure in the aftermath of the Gulf War, have resulted in one of the most pronounced economic reversals in the second half of the twentieth century. A combination of high inflation, lack of basic foodstuffs, and a contracting economy have driven some of the country's most highly trained professionals into the streets selling trinkets and ice cream in order to survive. Although the situation in neighboring Iran is not as dismal, this nation's economy has been depressed because of the global oil glut in the mid- to late 1990s. With 85 percent of its hard currency coming from crude oil exports, Iran faced a $6 billion shortfall, or one-third of the nation's annual budget in 1998 ("Reaching Out, if He Can," 1998). The state owns approximately 80 percent of the highly regulated Iranian economy, a situation that has thwarted much-needed foreign investment.

An agricultural society when it first came into existence in 1948, Israel has transformed itself into an economically successful, modern state. With a gross national product that rose some 6 percent for much of the 1990s, this Middle Eastern country's per capita GDP was over $17,000 in 1998, a figure equivalent to that of the United Kingdom and approaching the economic well-being of Italy. A high-tech center for computer software, telecommunications, and biomedical equipment, some parts of Israel are now indistinguishable from California's "Silicon Valley" (Thanos, 1998).

The first and largest nation to make peace with Israel, Egypt is also on the economic upswing. Tourism, a growing textile industry, a center for regional financial services, and high-tech industries have brought this "emerging-market" nation a 5 percent annual economic growth rate in recent years ("Egypt: Wonder of the Past, Investment of the Future," 1998).

Once considered a rising star, Jordan's financial future is uncertain as the unemployment rate is over 18 percent and economic growth has slowed substantially. The Palestinian economy is in the doldrums with high unemployment and investment capital reduced to almost nothing. In Algeria, as many as 120,000 people were killed between 1992 and 1998 as Islamic extremists, criminal elements, and a military-backed government have battled for political supremacy and legitimacy. In an atmosphere of intense fear, hatred, and indiscriminate violence, it is virtually impossible for a nation to develop economically.

Peace and political stability are the keys to economic success and overall modernization in North Africa and the Middle East. If internal class warfare and religious strife (fundamentalist Muslims versus moderate Muslims) can be minimalized (or avoided), and reconciliation with Israel on the part of more Islamic nations becomes a reality, sustained economic growth can occur in one of the poorest regions of the world.

Europe: Changes East and West Beginning in the late 1980s, most of the world cheered as one eastern European country after another and, finally, the U.S.S.R. itself emerged from the domination of Soviet-style communist regimes. However, when the joyful celebrations ended, the extremely difficult task of making the transition from centrally planned "command" economies (in which both the amount and price of goods produced are determined by the state) to "free-market" economies (in which the number of goods produced and their cost are a result of "supply and demand") was undertaken in each of these countries. Unfortunately, the initial period of change was even more difficult than most experts had anticipated. When the Cold War ended, eastern European nations plunged into the second great depression of this century (PlanEcon Inc, in Marshall and Williams, 1993). Almost overnight, rates of unemployment and inflation increased dramatically, while industrial output plummeted. In the region as a whole, domestic production fell by 10 percent in 1990 and 19 percent during the "collapse" of 1991. The decline in industrial output ranged from 12 percent in Poland to a high of 60 percent in Albania (*Economic Survey of Europe in 1991–1992*, 1992).

By 1995 Poland was the regional leader in making the transition from a centrally planned socialist economy to a capitalist market system, with over 50 percent of the nation's gross domestic product generated by the private sector (Burke, 1995). In the mid- to late 1990s, Poland's economy received a boost when General Motors, Ford Motor Company, Fiat Motors, Adam Opel (Germany), and South Korea's Daewoo Motor Company all built manufacturing plants in

The Eastern European nations of Poland, Hungary, and Czech Republic are expected to be among the first nations in that region to become members of the European Union. Whereas the shelves of stores in these former communist countries were devoid of all but the bare necessities prior to 1989, these shoppers in a Budapest mall have no trouble finding almost anything they want.

that country (Piatt, 1997). In 2000 Polish consumers were expected to buy 500,000 new automobiles, a sign of the economy's vitality in a nation of 39 million people. One observer noted that "Poland today more closely resembles Spain or Portugal than it does most former Eastern Bloc nations" ("A 'Normal' Poland," 1997).

Along with Poland, the Czech Republic and Hungary are on the "economic fast track," as these nations continue to attract foreign investment, privatize more industries, and control inflation while the financial well-being of their citizens increases. With a pre–World War II history of democratic governments and present-day political stability, these nations are hopeful of joining the European Economic Union as they strive to become fully integrated (and accepted) members of the modern European community.

Plagued with varying degrees of political instability and economic uncertainty, the future of eastern Europe's "slow track" countries (Romania, Bulgaria, Slovakia, Albania, and most of the former Soviet Republics) is less optimistic. Although numerous industries have been privatized, agriculture and a once significant weapons industry are stagnant in the Ukraine. While this nation of 51 million people looks longingly at the success of neighboring Poland, it appears to be following the economic policy of much-troubled Russia. A former accountant who now sells

coffee and cookies to survive in an outdoor market said, "What I notice in Poland is not that the people are better off. Many dress much like we do. I see that in their faces there is a tranquility. They know where they are going. We do not" (in Williams, 1998).

In Russia, the transition from a centrally planned economy to capitalism has been unpredictable, chaotic, and is ushering in a system of inequality last seen in that nation during the reign of the last Czar prior to the revolution of 1917. The former communist republic is turning toward "oligarchic capitalism" characterized by giant conglomerates. Run by a small group of individuals who receive preferential treatment because of their relationship with the government, this arrangement is little more than "crony capitalism," Russian style (Hoffman, 1998a). Foreign correspondent David Hoffman notes that "With silk ties . . . armor-plated Mercedez Benzes and lavish country *dachas,*" these individuals "have become the most conspicuous advertisement for the success—and excess—of Russia's switch to market capitalism" (p. 15).

As a result of a national tax system that is continually changing (and widely perceived to be unfair) and subject to bribe-taking officials, tax cheating is akin to a national sport. Two recent studies concluded that approximately half of Russia's gross domestic product (often referred to as the "shadow economy") is subject to tax evasion (in Caryl, 1998). As a result, the government is short some $100 billion a year and must borrow money (typically at high interest rates) to meet its financial obligations. When and where the government does collect taxes can bankrupt marginal businesses and contribute to the nation's already high unemployment rate (Hoffman, 1998b; Caryl, 1998). (The irony is that many of these factories—holdovers from the communist era—spend $3 to produce an item that sells for $2 [Weinstein, 1998].) The tax collection problem (one poll found that 80 percent of the population believe that there is nothing wrong with tax evasion) is a major reason why Russia has been forced to borrow tens of billions of dollars from the International Monetary Fund.

An economy in constant turmoil has produced what money traders call "ruble whiplash"; that is, the wildly bouncing value of the Russian ruble as measured against other currencies. When the ruble lost half of its value in July 1998, inflation increased 15 percent the following month as the cost of basic foods (potatoes, cabbage, and beef) escalated in price from 60 to 85 percent (Nelan, 1998). Some individuals receive only a portion of their salary in rubles, as is the case for factory workers in Zlatoust who are compensated primarily with company coupons which can be used only in local stores (Hoffman, 1998b). After rejecting "funeral supplies" and toilet paper, school teachers in one town agreed on a salary of 15 bottles of vodka a month (*Marketplace,* 1998).

In spite of all of these problems, there is an upside to the Russian economy. A study conducted by two Moscow economists found that 27 percent of the population could be classified as rich or middle class, 48 percent as "tolerably well off," and 25 percent as poor (in Caryl, 1998). While this latter figure represents a poverty statistic twice that of the United States, it could be considered relatively low in light of the fact that so many Russians were poor when the transition from socialism to capitalism began. Although the nation's gross domestic product decreased by about 50 percent between 1991 and 1998 (Weir, 1998), the number of Russians with automobiles more than doubled to just under 17 million (one-third of all households) from 1992 to 1998. The number of families with telephones and computers has also increased significantly over the last few years.

In the early 1990s, western Europe was experiencing its worst depression since the mid-1950s as many of the world's wealthiest nations were mired in a kind of global paralysis (Thomas, 1992). Although some experts pointed to more of the same for the decade, the economic health of the region began to change for the better by the mid-1994. By 1999 the recovery was well under way. However, the problem of nagging unemployment continued, with the jobless rate ranging from 9.3 to over 18 percent in Germany, France, Italy, and Spain, four of the continent's most populous nations (Seward, 1999). Western Europe's unemployment problems have been compounded by people from now politically free eastern European countries streaming across their borders in search of work. Short of implementing "the dreaded American model"—low-wage, service-sector jobs, little if any job security, and high income inequality—no one had formulated a plan to put more people to work (Walsh, 1997).

Unemployment is no longer an issue in Norway, a nation whose only economic difficulties have been "luxury problems." The world's second-largest producer of oil (Saudi Arabia is number one), the Norwegian government has enough money to provide 70 percent of its citizens funds or subsidies in the form of free universal health care, "cheap" university education, and 10 months of maternity leave (at full pay) for all new mothers, to name but a few programs (Walsh, 1997). The jobless rate is so low that workers have to be brought in from nearby Sweden. If estimates of Norway's oil reserves are correct, all of this wealth is merely the beginning, according to a Norwegian political consultant who noted, "We are going to be filthy rich" (Geelmuyden, in Walsh, 1997, p. A1).

On January 1, 1999, eleven members of the European Union (Austria, Belgium, Finland, France, Germany, Ireland, Italy, Luxembourg, Netherlands, Portugal, and Spain) made economic history when they adopted a common currency—the "euro." England, Denmark, and Sweden decided to forgo the euro, while Greece failed to meet the necessary economic criteria. Although member nations will not begin using the actual bills and coins until 2002, currency values will be posted in both the local currency and the euro for a three-year period. Proponents of the euro see at least three major advantages to this new currency: (1) Individuals and businesses will no longer lose money (commission costs) when funds have to be changed from one currency to another—from Italian lira to French francs, for example. (2) Without currency fluctuations, buying across borders will be cheaper, thereby stimulating trade among countries using the euro. According to one estimate, by the year 2001, the number of cross-border, business-to-business transactions among euro nations will increase between 60 and 100 percent. (3) With almost 300 million inhabitants, the "euro zone" will account for almost 20 percent of world trade. Having a combined economy greater than that of the United States, euro nations will have a currency to compete with the American dollar as the world's main reserve currency (Radosevich, 1998; Sanchez-Klein, 1998).

POLITICS AS A SOCIAL INSTITUTION

From ancient times to the present, people have had to make important decisions about how to spend their time and resources. These decisions have often had crucial consequences for the survival and well-being of the society. Do we remain faithful to our traditional was of life or do we embrace new technologies that promise (or threaten) to change that way? Do we welcome immigrants seeking refuge in our land, or do we keep that land for ourselves? Do we employ economic boycotts to change the unwelcome behaviors of people in neighboring societies, or do we threaten them with military invasion? Do we take sides when neighboring societies go to war with one another or do we try to remain out of the conflict?

When people show significant differences in their beliefs about the desirability or correctness of one choice compared to another, they must come to some agreement about how final decisions will be made in their society. The alternative, as the philosopher Thomas Hobbes concluded centuries ago, would be chaos and anarchy: a war "of every man, against every man" (1881, p. 93). Individuals and groups would be locked in open and constant conflicts as they tried to wield power over one another.

Regardless of which particular form they happen to assume in a given society, these agreements to regulate the exercise of power and decision making represent the creation of some sort of political institution. Such institutions are an ancient and enduring fact of human societal life whose importance has grown with the increasing complexity of social organization.

In modern or developed societies such as the United States and Canada, and in many developing societies such as Mexico and Korea, final decision making and other political activities rest with the state, the institution that holds a monopoly over the legitimate use of force in society and exercises governing power. Sociologists of all theoretical schools are in agreement about the pervasive and critical impact of the state in most contemporary societies. However, as might be anticipated, they are in sharp disagreement about how the state's activities affect those societies and their populations.

Theoretical Interpretations of Political Institutions

The Functionalist Perspective Sociologists in the structural-functional tradition have tried to understand and explain the growth of modern political institutions in terms of their contributions to societal survival. Functionalist theorists claim that the state (or **polity,** as they call it) plays a critical societal role in what Talcott Parsons (1971) referred to as *goal-attainment* activities.

According to this argument, every society possessing a surplus of economic resources must decide how that surplus will be used. Societal goals (for example, universal adult literacy) must be established and communicated to population members. Specific groups (public and private elementary and secondary schools, junior and community colleges) must be assigned responsibility for particular objectives and provided with the resources (monetary funds, books, teachers, lesson plans) necessary for their successful attainment. Individuals must be mobilized to join the specific goal-oriented groups and carry out assigned group responsibilities (for example, free tuition, special tax credits, and free childcare offers to adults returning to school). Finally, people's behaviors and beliefs must be controlled and directed toward the fulfillment of these goals (for example, the state may extend existing compul-

sory education requirements or establish new literacy requirements for civil service and other government jobs). This cluster of activities, according to functionalists, constitutes the essence of institutionalized political behavior in any society. The polity decides what, when, where, how, and by whom important societal actions will be carried out. In so doing, it helps to ensure that activities necessary for developing and maintaining society will be performed efficiently.

The Conflict Perspective Whereas functionalists emphasize the role of political institutions in establishing and coordinating societal goals for collective well-being, conflict theorists focus on the coercive and divisive aspects of the polity. For sociologists in this perspective, the state, as the ultimate source of power in society, is an important resource employed by some groups to gain and maintain control over other groups. As with so many other aspects of conflict theory, the classic statement was made by Karl Marx.

As you may recall from earlier discussions, Marx regarded the political apparatus in capitalist societies—the state—as the ultimate instrument of class oppression. Like other superstructural elements, political institutions reflect the underlying economic substructure on which they are founded. However, more than most other derived social or cultural elements, the state plays a direct and active role in maintaining bourgeois dominance and proletarian subordination. The state generates legislation (e.g., tax and inheritance laws in the U.S.) that keeps both owners and workers in their respective places. It makes daily decisions and establishes societal policies (for example, the taxpayer-funded bailouts of banks in the United States in the late 1980s, and in Japan and Mexico throughout the late 1990s) that favor the advantaged and add to the burdens of the disadvantaged. When necessary, the state supplies the physical force to reassert the rule of the ownership class and squash proletarian attempts to gain justice (for example, the U.S. criminal justice system's tendency to punish lower-class crimes severely and to give white-collar or corporate criminals only token punishment).

Avoiding some of Marx's rhetoric, modern conflict theorists maintain the assertion that the polity and the economy are intertwined in a symbiotic or mutually supportive relationship (Collins, 1988b). They speak of a "political economy" that supports and furthers existing social inequality arrangements. As Turner (1997, p. 155) notes, "When power is consolidated and concentrated, inequalities increase, for power is not only a resource in itself, it can be used to extract the resources of others. Those who can coerce, symbolically control, materially manipulate, or administratively dictate are all in a position to increase their resources at the expense of others." Control of the polity is recognized by those both in and out of power as a prize with enormous consequences for economic and social advancement. It is hardly an accident that the history of various minority group movements in the United States has been one of growing political activism and attempted political takeover. For conflict theorists, the cynical version of the Golden Rule—the one who has the gold makes the rules—has an equally cynical converse: the one who has the rule makes the gold. In societies lacking long-standing traditions of orderly political competition, getting the rule (and the gold) can result in unrestrained bloodshed between contending power-seeking groups.

The U.S. Political System

Freedom and the Constitution The promise of freedom has been a large part of the historic appeal of the United States to tens of millions of immigrants who have swollen our ranks over the last two centuries. Our culture's strong emphasis on individual liberty is a reminder of the fact that this society was created as a political experiment, a truly New World where people could escape the tyranny of Old World monarchies and shape the conditions of their own lives. A government "of the people, by the people, and for the people" is what the framers of our Constitution had in mind. They attempted to embody that concept in a democratic political system that disbursed power evenly among the many different segments of the population. The extent to which they succeeded has been a matter of continuing debate among political sociologists and other observers of the U.S. political scene for many years. The major issue in this debate centers on how closely the reality of the U.S. political structure fits the model outlined in the Constitution and in other official documents. Attempts to address the issue focus on two related aspects of political life: the distribution of power within and among population segments, and the extent and depth of people's involvement in political activities.

The Structure of Political Power In his farewell address to the nation before stepping down from office in 1961, President Dwight D. Eisenhower warned the American public of a growing "military-industrial complex" that threatened to take control of government and subvert the democratic process. Although hardly what one would call a conflict theorist or a radical social critic, the outgoing chief executive was echoing the words of someone who was both.

Five years before Eisenhower's famous speech, sociologist C. Wright Mills had argued that the takeover of the U.S. political system by what he termed a *power elite* was already an accomplished fact. As described by Mills, this **power elite** was a coalition of high-ranking officials from the largest corporations ("corporate chieftains"), the branches of the military services ("warlords"), and the executive branch of the federal government ("political directorate"). The members of this coalition formed a "higher circle of power" that effectively controlled the running of the political system and dominated all aspects of important societal decision making (Mills, 1956, pp. 3–4). Their ascension to the highest levels of political influence reflected the enormous power of the large formal organizations that now structured and controlled most societal activities in the United States. It also signified the growing loss of control over most daily activities by individuals. This power elite, Mills claimed, formed the apex or top level of a pyramid of political power in our society. However, despite the magnitude of its impact on societal and political affairs, this group's existence remained unknown to the general population.

Directly below the power elite lay the group that, according to Mills, was believed by the people to have control: the elected officials who make up the Congress and the other offices of government. Referring to this group as the "middle level of power" (p. 4), Mills claimed that their actual influence was restricted to relatively unimportant issues and was further weakened by their lack of overall coordination and consensus. Their primary role was to serve as a front for the power elite by providing the illusion of democracy for the benefit of the larger population.

Mills argued that this larger population was fragmented and alienated into a **mass society** consisting of millions of individuals who, for the most part, were uninterested and uninvolved in political affairs. The combination of their own apathy and the manipulations of the power elite left the masses virtually powerless. In the vacuum created by their withdrawal from the political sphere and the limited activities of the middle levels of power, members of the corporate, military, and political elite could and did exercise a stranglehold over the U.S. political system. This was hardly the democracy envisioned by the founding fathers or described in high school civics textbooks.

The Pluralist Model Mills's portrayal of an American political system run by and for a small group accountable neither to the public nor the formal system of government checks and balances generated an immediate and heated response. Some Marxists criticized Mills for failing to recognize the social class basis of the composition and operation of the U.S. political structure, and most critics blasted him for his assertion that democracy of any sort in this society was a myth (Domhoff and Ballard, 1968, assembled a number of these critiques). On the contrary, they asserted, democratic political rule was alive and well in this society, although in a different form from that commonly imagined.

Proponents of this so-called **pluralist perspective** concede that political power in the United States is in the hands of large organized groups rather than individuals. But they contend that the number of such groups and the different interests they represent prevent any single group or coalition of groups from acquiring controlling power over the system. Rather, these groups act as "veto groups" (Riesman, 1961) that shift according to the specific issues at hand. They restrain one another's power and limiting each other's influence to particular situations. In this model, individuals retain final political power by joining and becoming involved in the various organized interest groups.

For example, in a large city, individual residents exercise very little power or control over the governing of the metropolis. But the organized groups to which these individuals belong—community planning groups, taxpayers' associations, and business or service clubs—may possess some clout in shaping the course of urban affairs. At times, the interests of these groups may coincide, and so they can form a coalition that will have an even louder voice in political decision making. For example, both citizens' and business groups may rally around plans to improve a community park in their neighborhood, believing that safe, attractive recreational facilities will encourage people to live and shop in the area. However, at other times, their interests may diverge, and so each group finds itself speaking out against the others. Plans to rezone single-family neighborhoods to allow the development of apartment and condominium complexes often generate heated disputes between neighborhood groups and business interests. In this case, the effective power of each group may be weakened considerably by opposition from the other.

U.S. Society—A Power Elite System?

Recent studies of the U.S. power structure provide evidence that the power elite interpretation may have greater validity than the pluralist model, although neither provides a completely accurate picture of power in this society. In a continuing series of analyses conducted over the past two decades, for example, Thomas Dye (1995) examined the institutionalized centers of power in this country (political bodies, the mass media, corporations, major universities, top legal firms, civic and cultural organizations) and the social origins of the people who occupy key positions in these institutions. His findings indicate a strong concentration of power in the hands of a relatively small number of highly influential organizations and a pattern of common socioeconomic class backgrounds for key officeholders across the different institutional sectors.

However, at the same time, data show that the social origins and political interests of elites in the various sectors are not identical. Although corporate leaders, top political officials, and directors of large research foundations (among other elites) at times may see the world in similar terms, they often display significant disagreements among themselves on particular issues. These internal divisions keep these powerful groups from forming the kind of completely unified power elite described by Mills. But, overall, these elites' shared world view makes them more like one another than like the nonelites who make up the bulk of the population. The paths of entry into their positions also make it very difficult for individuals from lower-, working-, and, in many cases, middle-class backgrounds to add new and different visions to the top rungs of power. The result is a power structure, as well as social and political policies, that generally reflects compatible (though not necessarily identical) definitions of social and political reality. Recent events in this society would seem to lend support to this conclusion.

Perhaps more than those of most other presidential administrations in recent U.S. history, the years of Ronald Reagan's and George Bush's tenure in the White House were marked by a close, friendly working relationship between the federal government and big business. During this time, many federal regulatory agencies were disbanded entirely or had their operations curtailed so that corporations could do what they did best—make profits. These profits, in turn, were to be plowed back into the economy. Eventually, they would trickle down and throughout the various social layers, fostering growth and prosperity as they trickled. In the end, all segments of the society would benefit. Seldom during the past half-century have the visions of the political and economic sectors seemed so closely aligned. It was a time of unrestrained capitalism and exuberant affluence—for some.

As the Reagan-Bush era came to a close, mounting evidence began to indicate that the shared vision of federal government and corporate leaders had worked to the best advantage of a much smaller population group than originally projected (Phillips,

1990a). During the decade of the 1980s, the economic position of the wealthiest segment of the U.S. population improved, while that of virtually all other groups either dropped or remained stagnant. Racial and ethnic minority group members, in particular, lost economic ground (U.S. Bureau of the Census, 1998a). Tax reforms passed during this period seemed to increase top income-receiving groups' share of after-tax revenues and fall most heavily on lower- and middle-income groups (Pearlstein, 1995; Phillips, 1990b). Snowballing savings and loan association collapses and a deepening federal deficit dug deeply into middle- and lower-income taxpayers' pockets, seemingly leaving upper-income groups untouched. The gap between the haves and the have nots widened, with many more individuals sinking into the latter category. If we assume that the outcomes of social and political policies reflect *someone's* interests, these patterns are more indicative of a special-interest than a public-interest political structure, a power elite–like rather than a pluralist system.

Patterns of Political Participation   Evidence regarding the distribution of political power in this society is ambiguous enough to permit a number of different conclusions about the true shape of power in the United States. In contrast, data concerning the involvement of the American people in their political system are clear and consistent. Among the political democracies in the contemporary world, this country ranks close to the bottom in terms of its citizens' involvement in electoral politics (see Table 11.1). According to the International Institute for Democracy and Electoral Assistance's (IDEA) comprehensive study of voter turnout in more than 1,400 parlimentary and presidential elections held across the globe between 1945 and 1997, the United State's overall average of 48.3 percent ranks 139th among the 172 countries studied. Of all the advanced democracies of the world, only Switzerland, with an average voter participation rate of 49.3 percent, come close to matching the U.S.'s dismal record. For all other advanced industrial societies with established democracies, voter turnout averaged 80.4 percent (Rose, 1997). For most Americans, most of the time, politics remains a matter of only passing and passive interest.

Of all the different ways in which people living in a democratic society might express involvement in political affairs, voting in national, state, and local elections would seem to be the most obvious and most important. After all, it is precisely the legal right to vote that distinguishes democracies from other types of political systems. The people who founded this society fought a revolutionary war to establish the right to elect their leaders. Over the

Source: International Institute for Democracy and Electoral Assistance, *Voter Turnout from 1945–1997: A Global Report on Political Participation* (Stockholm: International Institute for Democracy and Electoral Assistance, 1997).

years, their successors, including many members of present generations, fought other wars to preserve that right. In our system of cultural beliefs, voting is as much a moral obligation as a civil right. Failure to exercise it is often regarded as failure to meet the minimum requirements of citizenship.

If there is any validity to this belief, a significant number of people in this society are not very "good" citizens. Their involvement in the political life of society does not extend as far as the simple act of casting a ballot in the elections through which government leaders formally enter and leave office. This pattern of widespread nonvoting is true even in presidential elections.

Since 1932, voter turnout in presidential elections has failed to exceed 63 percent of the registered, voting-age population (U.S. Bureau of the Census, 1998c). Most often, the figures have averaged in the low to mid-50 percent range. In the 1988 election, for example, only about half (50.2 percent) of all eligible voters turned out to elect George Bush president over Michael Dukakis. In 1992, the chance to choose among Bush, Clinton, and Perot drew a record number (104.4 million) of voters. But even that number represented only 55.5 percent of all eligible voters in the country that year. In the 1996 election, only 49 percent of voters, the lowest percentage in over 65 years, turned out to reelect Bill Clinton over Bob Dole (U.S. Bureau of the Census, 1998c, Table 485). Voting percentages for off-year (that is, nonpresidential) congressional elections for the same time period are even smaller, as low as 33 percent in 1942. In 1998, just slightly over 36 percent of those eligible cast votes in congressional races, the lowest turnout percentage since 1942 (Committee for the Study of the American Electorate, 1999a). And, in the 36 statewide 1998 primary elections in which the two major parties had gubernatorial and/or U.S. Senate contests at stake, a record low 17.4 percent turned out to cast their votes. Commenting on the progressive decline of primary election turnouts, Curtis Gans, president of the Committee for the Study of the American Electorate, observes, "What we are witnessing is a progressive meltdown in civic engagement, a major danger to American democracy. . . . Primaries are and have been for the active and interested in each political party, but when you have a situation where an average of less than five percent of the electorate can determine the nominees and direction of either major political party, you are inviting intense factions to take over one or both parties and skew the public agenda" (Committee for the Study of the American Electorate, 1998, p. 2).

Studies of voting patterns and the social correlates of voting are consistent in their findings of who votes and who doesn't. The likelihood of voting increases with age, people between the ages of 30 and 65 being more likely to vote than younger and older groups (see Table 11.2).

As Table 11.2 indicates, members of higher socioeconomic status (SES) groups vote with much greater frequency than members of lower SES groups. Formal educational level, in particular, appears to be the critical class-related factor influencing participation in the electoral process. In the 1996 elections, 28 percent of people with an eighth-grade education or below

TABLE 11.2

Self-Reported Voting in Presidential Elections by Sex, Race, Age, and Education (in percentages)

Characteristic	Election Year				
	1980	1984	1988	1992	1996
Sex					
Male	59.1	59.0	56.4	60.2	52.8
Female	59.4	60.8	58.3	62.3	55.5
Race—Ethnicity					
White	60.9	61.4	59.1	63.6	56.0
African American	50.5	55.8	51.5	54.0	50.6
Hispanic	29.9	32.6	28.8	28.9	26.7
Age (years)					
18–20	35.7	36.7	33.2	38.5	31.2
21–24	43.1	43.5	38.3	45.7	33.4
25–34	54.6	54.5	48.0	53.2	43.1
35–44	64.4	63.5	61.3	63.6	54.9
45–64	69.3	69.8	67.9	70.0	(N.A.)
65 and over	65.1	67.7	68.8	70.1	(N.A.)
Education					
8 years or less	42.6	42.9	36.7	35.1	28.1
High school					
1–3 years	45.6	44.4	41.3	41.2	33.8
4 years	58.9	58.7	54.7	57.5	49.1
College					
1–3 years	67.2	67.5	64.5	68.7	60.5
4 years or more	79.9	79.1	77.6	81.0	73.0

Source: Adapted from U.S. Bureau of the Census, *Statistical Abstract of the United States: 1998* (Washington, DC: U.S. Government Printing Office, 1998), Table 483.

reported voting, compared to 73 percent of college graduates. Race and ethnicity are also important factors in voting, with non-Hispanic whites having higher levels of participation than either African Americans or Hispanics. Hispanics are only about half as likely to vote as either whites or African Americans.

Gender differences are reflected somewhat in presidential and congressional elections over the past two decades. Since the 1980 presidential election, women have had slightly higher voting turnouts than men. For example, in 1996, 55.5 percent of women reported casting a presidential vote, compared to 52.8 percent of men. Women comprised 53.4 percent of all voters in that election, and they voted for Clinton (54 percent) over Dole (38 percent) and Perot (7 percent) (Center for the American Woman and Politics, 1997).

Other forms of political involvement such as following campaigns and campaign issues, discussing politics with other people, becoming active in a campaign (working for a candidate, making telephone calls, wearing campaign pins, etc.), and contributing money to a candidate or campaign show similar social and demographic patterning. Though perhaps difficult to imagine, the levels of participation in these political activities are substantially lower than voting levels (Conway, 1991).

This widespread disengagement from the political process has been subject to a number of interpretations, ranging from contentment with the system ("Things are working just fine; I don't need to get involved") to disgust ("Things are rigged; why waste time getting involved?"). The definitive explanation has yet to be written, but evidence points to a growing cynicism in people's perceptions of how politics works and a sense that individuals make little or no real difference in a mass-based polity. For example, one 1999 survey found that only 7 percent of respondents felt that, in overall matters of policy, government officials most often respond to the public's wishes when making decisions for the country. In sharp contrast, 64 percent felt that special-interest groups and lobbyists had the most influence. Interpreting the results of this survey, researchers concluded that "Although government officials regularly claim to speak for 'the American people,' the public does not buy it. . . . In a country that rests on the democratic principle of popular sovereignty, large majorities of the citizenry see special interests and politicians as running the show and casting them to the side" (in Morin, 1999).

These feelings may or may not be an accurate reflection of the reality of U.S. politics. The danger is that, with so many people holding these feelings and acting—or, rather, not acting—on them, what they believe to be true may become true. If those who believe in the existence of some kind of controlling elite structure let that belief remove them from active political participation of any sort, they may very well have a hand in confirming their own worst fears.

Politics in a Changing World

If human social patterns are at all subject to general laws, the one law that would seem to apply in the case of politics is that anything and all things are possible. Modern nation-states and their complex political structures arose from the widespread technological and economic changes that swept through traditional societies, turning their worlds upside down. As the center of planning and decision making for these developing (and now developed) societies, the state attempted to gain control over the forces of social and cultural change so that stability could be regained. In the process, what had been political rule by physical force—the king's army—was transformed into what Max Weber (1978/1921) called **rule by authority.** Raw power was replaced by a sense of moral obligation as the basis for the orders and decisions of political leaders being followed by members of the population. As both the rationalization and secularization of societies grew, **charismatic authority** (rule based on some extraordinary personal quality of the political leader) and **traditional authority** (rule based on long-standing customs) were replaced by what Weber called **rational-legal authority** (rule based on the reasonableness of laws and the acceptability of law-making procedures). The growth of these large-scale, legitimate political systems promoted and reflected continuing economic and societal development, ushering in the modern era.

But significant political change did not end with the emergence of the modern state; nor do political changes in the modern world follow any single route. Events taking place during the past few decades and in the current one point out the weaknesses of assuming, as some sociologists once did, that either social or political development unfolds according to some natural, inevitable sequence.

The Collapse of Soviet Communism   In a 1960 visit to the United States, then-Soviet Premier Nikita Khrushchev predicted that in the near future, communism would bury capitalist societies such as the United States. At the time, Soviet-style government appeared to be on the move. Both eastern Europe and the People's Republic of China were in the communist camp, and portions of Latin America were leaning in the same direction. However, not quite forty years later, Sergei Khrushchev was sworn in as a U.S. citizen, having survived the deaths and burials of both his father and the U.S.S.R. ("Khrushchev's Son Buries Ghost of Cold War," 1999). On December 25, 1991, Soviet president Mikhail Gorbachev announced his immediate resignation as head of the Union of Soviet Socialist Republics. His departure paved the way for the newly formed Commonwealth of Independent States under the informal leadership of Russian president Boris Yeltsin, thus effectively putting an end to the Soviet Union (Clines, 1991). One of the most significant world political events of the early twentieth century had been eclipsed by what is undoubtedly the major political event of the late twentieth century.

The collapse of the Soviet Union had been in the making for some time. In large part, it was a result of the inability of Soviet political leaders to bring about significant changes in the depressed economic conditions that plagued most of its member republics. As sociologist Seymour Martin Lipset (1963) once observed, successful political rule depends as much on government being perceived by citizens as effective as it does on granting legitimacy to political leaders.

The Soviet breakup was further hastened by a growing spirit of **nationalism**—an ideology that emphasizes national identity and the importance of self-governance—within the different republics. In 1990, the Baltic republic of Lithuania proclaimed its independence from the Soviet Union, declaring that it had been illegally annexed into the U.S.S.R. as part of a secret deal between Stalin and Hitler during World War II. The two other Baltic republics—Latvia and Estonia—soon followed, and the fragmentation of the Soviet state had begun.

Post-Soviet Blues The breakup of the Soviet Union has been hailed as a smashing triumph for democracy, capitalism, and even Christianity. (Then-President Ronald Reagan once described the U.S.S.R. as "the evil empire.") But these joyous celebrations may turn out to be a bit premature. To date, political democracies in the now-independent post-Soviet republics have been sickly at best. As discussed earlier in this chapter, for the most part, their economies remain unable to create and maintain the higher standards that many of their people had come to believe would automatically follow political liberation. Thus, they find themselves subject to the same internal pressures that spelled the doom of the Soviet Union. Unless and until their lagging economies perk up, democratic political rule will remain in jeopardy. Analyses of fledgling democracies in eastern Europe and in other parts of the world indicate that political democracy seemingly cannot survive without economic health. "Poverty is probably the principal obstacle to democratic development. The future of democracy depends on the future of economic development" (Huntington, in R. Wright, 1992a).

Ironically, Lithuania, the first republic to declare its independence from communism and the Soviet Union, has been the first to restore many communists to political power. As a result of disastrous agricultural changes instituted by reform leaders, Lithuanian voters in 1992 gave the country's new Communist Party a majority win in Parliament. On February 14, 1993, Lithuania became the first of the breakaway republics to elect a former Communist Party leader as its president (Goldberg, 1993). Since then, there has been a "resurrection" of ex-Communists in the governments of Bulgaria, the Czech Republic, Romania, Slovakia, and elsewhere throughout eastern Europe ("Ex-Communists Are Back," 1994). The Soviet Union may be history, but communism itself may yet be heard from again. People may be more loyal to concrete economic and social improvements in their lives than to abstract political ideologies.

Nationalism in the Developing World With the death of the Soviet Union and the apparent decline of developed societies such as Japan, some developing societies may be on the rise. With control over supplies of petroleum and other resources vital to the industrial and postindustrial economies of the current superpowers, they are in a position to exert considerable influence and leverage over international political and economic markets.

In some cases, developing societies have rejected modern social and cultural forms altogether, overthrowing established leaders in an attempt to return to a simpler and purer traditional way of life. The successful Shiite-led revolution against the Shah of Iran in 1979 and the establishment of postrevolutionary fundamentalist government in that country, as well as the rise of fundamentalist Islamic forces in Afghanistan and Algeria, illustrate the fact that not all societal populations accept the view that Western-style modernization necessarily represents human progress. The disenchantment of Christian fundamentalist groups with societal trends and the rise of the new conservative religious-political movement in the United States during the past two decades may indicate that not all members of our own society equate modernization with progress.

At other times, resistance to modernization has reflected a growing nationalistic spirit that rejects any form of social or political structure, whether democratic or socialist, imposed from the outside. Nationalism has been and is a significant force in many developing societies, as witness the intensity with which Serbs in Yugoslavia and the Taliban in Afghanistan have fought NATO, the United Nations, and other efforts to end their militaristic and terrorist campaigns.

Devolution and the Rise of Nationalism Nationalism has been an especially powerful unifying political force, as well as the source of many violent and bloody conflicts, in countries that once were colonial territories (Lenski, Nolan, and Lenski, 1995). According to Bernard Nietschmann (1988), World War III has been fought on a continuing basis since 1948 and has already claimed the lives of millions of people. The antagonists in these "dirty little wars" are fighting not over competing political ideologies or territory, but over issues of autonomy and independence. These conflicts revolve around a process that political scientists call **devolution**—the surrender of powers to local authorities by the central government—and are often rooted in specific historical events. As a result of the Congress of Berlin and European colonization, more than 2,000 tribes and ethnic groups became members of political states arbitrarily created by their European masters. The consequences of this partitioning were felt in the years after World War II and in the demise of imperialism.

Vanquished colonial governments were often replaced by bureaucrats who showed little concern for the diverse ethnic, linguistic, religious, and overall sociocultural composition of their newly independent populations. When local officials decided that existing political boundaries should be redrawn to reflect these cultural divisions more accurately, the fighting began.

Another way of viewing this situation is that World War III is now an over-forty-year-long second or advanced colonial revolution. The initial colonial wars led to the overthrow of foreign masters who not only dominated indigenous populations, but refused to recognize and respect their individuality. The second part of this war of independence is the continuing struggle on the part of millions of people to win their freedom from homegrown leaders who also refuse to recognize these differences and grant minority populations more autonomy or complete self-determination. Nietschmann (1988, p. 88) wrote that in the years after World War II, people throughout Africa sought decolonization but were forced to settle for recolonization "with brown and black colonial rulers instead of white." World War III, therefore, is a struggle between nations and states.

A **state,** as we saw earlier, is a political entity occupying a designated territory, with a government that has the authority and ability to use physical violence against citizens who resist its laws. A **nation** is a group of people with a common history and culture. In the developing world today, a significant number of nations are attempting to withdraw from existing states and create their own independent political entities.

One of the most bitter state-nation confrontations was the battle between Nigeria (a former British colony) and the indigenous Biafran nation. In a three-year period (1967–1970), over 1 million people were killed, and the Nigerian economy was reduced to a shambles from which it has yet to recover fully. That figure represents more than twice the number of fatalities suffered by U.S. troops in World War II and Vietnam combined. In Zaire (formerly the Belgian Congo), the province of Katanga has been fighting since 1960 to become a separate state. With independence in 1947, the Indian subcontinent was partitioned, and the newly independent state of Pakistan was created. As a result of this division, millions of Sikhs and Hindus were trapped in predominantly Muslim Pakistan, while an almost equal number of

Although Nigeria emerged as one of the world's leading producers of oil in the 1970s, a significant portion of the money made from this critical resource was lost via widespread corruption and mismanaged programs. With an annual per capita income of less than $300, the people of this sub-Saharan African country are among the poorest in the world. Markets such as this one in the Nigerian city of Ibadan are the shopping centers of the developing world where mostly impoverished people provide goods and services for other poor individuals.

From the Conflict Theory perspective, politics is a mechanism for the exercise of power and resolution of conflicts among groups or populations with different self-interests. Here, Indian Muslim women shout anti-Pakistan slogans near the Pakistan embassy in New Delhi, In June, 1999. Hundreds of people demonstrated against Pakistani-backed armed intrusion into India's side of Kashmir.

Muslims were trapped in primarily Hindu India. Almost 1 million people were killed in especially brutal fighting as the two groups attempted to leave India and Pakistan and join their religious brethren. In 1971, residents of East Pakistan, whose only link with citizens of West Pakistan was their common Islamic faith, staged a successful revolt that resulted in the formation of Bangladesh. Since 1980, the Indian government has had a series of bloody confrontations with Sikh separatists who want to secede and create the independent state of Khalistan.

Nietschmann (1988, p. 88) pointed out that nations fighting for independence are rarely known or identified by their real names; "instead they are referred to as rebels, separatists, extremists, dissidents, terrorists, tribes, minorities, or ethnic groups." For example, the Oromo in Ethiopia are called Ethiopian rebels, and the 5 million Karen people of Burma are known as terrorists. Nietschmann claimed that, in an effort to cultivate and maintain political allies, superpowers like the United States almost always side with the state in its attempts to suppress nationalistic movements.

Although wars of devolution are well underway in developing countries, industrial states are hardly immune from these conflicts. As discussed in Chapter 6, Canada faces recurring demands for an independent Quebec from French-speaking separatists whose influence continues to grow. In November 1995, voters in Quebec elected to remain in the Canadian federation by a margin of less than 1 percent, and the issue is almost certain to surface again in the future (Farnsworth, 1995). The United Kingdom may have only a short future as a political entity, as British Prime Minister Tony Blair has authorized the creation of "devolved" legislatures in Northern Ireland, Scotland, and Wales, stimulating renewed efforts for complete self-determination from those three countries. According to one observer, "Although it was never Blair's intention to set in motion a possible dissolution of the United Kingdom itself, the law of unintended consequences seems to be operating with full force" (Miller, 1998). The Basques of northern Spain were crushed by Francisco Franco's army in the 1930s, but some Spanish and French Basques are still fighting a sporadic guerilla war with their respective nations. But the most notorious examples of nationalistic-based conflicts in developed societies may be the former Soviet-bloc states of eastern Europe.

The former state of Czechoslovakia was able to negotiate an amicable "divorce" that led to the peaceful dissolution of the state and the creation of the Czech Republic and Slovakia on January 1, 1993 (Porubcansky, 1993). But, this pattern has been the exception to an otherwise bloody rule. Far more often, the area that includes the Balkans has for decades been rocked by ferocious conflicts among various ethnic groups seeking to reestablish political sovereignty over traditional ancestral homelands. (Recall our discussion in "Focus on Yugoslavia" in Chapter 6.) Similar problems have emerged throughout the former Soviet republics as old ethnic identities and hatreds have resurfaced after decades of dormancy under Soviet rule. This "explosion of tribalism" (Nye, 1992) has shaken these newly formed democracies and called into question both the viability and the desirability of unlimited self-determination for the various peoples of the world.

We live in an era when the spirit of freedom and the drive for self-determination are especially strong. Enough nationalist movements have been successful in recent history to serve as examples for all those with dreams and visions of independence. Although the rightness or wrongness of these movements can be debated on an individual or collective basis, one thing seems remarkably clear and certain: in the short term, millions of desperately poor people on both sides of these struggles will suffer as countries spend badly needed funds to try to defeat separatist movements.

Contemporary populations show tremendous social, cultural, economic, religious, historical, and geographical diversity. Given these vast differences, continuing political diversity and change are about as close to a certainty as one is likely to encounter. The assumption that any specific system represents a final, highest state of political or societal evolution reflects ethnocentrism (or at least a mistaken belief in stability) far more than social science observation. In the world of human politics, anything and all things are possible.

SUMMARY AND REVIEW

Economy as a Social Institution

1. *From a functionalist perspective, what is the role of the economy in any human society?*

From the functionalist perspective, the economy is a critical institution that allows populations to adapt to their environments by extracting resources needed for survival. With economic success, larger and more complex social organization becomes possible. (P. 246)

2. *How do conflict theorists view economy as a social institution?*

Conflict theorists such as Marx saw economies as forming the basic substructure of all societies. Economic power was the basis for social, political, and cultural power and the source of oppression of the many by the few. (P. 246)

3. *What are the four major types of economic systems found in the world today?*

Pure capitalist economies are defined by private property ownership and free markets. In welfare capitalist systems, states provide minimum market regulation to promote social stability, while otherwise permitting private enterprise. Pure socialist economies are distinguished by collective ownership of properties and regulated markets. Democratic socialist systems feature government-directed markets but widespread private property ownership. (P. 247)

4. *What is the relationship between economic development and political democracy?*

Successful economic development appears to be a necessary condition for the maintenance of political democracy. Many newly free nations in the Third World and eastern Europe face the prospects of political upheaval as their populations remain poor. (P. 247)

5. *How is the U.S. economic system currently structured?*

The U.S. economy is dominated by large, powerful corporations that control markets in manufacturing and other areas. They form the "core" of the economy, whereas smaller companies make up the "periphery." Over the past twenty years, the U.S. economy has seen a loss of manufacturing and other skilled blue-collar jobs and a rapid growth of technical and service jobs. This change has been cited as evidence of movement into a "postindustrial" form of organization, although other associated trends such as rising affluence for the workforce are not yet apparent. With the onset of a global economy, the U.S. system has become much more international. The North American Free Trade Agreement (NAFTA) has created a hemispheric trading bloc of the United States, Canada, and Mexico. (Pp. 248–249)

6. *What are the major trends in the world economy as we approach the twenty-first century?*

There are at least three trends: (1) A widening international income gap with the rich getting richer and many of the poor sinking deeper into poverty. The wealth gap between the haves and have nots of the world has doubled since 1960 and continues to grow. (2) Continuing high rates of unemployment and underemployment in a world where one in three workers does not have a job or does not earn subsistence wages (3) A possible collapse of the capitalist global system as the world faces the greatest financial challenge of the past 50 years. One reason for this dire forecast is the global overproduction of goods and services across numerous industries. (Pp. 249–250)

7. *Why have the four little dragons experienced such rapid economic growth?*

Since 1960, economic growth in Hong Kong, Taiwan, South Korea, and Singapore has surpassed that of any other developing nation. Taken as a group, these nations (in the case of Hong Kong, before it became part of China in 1997) (a) emphasize education, especially in the physical sciences and engineering, (b) have a high rate of national savings that is used for investment, (c) have stable (although not always democratic) political systems, (d) have export-based economies, and (e) have benefited from a successful Asian role model: Japan. (P. 251)

8. *What is the state of Chinese and Indian economies?*

As a result of the "responsibility system," farmers in China have earned more money than urban workers. This rural-to-urban income discrepancy contribute to the formation of the pro-democracy movement that was ruthlessly crushed by the People's Liberation Army in June, 1989. From 1980 to the late 1990s, the Chinese economy grew at a rate of almost 10 percent a year. The problem of political stability, or the collision between freewheeling capitalism and an authoritarian state will come to a head if this substantial economic growth continues.

Close to bankruptcy in 1991, the Indian economy rebounded and expanded at a healthy pace for most of the 1990s. Issues of foreign investment and the presence of multinational corporations are very controversial issues in India. How these issues are resolved will be central to the nation's economic future. (Pp. 255–257)

9. *How have Latin American countries fared economically since the end of World War II?*

Latin American countries participated in the postwar global economic upswing of the 1970s. However, the ten-year period between 1980 and 1990 (sometimes called the "lost decade") witnessed a complete reversal of economic fortunes in this region. Beginning in 1991, numerous Latin American countries (especially Mexico and Chile) made significant economic headway. By the end of the decade, Brazil's economy was near collapse and required a substantial infusion of money from the International Monetary Fund to remain solvent. In 1998, Hurricane Mitch devastated Honduras and Nicaragua, two of the poorer countries in Central America. According to some estimates, it will take these nations 50 years to recover economically. (Pp. 257–258)

10. *What is the economic forecast for sub-Saharan Africa?*

With a population of over 650 million people, sub-Saharan Africa is the fastest-growing region of the world. It is also the poorest, and prospects for significant economic growth are not encouraging. The economies of most of these countries are in shambles, unable to keep pace with current population growth much less contribute to the modernization process. Many of these nations have also been plagued by political corruption and/or internal or external conflict and war. However, there is some reason for optimism as a few nations have progressed economically, forerunners in what some have hopefully referred to as an "African Renaissance." (Pp. 258–259)

11. *What is the economic situation in Europe?*

With the demise of repressive Soviet-style regimes in eastern Europe, the nations of this region were plunged into the second great depression of the twentieth century. Economic recovery is much farther along in the "fast track" countries of Poland, Hungary, and the Czech Republic than in the remaining "slow track" nations of this region. In Russia, the transition from a centrally planned economy to capitalism has been unpredictable and chaotic as a system of inequality is forming not seen since the days of the Czar prior to the revolution of 1917.

In the early 1990s, western Europe was experiencing its worst depression since the mid-1950s although a substantial economic recovery was underway by the latter part of the decade. In January, 1999, eleven members of the European Union adopted a common currency called the "euro." Proponents of this new medium of exchange were of the opinion that it would provide a significant boost to the European Union, and that the euro would eventually rival the U.S. dollar as the world's major reserve currency. (Pp. 260–262)

Politics as a Social Institution

12. *What is the primary role of political institutions in any human society?*

In all human societies, political institutions regulate the exercise of power by various social groups. Of the various political structures in modern societies, the most significant is the state, the institution having a monopoly over the use of coercive force. (P. 263)

13. *What is "goal attainment?"*

For functionalists, the state or polity plays a critical role in "goal attainment," the process by which important societal objectives are defined, resources are allocated and mobilized toward the realization of these goals, and social control is exercised over individual actions. From this perspective, without the state, society would remain directionless and foundering, torn by widespread conflicts. (P. 263)

14. *How do Marxist conflict theorists view political structures?*

For conflict theorists such as Karl Marx, the state and other political institutions are powerful weapons used by ruling classes to preserve their own advantaged positions in the economic and social order. Laws passed and enforced by the state are seldom neutral; rather, they reflect the power and the interests of the owning classes. The net effect of the political apparatus is the protection of the societal status quo and the preservation of vested interests. (P. 263)

15. *How is political power structured in the contemporary United States?*

Sociologists have disagreed sharply on the question of how political power is structured in the United States. Radical conflict theorist C. Wright Mills saw evidence of a power elite composed of corporate, political, and military chieftains who effectively controlled decision making and dominated higher-level government. Pluralists such as David Riesman viewed political power in the United States as being dispersed among a number of groups and organizations that act as veto groups, preventing any single group or coalition from becoming dominant. Although empirical evidence often is far from conclusive, data do seem to point to a significant concentration of national and local political power in the hands of a relatively small segment of the population, drawn primarily from upper-SES (socioeconomic status) ranks. (Pp. 264–266)

16. *To what extend do people in the United States participate in the political processes of their society?*

With respect to political participation in the United States, existing data indicate a clear pattern of widespread disinterest and noninvolvement in voting, campaign activities, and other forms of political expression, especially among minorities, the young, and members of lower-SES groups. This massive apathy might be interpreted as cynicism and distrust of politics, and it creates the kind of climate in which nondemocratic, self-interested power can be exercised. (Pp. 266–268)

17. *How has modernization affected political governance?*

As societies modernized, political rule based on force and power gave way to rule based on charismatic, traditional, or rational-legal moral authority. Recent events throughout the world point to the potential instability of any political system. The Soviet Union has collapsed, and some developing societies are rising under the twin impulses of strategic resources and nationalistic movements. (Pp. 268–269)

18. *What is "devolution"?*

In the developing world, many nations are attempting to withdraw from existing political states. Violent clashes between groups seeking more independence and governments blocking such devolution have claimed the lives of millions of people over the past forty years. These confrontations are likely to continue as the spirit of freedom and self-determination spreads throughout the world. (Pp. 270–271)

12

Population, Health Care, and the Environment

Because of conflicting trends regarding the spread and treatment of numerous diseases, and the vast disparity of medical resources between rich and poor nations, the overall health of humanity is difficult if not impossible to neatly summarize. On the one hand, as Leslie Roberts (in Kemps, 1998, p. 3) of the World Resources Institute stated, "Global health is better than ever before . . . " More people than at any time in history are living longer, healthier, and more productive lives.

On the other hand, billions of people each year in developed and developing countries (especially the latter) are at risk of falling victim to both old and new, or "emerging" diseases. Three million people (mostly children) die each year from malaria, while hundreds of thousands more succumb to yellow fever and dengue fever. These airborne maladies are spread by mosquitoes, an insect the World Health Organization (WHO) has called "public-enemy-number-one." Residents of many developing countries face a dual health problem as they are subjected to diseases spread by polluted water and inadequate sanitation as well as sickness and death resulting from industrial pollution in the past 20 to 30 years (Kemps, 1998).

Physician and medical writer Laurie Garrett (1996) notes that, until recently, the medical community was of the opinion that infectious, communicable diseases could be eradicated the world over. This optimism was based on the false assumption that humankind's viral, bacterial, and parasitic enemies were "stationary targets" that could be identified and contained in a geographical area and then destroyed. In 1969, then–U.S. Surgeon General William Stewart (in Cheevers, 1995, p. A1), stated that medical researchers could "close the books on infectious diseases" and concentrate on other maladies. In other words, humanity was passing through a "health transition" as we left infectious diseases (permanently) behind, and contracted illnesses—such as heart disease, Alzheimer's disease, and cancer—that are associated with longer-lived populations in modern countries (Garrett, 1998).

The medical community has learned that some of the microbes responsible for infectious diseases have RNA and DNA codes that change under stress and can now survive doses of penicillin significantly higher than that which was needed to kill them 50 years ago. Some strains of tuberculosis (a disease many thought would be eliminated by the year 2000) are immune to 11 different drugs. Drug-resistant forms of this disease have spread to almost every nation (Cheevers, 1995; Garret, 1996). Pneumonia is increasingly becoming resistant to antibiotics as are inner-ear infections that routinely plague children. Antibiotics are rapidly losing their effectiveness in combating infectious diseases, and one physician noted that "The number of deaths in humans due to drug resistance is going to get worse before it gets better" (Levy in Cheevers, 1995, p. A1).

In a paper entitled "The Return of Infectious Diseases," Garrett (1996) stated that not only have researchers run out of ideas on how to effectively combat these deadly life forms but also, as a result of minimal profit margins, drug companies have cut back trying to discover effective mechanisms for fighting maladies that are predominantly found in developing countries. With international travel faster, less expensive, and easier today that ever before, residents of rich countries can take little comfort in the fact that the infectious disease-killing ground has, to date, been limited to the developing world. During a 1994 plague outbreak in India, more than 2,000 airline passengers arrived each day in New York City from that country (Woodall, 1997). Long before air travel became routine, the swine flu epidemic of 1918–1919 that killed millions of people worldwide traveled around the globe five times (Garrett, 1996).

If the 20 diseases that have reemerged in a deadlier, more drug-resistant form between 1973 and 1996 signal a major health problem, the 29 previously unknown or "emerging" sicknesses that have appeared during this period may well bring about a global health crisis. To date, the most well known of these diseases are HIV, hantaviruses, new strains of cholera, and Ebola (Woodall, 1997). In 1976, the Ebola virus (named after a small river in the Congo [formerly Zaire] where it was first recorded) killed 290 of the 318 people it infected—a mortality rate of 90 percent ("The Hobbled Horesman," 1995). Apart from the very high death rate, what alarmed health officials was the short incubation period—the phase in the development of a disease between initial infection and first symptoms—of from seven to twenty-one days. In addition, victims of the Ebola virus died an agonizing death. After flu-like symptoms of a headache and muscle aches, victims had severe diarrhea, vomited blood, and experienced internal hemorrhaging to such an extent that their organs turned into mush.

Whereas viruses such as Ebola and HIV were once thought of as genetic mutations, many health experts are of the opinion that these organisms have existed for decades, if not centuries. Prior to about 1960, they lay dormant, hidden away in remote jungles and rainforests. However, with rapidly increasing populations in some of the world's poorest countries, millions of acres of previously undisturbed vegetation were cleared and settled as humanity inadvertently opened up a most deadly biological Pandora's Box. Ebola-like viruses are teaching us a painful lesson: transforming Planet Earth also brings changes in the "invisible ecology" of viruses and their prey ("The Hobbled Horesman," 1995).

Wars and famines in developing countries (also caused in whole or part by overpopulation) can lead to mass migrations as people flee their impoverished surroundings. As individuals carrying emerging diseases take their maladies with them to heavily populated cities and/or push into previously uninhabited areas they exacerbate the problem. If these diseases are caused by humankind moving into the remotest areas of the planet and fueled by grinding poverty, AIDS and Ebola may only be the first of a long line of even deadlier viruses unleashed on human populations. As one prominent virologist stated regarding emerging diseases, "The primary problem is no longer virological but social" (Morese, in Cowley, 1995, p. 53).

In addition to examining the health care system in the United States and a number of environmental issues, the major focus of this chapter is the investigation of human populations. **Demography**—the scientific study of population—is an interdisciplinary subject with ties to sociology, economics, geography, business, biology, and medicine. It is used in all these disciplines to address different sets of questions and issues. As students of sociology we are primarily interested in (1) population processes (fertility, mortality, and migration), (2) the size and distribution of a population, and (3) the structure and characteristics of a population. Demography is crucial to our understanding of some of the most significant global trends over the past 250 years, such as unprecedented population growth, urbanization, and the modernization of societies across all major institutions. A knowledge of demographic trends also provides some insight into how population variables will affect societies around the world in the years to come.

Questions to Consider

1. What are the major communicable diseases in the Third World that kill tens of thousands of people each year?
2. What is the **crude birth rate,** and why is it a "crude" measure of fertility?
3. To what extent will the worldwide AIDS epidemic spread in the coming years? What countries will be most seriously affected? What subgroups of the population in the United States are most likely to contract the AIDS virus?
4. Historically, what are the most important push and pull factors affecting rural-to-urban migration?
5. What is the Malthusian theory of population growth? Was Malthus correct?
6. What is the theory of the demographic transition? Why and in what stage of the transition are most Third World countries "stuck"?
7. What are some of the major problems resulting from overpopulation in less developed countries? Can these problems be solved?
8. Why is the fertility rate declining in some developed nations?
9. Why do many people believe that "world hunger" (chronic malnutrition and starvation) is primarily a political and economic problem?
10. Why is health care in the United States so expensive? What if anything can be done about rising medical costs?
11. How does economic development contribute to environmental problems?
12. With so much water on the planet, why is the world facing a growing water scarcity problem?
13. What is *desertification* and what are its main causes?
14. What are *greenhouse gases* and what are their effects on the global environment?
15. Why is radioactive waste such a serious threat to human well-being?
16. What is *sustainable development*?

FERTILITY

The term **fertility** refers to the number of children born to women in a given population. The fertility rate is a function of two factors, one biological and the other social. The biological component is called **fecundity;** that is, the physical ability to conceive and bear children. For most women, this period lasts approximately thirty-three years, between the ages of 12 and 45. Fecundity may be thought of as a necessary but not sufficient condition of fertility. In other words, the fact that a woman is able to give birth does not mean that she will, nor does it determine how many children she will bear.

The number of children to whom a woman will give birth is related to a series of psychological and, especially, social factors in her environment. Kingsley Davis and Judith Blake (1956) cited social factors such as race, religion, and education that are powerful yet indirect influences on fertility. Their effects are filtered through a group of intermediate variables such as age at first intercourse, the use of contraception, and induced abortion. William Pratt and colleagues (1984) modified the Davis and Blake schema and devised three sets of intermediate variables. **Intercourse variables** concern the commencement of and frequency of sexual activity over a given period of time. For example, the more time spent in marriage, the more likely a woman will become pregnant. Data for the United States indicate that if a marriage is broken, a woman's fertility will be lower than if the union had remained intact (Weeks, 1999).

Similarly, the longer marriage is postponed, the fewer children a woman is likely to have. Beginning in the 1960s and 1970s, large numbers of American women pursued a college education (and advanced degrees) and had high occupational goals, resulting in both delayed marriage and a lower rate of fertility. Because they postponed starting a family in favor of having a career, many women in their late thirties and forties are now worried that their "biological clock" is rapidly winding down and they will never have children. The term **biological clock** refers to the ages between which women are physically able to conceive; it is said to wind down when women reach the upper limits of fecundity, approximately 45 years of age.

Fertility is also influenced by a number of **conception variables,** especially contraception. It is common knowledge that the widespread use of contraceptive devices (artificial infertility) reduces the number of live births in a given population. The oral contraceptive pill, intrauterine device, condom, and diaphragm are all considered highly effective methods of birth control and have been used by tens of millions of people (especially in modern, industrial societies). The presence (and duration) or absence of breast-feeding can also have a significant impact on fertility. The average woman will not become pregnant for about two months (a period of infecundity) after the birth of a child; however, a woman who is breast-feeding her children might not conceive for between ten and eighteen months. Fertility rates in many areas of the less developed world would be significantly higher were it not for this innate yet socially determined method of birth control. In other words, the length of time a woman breast-feeds her child (if she does at all) is largely a function of the customs of her social group.

Pregnancy or **gestation variables** (miscarriage, stillbirth, induced abortion) determine whether a fetus will come to term resulting in a live birth. Induced abortion is undoubtedly humanity's oldest and most frequently used form of birth control. The number of legally induced abortions in the United States increased from 750,000 in 1973 to almost 1.6 million in 1988 before declining to 1.27 million in 1994 (O'Connor, 1998). Women between the ages of 20 and 24 account for approximately 33 percent of abortions performed annually, with the next most numerous age bracket for ending a pregnancy by this method 25 to 29 years of age (22 percent of abortions). About 78 percent of females obtaining an abortion in any given year are unmarried, with black women having an abortion rate in 1994 that was more than three times as high as that of white women (43 abortions per 1,000 as opposed to 13 abortions per 1,000 women). Inasmuch as an unknown number of abortions are not officially recorded (so called "backalley" abortions) each year, abortion statistics released by the Centers for Disease Control are "conservative estimates" and, therefore, lower than the actual number performed (O'Connor, 1998).

Fertility Measures

Now that we have seen how birth rates can be affected by numerous social factors and intervening variables, it is time to examine how demographers measure fertility. The most commonly used statistic is the *crude birth rate (CBR)*—the number of births per year per every 1,000 members of the population. This statistic is aptly called crude because it does not take into consideration a society's age structure or, more specifically, the number of people in a given population who are actually at risk of having children. For example, a typical rich industrial nation may have 15 percent of its population in the childbearing years (15 to 45), whereas in a poor, underdeveloped country that figure may be 30 percent. An actual CBR of 20 would be *high* for the developed nation (in which only 15 percent of the population were in their reproductive years), while the same figure would be *low* for the developing country (in which twice that number were at risk of having children). The poor countries of the world have much younger populations and, consequently, a larger percentage of women of childbearing age. The CBRs of these countries as a group is 26 (births per 1,000 people) with some nations having rates of 50 or more (Chad, Mali, and Somalia). In contrast, some European nations with much older populations have CBRs as low as 8 (Latvia) and 9 (Russia, the Czech Republic, and Italy).

MORTALITY

The size and structure of the population are also affected by the number of people who die. The three major reasons why individuals die in any society are that they degenerate, they are killed by communicable diseases, and they are killed by products of the social and physical environment. The term *degeneration* refers to the biological deterioration of the body. In modern societies such as the United States, the primary degenerative diseases are cardiovascular or heart disease and cancer (see Table 12.1). These two maladies, as Joseph McFalls (1998, p. 14) notes, "are in a league by themselves" and account for approximately 55 percent of all deaths in the United States each year.

Physical degeneration leading to death can be accelerated by an individual's lifestyle and personal habits. For example, the World Health Organization estimates that tobacco products kill about two million people annually in the developed world, a figure that will increase to roughly three million individuals a year in 2020. During this same time period, cigarette-smoking-related deaths in developing nations will grow from one to seven million a year. A World Bank Development Report (in Frankel, 1996, p. 11) stated that "Unless smoking behavior changes, three decades from now, premature deaths caused by tobacco in the developing world will exceed the expected deaths from AIDS, tuberculosis, and the complications of childbirth combined." A study entitled the "Global Burden of Disease," the first comprehensive investigation of how people die, estimated that by 2020, 8.4 million people will be dying annually from cigarette-smoking-related diseases, making it the single largest cause of death across the world (in Maugh III, 1996). Smoking kills more people in this country each year (approximately 440,000) than the total number of Americans who died in battle during World War II and Vietnam combined.

One of the more interesting and relevant areas of research concerning mortality is the relationship be-

TABLE 12.1

The 15 Major Causes of Death: United States, 1995

			Ratio of Rates	
Cause of Death	Deaths per 100,000	Percent of all deaths	Male to female	Black to white
1. Heart Disease	280.7	31.9	1.8	1.5
2. Cancer	204.9	23.3	1.4	1.4
3. Stroke	60.1	6.8	1.2	1.8
4. Lung disease	39.2	4.5	1.5	0.8
5. Accidents[a]	35.5	4.0	2.5	1.3
6. Pneumonia and influenza	31.6	3.6	1.6	1.4
7. Diabetes	22.6	2.6	1.2	2.4
8. HIV/AIDS	16.4	1.9	5.0	4.7
9. Suicide	11.9	1.4	4.5	0.6
10. Liver disease	9.6	1.1	2.4	1.3
11. Kidney disease	9.0	1.0	1.5	2.8
12. Homicide/legal intervention	8.7	1.0	3.7	6.1
13. Septicemia	8.0	0.9	1.2	2.7
14. Alzheimer's disease	7.8	0.9	1.0	0.7
15. Atherosclerosis	6.4	0.7	1.4	1.0

[a]Unintentional injuries

Note: the male/female and black/white ratios are for age-adjusted rates.

Source: National Center for Health Statistics. *Monthly Vital Statistics Report* 45, no. 11. Supplement 2 (June 12, 1997): tables 6, 7, 10, and 12. In "Population: A Lively Introduction," by Joseph A. McFalls, Jr. Population Reference Bureau 1998, Washington, DC.

Chapter 12 • Population, Health Care, and the Environment

tween economic inequality and health/mortality. Investigators in the United States, Canada, and Britain have discovered that societies with a high degree of economic inequality are more unhealthy (and have higher death rates) than are societies characterized by less economic inequality. Higher death rates in societies of the first type are not found just in the lower classes (as one might expect), but for the "bulk" of the population (Lardner, 1998b). In Japan, for example, a nation with a relatively small gap between rich and poor, people live longer than in any other country in the world even though Japanese men are twice as likely to smoke (and have lower rates of cancer) than American men. Great Britain and the United States have the highest degree of economic inequality among developed nations and the lowest life expectancy of countries in that group. By way of an explanation for this relation, James Lardner (1998b, p. 22) speculates that "when a society creates steep discrepancies in income and wealth, it excites a preoccupation with material pleasures, money, and status, and aggravates feelings of anxiety and inferiority that (it is all too accurate to say) eat away at people."

In a small Pennsylvania town in the 1950s, the mostly Italian immigrants who lived there had a very low incidence of heart attacks although they smoked heavily and cooked with lard (high in saturated fats) on a regular basis. The lifestyle of these people was one of strong in-group solidarity and closeness. Engaged in a more individualistic, materialistic life style, the sons and daughters of these immigrants had a heart-attack fatality rate that was as high as that of people in neighboring towns (Larder, 1998b).

Medical experts disagree on (1) the upper limits of human longevity, and (2) if it is possible by way of medical technology and bioengineering to extend these limits. Although there have been claims of people living to age 130 and longer, none of these cases have been substantiated. The longest-lived person (authenticated case) was a French woman who died in 1997 at the age of 122 years and five months (McFalls, 1998).

The Specter of AIDS

Acquired immune deficiency syndrome (AIDS) is a communicable disease contracted directly from another person through sexual activity or by contact with infected blood (usually through a transfusion or intravenous drug use). Pregnant women infected with the virus can transfer the disease to their babies; HIV is also transmitted from mother to child via breastmilk. AIDS is caused by the human immunodefiency virus (HIV), new strains of which continue to be discovered.

The Centers for Disease Control (CDC) in Atlanta estimated that worldwide more than 30 million people were living with the HIV/AIDS virus in 1999. According to projections of the Global Policy Coalition, between 60 and 70 million people will be HIV positive in the year 2000 ("AIDS Information," 1998). By the year 2001 the direct (medical) and indirect (loss of productivity) costs of the disease are expected to be more than $50 billion (Garrett, 1996). Since the epidemic was first diagnosed in the 1980s, through December 1999, 16.3 million people have died from AIDS. Of this number, 84 percent (13.7 million) resided in Sub-Saharan Africa, the continent hit hardest by this disease (Bartholet, 2000). Of the current infected population, 41 percent are females and 3.6 percent are children under 15 years of age.

Over the past 15 years the AIDS epidemic appears to be stabilizing in some countries (the United

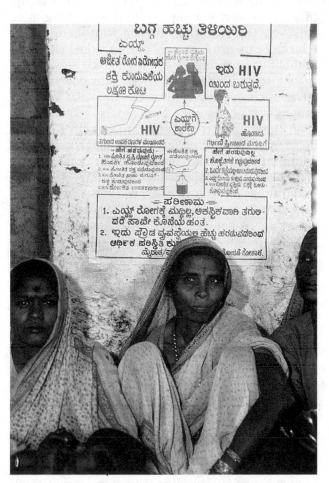

AIDS is rapidly becoming a major health problem in India. These women in a local health clinic sit below a poster stating that the HIV virus is spread via sexual intercourse, intravenous drug use, and contaminated blood. For lower class and caste AIDS victims in the poorest countries of the world, medical help for their malady is all but nonexistent.

States), declining in others (Thailand and Uganda), while increasing rapidly in still other nations and regions (Africa, India, and China) (Altman, 1996; Altman, 1997; Horowitz, 1998). In nine Sub-Saharan countries 12 percent or more of the population of adults 15 to 49 years of age are living with HIV/AIDS. In Botswana and Zimbabwe, the nations with the most serious AIDS problem, those numbers are 25 and 26 percent respectively (Bartholet, 2000). Since the epidemic first struck that country, life expectancy in Botswana has declined from 70 years to 41 years with that figure expected to plummet to 33 years, approximately the same as that for the global population at the time of Christ.

In 2000, there were 10.4 million African children under 15 who had lost their mothers or both parents to AIDS. By the year 2010, there could be as many as 40 million such orphans. In Rwanda, where a bloody civil war in the mid-1990s claimed up to one million lives, many women who lost their husbands in the fighting are now sharing men in order to have more children. This behavior, coupled with the Church's reluctance to distribute condoms in a predominantly Catholic country, has greatly facilitated the spread of AIDS ("Millions of Rwandans Threatened by AIDS," 1998). As is the case in Rwanda, HIV/AIDS is spread primarily via heterosexual intercourse in Africa.

In Russia and the Ukraine, the number of HIV-infected people has increased dramatically after the fall of the Soviet Union in 1991. Most of the victims contracted this disease through intravenously injected drugs or heterosexual prostitution, two activities that became much more prevalent once the Soviet police-state collapsed. The unofficial number of Russians infected may be 10 times as high as the official statistics claim, since the country cannot pay its soldiers and retirees, much less put money into AIDS prevention and treatment programs (Kaminski and Palchikoff, 1997). Speaking of the AIDS problem in his country, one Russian medical researcher stated, "It's as if we're standing on the beach and watching a giant wave coming right at us. We know it, we see it, and we can do almost nothing about it. We're just going to get swept away" (Kaminski and Palchikoff, 1997, p. 45).

As of December 1998, just over 688,000 people in the United States were known to have the AIDS virus, and 413,576 Americans have died from the disease. Between 650,000 to 900,000 individuals are thought to be HIV positive. This translates to about 0.3 percent of the population, or 1 in 300 Americans of all ages. New York, California, Florida, Texas, and New Jersey combined account for almost 58 percent of all the AIDS cases in this country, with New York City alone contributing just under 16 percent to the

TABLE 12.2

AIDS Cases by Race or Ethnicity

Race or Ethnicity	# of AIDS Cases	% of Aids Cases
White, not Hispanic	288,541	45.00
Black, not Hispanic	230,029	35.90
Hispanic	115,354	18.00
Asian/Pacific Islander	4,589	.01
American Indian/ Alaska Native	1,783	.007
Race/ethnicity unknown	790	.001
Total	641,086	99.0*

*Does not add up to 100% because percentages were rounded off.

Source: Centers for Disease Control, 1998.

national total. ("Magnitude of the Epidemic" 1998; "Statistical Projections/Trends" 2000).

Of the total number of AIDS cases known to the CDC, at the time of diagnosis 75.2 percent were between the ages of 25 and 44. While young to middle-aged adults are most likely to be AIDS victims in the U.S., so too are members of particular minority communities (see Table 12.2). Although they comprise only 13 percent of the population, African Americans account for 35.9 of known AIDS cases. Similarly, 18 percent of known AIDS victims are Hispanic Americans while that ethnic group makes up only 11 percent of the nation's population. An examination of the AIDS-infected population by race and gender yields the following profile ("A Closer Look at Trends by Race and Gender," 1998):

African-American Men   Of the over 17,000 individuals in this category diagnosed with the disease in 1996, 40 percent were men who had sex with men (MSM), 38 percent contracted AIDS by way of intravenous drug use (IDU), and 13 percent were infected via heterosexual intercourse.

African-American Women   Of the 6,750 women in this category, 53 percent were infected through IDU and 43 percent via heterosexual intercourse. Most of the women in this latter group who contracted the disease were infected by male intravenous drug users.

Hispanic Men 8,680 men were diagnosed with AIDS in 1996, with 45 percent classified as MSM, and 38 percent getting the disease by injecting drugs.

Hispanic Women   The approximately 2,200 Hispanic women diagnosed with AIDS in 1996 contracted the malady by heterosexual contact (60 percent) and IDU (37 percent).

White Men Almost 19,000 white males were diagnosed with AIDS in 1996. Seventy-five percent of the infections were attributed to MSM, 8 percent to IDU, and 3 percent to heterosexual intercourse. The latter two categories have accounted for an increasing number of AIDS cases among white males over the past 10 years.

White Females Although they comprise a significant portion of the total population, white females accounted for only 2,390 of the reported AIDS cases in 1996. Fifty-one percent of these women were infected via heterosexual intercourse and 43 percent by way of IDU.

While AIDS is increasing among minorities and low-income women, 1996 marked the first year the disease decreased with new cases down 6 percent from the previous year and deaths having declined 25 percent from 1995 to 1996. Approximately one of every 300 Americans is infected with HIV. New treatments have slowed both the progression from HIV to AIDS as well as from AIDS to death among the HIV-infected population ("Trends in the HIV and AIDS Epidemic, 1998," 1998). The decline in AIDS deaths is due in large measure to a new group of drugs (protease inhibitors) that slow the progression of HIV. Unfortunately, the drugs are difficult to take (requiring as many as 20 daily doses on a precise schedule), can result in unpleasant side effects, and do not work for everyone (Haney, 1998; Schultz, 1998). Protease inhibitors are also very expensive with the cost of the drug including tests and related expenses running as high as $20,000 annually (Clark and Knestout, 1997).

Researchers have discovered that although some individuals are routinely exposed to HIV, they do not contract the disease, that is, their bodies seem to have some natural immunity. When combined, two known genetic mutations in the same individual are believed to provide resistance to HIV. Some scientists are of the opinion this is the same mutation that protected some people from the bubonic plague of the fourteenth century—a plague that killed millions of people as it ravaged Europe and parts of Asia. Up to 15 percent of the white population may have this mutation that appears to be absent among blacks and Asians ("Mutations May Have Foiled Plague," 1998). Researchers are trying to re-create this genetic tendency in laboratory animals as a first step toward developing a vaccine that will prevent HIV from taking hold in humans (Schultz, 1998). According to this strategy, inasmuch as the virus cannot be eliminated, it may be successfully contained.

Whereas mutations in the human population offer new hope in combatting AIDS, the virus is mutating as well, making it that much harder to control. At the twelfth International AIDS Conference in Geneva in 1998, scientists presented evidence of a new HIV/AIDs "superbug" that is "potentially untouchable" by new drugs and that can be readily transmitted from person to person (Krieger, 1998; Schultz, 1998). As one observer noted regarding the "inventive AIDS virus," "It dodges. It hides. When cornered, it simply re-creates itself" (Krieger, 1998).

Mortality Measures

Demographers also have a series of statistics for measuring mortality. The most frequently cited is the **crude death rate (CDR)**—the number of deaths per year for every 1,000 members of the population. Like the crude birth rate, the CDR does not take into account the age composition of the population. The rates in developed countries like the United States, Japan, and France are relatively low, even though these nations have older populations. These rates are the result of high-quality medical care, few deaths resulting from nutritional deficiencies, and the ability to control communicable diseases like cholera and diphtheria. The CDR of the world's developed *and* developing nations in 1999 was 9 (per 1,000) population.

In developing nations the CDR ranged from a low of 2 in Jordan and Qatar, to 24 in Malawi and 30 in Sierra Leone. In other words, the poor nations of the world have CBRs both *lower* and *higher* than those of the rich nations. The low rates are the result of two factors. First, because they are growing so rapidly, developing nations have very young populations, with up to 50 percent of their citizens (Libya) under 15 years of age. Young people die at a much lower rate than older individuals. Second, communicable diseases have been controlled effectively in much of the Third World. The ability to minimize death from epidemics is a function of modernization and the work of agencies like the World Health Organization—for example, the immunization of millions of people from infectious diseases in the years after World War II. However, mortality did not fall at the same rate in all Third World countries. For a variety of reasons (political, economic, and environmental), the CBR of countries like Malawi and Sierra Leone are still high. But on the whole, the death rate in these developing nations has declined significantly in a short period of time. Between the early 1960s and 1970s (excluding China), it fell from 17 to 12, and by 1999 it was down to 9.

Another often-cited mortality statistic is the *infant mortality rate,* the number of deaths in the first year of life per 1,000 live births. This statistic clearly and tragically indicates the differences in income, education, health care, and nutrition that exist between

In many societies funerals are elaborate events marking the transition from one form of existence to another. This corpse being carried through the streets of an Indian city will probably be cremated on a funeral pyre. Inasmuch as only wealthy families can afford this ceremony in a nation where wood is very expensive, the bodies of poor people are typically wrapped in a clean white cloth and slipped into a river.

rich and poor nations. For example, the infant mortality rate for developed countries in 1998 is 8, being especially low in nations like Finland (3.5) and Japan (3.8). The U.S. rate is 7.0, a figure that differs significantly by social class. Children born to poor females in this country are much more likely to die in the their first year than are children of more affluent mothers. Although infant mortality has continued to drop in developing nations, children in Third World countries are much more likely to die in the first year of life than those in rich countries. In 1998, developing nations had an infant mortality rate of 64 per 1,000 (down from 84 in 1988), with twenty-one African nations having rates over 100 in that same year. The infant mortality rate in Sierra Leone (195) was 56 times higher than the rate in Finland (3.5).

Social Correlates of Mortality

In our discussion of mortality, we have examined some of the major causes of death in the United States. By way of conclusion, we will look at a number of social correlates of death in this country. Although death may appear to be a random phenomenon, data indicate that mortality rates differ significantly from one segment of the population to another. Studies from which the following summary statistic statements are drawn were compiled by McFalls, (1998, pp. 14–16), Weeks, (1999), and Sobieraj (1998):

1. As education, occupational prestige, and income increase, death rates decrease. This relationship between social status and mortality exists in virtually all societies. In the United States, white males with at least one year of college have a lower risk of death than men with lesser educational achievements. The difference between these two groups was greatest for accidental deaths. Weeks (1999) notes that educated men are more likely to avoid dangerous, high-risk situations.

2. Primarily because they are often economically disadvantaged, racial and ethnic minorities typically have higher mortality rates than white Americans. With one-third of African Americans living below the poverty line, many blacks do not have job-related health insurance nor can they afford to pay for medical treatment out of pocket. Undiagnosed illnesses are more likely to turn into life-threatening situations. Minority death rates may also be a function of lifestyle and diet. Hispanic men are a two to three times more likely to die of stomach cancer than white men. In 1900, whites lived about 15 years longer than blacks, with the gap between the two races reduced to seven years by 1996. Native Americans live on average four fewer years than whites while Hispanic longevity is about the same as the national average. Asian Americans born in this country live significantly longer than whites.

3. As in most other countries, married people in the U.S. tend to outlive their unmarried counterparts. One (partial) explanation for this finding is that physically ill and handicapped people are less likely to marry as well as have a higher risk of death because of their health problems. Single individuals also have a higher rate of consumption of "socially approved narcotics" such as alcohol and cigarettes, drugs that can significantly shorten one's life.

4. As a group, women live almost seven years longer than men. While a portion of this longevity discrepancy is a function of lifestyle (for example, more men than women smoke), one component of this gender gap is the possibility that "a real biological superiority exists for women"—that is, women may have a superior immune system related to the hormone estrogen (Weeks, 1999).

This final statement has to do with life expectancy—the statistical average length of time a person in a given population can expect to live. In the developed world, life expectancy is 75 years, in the developing nations, it is 63 (52 in sub-Saharan Africa). A female born in Japan in 1998 can expect to live eighty-four years (the highest in the world) compared to 36 (for both sexes) in Malawi (the lowest in the world). Of course many people in that African nation are over 36 years of age; however, the *average* life span of an individual in Malawi is drastically reduced if all of the children who die in the first year of life are factored into the equation. Once a child makes it through that first dangerous year, his/her chances of living past age 36 increase dramatically. Those who reach their fifth birthday (another significant milestone) will live even longer.

Inasmuch as the life expectancy of an individual is affected by both biological and social variables, the fact that the Japanese as a group can expect to live over twice as long as people in Malawi is best explained by a number of socioeconomic factors. Levels of income, technology, nutrition, education, and health care are vastly superior in a country such as Japan. Another important reason for longevity differences between developed and developing nations in the high rate of infant mortality in the latter.

MIGRATION

We tend to think of population growth solely in terms of the relation between fertility and mortality. However, the movement of people from one location to another affects not only the rate of growth, but also the distribution of the population. The study of geographic mobility or migration is one of the major subareas of demography. **Migration** is defined as the relatively permanent movement of people from one place to another.

As students of society, sociologists are concerned with the reasons people move, as well as the number of individuals who change their place of residence. Migration is usually the result of social, political, or economic conditions. One or more of these conditions may push or pull individuals and groups, resulting in streams of migrants moving within or across national boundaries. **Push factors** serve to drive off or send a stream of migrants from a particular locale. **Pull factors** are socioeconomic magnets and draw migrants to a given geographical area. Historically, some of the more important push factors have been the decline of natural resources in an area, loss of employment, persecution (racial, religious, political), and natural disasters (flood, fire, drought, famine). When people decide to leave an area, they search for a location that will enhance life chances for themselves and their children. The most important pull factors are increased opportunity for employment and income, better living conditions (climate, housing, schools, health), and the possibility of new and different activities (Bogue, 1969).

Internal and International Migration

Demographers make a distinction between internal and international migration. **Internal migration** is the movement of one group of people within a political state or country. The United States, Gober (1993, p. 2) notes, has always been a nation of movers as "geographic mobility is embedded in the America national character. In the United States, moving has always been synonymous with moving on." The average American will move about 11 times during the course of a lifetime, a slight decline from prior periods of our history. Demographer Joseph McFalls (1998) notes that an increase in the number of people who own their homes, coupled with a rise in housing costs and an aging population, are all factors associated with this decrease in movement.

Migration is a selective process along a number of dimensions. People are more likely to move at certain stages of their lives—upon getting married, divorced, or retiring, for example—than at others. Although African Americans and Hispanic Americans move more often than whites, the former groups tend to move shorter distances than the latter (McFalls, 1998). Individuals with the highest and lowest levels of educational achievement (measured by years of school completed) are more likely to move than people in the academic mid-range. College-educated people tend to make long-distance moves, while people with less than a high school education are apt to make local moves. This is why African Americans and Hispanic Americans (as a whole) with less formal education than white Americans make more local and relatively short-distance moves that white Americans (McFalls, 1998). Finally, young people between the late teenage years and early 30s have the highest rate of geographic movement as these individuals leave home to marry, attend school, find jobs, or in some way strike out on their own (McFalls, 1998).

Large-scale **international migration**—the movement of people across political states—is a relatively recent phenomenon in human history, occurring for the most part over the past 400 years (Bouvier and Gardner, 1986). One of the largest migrations in history began in the 1800s and continued for the remainder of the century when approximately 60 million Europeans left their homelands and embarked for the "New World," with the majority of these travelers heading for the United States. Demographer Hal Kane (1995, p. 25) argues that we are entering a historical period of accelerated migration when "as many people can move in one year as moved in entire centuries."

This unprecedented movement of people is the result of numerous factors including (1) The demise of the former Soviet Union and the stranglehold it had on eastern European countries such as Poland and Hungary. Political freedom in these nations means that people are able to pursue economic opportunity in more affluent neighboring countries, notably Germany and Austria. (2) Wars that produce refugees, especially in the developing regions where 92 percent of post–World War II conflicts have occurred. For example, in the mid-1990s, tens of thousands of Rwandan refugees fled their war-ravaged country for safety in Zaire and Tanzania. (3) Rapid population growth in developing countries has led to environmental degradation (producing "environmental refugees"). (4) Other population-related problems such as high unemployment, high rates of violent crime, dilapidated housing, or no housing at all have driven people from their homelands. (5) Natural disasters, most notably famines and floods, have forced people to seek more hospitable areas.

Illegal Immigration

Each year almost 800,000 foreign-born people enter the United States (to live and work) legally, while another 200,000 to 300,000 individuals make their way into this country illegally for the same reasons (Bayer, 1997). As a result of rapid population growth and a myriad of related problems, hundreds of thousands of Mexican nationals as well as people from Central American countries were "pushed" from their homelands and "pulled" to the United States in search of greater economic and social opportunities. In 1960, there were slightly fewer than 600,000 Mexican-born people residing in the United States, a number that increased to over 7 million in the mid-1990s. While many of these people arrived via an unlawful entry, most are now in the United States legally as a result of the federal amnesty program of 1987–1988 (McDonnell, 1998a, 1998b). The approximately $4 *billion* Mexicans in the U.S. (both legally and illegally) send home each year is their country's second-largest source of foreign capital behind oil-generated revenue.

Table 12.3 is an estimate of the number of illegal immigrants in the United States from the top 20

TABLE 12.3

Estimated United States Illegal Immigrant Population for Top Twenty Countries of Origin and Top Twenty States of Residence: October 1996

Country of Origin	Population	State of Residence	Population
All Countries	5,000,000	All States	5,000,000
1. Mexico	2,700,000	1. California	2,000,000
2. El Salvador	335,000	2. Texas	700,000
3. Guatemala	165,000	3. New York	540,000
4. Canada	120,000	4. Florida	350,000
5. Haiti	105,000	5. Illinois	290,000
6. Philippines	95,000	6. New Jersey	135,000
7. Honduras	90,000	7. Arizona	115,000
8. Poland	70,000	8. Massachusetts	85,000
9. Nicaragua	70,000	9. Virginia	55,000
10. Bahamas	70,000	10. Washington	52,000
11. Colombia	65,000	11. Colorado	45,000
12. Ecuador	55,000	12. Maryland	44,000
13. Dominican Republic	50,000	13. Michigan	37,000
14. Trinidad & Tobago	50,000	14. Pennsylvania	37,000
15. Jamaica	50,000	15. New Mexico	37,000
16. Pakistan	41,000	16. Oregon	33,000
17. India	33,000	17. Georgia	32,000
18. Dominica	32,000	18. District of Columbia	30,000
19. Peru	30,000	19. Connecticut	29,000
20. Korea	30,000	20. Nevada	24,000
Other	744,000	Other	330,000

Source: United States Department of Justice, 1998

countries of origin as well as their top 20 states of residence once they arrive in this country. For example, of the 5 million people in this country illegally in 1996, 2.7 million came from Mexico. California has the largest illegal immigrant population with 2 million such individuals followed by Texas with 700,000 undocumented residents. The Bureau of the Census recognizes three categories of people who are in the United States illegally: *Settlers* come to the United States on a more permanent basis; *sojourners* such as farm laborers do seasonal work and then return home; and *commuters* cross the border on a daily basis (Bouvier and Gardner 1986). Settlers often come to the United States by way of "chain migration." That is, a small number of immigrants establish themselves in a particular community, and then send for, or inform individuals back home of their presence. The newcomers now have a destination where friends and relatives are somewhat established. Chain migration occurs for both legal and illegal as well as international and internal migrants (McFalls, 1998; McDonnell 1998a).

POPULATION COMPOSITION

The Sex Ratio

Demographers are interested in the composition of a population as well as its size and rate of growth. A simple summary statistic that tells us a great deal about a given society is the **sex ratio (SR)**—the number of males per 100 females in a population. A sex ratio of 100 (balanced) means that there are an equal number of males and females. In 1910, the SR of the United States was 106, indicating a surplus of males (106 males for every 100 females). This imbalance was due in large part to the disproportionate number of males who immigrated to America around the turn of the century. By 1986, the SR had declined to 95.2, revealing a surplus of females and indicating the fact that women live longer than men in the United States as they do in almost every society.

The SR and population growth rate can also tell us something about people's chances of getting married in a given society. More males are born than females; but because males also have a higher mortality rate, by age 20 to 24 years, the SR is "balanced" (100). From age 25 and up, there is a surplus of females; and because American women marry men two or three years older than themselves, there are not enough men to go around. During the baby boom years (1946–1964), each year's crop of babies was bigger that the year before, meaning that still

fewer males two or three older were available for American women to choose from when they were of marriageable age.

The Age-Sex or Population Pyramid

Another important device for understanding the composition of a population is an **age-sex** or **population pyramid,** which summarizes the age and sex characteristics of a given society. Figure 12.1 presents age-sex pyramids for Kenya, the United States, and Italy. The Kenyan pyramid is also called a "true" pyramid and indicates a rapidly growing population with each cohort (group) larger than the preceding one. Societies with age-sex pyramids like that of Kenya (most developing nations) will continue to grow for the foreseeable future. In fifteen years all of the females 14 years of age and younger will be between 15 and 29, their peek reproductive years. There are so many young people in a nation like Kenya that if each couple were to have only two children (replacement level), the population would continue to grow for many years. The narrowing near the top of the Kenyan pyramid indicates that the death rate in developing countries for middle-aged and older people is much higher than the death rate in rich countries.

The age pyramids of the United States and Italy tell a very different story. They illustrate populations that are aging and have a slow rate of growth (the United States), or negative growth (Italy). Regarding Italy, the 1990–1994 cohort was only half the size of the 1965–1969 group (McFalls, 1998). With a relatively small percentage of females (potential mothers) under age 19, fertility rates in countries like the U.S. and (especially) Italy will remain low for at least a generation. The large cohorts in the U.S. pyramid represent the baby boomers born between 1946 and 1964. The aging of this large group (80 million people) combined with a low fertility rate indicates that the U.S. population is growing old. The median age in this country in 1970 was 27.9, meaning that half of the population were younger and half were older than this number. By 1997, increased longevity and the aging of boomers raised the median age to 34.9 years. In slow-growth Sweden the median age is 38, while in the rapidly growing African nation of Niger the median age of the population is only 16.

The U.S. Bureau of the Census predicts that the number of elderly individuals will continue to increase until at least the year 2050, when the median age of the population could be as high as 48.2 years. Beginning in 2010, the baby boom generation will trigger a "senior boom," with more than 50 million Americans over the age 65 by the year 2020. The estimate

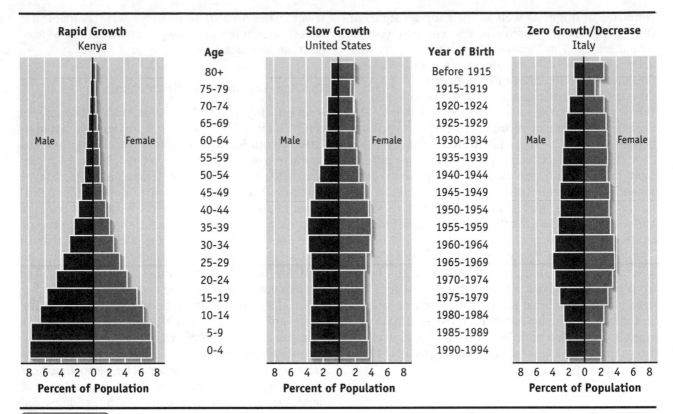

Rapid Growth	Age	Slow Growth	Year of Birth	Zero Growth/Decrease
Kenya		United States		Italy
	80+		Before 1915	
	75-79		1915-1919	
	70-74		1920-1924	
	65-69		1925-1929	
Male Female	60-64	Male Female	1930-1934	Male Female
	55-59		1935-1939	
	50-54		1940-1944	
	45-49		1945-1949	
	40-44		1950-1954	
	35-39		1955-1959	
	30-34		1960-1964	
	25-29		1965-1969	
	20-24		1970-1974	
	15-19		1975-1979	
	10-14		1980-1984	
	5-9		1985-1989	
	0-4		1990-1994	

8 6 4 2 0 2 4 6 8 — **Percent of Population** 8 6 4 2 0 2 4 6 8 — **Percent of Population** 8 6 4 2 0 2 4 6 8 — **Percent of Population**

FIGURE 12.1

Population Pyramids: Kenya, United States, and Italy, 1995

Sources: U.S. Bureau of the Census. "U.S. Population Estimates by Age, Sex, Race, and Hispanic Origin: 1990 to 1995," PPL-41 (Feb. 14, 1996); (United States): Council of Europe, *Recent Demographic Developments in Europe* 1997:Table 1-1 (Italy) United Nations: *The Sex and Age Distribution of the World Populations—The 1996 Revision: 500–1* (Kenya). *In* "Population: A Lively Introduction," by Joseph A. McFalls, Jr. Population Reference Bureau, 1998, (Washington, DC).

of the number of elderly people in the first half of the twenty-first century is probably accurate because these people are alive today, and only mortality rates need be considered (Soldo and Agree, 1988). Predicting the median age of the population in the next 50 years is much more difficult because (unknown) fertility rates must be estimated and factored into the equation.

POPULATION OF THE UNITED STATES

Over the past 30 years there have been at least four significant (and ongoing) population trends in the United States, the third largest country in the world with 275 million inhabitants in the year 2000: (1) a movement of people from cities to suburbs (to be discussed in the next chapter); (2) a movement of millions of Americans south and west in the 1980s and 1990s, continuing a pattern of migration that began in the 1970s; (3) in some areas of the country, a rapidly increasing minority population; and (4) the

aging of the nation. Nine of the ten states with the largest population increase in the 1980s were in the southern and western regions of the country. In the 1990s, this trend continued, with growth in the mountain and western states ranging from 14 percent in New Mexico to 40 percent in Nevada (Van Slambrouck, 1998). According to one projection, California's population is expected to increase by some 18 million individuals (approximately the size of New York State) from 33 million in 1998 to 51 million in 2025. As one observer noted, "We know that California, Texas, and Florida are the mega-states of today and tomorrow . . . " (Mann, in Wilgoren, 1998, p. A24). The movement of people to the south and west also results in a shift of political power as congressional seats are lost by eastern and midwestern states and gained by Sunbelt states.

While the overall quality of life in the suburbs is usually thought to be superior to that of the cities (especially the inner cities), this is not always the case. Some suburban areas are now part slum and part suburb, and constitute a new residential pattern that

Edwin Bailey (in Clifford, Roark, and Horstman, 1991) calls a **sluburb.** A partial explanation for this phenomenon is that suburbs are becoming ports of entry for poor (mainly minority-group) immigrants. In other words, the path of residential mobility from the central city to suburbs typical of movement in years past is no longer the only road to the outer environs. This rapid influx of relatively poor people to the suburbs is putting a tremendous strain on social services (schools in particular) in some communities.

Whereas millions of African Americans migrated from the South to cities of the North and Midwest during the Great Depression of the 1930s, starting in the 1970s there has been a return or "counterstream" of blacks moving back to the South (McFalls, 1998). Between 1990 and 1996, there was a net gain of blacks in the South as more African Americans moved into that region then departed for the Northeast, the Midwest, and the West. Seven of the ten urban areas that gained the most black residents during this period were in the South. African Americans of all ages and socioeconomic levels moved to the South to take advantage of diversified economic growth in that region (Frey, 1998).

The Census Bureau predicts that each year between 1997 and 2050, more than half of the population growth in this country will come from three groups: Hispanics, Asians, and Pacific Islanders. In 1998, the nation's just over 30 million Hispanics accounted for 11 percent of the total population. As a result of immigration and high fertility, individuals in this ethnic group are expected to numerically surpass African American in the year 2005 as they become the country's largest minority group. At that time, the Hispanic population (which will have doubled since 1980) will total 36 million people, while the number of African Americans is anticipated to be about 35.5 million. A decrease in black fertility is also a factor in the juxtaposition of these two groups, as the number of Hispanic children in the United States is already greater than the number of African-American children ("Hispanic Population Nearing 30 Million," 1998).

The Census Bureau also predicts an increasingly long-lived and aging U.S. population (see Figure 12.2). Life expectancy at birth in 1998 was 76 years (79 for women and 73 for men), up from 74.9 in 1988). The number of people over 65 has increased more than elevenfold since 1900 from approximately 3 million to 35 million. As baby boomers and their children age in a more health-conscious society, the number of people 85 years of age and older, the so-called "oldest old" (already the fastest-growing elderly age group), will increase dramatically. Their

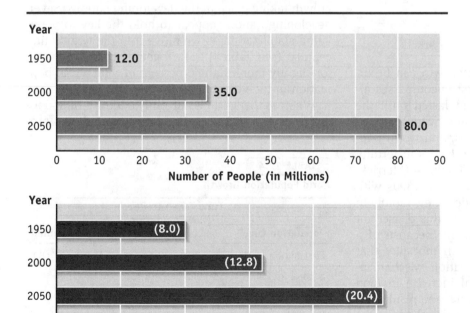

FIGURE 12.2

Number and Percentage of Americans Age 65 or Older for Selected Years

Source: Adapted from *Older Americans in the 1990s and Beyond* by Judith Treas. Population Reference Bureau (1995), p. 4. Used by permission.

numbers will rise from about 3.5 million in the late 1990s to 7 million in 2020. The 65-and-over population will double in eight states (Nevada, Arizona, Colorado, Georgia, Washington, Alaska, Utah, and California) between 1993 and 2000. Kevin Kinsella (in "Census Bureau Predicts, 1996" p. 2) noted "These data are important because they confirm that states need to prepare their resources for an increasingly elderly population." This age group (or "cohort" in demographic terms) will consume vast financial and health-related resources, as well as affect the personal lives of their loved ones.

A final, emerging population trend is worth noting. For many years, dozens of rural counties in the Midwest and Great Plains have been losing population as people migrated to cities. However, while a significant number of these counties continue to lose residents, between 1990 and 1995, 1.6 million more people moved to rural areas from cities and suburbs than went in the other direction. This "rural rebound" has been fueled by affluent retirees, professionals who can work from home via computers, aging baby boomers looking for a more tranquil lifestyle, and the construction of factories in nonmetropolitan areas (Johnson, 1996; McFalls, 1998). Some demographers view this partial change in the direction of migration in the 1990s as "a rebirth of rural America" (McFalls, 1998).

WORLD POPULATION

The history of world population growth can be divided into three periods. The first encompasses almost all of human existence and lasted until the eighteenth century. High birth rates were matched by almost equally high death rates, and world population grew slowly. Any regional spurts in fertility were nullified by plagues and famines (Merrick, 1986). The second period began in the 1800s with the Industrial Revolution. Population grew rapidly in Europe and the United States during this phase, not as a result of increased fertility, but because of a rapid and unprecedented decline in mortality that was directly related to industrialization. Mechanization brought about a substantial increase in food supplies, reduced dangers of famine, and resulted in a healthier population. When nutritional needs are met, people are more resilient to disease. Parallel advances in medical knowledge and technology helped prolong life, and infant mortality was reduced. This European-based population increase (the "first population explosion") lasted until the end of World War II and the beginning of third stage of world population growth.

This latter phase is sometimes referred to as the "second population explosion" and is currently taking place in the developing world. Whereas substantial growth in Europe and regions of the world populated by Europeans took almost 200 years, an enormous surge of growth occurred in the developing nations in only a few decades. Unfortunately, the poor nations of the world benefited only selectively from the rich countries. Their economies grew at a meager rate, and the infusion of medicine and public health systems from the West resulted in a substantial reduction in mortality. Antibiotics, sanitation, immunization, and insecticides checked the heretofore widespread misery and death brought about by malaria, smallpox, and a host of other diseases (Murphy, 1985). Increased food production via the "Green Revolution" resulted in longer life expectancy and a reduction in death rates ("World Population Data Sheet—1998," 1998). Although mortality was dropping rapidly, fertility rates that had been high for hundreds of years declined only slightly.

An overarching view of world population history is shown in Table 12.4. It took from 2 to 5 million years for the population to reach the first billion, but less than 200 years more to hit 5 billion. Currently the world is increasing by 220,000 every day, or just over 80 million people a year (approximately the population of Germany) with 98 percent of that growth taking place in the developing nations. Seven developing nations appear to hold the key to population stabilization as we move into the twenty-first century (see Table 12.5). Together they accounted for slightly more than 50 percent of total world population in the year 2000.

Whereas the world is currently adding a billion individuals every 12 years, long-range population pro-

TABLE 12.4

World Population Growth

Population Level	Time Taken to Reach New Population Level (years)	Year Attained
First billion	2–5 million	About A.D. 1800
Second billion	Approximately 130	1930
Third billion	30	1960
Fourth billion	15	1975
Fifth billion	12	1987
Sixth billion	12	1999

Note: It took 2 to 5 million years for world population to reach 1 billion. The second billion took approximately thirty years, and the last 4 billion people were added in the span of one lifetime—sixty-nine years.

Source: Population Reference Bureau, Inc. Washington DC.

TABLE 12.5

Population Giants in the Developing World

Country	Percentage of World Population (1999)
China	20.9%
India	16.5
Indonesia	3.5
Brazil	2.9
Pakistan	2.4
Bangladesh	2.1
Nigeria	1.9
Total	50.1 percent

Note: Seven developing countries accounted for 50 percent of the world's population in 1998. Their future growth rates (especially China and India which together comprise 37.5 percent of global population) will determine, to a great extent, world population in the twenty-first century.

Source: Adapted from Population Reference Bureau, Inc., *World Population Data Sheet* (1998).

jections are difficult (if not impossible) to make because we cannot predict with a high degree of accuracy what people's childbearing plans will be. Family-size decisions of the "critical cohort"—those 2 billion people currently under 20 years of age—will go a long way toward determining how many people inhabit Planet Earth 50 to 150 years from now (see Figure 12.3). If overall fertility were to decline to 1.7 children per woman, world population could decline to less than 5 billion people. At the other extreme, if

fertility remains high (2.5 children per woman) world population could theoretically top 25 billion by the middle of the 22nd century. In 1999, the world fertility rate was 2.9 children per woman. Changes in life expectancy (an increase), especially in developing countries would also impact world population ("World Population Data Sheet—1998," 1998).

As a result of declining fertility rates in the developed nations (see "Focus on Europe" in this chapter), many people are under the mistaken impression that the era of rapid population growth has come to an end. However, as demographers Alene Gelbard and Carl Haub (1998) point out, Germany and Italy are not India and Ethiopia; today there are two very different worlds of population growth. The "two-children-or-fewer-world" is comprised of Europe, the United States, Canada, Japan, and a number of newly industrializing countries such as South Korea and China (the latter because of its stringent population control measures). The "rapid-growth-world" is made up of most of the nations of Asia, Africa, and Latin America. Accounting for more than 50 percent of the world's population, women in these nations currently average four children each (Gelbard and Haub, 1998). Zero population growth in Europe as a whole, and slow growth in the remainder of the industrialized nations represent little more than a demographic speed bump as world population continues to race forward.

A final note concerning population growth: it is important to understand that (discounting migration) population growth is the relation between fertility and mortality. Neither high fertility nor low fertility

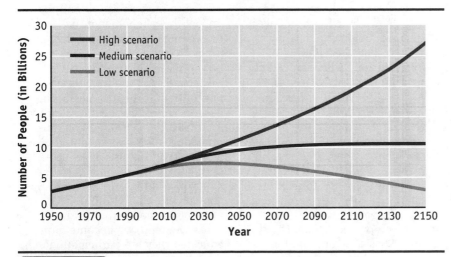

FIGURE 12.3

World Population, 1950–2150
Three Possible Futures

Source: United Nations Population Division, 1998. In *World Population Data Sheet—1998*, Population Reference Bureau, Washington, DC.

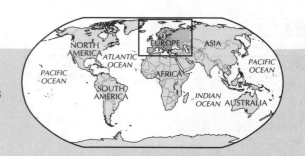

Population: 728,000,000
Life Expectancy at Birth (years): Male—69; Female—78
Forms of Government: Mostly Democratic Republics
Major religions: Primarily Christian; Significant Muslim population in some countries
Population Double Time: Zero Population Growth
Per Capita GNP (1997 U.S. Dollars): $13,890
Principal Economic Activities: Manufacturing; Mining; Agriculture
Colonial Experience: Many nations were colonial powers
Adult Literacy: At or near 100 percent across continent

Underpopulation and the "Gray Continent"

While the governments of most developing nations are struggling with a host of problems related to rapidly increasing populations, leaders in many developed countries are concerned with the implications of zero and negative population growth. This is especially so in Europe where 13 of 42 countries have declining populations and the continent as a whole is experiencing zero population growth.

By way of comparison, at present rates of growth the populations of Africa and Europe, which were approximately the same in 1998 (743 million for the former and 729 million for the latter), will be radically different by the middle of the twenty-first century as Africa would have three times as many people as Europe. Whereas 4 out of 5 people currently live in developing nations, that figure will increase to more than 9 out of 10 in the year 2050.

Contracting and aging populations in wealthy countries are primarily the result of a drop in the **total fertility rate** or **TFR** (average number of lifetime births per woman) in these nations that have fallen from 1.7 in the early 1990s to 1.4 at the end of the decade. At this rate of decline, the TFR would drop to 1.3 in another 10 years.

With a birth rate of 1.2 children per woman (one of the lowest in the world), Italy is a prime example of the consequences of negative population growth. Italian demographer W. D. Montalbano (1994) predicted that if this trend continues his country's population will decline from 57.7 million (1998) to about 15 million in 2100. In 1995 the median age (half of the population is younger and half older than this number) of Europe and the United States were 36 and 34 respectively. According to the Census Bureau, by the year 2015 the median age of the U.S. population will be 37 while in Europe that figure will jump to 45 years. With a median age of 50, Italy's population will be even older with one quarter of its citizens over 64 years of age (Francese, 1998).

At current rates of growth, women in Italy will average only one child each in the year 2050. If this scenario comes to pass, almost 60 percent of Italian children will have no siblings, aunts or uncles; they will have only parents, grandparents, and possibly great-grandparents (Eberstadt, 1997). Although the time frame will be extended, the scenario is much the same for other European nations, most notably Germany, Russia, Spain, and the Czech Republic.

Several European countries have taken steps to increase fertility rates. Italy formed a parliamentary committee to explore alternatives that would permit women to simultaneously have children and pursue careers. This is especially important in light of sociologist Carla Collicelli's (in Montalbano, 1994) observation that for many working women in Italy, having a job is not only an economic activity but also a way of achieving a social identity. The French government pays a child allowance as well as providing social services to families willing to have additional children (Crossette, 1997). Germany also grants monetary incentives toward the end of increasing the country's fertility rate. To date none of these programs has proved to be effective as the region's birth rate continues to plummet.

Numerous explanations have been offered to explain the "birth dearth" in Europe and other developed nations. Most of them are related to modernization and the impact this phenomenon has had on women. The esteemed demographer Kingsley Davis (1986) observed that rising divorce rates associated with the transformation of traditional societies to industrial states has lowered fertility in at least two ways. First it simply reduces the time men and women spend in marriage. Second, a high divorce rate is indicative of marital instability, and people with marital problems often postpone having children.

As women have become more educated they are participating in the labor force in record numbers. For Davis (1986, p. 58) the tens of millions of working wives in developed nations have had a "chilling effect on fertility in several

These elderly men in Rome pass the time of day in each other's company. Scenes like this are increasingly common throughout Europe as approximately one-third of the nations on that continent are experiencing negative population growth. In a country with more deaths than births and a shortage of people moving into their working years, where is the money needed to support these people in their old age going to come from?

ways." For example, to get better-paying, more prestigious jobs, single women often postpone marriage in favor of continuing their education. Facing more competition from increasingly better-educated women, men also delay marriage and stay in school. When two working people marry, the husband is in no position to demand that his wife quit her job. The employment of married women also contributes to marital instability. "By giving the wife an income of her own, it lessens her need for a husband; by providing social contacts at the workplace, it enables her to meet other men . . . " (Davis, 1986, p. 58). In addition, work outside of the home provides meaning in women's lives other than that of mother and homemaker.

For Peter Drucker (1997) Europe's fertility woes are a consequence of increased longevity and the cost of caring for an aging population. It is no accident that the "gray continent's" lowest rates of fertility are found in those nations that have the earliest retirement ages and offer the most generous retirement benefits. Squeezed by the financial burden of supporting a dependent, elderly population and the high cost of raising children in a modern, in-

dustrial society, a growing number of young people are opting to save money by having a small family, or no family at all.

High rates of youth unemployment—26 percent in France and 33 percent in Italy—have also been mentioned as a factor in explaining Europe's low fertility rate (Francese, 1998). Just as birth rates decreased during the worldwide depression of the 1930s, economic uncertainty regarding job opportunities for the next generation is thought to deter many people from having children. Although the employment situation in Europe is hardly as bleak as it was in the depression years, economic uncertainty is still considered a major reason why so few people desire large families.

Government-funded social programs that support people in large measure from "the cradle to the grave" in many European countries will have to be scaled back as the number of young people entering the work force declines annually. As the ratio of working-age, productive employees to retirees falls, society has only three alternatives if these wide-ranging financial and social support programs are to remain solvent, even in some modified (reduced) capacity (Eberstadt,

1997): (1) reduce pension benefits, (2) restrict eligibility by raising the age at which people can start drawing benefits, and (3) raise the taxes of the working population. If the third alternative is adopted, and the financial costs of having children are in fact a reason for declining fertility in Europe, an already low birth rate will certainly continue to decline, perhaps falling below one child per family in the not too distant future.

For Drucker (1997), the process of "collective demographic suicide" that European nations and other developed countries are committing (most notably Japan, and to a lesser extent the United States and Canada) will have consequences for the entire world. Economic growth has traditionally come from increasing consumer demand (in an expanding population) and the corresponding creation of jobs to meet that demand. In societies experiencing negative population growth this manner of economic stimulus is all but impossible. Similarly, Joseph Chamie (in Crossette, 1997, p. 4–1) states that as "engines of economic growth," developed countries "have a particularly important role because they provide a great deal of economic leadership and social leadership." Developing nations export their products primarily to North America and Europe, and if demand from these regions of the world slows, so too will the modernization process in the poorer countries of the world.

Other observers have focused on the positive aspects of declining European population. Individuals in these nations consume a tremendous (and disproportionate) amount of the earth's resources which in turn pollutes the air and water and contributes to global warming. People in rich counties also generate enormous amounts of garbage via the products they consume and eventually discard. Fewer individuals in these pollution/garbage-producing societies will result in a cleaner, more liveable planet.

Jean Bourgeois-Pichat (1986) believes that below-replacement-level fertility and the impending population "implosion" will soon replace the population explosion as our primary demographic concern. However, for Kingsley Davis (1986) low levels of fertility in Europe and other developed areas of the world is a blessing and not a calamity. "It is a solution to a major problem, not the problem itself" (p. 62). Smaller and older societies will help (if only slightly) reduce the high rate of global population growth.

---

alone will result in rapid increases. Table 12.6 shows three hypothetical countries with different crude birth and death rates. All of these countries, however, have the same growth rate, 2.0 per annum.

Malthus and Marx

The first major attempt to explain and project population growth and its consequences was undertaken by the English economist and clergyman Thomas Malthus (1766–1834). In "An Essay on the Principle of Population," published in 1798, Malthus predicted that humankind was in for big trouble, to say the least. He reasoned that food supply increased arithmetically (one—two—three—four, etc.), whereas population increased geometrically (two—four—eight—sixteen, etc.). It was only a matter of time before humans outstripped what contemporary biologists call "carrying capacity," the point at which the environment can no longer sustain the population. When this point is reached, the result will be widespread misery, famine, and death. Malthus realized that before people starved to death, however, they would be killed off by disease, war, and famine. He referred to these growth limits as *positive checks.* This horrible scenario could be avoided if people used *preventive checks* (delayed marriage or moral restraint, i.e., celibacy) to control their fertility. A conservative clergyman, Malthus rejected any form of contraception, abortion, or infanticide.

Malthus's theory attracted much attention and was roundly criticized. Weeks (1999) described three of its major shortcomings. First, the idea that food production could not keep up with the population was wrong. The Industrial Revolution brought about dramatic increases in food production and agricultural knowledge. Today, enough food is available in the world to provide every human being with 3,600 calories per day. The problem is not one of production but one of distribution. Second, the belief that preventive checks (moral restraint) are the only way to reduce fertility is a moral position and not a scientific one. Effective mechanisms of birth control using various methods of contraception and abortion are practiced in many nations of the world. Finally, the conclusion that poverty is the inevitable result of population growth is false. Recall that population increases in Europe and North America brought about by the Industrial Revolution resulted in a higher, not lower, standard of living.

One of the harshest critics of Malthus was Karl Marx, who argued that the work of the "Parson of

TABLE 12.6

Rate of Population Growth

	Country		
	A	**B**	**C**
Crude birth rate	50	40	30
Crude death rate	30	20	10
Difference	20	20	20
Rate of growth (%)	2.0%	2.0%	2.0%

Note: Although these countries have the same rate of growth—2.0 percent per annum—they have different rates of birth and death. Keep in mind that population growth is not the result of either a high birth rate or a low death rate but the *difference* between these two variables. This example does not take into account inmigration or outmigration, either of which could dramatically affect population growth.

Doom" (as Malthus was often called) was superficial, unimaginative, and just plain wrong. Marx thought that problems like poverty due to overpopulation were the result not of any natural laws (arithmetic and geometric progressions of food and people), but of an oppressive, exploitive capitalist system. The solution was not moral restraint but socialism, an economic system that would outproduce capitalism and ensure an equitable distribution of food, material goods, and services. Under socialism, birth rates would also decline because of a rising standard of living and a reduction of child labor. The Marxist position, in turn, has been criticized for being long on faith and short on scientific research.

The Demographic Transition

The inability of Malthus, Marx, and others to adequately explain population dynamics in the modern world led to the **demographic transition theory.** This perspective was developed by Warren Thompson in 1929 and later expanded by Frank Notesien in 1945. According to the theory, birth and death rates of a country will change as they pass through three stages (Figure 12.4).

Stage 1 lasted for tens of thousands of years and was characterized by high birth and death rates.

Birth rates were high because human labor was a necessary and valued commodity. Death rates (including infant mortality) were high because of an overall low standard of living and lack of medical knowledge. Population growth during this period was modest and slow. Because of high birth rates, Notesien referred to this stage as one of *high growth potential.*

Stage 2 was a period of *transitional growth* that began with the Industrial Revolution and had high birth and rapidly declining death rates. With advances in medicine and better nutrition, mortality rates (especially infant mortality) fell dramatically. This was a period of explosive population growth.

In the latter part of this stage, fertility began to "catch down" with mortality as people gained both the desire and ability (contraception) to control fertility. Up to this point in the evolution of human societies, children were almost always regarded as economic assets to the family. As Caldwell (1980) noted, "The flow of wealth is upward from children to parents and even grandparents, and high fertility is profitable, at least in the long run to parents" (p. 225). Children supported elderly parents financially and also treated them with considerable respect—two significant reasons for having large families. As nations began to modernize, however,

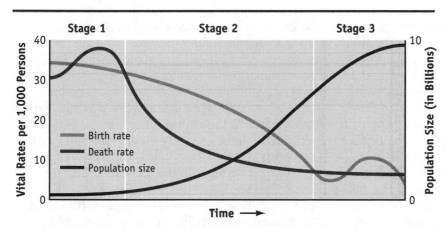

Note: The demographic transition is divided roughly into three stages. In the first stage there is high growth potential because both birth and death rates are high. The second stage is the transition from high to low birth and death rates. During this stage the growth potential is realized as the death rate drops before the birth rate drops, resulting in rapid population growth. Finally, the last stage is a time when death rates are as low as they are likely to go, while fertility may continue to decline to the point that the population might eventually decline in numbers. In the developed countries, the full transition took place essentially as schematized. However, most less developed nations have not yet followed the full pattern of change.

FIGURE 12.4

Stages of the Demographic Transition

Source: Adapted from *Population: An Introduction to Concepts and Issues,* Seventh Edition, by John R. Weeks. Copyright © 1999 by Wadsworth, Inc. Reprinted by permission of the publisher.

children became an economic liability, and fertility began to decline.

Stage 3 is that of *incipient decline,* with low fertility and mortality and therefore low population growth. Contraceptive use is extensive and socially acceptable. Women have gained economic and political rights and work outside of the home, and children are increasingly viewed as an economic liability. The developed nations of the world have completed the demographic transition and are in this final stage.

Societies may differ somewhat in the time it takes to complete the transition, but once the process has begun, it is irreversible. Developing nations are in stage 2 of the transition, accounting for approximately 90 percent of world population growth. Death rates dropped much faster in stage 2 for the developing nations in the years after World War II than they did for the developing countries after the Industrial Revolution. Because of this time factor and lack of economic development, the birth rate in poor countries has not declined as fast, hence the population explosion in the nations least able to cope with it.

The demographic transition theory has been criticized for not being able to predict when fertility will decline (stage 2) and for its ethnocentrism (Weeks, 1999). Concerning the first, demographers were of the opinion that fertility decline was dependent on the spread of industrialization or the rate of economic development. However, in an important restatement of demographic transition theory, John C. Caldwell (1976) stated, "Fertility decline is more likely to precede industrialization and to help bring it about than to follow it" (p. 358). Regarding the criticism of ethnocentrism, the assumption was that since the developed nations completed the transition in a particular manner and time frame, the developing countries would do the same. To date, they have not. It is easy to fall into the trap of believing that what transpired and benefited the industrialized nations will also take place in, and be good for, the rest of the world.

CONTROLLING FERTILITY

As we have seen, population growth in developing nations is the result of rapidly declining mortality in the years after World War II. The three ways in which this growth can be slowed are to decrease fertility, increase mortality, or employ some combination of these. Since increasing mortality is not realistic for a number of moral, religious, and practical reasons, the second and third alternatives can be dismissed. This leaves us with controlling fertility as the only acceptable way of reducing the rate of population increase. Unfortunately, population growth was not even viewed as a problem until the 1950s, and then by only a few countries. On the contrary, large populations were seen as a source of strength (more labor power) and therefore a boon to modernization. Socialist countries like China were loath to admit they had population difficulties, viewing such an admission as tantamount to saying their economic system (communism) was less than perfect, unable to meet the needs of an expanding society.

In 1952, the Indian government implemented the Third World's first major program to limit birth rates. By the late 1970s, U.N. surveys indicated that 81 percent of Third World people lived in countries whose governments wanted to curb rates of growth (Loup, 1983). Undoubtedly, the most ambitious and controversial population policy was introduced by China in 1979. Using a system of rewards and punishments and a nationwide propaganda campaign, the government hoped to limit families to only one child. Although highly criticized in the West, this program has reduced the Chinese birth rate to a level comparable to many developed countries. Less controversial strategies have met with some success in other nations, and in the past 40 years the number of children that women in the developing world (excluding China) have has declined from over 6 to 3.8.

Demographer John Weeks (1999) observed that the desire to have children is rarely an end in itself, but a means to some other goal(s). One important reason people in developing nations want children is for the labor they provide. As E. Boserp (in Weeks, 1999, p. 200) noted, "In most African countries, a large share of the agricultural work was and is done by women and the children, even very young ones, perform numerous tasks in rural areas." Individuals also want children (especially sons) for social and religious concerns. In India, Hinduism requires that parents be buried by their sons (Weeks, 1999). It follows from these examples that if the birth rate is to be reduced voluntarily, the motivation to have a large family must also be lowered. This may be accomplished in part through alterations in religious practices and traditions, and education (alerting people to the dangers of overpopulation).

Research from numerous developing countries indicates that there is an inverse relation between the level of women's education (often measured in terms of literacy) and fertility rates. In other words, as the level of education of these women increases, their rate of fertility decreases. One reason for this finding is that the longer females stay in school the older they tend to be upon marrying, which translates into a reduction in the number of years they can become pregnant (Moffet, 1994). In India and Ethiopia where only 38 percent and 11 percent of females of high school age were enrolled at school, the average number of births per woman (1996) was 3.4 and 6.8. By way of contrast, in Argentina and Cuba the corresponding figures were 75 percent and 81 percent for school enrollment, and fertility rates of 2.7 and 1.5 respectively.

If a nation's fertility rate is to be significantly reduced it appears that widespread government intervention is some form is mandatory. By the early 1970s, the government of Bangladesh viewed population control as a matter of national survival. A public relations campaign that enlisted the help of the clergy in this Islamic country was instituted, along with counseling services provided by 35,000 female family-planning workers who went into the countryside and talked about spacing the birth of children, among other matters (Anderson, 1994). As a result of this fertility-reducing strategy, the number of births per woman in Bangladesh fell from 7.4 in 1975 to 3.3 in 1998, a dramatic reduction in a short period of time.

Inasmuch as reducing fertility in developing nations is most likely to be accomplished voluntarily, the availability of affordable contraceptives is crucial. Although the number of women in the world using some form of birth control increased sharply from 10 percent in 1959 to 56 percent in 1998, hundreds of millions more women will have to control their fertility if rapid population increase in the developing regions is to be slowed. According to one estimate, 150 million women in poor countries want to delay or stop bearing children but are not engaged in any family planning strategies ("Family Planning's Role," 1998).

World Hunger

In 1969–1970 more than one-third of the developing world's people—approximately 918 million individuals—were estimated to be malnourished. By the late 1990s, that number had fallen to 840 million in a world with about 2 billion more people. Almost one-third of the current group of chronically underfed people reside in sub-Saharan Africa (Bender and Smith, 1997). There are two major reasons for the reduction of malnutrition over the past 30 years. Millions of people were lifted from the deepest recesses of poverty and could afford to buy food, and the world's farmers doubled food production since 1975 (Nichols, 1996).

About 25 percent of those malnourished today are children, and hunger-related problems often begin for these individuals while they are still in the womb. Malnourished pregnant women are likely to have underweight, physically weaker babies that are vulnerable to a variety of diseases. Survivors of these childhood maladies are subject to numerous physical problems including stunted growth. As many as 60 percent of Southeast Asian children are shorter and weigh less than more adequately fed young people (Bender and Smith, 1997).

The causes of widespread hunger are twofold: natural and man-made. Both components were evident in the North Korean famine, which claimed the lives of between 1 and 5 million people from the mid- to late 1990s (Chu, 1998; Mackenzie, 1998). Natural disasters took a significant toll on food production as the country endured two years of torrential rains and flooding, followed by a drought. However, there are also significant man-made components to this tragedy. A failed agricultural policy dating back to 1989 limited food production, and with the demise of the Soviet Union a primary source of economic aid was no longer available. A nation with a strong military posture, North Korea was adding weapons to its arsenal in the midst of this tragedy.

While natural disasters will always destroy crops and bring about starvation, disease, and death (especially in the developing world), the principal cause of hunger and malnutrition is chronic poverty. Poor nations that cannot feed themselves typically lack the funds to purchase sufficient foodstuffs on the world market. When food is available, tens of millions of impoverished people cannot afford to feed their families. People in rural areas are more apt to go hungry because they are more likely to be poor, with as much as 80 percent of extreme poverty concentrated in the countryside (Bender and Smith, 1997). Even when food is available tens of thousands of people may starve. In the aftermath of floods in Bangladesh in 1974, farmers in some regions of the country lost their crops. They had nothing to eat and no money to purchase food from people in other parts of the country (Bender and Smith, 1997).

What, if anything, can be done to alleviate chronic hunger/malnutrition-related diseases that affect 14 percent of humanity? The following is a list of solutions most often put forth by experts from a variety of backgrounds:

1. Reduce fertility and slow population growth. While this strategy will not eliminate hunger in the short run, it will prevent the problem from getting substantially worse.

2. Take the necessary political and economic steps to bring about a more equitable distribution of the world's wealth.

3. Change our collective eating habits. Enough food is produced annually to feed a world of 10 billion vegetarians. However, a significant amount of grains, corn, and other crops goes to feed cattle, pigs, and chickens; animals later consumed by the planet's most affluent people.

4. Increase the food supply. According to one estimate, the current global food supply will have to double by 2025 to keep up with population growth. A report by the United Nations Food and Agricultural Organization concluded that to feed its citizens in the year 2050, Africa would have to increase food production by 300 percent, Latin America by 80 percent, and Asia by 70 percent. Even the relatively slow-growing nations (in terms of population) of North America would have to step up food production by 30 percent to feed their own people ("Future Population May Overwhelm," 1997)

While the Green Revolution that began over 50 years ago resulted in spectacular increases in food production, a much-debated question among agricultural experts concerns the limit of our capability to produce foodstuffs. More specifically, what is the limit and how close are we to that biological capacity? While global population is increasing, cropland is decreasing. As societies modernize, homes, office buildings, factories, schools, roads, parks, and recreation areas inevitably use more and more land that was formerly used to produce food. Existing cropland is plagued by erosion, desertification (especially in sub-Saharan Africa), and salinization.

If the man-made causes of malnutrition are not alleviated (at least partially), not only will the gains in reducing chronic hunger made over the previous 30 years be wiped out, but the problem will become significantly worse. Unfortunately, the prognosis is not encouraging. The potential for "major famines" is especially high in a number of African countries on the "brink of a major breakdown" (Bouvier, 1995, p. 2), and food shortages are expected in India, the world's second most populous country (Brown, 1994).

HEALTH CARE IN THE UNITED STATES

Depending on who you are, the U.S. may well be the best place in the industrialized world to live should medical attention (especially for a life-threatening illness or accident) be required, or the absolute worst of all such nations to reside. An argument

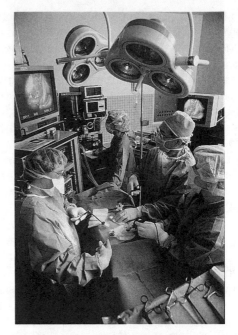

In modern societies the practice of medicine is intertwined with sophisticated technology. Unlike almost every other affluent nation where "universal health care" is provided by the state in some manner, millions of people in the United States are not covered by any form of private or public health insurance. For these individuals high-tech medicine has little meaning.

could be made that the combination of sophisticated medical talent and high technology available in this country is simply unrivaled. Medical advancements are almost routine events and a variety of new drugs, surgical techniques, as well as physical and mental therapies have "extended the lives of millions of people" and "improved the quality of life of millions more" (*Health Care Crisis,* 1992, p. 14). The American health care establishment has contributed to an increase in longevity of approximately 30 years (for the U.S. population) since 1900.

Unfortunately, the overall structure, complexity, and implementation of this gigantic health care system is riddled with a host of problems, the most serious of these being cost, equity (as measured by availability), and the distribution of services (Cockerham, 1998). Whereas health care cost the nation $60 billion 1980, total medical expenditures topped $1 *trillion* in 1994, and $1.5 trillion in 1998. According to estimates made by the Department of Health and Human Services, the national medical bill could reach $2 trillion in the year 2007 (Forbes, 1998). This latter figure would represent a thirty-three fold increase in only 37 years (1970 to 2007). If the price of automobiles escalated at this rate, a car that sold for $5,000 in 1970 would cost $165,000 in 2007.

This incredible expenditure of money has resulted in the most expensive health care system in the world. Despite its high cost, our medical enterprise excludes a sizeable portion of the population, and when compared with the health systems of other industrial nations, provides inferior service. In 1998, an estimated 44.3 million people (including 11.1 million children) or 16.3 percent of the U.S. population had no health insurance coverage. In recent years both the absolute number of people, and individuals as a percentage of the total population without medical coverage have increased. People without health coverage are most likely to come from the following segments of society: (1) low-education and low-income, (2) young adults between 18 and 24 years old, (3) individuals of Hispanic origin, (4) foreign-born individuals, and (5) people who change jobs frequently, inasmuch as health insurance is often employer provided. It follows from this categorization that the number of people without health insurance will vary by state and region. For example, in Texas, a state with a sizeable Hispanic population, 24.3 percent of the population (on average) lacked health insurance between 1994 and 1996. In Wisconsin, a state with fewer poor, lower-educated minorities, 8.2 percent of the residents did not have health coverage during this same period.

Access to medical treatment is also related to the distribution of physicians and hospitals. Areas with fewer than one primary care physician for every 3,500 people are designated "shortage areas" by the federal government. Located primarily in rural America, there were 2,663 such areas in 1994 that accounted for 18 percent of the population or 47 million people (Schroeder and Beachler, 1995). One of every 20 counties does not have a single physician, while more than 50 percent of all U.S. counties do not have a pediatrician (Cockerham, 1998). There are numerous reasons for this shortage of medical doctors in rural areas (Cockerham, 1998; Schroeder and Beachler, 1995).

To begin, while medical students raised in nonurban areas are more likely to return home after graduation, proportionately fewer rural individuals attend medical school. A primary advantage of cities is that they have the resources generally considered important to physicians, including well-equipped hospitals with up-to-date clinics, laboratories, and a well-trained support staff. Colleagues who share one's medical expertise and interests are much more likely to be found in an urban as opposed to a rural setting. After attending medical school in a city, people get used to the educational, recreational, and cul-tural facilities and lifestyle of an urban environment. Finally, physicians who practice in cities (especially big cities) make more money than their rural counterparts. This problem of distribution has been lessened to some extent as a result of a recently instituted federal government program. The National Health Service Corps is attempting to redistribute physicians to rural and poor inner city areas by paying students' medical school tuition and providing a small stipend (income) in exchange for a commitment to work in shortage areas for a specified time, typically four years.

A related problem is that of overspecialization. As modern medicine has become increasingly complex, more medical students are choosing to specialize in one or more of 52 subareas such as neurology or orthopedic surgery. According to one estimate, in the year 2000, the U.S. had 139,000 specialty physicians too many. At the same time there was a shortage of primary physicians or general practitioners. William Cockerham (1998) has noted that while the move toward medical specialization has produced positive benefits by allowing medical doctors to focus on specific parts of the body, it has also contributed to a lack of practitioners who "take on continuing responsibility for the 'whole' patient." Medical specialization has also produced an oversupply of surgeons, which has resulted in a sharp increase in the number of surgeries performed, many of which, according to critics, are unnecessary. More operations are performed in the United States than in a number of other industrial nations (Cockerham, 1998). While the poor receive "too little" health care, more affluent Americans may well be the recipients of "too much" medical intervention.

Returning to the high cost of medical care, there are a number of factors that contribute to the nation's ever-increasing health bill. Hospital costs are the single largest component of health care in the United States. With high operating expenses, hospitals routinely pass on their overhead costs to patients and/or the health care plans that insure them. In one typical case an Alabama woman was charged over $37,000 for a one-week hospital stay for a perforated colon, and the bill did not include the treating physician's expenses. Among other items, the patient was charged $16.67 for surgical latex gloves, $4.15 for a disposable razor and $170.91 for an X ray that was never performed. The senior vice president for policy at the American Hospital Association called hospital billing systems in the U.S. "crazy" (Bentley, in Sharpe, 1997).

Another very serious health care problem was recently brought to light by the National Academy of Sciences which estimated that each year between

44,000 and 98,000 people die as a consequence of medical mistakes in hospitals. Included in these figures are approximately 7,000 deaths resulting from medication errors (Greider, 2000). To put these numbers in perspective, consider that in 1998 there were approximately 17,000 criminal homicides known to police in this country.

Health Care and Crime

The Government Accounting Office estimates that 10 percent of the nation's annual health care expenditure is lost to fraud and abuse. However, Malcolm Sparrow (1996), who has written extensively on this subject, notes that the "true level of fraud losses" could be lower or significantly higher than this figure. If the 10 percent estimation is accurate, it means that of the $1.5 trillion spent on health care in 1998, $150 billion was lost to criminal activity. This is almost twice the amount of money spent each year to fund the entire criminal justice system (the police, the courts, and the prisons). The techniques utilized to extract money from health care providers are almost endless, with new "scams" appearing on a regular basis. Starting with the most basic form of insurance fraud, physicians, clinics, and hospitals charge for services not rendered or only partially rendered. For example, a psychiatrist was recently convicted and sent to prison for 46 months for filing false claims. "If he saw you 12 times, he billed for 100. If he saw you alone for 40 minutes, he billed for a group or family therapy for 90 minutes. When he exhausted our policy's benefits, he would make up claims in the names of your family members" (Mahon, in White, 1998, p. 33).

Law enforcement officials have noticed a movement of people from the illegal drug trade into health insurance fraud because the latter activity can result in enormous profits (higher than drug trafficking) and the penalties (if arrested and convicted) are low. One individual with experience in both criminal enterprises stated that "The drug business was very dangerous," whereas health care fraud "was easy money and there was no risk" (Hernandez, in Hedges, 1998, p. 47). Criminals have set up thousands of phony clinics, medical-equipment outlets, and laboratories, in their attempt to defraud health care providers.

In a pharmaceutical-recycling scheme outlined by Sparrow (1996), physicians and their partners open a clinic in a large city where they employ "runners" to recruit poor, homeless, and drug-addicted individuals who are often all too willing to spend an hour of their time in exchange for cash. The recruits/patients are led to the clinic where they are diagnosed with some nonexistent malady that requires expensive prescription drugs. The physician then bills the federal government Medicaid program for a one-hour consultation for each recruit.

"The 'patient' is then taken (or sent) to a local pharmacy to have the prescription filled—again, at the government's expense. Upon leaving the pharmacy the patient finds someone outside with his/her car trunk open, waiting to buy the drugs back from the patient for $10 or $15. The recruited patients are pleased to accept the cash and they may return the next day for a repeat performance. The buyers are known as 'non-men,' because they deal in noncontrolled drugs. Through the non-men, the drugs are repackaged and fed back into the pharmacy supply chain, with the recyclers reaping enormous profits, once again at the insurer's expense" (p. 3).

In an effort to combat health care fraud, the Federal Bureau of Investigation increased the number of full-time agents devoted to this type of criminal activity from approximately 100 to 375 in 1998 (Lau, 1998). The government collected $1 billion in health care fraud-related fines and settlements in 1997, a dollar amount that is sure to increase as a result of more aggressive enforcement.

Paul Starr (1994), author of *The Logic of Health Care Reform* argues that the increase in the number of physicians (especially surgeons and other specialists) over the past 40 years has contributed to rising health care costs. Starr notes that more physicians will find more things to do, "more tests to run, more need for surgery, more patients requiring followups" (p. 33). This increase in the number of physicians equals an increase in the number (and cost) of medical interventions in what economists call "supplier induced demand" (Starr, 1994). A former editor of the prestigious *New England Journal of Medicine* believes that approximately one-third of all health care expenditures in this country are unnecessary (Relman, in Starr, 1994). If this estimation is correct, the health care bill could be cut by tens of *billions* of dollars annually with no adverse impact on the country's overall medical well-being.

As much as one-third of the nation's total health care bill is related to self-inflicted wounds, so to speak. Dr. Monroe Trout (1994) estimates that we spend $20 billion each year on medical treatment due to violence caused by guns, $44 billion for treating drug abuse, $65 billion a year for medical problems caused by tobacco, and $136 billion annually on people who abuse alcohol. Regarding gunshot wounds, one study found that children injured by gunfire had hospital costs averaging $14,434, a figure that did not include doctors bills or a lifetime of rehabilitation for those individuals permanently crippled ("High Cost of Treating Wounded Youths," 1995).

The Health Care Delivery System

As medical sociologist William Cockerham (1998) has noted, the health care delivery system in the U.S. is a "conglomerate" of both private and public practitioners, agencies, and institutions that exist independent of one another. The following is a brief summary of some of the more important components of this system (Cockerham, 1998).

Invented in California, *Health Maintenance Organizations* or HMOs, are among the fastest-growing medical providers in the country. HMOs are prepaid group practices (hospitals and clinics) wherein individuals (usually via their place of employment) pay a monthly fee for "comprehensive" health coverage. For example, most if not all employees of a particular company will have their health coverage with one HMO. Patients are entitled to a full range of health services that often includes a discount on prescription drugs. These organizations derive profits by keeping members healthy, thereby minimizing medical expenses. With *Preferred Health Providers* (PPOs), employers purchase group health insurance and agree to send their employees to a set list of physicians and hospitals in return for discounts. That is, PPOs charge members less than nonmembers for identical services. In exchange for reduced fees, PPOs are assured of a relatively constant stream of patients (Cockerham, 1998).

Medicare is a federally administered health care program that provides supplemental medical insurance and hospital insurance for people *over* 65 years of age regardless of their financial situation, disabled individuals *under* 65 receiving cash benefits from Social Security or railroad retirements programs, and some individuals with persistent kidney disease. *Medicaid,* as Cockerham (1998) notes, is basically a medical welfare program designed to provide health care to the poor. Funding comes form the federal and state governments. The combination of a "hassle free" billing system and a staggering 800 *million* claims a year has made Medicare a prime target for health care fraud (Hedges, 1998). Much the same could be said for Medicaid.

HMOs have been increasingly criticized by their members/patients. The dissatisfaction with these health care providers is primarily focused on the following three concerns:

1. Exclusion of members most likely to use medical services. This happens in a number of ways. In what has been referred to as "cherry picking," HMOs recruit people from those populations least likely to need expensive health care (Winslow, 1998). In order to sign up only the healthiest elderly individuals, "senior ambassadors" of some HMOs give their sales talks at locations accessible to only the more robust individuals over 65 years of age; golf courses, shuffle board courts, and the second floor of two-story buildings with no elevators (Court, 1998).

2. Denial of medical services such as admission to hospitals, X rays, laboratory tests, and visits to specialists. The decision to deny care is often made by someone with no medical background or an administrative physician who has never seen the patient. One doctor noted that when she was the medical director of a managed care hospital, it was her job as the "company doctor" to decide what patients were entitled to what services. "I had the final medical word . . . it simply means that I practiced medicine on patients I never saw, touched or heard." She added that "Employees with little more than a high school education were making complex, urgent medical decisions" (Peeno, 1998, p. B9). As of late, a number of states have adopted, or are in the process of adopting, laws that will restrict HMOs from limiting services to their patients (Hilzenrath, 1998).

3. A provision of the Employee Retirement Income Security Act (ERISA) of 1974 prohibits approximately 125 million people from suing HMOs for damages resulting from the denial of services. For example, if a patient dies of cancer because that disease was not detected for lack of an MRI exam (that was denied by an HMO), surviving family members are entitled to sue for no more than the cost of the MRI exam (Peeno, 1998). As the law currently stands, ERISA shields much of the HMO industry from malpractice suits. Whereas Texas and Missouri passed legislation extending malpractice liability to HMOs, a spokeperson for one of the country's largest HMOs said that any such proposed legislation at the national level will be fought "to the death" (Rundle, 1998).

Efforts to reform or completely overhaul the health care system in this country have met with limited success. President Truman's proposal for national health care insurance that would provide medical coverage for all citizens was strongly opposed by the American Medical Association. President Nixon's attempt at a more inclusive national health care program was thwarted by his involvement in the Watergate Scandal. The only measure of success in this area came during the Johnson administration with the creation of Medicare and Medicaid (Cockerham, 1998). President Clinton's proposal to provide medical coverage for all Americans was met with such opposition and open hostility that it is doubtful if any high ranking political official will make a concerted effort in that direction in the near future.

THE ENVIRONMENT AND ENVIRONMENTAL ISSUES

As we saw in the last chapter, the environment presents human groups with one of their earliest and most serious challenges—that of adapting to the possibilities offered and the limitations imposed by the characteristics of their physical surroundings. Until populations develop an economy that will allow them to extract adequate supplies of food and other life-maintaining resources from their local environments, they have no real hope of long-term survival. It is only after a population's minimal physical needs have been satisfied, and a surplus of resources created, that true societal development can begin.

But the imperative that a society arrive at a viable working relationship with its physical environment does not end with the formation of a successful economy and the ensuing processes of population expansion and societal elaboration. On the contrary: population growth and the host of new and enlarged activities needed to sustain that population have significant impacts on local environments. In his evolutionary theory of societal development, Gerhard Lenski (recall our discussion of Lenski's theory in Chapter 3), argued that technological changes pave the way for economic development that, in turn, makes it possible to support increasing numbers of people at increasingly higher levels of material comfort. What he left out of his analysis, however, was the fact that the increasing resource depletion, environmental destruction, and disposal of wastes that accompany economic development constitute a real (perhaps fatal) threat to the environment's **carrying capacity;** that is, to its ability to support plant and animal life over the long run without being degraded or destroyed ("Threats to Earth," 1992). Judging by mounting evidence from the United States and from other societies around the world, we may be dangerously close to exceeding the carrying capacity not just of local environments, but of the global environment as well.

Environmental Resource Depletion

Human exploitation of natural resources has been a fact of life since the time of the earliest societies. In their day-to-day quest for survival, populations have always made use of whatever materials local environments have had to offer. For the most part, the amount and speed of past consumption was low

enough and slow enough that *renewable resources* such as water, land, and forests could be replenished, and *nonrenewable resources* such as coal, oil, and other fossil fuels were in little or no danger of being exhausted. But the 6 billion people who make up the current world population are putting such historically unprecedented demands on the environment that even the most basic and plentiful of resources—water and land—are in serious peril.

Water Shortages   The appearance that the earth is literally swimming in water is somewhat misleading. Although 70 percent of the planet's surface is covered by water and the total volume of water is about 335 million cubic miles ("Speaking of Water," 1993), only about 2.5 percent of that amount is drinkable or otherwise usable fresh water. And about two-thirds of that fresh water is frozen in glaciers and ice caps, out of easy human reach, leaving populations dependent on streams, rivers, lakes, rainfall, and groundwater supplies (aquifers) for their residential, industrial, and agricultural needs. Those needs have risen so fast—to about 2,713 cubic miles a year in 1996, more than triple the 1950 usage—that a growing water scarcity in various parts of the world has become "a major impediment to food production, ecosystem health, social stability, and peace among nations" (Postel, 1996, p. 6). This may be particularly true in the Middle East, an explosive area in which, according to then–Israeli Premier Benjamin Netanyahu, (in Prusher, 1998a, p. 1), "for the last 5,000 years, most of the wars have been fought over water." More than 80 countries around the world have acute water shortages, and about 2 billion people—roughly one-third the entire world population—are without clean drinking water ("Water's Scarcity," 1998).

This alarming depletion of the earth's fresh water supply is the net result not only of global and regional population growth, but also of the growth of agricultural and industrial economies over the past half-century. Large-scale farming and large-scale industry are both very water-intensive economic pursuits: on average, about 65 percent of the world's water is used for irrigation and other agricultural purposes, and another 22 percent for industrial activities. Only about 7 percent of all fresh water is used for domestic or household purposes ("Speaking of Water," 1993). Some observers argue that, in many cases, water employed for agricultural use is wasted on a sector that does not return benefits to society in proportion to its costs. For example, in Israel, agriculture consumes 57 percent of all water but accounts for just 3 percent of the country's gross domestic product; in Jordan, agriculture uses 72 percent of the water but contributes only 6 percent of the GDP (Orme, Jr., 1999).

Land and Soil Depletion   According to some estimates, since 1945, about 4.9 billion acres of once-productive land has been lost worldwide as a result of damage caused by humans (Postel, 1994). Of this amount, about 215 million acres have been depleted so badly that they are either completely beyond restoration or would require major engineering work to restore them to productivity. Since 1990, the amount of land taken out of agricultural production because of soil degradation has increased to over 12.5 million acres per year (Gardner, 1996). About two-thirds of the world's most seriously depleted land lies in poverty-stricken areas of Africa and Asia, where malnutrition and starvation already are widespread. According to the United Nations Development Program (1998, p. 5), almost half the world's poorest people—more than 500 million—live on marginal lands. These lands represent the consequence of a process known as **desertification**—the process of having literally been turned into desert.

Scientists have identified three major factors that, in combination, account for about 93 percent of all land lost to desertification: *overgrazing* by livestock, which compacts the soil, strips it of vegetation, and contributes greatly to soil erosion; the *deforestation* or clear-cutting of approximately 28 million acres of forest land each year, a process that contributes to erosion, droughts, and flooding; and *unsuitable agricultural practices* such as hillside cultivation and poor plowing, which promote soil erosion, and the overuse of fertilizers that acidify the soil (Postel, 1994). In Brazil alone, over 200,000 square miles of

the Amazon rainforest have been destroyed since the late 1970s ("Amazon Destruction Continues Unchecked," 1999).

Noting that world private and public consumption expenditures reached $24 trillion in 1998, twice the level of 1975 and six times the 1950 level, the United Nations Development Program (1998, pp. 1–2) has cited "runaway growth in consumption in the past 50 years," especially in the wealthy industrialized nations, as the single most significant factor undermining the environmental resource base. In industrialized nations, this overuse of resources takes the form of "consumption for conspicuous display"; that is, consumption of resources for non-essential goods and services intended to enhance one's prestige or social standing. According to the UNDP (1998, p. 5), the 20 percent of the world's people living in the highest-income countries account for 86 percent of total private consumption expenditures. Among other things, they own 87 percent of the world's vehicle fleet, consume 84 percent of all paper, have 74 percent of all telephone lines, and consume 58 percent of total world energy, as well as 45 percent of all meat and fish—all at enormous environmental resource costs.

In contrast, in developing countries, environmentally destructive consumption occurs for far different reasons: "[in] the absence of other alternatives, a swelling number of poor and landless people are putting unprecedented pressures on the natural resource base as they struggle to survive. . . . Poor people are forced to deplete resources to survive; this degradation of the environment further impoverishes them" (United Nations Development Program, 1998, p. 5).

According to United Nations' estimates, in the past half-century, approximately 5 billion acres of one-productive land has been destroyed by logging, mining, and other activities associated with rapid, poorly-planned development. Much of this destruction has taken place in what are already poverty stricken areas of Africa and Asia, as is the case pictured here—in the Indonesian province of West Kalimantan, deforestation continues unchecked. In the eyes of many developing nations, environmental protection is a luxury that must be deferred until economic success has first been attained.

Fossil Fuel Depletion   Many of the contemporary societies of the world are either fully industrialized (some, postindustrialized) or in the process of industrializing. Whereas agricultural and other nonindustrial economies are labor-intensive, running on animal and human power, industrial and postindustrial systems are machine-intensive. They run on mechanical power, and those machines, whether they happen to be drill presses or personal computers, run on electricity or some other form of energy. Over the space of the last three centuries, as more and more societies have been swept up in the Industrial Revolution, local, regional, and global demands for energy have skyrocketed, leading to rapid increases in the extraction of energy resources. For the most part, "energy resources" means fossil fuels such as oil, coal, and natural gas. Together, these three fuels currently supply over 85 percent of the world's energy and are projected to continue doing so over the next several decades (see Table 12.7).

Exploding global usage of fossil fuels, coupled with a 1973–74 OPEC (Oil Producing and Exporting Countries) embargo on the shipment of petroleum products to industrial nations and a series of resulting energy crises, led some observers to conclude that world reserves of oil were dangerously low and would be exhausted by as early as 1997 and no later than 2017, leaving the world without its primary source of energy (Courtney, 1993). However, it now appears that, thanks to the discovery of new reserves and the combined effects of lower rates of energy demand, greater energy efficiency, recycling, and several other conservation factors, there is no immediate danger of oil and other fossil fuels being exhausted (Energy Information Administration, 1999b; United Nations Development Program, 1998). Oil, in particular, will remain available in the foreseeable future, though perhaps at highly inflated prices.

Rather than looming depletion, the most serious problem related to continued fossil fuel use is its association with environmental destruction, in the form of pollution.

Problems of Environmental Pollution

According to a 1998 Cornell University study of population trends, climate change, increasing pollution, and emerging diseases, "Life on Earth is killing us. An estimated 40 percent of world deaths can now be attributed to various environmental factors, especially organic and chemical pollutants" (in Segelken, 1998). As a consequence of the modernization process (discussed in the next chapter), more and more humans are living in crowded, polluted urban ecosystems "that are ideal for the resurgence of old diseases and the development of new diseases . . . we humans are further stressed—and disease prevalence is worsened—by widespread malnutrition and the unprecedented increase in air, water and soil pollutants" (Pimentel, in Segelken, 1998).

Air Pollution   Since the coming of the Modern Age and the industrialization of the world's societies, the earth's natural ability to cleanse itself of atmospheric pollutants has been strained to the point of collapse. In many parts of the world, the hackneyed old phrase "the air was so thick you could cut it with a knife" is on the verge of becoming literally true, as both developed and developing countries discharge millions of tons of toxic pollutants into the air each year. According to the United Nations Development Program (1998, p. 5), an estimated 2.7 million people die annually from air pollution, 80 percent of whom are rural poor in developing nations. In the People's Republic of China, a country with the dubious distinction of possessing five of the world's ten most

---

TABLE 12.7

Total World Energy Consumption by Fuel, 1990–2020 (Quadrillion Btu)

Fuel	History					Projections		
	1990	1995	1996	2000	2005	2010	2015	2020
Oil	134.9	142.5	145.7	157.7	172.7	190.4	207.5	224.6
Natural Gas	72.0	78.1	82.2	90.1	111.3	130.8	153.6	177.5
Coal	90.6	91.6	92.8	97.7	107.1	116.0	124.8	138.3
Nuclear	20.4	23.3	24.1	24.5	24.9	25.2	23.6	21.7
Other	25.9	30.1	30.7	32.7	38.3	41.9	45.6	49.7
Total	343.8	365.6	375.5	402.7	454.3	504.2	555.1	611.8

Source: U.S. Energy Information Administration, *International Energy Outlook 1999.* (Washington. DC: U.S. Department of Energy/Energy Information Administration, 1999). Adapted from Table A2.

TABLE 12.8

Air Pollutant Emissions in the United States, by Pollutant and Source: 1995 (in thousands of tons)

Pollutant	Total Emissions	Transportation	Fuel Combustion[a]	Industrial Process	Solid Waste Disposal	Miscellaneous
Carbon monoxide	92.1	74.2	3.9	5.6	1.8	6.4
Sulfur dioxide	21.3	0.6	18.3	2.0	0.4	0.0
Volatile organic compounds	22.9	8.3	0.7	2.7	2.4	0.4
Particulates	46.6	0.7	0.9	0.6	0.2	40.1
Nitrogen oxides	21.8	10.6	10.1	0.8	0.1	0.2
Lead	5.0	1.5	0.5	2.1	0.8	—

[a]Stationary sources.

Source: Adapted from *Statistical Abstract of the United States: 1997,* Table 380.

polluted cities, bad air is believed to be responsible for 178,000 premature deaths a year (Rosenthal, 1998).

But pollution-induced sicknesses and deaths are not confined to the developing world. In the United States, according to a 1998 report prepared by Greater Boston Physicians for Social Responsibility, as of 1996, 46 million people lived in areas not meeting the U.S. Environmental Protection Agency's National Ambient Air Quality Standards. The result is "Thousands of deaths every year . . . increased incidence of illnesses, increased absence from work and school, decreased lung function, and increased hospital visits" (Dickey, 1998). In California, a 10-year-long study of the effects of smog on children has shown clear links between elevated pollution levels and reduced breathing capacity in girls, as well as increased respiratory illnesses in boys (Marquis, 1999). The primary sources of this pollution are the industrial processes, fossil fuel combustion in energy production and transportation, and solid waste disposal that represent the inevitable by-products of an advanced industrial economy intended to raise its population's standard of living (see Table 12.8).

Global Warming and the Greenhouse Effect As serious as are the health consequences of air pollution, they may not represent the worst that such pollution has to offer. According to many scientists, the most serious threat to humans from air pollution is that posed by so-called *greenhouse gases*—primarily, carbon dioxide, methane, and nitrous oxide. These gases trap heat reflected from the earth's surface in the atmosphere, much as the glass in a greenhouse traps heat reflected from that structure's floor. In both cases, the result is the same: increased temperatures inside the enclosure. But, whereas the higher

temperatures inside a greenhouse are desirable and beneficial for the raising of plants or flowers, higher temperatures on the earth's surface are neither desirable nor beneficial. Even modest increases of 4 to 8 degrees in global temperatures would generate a series of catastrophic outcomes including polar ice cap melting, rising sea levels and the consequent destruction of many densely populated areas across the world, frequent droughts, and the extinction of many plant and animal species (Cylke, 1993).

Concerned by data showing steady rises in global average temperatures over the past century, delegates at the 1992 Earth Summit at Rio de Janeiro, Brazil, adopted a Climate Change Treaty that sought to curb emissions of greenhouse gases in both developing and developed societies. However, the treaty was never fully embraced by the United States, which was concerned about the extraordinarily high costs of changing the industrial processes responsible for greenhouse emissions in this country. It was also opposed by China and India, the world's two most populous developing countries, on the grounds that compliance with the treaty would be disastrous for their continued industrialization.

In December 1997, representatives from over 150 nations passed the Kyoto Protocol, an international treaty establishing legally binding targets for reducing greenhouse emissions by 38 industrial nations. This treaty would take effect after being ratified by at least 55 nations and would be binding on individual countries only after being ratified by their governments. Under its terms, by the year 2012, Japan, the United States, and the industrialized nations of Europe would have to reduce their emissions of greenhouse gases to 6 percent, 7 percent, and 8 percent, respectively, below their 1990 levels. These mandated levels would not apply to China, India, and other developing nations. Those countries would be encouraged to curb their greenhouse emissions voluntarily, but would not be subject to sanctions should they choose not to (Stevens, 1997).

Like the 1992 treaty, the Kyoto Climate Change Protocol has met with strong resistance. Although 83 countries had signed the treaty as of mid-March 1999 none of the major industrial societies had ratified it by that date, and their greenhouse emissions continued to grow (Energy Information Administration, 1999b). In the United States, for example, carbon emissions from the burning of fossil fuels rose from 1,346 million metric tons in 1990 to an estimated 1,484 million metric tons in 1998—an increase of 10 percent (Energy Information Administration, 1999a). Perhaps not coincidentally, 1998 was also the warmest year on record, with six of the first eight months of the year exceeding the monthly global average temperature figures recorded in the 139 years that such figures have been tracked (Flavin, 1998). Some scientists see the potential for a "runaway" greenhouse effect, with catastrophic consequences for the global ecosystem, if fossil fuel use is not substantially reduced in the next half-century (in Brown and Flavin, 1999). But even this grim scenario has not been sufficient to goad the United States into significant positive action. After a 95–0 Senate vote against ratification of the Kyoto treaty, rather than encouraging further research on climate changes or on the development of nonpolluting alternative energy sources, the U.S. Congress—described by one observer as being "completely dysfunctional" on global warming issues (Cochran, in Thompson, 1999, p. 57)—in 1999 cut funding for these programs by 8 percent.

Problems of Waste Disposal

Modern economies depend on mass production and mass consumption, and those mass production and consumption activities lead to massive amounts of waste. To the extent that both developed and developing societies extract and process numerous raw materials for later economic or social uses, these actions create waste products that somehow must be disposed of safely. To the extent that the conversion of these raw resources into finished consumer products also creates waste by-products, these materials likewise must be disposed of. And, finally, to the extent that the eventual use of finished products results in additional waste materials, these, too, become part of a disposal problem. Determining how to rid ourselves of these wastes without doing serious harm to the environment or to ourselves has become a problem of epic and growing dimensions.

Solid Wastes   The term **solid wastes** refers to the glass, metal, plastic, paper, cardboard, wood, food, plant material, and other residues of daily living that typically end up in the nation's and the world's landfills. As the sheer number of people in developed and developing countries using greater amounts and kinds of resources in the pursuit of more comfortable lives has increased, so also has the volume of solid wastes—much more so than the number of landfill or "dump" sites deemed suitable enough or safe enough to handle these municipal and industrial castoffs. In the United States, for example, municipal solid waste generation rose by over one-third between 1980 and 1996, climbing from 151.5 million tons to 208.7 million tons per year. At the individual level, these figures represented an increase from 3.7 pounds to 4.3 pounds of "garbage" per person per day (U.S. Bureau of the Census, 1998c, Tables 402 and 403). And, although a much higher amount of this solid waste is being recovered than ever before—27.3 percent in 1996 compared to only 9.6 percent in 1980 (U.S. Bureau of the Census, 1998c, Table 403)—existing and projected landfills simply cannot keep up with the sheer bulk of the remaining solid wastes. Successful landfill development has become a much more difficult and lengthy process, even for waste disposal companies employing state-of-the-art landfill technologies. The average "permitting" time now stands at approximately 10 years from initial site identification to on-line operational status (Soroka, 1999). In Japan, an island nation whose topography severely limits the development of new landfills and whose industrial solid wastes reached 400 million metric tons in 1997, it has been estimated that all of the country's solid waste disposal sites will have been completely filled by the end of the twentieth century (Pollack, 1997). That society, and many others, may soon be literally buried in an avalanche of solid wastes.

Toxic Wastes   The growing mountains of municipal and industrial solid wastes that litter the world constitute a very real threat to contemporary societies if for no other reason than their sheer volume. But there are other varieties of industrial and household waste materials that are infinitely more dangerous—the liquid, solid, and gaseous toxic chemical wastes representing the unintended but nonetheless very real and very lethal by-products of industrial economies.

No one knows exactly how much hazardous waste must be disposed of throughout the world each year, but it is undoubtedly a mind-boggling amount. According to one estimate (Fogel, 1993), the two dozen most industrialized nations of the world produce 98 percent of all hazardous wastes and collectively generate about 300 million to 400 million tons of such materials each year. More recently, in its annual *Toxics Release Inventory,* the U.S. Environmental Protection Agency (1999) reported that 2.6 billion pounds of toxic chemicals were released, transferred, or otherwise disposed of by reporting facilities across the United States in 1997, an increase of some 100 million pounds from the previous year. And these figures do not include the unknown amount of toxic industrial wastes that were illegally disposed of and went unreported that year.

But civilian hazardous wastes are hardly the only toxic chemical threat. As an artifact of a nearly 50-year-long Cold War, the U.S. and the former U.S.S.R. are both home to significant amounts of chemical weapons that pose a real danger to their respective populations. In the United States, work has already begun on destroying the military's stockpile of 32,000 tons of chemical weapons, a job ultimately expected to cost an estimated $13 billion. In Russia, final resting place for the bulk of the former Soviet Union's declared chemical arsenal of 40,000 tons, the liquidation would cost at least $5.5 billion, a figure well beyond the reach of that country's struggling economy. And, according to many observers, there may be as much as another 500,000 tons of undeclared chemical weapons abandoned across Russia, the legacy of decades of ultra-secret military testing (Hoffman, 1998b).

Faced with more stringent domestic waste disposal laws and higher domestic waste disposal prices, many developed countries have been exporting their hazardous chemical wastes to cheaper (and safely distant) sites in developing nations, adding to those countries' existing environmental and health problems. Concerned by this growing menace, by the mid-1990s over 100 developing nations had banned the importation of hazardous waste materials and called upon the major industrial societies to halt their practice of dumping locally produced toxins in foreign countries (Satchell, 1994). But many industrial countries have continued this practice, as their stockpiles of hazardous wastes continue to grow and the amount of available domestic landfill space continues to shrink.

Radioactive Waste   In 1996, the United States' 424 commercial nuclear reactors produced an estimated 2,174 metric tons of spent nuclear fuel (U.S. Bureau of the Census, 1998c, Table 978), thus adding to what may well be the world's most serious waste disposal problem: radioactive waste. As hazardous as (or more hazardous than) toxic chemicals, radioactive wastes remain lethal to humans for a much longer time—in some cases, for thousands of years.

The U.S. federal government, which was supposed to have begun accepting and disposing of the country's commercial nuclear wastes by 1998, has been unable to do so, leaving these materials largely stored on-site at individual power plants, hospitals, and other points of origin. Thousands more tons of dangerous military-related radioactive materials, another legacy of the Cold War era, must also be dealt with as U.S. nuclear weapons are phased out in the aftermath of the death of the Soviet Union (Knickerbocker, 1992). One U.S. Department of Energy estimate (in Levy, 1993) claimed that the final cost of cleaning up the *known* radioactive waste sites across the country will exceed $200 billion.

As was also the case with regard to toxic chemical wastes, the breakup of the U.S.S.R. has revealed radioactive waste problems of catastrophic proportions in economically strapped countries (primarily Russia) financially unable to deal with them. Decades of plutonium production and atomic bomb testing have left vast areas in Siberia and other regions of Russia with massive amounts of water and soil contamination that threaten the lives of tens of thousands of citizens now and for years to come (Hoffman, 1998a). Radioactive contaminants from spent nuclear fuel and spent reactors that were simply dumped in the Kara Sea and the Sea of Japan present a very real danger of leaking into international waters and, from there, into the global food chain (Bogert, 1992; Knickerbocker, 1993).

Addressing Environmental Problems

Although most people in the United States and across the world might be painfully aware that we all face serious environmental problems, many would disagree on the question of what can and should be done to address those problems. In a large number of cases, opposition to proposed environmental policies rests squarely on economic grounds. In developed societies, the sticking point is the extraordinarily high costs so often associated with emissions reductions, pollution cleanups, alternative energy startups, and other environmentally friendly changes to the status quo. In developing societies, the stumbling block is the slowed or halted economic development that presumably would result from a more benign environmental perspective. Simply put, societies that view economic development and modernization as their best or only path to long-term survival are not about to jeopardize that survival. If short-term environmental sacrifices are the price of ultimate development and survival, then so be it.

In too many cases, it seems, questions of economic well-being and environmental well-being are framed in an "either/or" or "zero-sum game" format: Either economic development or environmental preservation will result from a particular course of action, but not both. If the economy gains, the environment loses; if the environment gains, the economy loses. If individuals, groups, nations, and the world-at-large are ever to adopt a "green ethic"; that is, a higher level of concern for global, as well as local environments, they must be shown that such an ethos is not necessarily antithetical to the nuts-and-bolts process of making a living.

Sustainable Development

Since 1900, the number of people on earth has almost quadrupled, while the world economy has expanded more than twentyfold. This incredible growth of both populations and economies has been fueled by a more than thirtyfold increase in the consumption of oil and natural gas, almost all of which has been used by the developed nations (MacNeil, 1989). With approximately 20 percent of the planet's population, rich countries consume about 86 percent of the world's industrial productivity and natural resources, and are responsible for more than half of all carbon dioxide emissions. According to one observer (Hayes, in Murphy, 1994), with an American-style level of high consumption and high pollution, the earth's carrying capacity is about 2 billion people, or one-third of the current total world's population.

Inasmuch as most developing nations and large sectors of primarily industrial states have resource-based economies (economies whose productivity is dependent on the use of soil, forests, fisheries, water, and the export of raw materials), can all the nations of the world modernize without seriously, if not completely, depleting these resources? Is **sustainable development** possible? That is, can we continue to make economic and social progress and meet "the needs of the current generation without compromising the needs of future generations" (Smith, 1997, p. 2)? William Catton (in Rossides, 1990) noted that developed nations became wealthy by relying on resources from "elsewhere." Today, both rich and poor nations are borrowing more and more resources from "elsewhen." The fivefold to tenfold increase in economic activity necessary to meet the demands of a growing world population over the next 50 years will put an incredible strain on the earth's natural resources. The modernization of Third World countries, as well as the continued prosperity of now-rich nations, raises questions not only of what *can* be done, but also of what *should* be done. For example, do we have the right to jeopardize the well-being of future generations so that we may prosper and live comfortably during our own lifetimes? Do the developed nations of the world have the right to ask or tell developing countries to conserve resources and not pollute when they themselves became wealthy and powerful by freely using any and all available resources, polluting the planet with little regard for anybody or anything?

Key factors in any global move toward reaching sustainable development will be the production, marketing, and waste disposal strategies of large national companies and multinational corporations. A survey of 481 companies worldwide revealed that the chief executive officers of most of these organizations understood that environmental issues will have to be addressed (Sissell, 1998). However, many environmentalists are fearful that sustainable development will become a priority in the international business community only if it can be made profitable. Hiding behind a "green screen" of "eco-efficiency," multinational corporations could ultimately do more harm than good. What is needed, say critics, is the introduction of another system that relies on alternate sources of energy and results in the creation of innovative, non-toxic products. Michael Braungart of Greenpeace stated (in Sissell, 1998, p. 56), "If you make the wrong system more efficient, it's simply more deadly."

For Fraser Smith (1997, pp. 5–6), sustainable development on the part of rich countries means subscribing to one or more of the following:

1. A nation's economy should not increase in size, or if it does, "only by a small amount."
2. A nation should embrace equity in the distribution of goods and services, as well as a conservation ethic.
3. Manufactured goods should not harm the environment, and individuals should choose their jobs and professions with this in mind.
4. Economic incentives (taxes and quotas, for example) should be implemented toward the goal of sustainable development.

In line with these policies, Donella Meadows (1992) argues that if we are to support all of the world's people, both now and in the future, at a sufficient standard of living within the environmental constraints of the earth, people will have to stop seeking more and be satisfied with what they have. After a nation has achieved environmental "efficiency," the next step is sufficiency," the idea of having enough. This is especially true in the rich nations of the world where, historically, economic growth and expansion have been a central or core value in both capitalist and socialist states.

Inasmuch as the economy and the environment are interdependent components of the societal development process, sustainable development in its beginning, intermediate, and advanced stages must be the central focus of our attention as we move into the twenty-first century. The words of naturalist Henry David Thoreau (1817–1862) should be uppermost in our minds:"We do not inherit this planet; we are keepers of it for our children."

<hr>

SUMMARY AND REVIEW

Fertility and Mortality

1. *What aspects of the population are demographers most interested in?*

Demographers in the field of sociology are interested in (a) fundamental population processes such as fertility, mortality, and migration; (b) the size and spatial distribution of a population; and (c) the structure and characteristics of a population. (P. 276)

2. *What "intermediate variables" determine how many children a woman will have?*

The number of children to whom a woman will give birth is a function of three sets of intermediate variables. Intercourse variables are the commencement and frequency of sexual activity over a period of time. Conception variables concern the use of items and strategies that may inhibit conception, such as birth control devices and breast feeding. Pregnancy or gestation variables (miscarriage, stillbirth, induced abortion) determine whether a fetus will come to term and be born. (P. 277)

3. *What are the major causes of death in society?*

There are three major reasons that people die in any society: (a) they degenerate, (b) they are killed by communicable diseases, and (c) they are killed by products of the social and economic environment. (P. 278)

4. *Is the crude death rate in developing nations higher or lower than the crude death rate in developed countries?*

In Third World nations, the crude death rate (CDR) is both lower and higher than the CDR in developed nations. Low CDRs in the developing world are a result of two factors. These nations have very young populations, with as many as 50 percent of their citizens under 15 years of age; young people die at a much lower rate than older individuals. For a variety of political, economic, and social reasons, some nations continue to have a high death rate. (P. 281)

5. *What are the major social correlates of mortality in the United States?*

Although death may appear to be a random phenomenon, mortality rates differ significantly from one segment of a population to another. In the United States, mortality rates are related to variables such as occupation, gender, race, and marital status. (P. 282)

6. *What groups of people are at greatest risk of contracting the AIDS virus?*

AIDS has become a "global epidemic" with up to 70 million people HIV positive in the year 2000. Nine out of ten HIV-positive people are in Africa and seven out of ten people who have died from the AIDS virus are Africans. In the United States 75 percent of all people diagnosed with AIDS are between 25 and 44 years of age. Although they comprise just under 13 percent of the population, African Americans account for 35.9 percent of known AIDS cases. Hispanic Americans make up 11 percent of the population and account for 18 percent of people in this country with AIDS. (Pp. 279–281)

Migration and Population Composition

7. *What are the three major categories of illegal immigrants to the United States?*

The Bureau of the Census has three categories of illegal immigrants to the United States: (a) *settlers* arrive on a more or less permanent basis, (b) *sojourners* do seasonal work and then return to their country of origin, and (c) *commuters* cross the border on a daily basis. Some people argue that illegal aliens help the U.S. economy by taking the lowest-paid jobs no one else will do. Others believe illegals take jobs from U.S. citizens as well as depress the wage scale in this country. (P. 285)

8. *What is a population pyramid?*

A population pyramid is a visual summary of the age and sex distribution of a given society. So-called "true" pyramids with a wide base and a narrow top signify a rapidly growing population that is typical of developing countries. The relatively narrow base of the U.S. pyramid indicates a population with a slow rate of growth. The rather wide top of the pyramid (the oldest age cohorts) illustrates an aging population where longevity is high. (P. 285)

9. *According to Malthus, how would world population growth be checked?*

Thomas Malthus reasoned that it was only a matter of time before population growth (geometric increase) outstripped the earth's food supply (arithmetic increase). *Positive checks* such as war, disease, and vice would eventually halt the rate of growth. *Preventive checks* of delayed marriage and celibacy would reduce population growth without the tremendous suffering that accompanies the positive checks. (P. 292)

U.S. and World Population

10. *What are the three stages of the demographic transition?*

According to the theory of the demographic transition, every country will eventually pass through three demographic states: (a) *high potential growth* characterized by high birth rates and high death rates; (b) *transitional growth* of high birth rates and declining birth rates (currently, most less developed nations are stuck in this phase), and (c) *incipient decline* with low birth and death rates. Developed countries are in this final stage of the transition. (Pp. 293–294)

11. *What are the major population trends in the United States?*

As we enter the new millennium there are four major population trends in this country: (1) movement of people from cities to suburbs, (2) a continuation of individuals moving to the southern and western regions of the country, (3) in some areas of the nation a rapidly increasing minority population, and (4) the aging of the United States. (P. 286)

12. *Why are some nations facing a future with the prospect of too few people in society?*

Some modern nations are facing a population decrease as they move toward the end of the century. A problem of underpopulation comes about when people are having fewer than the 2.1 children per couple necessary to maintain a stable population over time. (Pp. 290–292)

Controlling Fertility and World Hunger

13. *What strategies to limit fertility in the developing world have been the most successful?*

Attempts to limit fertility in the poorer nations of the world have met with some success. These strategies include China's policy of one child per family and forced sterilization. Many nations have used media campaigns aimed at convincing people that having fewer children is to everyone's advantage. Governments have made various contraceptive devices available at low enough costs (or for free) so that even poor people can afford them. Educating women via formal schooling appears to be one of the most effective ways of lowering fertility. (Pp. 294–295)

14. *What are the primary causes of the world's food shortage?*

The world's food shortage is related to the following factors: (a) *ecology*-related causes of food shortage include bad weather conditions, poor soil, soil erosion, and pests; and (b) *political and economic variables* determine how food is distributed. (P. 295)

Health Care in the U.S.

15. *Why is health care in the United States so expensive?*

Advancements in medical technology and the proliferation of highly trained health care professionals have resulted in a healthier, longer-living population in the United States. However, the overall medical bill was approximately $1.5 *trillion* in 1998 (and climbing) making it by far the most costly health care system in the world. Health care costs are driven up tens of billions of dollars each year by fraud and other forms of criminal activity as well as unnecessary treatments and operations, duplication of services, high-priced medical specialists, the expense of billing some 1,500 providers, and the medical needs of a rapidly aging population. Approximately 16 percent of the population (35 million people) have no medical insurance or coverage. Middle-aged and elderly women, as well as children, are disproportionately represented in this uninsured group.

Millions more are underinsured and face financial ruin if they become seriously ill. *Medicare* is a federally administered health care program that provides medical insurance and hospital care for people over 65 years of age and disabled people under 65. *Medicaid* is a medical welfare program designed to provide health care to the poor. (Pp. 296–299)

The Environment and Environmental Issues

16. *How are societal development and the environment related?*

Societal development is possible only after a population has created an economy capable of meeting basic survival needs and providing a surplus of resources. In turn, increasing population growth and societal development place increasing strains on the environment in the forms of resource depletion, pollution, and growing solid, toxic, and radioactive wastes. (P. 300)

17. *Why is the world facing a crisis with regard to such renewable resources as water and land?*

Although world water and land resources are extensive and, in theory, renewable, they are rapidly being depleted to meet the needs of expanding populations attempting to lead more comfortable lifestyles (in the case of developed nations) or simply trying to survive (in the case of developing countries). About 93 percent of world water use is directed to agricultural and industrial economies. At the same time that rivers, lakes, and aquifers are being drained of their supplies, millions of acres of land are undergoing desertification each year as a result of overgrazing by livestock, deforestation, and unsuitable agricultural practices. Though modern economies consume an enormous amount of oil and other fossil fuels, these resources do not seen to be in immediate danger of being exhausted. (Pp. 300–302)

18. *Why has air pollution become such a serious problem across the world?*

Continued world reliance on oil, coal, and other fossil fuels for energy production and other industrial purposes has created enormous air pollution problems, leading to the premature deaths of millions of people each year and health problems for tens of millions more. Rising global temperatures as a result of so-called greenhouse gases place the world at risk for catastrophic climate changes, but few countries so far seem willing to absorb the colossal economic costs that would be required to reduce the fossil fuel emissions responsible for this greenhouse effect. (Pp. 302–304)

19. *Why has the disposal of solid, toxic, and radioactive wastes become such a serious problem?*

Industrial economies are resource-intensive systems that create enormous amounts of waste by-products in the process of extracting raw materials and converting them into finished products. The consumption of these goods and services also generates mountains of wastes. Paper, plastic, metal, plant materials, and other solid wastes have become a serious problem simply by virtue of their sheer volume which is running ahead of landfill availability. Toxic chemical wastes present a serious threat because of their harmful effects on human health. Nuclear or radioactive wastes produced by commercial and military operations are not only extremely hazardous to human health, but remain potentially lethal for centuries. Disposing of these materials may be among the most serious environmental problems facing humankind. (Pp. 304–305)

20. *What are the prospects for attaining sustainable development in the coming century?*

Sustainable development is the creation of economic and social systems that meet the needs of current generations without endangering the prospects of future generations or of the environment on which they are based. If sustainable development is to become a reality, the developed nations will have to adopt a "less is enough" ethos that considers the harmful environmental effects of their mass-production, mass-consumption economies. As a way of encouraging developing countries, the more-affluent nations must also be willing to share their resources more equitably. Finally, both developed and developing societies need to adopt alternative, more environmentally friendly energy sources, recognizing that the long-term environmental and health costs of not doing so will far outweigh the short-term economic costs of embracing these new technologies. (Pp. 306–307)

13 *Urbanization and Modernization*

Whereas the majority of people in developed countries live in cities, developing nations (with the exceptions of Central and South American countries) are still primarily rural, agricultural societies. Tens of millions of people in the world's poor countries are residents of *primate cities*—cities that have at least twice the population of that nation's next largest urban area. In some cases the size discrepancy between cities number one and two are overwhelming, as in the case of Thailand's capital of Bangkok and the city of Chang Mai, with the former being 30 times more populous than the latter. A country's primate city, as J. John Palen (1992) has stated, is often "the only city of note."

Primate cities dominate their respective nations economically, politically, and socially. For example, half of Mexico's gross domestic product (GDP) is generated within a 100-mile radius of downtown Mexico City ("Mexico's New Frontier," 1997). Besides being the nation's capital, a primate city typically boasts the country's best university and is the center of a society's cultural life (the theater, music, museums, the best restaurants, etc.). As is the case in other primate cities, the Mexican capital attracts migrants from throughout the country who leave rural areas in search of a better quality of life for themselves and their children.

Herein lies the reason why primate cities grow so rapidly. Population expansion in these giants is not only a result of natural increase (birth over deaths), but city size is greatly enhanced by a steady stream of rural-to-urban migrants. Between 1950 and 1980, 5.43 million people moved to Mexico City at an average rate of 510 migrants a day. This tremendous influx of people was responsible for 38 percent of the city's growth in a 30-year period. Not only do these disproportionately young people (mostly under 35 years of age) contribute their own numbers to primate cities, but in later years, the numbers of their children as well.

Common to all primate cities, problems such as inadequate housing, traffic congestion, noise, and water and air pollution are staggering. The often unmeasurable impact living in giant cities has on the mental and physical health of residents decreases their productivity and significantly lowers the overall quality of life. Something as mundane as getting a clean glass of drinking water is increasingly problematic for even some relatively affluent residents of primate cities. With an overall usage rate of 63 cubic feet *per second,* Mexico City requires millions of gallons of water each day. To meet this demand, the municipality has been drawing water from depleting underground aquifers for decades. In some areas of the capital the ground is sinking at a rate of up to one and one-half inches a year, while in downtown Mexico City land has sunk as much as 30 feet since the early 1900s (Ezcurra and Mazari-Hirriart, 1996).

In recent years the flow of migrants into Mexico City (population 17 million) has slowed as a sizeable number of people have moved to *la frontera,* those Mexican states that border the U.S. Since 1950, the population of border states has increased fivefold as people come to work in the over 2,300 *maquiladora* factories that have become a cornerstone of northern Mexico's drive toward modernization. In an effort to attract outside investment, Mexico embarked on the *maquiladora* program in 1965. Also known as the twin plants approach, components manufactured in the United States (the first plant) are shipped duty free to a factory in Mexico (the second plant) where they are assembled or turned into finished products (e.g., running shoes, televisions, clothing) and sent back to the United States. Customs duty is assessed *only* on the value added in Mexico; that is, the cost of the finished product minus the cost of the components. For much of the 1980s and 1990s, these plants represented the fastest-growing sector of the Mexican economy. One rarely speaks of modernization in Mexico without discussing *maquiladoras* in the cities of *la frontera.*

As we saw in Chapter 1, the word **modernization** describes the transformation from a traditional, usually agrarian society to a contemporary, industry-based state. Inasmuch as developed societies like the United States and Japan are wealthy, modernization research has focused more on economic growth than on the development of other institutions and patterns of behavior. The economic development of today's now-rich countries (NRCs), is related to four primary aspects of industrialization as outlined by Harper (1989): (1) economic growth through transformation in energy (from human and animal power to machines), (2) a shift from primary production (agriculture and mining) to secondary production (manufacturing), (3) growth in per capita income, and (4) an increase in the division of labor (diversification of occupations). To this list we can add a final aspect of industrialization, that is, the growth of cities. No country has ever successfully industrialized without a dramatic increase in the number of people who live and work in urban areas.

Industrialization is a powerful mechanism of change affecting the intellectual, political, social, and psychological aspects of society. In turn, industrialization itself is affected by these same dimensions. Once the process of change and development is accelerated by a momentous incident (e.g., war) or a continuing factor (e.g., the industrial revolution), the major institutions, values, and patterns of behavior become both independent and dependent variables, causing and being affected by change. Modernization, therefore, is a very uneven process of development, with some institutions changing faster and to a greater degree than other institutions, social values, and modes of interaction to which they are related.

In this chapter we examine cities and the process of urbanization in both rich and developing countries. Next, we explore classical and contemporary theories of modernization in our effort to understand why some countries successfully industrialize, while many others remain relatively poor.

Questions to Consider

1. What is the relationship between urbanization and modernization?
2. What are the major theories of the human ecology school?
3. When and why did suburbanization begin in the United States?
4. What accounted for the growth of sunbelt cities?
5. Why have the populations of so many winter cities declined over the past thirty years?
6. Why are Third World cities growing at such an unprecedented rate?
7. What are the personal qualities and characteristics of modern humans?
8. How did the biological sciences influence nineteenth-century theories of social change?
9. What do evolutionary and modernization theories have in common?
10. What are the major criticisms of modernization theories?
11. What assumptions does world system theory make about the modern world?
12. What is neocapitalism, and how does it affect economic development in the Third World?
13. How has modernization affected women in the developing world?

CITIES IN THE MODERN WORLD

From ancient times until the beginning of the Industrial Revolution, cities remained essentially the same. Peasants provided the agricultural surplus, which made specialization and a more complex division of labor possible, and the entire community was integrated into an urban social system characteristic of Emile Durkheim's "mechanical solidarity" (see Chapter 1) (Berger, 1978). However, the Industrial Revolution significantly changed the size, structure, and composition of European and American cities. On the eve of this revolution in 1800, England had 106 towns with 5,000 or more inhabitants. By 1891, this figure had increased to 622 with nearly 20 million people (Hosken, 1985). With a concentration of workers and potential workers (nearby agriculturalists), as well as being situated on trade routes and waterways, these towns were the perfect places to build factories. Labor shortages were quickly alleviated by the influx of peasants who left their farms in the hope of finding a better life in the city. Unfortunately, most simply traded rural for urban poverty. Jammed into hastily built, overcrowded apartments, they lived in squalor and despair. Sanitary conditions were abysmal, and untold thousands died during typhoid, cholera, and dysentery epidemics (Hosken, 1985).

Urban life significantly changed the way people related to one another. Traditional patterns of interaction with family, friends, and organizations such as the church were altered. Informal mechanisms of social control that had been effective in keeping people from engaging in deviant behavior were disrupted and, for some, permanently severed. As a result, many of the social problems now associated with cities (especially crime) began to rise dramatically. In the United States, these problems were exacerbated by the arrival of large numbers of immigrants from Poland, Germany, Italy, and Ireland beginning in the middle of the nineteenth century. The values and behavior of these people clashed (often literally) as they were crowded together in one area of the city: the slum. Big cities also brought big government. Political corruption and incompetence were rampant. In many cases, public officials were part of a long list of problems rather than their solutions. Zastrow and Bowker (1984) noted that, although "machine politics" and corruption were not invented in the middle of the nineteenth century, the latter was "brought to a higher level of development" (p. 420).

Despite increasing social problems and the wretchedness of urban life for the masses, many people prospered as cities in the United States, Europe, and other parts of the world grew rapidly. Between 1800 and 1970, the world's urban population increased by 4,750 percent—twelve times faster than its population increased (Light, 1983). This was a period of rapid *urbanization*, that is, growth in the proportion of people in a given society residing in urban areas. Note that the population of a society could remain stable while that society underwent urbanization. For example, at one point in time 50 million people of the 100 million in society A lived in cities. Years later, after considerable rural-to-urban migration, 75 million of the 100 million individuals in that society lived in urban areas. What typically happens, however, (especially in the developing world) is that the population of a country increases *and* it becomes more urban simultaneously. By way of example, the population of Bangladesh escalated from 116.6 million in 1994 to 119.9 million in 1995 while the percentage of people residing in cities during that same time frame increased from 14 to 16 percent.

Societies differ as to the *number* and *proportion* of individuals residing in urban areas. Approximately 26 percent, or 260 million, of India's 1 billion people live in cities. In the United States in that same year (1999) the figures are 75 percent, or 203.8 million of the country's 271.8 million people. Even though India has more people living in cities, the United States,

with a higher proportion of city dwellers (75 percent to 26 percent), is a much more urban society.

Over the past one hundred years, the world has become increasingly urban. In 1900, an estimated 10 percent of the population lived in cities, a figure that reached 44 percent in 1999. By the year 2010, over half of the world's population is expected to reside in urban areas. The global urban population will almost double from 2.6 billion in 1995, to 5.1 billion in the year 2030 (*World Urbanization Prospects: The 1996 Revision*, 1997). No doubt it was with these statistics in mind that Wally N' Dow (in Wright, 1994, p. A17) of the United Nations Center for Human Settlement stated, "the twenty-first century will be the first urban century."

HUMAN ECOLOGY AND THE CITY

In their 1921 book, *An Introduction to the Science of Sociology*, Robert Park and E. W. Burgess first used the term *human ecology*. Broadly speaking, ecology is the study of the relationship between organisms (plant, animal, and human) and their environment. Following Darwin, ecologists focus on the manner in which organisms relate to each other as they struggle to survive. Recognizing the "fundamental unity of animal nature," **human ecology** concentrates on

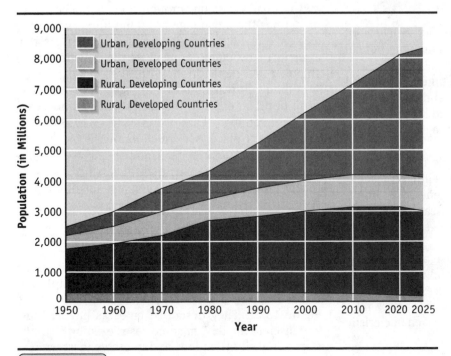

Between 1950 and 1999, the world's urban population more than tripled to 2.7 billion. In the 1990s, the world's urban population grew at the rate of 10 Paris-sized cities a year. (This chart is based on medium–fertility projection.)

FIGURE 13.1

Urban and Rural Growth Projections to 2025

Source: VanPelt in *The Christian Science Monitor* © 1992 The Christian Science Publishing Society.

the "form and development of the community in human populations" (Hawley, 1950, p. 8).

Human beings have much in common with other living creatures but are capable of behavior that other life forms are not. For example, unlike any other animal, we have the ability to construct and modify our physical and social environment. Once altered, the environment may result in new ideas, values, and patterns of behavior. Just as we change the environment, our behavior is altered as we respond to these changes. To test their theories and observe the relation between humans and the world they constructed, ecologists used the city as a vast, natural laboratory. They posed (and attempted to answer) two fundamental questions: (1) Do cities tend to develop a common, general physical form? (2) What accounts for this form? (Shannon, 1989).

The Concentric Zone Model

One of the first and most important contributions of human ecological theory was the **concentric zone model** (see Figure 13.2). This model views the city as a series of zones emanating from the center, each one being characterized by a different group of people (or institutions) and activity. It assumes that cities have one center and have a heterogeneous population (Berger, 1978) competing for livable space as well as jobs. According to Burgess's (1925) version of the concentric zone model, the city has five distinct zones.

Zone 1 The central business district consists of stores, offices, light industry, and commercial establishments.

Zone 2 The zone of transition has some business and commerce as a result of growth and expansion in zone 1. It is also home to unskilled laborers (often first-generation immigrants), who live in poorly maintained tenements.

Zone 3 The zone of working people is made up of simple one- and two-family dwellings of semi-skilled workers (often second-generation immigrants) who have managed to escape from zone 2. This is the area of ethnic enclaves; Deutschland and Little Italy, for example.

Zones 4 and 5 The apartment house and commuter zones are inhabited by middle- and upper-middle-class people, the city's more successful and permanent residents. These neighborhoods are relatively free of the crime and deviance characteristic of the poorer areas of the city.

Ecologists were studying the city when rates of population growth (primarily as a result of in-migration) were high. Steady growth pushed city limits outward as zone 1 encroached on zone 2, which in turn moved into zone 3, and so forth. This dynamic process of expansion was caused by a phenomenon called *invasion and succession*. Newly arrived immigrants would settle in the zone of transition (invasion) and take the place (succession) of those more upwardly mobile residents who were moving to the next zone. Over the years, the concentric zone model has been criticized for being simplistic, overgeneralized, and inaccurate (zones do not really exist). Nevertheless, it has maintained its popularity and importance and appears in virtually all urban geography texts.

The Sector Model

As a result of studying the composition and configuration of 142 cities in 1900, 1915, and 1936, Homer Hoyt (1939) rejected the notion that cities were arranged in concentric zones and advanced his own spatial interpretation of urban America known as the **sector model** (see Figure 13.2). Rather than a bull's-eye layout, Hoyt argued that urban zones were pie- or wedge-shaped sectors radiating outward from the **central business district (CBD),** the major shopping and commercial area of a city. More exclusive neighborhoods were usually found along transportation lines or high ground near lakes and rivers, forming a sector that ran from the center city to the suburbs. Similarly, industries developed in sectors with rivers and railroads passing through the CBD. The sector model has the advantage of taking into account the existence of hills, mountain ridges, and rivers that exist in many cities, as well as the significance of shipping and transportation lines.

Although it was an important step in the development of urban ecology, the sector model is not without shortcomings. Larkin and Peters (1983) maintained that it places too much emphasis on the role of the upper classes in determining spatial organization and neglects the part played by other socioeconomic groups in understanding the distribution of space.

The Multiple-Nuclei Model

Rejecting the notion of a single CBD in any given city, Harris and Ullman introduced the **multiple-nuclei model** of urban spatial organization in 1945 (see Figure 13.2). They described cities as having "several discrete nuclei," in some cases existing from the start of the city (London) and in others increasing as the city grew and diversified (Chicago). Nuclei may develop around a number of activities, including manufacturing, retailing, wholesaling, and education.

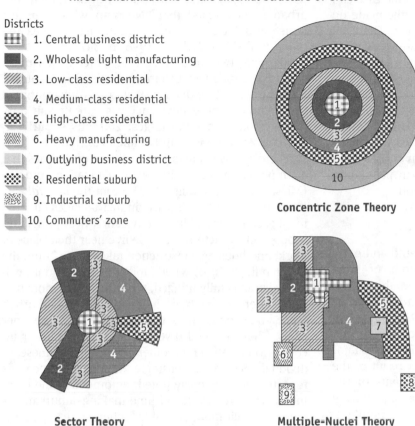

Three Generalizations of the Internal Structure of Cities

Districts

1. Central business district
2. Wholesale light manufacturing
3. Low-class residential
4. Medium-class residential
5. High-class residential
6. Heavy manufacturing
7. Outlying business district
8. Residential suburb
9. Industrial suburb
10. Commuters' zone

For Harris and Ullman (1945), the concentric zone model is a generalization for all cities. The arrangement of the sectors in the sector model varies from city to city. The diagram for multiple nuclei represents one possible pattern among innumerable variations.

Concentric Zone Theory

Sector Theory

Multiple-Nuclei Theory

FIGURE 13.2

The Nature of Cities

Source: Reprinted from Chauncy D. Harris and Edward L. Ullman, "The Nature of Cities," *The Annals of the American Academy of Political and Social Sciences,* 242. © 1945. Reprinted by permission of Sage Publications, Inc.

The type and number of these nuclei differ for two reasons: Certain areas of the city are more suitable for some activities than others because of terrain and transportation, and, as in Los Angeles and Chicago, multiple nuclei are a function of growth; they simply incorporate a host of smaller cities. The major criticism of the multiple-nuclei model is that most cities really have only one center and the other nuclei are merely subcenters (Parker, 1982).

FROM JAMESTOWN TO MANHATTAN AND BACK

With the settlement of Jamestown, Virginia, by the British in 1607, the initial step leading to the eventual urbanization of America was taken. By the end of the seventeenth century, New York, Boston, and Philadelphia were relatively small, although prosperous, colonial cities. Located on rivers and seacoasts, many of these early cities were centers for the export of raw materials to Europe (Spates and Macionis, 1987). Until the early 1800s, most were free of congested areas and serious social problems, although slums emerged soon after in New York and Boston (Butler, 1976). Even though the number of Americans living in urban areas was increasing, not everybody viewed cities in a positive light. Some were of the opinion that cities were a potential threat to political stability. Thomas Jefferson believed that they were "ulcers on the body politic," places where "mobs" could undermine good government (Jones and Van Zandt, 1974, p. 112).

Cities played an important role in the country's westward expansion. Completed in 1825, the Erie Canal, running from New York City to Buffalo, opened the Great Lakes and much of Canada for trade. Between 1820 and the start of the Civil War in 1860, the

U.S. population doubled, and city growth increased 500 percent. A significant portion of this increase can be attributed to European immigrants, who made up 19 percent of the northeastern population. The Civil War era was a landmark period in the evolution of American cities. Before the war, most cities were commercial centers; however, with the completion of hostilities and shift toward manufacturing, the United States was catapulted into the Industrial Age. The economic and social transformation of the United States, especially its urban areas, was underway. Between 1860 and 1910, the nation's population increased from 31 million to 92 million, with the urban population rising from 6 million to almost 45 million.

Suburbanization

The industrial cities of the late nineteenth and early twentieth centuries were concentrations of large numbers of people in small places. In the 1920s, however, a process of decentralization began. During the ten-year period ending in 1930, suburban population growth outstripped that of the central cities for the first time in U.S. history. The first major period of suburbanization was a direct result of the prosperity and technological advancements of the Roaring Twenties. Automobile ownership during these ten years jumped from 9 million to 26 million, and the total monetary expenditure for road construction in 1930 topped $1 billion for the first time (Ebner, 1987). The number of commuter trains running from central cities to the suburbs was also a major factor in the surbanization process. Access to outlying areas, coupled with affordable homes, made this early exodus possible.

With the Great Depression in the 1930s, both the good times and the spurt in suburban growth came to a halt. When World War II ended and the U.S. economy was converted from a wartime to a peacetime posture, the suburbanization of the country resumed at an accelerated pace. Joel Garreau (1996, p. 23) has chronicled surbanization in the U.S. in the post-war era:

> In the first wave of urban change after World War II, we moved our homes out past the old downtown. That was classic suburbanization. Then, in the second wave, we got sick of going downtown to shop so we moved an important urban function, the distribution of all our worldy goods, to where we lived . . . In the third wave during the 80s we moved our jobs and our means of creating wealth out to where we had been living and shopping for two generations.

By the 1950s suburbs were hailed as the "New America," and this move to home ownership in the outskirts even became part of our Cold War beliefs (Carlson, 1996). Bill Levitt, builder of Levittown suburban homes stated that "No man who owns his house and lot could be a communist. He has too much to do" (in Carlson, 1996, p. 34). By the mid-1990s, over two-thirds of the 75 percent of Americans that resided in urban areas lived in suburbs. Joel Garreau (*Economist*, 1994, p. 26) has argued that many of these new enclaves "aren't sub anything," noting that the largest 200-plus suburbs in this country are more aptly called *edge cities*.

There are two categories or classes of theories that attempt to explain the suburbanization process (Mieszkowski and Mills, 1993). From the *natural evolutionary perspective,* in early industrial cities employment is concentrated in the city center near ports, railheads, and/or factories. People live near their place of work, and housing construction takes place "from the inside out." That is, when land near the central business district is fully utilized, typically larger, more luxurious homes are built in peripheral or suburban areas, and people who can afford them leave the inner cities. These vacated dwellings are sold to lower income groups, often newcomers to the city. As these individuals become increasingly affluent the process is repeated. As previously noted, automobiles and commuter trains reduce travel time making suburban living that much more desirable. When stores, theaters, restaurants, and finally employers moved to the suburbs, the process is complete.

A second set of explanations, the (white) *flight from blight* perspective focuses on the problems associated with living in central cities: high taxes, low-quality public education, high crime rates, traffic congestion, air pollution, and an overall lower environmental quality of life. These problems serve as "push" factors resulting in the most affluent central city residents moving to the suburbs. This leads to further deterioration of inner cities as the tax base is eroded and businesses of all kinds follow their richer clientele (Mieszkowski and Mills, 1993).

Discrimination and a lack of buying power kept African Americans out of the suburbs in any substantial number until the 1970s. Although the suburbanization of blacks has increased significantly since that time, African-American suburbanites tend to live in primarily black suburbs (Logan, Alba, and Leung, 1996). One reason for this phenomenon is a dual housing market, one that operates for whites, and another that operates for blacks as well as other minorities. Real estate agents, mortgage lenders, and even local governments have engaged in discriminatory practices (South and Crowder, 1997). A 1979 study conducted by the Department of Housing and Urban Development (HUD) concluded

Some inner city neighborhoods in this country do not look much different than bomb-destroyed war zones. This vacant building in the South Bronx, New York, City, stands next to a structure that has recently been leveled. From a Conflict Theory perspective, decaying inner cities are a testament to the ongoing exploitation of, and indifference to the nation's poor, even in a period of economic prosperity.

that "discrimination is extensive and pervades metropolitan areas throughout the country" (Wienk et al., 1979). A 1989 HUD study (in Yinger, 1995) used matched pairs of white and matched pairs of black investigators who inquired about advertised properties in 25 metropolitan areas. Realtors withheld all information about some available units in 5 to 10 percent of the cases, and were much more likely to show additional available homes to the non-Hispanic, white researchers. Inasmuch as many whites do not want their children to attend integrated schools, "housing agents clearly discriminate more against black and Hispanic households with children" (Yinger, 1995, p. 185).

Because of ongoing housing discrimination, most African Americans live in neighborhoods that are comprised predominantly of minority groups, while most whites reside in neighborhoods that are predominantly if not exclusively white (Stegman and Turner, 1996). Residential segregation is most severe in central cities and suburbs (the latter being the most segregated residential areas in the nation), especially in the largest metropolitan areas of the Northeast and Midwest. In New York City, approximately 20 percent of the population lives in poverty, almost triple the suburban poverty rate of 6.5 percent. Whereas 30.2 percent of Detroit's residents live in poverty, only 6.5 percent of that city's suburban inhabitants are poor (Stegman and Turner, 1996).

SUNBELT CITIES

In a 1969 book analyzing national political trends, Kevin Phillips coined the term *sunbelt*. Although not in vogue until the mid-1970s, this loosely defined word has come to represent the vast southern region of the United States stretching from the Carolinas to California. The 1970s witnessed a significant shift in population as millions of Americans left northeastern and north central states and moved south and west. States with the most significant population increase between 1970 and 1980 were California (3.7 million), Texas (3 million), Florida (3 million), Arizona (1 million), and Georgia (875,000). The population of most eastern and central states increased only slightly during this period, and two states, New York and Rhode Island, even lost population. In the mid-1980s, four of the ten largest cities in the nation were "winter cities" (those cities located in the Northeast and Midwest regions of the country). By the late 1990s, only New York and Chicago remained on that list. Between 1990 and 1994 the metropolitan areas of Dallas, Houston, El Paso, Miami, Atlanta, Orlando, Nashville, Phoenix, Tucson, Tulsa, and Albuquerque (among others) recorded population increases of between 8.1 and 12.4 percent. During this same brief period, the population of Las Vegas grew by 26.2 percent. Apart from in-migration, cities in this region grew rapidly by expanding geographically, in some cases, dramatically. For example, between 1950 and 1990 Tuscon grew from 10 to 156 square miles, while neighboring Phoenix increased in size from 17 to 420 square miles (Finc, 1993). Towns and smaller cities in these areas of expansion were incorporated into, and became part of Arizona's two largest cities.

While sunbelt cities as a group have been doing well over the past 25 years, population growth has been minimal or nonexistent in other warm-weather municipalities such as New Orleans, Louisville, and Richmond. This slowdown in sunbelt population increase has been greeted with enthusiasm by many residents of this region who strongly oppose uncontrolled urban expansion. In his book, *Fighting Sprawl and City Hall: Resistance to Urban Growth in the Southwest,* Michael Logan (1995) notes that urban growth has been contested by concerned citizens groups and environmentalists beginning in the late 1940s and the post–world War II economic boom.

Explanations for the rapid growth of sunbelt cities and the concomitant decline of frostbelt cities are often complex. Thomas Shannon (1989) outlined five general explanations for this population shift.

1. *Wage rates* Because of a more conservative political environment, sunbelt states have always had lower wage rates than eastern states. The large number of illegal workers from Mexico and Central America also tends to depress wages. Inasmuch as labor costs are a significant part of overall production expenses, industries began closing up shop in snowbelt cities and relocating to a warmer (and less expensive) part of the country. This runaway plant phenomenon resulted in the loss of 4 million jobs in the frostbelt between 1966 and 1975. Millions more manufacturing positions would disappear in the next 25 years.

2. *Avoiding unionization* The major reason labor costs are relatively low in sunbelt states is because unions have had little success in organizing workers. Right-to-work laws have effectively locked unions out, and conservative law enforcement officials are more likely to view labor disputes from management's perspective. These observations have not been lost on foreign-based, multinational corporations that are more likely to build their American-based plants in the sunbelt than in the frostbelt.

3. *Tax incentives* Because they pay their employees higher wages and have more extensive social service and welfare programs, northern cities have the highest tax rates in the country. Lower rates of taxation can be a powerful incentive to move for both individuals and, especially, industry. In fact, lower corporate tax rates act as a kind of government subsidy, partially offsetting the cost of relocating a company to the sunbelt.

4. *Federal Expenditure Patterns* A significant number of senior members of Congress come from the sunbelt. As a result of their influence and position, a large share of pork-barreled projects have found their way to warm-weather states. Many of these projects not only create jobs, but encourage industry and commerce. Defense spending has also been important in this increasingly high-technology aerospace region, much of which is located in the so called "military arch."

5. *Changing structure of the economy* In a very real sense, the sunbelt was in the right place at the right time. The South, Southwest, and Mountain regions benefited as the nation began a gradual (and often painful) transition from a heavy-industry, manufacturing economy to a postindustrial economy based on high technology, information processing, and light manufacturing. Anchored in the old economic order, winter cities had a much more difficult time making the transition to new economic activities.

The growth of sunbelt cities is not limited to matters of dollars and cents, however. Warm weather is important to retirees and tourists who have more leisure time and/or are increasingly concerned with health and physical fitness. For some the warm weather is merely a pleasant bonus. These individuals come to the sunbelt with thoughts of leaving behind the crime, pollution, and congestion of industrial states.

But paradise found may be rapidly turning into paradise lost. Heavyweight champion Joe Louis said of one of his opponents before a fight, "He can run but he can't hide." The same may be true of urban problems, which appear endemic to cities. Crime is high in many sunbelt cities as economic prosperity has increased opportunities for both street criminals and white-collar workers. For example, in 1997, rates of violent crime (the number of offenses known to police per 100,000 residents) were significantly higher in Dallas (717), Albuquerque (1,088), New Orleans (1,093), Los Angeles (1,135) and Miami (1,692) than they were in the winter cities of Columbus (575), Boston (540), Milwaukee (521), Hartford (345), and Pittsburgh (303).

Pollution levels in a number of sunbelt cities are among the worst in the nation, and gridlock on the streets and highways of many warm weather urban areas is already severe. Economic prosperity has been a hallmark of the sunbelt, but not everybody has shared in the wealth. Although Phoenix and Atlanta added a combined total of 700,000 new jobs between 1991 and 1996 (Daniels, 1996), a significant number of these positions are entry-level, minimum-wage jobs. Low wages in the region have fostered what has been referred to as "sunbelt poverty," a condition that affects millions of lower-class laborers and their families.

The most serious issue threatening the continued prosperity and growth of cities and states in the arid West and Southwest is the lack of water. Because most of the sources of water in the region (the Colorado River, for example) have been "fully exploited," the strategy for ensuring a continual supply of this life-sustaining resource have changed from "increasing *supply* to managing *demand*." (Shannon, 1997 p. 222). The success or failure of water conservation will certainly be a crucial factor in the economic well-being/future of many sunbelt cities.

WINTER CITIES

For Thomas Shannon and his colleagues (Shannon, Kleniewski, and Cross, 1997), the frostiest states of the Northeast and Midwest consist of two areas: the highly industrialized sections bordering the five Great Lakes and the Atlantic Ocean; and the rural farming areas stretching from central Ohio to the Midwestern plains. In the 1960s and the 1970s, urban economic growth in the United States appeared to resemble a zero-sum game, with the prosperity of sunbelt cities coming at the expense of frostbelt cities. As a consequence of the changing dynamics of the American economy, the concentration of poverty has been especially high in Northeastern cities beginning in the 1970s, and Midwest cities starting in the 1980s (Krivo et al., 1998). These cities lost a significant number of manufacturing jobs to the suburbs, sunbelt cities, and developing countries. Lauren J. Kirvo notes that rather than being disbursed randomly or evenly throughout the city, poverty tends to be localized. For example, African Americans in winter cities (most of whom reside in the central or "inner" city) have suffered disproportionately as a result of this economic transition with the percentage of blacks living in "extreme poverty" areas increasing from 15.5 percent in 1970 to 24.2 percent in 1990. Kirvo and colleagues use the term *concentrated disadvantage* to describe "the degree to which poverty and other disadvantages are confined to a limited number of neighborhoods within a city" (p. 62).

One explanation for the recent ascendancy of sunbelt cities is that these urban areas are finally catching up to Northeastern and Midwest cities. However, domination of certain economic activities by sunbelt cities represents a temporary shift in the overall U.S. economy, and is not a permanent regional transformation. According to this perspective, an eventual "convergence" or evening out of urban economies will take place across the country (Shannon, 1989). A contrasting point of view is that the nation's economic growth is uneven, with each region developing in a specific manner and time. Specializing in heavy industry and manufacturing, winter cities were dominant during the heyday of the Industrial Revolution. They erected "development barriers," successfully preventing other areas of the country

from competing with them in their areas of specialization. However, when the United States moved into the postindustrial era with the emphasis now on high technology and light industry, the major sphere of economic activity shifted to the sunbelt. Rather than convergence at some future date, the theory of uneven development suggests that if winter cities are to be prosperous again, they will have to cultivate new economic activities.

Thomas Shannon and his colleagues (Shannon, Kleniewski, and Cross, 1997) remind us that regional economies are no longer solely affected by political/economic events occurring in the United States. Because of the globalization of the marketplace, distinct components of our economy (located in different sections of the country) are more or less related to other nations. For example, now part of the Pacific Rim, California is increasingly tied to the economic fortunes of Asia. Metropolitan Miami is a center for banking, commerce, and tourism for Central America, South America, and some Caribbean countries. The Texas economy is intertwined with and contingent upon the economic health of Mexico (Shannon, Kleniewski, and Cross, 1997). Although hit hard by the loss of thousands of manufacturing jobs in the postindustrial era, Buffalo's economy has remained stable because of its proximity to neighboring Canada and the relatively affluent cities of Hamilton and (especially) Toronto.

While most observers would agree that winter cities were in a period of decline (at least relative to sunbelt cities) in the 1970s and 1980s, there is evidence that numerous urban areas in the frostbelt are recovering. Boston and other New England cities are leaders in the microcomputer industry, with the largest city in Massachusetts having a rate of unemployment of only 3.4 percent in 1998. New York City has experienced solid growth although unemployment was relatively high at just under 9 percent in the late 1990s. Economic growth in Columbus, Ohio, has been described as "excellent" with unemployment rates as low as 2.4 percent. Economic expansion in Chicago is strong with only 2 percent of the residents of that city out of work. The continued success of these and other winter cities will depend on the internal political/economic dynamics of each city, the overall well-being of the U.S. economy, and the position of these metropolitan areas in the global economy.

URBAN COMPOSITION AND LIFESTYLES

Cities not only are larger than towns and villages, but also differ in their makeup or composition on at least

The world's urban population is expected to increase by 1.5 billion over the next 20 years. Almost all of this growth will be in developing nations, where cities often resemble islands of relative affluence surrounded by a vast sea of poverty.

three dimensions (Fischer, 1976). First, urban residents are on average younger than nonurban persons. They are also less likely to be married, and if married, they are less likely to have children. Second, as city size increases, the number of racial, ethnic, and religious minorities increases. In other words, minority group members are attracted to, and usually concentrated in, cities. Finally, on average, the larger the community, the higher the mean educational, occupational, and income levels of the population.

Early Theorists

Early- to middle-twentieth-century sociologists believed that to the extent that the composition and structure of urban America differed from small-town and rural areas, so too would the values and patterns of behavior of urban residents. George Simmel (1858–1918) examined the influence urban structures had on individuals, and Louis Wirth (1857–1952) was interested in everyday, observable patterns of interaction in cities (Berger, 1978). For Simmel, life in the city forced people to respond selectively to the almost overwhelming amount of stimuli they are bombarded with in a rapidly changing, culturally diverse environment. Because of such overstimulation, people interact with one another more superficially; that is, as members of a particular social class or category rather than as individuals. The result is a nation of detached, self-serving urban residents living in what Davis (1949) called "the world of physically close but socially distant strangers" (p. 331). For Wirth (1938), the greater size, heterogeneity, and density of city life led to numerous, impersonal, "secondary" relations, as opposed to the warm, intimate, personal contacts

or "primary" relations characteristic of rural life. Fewer primary relations (the exception being close friends and family) lead to a variety of individual maladies, including anomie, alienation, and psychological stress. These, in turn, are responsible for a long list of problems including crime, alcoholism, drug abuse, broken families, mental illness, and the extremes of apathy and aggression.

The view of the city as a major source of evil in the modern world may tell us more about the researchers' bias than the phenomenon they were trying to understand. This antiurban sentiment, coupled with a nostalgic longing for a wholesome, unspoiled rural life, has a long tradition in American thought. Disdain for cities is a common theme in both our history and fiction dating back to the days of Thomas Jefferson. However, attempts to show that urban life is a singularly stressful, anomic, or alienating condition or that urbanites are more unhappy than rural people have been ambiguous or unsuccessful (Shannon, 1989). For example, Fischer (1976) found that people have approximately the same levels of mental health regardless of where they live. Rates of deviance may be higher in urban areas because these types of behavior are more visible and accurately recorded. It is also probable that rural people with problems (e.g., alcoholism) or less socially acceptable lifestyles move to the city to be with others like themselves (Fischer, 1976). Even the commonly held notion that small cities are friendlier than large ones is in doubt. Whyte (1988) found that as far as the frequency of interchange is concerned, "the streets of the big city are notably more sociable than those of smaller ones" (p. 6).

It appears that the rural—urban (gemeinschaft—gesellschaft) dichotomy of Tönnies (see Chapter 3) and others is at best only partially true. To the extent that urban residents live in "ethnic enclaves" or are bound together by some common trait or interest, they can create a "quasi-gemeinschaft" community with personal relations much closer and warmer than either Simmel or Wirth would have predicted (Berger, 1978, p. 170). In effect, urban neighborhoods can be so many small towns loosely bound together by the same political and economic entity—the city.

Contemporary Urban Researchers

In the tradition of Wirth and Simmel, contemporary urban investigators have observed patterns of interaction on city streets. For example, Dabbs and Stokes III (1975) discovered that the amount of room pedestrians gave each other as they passed was related to, among other things, beauty. During the course of an experiment, a woman wearing tight clothes and attractive makeup was given more room as she passed, by both males and females, than the same woman wearing baggy clothes and no makeup. The researchers interpreted their findings in terms of social power, with people deferring to those farther up on the scale of beauty. Longtime urban researcher William Whyte (1988) observed that pedestrians in great metropolitan centers from different countries act more like one another than like people from smaller cities in their own cultures. They walk fast and aggressively and tend to cluster in the middle of the sidewalk. For Whyte, this is not surprising because people in giant cities are "responding to high-density situations and to a range of stimuli not found in smaller cities" (pp. 23–24). Because of their size, structure, and relatively fast-paced lifestyle, large cities may have a homogenizing or leveling effect on certain aspects of people's lives.

Herbert Gans As a result of its cultural diversity, rapid turnover of residents (invasion and succession), and high rates of deviance and crime, the inner city has been well researched by sociologists since the early days of human ecology in the 1920s at the University of Chicago. In a 1962 article, Herbert Gans constructed a typology of inner-city residents that is still useful. *Cosmopolites* are intellectuals and professionals as well as students, writers, and artists who live in the inner city to be near special cultural facilities. In the 1980s and early 1990s, people contributing to the gentrification of inner cities made up a sizable portion of cosmopolites. The *unmarried* or *childless* consist of two subgroups, those who move to the outer city when they can afford to, and those permanent, low-income individuals who live in this zone of transition for the rest of their lives. *Ethnic*

villagers are those residing in quasi-gemeinschaft neighborhoods who successfully isolate themselves from the anonymity of big-city life and find a good deal of satisfaction in intraethnic, primary group relations. The *deprived* and the *trapped and downwardly mobile* are the very poor, emotionally disturbed, and handicapped residents. This primarily nonwhite population makes up the growing underclass in urban America—those who are unemployed and unemployable. Sometimes called America's Third World population, these individuals are only marginally integrated into the larger society and lead difficult, unfulfilling lives.

Elijah Anderson Sociologist Elijah Anderson is arguably the preeminent urban ethnographer in the U.S. today. **Ethnography** is the direct observation of a group of people, an organization or small society, and the written description that results from this observation (Jary and Jary, 1991). For 14 years, Anderson observed and interviewed residents of two communities in a large Eastern city. One neighborhood was comprised of very poor to low income African Americans, while the other was a racially mixed setting with a growing number of affluent white inhabitants. **Streetwise** (Anderson, 1992) is a detailed, analytical examination of what has been called the sociology of everyday life. Anderson focused on the "nature of street life and public culture—how this diverse group of people 'got it on' or related to one another in public" (p. IX). In chapters titled "Sex Codes and Family Life" and "Street Etiquette and Street Wisdom," the author gives us a sociological interpretation of the lives of people who live in big-city America.

"The Impact of Drugs," another chapter, reveals how mind-altering substances have affected the lives of neighborhood users and non-users. Because "meaningful employment" has all but disappeared for young black males, many of these individuals have turned to crime and drugs. Relatively inexpensive crack cocaine has been the drug of choice for an untold number of poor, inner-city residents. Crack is a highly addictive substance that produces a "brief euphoria, then a sudden 'crash' that leaves the user with an intense craving . . . for more" (Anderson, 1992, p. 87). Inasmuch as this drug is commonly ingested via smoking a glass pipe, individuals whose lives are dedicated to staying high are called pipers. Crack addicts who search for anything of value— sometimes scouring the ground on their hands and knees—that can be turned into their "next blast" of the drug are known as "zombies."

After dealers convince a female to try crack, they may encourage her to engage in prostitution as a way of paying for additional drugs. Anderson explains how "crack whores" become agents for drug dealers, "hooking" men during sexual encounters and providing dealers with new customers. As she moves from one male client to another, the new addict may prostitute herself not primarily for making money, but as a mechanism for maintaining her drug habit.

One of the strengths of ethnographic research is the ability to understand some pattern of behavior from the perspective of those individuals who are intimately involved with it. Consider this description of a crack-addicted mother provided by a taxi driver (Anderson, 1992, p. 90):

> I've had my share of run-ins with these women on crack. They get in the cab, and wanna give you sex instead of the fare . . . One night a woman flagged me down . . . and I could tell right away she wasn't right . . . she was a piper . . . she had this little baby with her . . . The little baby stank like piss, and the Pampers hadn't been changed for a long time . . . All they [crack addicts] care about is getting that pipe . . . They don't have any feelings. And they'll do you in for your money. But she looked so bad, dragging that little baby around.

URBAN EXPLOSION IN DEVELOPING NATIONS

The Industrial Revolution was responsible for the initial and continued growth of scores of cities in Europe and North America. The growth of cities as Hoselitz (1954–1955) pointed out nearly a half-century ago, "is a necessary condition of economic development" (p. 278). It is no surprise, therefore, that modernization in the Third World would be accompanied by high rates of urban growth. What is astonishing is the incredible and unparalleled rate of population increase in these cities. In 1950 there was a total of 75 cities with populations between 1 million and 5 million people, with most of these urban areas located in developed countries. By 2015 there will be an estimated 463 world cities in this population category of which 345, or 75 percent will be in the poorer nations of the world.

An examination of **megacities,** that is, urban areas with 10 million or more inhabitants, is even more indicative of the growth of cities in developing nations. In 1950, New York City was the world's only megacity (see Table 13.1). By 2000, 12 of the 15 cities with 10 million plus residents were located in the developing world. The United Nations (*World Urbanization Prospects: The 1996 Revision,* 1997) estimates that of 26 megacities in the year 2015, only 4 will be the in rich nations. Eighteen of these giants will be Asian cities, including 2 in Japan (Table 13.2).

As noted in the chapter introduction, some megacities are primate cities, sprawling urban areas that are at least twice as big as the nation's second largest city and serve as a country's economic, political, and cultural hub. Mexico City, Lima (Peru), Cairo (Egypt), and Dacca (Bangladesh) are primate cities. Some observers are of the opinion that primate cities are good for a nation's urban development because of the trickle-down effect of advanced technology and overall economic momentum from these urban giants to smaller cities. Others insist that the concentration of resources in primate cities effectively slows down the development of middle-size urban areas. Primate cities can become so overpopulated and congested that vital economic and political functions are severely impeded (Spates and Macionis, 1987).

Urban population projections (especially megacities) may seem far-fetched until one realizes that a city such as Cairo adds an additional 2,050 people *each day,* or almost three-quarters of a million people a year (Murphy, 1992). A significant component of this explosive growth is a function of *rural-to-urban migration.* As noted in the previous chapter, migration is a function of push and pull factors. Regarding the rapid growth of cities in the developing world, people are pushed out of rural areas because of high unemployment and few if any chances for an improved standard of living, and drawn or pulled to cities because of a perception of greater economic opportunities and a better overall quality of life for themselves and their children.

In his book *Inside the Third World,* Paul Harrison (1984) said that "hell is a city." This is an obvious exaggeration, but urban slums in developing nations are densely packed areas of human misery and suffering, quite unimaginable to most people living in the developed world. Harrison described his first impressions of Calcutta as follows:

> I had seen a good deal of India and of the Third World before I visited Calcutta. But it was still a culture shock to arrive there, in a hot and damp rush hour, as dusk fell. It is the nearest human thing to an ant heap, a dense sea of people washing over roads hopelessly jammed as taxis swerve round hand pulled rickshaws, buses run into handcarts, pony stagecoaches and private cars and even flock of goats fight it out for the limited space . . . A young woman in a sari, her head leaning on her hand with a sleepy air of melancholia, reached for breath out the window, though the air outside was almost as dank and malodorous as inside. (pp. 165–166)

TABLE 13.1

The 15 Largest Urban Agglomerations Ranked by Population Size (in millions), 1950–2000–2015

	1950			2000			2015	
Rank	Agglomeration and country	Population	Rank	Agglomeration and country	Population	Rank	Agglomeration and country	Population
1	New York, United States of America	12.3	1	Tokyo, Japan	28.0	1	Toyko, Japan	28.9
2	London, United Kingdom	8.7	2	Mexico City, Mexico	18.1	2	Bombay, India	26.2
3	Tokyo, Japan	6.9	3	Bombay, India	18.0	3	Lagos, Nigeria	24.6
4	Paris, France	5.4	4	Sao Paulo, Brazil	17.7	4	Sao Paulo, Brazil	20.3
5	Moscow, Russia Federation	5.4	5	New York, United States of America	16.6	5	Dhaka, Bangladesh	19.5
6	Shanghai, China	5.3	6	Shanghai, China	14.2	6	Karachi, Pakistan	19.4
7	Essen, Germany	5.3	7	Lagos, Nigeria	13.5	7	Mexico City, Mexico	19.2
8	Buenos Aires, Argentina	5.0	8	Los Angeles, United States of America	13.1	8	Shanghai, China	18.0
9	Chicago, United States of America	4.9	9	Calcutta, India	12.9	9	New York, United States of America	17.6
10	Calcutta, India	4.4	10	Buenos Aires, Argentina	12.4	10	Calcutta, India	17.3
11	Osaka, Japan	4.1	11	Seoul, Republic of Korea	12.2	11	Delhi, India	16.9
12	Los Angeles, United States of America	4.0	12	Beijing, China	12.0	12	Beijing, China	15.6
13	Beijing, China	3.9	13	Karachi, Pakistan	11.8	13	Metro Manila, Philippines	14.7
14	Milan, Italy	3.6	14	Delhi, India	11.7	14	Cairo, Egypt	14.4
15	Berlin, Germany	3.3	15	Dhaka, Bangladesh	11.0	15	Los Angeles, United States of America	14.2

Source: World Urbanization Prospects: The 1996 Revision, United Nations Secretariat, Department of Economics and Social Affairs, Population Division. DRAFT. December 1997, New York.

TABLE 13.2

Number of Megacities in 1975, 1995, and 2015

Region	1975	1995	2015
World	5	14	26
Less developed regions	3	10	22
Africa	0	1	2
Asia*	1	5	16
Latin America and the Caribbean	2	4	4
More developed regions**	2	4	4
Northern America	1	2	2
Japan	1	2	2

* Excluding Japan

** Including Japan

Source: World Urbanization Prospects: The 1996 Revision, United Nations Secretariat, Department of Economics and Social Affairs, Population Division. DRAFT. December 1997, New York.

Since Harrison wrote that passage over 15 years ago, Calcutta has added some three million people to reach the 12.9 million mark, and is expected to have approximately 17.3 million inhabitants in the year 2015.

In 1994, the World Health Organization and the United Nations Environmental Program began a "detailed study" of the air quality in 20 megacities. The study concluded that in many of these urban areas "air pollution is a major health and environmental concern" ("Air Pollution in the World's Megacities," 1994, p. 13). Toxic chemicals in the air come from a variety of sources including waste incinerators, sewage treatment plants, factories, dry cleaning establishments, and motor vehicles. In all of the cities examined, lead from motor vehicle exhaust systems was a major source of pollution, and in half of them it is the most prominent source. As people become increasingly affluent in cities of the developing world, they will purchase more cars, trucks, and motor scooters making an already serious problem that much worse.

Because of ever-increasing air pollution, some Chinese cities are no longer visible when photographed from satellites. A recent study concluded that the air quality in Beijing was at a "level 4" with "level 5" being the worst ("Heavy Breathing in China," 1998). Some school children in Mexico City and Taipei wear surgical masks to protect them from a variety of pollutants as do many residents of Beijing. The U.S. State Department advises women assigned to Mexico City not to become pregnant lest their children suffer brain damage while still in the womb as a result of high rates of airborne toxins. A

World Health Organization study in the Mexican capital found blood toxicity in 70 percent of the fetuses examined (Gardels and Snell, 1989). Another study discovered levels of lead in 41 percent of newborn babies (Walker, 1993). Lead levels of this magnitude could reduce the intelligence quotient (IQ) of an individual by as much as 10 percent. A Mexican lung specialist stated, "If we continue this way, Mexico will have very few intellectuals (Sanchez, in Rodriguez, 1992, p. D7).

Apart from air pollution, there is a long list of problems facing cities in the developing world: high rates of unemployment and underemployment; water and noise pollution; water, food, and power shortages; not enough schools and hospitals; and quite often, massive corruption at every level of private and government bureaucracies. However, the most debilitating of these problems is the lack of housing. In the developing world slums are increasing at twice the rate of rapidly growing cities as a whole. Whereas the number of dwellings constructed annually in Third World nations is between 2 and 4 per 1,000 individuals, the urban population in these nations is increasing at between 25 and 60 persons per 1,000 (Hardoy and Satterthwaite, 1997). The housing shortage is so acute in many poor countries that in all likelihood it will never be resolved. For example, in Kenya, three million new units would have to be built each year to accommodate that country's urban growth. In Cairo, between 200,000 and 500,000 people live in cemeteries; and some residents of the infamous "City of the Dead" even have running water and electricity. Approximately 500 million urban dwellers (or one of every 12 people) worldwide

Available land is a scarce commodity in overcrowded cities throughout the developing world. These dwellings among heaps of garbage are home to thousands of people in Cairo's infamous "City of the Dead." In the not-too-distant future even the cemeteries of many urban giants will be overflowing with people, both living and dead.

Focus on
India

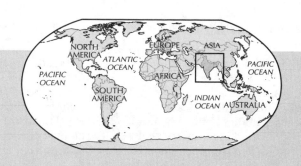

Population: 1,004,000,000
Life Expectancy at Birth (years): Male—62.54;
  Female—64.29
Form of Government: Federal Republic (Democracy)
Major Religions: Hindu (80%); Muslim (14%);
  Christian (2%); Sikh (2%)
Major Racial and Ethnic Groups: Indo-Aryan (72%);
  Dravidian (25%)
Population Doubling Time: 37 years
Per Capita GNP (1997 U.S. dollars): $370
Principal Economic Activities: Agriculture; Industry
Colonial Experience: Former British Colony
Adult Literacy Rate: 52% Male—65.5%; Female—37.7%

Megacities in a Developing World

India is not usually thought of as an urban nation, and that supposition is correct when one considers that only 26 percent of its citizens reside in cities. However, 26 percent of one billion people is approximately 260 million, a figure only slightly less than the entire population of the United States. For most of its 4,000-year history, India has been a rural society, and as recently as 1901, only 26 million people residing in modern-day Indian territory, or 11 percent of the population, lived in cities (Nagpaul, 1988). The growth, therefore, to 260 million urban dwellers represents a tenfold increase in 100 years as the number of cities with populations of 100,000 or more jumped from 24 to well over 300 in the same period.

As incredible as India's urban evolution has been, growth projections for the first quarter of the twenty-first century are nothing less than mind-boggling. By the year 2025, approximately one-half of the country's projected 1.384 billion people will be urban residents (Dogan and Kasarda, 1988). This translates into 629 million city dwellers, only 37 million people fewer than the combined population of all 40 European nations in the year 2000. Currently, of the nation's 23 urban centers with a million or more people, the "big-four" megacities of Bombay, Delhi, Madras, and Calcutta are the largest. Between 1981 and 1991, their population increased by 66, 46, 25, and 19 percent respectively (most of the increase in Bombay's population was due to the incorporation of five neighboring political units) (Dutt and Sen, 1992). India's National Capital region, which is comprised of Delhi and a constellation of smaller cities, has a population of approximately 32.5 million (approximately the number of California residents in 1999) living in an area the size of Maryland.

Like the inhabitants of other poor countries, residents of India have a life expectancy (59 years) significantly shorter than that of individuals living in developed nations (75 years). Health problems are especially severe for the most destitute residents of urban areas, commonly known as squatters, pavement dwellers, or slum ("jhuggie") dwellers. Undernourished if not chronically malnourished, these individuals are susceptible to a host of illnesses. Because tens of millions of pavement dwellers across the country have no access to basic facilities, they urinate and defecate in the streets, open gutters, and unattended fields, creating human waste that pollutes the air and water and spreads disease-causing microbes. These urban untouchables "ultimately touch everyone, including the upper class, no matter how hard this group tries to maintain their purity within their upper-income clubs, and Lysol disinfected homes" (Banjeree, 1996, p. 232).

Although their poverty generates disease-producing behavior, the urban poor consume much less water, much less energy, and produce significantly less solid waste than members of the affluent classes. Collectively, the residents of Calcutta, Bombay, Madras, and Delhi generate 15,855 tons of garbage a *day*, 12,660 tons of which is cleared and disposed of. This leaves a deficit of 3,195 tons (or 6,390,000 pounds) a day that accumulate in city streets. Similar figures for the "uncleared" sewage deficit in these cities run into the tens of millions of liters per day (Banjeree, 1996). The undisposed garbage and sewage attracts mosquitoes, cockroaches, rats, fleas, flies, and a variety of insects that spread bacteria-causing diseases such as malaria, dengue fever, encephalitis, dysentery, cholera, amoebiasis, and poliomyelitis. The situation is especially problematic during the monsoon season when torrential rains quickly back up antiquated sewer systems and many streets (as well as entire neighborhoods) are flooded and awash in raw sewage.

Urban and regional planning specialist Tridib Banjeree (1996) reminds us that although they are often examined individually, poverty, pollution, public health, and productivity are interrelated and interdependent phenomena. In the fall of 1994, an epidemic in the Indian city of Surat killed 5,000 people (and caused the mass exodus of 500,000 more) and was attributed to urban squalor and the unsanitary living conditions of pavement dwellers. Fearful of a plague spreading to their shores, India's trading partners banned the importation of all products from that country for two weeks (Banjeree, 1996). The loss of export revenue cost India over $1 billion, a significant amount of money for a developing nation.

In 1982, Indian environmentalists estimated that just breathing the air in Calcutta was equivalent to smoking one pack of cigarettes a day. Today, with millions more people living in the metropolitan area, residents of Calcutta are no doubt inflicting damage upon their lungs comparable to two-plus packs of cigarettes a day. India's air pollution problems are a direct result of motor vehicle emissions, power plants, and the engines that fuel heavy industry. As long as cities increase in size, and the middle class expands, the growing number of motor scooters, cars, and trucks will make the foul-smelling, noxious air even more toxic. Like other developing nations, India is polluting the physical environment in its effort to modernize as quickly as possible.

Another major health problem in India with a predominantly urban locus is AIDS. In the mid-1990s, an estimated 5 million people were HIV positive, a figure that I. H. Gilda (in Key et al., 1996, p. 12) of the Indian Health Organization stated is "likely to go up to 20 million in a best-case scenario and 50 million in worst-case scenario" in the next few

years. According to one particularly grim forecast, by the year 2006, as many as 160 million Indians could be infected with this disease (Friedman, 1996).

The overwhelming number of people who contract AIDS in India do so via heterosexual intercourse, with most of the victims living in Maharashtra, especially the capital of that western state, Bombay. India's financial center, Bombay has approximately 100,000 female prostitutes (of an estimated 10 million prostitutes in the entire nation), over 50 percent of whom are believed to be carrying the AIDS-causing virus (Friedman, 1996). Truck drivers, who frequently exchange money for sex, transmit the disease from one urban center to another, while migrants to the cities (predominantly young males) infect their wives when they return home, or when their spouses eventually join them in the city (Purvis, 1997; "India Wakes Up to AIDS," 1998).

Prostitution is legal in India, although operating a brothel and living off the money from the sexual transactions of a second party are punishable offenses. However, because this activity generates in excess of $400 million annually in Bombay alone, organized crime syndicates in league with local politicians and criminal justice officials are not likely to be deterred from making money via the "fabulously lucrative flesh trade," no matter what the heath risk to all concerned may be (Friedman, 1996). With as many as 10,000 AIDS-related deaths a month in Bombay, the city is spending a sizeable percentage of its limited health budget on this single malady.

Each of the big-four cities is the primary metropolitan center in a geographical region of the country (north, south, east, and west). As such they attract a significant number of migrants who gravitate to these urban giants in

search of economic opportunities and an overall improvement in their standard of living. Whereas population growth in rural India has been at the rate of 2 percent per year recently, the growth rate in urban India has been closer to 3.5 percent. The difference in these two figures is the result of rural-to-urban migration. One Indian sociologist described the influx of rural peasants to the cities each year as "several thousand lifeboats heading for few islands" (Chengappa, 1988, p. 57). A Calcutta newspaper publisher noted, "Survival is why all these people come. Whatever little they can earn is more than they could in the villages where they were born" (in Kaylor, 1984, p. 86). As is the case in other developing nations, the movement of so many people from primarily impoverished rural areas to Indian cities is in large measure a function of an uneven policy of development that has favored cities at the expense of the agricultural sector.

Movement from the countryside to cities is selective by sex, that is, more males than females make their way to urban India. As a consequence, the *sex ratio* (the number of males per 100 females) is highly skewed with just over 120 males residing in cities of over 100,000 for every 100 females. This surplus of young males in urban areas has undoubtedly contributed to the spread of AIDS, as young men now far removed from the network of informal social control that exists in the villages frequent prostitutes. Rural-to-urban migration also contributes to the rural "brain drain" as people who migrate tend to be the most productive and skilled workers in the countryside.

Approximately 30 to 40 percent of the residents of India's major cities (both recent migrants as well as people born in urban areas) are members of what McGee (1997) calls the "proto-

India's untouchables do the nation's hardest and most demeaning work. Mohandas Gandhi (1869–1948) was largely unsuccessful in his effort to elevate the status of untouchables, or as he often called them, "harijans" (children of God). The Indian government's attempt to "reserve" a designated number of spots for untouchables in schools, universities, and public sector jobs has often been met with violent opposition on the part of upper caste members.

proletariat"—people who are neither salaried wage earners nor peasants. Rather, they are engaged in individual or family enterprises (legal and illegal) in what has been referred to as the "lower circuit, informal, or bazaar economy." All manner of foodstuffs, clothing, cheap household goods, inexpensive religious items, toys, and books are sold, oftentimes displayed on a blanket strewn over one or two square yards of sidewalk with the owner's entire stock of inventory costing less than $100. Services include washing and cutting hair, repairing shoes, fixing small appliances, transporting individuals and goods via bicycles and carts, pumping air into tires, and removing wax from people's ears. These services are routinely provided on the streets without the benefit of privacy. The proto-proletariat are vital members of the urban economy. Not only do these individuals provide necessary goods and services for other poor people, but by so doing, they contribute to the political stability of the cities. Tens of thousands of people without the wherewithal to make a living

are likely to engage in collective violence (riots), and are prime candidates for more organized (potentially revolutionary) political behavior that is strongly opposed to the status quo.

Apart from the serious problems associated with the tremendous growth of Indian cities, many individuals have been concerned with the impact urbanization/modernization is having on the traditional aspects of Indian society. Mohandas Gandhi (1869–1948) believed that Indian growth and industrialization would slowly but surely destroy traditional culture in his country. However, others are quick to point out that India has survived serious challenges (including over four hundred years of European colonization) to its social/cultural integrity and still remains overwhelmingly "Indian." One need only visit a few of the nation's over 600,000 villages to see the evidence of this firsthand.

While village life remains vibrant in contemporary India, it has been affected by rural-to-urban migration. The lives of people who move to the cities are no

longer circumscribed by family and the dynamics of caste relations in a locale that was the center of their universe. Jay Weinstein (1991, p. 19) notes that "when village life is challenged . . . the effects reverberate throughout the social structure." For Weinstein, urban growth in India has not been characterized by the replacement of traditional values with modern ones; rather the process has been "seemingly paradoxical mixtures, combinations, compromises, and synthesis" (p. 20).

When rural Indians who moved to cities began working in factories, plant managers had to make changes that would accommodate a "rural reality." For example, the work calendar was modified to include days off for Hindu religious festivals, and employees had to be situated in positions that were compatible with caste membership and relations. Altars and shrines are routinely found in work areas, and some large manufacturing companies have dozens of places of worship scattered throughout the work environment. Although the interpenetrations of family, work, caste, and religion may not be as significant and far-reaching in urban India as in the countryside, that relationship is hardly absent.

To date, traditional Indian culture has been able to "endure resist, and even combat" the impact of urban growth to a degree that had not been anticipated by numerous scholars and political leaders (Weinstein, 1991, p. 20). It remains to be seen if this pattern will persist, or if the forces of urbanization and modernization will destroy much of traditional Indian society as Gandhi predicted. At the current rate of change, if the latter occurs it will not be happen quickly, but if this transformation does come about, a way of life that persisted for more than 4,000 years will be gone forever.

(mostly in developing nations) are homeless or lack adequate housing (Harper, 1998). According to a United Nations report, an estimated 10 million people die each year in densely populated urban areas as a result of health problems brought about by substandard housing and poor sanitation (Wright, 1994).

A partial solution to the housing shortage is for people to construct dwellings "illegally or informally." Hardoy and Satterthwaite (1997) note that it is not uncommon for 30 percent of a city's population to be housed in such a manner, with dwellings constructed by people who have "demonstrated remarkable ingenuity in developing their own homes and new residential areas" (p. 267).

MODERN PEOPLE

Discussions of modernization are usually focused at the institutional level; that is, the transformation of a society's political, cultural, and, especially, economic organizations. However, the fundamental unit of change in any group or social system is the individual. So before launching into an investigation of how and why modernization occurs, we have to determine the respects in which modern people differ from their traditional counterparts and the circumstances under which this change from the old to the new takes place.

Alex Inkles (1973) identified a set of personal qualities he believed accurately characterize modern individuals. The most important of these are (1) openness to new experience both with others and with ways of doing things, (2) increasing independence from traditional authority figures such as parents and priests, (3) belief in the power and effectiveness of science and medicine with a corresponding disregard of a fatalistic view of life, (4) ambition for oneself and one's children to be upwardly mobile and successful, and (5) a strong interest in community activities as well as local, national, and international affairs (see Figure 13.3).

To see whether the process of modernization had an effect on the values and behaviors of people in developing nations, Inkles and his research assistants (1973) interviewed 6,000 people in Argentina, Chile, India, Israel, Nigeria, and East Pakistan (now Bangladesh). They concluded that people in these countries did in fact take on the preceding characteristics, and the term " 'modern man' is not just a construct in the mind of social theorists" (p. 345). Indeed, the personality and behavioral characteristics of modern individuals were the same in all six societies. On the basis of this finding, Inkles speculated on a psychic "unity of mankind." "There is evidently a system of inner, or what might be called structural, constraints on the organization of the human personality which increase the probability that those individuals—whatever their culture—who have certain personality traits will also more likely have others which 'go with' some basic personality system" (p. 347). Data also indicated that formal education was the most powerful variable in determining how an individual scored on the modernization scale.

1. What is the ideal amount of schooling for children like yours?   low to *high years*
2. If a boy suggests a new idea for farming, should father *approve*/disapprove?
3. Which should most qualify a man for higher office? *education*/popularity/family/ tradition
4. One's position in life depends on fate always to *own effort always*.
5. Do you prefer a job with *many*/few/no responsibilities?
6. Will we someday understand nature?   *fully*/never can
7. Limiting the size of families is *necessary*/wrong.
8. Do you consider yourself primarily a citizen of a *nation*/region/state/city?
9. How often do you get news from newspapers?   *daily*/often/rarely/never
10. Would you prefer a rural life/*urban life?*
11. Can a person be good without religion?   *yes*/no
12. Would you choose a spouse to suit your parents always/*yourself always?*

FIGURE 13.3

Selected Abbreviated Questions from Scales Measuring Individual Modernity (italic alternative indicates modernity)

Source: Adapted from Alex Inkles, 1983, EXPLORING INDIVIDUAL MODERNITY. © 1983 by Columbia University Press. Reprinted with permission of the publisher.

School, therefore, is not only a place where individuals learn a set of facts and skills, it is also an institution that changes the way people think of themselves, others, and the society in which they live.

The factory was the second most important organization in changing a person's personality or character, "serving as a general school in attitudes, values, and ways of behaving which are more adaptive for life in a modern society" (Inkles, 1973, p. 348). Significant changes arising in the workplace even occurred when individuals were adults. Commenting on the findings of Inkles, Robert Lauer (1982) noted that no claim is made that modern societies make modern individuals or vice versa. "Rather, there is interaction with individual modernity facilitating societal modernity and, in turn, modernization generating greater numbers of modern individuals" (p. 103).

MODERNIZATION THEORIES

Evolutionary Models

Theories of modernization that attempted to explain the industrialization and development of Africa, Asia, and Latin America were directly related to nineteenth-century evolutionary explanations (Applebaum, 1970). These, in turn, were influenced by Darwin's monumental works, *On the Origin of Species* and *The Descent of Man*. The founders of sociology reasoned that if biological laws could explain the evolution of animals (including humans), an identifiable set of social laws must be responsible for the development and progress of human societies. Much of the work of this period was an attempt to discover and articulate these "social laws." Not only did nineteenth-century sociologists incorporate much of the philosophy of the biological sciences (the search for laws, emphasis on experimentation and observation), but they also began to think of society as a living organism. Using an organic analogy, they viewed society as an organism that continually develops and matures as it passes or grows through a number of stages. Cyclical theorists eventually added stages of decay, decline, and death to their grand schemes of social change (Applebaum, 1970).

Auguste Comte and Herbert Spencer Auguste Comte believed that societies evolved as they passed through three stages and that their development was "natural and unavoidable." Societies invariably change because of the human being's instinctive quest for self-perfection. This evolutionary movement toward a final state of perfection was smooth and uniform. Comte viewed society as "the Great Being" that be-

came increasingly complex, interdependent, and subject to central authority (Applebaum, 1970, p. 210).

English sociologist Herbert Spencer depicted societies as passing through a series of stages as they became increasingly complex and interdependent. Depending on the presence or absence of external conflict, they were either militant or industrial in response to their social and natural environments (Coser, 1971).

Ferdinand Tönnies For Ferdinand Tönnies, the two societal types were gemeinschaft and gesellschaft. Gemeinschaft, or community, denotes societies that are informal, traditional, and based on primary as opposed to secondary relations. Family and kinship relations are paramount, and social control is a function of shared values, norms (folkways and mores), and religious beliefs (Martindale, 1981). Gesellschaft means association or society and refers to relations that are "contractual, impersonal, voluntary and limited" (p. 98). These large, urban societies are dominated by economic institutions and the quest for material success. The principal forms of social control are public opinion and the law. Tönnies predicted the rapid demise of gemeinschaft societies and the corresponding ascendancy of gesellschaft ones. This troubled him, as it could lead to the death of culture itself if some gemeinschaft traditions were not kept alive.

Emile Durkheim Durkheim, as you will recall, was concerned with the social and psychological factors that bonded individuals and groups together to form a common entity, or society. In societies characterized by "mechanical solidarity" with a minimal division of labor and little role specialization, people share a common world view or "collective conscience" (Durkheim, 1933/1895). Lacking an opportunity for individual experiences, members of society are bound together by their sameness and devotion to common values. The polar opposite, "organic solidarity," is found in large, complex societies with a significant division of labor. Specialization in the workplace means that people have different experiences and are less likely to view and interpret events in the same manner. In societies of the organic type (the modern world), the "individual conscience" is well developed, resulting in fewer shared values. Social solidarity, therefore, is a function of mutual dependence: people need the skills and services that others provide in their daily lives. For Durkheim, a growing population and the corresponding increase in interaction ("moral density") were major factors in the transition from mechanical to organic solidarity.

Impact of Classical Theorists

Nineteenth-century evolutionary thinkers like Durkheim and Spencer had a significant impact on contemporary modernization theorists. According to most of these **unilinear theories of change,** societies would undergo a similar (if not identical) set of transformations, resulting in the same end product: the modern industrial state. Modernization was also considered a universal and highly predictable event (Applebaum, 1970). Writing in the evolutionary tradition, contemporary sociologist Neil Smelser (1973) saw modernization primarily in terms of economic development. Notice the dual-stage model implicit in his view of the "technical, economic, and ecological processes frequently accompanying development" (p. 269). In other words, development is the transition from traditional societies (stage 1) to modern societies (stage 2) on four dimensions. Concerning technology, a change occurs from the simple and traditional toward the use of scientific knowledge. In agriculture, the transformation is from subsistence farming to specialization in cash crops and the use of wage labor for agricultural work. In industry, the transition is from human and animal power to machines for the purpose of mass production and making a profit. Demographically, the movement is of people from farms and villages to urban centers.

These processes have a significant impact on the entire society, and one of their results is that human groups become increasingly differentiated; that is, there are more specialized and "autonomous social units." For example, education is no longer carried out informally by the family but is conducted in schools by trained professionals. With modernization and the expanding division of labor, a highly specialized system of education is necessary to train doctors, lawyers, and engineers, as well as workers in the hundreds of other occupations that make up the industrial workforce. This increased specialization and differentiation renders the "old social order" or patterns of integration obsolete.

Smelser cautioned that the transformation from a traditional to a modern society does not occur without paying a price. Social disturbances such as "mass hysteria, outbursts of violence, and religious and political movements" (1973, p. 279) reflect the unevenness of large-scale social change. These disturbances also occur because people are fearful of new social arrangements or have a vested interest in maintaining the existing system of stratification.

Criticisms of Evolutionary Models

Evolutionary models have expanded our knowledge and understanding of the modernization process, but they are not without shortcomings. The most damaging criticism is that they are long on description and short on explanation. In other words, they do a good job of telling us *how* the process of modernization takes place and unfolds but not *why* it occurs in the first place. Sociologist Alejandro Portes (1976) suggested that these theories "beg the entire question" (p. 64) of large-scale (macro) social change. For example, they do not tell us why social transformation happens in some societies and not others, why differentiation takes place at various rates, and whether and when the process can be reversed. Another fundamental criticism is that change is generally viewed as smooth and gradual. However, a cursory view of development in many (if not most) Third World nations reveals that modernization is anything but slow and even; rather, it is a process fraught with strife, conflict, and, too often, the loss of life. These evolutionary or modernization theories also ignored the possibility that patterns of development in the twentieth century were distinctly different from those experienced by NRCs when they began industrializing over 150 years ago (Evans and Stephens, 1988).

The distinguished scholar Samuel Huntington (1996) has commented on two beliefs often associated with modernization that he believes are "misguided, arrogant, false, and dangerous" to varying degrees. The "Coca-colonization thesis" is the view that developing nations are embracing American popular culture, a culture that is rapidly "enveloping the world." For Huntington, proponents of this position are confusing the heart of a nations's culture (language, religion, traditions, etc.) with material consumption. "Drinking Coca-Cola does not make Russians think like Americans any more than eating sushi makes Americans think like Japanese" (p. 28–29). Closely related to this view is the equally false perspective that as nations modernize they automatically Westernize, abandoning traditional cultures for prevailing ideas from rich industrial states. Huntington flatly asserts that "Modernization and economic development neither require nor produce Westernization" (p. 37).

Yet another shortcoming of these theories is that their explanations often seem "actorless." The processes of "urbanization, bureaucratization, and the other components of modernization appeared driven by inexorable forces rather than by the interests and actions of states, classes and other social actors" (Evans and Stephens, 1988, p. 739). Just as evolutionary or modernization theories tend to ignore the actions of human beings as causal agents of change, they also remove societies from the international context within which they exist. That is, they focus almost exclusively on the *internal* mechanisms of social change and neglect the "interrelationships among nations and the impact of such factors on the internal structures of each" (Portes, 1976, p. 66).

This leads to a final criticism, that evolutionary or modernization theory is ahistorical. Social change, especially something as far-reaching as modernization, does not happen in a sociohistorical vacuum. Although many similarities across nations exist regarding their social development, each nation has a unique history that must be taken into account in explaining and predicting the country's social, political, and economic advancement. Whereas sociology attempts to make general statements about a particular category of events (e.g., modernization), and some things may be said about all the countries in this category (energy changes from muscle to machine power), we cannot ignore the fact that a given country's cumulative experience will affect its path and speed of modernization. For example, we need consider only India, China, and Mexico to see how each nation's individual historical record has affected its development process. Modernization theory all but ignores the impact (trade, colonization, military intervention) that European powers and the United States had on poor nations of the world for hundreds of years (Shannon, 1996).

In spite of these many criticisms, evolutionary or modernization theories cannot be dismissed en masse. As we have seen, they were an integral part of the development of sociology. Pioneering sociologists were spectators during the first wave of industrialization that began in the nineteenth century and sought a general, theoretical explanation for the changes they were witnessing. Flawed as they were, these early theories demonstrated that systemic social change could be explained only from a scientific discipline that considered the interplay of all the major institutions in society. Such a discipline was sociology. In the post—World War II era, modernization theorists challenged social scientists and historians to explain development that was occurring in the so-called Third World. This helped broaden the base of inquiry as researchers focused their attention on the developing as well as the developed nations of the world. A renewed interest in the process of development partially set in motion work by sociologists with a completely different view of modernization: world system theory.

WORLD SYSTEM THEORY

At the end of World War II, most African and Southeast Asian countries were members of European-dominated colonial empires. In the aftermath of a war that took such a heavy toll in lives and money, even victorious nations such as England and France were unable and/or unwilling to put down movements for independence sweeping across their colonies. The eventual success of these movements resulted in a heightened awareness and concern in the United States regarding the future of Third World nations. A major worry was that these newly independent states would turn communist. The Cold War of the 1950s saw the world divided into two hostile camps: East and West, communist and capitalist. To keep former colonized nations political allies of the West and ensure that economic development followed a capitalist rather than socialist path, a substantial amount of foreign aid was pumped into Third World countries. According to Chirot (1977, p. 3), this aid was to accomplish four goals:

1. Outdated traditional values in Third World countries that inhibited savings, investment, and a rational organization of the economy had to be changed.
2. Antiquated, insufficiently democratic political structures had to be modernized to encourage progress and effectively undermine leftist revolutions.
3. People had to be trained in order to provide an adequate supply of skilled labor and managerial personnel.
4. Money in the form of loans and gifts had to be made available to speed up the development process.

These goals were based on a fundamental assumption of evolutionary theory; that is, that modernization occurs gradually and uniformly along a relatively smooth path. Post—World War II theorists and policymakers assumed that the realization of these goals would accelerate the development process. They believed that money and technical assistance from the United States would prime the modernization pump, and economic development would quickly come pouring out.

But the water never did flow, and the plight of many Third World countries did not improve; on the contrary, in some, the conditions deteriorated. So what went wrong? A new generation of scholars called world system theorists argued that the fundamental assumptions of modernization theory were wrong and that the theory totally ignored the destructive side of capitalism (Apter, 1986). They offered an alternative view of the development process based on a new interpretation of history. This particular view of modernization, therefore, is as much an interpretation of history as it is a sociological theory.

Immanuel Wallerstein and His Followers

Foremost world system theorist Immanuel Wallerstein made three assumptions about the modern world (Harper, 1989). First, since approximately 1500, the modernizing countries of Europe had contact with most of the nations of the world, contact after 1800 taking the form of colonial empires and colonized nations. Second, after 1900, these empires gradually dissolved, although they maintained control as a result of their domination of world trade. Third, in the contemporary world, global economics are dominated by an interdependent, capitalist *world economic system* of trade and investment.

The colonial periods outlined in the first two assumptions are of crucial importance to an understanding of **world system theory (WST)** and require additional explanation. Before proceeding with this explanation, however, we must examine the international stratification system from the WST perspective. A central component is the Marxist notion of classes and class conflict; that is, capitalist societies consist of two antagonistic groups of classes, the bourgeoisie and the proletariat. WST extended this notion to a global level and, in a sense, viewed the world as one large, interrelated, interdependent society with upper, middle, and lower classes. On the global level, however, classes are made up not of groups of people, but of countries. The international upper class is called the **core,** the lower class the **periphery,** and the international middle class is known as the **semiperiphery** (see Figure 13.4). Sociologist Thomas Shannon (1996, p. 33) has spelled out how the core, periphery, and semiperiphery are interrelated in the capitalist world-economy. Peripheral countries produce and export labor-intensive, low-technology goods (toys, clothing, etc) that are in demand in both core and semiperipheral states. Core nations produce capital-intensive, high technology goods that are sold primarily to other core states. However, some of these products are also sold to peripheral and semiperipheral countries. The semiperiphery produces and exports peripheral-like goods to the core, and core-type goods to poorer peripheral states. In return, semiperipheral countries receive goods produced with labor-intensive, low-technology methods from the periphery and capital inten-

---

The Capitalist World System in the Early 1900s

Core societies were industrial, economically diversified, rich, powerful nations relatively independent of outside control. They were the United Kingdom, Germany, United States, and France.

Lesser core societies were not as powerful or as influential as the major core nations, including Belgium, Sweden, the Netherlands, Denmark, and Switzerland.

Semiperipheral societies were midway between the core and the periphery. These nations were trying to industrialize and diversify their economies, and were not as subject to outside manipulation as peripheral societies. They were Spain, Russia, Austria-Hungary, Japan, and Italy.

Peripheral societies were economically overspecialized, relatively poor, and weak societies subject to the manipulation or direct control by the core. The rest of the world made up these societies.

The Capitalist World System Today

Core societies are the United States, western and northern Europe, Japan, Canada, Australia, and New Zealand.

Semiperipheral and peripheral states make up the rest of the world. These categories are not as sharply defined today as they were at the beginning of the century. They include some oil-rich countries and newly industrializing states, as well as nations that are poor but increasingly important regional powers because of their large populations. These countries are relatively independent of the core. Examples are Saudi Arabia, India, Iran, Turkey, Israel, Indonesia, Mexico, Argentina, Egypt, Taiwan, South Korea, and Singapore.

Truly peripheral societies are peripheral in the old (1900) sense of the world. Today they include communist as well as capitalist countries. Most of sub-Saharan Africa, smaller countries of Latin America and the Caribbean, and some South and Southeast Asian nations are in this group.

FIGURE 13.4

The Capitalist World System

Source: Adapted from Daniel Chirot, *Social Change in the Twentieth Century* (New York: Harcourt Brace Jovanovich, 1977), pp. 24–25; Daniel Chirot, *Social Change in the Modern Era* (San Diego: Harcourt Brace Jovanovich, 1986), pp. 232–233.

sive, high-technology methods from the core. The result of this stratification is an international division of labor in which lower-class countries work at the least desirable jobs for low wages and enrich upper-class societies.

But how did this international system of stratification come about? According to WST, the answer is colonization. Bergeson (1980) posited that "formal" core domination of the periphery occurred in two waves. The first wave was centered in North and South America and lasted from the sixteenth to the early nineteenth century. The European powers (France, England, Spain, Portugal) destroyed or forcibly moved indigenous Native American populations to make way for settlers and institutions from the core and the transplanting of slaves from Africa. The second period of colonization was centered in the Americas once again, as well as in Africa and Asia, and lasted from the late nineteenth century to the mid-twentieth century. This wave was less a matter of conquering and displacing local populations "and more a question of domination and control through political occupation" (Bergeson, 1980, p. 122). A third wave (beginning in the early 1970s) that *does not* involve formal colonial rule, but economic and arms dependence of peripheral countries, is less severe (for the peripheral nations) than the first two periods.

In 1994, developing nations spent $12.5 billion for armaments with much of this money flowing to arms dealers in the developed world. Countries such as India and Pakistan have formidable, well-equipped armies as a result of these purchases. In 1991, a U. N. coalition of over 500,000 troops was required to drive Iraq out of Kuwait. Iraq is a relatively poor nation that used its oil money to assemble the world's fourth-largest army. That army was built through arms purchases from numerous industrial countries, especially the Soviet Union and France.

The second period of formal colonization (1870–1945) is the most important for our understanding of development currently taking place in Third World nations. Chirot (1977) maintained that in the 1870s, the "French, the Germans, and the British set out on a hysterical race to divide up what was left of the world (and there was still quite a lot left at that time)" (p. 49). This mad scramble for territory was a result of the mistaken belief that the world was running short of raw materials and agricultural products. However, capitalism is predicated on a profit motive requiring continual growth and expansion, so even if the world was not running out of natural resources, colonies became lucrative areas where capital could be invested at a high rate of return. According to V. I. Lenin, the core's imperialistic ventures signaled the final, or most mature, phase of

capitalism. Lenin wrote that profits in "backward countries are usually high, for capital is scarce, the price of land is relatively low, wages are low, raw materials are cheap" (in Szymanski, 1981, p. 37).

The years of colonial expansion and high profits came to an end in 1910, when the world was essentially "filled up"; that is, there were no new, easy countries left to conquer and dominate. The demand for raw materials and new markets, coupled with an arms buildup that had been taking place for decades, led to a giant explosion: World War I (Chirot, 1977). After a brief postwar economic recovery, the world capitalist system was on the verge of collapse in the 1930s. The international economic system was in a shambles as a result of a terrible depression that ravaged the United States and other core nations. Germany, Italy, and Japan had turned fascist, and Germany was attempting to regain core status after its defeat in World War I. Japan and the Soviet Union (semiperipheral states at the time) were also trying to get into the core. It follows from Chirot's perspective that World War II was not an ideological struggle, but an attempt to control and alter the world system. In its aftermath and the destruction of the Japanese and German empires, the United States emerged as the undisputed leader of the capitalist world system. However, revolutions in the periphery (the colonies), beginning with the independence of India in 1947, signaled that the age of imperialism was coming to an end.

As this discussion indicates, Third World nations (especially former colonies) did not benefit from contact with the West as modernization theory assumes, but took a significant economic step backward. Thus, "underdevelopment in the less- developed countries arose at the same time and by the same process as did development in the richer industrial nations" (Harper, 1999, p. 244). In other words, underdevelopment and development are not two separate stages or phases, as some modernization theorists believe, but two sides of the same coin. Andre Gunder Frank (in Harper, 1998) stated, "The rich countries could not have become that way without exploiting the poor ones, so that underdevelopment is simply the reverse side of development" (p. 244). Speaking of WST, Portes (1976) stated that underdevelopment is not a backward, more primitive state prior to capitalism, but a variant of capitalism and "a necessary consequence of its evolution" (p. 74). It is important to keep in mind, however, that in spite of the exploitative relationship between the core and periphery, the core did not cause the *initial* poverty in these countries; it existed prior to their arrival. The core did, however, "create peculiarly lopsided economies and a slow pace in economic diversification" (Chirot, 1977, p. 36).

Colonialism and Modernization

The importance of the colonial period in understanding modernization today cannot be overemphasized. According to one variation of WST, the world modernized in the latter half of the nineteenth century and the first half of the twentieth century. At the end of this period, there were economic winners and losers. The core countries obviously won, and the losing peripheral nations would never successfully transform their economies to core level no matter how long and hard they worked. One reason for this inability to modernize fully is that exploitation did not end with the demise of colonialism in the post—World War II era. Even though many of the world's less developed nations gained political independence between 1946 and 1987, the majority (if not all) of them remain economically dependent on industrialized states to a significant degree. For example, coffee produced in the African nations of Kenya, Tanzania, and Ethiopia, as well as in most Latin American countries, is sold to a handful of multinational corporations. Inasmuch as these corporations control the price of coffee in a buyer's market, the producers have little choice but to sell their crops for whatever they are offered (Harper, 1989).

This neocolonialsim in the form of economic domination by multinational corporations ensures that modernization in the developing world can never be more than moderately successful. Consider the following example from the clothing industry. A dozen Paris-designed shirts can be manufactured in Bangladesh for as little as $38, or just over $3 apiece (see Table 13.3). The gross markup is $228, with the 12 shirts now selling at retail for $266 ($228 plus $38), or approximately $22 apiece (Chossudovsky, 1997). One reason for the huge profit margin on this merchandise is the (low) cost of labor in developing countries. Whereas a garment worker in the United States or Canada is paid between $6 and $10 an hour, laborers in a Bangladesh clothing factory earn between $1.20 and $1.60 a *day*. Over the past 30 years an increasingly large share of world manufacturing has been moved to cheap labor countries in Asia, Latin America, and eastern Europe.

Reducing the cost of labor is one of the ways that companies compete with each other. That is, if company A can pay its employees less than company B for doing the same work, company A can lower the price of its goods and sell more items than company B while still maintaining the same profit margin (the difference between the overall cost of producing an item and the selling price).

According to WST, multi-national corporations operate to further their own growth and profits and have little interest in the economic or social development of their host nations. These companies will continue down the path of cheap labor and pay impoverished people in poor countries as little as pos-

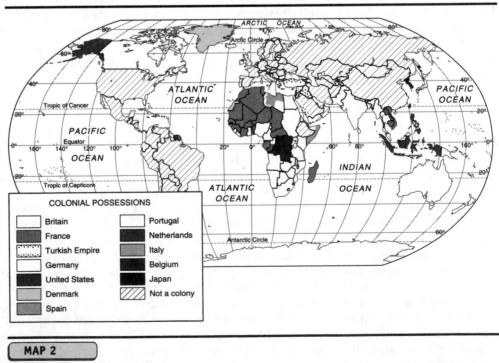

COLONIAL POSSESSIONS

- Britain
- France
- Turkish Empire
- Germany
- United States
- Denmark
- Spain
- Portugal
- Netherlands
- Italy
- Belgium
- Japan
- Not a colony

MAP 2

The Colonial World in 1914

TABLE 13.3

Cost Structure Third World Garment Exporter (U.S. dollars)

Materials and accessories (imported)	27
Depreciation on equipment	3
Wages	5
Net industrial profit	3
Factory price (one dozen shirts)	38
Gross mark-up	228
Retail price (per dozen) in the advanced countries	266
Retail price including sales tax (10 percent)	292.60

Note: Based on cost structure and sale prices of Bangladesh garment factory, 1992.

Source: The Globalization of Poverty—Impacts of IMF and World Bank Reforms, by Michel Chossudovsky, Zed Books Ltd, London, and New Jersey, p. 90, 1997.

sible. The power and scope of these organizations is as follows (Rohde, 1994a):

- Approximately one-third of the world's economic output is controlled by these organizations.
- These organizations employ (directly or indirectly) 150 million people, or 20 percent of the world's nonagricultural workforce.
- The richest 100 multinationals have $3.4 *trillion* in total assets.
- One-third of world trade is controlled by multinational corporations.

The presence of multinational corporations in Third World countries perpetuates a system in which the rich get richer and the poor get poorer. Michael Parenti (1989) has even rejected the label *developing countries,* stating the term is false and misleading. Many Third World nations are neither underdeveloped nor developing. Instead, they are more impoverished than ever and should be labeled *overexploited and maldeveloped.*

The economic situation of the world's poor countries is further complicated by the tremendous amount of money they owe First World banks and organizations like the International Monetary Fund (IMF). The collective foreign debt of developing nations increased from $62 billion in 1970, to over $2.2 *trillion* in 1998. With some of these countries spending between 35 and 50 percent of their export earnings just to pay the interest on the money they owe, economic development is severely hindered. Every dollar spent servicing the debt is one dollar less that can be used for developing a nation's infrastructure (schools, transportation, communication, health care, etc.) the foundation for economic growth.

Overspecialization

As a result of having been developed in a lopsided manner that benefited the core, many former colonies are economically overspecialized. Their economies are centered on the production of one or two cash crops or raw materials that they trade and sell in the international marketplace. When the price of coffee, cotton, aluminum, copper, rubber, tin, and oil begin to fall, countries that are economically dependent on these products can experience a rapid and severe decline in revenue. For example, farmers who attempt to make up for monetary losses by growing more coffee the following year may be rewarded by even lower prices if supplies increase (other growers are doing the same thing) and demand remains steady. Jacques Delacroix (1977) claimed that developed countries help to keep underdeveloped nations in the position of raw material exporters by controlling their access to technology and capital from the outside world. Acting as "gatekeepers," developed nations block the importation of money, goods, and the technological know-how necessary for industrialization and prevent poor countries from "becoming either self-sufficient or exporters of processed goods" (p. 96).

Another problem with agricultural overspecialization is that many primary food-producing countries cannot hope to see their markets expand significantly, no matter how healthy the economy of the developed world. For example, someone in the United States who sees his or her income double in the course of a year may buy twice as much sophisticated camera equipment, thereby helping the economy of some industrial nation. However, this person is highly unlikely to start eating twice as many bananas and thus significantly boost the earnings of a Ecuadorian farmer. WST contends that core nations will "only" provide loans and foreign aid to peripheral countries to invest in the mining of raw materials and the production of agriculture products that they (core nations) want to buy. This policy both perpetuates overspecialization on the part of poor countries and increases their dependency on rich nations (Shannon, 1996). There is also the danger that an increasing number of natural commodities like rubber and hemp will be partially if not totally replaced by synthetic products (Harper, 1989).

The Uncertain Future

With the demise of communism in the former Soviet Union and eastern block countries, as well as the growing economic might of Japan, China, numerous European nations, and the "four dragons," what does the future hold for the capitalist world system? Wallerstein (1996) is of the opinion that the United

States, Japan, and the European Community (EC) will struggle for "quasimonopolistic control over new leading industries" (p. 495). He argues that Japan has a "good chance" of winning this competition and will form an economic alliance with the United States, the latter playing the role of a "junior partner." A major sphere of influence for this alliance will be China, while the EC will have economic sway over Russia.

Politically, Wallerstein (1996) envisions three primary sources of instability in the world system over the next half century. In what he calls the "Khomeini option" (named for the Ayatollah Khomeini who controlled Iran from 1981 to 1989), one or more countries in the periphery will refuse to play by the rules and "geopolitical norms governing the world system" (p. 496). A second and more dangerous source of trouble is the "Saddam Hussein option." In this scenario a peripheral state challenges the military might of the rich nations. While Iraq was quickly brought to its knees in the Persian Gulf War, an enormous military mobilization was required on the part of the United States and its allies to achieve this end. Wallerstein notes that since the United States cannot sustain its armed forces at current levels either financially or politically into the next century, another Hussein-like challenge (especially if a number of them occur simultaneously) will be much more difficult to subdue. We might also add that terrorists using biological and/or nuclear weapons could bring about more havoc in the international capitalist system then a conventional war. The death of perhaps tens of thousands of people in core nations and the destruction of centers of business, communication, and transportation could cripple worldwide trade for a prolonged period of time.

Finally, there will be an "unstoppable mass movement of people" from poor countries of the south to rich countries of the north (including Japan). Political instability is likely to occur as a result of pressures from right-wing anti-immigrant groups and the demands of the immigrants themselves. Immigration-related problems will be difficult to solve inasmuch as many, if not most, people will have lost faith in the ability of the state to reconcile social inequities.

Criticism of World System Theory

A theory as all-encompassing and ruthless in its assessment of capitalism as WST is not without critics. Carlos Rangel (1989) maintained that even the poorest and most backward countries in the world have progressed as a result of international capitalism. They are better off "in measurable indexes of economic growth, public health, education, consump-

tion, and better off in something not measurable but essential: spiritual tone, the condition of being awake, alert and demanding" (p. 31). Rangel cited the four "little dragons" (Japan is the big one) of the Far East—South Korea, Singapore, Taiwan, and Hong Kong (now part of China)—as benefiting significantly from contact with capitalist countries. Critics of WST would also contend that as a result of the North America Free Trade Agreement (NAFTA), Mexico has realized substantial economic gains, perhaps even more so than the other two parties to the treaty, the United States and Canada.

Thomas Sowell (1983) claimed that explanations of colonial and neocolonial exploitation for underdevelopment beg the central question of why these countries were poor in the first place, long before the arrival of the European powers. Even if colonialism is a major factor in underdevelopment, how long can this explanation (excuse?) be used? South and Central American countries have been free of their colonial masters for over 175 years yet remain relatively poor. Sowell and others reasoned that the sad state of affairs in so many Third World nations is more a factor of *internal* problems (inefficient, corrupt governments, excessive military spending, etc.) than of *external* exploitation. Whereas WST is correct in its criticism of modernization theory for neglecting a country's ties to the outside world, it errs in the opposite direction by not taking into consideration numerous internal mechanisms of change. Finally, WST is criticized from a scientific perspective. Because it is not made up of interrelated propositions, it cannot be tested easily. Rather, it is a grand historical vision, a sociohistorical model meant to apply to a plurality of situations. It is a catchall explanation for everything that is wrong with the Third World. Shannon (1996, p. 21) notes that for many scholars "the entire intellectual approach of world system theory is questionable."

Regardless of the validity of these criticisms, WST has made valuable contributions to our understanding of the modernization process, especially the relationship between developing and developed nations. It rejected the assumption of modernization theorists that increased contact between the core and periphery would further development in the periphery. Although the idea that contact between rich and poor nations is *always* to the detriment of poor nations may be equally false, WST was correct in calling for a careful examination of this relationship. Unlike modernization theories that view internal class struggles as minor aberrations in need of "adjustment" (Evans and Stephens, 1988), WST correctly points out that these antagonistic relationships are *long-term* affairs with major political, economic,

These Palestinian women hold banners asking for freedom of speech and equality with men during a protest march at the Palestinian Legislative Council in Gaza City. A recent United Nations publication stated that "women comprise about half the world's population, perform approximately two-thirds of its work, receive only one-tenth of its income, and own less than one-hundredth of world assets."

and social consequences for all concerned. The theory examines the modernization process in the real world of continuing competition, conflict, and violence, both domestically and in the international political-economic arena.

Finally, WST draws our attention to questions that can only be addressed from a macro, sociohistorical perspective. Some of these questions, as Thomas Shannon (1996, p. 212) notes are: What accounts for the initial rise of capitalism and the economic success of core states? What explains the rise and fall of the great core powers? Why have most countries in the periphery failed to achieve sustained economic development?

WOMEN IN THE DEVELOPING WORLD

In the early 1970s, a cigarette advertisement featured a fashionably dressed young woman smoking with the caption reading "You've come a long way, baby." The distance women (babies?) in the United States have traveled in their struggle for equality is certainly debatable. However, the journey for Third World women in many countries is just beginning. Consider the following summary statements and situations regarding females in developing nations (Sivard, 1985; Heise, 1989; Jacobson, 1992; Gannon, 1994; "World Health Organization: Women's Health and Family Violence, 1997; "Women of Our World," 1998):

- Rural women produce more than half the food produced in developing nations, and as much as 80 percent in Africa.
- About two-thirds of the women over age 25 (and about half the men) have never been to school.

- Forty-three percent of males and 29 percent of females of the appropriate age are enrolled in secondary schools.
- In the developed world 14 of every 100 parliament/congressional seats are held by a woman. For the developing world those numbers are 10 out of every 100.
- Approximately 450 million women throughout the world (mostly in developing nations), as opposed to 400 million men, are stunted in growth because of malnutrition. One researcher found that boys in India were fifty times more likely to be treated for malnutrition than were girls, even though the condition was four or five times more prevalent in girls.
- In Peru, 70 percent of all crimes reported to police are of women beaten by their husbands.
- Forty-two percent of all Kenyan woman surveyed said they were beaten "regularly" by their husbands.
- In Kenya in 1991, the boys at a boarding school went on a rampage in the girls' dormitory, raping seventy-one and killing nineteen. Afterward the principal reportedly stated, "The boys never meant any harm to the girls. They just wanted to rape" (in Holloway, 1994, p. 78).
- A women's rights advocate in Pakistan noted that men in her country are rarely prosecuted for taking a female's life; "Killing a woman is like killing a cow or a goat or a chicken" (Sharif, in Gannon, 1994, p. 19).

Although women in developed nations are also exploited and physically abused by males, the rate and intensity of degradation at the hands of men are significantly greater in the Third World. For example, consider the grotesque and needless tragedy of dowry deaths, or bride burning, in India. At the time of marriage, the bride's family pays a dowry of money or goods to the groom as part of the nuptial agreement. This practice is increasingly viewed as a get-rich scheme on the part of husbands, with young brides meeting tragic deaths if the agreed-on dowry is not delivered (Heise, 1989). One of the most common ways of killing these women is burning them alive, later claiming the fiery death was an unavoidable "kitchen accident." The bereaved widower is now free to try for another marriage and another dowry. Indian police statistics indicate that in a recent year there were 4,835 dowry deaths in the entire country. However, a women's action group estimated that there are 1,000 annually in the state of Gujurat alone ("World Health Organization: Women's Health and Family Violence," 1997). Bombay officials report that one of four deaths in women between the ages of 15 and 24 is the result of "accidental" burning (Holloway, 1994).

Females are even discriminated against before they are born. Until forced to stop as a result of political pressure, an Indian sex detection clinic (using amniocentesis) advertised that it was better to spend $38 for aborting a female pregnancy now than spend $3,800 later on the young woman's dowry. One study examined 8,000 fetuses in six Bombay abortion clinics; 7,999 were female (Heise, 1989).

Reproductive Capacity and Control

That women give birth is an obvious fact of life. Not so obvious, however, is the way in which their reproductive capacity is socially defined and controlled. In developed countries, the number of children a woman has is most likely the result of a decision made jointly with her husband. In addition, although having a family may still be the most socially acceptable lifestyle in rich nations, little if any stigma is attached to being childless. Gender relations are significantly different in more traditional societies. Tens of millions of women are under enormous economic and cultural pressure to have large families. In many Asian countries, for example, a woman gains security and respect by bearing sons who will take care of her when she is old. Having daughters is preferable only to having no children at all; in Muslim societies, however, the failure to bear sons is cause for a man to consider finding a new wife.

Pregnant women in the United States are usually given special attention and thought to be particularly "cute" and feminine when they are "with child." In developing countries, however, having a baby is more likely to be a physically draining, possibly life-threatening ordeal than a time of excitement and anticipation. A pregnant woman living in a developed nation is surrounded by friends who shower her with attention. In the Third World, she is surrounded by other pregnant women who share her poverty. Numerous pregnancies over a short period of time, coupled with an inadequate diet, pose serious health problems for these women. Every pregnancy is a tremendous drain on a woman's body, requiring approximately 100,000 calories of nourishment (Sivard, 1985). Whereas it might be assumed that these women would be given nutritional priority because of their biologically demanding condition, the exact opposite is often true. In many societies, it is customary for men to eat first, boys next, then girls, and finally women. A pregnant woman residing in a protein-deficient environment is a prime candidate for malnutrition and anemia (a poverty-related disease that saps people's strength and increases their chances of becoming ill). Inasmuch as 50 percent of pregnant women in developing nations have anemia, it is not surprising that maternal mortality rates are so high. A woman's risk of dying during pregnancy or childbirth is 1 in 4,000 in northern Europe, 1 in 130 in Latin American/Caribbean countries, 1 in 65 in Asia, and 1 in 16 in Africa. Of the roughly 600,000 women who die each year from causes related to pregnancy, childbirth, is abortion, the overwhelming majority reside in developing countries. The implementation of two factors can help reduce these deaths: (1) family planning, which would help females delay having children as well as prevent unwanted pregnancies and abortions, and (2) Increased access to prenatal, delivery, and postpartum health care ("Women of Our World," 1998).

Effects of Modernization

Modernization has undoubtedly been a positive force in the lives of millions of Third World women, especially in terms of education and general health care. Although they still lag behind men on most indicators of well-being, the gap is not as wide as it was just a generation ago. Development is a double-edged sword, however, and its effect on females cuts both ways. For example, in Bangladesh, rural males who migrate to the cities in search of employment often abandon women and children, who must fend for themselves in economically depressed rural areas. Faced with the task of surviving alone in a poor village, women are often victimized yet a second time by the forces of modernization. In recent years, traditional markets for domestic handicrafts have been severely undercut by mass-produced factory items. In those factories where women work beside men, they often do so for significantly less money. In South Korea, for example, women receive only 60 percent of men's wages. Young women are often treated as disposable objects by some multinational corporations—organizations that work females hard for subsistence wages and then replace them when they are no longer as productive as a new group of desperately poor (younger) females.

Over the past twenty-five years, the number of rural women living in poverty has increased by almost 50 percent, while the corresponding increase for men has been only three percent. According to some observers, we are witnessing "the feminization of the Third World countryside"—a region disproportionately populated by women that is sliding into poverty (Power, 1992, p. B5). For Priscilla Gonzalez (1998, p. 5), the feminization of poverty refers to the "unique hardships" that females face worldwide. This phenomenon is "both a *cause* and *effect* of low birthweight, malnutrition, illiteracy and poor primary education."

Many African women are calling for an end to "gender apartheid," those discriminatory practices across social, economic, and political institutions that have kept females trapped in the lowest strata of society, subservient to males. In some Third World countries adult women have the status of "legal minors," that is, they are not permitted to own property or enter into contracts. Even when these legal barriers are absent, as a result of limited income and few economic opportunities, females very often do not have the money to purchase land ("Women's Access to Land Still Restricted by Tradition," 1996) The development process not only may increase the existing disparity in wealth, status, and power between the sexes, but can function to legitimate these inequalities as well.

The amount, pace, and direction of change associated with modernization can be very difficult for people in the developing world (as it was in the United States when we were modernizing) and for women in particular, who toil in centuries-old, male dominated societies. If males extend and consolidate their power over females as a by-product of the development process, a significant number of women may find themselves living in societies with the material trappings of modernization but the social, political, and economic reality of an even stronger patriarchal system.

SUMMARY AND REVIEW

Cities in the Modern World

1. *What impact did the Industrial Revolution have on cities?*

With the Industrial Revolution, both the number and size of cities in the United States and Europe grew rapidly. People flowed into urban areas from the countryside and typically lived in hastily built, overcrowded, unsanitary apartments. Tens of thousands of immigrants from Europe also relocated to American cities in the middle of the nineteenth century. (P. 312)

Human Ecology and the City

2. *How do human ecologists view cities?*

Human ecologists constructed theories explaining the relationship between humans and the social and physical world they constructed, especially cities. Concentric zone theory views the city as a series of zones emanating from the center, each one characterized by a different group of people and activity. Sector theory envisions urban areas as pie- or wedge-shaped sectors radiating outward from the central business district. According to the multiple-nuclei theory, cities have not one major center, but several nuclei or centers scattered throughout the urban area. (Pp. 314–315)

Suburbanization, Winter Cities, and Sunbelt Cities

3. *When and under what conditions did suburbanization occur in the United States?*

In the 1920s, U.S. cities began to decentralize as the growth of the suburbs exceeded that of the central cities. Suburbanization slowed considerably during the Great Depression and resumed with the end of World War II in 1945. White working-class families followed many businesses and industries to the suburbs, while minority groups were left behind. (P. 316)

4. *Why did sunbelt cities grow rapidly in the 1970s?*

In the early 1970s, the sunbelt began to grow for at least five reasons: (a) Conservative legislation and illegal workers from Mexico and Central America kept the cost of labor down, making the region attractive to business; (b) industries began leaving the Northeast to escape the relatively high cost of union labor in that region; (c) local governments started subsidizing new industries by giving them generous tax breaks; (d) influential sunbelt politicians were successful in winning big military contracts and physical improvements such as highway projects from the federal government; and (e) the region benefited as the economy changed from heavy industry and manufacturing to one based on high technology and information processing. (P. 318)

5. *Why are cities in the developing world growing so fast?*

Cities in Third World nations are growing much faster than urban areas in the developed world when the latter were modernizing. This tremendous growth is a product of two factors: a substantial, natural increase in urban populations (births over deaths), and unprecedented rural-to-urban migration as people leave the countryside in the hopes of finding employment and leading a better life in the cities. What they typically encounter is overcrowding, unemployment, pollution, and violence. (Pp. 322–324)

Modern People

6. *What difference, if any, is there between people who reside in traditional countries and individuals who live in modern nations?*

People in modern societies are different from those individuals in more traditional nations. They are open to new experiences; increasingly independent of traditional authority figures; less fatalistic and more inclined to accept science and modern medicine; ambitious, seeking to improve their standing in society; and interested in community, national, and international affairs. (P. 328)

Modernization Theories and World System Theory

7. *How did the founders of sociology view change at the societal level?*

The founders of sociology reasoned that if biological laws explained the physical evolution of animals and human beings, social laws could be identified that explained development and progress in human societies. These early theorists believed that societies evolved or passed through recognizable stages. (P. 329)

8. *What are the dual-stage theories of Tönnies and Durkheim?*

Ferdinand Tönnies and Emile Durkheim advanced dual-stage theories of social change. For Tönnies, gemeinschaft societies were traditional societies based on primary relations. Gesellschaft societies were contractual, impersonal, and characterized by secondary relations. For Durkheim, societies based on "mechanical solidarity" had a minimal division of labor. People in these nations had a common world view or collective conscience. Modern societies held together by organic solidarity have a complex division of labor. The individ-ual conscience in these nations is well developed, and people have fewer values in common. (P. 329)

9. *What is world system theory, and how do such theorists explain modernization?*

World system theory (WST) focuses on the political and especially economic interdependence of the world's nations. From a WST perspective, the developed societies of the world became rich and powerful by systematically exploiting poor and militarily weak countries. In the nineteenth and first half of the twentieth centuries, this was accomplished through colonization or imperialism. In the post—World War II era, economic domination of the periphery by the core continued through multinational corporations (neocolonialism). This long-lasting and continued economic domination of poor nations by rich states means that the modernization of Third World countries will never be more than moderately successful. (Pp. 332–333)

Women in the Third World

10. *What is the quality of life for females in developing countries?*

In most Third World nations, the political, economic, social, and physical well-being of women is significantly below that of men. As of result of their inferior status, women are often denied an education or have significantly less formal schooling than men. (P. 337)

11. *Has the modernization process helped or hindered Third World women?*

The modernization process has helped close the education gap and has also resulted in improved health care for millions of Third World women. However, technological and economic assistance programs have generally targeted males and made it even more difficult for women to succeed economically. Modernization, therefore, has both helped and hurt Third World women. (P. 338–339)

Sociology and the Future

THINGS TO COME?

Social scientists do not have a very good track record when it comes to predicting future events. For example, no political sociologists or political scientists that we are aware of accurately forecast the single most significant political event of the last eighty years, the demise and disintegration of the former Soviet Union in 1991. On the contrary, the experts in Soviet and Eastern European studies appeared to be caught off guard as the political and social events of that year and region unfolded. Similarly, although many criminologists predicted that crime rates would drop in the 1990s as the number of high-risk young males declined, no one was of the opinion that rates of criminal behavior—especially for violent crime—would drop so far and so fast.

One major reason for our inability to foretell events accurately is that one incident can trigger a whole series of occurrences. This means that the failure to predict the first incident almost guarantees that the subsequent occurrences will be missed as well. If the Soviet Union had not collapsed, Poland, Hungary, and the Czech Republic never would have become members of the North Atlantic Treaty Organization, a military alliance these three countries formerly opposed when they were part of the Warsaw Pact. Additionally, the end of the Soviet military threat has been cited as a major reason for reduced arms spending in the United States (the so-called "peace dividend") and concomitant greater spending on a wide range of domestic programs.

A second stumbling block to our ability to predict the future is that human behavior is extremely complex. Prior to World War II, sociologists sought in vain to discover *the* cause of crime. However, if we have learned nothing else in the past 50 years, we now realize that "one size does not fit all when it comes to an explanation of human actions." That is, the causal factors of some people's criminal use of drugs are apt to be quite different from those leading other individuals to commit computer crime. Sociology's shift from grand theories that attempt to explain virtually all aspects of human existence to middle-range theories emphasizing specific problem areas is a way of saying that we do not yet fully understand the interplay of social, economic, and political variables at the societal level. A limited understanding of what makes societies "tick" also means that we have a very limited ability to predict what the next day—or the next year or the next decade—will bring.

Lacking an all-knowing sociological "crystal ball," we can offer no more than projections regarding the future. Recall, from the population chapter, that demographers do not predict what global population

will be at some specified date—the year 2050, for example. Rather, they make projections based on high, medium, and low levels of fertility. If fertility rates remain high for the next half-century, world population will increase by "X" million; if fertility rates remain at a mid level, there will be "Y" more million people in the world; if fertility rates drop to a lower level, there will only be "Z" more million people. Similarly, our forecasting will be in similar terms: if "A," there is a high probability of "B" happening; or, if "C" occurs, we are not likely to experience "D." Any attempt to be more bold in discussing the future would be naive at best and downright foolhardy at worst.

Finally, keep in mind that whereas a rock dropped repeatedly from a tall building will always hurtle toward the ground at the same rate of acceleration, human beings, unlike inanimate objects, have the capacity to think and to change their behavior at a moment's notice for both logical and illogical reasons. This capacity (and humans' frequent tendency to exercise it) makes predicting their behavior much more difficult than forecasting events in the natural world. In this brief final chapter, we offer some projections concerning the future course of events as they will affect the United States, a select number of other societies, and—in some instances—the entire world. Our comments will follow the chapter outline in the text with the exception of the last two chapters. Because issues of population growth, health care, the environment, urbanization, and modernization are so interrelated, we will discuss these topics as a single unit.

CULTURE

Of the estimated 6,000 languages spoken throughout the world today, approximately 5,400 (90 percent) are in danger of disappearing. Most of the threatened languages have 5,000 or fewer speakers and are the native tongues of people in developing nations. Jared Diamond (1993) notes that languages are lost in one of three ways: (1) Native peoples who speak the language are annihilated. When Columbus reached the Americas, the indigenous people spoke about 1,000 different languages. Today, outside of Alaska, only 187 Native American forms of speech survive on the continent. When an entire tribe was wiped about by military conquest or by the diseases of the conquerors, those people's language died with them. Similarly, when the British colonized Tasmania (part of Australia), all of the native languages of that island disappeared in the space of little more than a generation. (2) People who speak the language are forced to assimilate into the dominant culture. Of the existing Native American languages, almost 80 percent are dying in large measure because, historically, Native American children were physically punished and/or humiliated for using their mother tongue. It was commonly believed that the best way to "civilize" the barbarians was to strip them of their culture, starting with their language. (3) Today, the world's "little" languages are being wiped out in a less brutal manner. The political unification of lands occupied by different groups of people who speak different languages often leads to increased mobility, intermarriage, and, in some cases an "official" language as designated by the government. The languages that are lost in the process can be viewed as casualties of modernization, a process that, to date, has been accompanied by nation-states that seek to instill people with a common identity and a common world view.

Inasmuch as language can be viewed as the bedrock of a people's culture, the loss of a language is concomitant with the loss of a culture. Diamond (1993, p.84) notes that, just as the destruction of most of the world's art and literature would be a tragedy of immense proportions, so, too, is the ongoing loss of humanity's languages, each the product of thousands of years of evolution, and each representing a different view of the social and physical world. There are no indicators that the death and dying of so many languages is being slowed. To the contrary: modernization and the all-to-often callous disregard for the ways of life of small indigenous groups could mean that, by the end of the twenty-first century, no more than 200 major languages will remain.

Along with the loss of languages, we are experiencing the loss of traditional cultures. Americans are increasingly defining themselves as members of subcultures that are oriented toward leisure and recreational activities. As modern industrial states become increasingly affluent, and middle-and-upper class individuals have more disposable income, they spend both more time and more money on pursuits they find enjoyable. This convergence of subcultures and popular culture has provided corporations and small entrepreneurs alike with new markets as they cater to the desires of consumers across a wide range of interests and activities. A visit to a local bookstore revealed over 300 different magazines and periodicals that regularly report on almost every type of (legal) activity imaginable. There were approximately 40 magazines about cars and trucks, 15 on motorcycles, 12 on guns and hunting, dozens devoted to computers, and an array of publications about financial investing. In the coming years, more individuals will be thinking of themselves in terms of leisure and sporting activities rather than their jobs and professions.

According to one argument, American popular culture has had a greater impact on the modern world than has the U.S. military over the past 50 years. There can be little doubt that American movies and television programs can be found in almost every nation in the world; in countries without a domestic entertainment industry of any magnitude, a significant portion of what people see in theaters and watch on television comes from Hollywood. While it is clear that American popular culture will be even more pervasive in the coming years, it is unclear what effect it will have on people, either at the individual or the societal level. In other words, to what extent will our customs, beliefs, activities, and way of life in general (as portrayed by the popular mass media) alter the thinking and behaviors of people around the world?

GROUPS AND SOCIAL STRUCTURE

Although modernization is typically portrayed as the ultimate objective or goal of the developing societies of the world, it should not necessarily be thought of as the ultimate or final stage in the process of societal evolution. As the developing nations have moved at differing speeds and with different degrees of success toward achieving "modernized" status in their economic, social, and cultural organization, the already-modernized nations have not been standing still. According to a growing number of observers (for example, Crook, Pakulski, and Waters, 1992; Harvey, 1989, Lash, 1990; Seidman and Wagner, 1992) societies such as the United States are, instead, evolving or developing into "postmodern" systems. Though an outgrowth of advanced industrial organization, postmodern societies represent a qualitatively different structural form than that envisioned by Daniel Bell (1973, 1976) and others in their early work on postindustrial societies. Jonathan Turner (1997, pp. 39–41) claims that, though there is no clear consensus among sociologists on exactly what distinguishes modernization from postmodernization, there do seem to be a number of observable trends in economic organization that, in combination, trigger a significant social restructuring. These trends are readily observable in the United States and will likely continue into the foreseeable future: (1) the *commodification* of objects, ideas, feelings, values, lifestyles, traditions, people, and other aspects of social life previously outside the scope of economic markets. As anything and everything comes to have a "price" and can be bought and sold, previously important symbols that had deep meaning to ethnic, religious, or other communities lose their original meaning and significance. For example, as a result of several long and bitter players' strikes in U.S. professional sports, baseball, basketball, and football have become, in the eyes of many formerly avid fans, just coldhearted businesses rather than the beloved "big kids' games" they once were. As news media carried stories of multimillionaire players complaining about their share of team and league revenues, and as players moved back and forth among teams in search of the most lucrative contracts, many fans were crushed to realize that their idols were in it for the money and not for the love of the game. Similarly, the U.S. Polo Association's attempt to publish a magazine devoted to that sport was thwarted after a lawsuit by designer Ralph Lauren, who had copyrighted the use of the word "Polo" in depicting a recognizable lifestyle, prevented the publication from legally using the term in its title. Ebay, the enormously popular Internet auction site, had to halt the sale of a human kidney after receiving complaints from several of its subscribers. Selling one's own organs is a federal crime in the United States, punishable by up to five years in prison or a $50,000 fine; however, before being stopped, bidding for the organ had reportedly reached $5.7 million ("Ebay Pulls the Plug," 1999). (2) the *hyperdifferentiation* or overelaboration of statuses, roles, activities, and organizations, leading to the *dedifferentiation* or weakening of boundaries among those categories. At some point, the seemingly endless array of job titles and occupational statuses found in contemporary societies becomes meaningless to people (think, for example, of the infinite number of "Vice-President" positions found in large banks and corporations), especially as the lifestyles and other badges of office once reserved for the members of these categories become increasingly accessible to others via the commodification process. The result is a breakdown of traditional distinctions and an increasing eclecticism or mixing of elements in fashion, decor, speech, music, and other cultural and social components. (3) the excessive or *hyperrationalization* of most economic and social activities, leading to increasing levels of formality, impersonality, and cost-calculations in virtually all aspects of human relations. In his study of the "McDonaldization" of U.S. society, sociologist George Ritzer (1996) argued, in the tradition of Max Weber's concept of the "iron cage of rationality," that this attempt to create greater speed and efficiency through increasing bureaucratization eventually will generate the opposite effects—for example, "fast food" restaurants whose service is anything but fast (and whose products, in many observers' opinion, are anything but food). Recognizing that outcome, corporations and other economic organizations ultimately will begin to debureaucratize, moving toward more novel, flexible work arrangements, the use of contingent (temporary) employees, and the contracting out or "out-

sourcing" of specialized tasks to consultants and service agencies external to the organization. Evidence that this trend is already well underway and likely will continue is provided by a 1999 Field Institute and University of California San Francisco study which found that only 1 in 3 California workers now hold traditional "9-to-5" jobs. According to that study, "Temporary workers, independent contractors, telecommuters and part-time workers are becoming the new norm" (Kinsman, 1999, p. A–1). But, while the erosion of traditional work arrangements may be unsettling to many people, "there has never been a time in our history when we've had the ability to create so many new ways of work (Toms, in Kinsman, 1999, p. A-1). These new ways of work may, indeed, afford people who "are hungry to return to family, extended family and community" (Blair, in Kinsman, 1999, p. A–15) the opportunity to satisfy that hunger by freeing them from former organizational constraints that monopolized the bulk of their time.

SOCIALIZATION

In August 1999, the American Academy of Pediatrics issued a report recommending that children under the age of 2 years not watch television at all; that older children be limited in their TV viewing and not have television sets in their bedrooms; and that pediatricians have parents fill out a "media history," along with a medical history, on office visits (Mifflin, 1999). Drawing on the accumulated findings of years of research conducted by the American Medical Association, the American Psychological Association, the American Academy of Child and Adolescent Psychiatry, and the National Institute of Mental Health (among other groups), these recommendations were based on the conclusion that television watching, especially of violent programming, can affect the mental, social, and physical health of young people. According to the report's lead author, "As pediatricians, we are taking all the research concerns into account, and trying to raise the bar a bit, as suggestions for optimal parenting" (Hogan, in Mifflin, 1999, p. A-1). The AAP report came at a time of renewed concern about the effects of television violence on young viewers, following a spate of shootings by adolescent gunmen that took the lives of over two dozen students and teachers at schools across the country (the most notorious of these killing sprees, at Columbine High School in Littleton, Colorado, had occurred just a little over three months prior to the report's publication). The U.S. public was demanding that something be done to stem the increasing tide of teen and preteen violence, and violent TV programming was identified as a likely significant causal factor.

Whether this demand translates into either voluntary or mandated limitations on the content of television programming remains to be seen. In the past, "freedom of speech" issues have effectively killed what have been defined as attempts at imposed censorship of the TV medium. But the recasting of the issue as a mental and physical health problem could conceivably generate the needed momentum for change, as happened in Canada (recall the "Focus on Canada" discussion in Chapter 4).

In recognition of the fact that personal computers and the Internet are rapidly overtaking television as the preferred entertainment medium in U.S. society, attempts have also been made to monitor and/or limit the content of cyberspace, particularly with regard to pornography. To date, these regulatory efforts have been unsuccessful. Passed by Congress in 1996, the first federal government attempt to police the Internet, the Communications Decency Act, was ruled unconstitutional by the U.S. Supreme Court on June 26, 1997. Though recognizing the likelihood that exposure to the graphic sexual materials available on the Internet is not in the best interests of young viewers, the Court nonetheless ruled that "the interest in encouraging freedom of expression in a democratic society outweighs any theoretical but unproven benefit of censorship" (Stevens, in "Supreme Court Rules CDA Unconstitutional," 1997). In 1998, Congress passed—and President Clinton signed—a second law aimed at restricting access of children and adolescents to Internet pornography, the Child Online Protection Act (COPA). Though structured in such a way as to overcome objections to the earlier Communications Decency Act of 1996, COPA nonetheless was declared unconstitutional by the U.S. Supreme Court in 1999, again on "freedom of expression" grounds.

Frustrated by Congressional failures to create legislation that successfully withstands court challenges and committed to the principle that "Individuals have a private right to control what comes into their home, school or workplace" (Wilson, in Fitzpatrick, 1999), a growing number of parents and teachers have begun marketing and utilizing Internet Service Providers (ISPS) that block violence, pornography, and hate-related sites. In the meantime, groups such as Morality in Media continue to search for a media-monitoring bill that could pass a Supreme Court review. However, given the sanctity of First Amendment guarantees of freedom of expression in U.S. history and culture, we do not foresee—short of a cyberporn or cyberviolence-spawned atrocity of such proportions that it galvanizes the U.S. population-at-large into making demands for action that cannot be ignored—the passage and successful implementation of any government attempts to regulate the Internet. In the absence of such an event, parents will be left up to their own devices in the matter of keeping their children out of harm's way when accessing the Internet.

INEQUALITY AND STRATIFICATION

During much of the 1990s, the United States experienced an almost unparalleled period of apparent economic well-being. Unemployment rates and home mortgage interest rates were low and, given an

Computer-based learning, including access to the myriad resources of the Internet, has already become the wave of the future in the socialization processes of modern societies such as the United States, as these first-graders in Berkeley, California, are discovering. Although children's computer use can be monitored in settings such as the one pictured here, concern over exactly what they may be accessing on the Internet in the absence of adult supervision remains high "Cybercensorship" is shaping up as one of the great mass media issues of the twenty-first century.

unusually healthy stock market, many people were becoming millionaires almost overnight. Thanks, in part, to the general public's feeling that they were, indeed, better off than they had been in prior years, President Clinton was able to weather an impeachment brought by the House of Representatives. Had the times not been so good, history may have recorded the ascent of Al Gore to the Presidency in 1999. The state of the nation's wallet, which brought Bill Clinton into office in 1993, allowed him to remain in office through the remainder of the decade.

However, beneath the apparent national affluence, not all was well. At the same time that some people were moving up the economic ladder, an equal or larger number of others remained locked in place and yet many others dropped several rungs. According to a report issued by the Congressional Budget Office in September, 1999, "The gap between rich and poor has grown into an economic chasm so wide that this year the richest 2.7 million Americans, the top 1 percent, will have as many after-tax dollars to spend as the bottom 100 million . . . In dollars, each [will] have about $620 billion" (Johnston, 1999). Data cited in the study showed that the share of total national income received by the bottom 80 percent of all U.S. households—about 217 million people—fell from 56 percent in 1997 to just under 50 percent in 1999. Of the 20 percent of households whose incomes grew between 1977 and 1999, more than 90 percent of the overall increase went to the richest 1 percent, whose 1999 after-tax incomes, according to estimates, averaged $515,600 (Johnston, 1999). Other studies indicated that one-third of all working-age adults, about 54 million people, describe themselves as having "just enough" or "not enough" money to meet basic living needs. And only an equal number (34 percent) are "very satisfied" with their current annual incomes (Williams and Otto, 1999). Affluence and inequality thus appear to be growing simultaneously, a phenomenon observed by the United Nations Development Program (1998) not just in the United States, but in many other developed and developing societies as well.

Whereas the current rate of poverty in the United States has dropped from previous years, nearly 36 million people remain poor in what is one of the world's wealthiest societies. But, as the United Nations Development Program notes in an examination of poverty in 17 industrial nations in its annual *Human Development Report* (1998, pp. 2, 29,), "Human poverty and deprivation remain a formidable challenge in both rich and poor countries . . . The extent of human poverty has little to do with the average level of income. The United States, with the highest per capita income measured in purchasing power parity (PPP) among the 17 countries, also has the highest human poverty."

Although the United States may continue to enjoy overall economic affluence in the next coming decade, we do not anticipate a significant lessening of the current unequal distributions of income and wealth in this society. On the contrary: if anything, we might project that those distributions will become even more unequal as a result of, among other things, trends in legal and illegal immigration.

According to a recent study by the Center for Immigration Studies, the number of immigrant households living in poverty in the United States more than tripled between 1979 and 1997, growing from 2.7 million to 7.7 million. Whereas the overall number of immigrant households in the country increased by 68 percent during this period, the number of poor immigrant households grew by 123 percent (Cantlupe, 1999). Recent immigrants to the United States generally are less educated and have fewer occupational skills than either native-born Americans or previous immigrant groups. Because of their lack of human capital factors, they most frequently are destined to low-paid, unskilled jobs offering little or no health, dental, or other benefits—and, thus, destined to poverty: "Clearly, as the level of immigration to the United States has increased in the last two decades, the poverty rate associated with immigrants has grown dramatically. A significant proportion of immigrants are unable to succeed in the modern American economy . . . If one is concerned about the poor already here, increasing the number of people in or near poverty through immigration is clearly counter-productive" (Camarota, in Cantlupe, 1999, p. A-19). However, to the extent that the United States will continue to serve as an immigration "magnet" in the coming years, attracting people from impoverished developing nations; and to the extent that the country's borders remain relatively open to these seekers of a better life, the income and wealth disparities that make this country the most economically unequal of all industrial societies are not likely to diminish appreciably. What will continue to diminish appreciably are the lives of the people trapped in the economic undercurrents of the supposed rising tide of affluence.

RACE AND ETHNICITY

In a mid-1999 *Newsweek* cover story on the current state of African Americans, journalist and social critic Ellis Cose (1999, p. 30) claimed "now is a great time—the best time ever—to be black in America." His assessment was based on an array of government statistics documenting the impressive gains made by African Americans in educational achievement, individual and family incomes, mobility into managerial, professional, and other white-collar occupations, home ownership, and a host of other quality-of-life indicators. Compared to the state of black America as recently as twenty-five years ago, this was, indeed, the best of times for many African Americans. But, much like the often-quoted opening passage from Charles Dickens' classic, *A Tale of Two Cities*, it was also the worst of times for many other members of this society's largest racial minority group, and for members of many other racial and ethnic minority groups as well.

At the same time that a growing number of their peers were moving into corporate boardrooms and up-scale housing developments, a disproportionately large number of black men were moving permanently into the nation's state and federal prisons. At the same time that more African Americans than ever before had gained access to expensive, world-class medical care, homicide remained the leading cause of death for the black male population-at-large. And, even as large numbers of black Americans relished the social and economic benefits that were finally coming their way, larger numbers evidenced concern that the ride would come to a sudden end should the booming U.S. economy experience a major slowdown or reversal. They felt that white Americans had not become significantly more color blind than they had been in the past, and might quickly revert to the kinds of prejudices and discriminatory acts that had been so prevalent in those times when economic conditions were less than booming ("Feeling Better About the Future," 1999). Judging by the stepped-up hate group activities of an increasing number of economically marginal whites in this society and by the rise of racist skinhead groups in Germany, England, Italy, France, and other economically challenged nations of western Europe, their fears may be well founded.

Whereas the fortunes of African Americans have improved dramatically for at least the short run, the same cannot be said of the fortunes of Hispanic Americans, the nation's fastest-growing—and, in many ways, the nation's poorest—ethnic or racial minority. As discussed both above and in Chapter 6, a very high percentage of this group's numerical and proportional growth within the U.S. population is the result of the millions of immigrants who have come to this country seeking a better life. Comparatively uneducated and unskilled, many of these arrivals have been shunted into low-paying, dead-end jobs. Once in these jobs, they find themselves increasingly excluded from formal educational and oc-

cupational training opportunities that might allow them to break out of the pattern. Competing against equally low-educated, low-skilled Anglos for manual labor and service-sector jobs, Hispanics have become the targets for often-violent acts of racism, especially in the southwestern states where their physical presence and other impacts are more immediately felt. We do not foresee any significant decrease in this inflammatory situation so long as the current high tide of Mexican and Central American immigrants continues. (Please bear in mind that we are *not* advocating a tightening or closing of the U.S. border to this flow of economic, political, religious, and environmental refugees. We are simply stating a causal sequence as we have observed it.)

According to the U.S. Commerce Department's 1999 report *Falling Through the Net*, the disparity of computer ownership and Internet usage between whites and black and Hispanic Americans is creating a "racial ravine" that threatens to turn the United States into a society in which "the 'haves' only become more information-rich . . . while the 'have-nots' are lagging even further behind" (quoted in Bridis, 1999). In the type of postmodern knowledge-based society that the United States has become, this information technology gap constitutes (with formal education, a resource in which Anglos also have a distinct advantage over African Americans and Hispanics) a significant dividing line between those most likely and those least likely to succeed. For the immediate future, until such time as they can more fully partake of the opportunities offered by formal education and the Internet, America's two largest minority groups will remain on the wrong side of that line.

SEX AND GENDER

On June 9, 1998, the Southern Baptist Convention, the nation's largest Protestant denomination at 16 million members, amended its essential statement of beliefs to include a declaration that a woman should "submit herself graciously" to her husband's leadership (Niebuhr, 1998). Though promoting a gender role model diametrically opposed to that espoused by most feminists, this addition to the *Baptist Faith and Message* did not generate the sort of widespread negative reaction from women that might have been expected. A little over a year later, the results of an annual study conducted by UCLA of more than 350,000 entering college and university students indicated that the percentage of young women in the United States supporting legalized abortion had dropped steadily each year for the previous nine years, from a high of 65.5 percent in 1989 to 49.5 percent in 1998 (Palmer, 1999). These figures raised concerns among abortion rights leaders for the future of the "post-Roe" generation, who "cannot imagine their right to an abortion would ever be taken away, perhaps because they didn't have to struggle to achieve it, or because they didn't have any direct experience with people who suffered a back-alley abortion or died from illegal abortion" (Michaelman, in Palmer, 1999, p. G–4). However, that right could very well be taken away, as conservative Christians and other anti-abortion/pro-life groups continue to exert pressure on individual states to restrict or eliminate abortions altogether. As of mid-1999, according to a national study conducted by a New York reproductive health think tank, abortion services were not available in 86 percent of counties in America (cited in Palmer, 1999).

Much of the seeming complacency of so-called Generation X women can perhaps be attributed to the fact that, on the surface, women in the United States appear to have made impressive gains in their quest for social equality. In 1999, the United States won the third annual Women's World Cup in soccer. The event drew hundreds of thousands of live fans and millions of television fans to watch the games at the Rose Bowl, and inspired untold thousands of girls and young women throughout the country to get involved in the previously male-dominated world of organized sports. For their unprecedented heroics, each member of the winning U.S. Women's Soccer Team received $12,500 in prize money. Had their counterparts on the U.S. men's team won the 1998 Men's World Cup, their (the men's) share of prize money would have been $388,000 each ("By Leaps and Bounds," 1999, p. 51). Also in 1999, businesswoman Carly Fiorina was named Chief Executive Officer of Hewlett-Packard Corporation, breaking the ultimate glass barrier to become the first woman CEO of a Dow 30 company. Her assumption of this highest-level corporate position was notable not only for the fact that "It's going to give young women, girls, a powerful message" (Wellington, in Greenfeld, 1999), but also for its rarity. In that same year, only 7 percent of top officers at Fortune 500 technology firms were female. Women in the United States, in Germany, in South Africa, and in many other nations have now surpassed men in opening up their own businesses (Maykuth, 1998; Sacirbey, 1998a). However, in many cases, their transformation from wage- or salary-workers to entrepreneurs has been the result of few or no employment opportunities in the labor market, depressed wages compared to men, sexual harassment, or other forms of gender discrimination. And, in attempting to secure start-up loans for their companies, many of these women face further discrimination, often having to resort to using personal credit cards to finance their businesses in the absence of funding from commercial banks (CNN Special Reports, 1992).

In Mexico and in Spain, two Latin countries whose gender relations have been shaped by the *machismo* cult of male superiority, there are signs of that long-standing syndrome's erosion. In Mexico, thousands of women throughout the country have flocked to see male striptease dancers perform in a show modeled after the popular 1997 English film *The Full Monty*, reveling in the opportunity to release their repressed sexuality (Walker, 1999). Once outside the nightclubs, however, their lives at home and at work remain substantially the same; namely, subordinated to the needs and wants of men. In Spain, where the phrase "I killed her because she was mine" once summed up many men's feelings about their female partners, a society wide campaign against *terrorismo familiar* (domestic violence) has succeeded in reducing the number of women murdered by abusive partners by 50 percent. However, many women throughout the country remain trapped in abusive relationships as a result of their employment in low-paying "female" jobs (Daly, 1999).

Given these trends, we have no reason to believe that the movement toward full gender equality in economic, occupational, familial, and other facets of societal life will experience a major or spectacular breakthrough in the immediate future. Progress in making sex and gender a decreasingly important factor in the shaping of individuals' lives will continue, but at the same pace as in the immediate past—slowly, perhaps grudgingly, one step at a time.

CRIME, DEVIANCE, AND SOCIAL CONTROL

Future rates of criminal activity provide a good illustration of the if "A" then "B" scenario. To the extent that crime—especially offenses like robbery and burglary—is a function of poverty, then crime rates will be contingent on the health of the economy. Just as low unemployment rates in the mid and late 1990s were somewhat responsible for the decline in street crime, if the nation were to experience a prolonged economic slow down (or depression) street crimes would be expected to increase. Inasmuch as the unemployed population typically includes a disproportionate number of poorly educated, semi-skilled or unskilled young males, and young males are the highest at risk crime group, then the economic well-being of the nation will be a significant factor in overall crime equation.

As the number and percentage of young people in the population increases substantially over the next ten years, the crime rate is expected to rise as well. Some observers are of the opinion that this period of decreased crime is the proverbial calm before the storm. If this tempest of criminal activity does in fact materialize, it may well be enhanced by a new crack cocaine–like epidemic that sweeps across urban America. This would result in not only more drug use, but a good deal of behavior associated with illegal drugs ranging from robbery and burglary (to pay for these substances) to gang wars as rival groups fight for access to territory and customers.

Although the murder rate declined to a 30-year low of seven criminal homicides per 100,000 population in 1997, it still remains "unacceptably high." Apart from guns being used in criminal acts, firearm injuries, suicides, and unintentional gunshot wounds take the lives of 38,000 people each year and are the eighth leading cause of death in this country. A teenager is more likely to die as result of a shooting than from natural causes of all diseases (Sheppard, 1999). Unless gun-reduction strategies are successfully implemented at the community level, the number of gun related deaths (both criminal and noncriminal) will remain high.

Criminologist Francis Ianni (1998) has noted that Italian domination of organized crime is beginning to give way to other groups, especially blacks and Hispanics. Sociologists have long argued that organized crime is best understood as a "process of ethnic succession," that is, this form of criminal activity is an important vehicle of upward mobility for minority groups whose path of advancement by way of legitimate channels (mainly education) is limited as a result of poverty and institutionalized discrimination. As "poverty and powerlessness are at the root of both community acceptance of organized crime and recruitment into its networks" (Ianni, 1998, p. 128), we can expect this brand of crime survive (in later years via other minority groups) well into the twenty-first century as we foresee no end to poverty and the powerlessness that accompanies the lives of racial and ethnic minorities.

As the first of the baby boomers turn 65 in the year 2011, the nation may well be faced with a new problem: the beginning of a senior citizens drug boom. Coming of age in the drug-culture, counter culture era of the 1960s and 1970s, millions of individuals in this generation experimented with and routinely used drugs. Taking drugs (both legal and illegal) became part of a lifestyle that they carried into middle age and will extend into old age as well. The minuscule number of senior citizens presently arrested for drug use can be expected to increase, perhaps dramatically.

Over the past 200 years crime trends throughout the world reveal a "generally consistent response to patterns of development" (Shelley, 1981, p. 137). Global-historical patterns of crime indicate that both the *process* and *achievement* of modernization are highly conducive to criminality. Not only will rates of crime in emerging nations increase and begin to approach those of industrialized countries, but the patterns of criminality in the former will begin to resemble the latter. For example, drug use and organized crime activity have increased significantly in eastern European countries since they embarked on the transition form totalitarian communism to democratic capitalism. Modernization results in a movement of millions of people from the countryside to urban areas where desperately poor individuals find themselves competing far too few jobs and places to live. Property crimes increase because there are now more things to steal that can be used directly or indirectly in the struggle to survive and more people to steal them.

MARRIAGE AND THE FAMILY

Although divorce rates in the United States have declined somewhat since 1980, they will remain at a relatively high level as millions of people continue to have few misgivings about ending a relationship they define as unworkable. However, Americans are firmly committed to the institution of matrimony as over one-half of all marriages each year are remarriages for one or both partners and the time period between divorce and remarriage has declined (Hutter, 1998). Remarriages create the ever increasing number of blended families in modern societies. Demographer Paul Glick estimates that more than 50 percent of the population have been, are currently, or will eventually be part of a stepfamily relationship (in Edmondson and Waldrop, 1993). Because of the post–World War II baby boom, there are currently more people in their thirties than there were a generation ago. This demographic fact combined with more people delaying childbirth until the third decade of life (especially among well-educated women) means "that the number of children born to older women will continue to increase" (Collins and Coltrane, 1995, p. 336). In addition, the number of women remaining permanently childless will rise.

Whereas the life expectancy of a child born in the U.S. in 1950 was less than fifty years, today's children expect to live into their mid to late 70s. Prior to the late twentieth century people rarely lived to be 100 years old. Of the 3.9 American children born in 2000, at least 70,000 of them will be alive in the year 2100

(Adler et al, 1998). The overall physical—and to some degree, psychological—well-being of these children is, to a great extent, linked to the socio-economic class in which they were born. While a number of indicators show life generally improving for the nation's children, not all children will share in this betterment. For example, almost 20 percent of America's youth live in poverty, with almost 40 percent of these individuals residing in "extreme" poverty, that is, in families earning less than 50 percent of the annually adjusted poverty threshold. The percent of children living with two parents continues to decline. This is important inasmuch as children in one parent families are much more likely to live in poverty than children who grow up in a home with two parents.

The number of children with no health insurance increased from 14 percent of all children in 1994 to 15 percent in 1995 ("America's Children: Key National Indicators of Well-Being, 1998). Even though the nation's economy has been strong as of late, the move toward hiring part-time workers and contract labor leads us to believe that because the health insurance of the majority of Americans is job related (and part-time workers are much less likely to have health benefits), both the number and percentage of children without health coverage will remain high. The lack of health coverage is especially problematic—and will remain so—among racial and ethnic minorities. While 85 percent of white children had access to health care in 1995 that number was 81 and 71 percent for Hispanic children ("America's Children," 1998).

At the other end of the age spectrum, because (1) men on the whole marry women younger than themselves, (2) women live longer than men, and (3) the first of the baby boomers will turn 65 in less than 15 years, there will be a significant increase in the number of widows in this country. Currently, in the age group 75 and older, 34 percent of men and 76 percent of women are living without a spouse (Coates, 1996). Eleven percent of all new AIDS victims are now people age 50 and older, and in the past few years new AIDS cases rose faster in people over 40 as opposed to under that age ("HIV, AIDS, and Older Adults," 1999). As a growing number of senior citizens stays sexually active longer (in part because of a rising divorce rate among the elderly) as a result of new sex therapies and drugs, the rate of sexually transmitted diseases in the population over 65 years of age is likely to increase.

Just as children in the 1980s and 1990s moved back home (primarily for economic reasons), this trend will be reversed as elderly parents return the favor and reside with their children in increasing numbers. Joseph Coates (1996, p.4) is of the opinion

that 'Granny flat' and mother-in-law apartments will be common additions to houses." Although elderly people are enjoying both longer and healthier lives, there comes a point when they must be cared for, and in many cases the "old old"—those people 85 years of age and older—require 24-hour attention. Taking care of elderly parents can be very stressful both economically and psychologically as people attempt to juggle the demands of their lives and the lives of an infirm mother or father as well. It remains to be seen how corporate America will respond, in terms of time off and "flex time," to the needs of employees who must tend to the needs of the people who brought them into this world.

EDUCATION AND RELIGION

On August 11, 1999, the ongoing, century-long battle between fundamentalist Christianity and public education in the United States came full circle. At that time, in an action later described by the state's governor as "a terrible, tragic, and embarrassing solution to a problem that did not exist" (Graves, in Leaming, 1999, p. 2), the Kansas Board of Education effectively ended the teaching of evolutionary theory in Kansas public schools. The entire topic, including the "Big Bang" theory, was summarily deleted from the state's science curriculum. The new science standards did not forbid the teaching of evolution, but they removed all aspects of evolution theory and evolutionary concepts from testing on statewide exams—"a virtual guarantee," according to renowned Harvard paleontologist Steven Jay Gould (1999), "that this central concept of biology will be diluted or eliminated, thus reducing courses to something like chemistry without the periodic table, or American history without Lincoln." Interestingly, it was the same issue—religious-based attacks against the teaching of evolutionary theory in public schools—that had led to what many observers once believed was the beginning of the end of fundamentalist religious influence on American public education, the famous (or, depending on one's perspective, the infamous) Scopes "Monkey Trial" of 1925. Though the Tennessee law banning the teaching of evolution was not at issue in the original Scopes trial, that law—and others like it—was later gutted and then overturned altogether on First Amendment "freedom of expression" grounds by Supreme Court decisions in 1968 and in 1987. The 1999 Kansas Board of Education action seemed designed to achieve the desired effect of getting evolution out of the classroom while avoiding the constitutional pitfalls of earlier fundamentalist-inspired legislation (Gould, 1999).

This latest attempt to shape public education in the image of a set of religious beliefs came at a time that the U.S. educational system was already under assault from a number of different quarters for its all-too-apparent failure to adequately educate its students—a time in which the continued survival of traditional public education was itself in doubt. Noting that "Outside a few universities owned by TV preachers, there is not a college or university in this country that does not teach evolution," one critic (Boston, in Leaming, 1999, p. 3), argued that "removing the evolution standards from secondary education in Kansas is a great disservice to the students." Echoing this sentiment, Gould (1999) claims, "as patriotic Americans, we should cringe in embarrassment that, at the dawn of a new, technological millennium, a jurisdiction in our heartland has opted to suppress one of the greatest triumphs of human discovery. Evolution is not a peripheral subject but the central organizing principle of all biological sciences . . . no one ignorant of evolution can understand science." And no one—or no nation—ignorant of science can hope to compete in a global arena largely grounded in the development and application of scientific principles.

Given the outcomes of previous fundamentalist intrusions into the secular school system and the enormity of the consequences the Kansas Board of Education's action would have on the quality of U.S. public education if it were allowed to stand, it seems almost certain to us that this decision will not survive the series of court challenges—including the eventual U.S. Supreme Court review—that surely will be brought against it. However, given the renewed growth and renewed political activities of the Christian right (and remember that the setting of the conditions and the content of public education is invariably as much of a political activity is a pedagogical one), it is highly unlikely that this episode will mark the final chapter and verse in the Christian fundamentalist "holy war" to capture the soul of American public education. Even though a large segment of the U.S. population expresses serious concern about the blending of religious beliefs and secular, tax-funded education, an equally large segment expresses a similar level of concern about the apparent inability of public schools to inculcate any sort of basic moral values in their students. Growing numbers of these concerned parents are choosing to send their children to sectarian or parochial schools rather than to traditional public schools at the same time that more of these alternatives are becoming financially available to them through charter school and school voucher programs. Faced with pressure from the public to do something about teaching morals and values

to students, and with a potentially fatal loss of students to religious-based schools, public schools might very well begin developing more morality-based curricula. If that particular scenario were to unfold, the critical questions that would have to be addressed would be those of *whose* moral beliefs would form the basis for the new curricula, and how those morals could be taught without doing serious injustice to the large number of students whose own religious beliefs do not coincide with those promulgated in their schools. Given the great religious diversity found in the United States and the fact that the fastest-growing religion in the country (Islam) falls well outside the society's historical Judaic-Christian framework, these questions may prove to have no easy answers.

ECONOMY AND POLITICS

At the same time that the nations of the world seem to be drawing closer together under the umbrella of global communications and a global economic market system, they also are being driven further apart politically by rising nationalism and the forces of devolution. According to the United Nations Development Program's 1998 *Human Development Report* (p. 36), of the 18 active conflicts throughout the world in 1997, "Nearly all are being fought within countries, where they tend to be smaller but more violent." Since that report, these intrastate hostilities have shown no signs of diminishing. On the contrary, new "hot spots" have flared up in Europe and in Central and Southeast Asia, among other regions.

As discussed in some detail in Chapter 6's "*Focus on Yugoslavia*," ethnic Albanian Kosovars' efforts to separate that province from the Yugoslavian Federation and establish political independence led to both Serbian military action and NATO counteractions that threatened to draw major world political powers into the conflict. In the course of NATO air strikes against Belgrade, the capital city of the Serbian-dominated Yugoslav government, the Chinese embassy was accidentally bombed, precipitating what might have turned out to be a very costly international incident.

Even as the Kosovo question was still being resolved, in the Russian North Caucasus province of Karachayevo-Cherkessiya the ethnic Cherkess minority group announced that it was forming its own autonomous republic following what it claimed was a "rigged" presidential election won by the rival ethnic Karachayev candidate ("Ethnic Strife Is Spreading," 1999). The region was already being torn by nationalist violence, as guerrillas attempting to set up an Islamic state in the nearby province of Dagestan battled troops sent by President Boris Yeltsin to maintain Russian rule. The Dagestan rebels, in turn, were being supported by allies from nearby Chechnya, which had gained de facto independence from Russia after an especially bloody conflict a few years earlier (Abdulayev, 1999). This "balkanization" of eastern Europe and of the Commonwealth of Independent States (the old republics of the former U.S.S.R) was precisely what the major international powers had feared would be the result if the Kosovo secession from Yugoslavia succeeded.

In East Timor, a former Portugese Southeast Asian colony seized by Indonesia in 1975, residents cast an overwhelming vote for political independence in a United Nations–sponsored 1999 referendum. This vote came after 24 years of iron-fisted Indonesian rule during which an estimated 200,000 East Timorese civilians had been killed by the military occupation force in recurring acts of violence and terrorism (Mydans, 1999). However, both during and following this historic vote, bands of anti-independence militias, with the support of the Indonesian military, killed hundreds of people and forcibly removed hundreds of thousands of others out of the area in an attempt "to terrorize the population with the most gruesome abuses of their fundamental rights" (Robinson, in Martinkus, 1999). Their apparent fear was that, if East Timor—which by this time had become "a symbol of the resistance of small territories against foreign occupation" (Mydans, 1999)—gained its independence, other rebel movements would arise in the 17,000-island Indonesian archipelago (Martinkus, 1999).

In spite of the willingness of ruling governments to use violence of the highest caliber to squash nascent independence movements, we do not believe that people's nationalist impulses and yearnings for political freedom can be stymied indefinitely. The breakup of regional or continental regimes such as the Soviet Union has removed repressive forces that, in the past, were strong enough (and ruthless enough) to keep centrifugal political tendencies in check. Now that those repressive forces have been removed—and with the perceived inability of many multinational states to provide satisfactorily for the economic and other needs of their constituent ethnic populations—we anticipate that current republics, provinces, and other subunits of existing political states will attempt to strike off on their own. In a similar vein, Robert Kaplan argues that modern nations will continue to weaken politically in the 21st century, and by the year 2100 "the organizing principle of the world will be the "city state" along with "urban radials of prosperity that will follow major trade routes" (1999, p. A23). Loyalty to the city will gradually overwhelm national patriotism as cities and their adjoining areas make alliances and fight

Following an overwhelming vote for political independence from Indonesia by residents of East Timor, bands of Indonesian military-backed militias and police embarked on what amounted to a reign of terror throughout the region. In countless violent confrontations such as the one pictured here, hundreds of people were killed and hundreds of thousands of others were forcibly removed from their homes. Authorities apparently feared that a successful break-away by East Timor would encourage similar movements in other Indonesian provinces. It is quite possible that such movements toward political independence by ethnic, racial, and nationalist groups will become more widespread over the coming century.

wars with one another not so much over territory as over "bandwidths in cyberspace and trade privileges." For Kaplan, North America will evolve into a loose confederation of urban regions—a modern version of ancient Greek city-states. "The next century will be the age of high-tech feudalism." What remains to be seen is if their independence can be achieved without the warfare and tremendous loss of life that have, unfortunately, typically accompanied such movements in the past.

POPULATION, URBANIZATION, MODERNIZATION, HEALTH, AND ENVIRONMENT

The crucial element in this final unit is population growth. Although the rate of increase will be affected by urbanization, the process and speed of modernization, as well as environmental issues, population growth is more likely to be in the position of an independent variable rather than a dependent variable. Regarding population growth and the near to mid-range future, we can be certain of at least two things: (1) In 1999, 32 countries that collectively account for 14 percent of global population have achieved population stability. In another 40 countries (including the United States and China) fertility has dropped to below two children or fewer. This latter group of nations (barring and radical reversal of fertility rates) is moving toward population stability. These modern and most advanced developing nations represent a trend that is beginning to slow global population growth. (2) However, in the developing world (excluding China) women are still averaging 3.8 children, a figure that contributes to a population doubling time for these nations of only 35 years. Because of "population momentum" we can be certain that overall global population will continue to increase for the foreseeable future. A major component of this momentum are the two billion people—one-third of humanity—under 20 years of age. The family planning decisions of this "critical cohort" will determine how many people there will on planet Earth before growth eventually stops and population size stabilizes or begins to decline (World Population Data Sheet 1998). Because there are so many women of childbearing age, even if fertility dropped to just over two children per family ("replacement level"), world population would increase to 8.6 billion people in the year 2060 before leveling off (Knodel, 1999).

As population increases so too will internal and international migration as people leave their place of birth in search of jobs, housing, and an overall better standard of living. The majority of movers will relocate to cities while others push further into what remains of the uninhabited countryside. Both of these courses of action have serious consequences for global health. A significant number of deaths in the developing world each year (55 percent in Africa and 41 percent in India) are the result of infectious and parasitic diseases (IPDs) such as cholera, malaria, AIDS, and tuberculosis. (In the developed world 5 percent of annual deaths are attributed to IPDs) (Olshansky et al, 1997).

As noted in the introduction to Chapter 12, "Population," infectious microbes that have laid dormant in rainforests and savannas for untold years will make their way into human populations. Once they reach cities, airborne diseases such as new, highly drug-resistant forms of tuberculosis can spread quickly among the poor who reside in overcrowded, squalid quarters. A waterborne malady like cholera can live in contaminated water (before that water is used for drinking) for prolonged periods of time. Fast growing cities in poor countries unable to afford sewage treatment facilities commensurate with population growth are especially prone to cholera like diseases where people have little choice but to use the only water that is available. Since 1995 a new strain of cholera has killed thousands of people in Africa and Asia. As we are currently live in an age characterized by the largest migration in human his-

Seen from the vantage point of outer space, Planet Earth shows a startling beauty that obscures the overdevelopment, environmental destruction, political conflicts, racial and ethnic clashes, and a host of other significant problems that threaten both individual societies and humankind in general. Preserving the increasingly fragile resources of our global home remains perhaps the single most important challenge facing us in both the near and the long-term future.

tory, IPDs related to population movement and the growth of cities are will almost certainly increase.

Biodemographer S. Jay Olshansky and his colleagues (Olshansky et al., 1997) note that, in most cases a "new" disease does not enter the human population via a mutation of a particular microbe; rather the disease causing agent finds a new pathway to a previously unexposed population. This new pathway can be introduced by way of changes in the physical, social, or biological environment. "Agriculture, deforestation, migration, and war all contribute to the introduction and dissemination of viruses and other infectious agents in new populations" (p. 22). And all of the changes are related to population growth.

Consider the relation between increasing populations, food production, and malaria. Rice farmers typically flood their rice fields or paddies which serve as breeding grounds for a variety of insects including malaria carrying mosquitoes. More people means more (to a limit) rice paddies, more mosquitoes and potentially a higher incidence of malaria (Olshansky et al., 1997).

Modernization and the environment will continue to be on a collision course. Lester Brown (1999, p. 15) of World Watch argues convincingly that the environment simply cannot support 6 billion-plus people with an American "fossil-fuel-based, automobile-centered, throwaway economy." If cars were used in globally at the same rate they are used in this country (one car for every two people), planet Earth would have three billion cars—six times the existing number of motor vehicles. The impact this worldwide fleet of cars would have on the environment in terms of pollution, global warming, and loss of cropland for streets, highways, and parking lots would be both catastrophic and unsustainable. If China alone were to consume oil at the same rate the United States does, that Asian nation would need 80 million barrels a day, significantly more than the world's total current production of 67 million barrels of oil a day (Brown, 1999).

One of China's most esteemed physicists, He Zuoxiu, stated that his country "just simply cannot sustain the development of a car economy" (in Brown, 1999, p16). It remains to be seen if China's leadership— as well as leaders in other developing countries—will persuaded by the logic He Zuoxiu and other like minded environmentalists and scientists. Our prediction is that most developing nations, both anxious to raise the living standards of growing populations as well as emulate the success of rich industrial countries will continue to pursue a highly materialistic "car economy." Leaders of many of these nations are apt to interpret a call for sustainable development from high energy consumption, environmentally unfriendly countries like the United States as nothing more than blatant hypocracy.

Brown is somewhat more optimistic regarding our environmental future when he states "there are some clear signs that the world does seem to be approaching a kind of paradigm shift in environmental consciousness," (1999, p. 14). Among other optimistic examples Brown notes that the CEO of British Petroleum "broke ranks" with the presidents of other oil companies who continue to dismiss worldwide climate changes as a consequence of global warming. In a similar vein Royal Dutch Shell (one of the world's largest petroleum companies) recently committed $500 million to the development of renewable resources.

Ted Turner, founder of CNN and owner of the Atlanta Braves, pledged $1 billion dollars to the United Nations (at the rate of $100 million a year). If some of the other approximately 600 billionaires in the world were to follow Turner's lead a tremendous amount of money could be funneled into poor countries that would help alleviate hunger, suffering, and poverty as well as start these nations down a path of sustainable development.

We sincerely hope that Lester Brown's environmental forecast is more accurate than ours and that the world wealth is more evenly distributed in the twenty-first century.

Glossary

absolute poverty   The inability to maintain physical survival on a long-term basis.

absolutist perspective   The view that deviance resides in the act itself and is wrong at all times (past, present, and future), and in all places.

age–sex or population pyramid   Summarizes the age and sex characteristics of a given population by five-year cohorts or groups. For example, a population pyramid of the United States would indicate the number of males and females ages 5 to 9, 10 to 14, and so on.

aggregate   Social collectivity whose members occupy the same physical space at the same time.

agricultural surplus theory   Theory stating that cities came into being as a result of a surplus of basic foodstuffs that allowed some people to develop occupations outside of agriculture.

altruistic suicide   The self-destructive act resulting from overinvolvement in a group. The individual takes his or her life for the good of the group.

amalgamation   Biological reproduction across different racial group lines.

Anglo conformity   The philosophy and policy that immigrants to the United States must abandon their old ways and conform to prevailing Anglo-Saxon cultural patterns.

anomic suicide   The self-destructive act that results from unregulated desires and ambition. It occurs in periods of rapid social change.

anomie   A word used by Durkheim to describe the breakdown of societal rules and norms that regulate human behavior. According to Merton, the gap between culturally acceptable goals and the culturally acceptable means of achieving them leads to deviant behavior. Overemphasis on goals in societies such as the United States also contributes to deviance.

anticipatory socialization   The early learning of appropriate behaviors and attitudes that will be required for some future social role.

apartheid   The legal system of racial segregation in South Africa.

ascription   The principle of filling social positions on the basis of personal qualities or characteristics.

assimilation   The process in which minority groups become absorbed or incorporated into the majority group's sociocultural system.

biological clock   Term referring to the ages between which women are physically able to conceive. The upper limits of fecundity occur at approximately 45 years of age.

biological drives   Drives experienced as a bodily imbalance or tension leading to activity that restores balance and reduces tension.

bourgeoisie   Marx's term for people who own and control the means of production in a capitalist society.

burakumin   Minority group in Japan whose members, although culturally and racially identical to the Japanese majority group, are regarded as ritually polluted and treated as outcasts.

bureaucracy   In Weber's formulation, an administrative device for maximizing human efficiency through the logical, orderly structuring of individual behaviors within a particular setting. Bureaucracies are characterized by well-defined spheres of responsibility and authority; standardized, impersonal procedures; recruitment and promotion on the basis of technical expertise; and a distinction between organizational and personal life.

category   Social collectivity whose members are clustered statistically on the basis of common or shared characteristics.

causal relationship   An empirical association between two or more variables in which change in one factor (the independent variable) is assumed to be responsible for changes occurring in the other factor(s) (the dependent variable[s]).

central business district (CBD)   The major shopping and commercial area of a city.

central place theory   Theory stating that cities emerged because farmers needed a central market to exchange and distribute their produce.

charismatic authority   Weber's term for political rule based on some extraordinary personal quality of the political leader.

class   In Weber's model, the position of individuals within the larger society characterized by a common level of life chances in the economic hierarchy.

class conflicts   Power struggles between unequal groups that, according to Marx, occurred in all stratified societies.

closed-caste structure   A society characterized by maximum inequalities of condition and of opportunity.

coercive organizations   In Etzioni's typology, organizations such as prisons or asylums that people join involuntarily and that restrain their members from normal contact with the larger society.

concentric zone model View of the city as a series of zones emanating from the center, with each zone characterized by a different group of people (or institution) and activity.

conception variables Factors that determine if a woman will become pregnant or not. The use of contraceptives and the presence or absence of breast-feeding have a significant impact on conception and, therefore, on society's fertility rate.

concrete operational stage In Piaget's cognitive development theory, the stage at which children begin to develop logical thought processes.

constructs Components or elements of the human world that do not have a direct empirical or physical existence.

continued subjugation Intergroup pattern in which minority groups are kept in a subordinate social and economic position.

control group In experimental research, the subject group whose members will not be exposed to the effects of the experimental condition (changes in the independent variable).

control theories of deviance Theories that take deviant motivation as a given, and attempt to explain why people do not engage in deviant behavior. According to this perspective, deviant motivation is contained by internal factors such as a positive self-image and external factors such as a supportive family and friends.

core In world system theory, industrial, economically diversified, rich, powerful nations relatively independent of outside control.

core values Values especially promoted by a particular culture, and often important identifying characteristics of that culture.

corporate crime A form of organizational crime committed by officials for their corporations, and crimes committed by the organization itself to maximize profits and enhance its position in the marketplace.

corporate dumping The sale to less developed nations of hazardous products that have been banned or are strictly regulated in the developed world.

corporations Organizations that have the legal right to engage in economic activities as though they were an individual person.

countercultures Groups whose members share values, norms, and a way of life that contradict the fundamental beliefs and lifestyle of the larger, more dominant culture.

criminal behavior Behavior in violation of society's laws that is not condemned by the norms of an individual's subculture.

cross-cultural research The gathering of comparable data from different societies.

crude birth rate (CBR) The number of births per year for every 1,000 members of the population. This statistic is crude because the age structure or distribution of the population is not considered.

crude death rate (CDR) The number of deaths per year for every 1,000 members of the population. This is a crude measure of mortality inasmuch as it does not take into account the age distribution of a population.

cult A new and distinctive religious organization that exists in a state of high tension with the established religions in society.

cultural anthropologists Researchers who study the social organization and patterns of behavior primarily of premodern people throughout the world.

cultural assimilation The giving up of established cultural patterns by a minority group and the acceptance of the majority group's cultural pattern.

cultural lag The process whereby one aspect of culture changes faster than another aspect of culture to which it is related. In modern societies, material culture (especially technology) typically changes faster than associated values, norms, and laws (nonmaterial culture).

cultural relativism The belief that there is no universal standard of good or bad, right or wrong; and that an aspect of any given culture can be judged only within the context of that culture.

culture A people's way of life or social heritage that includes values, norms, institutions, and artifacts that are passed from generation to generation by learning alone.

culture shock The experience of encountering people who do not share one's world view that leads to disorientation, frustration, and, on some occasions, revulsion.

Davis–Moore theory A functionalist interpretation of social stratification that attempted to explain social inequality in terms of its contribution to social survival.

debunking Looking for levels of reality other than those given in the everyday and official interpretations of society.

deconcentration explanation View of the slow-down and reversal of population growth in many of the country's largest cities as a fundamental break with past trends. More people are deciding to live in smaller cities and semirural areas.

decriminalization The reduction or elimination of penalties for a specific offense. For example, some individuals think the use of currently illegal drugs in the United States should be decriminalized.

de facto racism Discriminatory actions that exist in practice, but are not supported or required by law.

definition of the situation Concept developed by symbolic interaction theorist W. I. Thomas (1928) stating that "situations defined as real are real in their consequences" (p. 572).

de jure racism Discriminatory practices that are required or supported by law.

democratic socialism Economic system characterized by some private ownership of property but government regulation of all essential market activities.

demographic transition theory The perspective that explains population changes in the modern world. The theory divides this change into three stages: stage 1 (high growth potential) has high rates of birth and death, and slow growth; stage 2 (transitional growth) has a high birth rate and a low death rate, resulting in explosive population growth; stage 3 (incipient decline) has both low fertility and mortality, and therefore slow population growth.

demography The scientific study of population. Demographers are especially interested in population growth and how that growth is affected by birth, death, and migration rates.

denominations Formal religious organizations that are well integrated into their society and recognize religious pluralism.

developed, or northern, countries The more economically developed and politically democratic nations in the northern hemisphere of the contemporary world.

developing, or southern countries The contemporary nations currently undergoing societal modernization and located disproportionately in the southern hemisphere.

deviance Behavior contrary to a group's or society's norms of conduct or social expectations.

deviant and criminal behavior Behavior that violates both subcultural norms and society's laws.

deviant behavior Behavior that violates reference groups and/or subcultural norms, but not the legal code of the larger society.

devolution The surrender of powers to local authorities by the central government.

differential association Sutherland's theory stating that if definitions favorable to violations of the law are in excess of definitions unfavorable to violations of the law, the individual will engage in criminal behavior.

discrimination Unequal, unfair treatment toward members of some specific group.

doubling time The number of years it takes a given population to double in size.

dual labor or segmented labor market The division of an economy into an upper tier of high-paying, high-prestige jobs and a bottom tier of low-paying, low-prestige jobs.

dyad A social group consisting of two members.

ego In Freudian theory, that conscious part of the human personality that negotiates and mediates between the opposing forces of id and superego.

egoistic suicide Suicide that results from a lack of group integration and commitment to other people.

endogamy Social interaction system in which individuals are limited to forming relationships only with others in their own membership group.

ethnic group People who possess a distinctive, shared culture and a sense of common identification based on that culture.

ethnocentrism The tendency to believe that the norms and values of one's own culture are superior to those of others, and to use these norms as a standard when evaluating all other cultures.

ethnography The direct observation of a group of people, an organization or small society, and the written description of this account.

exogamy Social interaction system in which individuals are required to form relationships with others outside their own membership groups.

experimental group In experimental research, the subject group whose members will be exposed to the effects of the experimental condition (changes in the independent variable).

experimental research Causal research designed to explain observed social patterns or predict future ones.

expressive tasks Activities carried out on behalf of establishing or maintaining satisfying emotional relationships within a group.

extermination or **genocide** The attempted physical annihilation of a particular minority group.

external migration The movement of people from a given society to another society.

exurbanization The movement of people to towns beyond the ring of big-city suburbs. This process has been referred to as the suburbanization of the suburbs.

fatalistic suicide The result of overregulation and lack of control over one's life. It is the self-destructive act committed by slaves.

fecundity The physical ability of women to conceive and bear children.

feminization of poverty The increasing association between being female and being economically deprived.

fertility The number of children born to women in a given population.

folk religions Interpretations and modifications of more formalized religious traditions to meet the needs of specific population groups.

folkways The customary, habitual way a group does things; "the ways of the folks."

formal organizations Large, deliberately planned groups with established personnel, procedures, and rules for carrying out some objective or set of objectives.

formal operational stage In Piaget's cognitive development theory, the stage at which children become capable of employing abstract systems of reasoning.

functional illiteracy The lack of basic reading and writing skills necessary for everyday life.

game In G. H. Mead's theory, any organized group behavior that requires the child to interact with other people.

gemeinschaft According to Tönnies, a traditional type of communal relationship based on personal emotions and long-standing customs among the members of a population.

gender A system for classifying people as girl or boy, woman or man, based on physiological, psychological, and sociocultural characteristics.

gender assignment The process by which individuals are defined, typically at birth, as being either female or male.

gender roles Specific social roles assigned to individuals on the basis of sex.

gender socialization Social learning process through which individuals acquire and internalize the proper role of female or male as defined by their culture.

gender stereotypes Categorical portrayals of all members of a given sex as being alike in terms of basic nature and specific attributes.

gender stratification Social inequality hierarchies based on sex.

generalized other In G. H. Mead's theory, the surrounding social and cultural community of which the child is a member, that ultimately provides the frame of reference from which the child views the world and him- or herself.

genocide Deliberate and systematic destruction of a racial, ethnic, political, or religious group, in whole or significant part, by killing its members or imposing conditions detrimental to their survival.

gentrification The return of middle- and upper-class people to deteriorating central city neighborhoods.

gesellschaft According to Tönnies, a modern type of associational relationship based on impersonal, rational, secondary group relations among the members of a population.

gestation variables Factors (e.g., miscarriage, stillbirth, induced abortion) that determine if a fetus will come to term, resulting in a live birth.

goal displacement or **bureaucratic ritualism** Phenomenon often found within bureaucracies, in which adherence to organizational rules becomes more important than fulfilling the original objectives for which the organization was created.

grand theory A theory that deals with the universal aspects of social life and is usually grounded in basic assumptions (as opposed to data) concerning the nature of humans and society.

gross national product (GNP) The market value of all final goods and services produced by a society's economy during a given year.

group Social collectivity whose members possess a feeling of common identity and interact in a regular, patterned way.

Hawthorne effect The effect that knowledge of being part of a research study has on the subjects. People who know they are being studied often will attempt to be "good" subjects, behaving according to their perceptions of the researcher's expectations.

hispanization The forced adoption of Spanish cultural patterns by Indian and African population groups in colonial Mexico (similar to Anglo conformity policy in the United States).

homogamy The tendency for people to marry individuals like themselves physically, psychologically, and/or socially.

horizontal mobility Social movement within a given level in the stratification hierarchy.

human capital factors Resources such as education, interest, and aptitude that give individuals a better bargaining position to sell their labor in the occupational or job market.

human ecology The area of sociology concerned with the study of the spatial distribution and aspects of human life.

humanism The belief that humans, rather than God, are the center of their own destiny.

id In Freudian theory, that unconscious part of the human personality representing inherited aggressive and sexual impulses.

ideal types Logical constructions that present, in exaggerated and idealized form, the distinguishing features of some phenomenon.

imitation perspective The point of view that children learn to speak by repeating the spoken word of others.

infant mortality rate The number of deaths during the first year of life per 1,000 live births. It is often used as a measure of a country's economic well-being. Developed nations typically have low infant mortality rates, and poor nations have much higher rates.

informal organization The actual set of relationships developed by the members of formal organizations as they carry out the activities defined by organizational objectives and procedures.

innateness hypothesis According to this perspective of language acquisition, human beings learn to speak because our brains are biologically constructed or prewired to acquire language.

instincts Biologically inherited predispositions that impel most members of a species to react to a given stimulus in a specific way.

institutionalized racism A discriminatory pattern that has become embedded in prevailing societal structures.

instrumental tasks Activities carried out in pursuit of some specific group objective or goal.

intercourse variables Commencement and frequency of sexual activity over a given period of time.

intergenerational mobility Social movement from one generation to another; for example, the social position of sons compared to fathers.

internal migration The movement of people from one area to another area within the same society.

international migration The movement of people across political states.

interview Survey research procedure in which the researcher gains information through verbal interaction with the respondents.

intragenerational mobility Social movement of individuals within their own lifetimes.

labeling theory A theory stating that societies create deviance by making rules and laws whose infraction constitutes deviance, and then applying these rules and laws to certain individuals. Labeling theorists are interested in how and why some people are labeled, and how this label affects their future behavior.

latent functions Consequences of social behaviors and institutions that are neither intended nor recognized.

laws Norms that have been codified or formally written into a legal code.

liberation theology Interpretation of Christian faith and practice that focuses on the obligation of Christians to help free oppressed peoples from poverty and suffering. It is primarily a Third World Catholic theological stance.

life chances In Weber's model, the levels of access to basic opportunities and resources in the marketplace that defined individuals' positions in the economic inequality hierarchy.

lifestyle In Weber's model, a distinctive orientation or relationship to the social world that formed the basis for prestige or honor.

looking-glass self In Cooley's theory, the sense of personal identity individuals acquire through interactions with other people.

machismo The cult of masculinity in Spanish America that dates back to the days of the conquistadors.

macro-level Dealing with large-scale social phenomena such as societies.

majority group A recognizable group of people who occupy the dominant position in a given society.

manifest functions Consequences of social behaviors and institutions that are intended and/or recognized.

marital or **physical assimilation** Intermarriage and reproduction across majority—minority group lines leading to the gradual blurring of distinctive group differences.

Marxist theory of crime Theory stating that in a capitalist society, crime is the product of the struggle between the bourgeoisie and the proletariat. The ruling class commits crimes as a result of its effort to exploit and control the working class. Workers commit crimes as a result of their brutal treatment at the hands of the bourgeoisie and their effort to survive economically.

mass (society) Societal population consisting of millions of fragmented, alienated individuals who are uninterested and uninvolved in political affairs.

material culture That aspect of culture consisting of things people make and use in society.

maternal mortality rate The number of women who die in childbirth per 10,000 live births. In developed nations, maternal mortality rates are extremely low (2 or 3), whereas in poor countries complications and death during childbirth are still common.

maturation The process of neurological and physiological development necessary for successful socialization in humans.

mechanical solidarity Social cohesion in preindustrial societies resulting from a minimum division of labor, common experiences, and a strong collective conscience.

megacities Urban area with 10 million or more inhabitants.

melting pot Name for an image of racial and ethnic group relations in the United States in which individual immigrant groups each contribute to the creation of a new "American" cultural and physical end product through the process of amalgamation.

membership group Social group to which an individual belongs and participates in.

mestizoization The physical amalgamation of Spanish, Indian, and African populations in Mexico, resulting in a new physical type.

metaphysical stage In Comte's model of societal development, the stage at which knowledge is based on observation of specific events and rational speculation as to the nature of general events.

micro-level Dealing with small-scale social phenomena such as families and committees.

middle-range theories Theories that focus on relatively specific phenomena or problems in the social world. A theory of white-collar crime would be a middle-range theory.

migration The relatively permanent movement of people from one place to another.

minority group A recognizable group of people who occupy a subordinate position in a given society.

mode of production In Marxist theory, the mechanism by which wealth was produced in a given society.

modernization The transformation from a traditional, usually agrarian society to a contemporary, industrially based state.

mores Types of norms in any given society that must be obeyed. Members of society believe that obeying mores is essential to the well-being of the group.

multidimensional model An interpretation of stratification developed by Weber that argued that modern societies are characterized by several hierarchies of inequality.

multiple-nuclei model Model in which the city is seen as comprising multiple centers or nuclei. In some cases these nuclei have existed since the origin of the city, while in other instances they increased as the city grew and diversified.

nation A group of people with a common history and culture; a nation may or may not be a political state.

nationalism An ideology that emphasizes national identity and the importance of political self-governance.

neutral observation Research technique in which the researcher is identified to the subject group and remains removed or detached from the group while observations are being made.

nonexperimental or **descriptive research**   Non-causal research aimed most often at providing valid, reliable information about some aspect of social reality.

nonmaterial culture   That component of culture lacking a physical substance, although created by human beings. Ideas, religions, beliefs, customs, laws, and economic systems are examples.

normative organizations   Also called voluntary associations, in Etzioni's typology, public interest organizations such as Scouts or PTA groups that people join for nonmaterial reasons.

normative perspective   The view that deviance is the violation of a specific group's or society's rules at a particular time in history.

norms   Rules stating what human beings should or should not think, say, or do under given circumstances.

nuclear family   In modern societies, the typical family unit consisting of two spouses and their immediate offspring.

objective classes   In Marx's theory, groups defined on the basis of relationship to the economic system. In modern society, the two major classes are bourgeoisie (owners) and proletariat (workers).

objectivistic   Arguing that the tangible, objective facts of social reality are of primary importance in shaping people's lives and events.

observation study   Research technique in which the sociologist observes subjects' behaviors directly in order to form conclusions or make inferences about attitudes and values.

occupational crime   Law-violating behavior committed by individuals or small groups of people in connection with their work.

open-class society   A social system in which inequalities of condition and of opportunities are minimized.

operational definitions   Procedures that specify how phenomena having no direct empirical existence (constructs) are to be measured empirically.

organic solidarity   The social bond found in large industrial societies where people are dependent on one another because of a specialized, complex, highly developed division of labor.

organizational crimes   Offenses committed by individuals or groups to further the goal of a particular organization.

oversocialized conception of human beings   The mistaken view that all aspects of human lives are controlled by society through the socialization process.

participant observation   Research technique in which the researcher participates in the actions of the subject group while observations are being made. The researcher may be identified to the group (overt study) or the researcher's identity may be kept hidden from the group (covert study).

parties   In Weber's model, groups composed of individuals sharing a given level of power.

peer group or **peers**   People of approximately the same social position and same age as oneself.

period explanation   View of the slowdown and reversal of urban growth that began in the 1970s as a singular and therefore temporary distortion of metropolitan expansion resulting from the convergence of economic and demographic factors.

periphery   In world system theory, economically overspecialized, relatively poor, weak societies subject to the manipulation and direct control of core nations.

play   In G. H. Mead's theory, behavior in which children pretend to be parents or other specific people.

pluralism   The retention of minority group diversities and identities in a given society.

pluralist   Holding the view that political power in modern societies is dispersed among a variety of competing groups and organizations, with no single unit or combination of units dominating the system.

political economy   In modern societies, the essential interweaving of political and economic institutions.

political hierarchy   In Weber's model, an inequality hierarchy defined on the basis of power differences.

polity   In Parsonian functionalist terminology, another name for the state.

popular culture   The culture of everyday life as expressed through sport, music, hobbies, television, movies, books, magazines, comic books, and so on.

popular religions   Sets of beliefs that lie outside of or span the boundaries of recognized denominations and appeal to mass audiences drawn from a variety of backgrounds.

population   Name given collectively to all the members of a specific group being studied in a survey research design.

positivistic stage   In Comte's model of societal development, the stage at which knowledge is based on the scientific analysis of events.

poverty   The condition or situation of economic deprivation.

power   The ability of an individual or group to accomplish desired objectives even in the face of opposition from others.

power elite   Term used by radical conflict sociologist C. Wright Mills to describe a coalition of corporate, political, and military elites who, according to Mills, secretly control the state in the United States.

predestination   As part of the Protestant ethic, the belief that one's fate in the afterlife had been decided before or at one's birth, and could not be changed through prayer or good works.

prejudice   An irrational, negative feeling or belief about members of a certain group based on presumed characteristics of that group.

preoperational stage In Piaget's cognitive development theory, the stage at which children learn to use symbols and images.

prescriptive laws Laws that spell out what must be done. Income tax laws, traffic laws, and draft laws require people to do things at specific times and places, and under given circumstances.

prestige Reputation or social honor.

primary deviance The initial act, or first few incidents, of deviant behavior.

primary groups As described by Cooley, social groups such as one's family or close friends that are essential in the formation of individual self-identity.

primary socialization The first social learning experienced by individuals, typically in the setting of the family.

primate cities Sprawling urban areas that are at least twice as large (population) as the nation's second-largest city and serve as a country's economic, political, and cultural hub.

profane The commonplace, ordinary elements of everyday life.

proletariat Marx's term for the working class in a capitalist society. These people survive by selling their labor power to the bourgeoisie.

property Income, wealth, and other material resources.

proscriptive laws Laws that state what behavior is prohibited or forbidden. For example, laws against robbing people or harming them physically are proscriptive and carry some form of punishment administered by the state.

Protestant ethic Weber's term for the world view and values associated with the Protestant Christian religions that developed in western Europe during the sixteenth and seventeenth centuries.

pull factors Socioeconomic magnets that draw migrants to a given geographical location. They include increased opportunity for employment and better living conditions.

pure capitalist economy Economic system characterized by private property ownership and an unregulated, unrestricted market.

pure socialist economy Economic system characterized by collective ownership of property and government planning and regulation of all market activities.

push factors Factors that drive off or send a stream of migrants from a particular locale. These include little economic opportunity, and racial, religious, and political persecution.

questionnaire Survey research instrument in which questions are posed to respondents in writing for them to answer in writing.

race A classification of human beings that is based on genetic characteristics.

rational-legal authority Weber's term for political rule based on the reasonableness of laws and the acceptability of law-making procedures.

reactive perspective The view that behavior is not deviant until it has been recognized and condemned.

reference group Social group whose perspective is adopted by an individual as a frame of reference for personal behaviors and attitudes.

regional restructuring From this perspective the deindustrialization of many winter cities in the 1970s is a component of a new geography of urban growth. Cities will expand in different geographic regions of the country for reasons unrelated to past growth.

reinforcement theory The language acquisition theory stating that children are positively reinforced when they say something correctly, and negatively reinforced when they say something incorrectly.

relative poverty The condition of economic deprivation relative or compared to some other individual or group.

representative sample A smaller segment or sub-group of a particular population that reflects the attributes of that larger group. For the sample to be representative, each member of the population must have an equal chance of being included in the sample.

resocialization Rapid and dramatic secondary socialization experiences in which established behaviors and attitudes are removed and new patterns are created.

role conflict Contradictory role expectations arising from two or more statuses occupied by an individual at the same time.

role/formal role The set of expected behaviors and attitudes associated with a particular status in a group or society.

role performance An individual's actual behaviors and attitudes in response to role expectations.

role playing The process in which, during play, children begin to duplicate the behaviors and attitudes of the specific people being imitated.

role strain The inability to meet all the expectations attached to a particular social role.

role taking During play activities, the process in which children begin to view and evaluate the world from the perspective of the people being imitated.

rule by authority Political rule based on a sense of moral obligation, rather than raw power and force.

sacred Those extraordinary elements of life that inspire a sense of reverence, awe, and fear in people.

scapegoat An innocent, powerless target for a more powerful individual's or group's frustration and aggression.

secondary deviance Nonconforming behavior that occurs as a result of being labeled deviant.

secondary groups Social groups such as customers and clerks that are more formal, less inclusive, less emotional than primary groups, and typically organized for some specific purpose.

secondary socialization Social learning experienced during adolescence and, in particular, during adulthood.

sector model Model of the city in which urban zones are wedge-shaped sectors radiating out from the center, or central business district.

sects Religious subcultural or countercultural groups that offer their members a different vision of the social and the spiritual life.

secularization Societal transformation from a religious to a civil and worldly basis, with a significant decline of religion in people's everyday lives.

self An individual's awareness and concept of personal identity.

semiperiphery In world system theory, term describing nations midway between the core and the periphery that are attempting to industrialize and diversify their economies.

sensorimotor stage In Piaget's cognitive development theory, the stage at which children learn about the world through direct sensory contact.

sex A system for classifying people as female or male based on anatomical, chromosomal, and hormonal differences.

sex ratio The number of males per hundred females in a given population.

significant others People who are important in creating an individual's self-concept.

significant symbols Physical stimuli that have been assigned meaning and value by a social group. People respond to these symbols in terms of their meanings and values, rather than their actual physical properties.

sluburb A residential area part slum and part suburb.

social collectivity Any collection or situation involving more than one person.

social Darwinism A social and political philosophy, the proponents of which believed in the existence of natural laws of social evolution and argued for a hands-off approach to human social affairs.

social hierarchy In Weber's model, an inequality hierarchy based on prestige or social honor accorded to individuals by others.

social institutions Orderly, enduring, and established ways of arranging behavior and doing things.

socialization The social learning process through which individuals develop their human potentials and also acquire the established patterns of their culture.

socialization agents Parents, teachers, and other important groups involved in the socialization of individual societal members.

social marginality The condition of being caught or poised between two recognized societal groups without being fully a member of either.

social mobility The movement of individuals and groups within and between social levels in a stratified society.

social self In G. H. Mead's theory, the human personality structure that results from the individual's interaction with others through play and game activities.

social stratification The systematic division of a societal population into categories in which people are defined and treated as social unequals.

social structure The organization of a societal population into various groups, and the patterned relationships that exist within and among these groups.

societies Self-perpetuating groups of people who occupy a given territory and interact with one another on the basis of a shared culture.

sociology The study of the social organization and patterns of behavior of people in primarily large, complex, modern, industrial societies.

state The social institution that holds a monopoly over the legitimate use of force and exercises governing power in a given society.

status Any defined or recognized position within a group or society.

stereotype A preconceived (not based on experience), standardized, group-shared idea about the alleged essential nature of a whole category of persons without regard to the individual differences of those in the category.

stratum In Weber's model, a level in the social hierarchy occupied by individuals of a certain lifestyle.

structural assimilation The acceptance of minority group members into secondary and primary group relationships by members of the majority group.

structural mobility Social movement that results from changes in economic or other social structures.

subcultures Groups that hold norms, values, and patterns of behavior in common with the larger society, but also have their own design for living and world view.

subjective classes In Marx's theory, groups whose members were conscious and aware of their own collective position and interests in the mode of production.

subjectivistic Arguing that people's subjective perceptions and interpretations of reality are of primary importance in shaping their lives and events.

substructure In Marxist theory, the economic system that shaped all other significant material and nonmaterial aspects of societal life, such as political and religious institutions.

superego In Freudian theory, that unconscious part of the human personality representing internalized cultural values and norms.

superstructures In Marxist theory, social or cultural forms such as law, politics, and art that derived from and reflected the society's economic substructure.

survey research Type of nonexperimental study in which the researcher asks some defined group a series of questions relating to their behaviors or attitudes.

symbolic interactionism Sociological approach that examines the process by which members of a group or society come to define and assign meaning to their surrounding world, and the consequences or effects of the created world view.

theological stage   In Comte's model of societal development, the stage at which knowledge is based on imagination and the interpretation of events in terms of supernatural beings and their activities.

theory   A set of logically coherent interrelated concepts that attempts to explain some observable phenomenon or group of facts.

total fertility rate (TFR)   A measure of completed fertility, or the total number of children born per 1,000 women.

total institutions   Places such as prisons and monasteries, where large numbers of people who are cut off from the larger society have all aspects of their lives planned and controlled by agents of the institution. These total institutions often are the settings in which resocialization takes place.

trading theory   Theory of city growth stating that specialists were responsible for producing the surplus food vital for the growth of cities. Traders introduced new seeds and livestock that resulted in improved crops and a successful agricultural revolution. This revolution in turn permitted people to develop occupations other than farming.

traditional authority   Weber's term for political rule based on long-standing societal customs.

triad   A social group consisting of three members.

typologies   Ordering systems that classify individual phenomena into categories or types on the basis of distinguishing characteristics.

unilinear theories of change   Theories predicting that societies would undergo a similar (if not identical) set of transformations, resulting in the same end product: the modern industrial state.

urbanization   Growth in the proportion of people living in urban areas.

utilitarian organizations   In Etzioni's typology, organizations such as corporations or universities that individuals join for some practical, material reason.

vertical mobility   Social movement between different levels in the stratification hierarchy.

voluntary mobility   Social movement that results from individual efforts.

WASP   Acronym for *white Anglo-Saxon Protestant,* generally regarded as the majority or dominant group in the United States.

welfare capitalist economy   Economic system characterized by private property ownership and limited or partial government regulation of market activities.

world system theory (WST)   The perspective that examines the relationship between the developed and developing nations of the world. According to this theory, the developed nations became rich in large measure by systematically exploiting the poor and militarily weak nations of the world.

worldly asceticism   As part of the Protestant ethic, the denial of material self-indulgence under the belief that frugality was morally superior to concern for worldly pleasures.

xenophobia   The fear and avoidance of foreign people and things.

References

Abdallah, D. 1999. "Saudi Prince Calls for Women's Rights." *San Diego Union-Tribune,* June 13.

Abdulayev, N. 1999. "Islamic Rebels Begin New Dagestan Attack." *San Diego Union-Tribune,* September 6.

Abdullah, Z. 1998. "Afghanistan's Taliban Orders Closure of Schools for Girls." *San Diego Union-Tribune,* June 17.

Adams, C. T. and K. T. Winston. 1980. *Mothers at Work—Public Policies in the United States, Sweden and China.* New York: Longman.

Adeola, F. O. 1996. "Military Expenditures, Health, and Education: Bedfellows or Antagonists in Third World Development" *Armed Forces and Society* (Spring):441–469.

———. 1996. "The West Unique, Not Universal." *Foreign Affairs* (November/December):28–46.

Adler, J., P. Wingert, E. Angell, and M. Meyer. 1998. "Tomorrow's Child." *Newsweek* (November 2):54–62.

"Afghanistan: The Facts." 1999. < http://www.afghan-network.net/facts.html > Accessed August 19, 1999.

"After Venezuela's Flood." 1999. *Economist,* December 3l, pp. 19–20.

Aguilar, E. O. 1992. "Air Is So Polluted It's Hard to Talk." *Oakland Tribune,* April 10.

"AI Report 1999: Afghanistan." 1999. Amnesty International. < http://www.amnesty.org/ailib/aireport/ar/99/asa11.htm > Accessed August 16, 1999.

"AIDS Information." 1998. *Centers for Disease Control http://www.cdc.gov/nchtsp/hiv/aids/stats/topten.htm*

"AIDS Outlook Grim for Africa." 1995. *San Diego Union-Tribune,* October 3, pp. A11.

"Air Pollution in the World's Megacities." (1994) *Environment* (March):4–21.

Alba, R. D. 1992. "Ethnicity," in E. F. Borgotta and M. L. Borgotta, eds. *Encyclopedia of Sociology,* vol. 1. New York: Macmillan, pp. 575–584.

"All Good Things Must Slow Down." 1998. *Economist* (March 7):35–36.

Allinson, G. D. 1984. "Japanese Urban Society and Its Cultural Context," in J. Agnew, J. Mercer, and D. Sopher, eds. *The City in Cultural Conflict.* Boston: Allen and Unwin,pp. 163–185.

Allison, J. and L. Wrightsman. 1993. *Rape: The Misunderstood Crime.* Beverly Hills, CA: Sage.

Allport, G. W. 1958. *The Nature of Prejudice.* Abridged edition. New York: Doubleday.

Alsop, R. J., ed. 1998. *The Wall Street Journal Almanac, 1999.* New York: Ballantine Books.

Alter, J. 1998. "A Different Kind of War." *Newsweek* (August 3): p. 27.

Altman, L. K. 1996. "India Suddenly Leads in HIV, AIDS Meeting is Told." *The New York Times International,* July 8, p. A12.

Altman, L. K. 1997. "AIDS Surge is Forecast for China, India, and Eastern Europe." *New York Times,* November 4, p. A10.

Amanpour, C. 1997. "Tyranny of the Taliban." *Time World* 150(5).

"Amazon Destruction Continues Unchecked." 1999. *San Diego Union-Tribune,* February 13.

"America's Children: Key National Indicators of Well-Being, 1998." 1998. < http://www.childstats.gov >

Amnesty International U.S.A. 1991. *Amnesty International Report 1991.* New York.

Anderson, E. 1978. *A Place on the Corner.* Chicago: University of Chicago Press.

Anderson, E. 1992. *Streetwise* Chicago and London: University of Chicago Press.

Anderson, J. W. 1994. "Where Birth Control Is a Means of Survival." *Washington Post Weekly Edition,* September 5–11, p. 18.

Applebaum, R. P. 1970. *Theories of Social Change.* Chicago: Rand McNally.

Apter, D. E. 1986. *Rethinking Development, Modernization, Dependency and Post-Modern Politics.* Beverly Hills, CA: Sage.

Arvidson, C., and J. Leaming. 1999. "Congressmen Wouldn't Go Further Than Posting Ten Commandments in Schools." *free! The Freedom Forum Online* (June 21).

Ashford, N. A. 1974. *Crisis in the Workplace: Occupational Disease and Injury.* Cambridge, MA: M. I. T. Press.

"The Asian Flu." 1998. *Canada and the World Backgrounder* (October):22–25.

Astrachan, A. 1986. *How Men Feel: Their Responses to Women's Demands for Equality and Power.* New York: Doubleday.

Bachman, R. 1994. "Violence Against Women." *U.S. Department of Justice.* Washington DC: U.S. Government Printing Office.

Backhaus, T. N., P. B. Belden, and T. J. Espenshade. 1994. "AIDS, Low Birth Rates and Future Growth in Thailand." *Population Today* (October):4–5.

Bai, M., and V. E. Smith. 1999. "Evil to the End." *Newsweek,* (March 8).

Baird, W. 1998. " 'Dark side' of Elvis Focus of Conference." *San Diego Union-Tribune,* August 10, p. A7.

Baker, M. 1998. "Out with Confucius in Korea's Big Firms." *Christian Science Monitor,* March 11, p. 1.

Baldouf, S. 1998a. "Gov. Bush Leads Revolt Against Tribal Casinos." *Christian Science Monitor,* June 25.

———. 1998b. "Public Schools at a Crossroads." *Christian Science Monitor,* September 8.

———. 1998c. "Corporate Welfare." *Time* (November 9).

"Balkans." < http://suc.suc.org/ ~ kosta/tar/history/balkan/html > Accessed August 22, 1999.

Baltzell, E. D. 1958. *Philadelphia Gentlemen: The Making of a National Upper Class.* Glencoe, IL: Free Press.

Banjeree, T. 1996. "Role of Indicators in Monitoring Growing Urban Regions." *Journal of the American Planning Association* 62(2):222–235.

Barkan, S. E. 1997. *Criminology.* Upper Saddle, NJ: Prentice-Hall Inc.

Barlett, D. L., and J. B. Steele. 1991. "Between Rich & Poor Are the Pinched." *San Diego Union,* November 17.

Barr, C. 1995. "Violence Pushes Japan To Dig for More Order." *Christian Science Monitor,* May 15.

Barr, C. W. 1998. "Indonesians Brace for Rapid Descent into Poverty." *Christian Science Monitor,* October 6, p. 6.

Barret, M. J. 1990. "The Case for More School Days." *Atlantic Monthly* (November): 78–106.

Barrett, P. M. 1999. "Race Intrudes into a Lawyer's Career." *Wall Street Journal,* January 5.

Barry, K. 1979. *Female Sexual Slavery.* Englewood Cliffs, NJ: Prentice Hall.

Barth, R. P. 1991. "Sweden's Contact Family Program." *Public Welfare* 49(3):36–42.

Bartholet, J. 2000. "The Plague Years." *Newsweek,* January 17, pp. 32–37.

Basow, S. A. 1986. *Gender Stereotypes.* Pacific Grove, CA: Brooks/Cole.

Bassouni, F, 1998. "There Is No Contradiction Between Islam and Feminism." *Middle East Times,* June 12.

Baum, G. 1991. "Should These Women Have Gone Free?" *Los Angeles Times,* April 15.

Baumer, E., J. Lauritsen, and R. R. Wright. 1998. "The Influence of Crack Cocaine on Robbery, Burglary, and Homicide Rates: A Cross-City, Longitudinal Analysis." *Journal of Research in Crime and Delinquency* (August):316–340.

Bayer, A. 1997. "Immigrants Big Economy Boost, Study Says." *San Diego Union-Tribune,* May 18, p. A1.

Beaty, J. 1989. "Do Humans Need to Get High?" *Time* (August 21):58.

Becker, H. S. 1963. *Outsiders—Studies in the Sociology of Deviance.* New York: Free Press.

Becker, M., and J. Gordon. 1991. "A Dumping Ground for Granny." *Newsweek* (December 23):64.

Beeghley, L. 1996. *The Structure of Social Stratification in the United States,* 2nd ed. Boston: Allyn and Bacon.

Beirne, P., and J. Messerschmidt. 1991. *Criminology.* Fort Worth, TX: Harcourt Brace.

Bell, D. 1973. *The Coming of Post-Industrial Society.* New York: Basic Books.

———. 1976. *The Post-Industrial Society: A Venture in Social Forecasting.* New York: Basic Books.

Bellah, R. N. 1988. "Civil Religion in America." *Daedalus* 117:97–118.

Bellah, R. N., R. Madsen, W. G. Sullivan, A. Swidler, and S. M. Tipton. 1985. *Habits of the Heart.* New York: Harper & Row.

Belsie, L. 1999a. "Coaxing Youths into Church Pews." *Christian Science Monitor,* January 27.

———. 1999b. "America's New Not-Melting Pot." *Christian Science Monitor,* March 5.

Bender, W., and M. Smith. 1997. "Feeding the Future." *Population Today* (March):4–5.

Bennefield, R. L. 1998. "Health Insurance Coverage: 1997." *Current Population Reports:* P60-202. Washington, DC: U.S. Government Printing Office.

Bennet, N. 1989. "U.S. Man Shortage Is Over, Says Sociology Researcher." *Missoulan,* July 30.

Bennett, C. 1999. "*Comment:* Serbia's War With History." *Balkan Crisis Reports,* April 19.

Benokraitis, N. V. 1993. *Marriage and the Family.* Englewood Cliffs, NJ: Prentice Hall.

Berger, A. S. 1978. *The City—Urban Communities and Their Problems.* Dubuque, IA: Wm. C. Brown.

Berger, B. 1992. "Sources of Prosperity—Culture and Economics." *Current* (November):27–30.

Berger, D. 1998. "As Anti-foreigner Sentiment Rises, German Politics Follows." *Christian Science Monitor,* September 24.

———. 1999. "Germany Redefining Germans." *Christian Science Monitor,* January 11.

Berger, P. L. 1963. *An Invitation to Sociology.* Garden City, NY: Anchor Books, Doubleday.

———. 1967. *The Sacred Canopy: Elements of a Sociological Theory of Religion.* New York: Doubleday.

———. 1977. *Facing up to Modernity.* New York: Basic Books.

Bergeson, A. 1980. "Cycles of Formal Colonial Rule," in T. K. Hopkins and I. Wallerstein, eds. *Processes of the World System.* Beverly Hills, CA: Sage, pp. 119–126.

"Berlin Airlift Began Long Road to Freedom." 1998. *Daily News* (Jacksonville, N. C.), May 13.

"The Berlin Wall." 1999. *MSNBC TV News.* < http://www.msnbc.com/onair/msnbc/timeandagain/archive/berlin/default.asp > Accessed August 31, 1999.

Bernard, J. 1981. *The Female World.* New York: Free Press.

Berndt, T., and G. W. Ladd, eds. 1989. *Peer Relationships in Child Development.* New York: Wiley.

Bettenson, H. 1974. *Documents of the Christian Church.* New York: Oxford University Press.

Beyer, L. 1999. "The Price of Honor." *Time* (January 18).

Bianchi, S. M, and D. Spain. 1996. *Women, Work, and Family in America.* Population Bulletin Vol. 51, No. 3. Washington, DC: Population Reference Bureau.

Bielby, W. T., and J. N. Baron 1986. "Men and Women at Work: Sex Segregation and Statistical Discrimination." *American Journal of Sociology* 91:759–799.

Biele, K. 1998. "Utah's Image Sullied by Legacy of Polygamy," *Christian Science Monitor,* August 17, p. 3.

Black, C. E. 1966. *The Dynamics of Modernization—A Study in Comparative History.* New York: Harper & Row.

Black, J. A., and D. J. Champion. 1976. *Methods and Issues in Social Research.* New York: Wiley.

Blake, J., and K. Davis. 1964. "Norms, Values, and Sanctions," in R. L. Faris, ed. *Handbook of Modern Sociology.* Chicago: Rand McNally.

Blau, P. M., and M. W. Meyer. 1987. *Bureaucracy in Modern Society,* 3rd ed. New York: Random House.

Blau, P. M., and O. D. Duncan. 1967. *The American Occupational Structure.* New York: Wiley.

Block, R. 1999. "South African Justice: Bloodthirsty Ways to Fight Carjackers." *Wall Street Journal,* January 11, p. 1.

Blum, D. 1999. "What's the Difference Between Boys and Girls?" *Life* (July).

Blum, L., and V. Smith. 1988. "Women's Mobility in the Corporation: A Critique of the Politics of Optimism." *Signs* 13(3): 528–545.

Blumberg, P. 1981. *Inequality in an Age of Decline.* New York: Oxford University Press.

Blumer, H. 1969. *Symbolic Interactionism.* Englewood Cliffs, NJ: Prentice Hall.

Bodipo-Memba, A. 1999. "Wage Gap for Nonfluent Males Widens In States with 'Official English' Laws." *Wall Street Journal,* February 26.

Bogert, C. 1992. "Get out the Geiger Counters." *Newsweek* (November 2).

Bogue, D. J. 1969. *Principles of Demography.* New York: Wiley.

Bolte, A. 1998. "Do Wedding Dresses Come in Lavender? The Prospects and Implications of Same-Sex Marriages." *Social Theory and Practice* (Spring):111–130.

Bonacich, E. 1992. "Class and Race," in E. F. Borgotta and M. L. Borgotta, eds. *Encyclopedia of Sociology,* vol. 1. New York: Macmillan, pp. 204–208.

Bongaarts, J. 1982. "Why Fertility Rates Are So Low," in S. W. Menard and E. W. Mohen, eds. *Perspectives on Population: An Introduction to Concepts and Issues.* New York: Oxford University Press.

Bonner, R. 1999. "War Crimes Investigators Accuse Croatian Army of Atrocities in 1995 Assault." *San Diego Union-Tribune,* March 21.

Booth, W. 1998. "Diversity and Division." *Washington Post National Weekly Edition,* March 2, p. 6.

Bourgeois-Pichat, J. 1986. "Comment." *Population and Development Review* 12:243–244.

Bourrie, M. 1999. "Canadian-US Fight Over Magazines." *Black World Today,* (February 5).

Bouvier, L. 1995. "More African Famines in the Future?" Lessons for the U.S." *Carrying Capacity Network* (March):1–7.

Bouvier, L. F., and R. W. Gardner. 1986. *Immigration to the United States: The Unfinished Story.* Washington, DC: Population Reference Bureau.

Bowers, F. 1995. "Islamists Strike At Women In Algerian War." *Christian Science Monitor,* June 28.

Bowles, S., and H. Gintis. 1976. *Schooling in Capitalist America.* New York: Basic Books.

Bradshaw, Y. W., and R. Noonan, L. Gash, and C. B. Sershen. 1993. "Borrowing Against the Future: Children and Third World Indebtedness." *Social Forces* (March): 629–656.

Bradsher, K. 1995. "Gap Between Rich and Poor in U.S. Grows." *San Diego Union-Tribune,* April 17.

Braithwaite, J. 1981. "The Myth of Social Class and Criminality Reconsidered." *American Sociological Review* 46:36–47.

Brandao, C. 1995. "Street Children: More and More Killed Everyday." International Child Resource Institute Report, April 24.

Branigin, W. 1995. "Sweatshops Reborn." *Washington Post National Weekly Edition,* September 18–24.

Braungart, R. G., and M. M. Braungart. 1994. "Political Socialization." *The International Encyclopedia of Education,* 2nd ed. Ed. T. Husen and T. N. Postlethwaite. London: Pergamon Press.

"Brazil's At-Risk Children." 1999. *Projeto Casa Esperanca.* Nova Friburgo, Brazil.

Bremmer, B., and M. Tanikawa. 1998. "The Cities Are Sinking." *Business Week* (November 10):54–55.

Breznican, A. 1999. "Tension Over Ho Chi Minh Poster." *San Diego Union-Tribune,* February 16.

Bridis, T. 1999. "Racial Gap Seen in Computer, Internet Use." *San Diego Union-Tribune,* July 9.

Bromley, R. 1982. "Working the Streets: Survival Strategy, Necessity, or Unavoidable Evil?" in A. Gilbert, J. E. Hardy, and R. Ramirez, eds. *Urbanization in Contemporary Latin America.* New York: Wiley.

———. 1993. "Making Female Bodies the Battlefield." *Newsweek* (January 4):37.

Bronner, E. 1998a. "Wisconsin Court Backs Vouchers in Church Schools." *New York Times,* June 11.

———. 1998b. "U.S. Drops in Education Rankings." *San Diego Union-Tribune,* November 24.

Brooke, J. 1997. "Vital Mix in Viper Militia: Hatred Plus Love of Guns" in *Terrorism in the United States* F. McGuckin, ed. New York: The H. W. Wilson Company.

Brookoff, D., C. S. Cook, C. Williams, and C. S. Mann. 1994. "Testing Reckless Drivers for Cocaine and Marijuana." *New England Journal of Medicine* (331, No. 8):518–521.

Brooks, J. F. 1994. "In South Bay Judge Cannon Has a Long Memory." *San Diego Union-Tribune,* July 12, p. E1.

Brooks, N. R. 1994. "Study of Asians in U.S. Finds Many Struggling." *Los Angeles Times,* May 19.

Brown, L. 1999. "Crossing the Threshold." *World Watch* (March/April):12–22.

Broom, L., and P. Selznick. 1970. *Principles of Sociology.* New York: Harper & Row.

Brown, L. R. 1991. "The Environmental Crisis—A Humanist Call for Action." *The Humanist* (November/December):26–30.

———.1994. "Who Will Feed China?" *World Watch* (September—October):10–19.

Brown, L., and C. Flavin. 1999. "A New Economy for a New Century," in L. Starke, ed., *State of the World 1999.* New York: W. W. Norton.

Brown, P. 1990. "Africa's Growing AIDS Crisis." *New Scientist* (November 17):38–41.

Brown, R. O. 1973. *A First Language: The Early Stages.* Cambridge, MA: Harvard University Press.

Brownlee, S. 1998. "Baby Talk." *U.S. News & World Report* (June 15):48–55.

Brownmiller, S. 1975. *Against Our Will: Men, Women and Rape.* New York: Simon & Schuster.

Brunner, B., ed. 1998. *Time Almanac 1999.* Boston: Information Please LLC.

Bryjak, G. J. 1990. "Reducing Demand Is Our Only Hope." *USA Today,* July, pp. 20–22.

———. 1997. "Heaven's Gate Slammed Shut on Members' Free Will." *San Diego Union-Tribune* April 22, p. B5.

Bryjak, G. J., and M. P. Soroka. 1985. *Sociology: The Biological Factor.* Palo Alto, CA: Peek Publications.

Buechlman, K. T., J. M. Gottman, and L. F. Katz. 1992. "How a Couple Views Their Past Predicts Their Future: Predicting Divorce from an Oral History Interview." *Journal of Family Psychology* (March–June): 295–318.

Burgess, E. W. 1925. "The Growth of the City," in R. E. Park and E. W. Burgess, eds. *The City.* Chicago: University of Chicago Press, pp. 47–62.

Burke, J. 1993. "Russia's Orthodox Church Strives to Remain Above Political Fray." *Los Angeles Times,* April 7, p. 7.

———. 1995. "Polish Reforms: The Job Is Only Half Done." *Christian Science Monitor,* February 6, p. 9.

Bush, R. C. 1988. "Introduction," in R. C. Bush et al., eds. *The Religious World—Communities of Faith.* New York: Macmillan, pp. 1–11.

Butler, E. W. 1976. *Urban Sociology: A Systematic Approach.* New York: Harper & Row.

Butler, S. and J. Egan. 1997. "No Magic Won For Korea." *U.S. News & World Report,* December 12, pp. 26–27.

"By Leaps and Bounds." 1999. *Newsweek* (July 19).

Caldwell, J. C. 1976. "Toward a Restatement of Demographic Transition Theory." *Population and Development Review* 2(3–4):321–366.

———. 1980. "Mass Education as a Determinant of the Timing of Fertility Decline." *Population and Development Review* 6(2):225–256.

Callaghy, T. M. 1997. "Globalization and Marginalization: Debt and the International Underclass." *Current History* (November):392–396

Campbell, D. T., and J. C. Stanley. 1963. *Experimental and Quasi-Experimental Designs for Research.* Chicago: Rand McNally.

"Canada & TV Violence: Cooperation & Consensus." 1996. *CRTC Factsheet,* (March 14).

Cantlupe, J. 1999. "Poverty Rate of Immigrants up, Study Says." *San Diego Union-Tribune,* September 3.

Caplow, T. 1968. *Two Against One: Coalitions in Triads.* Englewood Cliffs, NJ: Prentice Hall.

Carlson, A. 1996. "Two Cheers for the Suburbs." *American Enterprise* (November/December):34–35.

Caron, A. H., and A. E. Jolicoeur. 1996. *Systematized Summary of Canadian Regulations Concerning Children and the Audiovisual Industry.* Montreal: University of Montreal.

Carroll, J. B. 1961. *The Study of Language.* Cambridge, MA: Harvard University Press.

Cart, J. 1998. "Tales of Abuse, Incest Frame 'Utah's Dirty Little Secret,' " *Los Angeles Times,* August 15, pp. 1A.

Caryl, C. 1998. "Only a Fool Pays Taxes in Capitalist Russia." *U.S. News and World Report* (March 30):38.

Cass, C. 1995. "Nearly 33% of Young Black Men Are Serving Criminal Sentences." *San Diego Union-Tribune,* October 5, p. A5.

Castilho, C. 1995. "Children to the slaughter." *WorldPaper,* (January).

"Catch Us if You Can." 1996. *Economist,* October 19, p. 68.

"Census Bureau Predicts 65 + Population to Double in Eight States by 2020." 1996. U.S. Census Bureau Press Release, May 20. < http://www.census.gov >

Center for the American Woman And Politics. 1997. "The Gender Gap." CAWP Fact Sheet. New Brunswick, NJ: Eagleton Institute of Politics, Rutgers University.

———. 1999. "Women in Elective Office 1999." CAWP Fact Sheet. New Brunswick, NJ: Eagleton Institute of Politics, Rutgers University.

Chaddock, G. R. 1998a. "U.S. 12th-Graders Miss the Mark." *Christian Science Monitor,* February 28.

———. 1998b. "Expelling Violence." *Christian Science Monitor,* May 26.

———. 1998c. "Help with 'R' No. 1." *Christian Science Monitor,* September 22.

———. 1999. "Reading Skills Rise for U.S. Students." *Christian Science Monitor,* February 11.

Chambers, A. 1998. "Privatization, Economic Stablization Go Hand-in-Hand in Latin America." *Power Engineering* (May):8–9.

Chanda, N. 1998. "Rebuilding Asia." *Far Eastern Economic Review* (February 12):46–50.

Chandler, C. 1994–1995. "And While We're on the Subject . . . Who Do They Mean When They Talk About 'the Middle Class'?" *Washington Post National Weekly Edition,* December 26—January 1.

Chandler, C. 1998. "A Market Tide That Isn't Lifting Everybody." *Washington Post National Weekly Edition,* April 13, p. 18.

Chang, M. S. 1988. " 'Women,' " in Y. Wu, F. Michael, J. F. Copper, T. Lee, M. S. Chang, and A. J. Gregor, eds. *Human Rights in the People's Republic of China.* Boulder, CO: Westview Press, pp. 250–267.

Charney, C. 1996. "Rockey Road." *New Statesmen* (December 2): 14–15.

Chase-Dunn, C. 1975. "The Effects of International Dependence on Development and Inequality: A Cross-National Study." *American Sociological Review* 40(December):720–738.

Chase-Dunn, C., and T. D. Hall. 1997. *Rise and Demise: Comparing World Systems* Boulder, CO: Westview Press.

Chaudhuri, P. 1992. "India—Economy." *The Far East and Australasia—1992.* London: Europa Publications, pp. 297–306.

Cheevers, J. 1995. "Drug-Resistant Bacteria Pose an Increasing Threat." *Los Angeles Times,* March 25, p. A1.

Chelala, C. 1998. "Egypt Takes Decisive Stance Against Female Genital Mutilation." *Lancet* 351(9096):120.

Chenault, K. 1996. "A Nation Under Seige." *Business Week* (September 30):54.

Chengappa, R. 1988. "India's Urban Chaos." *World Press Review,* August, p. 57.

Cherlin, A., F. F. Furnsterberger, Jr., P. L. Chase-Landsdale, K. E. Kiernan, P. K. Robins, D. R. Morrison, and J. O. Teitler. 1991. "Longitudinal Studies of Effects of Divorce on Children in Great Britain and the United States." *Science* 252(June 7):1386–1389.

"Child Abuse and Neglect Still A Widespread Problem in America." 1997. *Nation's Health* (May/June):9–10.

"China's Economy in the 1990s." 1992. *Beijing Review* (February 17–23):15–17.

Chipello, C. 1998. "Francophones Struggle Outside of Quebec." *Wall Street Journal,* February 26, p. A12.

Chirot, D. 1977. *Social Change in the Twentieth Century.* New York: Harcourt Brace Jovanovich.

Chiu, A. 1999. "Study Links Eating Disorders Among Fiji Girls to Television." *San Diego Union-Tribune,* May 20.

Choe, S. 1999. "Abuse Rife in Schools of South Korea." *San Diego Union-Tribune,* February 5.

Chomsky, N. 1965. *Aspects of the Theory of Syntax.* Cambridge, MA: M. I. T. Press.

Chong, J. 1998. "Crime Indicators for Alcohol and Drug Abuse," *Criminal Justice and Behavior* (September):283–305.

Chossudovsky, M. 1997. *The Globalization of Poverty.* London: Zed Books Ltd.

———. 1996. *An Introduction to the World-System Perspective.* Boulder, CO: Westview Press.

Christiansen, K. O. 1977. From lecture at University of Oklahoma.

"Chronology to a Crisis." 1999. *San Diego Union-Tribune,* February 7.

Chu, H. 1998. "U.S. Officials Report Horror of North Korea Famine." *Los Angeles Times,* August 20, p. A1.

Chudacoff, H. P. 1981. *The Evolution of American Urban Society.* Englewood Cliffs, NJ: Prentice Hall.

CIA World Factbook. 1998. < http://www.odci.gov/cia/publications/factbook/af.html > Accessed August 18, 1999.

Clark, J. B., and B. Knestout. 1997. "New Weapons Against AIDS—At a Price." *Kiplinger's Personal Finance Magazine* (February): 102–103.

Clay, J. W. 1991. "Respecting and Supporting Gay and Lesbian Parents." *Education Digest* (April):51–52.

Clayton, M. 1996. "Prostitution 'Circuit' Takes Girls Across North America" *Christian Science Monitor,* August 23, p. 10.

———. 1998. "No Test, No College Degree." *Christian Science Monitor,* September 22.

Cleelan, N. 1994. "Immigrants Are $30 Billion Plus for the Nation, Study Contends." *San Diego Union-Tribune,* May 25.

———.1995. "Peso's Effect on Illegal Immigration Puzzles Analysts." *San Diego Union-Tribune,* February 27.

Clifford, F. 1991. "Urban Areas Now Home to U.S. Majority." *Los Angeles Times,* February 2.

Clifford, F., A. C. Roark, and B. M. Horstman. 1991. "Census Finds Ethnic Boom in Suburbs, Rural Areas." *Los Angeles Times,* February 26.

Clifford, F., and A. C. Roark. 1991. "Big Cities Hit by Census Data Showing Declining Role." *Los Angeles Times,* January 24.

Clinard, M. B. 1974. *The Sociology of Deviant Behavior.* New York: Holt, Rinehart and Winston.

———. 1983a. *Corporate Ethics and Crime—The Role of Middle Management.* Beverly Hills, CA: Sage.

Clinard, M. B., and D. J. Abbott. 1977. "Crime in Developing Countries," in Sir L. Radzinowicz and M. E. Wolfgang, eds. *Crime and Justice.* Vol. 1, *The Criminal in Society.* New York: Basic Books, pp. 25–51.

Clinard, M. B., and P. C. Yeager. 1980. *Corporate Crime.* New York: Free Press.

Clinard, M. B., and R. F. Meier. 1992. *Sociology of Deviant Behavior.* Fort Worth, TX: Harcourt Brace Jovanovich.

Clinard, M. B., and R. Quinney. 1973. *Criminal Behavior Systems: A Typology.* New York: Holt, Rinehart and Winston.

"A Closer Look at Trends by Race and Gender." 1998. *Centers for Disease Control http://www.cdcnpin.org/geneva98/trends/ trends_6.htm*

Cloud, J. 1999. "A Halfway Win for Gay Couples" *Time,* December 31, p. 220.

CNN Special Reports. 1992. "Beyond the Glass Ceiling" Video. Atlanta, GA: Cable News Network.

Coakley, J. J. 1998. *The Sociology of Sport.* St. Louis: Mosby.

Coates, J. F. 1996. "Five Major Forces of Change." *Futurist* (September/October):1–8.

Cockerham, W. C. 1998. *Medical Sociology.* Englewood Cliffs, NJ: Prentice Hall.

Cohen, K. H. and M. Felson. 1979. "Social Change and Crime Rate Trends: A Routine Activities Approach" *American Sociological Review* 44 (August): 588–608.

Cohen, W. 1998. "The Couch Potato Factor." *U.S. News & World Report* (May 25):39–40.

Cole, W. T. 1995. *Ebola: A Documentary Novel of Its First Explosion.* New York: Ivy Books.

Coleman, B. 1997. "Survey Finds 14,000 Drivers an Hour in '93 Were Drunk." *Buffalo News,* January 8, p. A4.

Collins, R. 1971. "A Conflict Theory of Sexual Stratification." *Social Problems* 19(1):3–21.

———. 1975. *Conflict Sociology; Toward an Explanatory Science.* New York: Academic Press.

———. 1979. *The Credential Society: An Historical Sociology of Education and Stratification.* New York: Academic Press.

———. 1988a. *Sociology of Marriage and the Family,* 2nd ed. Chicago: Nelson-Hall.

———. 1988b. *Theoretical Sociology.* San Diego, CA: Harcourt Brace Jovanovich.

———. 1994. *Four Sociological Traditions.* New York: Oxford University Press.

Collins, R., and M. Makowsky. 1984. *The Discovery of Society.* New York: Random House.

Collins, R., and S. Coltrane. 1995. *Sociology of Marriage and the Family: Gender, Love, and Property.* Chicago: Nelson-Hall.

Committee for the Study of the American Electorate. 1999. *Final Post-Election Report,* February 9. < http://tap.epn.org/csae/ cgans5.html > Accessed July 31, 1999.

———. 1998. "Primary Turnout Falls to Record Low." Press Release, September 28.

Comte, A. 1877. *Early Essays.* London: Longmans, Green.

Conklin, J. E. 1972. *Robbery and the Criminal Justice System.* Philadelphia: Lippincott.

Connell, D. 1994. "An Island of Stability in Strife-Filled Africa." *Christian Science Monitor,* November 30, pp. 10–11.

Connolly, C., and D. Balz. 1998. "The Christian Coalition, Born Again." *Washington Post National Weekly Edition,* January 5, p. 16.

Constable, P. 1998. "A New Regional Rivalry Is Brewing." *Washington Post National Weekly Edition,* September 24, pp. 16–17.

Converse, H. S. 1988. "Hinduism," in R. C. Bush et al., eds. *The Religious World—Communities of Faith.* New York: Macmillan, pp. 52–112.

Conway, M. M. 1991. *Political Participation in the United States,* 2nd ed. Washington, DC: Congressional Quarterly.

Cooley, C. H. 1902. *Human Nature and the Social Order.* New York: Scribner's.

——. 1909. *Social Organization.* New York: Scribner's.

Cose, E. 1994. "Truths About Spouse Abuse." *Newsweek* (August 8):49.

——. 1999. "The Good News About Black America." *Newsweek* (June 7).

Coser, L. 1964. *The Functions of Social Conflict.* New York: Free Press.

——. 1971. *Masters of Sociological Thought.* New York: Harcourt Brace Jovanovich.

Council of Economic Advisors to the President's Initiative on Race. 1998. *Changing America: Indicators of Social and Economic Well-Being by Race and Hispanic Origin.* Washington, DC: U.S. Government Printing Office.

Court, J. 1998. "HMOs Dump Elders." *Los Angeles Times,* October 23, p. B9.

Courtney, H. 1993. "Energy and Population." *ZPG Reporter,* 25 (5).

Cowley, G. 1995. "The Outbreak of Fear." *Newsweek* (May 22):48–55.

Cox, F. D. 1992. *The AIDS Booklet.* Dubuque, IA: Brown.

Cox, H. 1965. *The Secular City.* New York: Macmillan.

Cox, O. C. 1948. *Caste, Class, and Race: A Study in Social Dynamics.* New York: Modern Reader Paperbacks.

Cressey, D. 1953. *Other People's Money: A Study in the Social Psychology of Embezzlement.* New York: Free Press.

Critchfield, R. 1992. "Sowing Success, Reaping Guns." *World Monitor* (July 24):24–30.

Crompton, R., and M. Mann, eds. 1986. *Gender and Stratification.* Cambridge, England: Polity Press.

Crook, S., J. Pakulski, and M. Waters. 1992. *Postmodernization: Change in Advanced Society.* London: Sage.

Crossette, B. 1997. "How to Fix a Crowded World: Add People." *New York Times,* November 2, Section 4, p. 1–2.

"Crossing the Threshold." 1997. *Intelligence Report: The Face of Terrorism* (Winter): Issue 47. A Project of the Southern Poverty Law Center, pp. 7–9.

"CRTC Announces Public Hearing and Regional Consultations on Approaches to Better Protect Children Against TV Violence." 1995. *CRTC News Release,* April 3.

"CRTC Pushes for More CanCon." 1998. *Toronto Globe and Mail,* May 1.

Cummings, P. and D. C. Grossman, F. P. Rivara, and T. D. Koepsell. 1997. "State Gun Safe Storage Laws and Child Morality Due to Firearms" *Journal of the American Medical Association* 278(13): 1084–1086.

Curry, C. D. and S. H. Decker. 1998. *Confronting Gangs: Crime and Community* Los Angeles: Roxbury Publishing Company.

Curtiss, S. 1977. *Genie: A Psycholinguistic Study of a Modern-Day "Wild Child."* New York: Academic Press.

Cylke, F. K., Jr. 1993. *The Environment.* New York: HarperCollins.

Dabbs, J. M., Jr., and N. A. Stokes, III. 1975. "Beauty Is Power: The Use of Space on a Sidewalk." *Sociometry* 38(4):551–557.

Dahrendorf, R. 1959. *Class and Class Conflict in Industrial Society.* Stanford, CA: Stanford University Press.

——. 1968. *Essays in the Theory of Society.* Stanford, CA: Stanford University Press.

Daley, S. 1996. "Drugs, Guns, and Vigilante Justice in South Africa." *New York Times,* September 20, p. A4.

Daly, E. 1999. "Spain works to change 'machismo' culture of abuse." *Christian Science Monitor,* January 19.

Daniels, M. R. 1997. "Warm Areas Continue Hottest Job Growth." *Monthly Labor Review* (July):43–44.

Daniloff, N. 1982. "For Russia's Women, Worst of Both Worlds." *U.S. News & World Report* (June 28):53–54.

Darling, J. 1992. "Latin American Debt Crisis Brings a Decade of Troubles and Progress." *Los Angeles Times,* August 30.

Davis, A., B. B. Gardner, and M. R. Gardner. 1941. *Deep South.* Chicago: University of Chicago Press.

Davis, K. 1940. "Extreme Social Isolation of a Child." *American Journal of Sociology* 45(4):554–565.

——. 1947. "Final Note on a Case of Extreme Isolation." *American Journal of Sociology* 52(5):432–437.

——. 1949. *Human Societies.* New York: Macmillan.

——. 1986. "Low Fertility in Evolutionary Perspective." *Population and Development Review* 12:46–48.

Davis, K., and J. Blake. 1956. "Social Structure and Fertility: An Analytic Framework." *Economic Development and Cultural Change* (April):211–235.

Davis, K., and W. E. Moore. 1945. "Some Principles of Stratification." *American Sociological Review* 10 (2):242–249.

Day, J. C., and A. E. Curry. 1998. "Educational Attainment in the United States: March 1998 (Update)." Current Population Reports: P20-513. Washington, DC: U.S. Government Printing Office.

De Bernardi, V. 1995. "Family Support Services in Sweden." *Journal of Comparative Family Studies* 26(3):459–467.

de Cerreño, A. L. C., and C. Pyle. 1996. *Education Reform in Latin America* (Studies Department Occasional Paper Series No. 1). New York: Council on Foreign Relations.

de lbarrola, M. 1996. *Education and Economic Growth: Creating a Culture of Education.* New York: Council on Foreign Relations Working Group on Educational Reform.

De Palma, A. 1999. "Culture wars: Trying to Stay Canadian Despite Giant to the South." *San Diego Union-Tribune,* August 8.

de Queiroz, M. I. P. 1989. "Afro-Brazilian Cults and Religious Change in Brazil," in J. A. Beckford and T. Luckman, eds. *The Changing Face of Religion.* Newbury Park, CA: Sage.

Deaux, K. 1992. "Sex Differences," in E. F. Borgotta and M. L. Borgotta, eds. *Encyclopedia of Sociology,* vol. 3. New York: Macmillan, pp. 1749–1753.

Deckard, B. S. 1983. *The Women's Movement: Political, Socioeconomic, and Psychological Issues,* 3rd ed. New York: Harper & Row.

"Defeating the Bad Guys." 1998. *Economist* (October 23):35–38.

Delacroix, J. 1977. "The Export of Raw Materials and Economic Growth: A Cross-National Study." *American Sociological Review* 42(October):795–808.

DePanfilis, D., and S. J. Zuravin. 1998. "Rates, Patterns, and Frequency of Child Maltreatment Recurrences Among Families Known to CPS." *Child Maltreatment* (February):27–43.

DeParle, J. 1994. "Census Report Sees Incomes in Decline and More Poverty." *New York Times,* October 7.

Dershowitz, A. M. 1998. "Why Johnny Shouldn't Learn to Shoot" *Los Angeles Times,* May 25, p. B5.

Desmond, E. W. 1998. "When Suicide Makes Sense—In Japan Anything's Better Than Bankruptcy." *Fortune* (May 25): 28–29.

Deutsch, L. 1999. "Cops Made No Racial Slurs, Lawyer Says." *San Diego Union-Tribune,* May 20.

Di Sabatino, D. 1997. "And a Moribidly Obese Man Shall Lead Them." *Alberta Report/Western Report* (September):38.

Diamond, J. 1993. "Speaking with a Single Tongue." *Discovery* (February): 78–84.

Dickey, J. H. 1998. *No Room To Breathe: Air Pollution and Primary Care Medicine.* Boston: Greater Boston PSR.

Dietrich, C. 1998. *People's China: A Brief History.* New York: Oxford University Press.

Dilulio, J. 1994. "The Question of Black Crime." *The Public Interest* (Fall):3–32.

Disney, A. 1992. "In One Day in One City, 1,846 Acts of TV Violence—That's Entertainment?" *Los Angeles Times,* September 10.

do Rosario, L. 1992. "Tokyo Pushes Its Limits." *World Press Review* (February):51.

Doherty, B. 1997. "Kiddie Cops." *Reason* (December):10.

Dolbee, S. 1999. "GOP Needs Us, Falwell Says." *San Diego Union-Tribune,* February 16.

Domestic Violence. 1991. Plano, TX: Information Aids.

Domhoff, G. W. 1998. *Who Rules America?: Power and Politics in the Year 2000.* 3rd ed. Mountain View, CA: Mayfield.

Domhoff, G. W., and H. B. Ballard, eds. 1968. *C. Wright Mills and the Power Elite.* Boston: Beacon Press.

"Doomed to Burn?" 1992. *Economist* (May 9):21–23.

Dornbusch, R. 1998. "On the Edge," in *Crash of '97,* Dan Biers, ed. Hong Kong: Review.

Dornbusch, S. M., and K. D. Gray. 1988. "Single-Parent Families," in S. M. Dornbusch and M. H. Strober, eds. *Feminism: Children and the New Families.* New York: Guilford Press.

Dorr, A. 1986. *Television for Children: A Special Medium for a Special Audience.* Beverly Hills, CA: Sage.

Douglas, J. 1991. "Suicide." *The Academic American Encyclopedia,* electronic version. Danbury, CT: Grolier.

Douglas, J. D. 1967. *The Social Meaning of Suicide.* Princeton, NJ: Princeton University Press.

———. 1976. *Investigative Field Research.* Beverly Hills, CA: Sage.

———. 1992b. "Born in Blood Bath, India Faces Replay of Holy War." *Los Angeles Times,* December 11.

Drozdiak, W. 1998. "The Power Shift in Germany." *Washington Post National Weekly Edition,* October 12, p. 23.

Drucker, P. E. 1997. "The Future That Has Already Happened." *Harvard Business Review* 75(5):20–22.

Dugger, C. W. 1998. "Data Say Immigrants Attain Parity in Income and Taxes." *New York Times,* April 30.

Duncan, G. J., T. M. Smeeding, and W. Rodgers. 1992. "The Incredible Shrinking Middle Class." *American Demographics* (May):34–38.

Dunn, K. 1998. "Mandela Hits White Wealth." *Christian Science Monitor,* February 26, p. A1.

Durkheim, E. 1933, original 1895. *The Division of Labor in Society.* New York: Macmillan.

———. 1938, original 1895. *The Rules of the Sociological Method.* New York: Macmillan.

———. 1951, original 1897. *Suicide.* New York: Free Press.

———. 1965, original 1915. *The Elementary Forms of the Religious Life.* New York: Free Press.

———. 1966, original 1895. *On the Division of Labor in Society.* G. Simpson, trans. New York: Free Press.

Dutt, A., and A. Sen. 1992. "Provisional Census of India 1991." *Geographical Review* 82(2):207–211.

Dye, T. R. 1995. *Who's Running America?: The Clinton Years.* Englewood Cliffs, NJ: Prentice Hall.

Dyer, G. 1985. *War.* New York: Crown Publishing.

"Ebay Pulls the Plug on Human Kidney Auction." 1999. *San Diego Union-Tribune,* September 3.

Eberstadt, N. 1997. "The Population Implosion." *Wall Street Journal,* October 16, p. A22.

———. 1998. "Longer Lives Create Newer Challenges." *Los Angeles Times,* May 14, p. B2.

Ebner, M. H. 1987. "Re-Reading Suburban America: Urban Population Deconcentration, 1810–1980," in H. Gillette Jr. and Z. L. Miller, eds. *American Urbanism: A Historical Review.* New York: Greenwood Press.

Eccles, J. S. 1987. "Adolescence: Gateway to Gender-Role Transcendance," in D. B. Carter, ed. *Current Conceptions of Sex Roles and Sex Typing.* New York: Praeger, pp. 225–242.

Economic Survey of Europe in 1991–1992. 1992. Secretariat of the Economic Commission for Europe Geneva, New York.

Economist. 1987. "The Proper Way to Behave." July 4, pp. 83–86.

———. 1989. "Mexico: From Boom to Bust." February 11, pp. 75–76.

Edgerton, R. B. 1976. *Deviance: A Cross-Cultural Perspective.* Menlo Park, CA: Robert B. Cummings.

Edmonds, P. 1993. "After War: 'Parade to Shelters.'" *USA Today,* June 1, p. A4.

Edmondson, B. 1998. "Elvis Lives Again." *American Demographics* (January):18–19.

Edmondson, B., and J. Waldrop. 1993. "Married With Children." *American Demographics* (December):31–33.

Efron, S. 1992. "Japan's Economic Boom Undermined by Baby Bust." *Los Angeles Times,* June 8.

———. 1998. "Seoul-Searching." *Los Angeles Times,* February 28, p. D1.

Eggebeen, D. J., A. R. Snyder, and W. D. Manning. 1996. "Children in Single-Father Families in Demographic Perspective." *Journal of Family Issues* (July):441–465.

Eggebeen, D. J., and D. T. Lichter. 1991. "Race, Family Structure, and Changing Poverty Among American Children." *American Sociological Review* 56(December):801–817.

"Egypt: Wonder of the Past, Investment of the Future." 1998. *Business Affairs* (March):13–17.

Einstein, P. A. 1996. "Korea, Poland, Typify Global Automotive Boom." *Christian Science Monitor,* January 18:8.

El Nasser, H. 1998. "Study Links Immigrants, Flight from Public Schools." *USA Today,* April 20.

Ellison, K. 1992. "Mexico Deaths Renew Questions on Police Tactics and Veracity." *Los Angeles Times,* September 18.

Elvy, P. 1987. *Buying Time.* Mystic, CT: Twenty-Third Publications.

Ember, C. R., and M. Ember. 1988. *Anthropology,* 5th ed. Englewood Cliffs, NJ: Prentice Hall.

Emery, R. E. 1989. "Family Violence." *American Psychologist* 44(2):321–328.

"The End of the Miracle." 1997. *Economist* (November 29):21–23.

Energy Information Administration. 1999a. *Emissions of Greenhouse Gases in the United States 1998.* Washington, DC: Department of Energy/Energy Information Administration.

———. 1999b. *International Energy Outlook 1999.* Washington, DC: Department of Energy/Energy Information Agency.

Engels, F. 1902, original 1884. *The Origin of the Family.* Chicago: Kerr.

England, P., and G. Farkas. 1986. *Households, Employment and Gender.* New York: Aldine.

Erikson, E. H. 1950. *Childhood and Society.* New York: Norton.

———. 1982. *The Life Cycle Completed: A Review.* New York: Norton.

Erikson, K. T. 1966. *Wayward Puritans.* New York: Wiley.

Eshleman, J. R. 1985. *Sociology of Marriage and the Family.* Chicago: Nelson-Hall.

———. 1991. *The Family: An Introduction,* 6th ed. Boston: Allyn and Bacon.

———. 1996. *The Family: An Introduction,* 8th ed. Boston: Allyn and Bacon.

"Ethnic strife is spreading." 1999. *San Diego Union-Tribune,* September 1.

Etzioni, A. 1975. *A Comparative Analysis of Complex Organizations,* rev. and enlarged edition. Glencoe, IL: Free Press.

Evans, H. 1995. "Poverty, Not Race, Is Critical Factor in Domestic Homicides, Study Finds." *Wall Street Journal,* June 15.

Evans, P. B., and J. D. Stephens. 1988. "Development and the World Economy," in N.J. Smelser, ed. *Handbook of Sociology.* Newbury Park, CA: Sage, pp. 739–773.

Evans, S. 1993. "Keeping Cool When the Baby Won't Stop Crying." *Los Angeles Times,* January 25.

"Ex-Communists Are Back in the Saddle Again." 1994. *Washington Post National Weekly Edition.* November 7–13.

Ezcurra, E., and M. Mazari-Hirriart. 1996. *Environment* 38(1):6–20.

Fagot, B. I., R. Hagan, M. D. Leinbach, and S. Kronsberg. 1985. "Differential Reactions to Assertive and Communicative Acts of Toddler Boys and Girls." *Child Development* 56:1499–1505.

Faltermayer, C. 1998. "What Is Justice for a Sixth Grade Killer?" *Time,* April 6, pp. 36–37.

"Family Planning's Role in Reducing Health Risks." 1998. *Population Today* (May):3.

Fareow, N. L. 1989. "Suicide," in R. Kastenbaum and B. Kastenbaum, eds. *The Encyclopedia of Death.* Phoenix, AZ: Oryx Press, pp. 227–230.

Farkas, G., R. P. Grobe, D. Sheehan, and Y. Shuan. 1990. "Cultural Resources and School Success: Gender, Ethnicity, and Poverty Groups Within an Urban School District." *American Sociological Review* 55:127–142.

Featherman, D. L., and R. M. Hauser. 1978. *Opportunity and Change.* New York: Academic Press.

"Feeling Better About the Future." 1999. *Newsweek* (June 7).

Feldmann, L. 1995. "Conservatives Question 'True Goal' of Goals 2000 Education Guidelines." *Christian Science Monitor,* June 8.

Finc, M. 1993. "Toward a Sunbelt Urban Design Manifesto." *Journal of the American Planning Association* (Summer): 320–333.

Fine, M. A., and D. R. Fine. 1994. "An Examination and Evaluation of Recent Changes in Divorce Laws in Five Western Countries: The Critical Role of Values." *Journal of Marriage and the Family* (May):249–263.

———. 1995. "Mexicans Hit Stores Before Tax Increase." *Los Angeles Times,* April 1, p. A5.

Fineman, M., and S. Rotella. 1995. "Former Mexico Prosecutor Linked to Drug Kickbacks." *Los Angeles Times,* March 10, p. A1.

Finkelhor, D., and K. Yllo. 1983. "Rape in Marriage: A Sociological Review," in D. Finkelhor, R. J. Gelles, G. T. Hotaling, and M. A. Straus, eds. *The Dark Side of Families: Current Family Violence Research,* Beverly Hills, CA: Sage.

Fischer, C. S. 1976. *The Urban Experience.* New York: Harcourt Brace Jovanovich.

Fitzpatrick, M. 1999. "Internet Servers Keep It Clean for the Kids." *San Diego Union-Tribune,* September 4.

Flavin, C. 1998. "Last Tango in Buenos Aires." *World Watch,* 11(6).

Fogel, C. 1993. "Break the Toxic Waste Habit." *Christian Science Monitor,* August 2.

Forbes, S. 1998. "Unhealthy." *Forbes* (October):31.

Francese, P. 1998. "The Gray Continent." *Wall Street Journal,* March 23, p. A22

Francis, D. E. 1998. "How Poor is Poor?" *Christian Science Monitor,* October 7.

Frank, R. 1998. "Europeans Search for a Shared Identity Amid Dark Memories." *Wall Street Journal,* October 19.

Frank, R. H., and P. J. Cook. 1995. "Too Many Superstar 'Wannabes.' " *USA Today,* October 9.

Frankel, G. 1996. "The Best Laid Plans . . . " *Washington Post National Weekly,* December 2–8, pp. 10–11.

Franklin, B. A. 1994. "We Are the Most Lethally Armed Nation on Earth." *Washington Spectator* (20, No. 2):1–4.

Freeman, D. G. 1998. "Determinants of Youth Suicide: The Easterlin-Holinger Cohort Hypothesis Re-Examined." *American Journal of Economics & Sociology* 57(2):183–199.

Freud, S. 1930. *Civilization and Its Discontents.* James Strachey, trans. New York: Norton.

Frey, W. H. 1998. "Black Migration to the South Reaches Record High in 1990s." *Population Today* (February):1–3.

Friedan, B. J. 1989. "The Downtown Job Puzzle." *Public Interest* (Fall):71–86.

Friedman, R. I. 1996. "India's Shame." *Nation* 262(14):11–18.

Fritz, M. 1998. "Violence: Schools Adopt a Variety of Ways to Tackle Problem" *Los Angeles Times,* May 23, p. A1.

Frivo, L. J., R. D. Peterson, H. Rizzo, and J. R. Reynolds. 1998. "Race, Segregation, and the Concentration of Disadvantage: 1980–1990." *Social Problems* (February):61–80.

Fromkin, V., and R. Rodman. 1988. *An Introduction to Language.* New York: Holt, Rinehart and Winston, pp. 375–398.

Fujimoto, K. 1991. "Working Their Way to a Sudden Death." *Japan Times Weekly International Edition,* January 14–20.

Fukutake, T. 1982. *The Japanese Social Structure: Its Evolution in the Modern Century.* Tokyo: University of Tokyo Press.

"Funding Rules Tightened for 'Canadian' Programs." 1998. *Ottawa Citizen,* December 12.

Furstenberg, F. F., and A. J. Cherlin. 1991. *Divided Families: What Happens to Children When Parents Part.* Cambridge MA: Harvard University Press.

Future Population May Overwhelm Food Supply" 1997. *Popline* (May/June):3.

Gagnon, J. H., and W. Simon. 1973. *Sexual Conduct: The Sources of Human Sexuality.* Chicago: Aldine.

Galbraith, J. 1979. *The Nature of Mass Poverty.* Cambridge, MA: Harvard University Press.

Galbraith, J. K. 1978. *The New Industrial State,* 3rd ed. Boston: Houghton Mifflin.

Gallagher, B. J., III, and C. J. Rita. 1995. *The Sociology of Mental Illness,* 3rd ed. Englewood Cliffs, NJ: Prentice Hall.

Gallagher, J. 1997. "Marriage Compromised." *Advocate,* May 27, p. 71.

Galston, W. A. 1996. "Divorce American Style." *Public Interest* (Summer):12–26.

"Gang Related Homicides in L. A. County at Epidemic Proportion." 1995. *San Diego Union-Tribune,* October 4, p. A11.

"Gangs in the Heartland." 1996. *Economist* May 25, pp. 29–30.

Gannon, K. 1994. "Wife-Torture Jailing Stuns Pakistan." *The Dominion* (New Zealand), July 19, p. 6.

Gans, H. 1962. "Urbanism and Suburbanism as Ways of Life: A Re-evaluation of Definitions," in A. M. Rose, ed. *Human Behavior and Social Process: An Interactional Perspective.* Boston: Houghton Mifflin, pp. 625–648.

Gans, H. 1983. "Popular Culture Defects as a Commercial Enterprise," in C. D. Geist and J. Nachbar, eds. *The Popular Culture Reader,* 3rd ed, Bowling Green, OH: Bowling Green University Popular Press, pp. 30–35.

———. 1980. *Deciding What's News: A Study of CBS Evening News, NBC Nightly News, Newsweek and Time.* New York: Vintage Press.

"GAO Says More Tots in Foster Care as a Result of Parental Drug Abuse." 1994. *San Diego Union-Tribune,* April 28, p. A16.

Gaouette, N. 1998. "Rules for Raising Japanese Kids." *Christian Science Monitor,* October 14.

Gardels, N., and M. B. Snell. 1989. "Breathing Fecal Dust in Mexico City." *Los Angeles Times Book Review,* April 23, p. 16.

Gardner, G. 1996. *Shrinking Fields: Cropland Loss in a World of Eight Billion.* World Watch Paper 131. Washington, DC: Worldwatch Institute.

Garfinkel, H. 1956. "Conditions of a Successful Degradation Ceremony." *American Journal of Sociology* 61:420–424.

Garreau, J. 1994. "Edge Cities in Profile." *American Demographics* 16(2): 24–33.

Garreau, J. 1996. "Civilization Comes to the Suburbs." *New Perspectives Quarterly* (Summer): 23–25.

Garrett, L. 1996. "The Return of Infectious Diseases." *Foreign Affairs* (January/February):67–79.

Gelbard, A., and C. Haub. 1998. "Population 'Explosion' Not Over for Half the World." *Population Today* (March):1–3.

Gelles, R. J. 1978. "Violence Toward Children in the United States." *American Journal of Orthopsychiatry* 48 (October): 580–592.

———.1980. "Violence in the Family: A Review of the Research in the Seventies." *Journal of Marriage and the Family* 42:873–885.

Gelles, R. J., and C. Pedrick-Cornell. 1990. *Intimate Violence in Families.* Newbury Park, CA: Sage.

Gelles, R. J., and J. R. Conte. 1990. "Domestic Violence and Sexual Abuse of Children: A Review of Research in the Eighties." *Journal of Marriage and the Family* 52(November):1045–1058.

"German Reunification." 1997. *Microsoft Encarta 97 Encyclopedia.*

"Germans from East Still Feel Estranged." 1998. *San Diego Union-Tribune,* September 4.

"Germany." 1994. *The Concise Columbia Encyclopedia. Third Edition.* New York: Columbia University Press.

"Germany." 1999. Information Please LLC. < http://kids.infoplease. lycos.com/ce5/ce020641.html > Accessed August 31, 1999.

Gibbons, D. C. 1997. "Review Essay: Race, Ethnicity, Crime, and Social Policy." *Crime and Delinquency* (July):358–379.

Gilbert, L. 1996. "Urban Violence and Health: South Africa 1995." *Social Science and Medicine* 43(5):873–886.

Gitlin, T. 985. *Inside Prime Time.* New York: Pantheon Books.

Glasberg, D. S., and D. L. Skidmore. 1998. "The Role of the State in the Criminogenesis of Corporate Crime: A Case Study of the Savings and Loan Crisis." *Social Science Quarterly* (March):110–126.

Glenn, N. D. 1998. "College Texts on Marriage: No Happy Endings." *Christian Science Monitor,* June 29, p. 11.

Gober, P. 1993. "Americans on the Move." *Population Bulletin* 48(3). Washington, DC: Population Reference Bureau.

Goffman, E. 1961. *Asylums: Essays on the Social Situation of Mental Patients and Other Inmates.* New York: Doubleday.

Goldberg, C. 1993. "Lithuania Voters Appear Poised to Reinstate a Moscow Minion." *Los Angeles Times,* February 14.

Golden, T. 1993. "Violently, Drug Trafficking in Mexico Rebounds." *New York Times International,* March 8, p. A1.

Gonzalez, P. Y. 1998. "Women: A Critical Link." *ZPG Reporter* (August):4–5.

———. 1995. "Urban Woes to Explode Along with Populations, U. N. Says." *Los Angeles Times,* December 16, p. A17.

Goode, E. 1990. *Deviant Behavior.* Englewood Cliffs, NJ: Prentice Hall.

Goode, E. 1999. "Along with Your Cholesterol Have Your Status Checked." *San Diego Union-Tribune,* June 9.

Goode, W. J. 1963. *World Revolution and Family Patterns.* New York: Free Press.

———. 1993. *World Changes in Divorce Patterns.* New Haven: Yale University Press.

Gordon, M. M. 1964. *Assimilation in American Life.* New York: Oxford University Press.

Gortmaker, S. L. 1979. "Poverty and Infant Mortality in the United States." *American Journal of Sociology* 44(2):280–297.

Gould, S. J. 1976. "Biological Potential vs. Biological Determinism." *Natural History* 85(5):12–22.

———. 1999. "Dorothy, It's Really Oz." *Time* (August 23).

———. 1981. *The Mismeasure of Man.* New York: Norton.

Gouldner, A. W. 1954a. *Patterns of Industrial Bureaucracy.* Glencoe, IL: Free Press.

———. 1954b. *Wildcat Strike.* Glencoe, IL: Free Press.

Gracey, H. L. 1977. "Learning the Student Role: Kindergarten as Academic Boot Camp," in D. H. Wrong and H. L. Gracey, eds. *Readings in Introductory Sociology,* 3rd ed. New York: Macmillan, pp. 215–226.

Graham, D. 1995. "Children Can Soak Up 2 Languages Simultaneously, Researcher Finds." *San Diego Union-Tribune,* February 18.

Graham, E. M. 1993. "Beyond Borders: On the Globalization of Business." *Harvard International Review* (Summer):8–11.

Graham, O. L., Jr., and R. Beck. 1992. "To Help Inner City, Cut Flow of Immigrants." *Los Angeles Times,* May 19.

Granelli, J. 1992. "Keating Receives 10-Year Sentence in S&L Fraud Case." *Los Angeles Times,* April 11.

Gray, J. 1992. *Men Are from Mars, Women Are from Venus.* New York: HarperCollins.

Gray, J. S. 1998. "Divorce-Law Changes, Household Bargaining, and Married Women's Labor Supply." *American Economic Review* (June):628–642.

Greenberg, J. H. 1968. *Anthropological Linguistics: An Introduction.* New York: Random House.

Greenfeld, K. T. 1999. "What Glass Ceiling?" *Time* (August 2).

Greenwald, J. 1999. "Who Needs a Tax Cut?" *Time* (August 2).

Greider, L. 2000. "His Advice: Speak Up to Avoid Medical Error." *AARP Bulletin* 41(1) p. 2.

Grier, P. 1995. "Why B-Students from the US Lag Behind European Peers." *Christian Science Monitor,* July 6.

Grier, P., and J. N. Thurman. 1999. "Impeachment's Cultural Divide." *Christian Science Monitor,* January 5.

Griffin, S. 1973. *Rape: The All-American Crime.* Andover, MA: Warner Modular Publications.

Groombridge, M. A. 1998. "Dragon Droop." *American Enterprise* (July/August):34–38.

Gross, G. 1993. "5 Cartels Control Drug Flow in Mexico." *San Diego Union-Tribune.* June 1, p. A1.

Gusfield, J. 1967. "Tradition and Modernity: Misplaced Polarities in the Study of Social Change." *American Journal of Sociology* (January):351–362.

Gwynne, S. 1992. "The Long Haul." *Time* (September 28):34–40.

Hacker, H. 1951. "Women as a Minority Group." *Social Forces* 30:60–69.

———. 1974. "Women as a Minority Group: 20 Years Later," in F. Denmark, ed. *Who Discriminates Against Women?* Beverly Hills, CA: Sage, pp. 124–134.

Hagan, F. E. 1986. *Introduction to Criminology—Theories, Methods, and Criminal Behavior.* Chicago: Nelson-Hall.

Hamberger, L. and J. M. Lohr, D. Bonge, D. F. Tolin. 1997. "An Empirical Classification of Motivations for Domestic Violence." *Violence Against Women* 3(4): 401–423.

Hamilton, J. 1997. "UN Condemns Female Circumcision." *British Medical Journal* 314(7088):1148.

Haney, D. Q. 1992. "Explosive, Disastrous AIDS Spread Predicted." *San Diego Union-Tribune,* June 4.

———. "Drug Treatment Virtually Eliminating HIV in Body Foreseen by AIDS Expert." *Buffalo News,* June 30, p. A10.

Hardgrave, R. L., Jr., and S. A. Kochanek. 1986. *India—Government and Politics in a Developing Nation.* San Diego, CA: Harcourt Brace Jovanovich.

Hardoy, J. E., and D. Satterthwaite. 1997. "Building Future Cities," in J. Gugler, ed. *Cities in the Developing World: Issues, Theory, and Policy,* 265–279. New York: Oxford University Press.

Harper, C. L. 1989. *Exploring Social Change.* Englewood Cliffs, NJ: Prentice Hall.

Harris, A. R., and L. R. Meidlinger. 1995. "Criminal Behavior: Race and Class," in J. P. Sheley, ed. *Criminology: A Contemporary Handbook.* Belmont CA: Wadsworth.

Harris, C. D., and E. L. Ullman. 1945. "The Nature of Cities." *Annals of the Academy of Political and Social Sciences* (November):7–17.

Harris, J. 1997. "Goodbye Dolly: The Ethics of Human Cloning." *Journal of Medical Ethics* (December):353–360.

Harris, J. R. 1998. *The Nurture Assumption: Why Children Turn Out the Way They Do; Parents Matter Less Than You Think and Peers Matter More.* New York: Free Press.

Harris, M. 1983. *Cultural Anthropology.* New York: Harper & Row.

———. 1989. *Our Kind.* New York: Harper Perennial.

Harris, R. 1994. "Brazil Introduces New Currency." *Los Angeles Times,* July 2, p. A16.

Harrison, P. 1984. *Inside the Third World.* New York: Penguin Books.

Hart-Landsberg, M. 1993. *The Rush to Development.* New York: Monthly Review Press.

Hartinger, B. 1991. "A Case for Gay Marriages." *Commonwealth* (November 22):681–683.

Hartman, B. 1994. "What Success Story?" *New York Times,* September 29, p. 17.

Harvey, D. 1989. *The Condition of Postmodernity: An Enquiry into the Origins of Cultural Change.* Oxford: Basil Blackwell.

Hass, L., and P. Hwang. 1995. "Company Culture and Men's Usage of Family Leave Benefits in Sweden." *Family Relations* 44(1):28–36.

Havemann, J. 1997. "A Nation of Violent Children." *Washington Post National Weekly Edition,* February 17, p. 34.

———. 1998a. "Bankrolling an Alternative to Public Classrooms." *Washington Post National Weekly Edition,* March 2, p. 32.

———. 1998b. "The Decline of Children Having Children." *Washington Post National Weekly,* May 18, p. 35.

Haviland, W. A. 1990. *Cultural Anthropology.* Fort Worth, TX: Holt, Rinehart and Winston.

Hawley, A. 1950. *Human Ecology: A Theory of Community Structure.* New York: Rosenthal Press.

Haworth, K., and D. Lederman. 1997. "President Vows to Make Education His Top Priority." *Chronicle of Higher Education,* February 14.

Hawton, K. 1986. *Suicide and Attempted Suicide Among Children and Adolescents.* Beverly Hills, CA: Sage.

Hayes, T. 1999. "Cop Convicted in Attack on Haitian." *San Diego Union-Tribune,* June 9.

———. 1998. "Russia's Time Bomb." *Washington Post National Weekly Edition,* November 16, pp. 8–9.

Hays, T. 1999. "Some Gun Makers Found Liable in NY Shootings; Others Cleared" *San Diego Union-Tribune* February 12, p. A13.

The Health Care Crisis: Containing Costs, Expanding Coverage. 1992. New York: McGraw-Hill.

Hearn, F., ed. 1988. *The Transformation of Industrial Organization.* Belmont, CA: Wadsworth.

Hearn, L. 1992. "Roe Survives Hard Blow by Split Supreme Court." *San Diego Union-Tribune,* June 30.

"Heavy Breathing in China." 1998. *Business Week* (April 13):31.

Hedges, S. J. 1998. "The New Face of Medicare." *U.S. News and World Report* (February 2):46–51.

Heise, L. 1989. "The Global War Against Women." *Utne Reader* (November—December):40–45.

Hemenway, D. and S. J. Solnick. 1998. "Firearms Training and Storage" *Journal of the American Medical Association* 273(1): 46–50.

Hendershott, A. 1995. *Moving for Work.* New York: University Press of America.

Herman-Giddens, M. E., J. B. Kotch, D. C. Browne, E. Ruina, J. R. Winsor, and J. Jung. 1998. "Childbearing Patterns In a Cohort of Women Sexually Abused as Children" *Journal of Interpersonal Violence* (August):504–603.

Herscherger, S. L. 1995. "A Twin Study of Male and Female Sexual Orientation." *Journal of Sex Research* 34(12): 212–222.

High Cost of Treating Wounded Youths." 1995. *Brown University Child & Adolescent Behavior Letter,* February, p. 4.

Hiltzik, M. 1991. "Africa Hit by 'Donor Fatigue.' " *Los Angeles Times,* March 8.

Hilzenrath, D. S. 1998. "Finding Something Left to Squeeze." *Washington Post National Weekly Edition,* July 14, p. 20.

———. 1999. "Test Hints That Body's Defense Can Limit HIV." *San Diego Union-Tribune,* February 5, p. A8.

Hirsch, E. D., Jr. 1987. *Cultural Literacy: What Every American Needs to Know.* Boston: Houghton Mifflin.

Hirschel, J. D. and I. W. Hutchinson. 1997. "The Failure of Arrest to Deter Spouse Abuse" *Journal of Research in Crime and Delinquency* 29(1): 7–33.

Hirschi, T. 1969. *Causes of Delinquency.* Berkeley: University of California Press.

Hirschi, T., and M. Gottfredson. 1983. "Age and the Explanation of Crime." *American Journal of Sociology* 89:552–584.

"Hispanic Population Nearing 30 Million." 1998. *San Diego Union-Tribune,* August 7, p. A2.

HIV, AIDS, and Older Adults." 1999. *Administration on Aging* < http://www.aoa.gov >

Hobbes, T. 1881. *Leviathan.* Oxford, England: James Thornton.

Hollander, D. 1997. "Female Circumcision in the U.S.?" *Family Planning Perspectives* 29(6):246.

Holley, J. 1994. "Confronting La Frontera." *Colombia Journalism Review* (May/June):46–48.

Holloway, M. 1994. "Trends in Women's Health—A Global View." *Scientific American* (August):76–83.

Holmes, R. M. and J. De Burger. 1988. *Serial Murder.* Beverly Hills, CA: Sage.

Holmstrom, D. 1994. "Census: Nuclear Family Fading." *Christian Science Monitor,* September 13, p. 2.

Hooper, B. 1991. "Chinese Youth: The Nineties Generation." *Current History* 90(557):264–269.

Hoover, S. M. 1988. *Mass Media Religion.* Newbury Park, CA: Sage.

Hopkins and I. Wallerstein, eds. *Processes of the World System.* Beverly Hills, CA: Sage, pp. 119–126.

Horgan, J. 1995. "Gay Genes, Revisited" *Scientific American* 273(5) p. 26. Horgan, J. 1995. "Gay Genes, Revisited." *Scientific America* (November):26.

Horowitz, J. M. 1998. "The Bad News." *Time* (May 4):20.

Hoselitz, B. F. 1954–1955. "Generative and Parasitic Cities." *Economic Development and Cultural Change* 3: 278–294.

Hosenball, M. 1999. "It Is Not the Act of a Few Bad Apples." *Newsweek* (May 17).

Hosken, F. P. 1985. *Academic American Encyclopedia,* vol. 5. Danbury, CT: Grolier, pp. 3–5.

Hotz, R. L. 1995. "Scientists Say Race Has No Biological Basis." *Los Angeles Times,* February 20.

Hoult, T. Ford. 1974. *Dictionary of Modern Sociology.* Totowa, NJ: Littlefield Adams.

Howard, M. C., and P. C. McKim. 1986. *Contemporary Cultural Anthropology.* Boston: Little, Brown.

Howe, C. 1992. "The People's Republic of China—Economy." *The Far East and Australasia—1992.* London: Europa Publications, pp. 198–207.

Hoyt, H. 1939. *The Structure and Growth of Residential Neighborhoods in American Cities.* Washington, DC: Federal Housing Administration.

Hsu, F. K. 1979. "The Cultural Problems of the Cultural Anthropologist." *American Anthropologist* 81:517–532.

"Human Rights Abuses Against Women." 1999. Amnesty International News Release, February 17.

Hun-Choe, S. 1997. "South Korean Restaurant Thriving on the sale of Dog Meat." *San Diego Union-Tribune,* May 10, p. A23.

"Hunger Myths and Facts." 1989. San Francisco: Institute for Food and Developmental Policy.

Hunt, A. R. 1998. "The Religious Right Is About Politics, Not Faith." *Wall Street Journal,* August 20.

Huntington, S. P. 1968. *Political Order in Changing Societies.* New Haven, CT: Yale University Press.

Huntington, S. P. 1969. *Political Order in Changing Societies.* New Haven, CT: Yale University.

———. 1992–1993. "What Cost Freedom?: Democracy and/or Economic Reform." *Harvard International Review* (Winter):8–13.

———. 1998. *The Clash of Civilizations and the Remaking of World Order.* New York: Touchstone.

Hutter, M. 1998. *The Changing Family.* Boston: Allyn and Bacon.

Ianni, F. 1998. "New Mafia: Black, Hispanic and Italian Styles." *Society* (January/February):115–129.

Imhoff, G. 1990. "The Position of U.S. English on Bilingual Education." *Annals of the American Academy of the Political and Social Sciences* 508:48–61.

"India Wakes Up to AIDS." 1998. *Economist* (December 20):50.

Ingwerson, M. 1994. "Both Conservatives and Liberals Decry Rapid Increase in Single-Parent Families." *Christian Science Monitor,* September 13, p. 1.

Inkles, A. 1973. "Making Man Modern: On the Causes and Consequences of Individual Change in Six Developing Countries," in A. Etzioni and E. Etzioni-Halvey, eds. *Social Change—Sources, Patterns and Consequences.* New York: Basic Books, pp. 342–361.

Institute for Social Research. 1994. "Televised Violence and Kids: A Public Health Problem?" *ISR Newsletter* 18(1):5–7.

Inter-American Development Bank. 1999. "Facing Up to Inequality in Latin America." *Report on Economic and Social Progress in Latin America, 1998–1999.* Washington, DC: Inter-American Development Bank.

International Bureau for Children's Rights. 1998. "Brazil: Beyond Prostitution and Sex Tourism." *Report of the Second Public Hearings of the International Tribunal for Children's Rights, August, 1998.* Montreal: International Bureau for Children's Rights.

International Child Resource Institute. 1995. "Brazil: Stop the Killings of Street Children." *Bulletin,* February 2.

Jacklin, C. N. 1989. "Female and Male: Issues of Gender." *American Psychologist* 44(2):127–133.

Jacobson, J. L. 1992. "Improving Women's Reproductive Health," in L. Starke, ed. *State of the World 1992.* New York: W. W. Norton.

———. 1993. "Global Dimensions of Forced Motherhood." *USA Today,* May, pp. 34–35.

Jaggar, A. M. 1983. *Feminist Politics and Human Nature.* Totowa, NJ: Rowman and Allanheld.

Japan Times Weekly International Edition. 1992a. "Land Price Spiral Comes Down to Earth." April 6–12.

———. 1992b. "Marriage? Girls Just Wanna Have Fun." July 13–19.

"Japan's Gangsters—Honourable Mob." 1990. *Economist,* April 21.

"Japanese-Owned Factories in California Often Resemble Sweatshops, Study Finds." 1992. *San Diego Union-Tribune,* April 7.

Jary, D., and J. Jary. 1991. *Dictionary of Sociology.* New York: Harper Perennial.

Jencks, C. 1994. *The Homeless.* Cambridge, MA: Harvard University Press.

Johnson, D. 1996. "Rural Regions, Depopulated in the 80s, Blossom Again." *San Diego Union-Tribune,* Dec 21st p. A30

Johnson, D. P. 1981. *Sociological Theory—Classical Founders and Contemporary Perspectives.* New York: Wiley.

Johnson, J. M. 1997. "Working to Stop Angry Men and Their Careers in Violence." *Applied Behavioral Review* 5(1): 59–66.

Johnson, K. 1998. "The Day the Music Died: Women and Girls in Afghanistan." *National NOW Times,* (March).

Johnson, P. 1983. *Modern Times—The World from the Twenties to the Eighties.* New York: Harper & Row.

Johnston, D. C. 1999. "Rich-Poor Gap in U.S. More Than Double 1977's, New Figures Show." *San Diego Union-Tribune,* September 5.

Johnston, O. 1991. "Bulk of Americans Living Longer but Blacks Are Not." *Los Angeles Times,* April 9.

Jones, B. 1997. "Venezuelan Economy Crushed by Bloated Bureaucracy." *San Diego Union-Tribune,* December 28.

Jones, C. 1992. "Introduction of Merit Pay Shocks Japanese." *Christian Science Monitor,* October 20.

Jones, E., and E. Van Zandt. 1974. *The City: Yesterday, Today and Tomorrow.* Garden City, NY: Doubleday.

Joseph, E. 1998. "Polygamy Now!" *Harper's* (February):26–28.

Josephson, W. L. 1987. "Television Violence and Children's Aggression: Testing the Priming, Social Script, and Disinhibition Predictors." *Journal of Personality and Social Psychology* 53(5):882–890.

Kagan, D. 1989. "How America Lost Its First Drug War." *Insight* 20:8–17.

Kallestad, B. 1999. "Florida Voucher Plan Will Let Students Leave Failing Schools." *San Diego Union-Tribune,* April 28.

Kaminski, M. and K. Palchikoff. 1997. "The Crisis to Come" *Newsweek,* April 14, pp. 44–46.

Kamm, S., A. J. Anderson, and M. Leek. 1994. "Latchkey Adults." *Library Journal* 119(12):58–59.

Kane, H. 1993. "Growing Fish in the Fields." *World Watch* (September—October):20–27

Kanei, S. 1995. "Aum Affair Reflects Japan's Spiritual Void." *Japan Times Weekly International Edition,* October 2–8, p. 8.

Kang, L. 1997. "Popular Culture and the Culture of the Masses in Contemporary China." *Boundary* 24(3):99–122.

Kanter, R. M. 1983. *The Change Masters: Innovation and Entrepreneurship in the American Corporation.* New York: Simon & Schuster.

———. 1985. "All That Is Entrepreneurial Is Not Gold." *Wall Street Journal,* July 22, p. 18.

Kantrowitz, B., and P. Wingert. 1992b. "One Nation, One Curriculum?" *Newsweek* (April 6):59–60.

Kantrowitz, B., with K. Springen and D. Foote. 1993. "Who Would Want This Job?" *Newsweek* (February 22):54, 56.

Kaplan, D. E., M. Tharpe, M. Madden, and G. Witkin. 1997. "Terrorism Threats at Home." *U.S. News & World Report* (December 27): 22–24.

Kaplan, J. 1995. "Right-Wing Terrorism in the United States," in T. Bjorgo, ed. *Terror From the Extreme Right.* London: Frank Cass, pp. 44–95.

Kaplan, R. D. 1999. "Could This Be the New World?" *New York Times,* December 27, p. A23.

Karp, J. 1998. "India Braces for Slowdown in Economic Growth." *Wall Street Journal,* March 26, p. A14.

Karp, J., and S. Sharma 1998. "India's Budget Aims to Restore Growth, Raise Import Tarifs and Boost Defense Outlays." *Wall Street Journal,* June 2, p. A16.

Kastenbaum, R., and B. Kastenbaum. 1989. *Suicide. Encyclopedia of Death.* Phoenix, AZ: Oryx Press.

Kaylor, R. 1984. "Calcutta: A City of 'Ruthless Passionate Love.' " *San Diego Union-Tribune,* February 14 p. A14.

Kemps, D. 1998. "Deaths, Disease Traced to Environment." *Popline* (May/June):3.

Kennedy, J. 1991. "Native Peoples in the United States and Canada," in M. J. Cohen and R. A. Hoehn, eds. *Hunger 1992: Second Annual Report on the State of World Hunger.* Washington, DC: Bread for the World Institute on Hunger and Development, pp. 155–157.

Kennedy, P. 1993. "Preparing for the 21st Century: Winners and Losers." *The New York Review of Books* (February 11):32–44.

"Kentucky School District Posts Ten Commandments in Classrooms." 1999. *free! The Freedom Forum Online* (August 12).

Kephart, W. M., and W. Z. Zellner. 1994. *Extraordinary Groups: An Examination of Unconventional Life-Styles.* New York: St. Martin's Press.

Kepp, M. 1991. "Loss of Land, White Encroachment Cited as Suicides Among Brazil's Indians Rise." *San Diego Union,* May 5.

Kerbo, H. R. 2000. *Social Stratification and Inequality: Class Conflict in Historical, Comparative, and Global Perspective,* 4th ed. Boston: McGraw-Hill.

Kesey, K. 1962. *One Flew Over the Cuckoo's Nest.* New York: Viking Press.

"Key Facts About Kosovo." 1999. < http://www.channel2OOO.com/news/kosovo_facts.html > Accessed August 23, 1999.

Key, K., D. J. DeNoon and S. Boyles. 1996. "India AIDS Situation Seen Out of Control by 2000." *AIDS Weekly Plus,* December 23–30, pp. 11–12.

"Khrushchev's Son Buries Ghost of Cold War to be U.S. Citizen." 1999. *San Diego Union-Tribune,* July 11.

Kifner, J. 1999. "Kosovo Body Count Rising Quickly." *San Diego Union-Tribune,* July 18.

Kim, L. 1998a. "German Special Squad Tackles Neo-Nazi Attacks, But Roots of Problem Remain." *Christian Science Monitor,* March 26.

———. 1998b. "Germany's Future Hangs on a Remnant of Its Past." *Christian Science Monitor,* June 25.

"The Kindness of Strangers." 1994. *Economist,* May 7, p. 19.

Kinsey, A. C., W. B. Pomeroy, and C. E. Martin. 1948. *Sexual Behavior in the Human Male.* Philadelphia: Saunders.

Kinsman, M. 1999. "Working 'traditional' 9-to-5? You're outnumbered, 2-1." *San Diego Union-Tribune,* September 6.

Kirchner, J. T. 1998. "Increase in Drug Abuse Among U.S. Adolescents." *American Family Physician,* July 1, pp. 233–234.

Kirn, W. 1997. "The Ties That Bind." *Time* (August 18):48–50.

Kirp, D. L., M. G. Yodof, and M. S. Franks. 1986. *Gender Justice.* Chicago: University of Chicago Press.

Knickerbocker, B. 1992. "Cost of Nuclear Waste Cleanup in the Billions." *Christian Science Monitor,* April 8.

———. 1993. "Ban on Dumping Nuclear Waste at Sea." *Christian Science Monitor,* November 15.

———1994a. "Managing Population Growth." *Christian Science Monitor,* April 6, p. 9.

———. 1994b. "Population Doubling Strains India's Environment, People." *Christian Science Monitor,* August 16, p. 11.

———. 1994c. "World Bank Turns from Saving Trees to Saving Cities." *Christian Science Monitor,* September 27, p. 13.

Knodel, J. 1999. "Deconstructing Population Momemtum." *Population Today* (March):3–4.

Koch, K. 1974. "Cultural Relativism," in *Encyclopedia of Sociology.* Guilford, CT: Dushkin Publishing Group.

Kohen, S. 1998. "Torn over Garments, Turkey Hurtles Toward a Showdown." *Christian Science Monitor,* March 25.

Kohn, M. L. 1976. "Interaction of Social Class and Other Factors in the Etiology of Schizophrenia." *American Journal of Psychiatry* 133(2):179–180.

Kolata, G. 1996. "Experts Are At Odds On How Best to Tackle Rise in Teenagers Drug Use" *New York Times,* September 18, p. B7.

"Kosova." < http://www.unpo.org/member/kosova/kosova.html > Accessed August 22, 1999.

"Kosovo and Metohija: History." < http://www.gov.yu/kosovo/history.html > Accessed August 22, 1999.

Koss, M., and M. Harvey. 1991. *The Rape Victim: Clinical and Community Interventions.* Beverly Hills, CA: Sage.

Kottak, C. 1994. *Cultural Anthropology,* 6th Ed. New York: McGraw-Hill.

Krieger, L. M. 1998. "Past Optimism is Missing at Start of International AIDS Conference." *Buffalo News,* June 28, p. A8.

Kronholz, J. 1998a. "U.S. 12th-Graders Rank Near Bottom In Math, Science." *Wall Street Journal,* February 25.

———. 1998b. "In Many Races, The Magic Word Was Education." *New York Times,* November 5.

———. 1999a. "Students Get Higher Scores In Reading Test." *Wall Street Journal,* February 11.

———. 1999b. "Charter Schools Begin to Prod Public Schools Toward Competition." *Wall Street Journal,* February 12.

Kuznets, S. 1955. "Economic Growth and Income Inequality." *American Economic Review* (March): 178–194.

Kwong, J. 1994. "Ideological Crisis Among China's Youth: Values and Official Ideology." *British Journal of Sociology* 45(2): 247–264.

————. 1995. "Despite Economic Upturn, Mexicans Say, 'It's the Tortilla Prices, Stupid.' " *Christian Science Monitor,* July 31, p. 7.

————. H. 1998a. "Brazil Trains Teachers via Satellite." *Christian Science Monitor,* April 22.

————. H. 1998b. "Rescuing Brazil: Why the U.S. has Big Stakes." *Christian Science Monitor,* October 26, p. 1.

————. 1998c. "Post-Mitch Risk—Abondon Farms, Teaming Cities" *Christian Science Monitor* (November 9): 1.

La Franchi, P., F. F. Stryer, and R. Gauthier. 1984. "The Emergence of Same Sex Affiliative Preferences Among Preschool Peers: A Development/Ethological Perspective." *Child Development* 55:1958–1965.

LaFee, S. 1992. "Learning a Language Harder Than Thought." *San Diego Union-Tribune,* February 11.

Lamb, D. 1984. *The Africans.* New York: Vintage Books.

Lampman, J. 1998. "Cloning's Double Trouble." *Christian Science Monitor,* August 13, p. B1.

Landes, J. B. 1979. "Women, Labor and Family Life," in R. Quinney, ed. *Capitalist Society—Readings for a Critical Sociology.* Homewood, IL: Dorsey Press, pp. 214–227.

Landler, M. 1998. "Riots Bare Ethnic Hatreds in Indonesia." *New York Times,* May 9.

Lane, C. 1998. "Disorderly Conduct." *New Republic* (November 24):21–26.

Langford, D. R. 1998. "Social Chaos and Danger As Context of Battered Women's Lives." *Journal of Family Nursing* (May):167–181.

Lanier, C. A., M. N. Elliot, D. W. Martin, and A. Kapadia. 1998. "Evaluation of an Interview to Change Attitudes Toward Date Rape." *College Teaching* (Spring):76–78.

Lapierre, D. 1985. *The City of Joy.* Garden City, NY: Doubleday.

Lardner, J. 1998a. "Criminals on Crime." *U.S. News & World Report* (May 25):37–39.

————. 1998b. "A New Health Hazard: Economic Inequality." *Washington Post National Weekly Edition,* August 24, p. 22.

Larkin, R. P., and G. L. Peters. 1983. *Dictionary of Concepts in Human Geography.* Westport, CT: Greenwood Press.

LaRocco, L. 1994. "How to Energize 'Deadbeat Parents.' " *Christian Science Monitor,* October 6, p. 19.

Lash, S. 1990. *Sociology of Postmodernism.* London: Routledge.

Laslett, B., and C. A. B. Warren. 1975. "Losing Weight: The Organizational Promotion of Behavior Change." *Social Problems* 23:69–80.

Lau, G. 1998. "Gotcha!" *Forbes* (May 5):130–131.

Lauer, J., and R. H. Lauer. 1985. "Marriages Made to Last." *Psychology Today* (June):22–26.

Lauer, R. H. 1982. *Perspectives on Social Change.* Boston: Allyn and Bacon.

Layng, A. 1990. "What Keeps Women 'in Their Place'?" in E. Angeloni, ed. *Anthropology 90/91.* Guilford, CT: Dushkin Publishing Group, pp. 148–151.

Leaming, J. 1999. "Kansas State School Board Adopts Standards That Ignore Evolution." *free! The Freedom Forum Online* (August 12).

Lee, C. S. 1998. "Kim Turns Up the Heat." *Far Eastern Economic Review* (February 19):61–62.

Leeds, A., and V. Dusek. 1981–1982. "Editors' Note." *Philosophical Forum* 13(2–3):i–xxxiv.

Lefkowitz, J. P. 1998. "Supreme Court on School Choice: 50 Years of Precedents." *Wall Street Journal,* November 23.

Lehman, S. 1999. "In Brazil, the Inflation Specter." *Orange County Register,* January 30, p. Business-3.

Lemert, E. M. 1951. *Social Pathology.* New York: McGraw-Hill.

Lenski, G. E. 1966. *Power and Privilege: A Theory of Social Stratification.* New York: McGraw-Hill.

Lenski, G., P. Nolan, and J. Lenski. 1995. *Human Societies: An Introduction to Macrosociology,* 7th ed. New York: McGraw-Hill.

Leslie, G. R., and S. K. Korman. 1989. *The Family in Social Context.* New York: Oxford University Press.

Levin, M. 1997. "Legal Claims Get Costly For Makers of Handguns" *Los Angeles Times,* December 27, p. A1.

Levine, S. B. 1980. "The Rise of American Boarding Schools and the Development of a National Upper Class." *Social Problems* 28(1):63–94.

Levy, F. 1988. *Dollars and Dreams: The Changing American Income Distribution.* New York: Norton.

Levy, J. R. 1993. "Firm Finds Green Solution to Nuclear Contamination." *Christian Science Monitor,* October 25.

Lewis, F. 1992. "Women First Must Pierce Glass Walls." *San Diego Union-Tribune,* April 27.

Lewis, O. 1960. *Tepoztlan: Village in Mexico.* New York: Holt, Rinehart and Winston.

————. 1966. "The Culture of Poverty." *Scientific American* (October):19–25.

Lewis, P. 1999. "After 20 years, U. N. Ban on Bias Against Women Gets Some Teeth." *San Diego Union-Tribune,* March 21.

Li, C. 1997. *Rediscovering China: Dynamics and Dilemmas of Reform.* London: Rowan and Littlefield.

Light, I. 1983. *Cities in World Perspective.* New York: Macmillan.

Lin, J. 1998. "Sex Entertainment is a Taxing Question for China" *San Diego Union-Tribune,* November 1, p. A29.

Lindner, E. W. (ed). 1999. *1999 Yearbook of American and Canadian Churches.* Nashville, TN: Abingdon Press.

Lindsey, R. 1987. "Colleges Accused of Bias to Stem Asians' Gains." *New York Times,* January 19.

Lipset, S. M. 1963. *Political Man: The Social Bases of Politics.* New York: Anchor Books.

Little, C. B. 1989. *Deviance and Control: Theory, Research, and Social Policy.* Itasca, IL: Peacock.

Liu, J. 1999. Conversations with Professor Liu at the University of San Diego, January 26.

Livingston, Jay. 1996. *Crime and Criminology.* Upper Saddle River, NJ: Prentice Hall.

Lloyd, J. 1998. "Rocky Mountain Backlash Against the Religious Right." *Christian Science Monitor,* August 11.

Lofland, J. 1977. *Doomsday Cult: A Study of Conversion, Proselytization and Maintenance of Faith.* New York: Irvington Publishers.

Logan, J. R., R. D. Alba, and S. Leung. 1996. *Social Forces* (March):841–881.

Logan, M. F. 1995. *Fighting Sprawl and City Hall: Resistance to Urban Growth in the Southwest.* Tucson, AZ: University of Arizona Press.

Lombroso-Ferrero, G. 1972. *Lombroso's Criminal Man.* Montclair, NY: Patterson Smith.

London, B., and B. Williams. 1988. "Multinational Corporate Penetration, Protest, and Basic Needs Provisions in Non-Core Nations: A Cross-National Analysis." *Social Forces* 66:747–773.

Longman, P., J. Egan, and M. Garrett. 1998. "Is Anyone in Charge?" *U.S. News & World Report* (October 28):50–52.

Lorber, J. 1992. "Gender," in E. F. Borgotta and M. L. Borgotta, eds. *Encyclopedia of Sociology,* vol. 2. New York: Macmillan, pp. 748–754.

Los Angeles Times. 1990. "Survey: Some Blacks Expect Too Much of Sport." November 15.

————. 1992. "Blacks' Earnings Up in '80s, Lag Other Groups' Income." July 25.

————. 1993. "Health Care Reform: Tough, but Stay with It." January 6.

Lott, J. R. Jr. 1998. "How to Stop Mass Public Shootings." *Los Angeles Times,* May 25, p. B5.

Loup, J. 1983. *Can the Third World Survive?* Baltimore: Johns Hopkins University Press.

Louw, A. 1997. "Surviving the Transistion: Trends and Perceptions of Crime in South Africa." *Social Indicators Research* 41:137–168.

————. 1997. "Video Helps Torpedo Trash Dumping at Sea." *Christian Science Monitor,* January 23, p. 10.

Low, P. 1993. "Trade and the Environment: What Worries the Developing Countries?" *Environmental Law* (April):705–709.

Lozada, M. 1996. "Searching for a Separate Peace." *Techniques: Making Education and Career Connections.* (October):14–20.

Lublin, J. S. 1996. "Women At Top Are Still Distant From CEO Jobs." *Wall Street Journal,* February 28.

Luckenbill, D. F. 1977. "Criminal Homicide as a Situated Transaction." *Social Problems* 25:176–186.

Luckenbill, D. F., and D. P. Doyle. 1989. "Structural Position and Violence: Developing a Cultural Explanation." *Criminology* 27:419–433.

Lutz, W. 1989. *Doublespeak.* New York: Harper Perennial.

Lyman, P. 1996. "South Africa's Promise." *Foreign Policy:* 105–119. (Spring) No. 102.

Lynch, J. 1995. "Chasing Deadbeat Parents." *Spokesman-Review* (Seattle), March 26, p. A1.

Lyon, D. 1988. *The Information Society: Issues and Illusions.* Cambridge, England: Polity Press.

MacFarquhar, E. 1995. "A Banking Lesson from Bangladesh." *U.S. News & World Report,* April 3, p. 41.

MacFarquhar, R. 1997. *The Origins of the Cultural Revolution 3: The Coming of the Cataclysm 1961–1966.* New York: Oxford University Press and Columbia University Press.

Macionis, J. 1989. *Sociology.* Englewood Cliffs, NJ: Prentice Hall.

Mackenzie, H. 1998. "Refugee's Report Suggest High Toll in North Korea." *Christian Science Monitor,* March 5, p. 1.

MacLeod, L. 1998a. "The Dying Fields." *Far Eastern Economic Review* (April 23)62–63.

———. 1998b. "Colombia U'wa Face Hazards of Oil Drilling." *Lancet* (July 18)209.

MacNeil, J. 1989. "Strategies for Sustainable Development." *Scientific American* (September):155–165.

Madge, J. 1962. *The Origins of Scientific Sociology.* New York: Free Press.

Madrid, A. 1990. "Official English: A False Policy Issue." *Annals of the American Academy of the Political and Social Sciences* 508:62–65.

Madsen, C. F., and G. Meyer. 1978. *Minorities in American Society.* New York: D. Van Nostrand, p. 244.

Madsen, W. 1964. *The Mexican-Americans of South Texas.* New York: Holt, Rinehart and Winston.

"Magnitude of the Epidemic." 1998. *Centers of Disease Control http://www.cdcnpin.org/geneva98/trends/trends_1htm*

Magnuson, E. 1981. "The Curse of Violent Crime." *Time* (March 23): 16–21.

"Mainline Churches Hit by Denominational Switching." 1994. *Christian Science Monitor,* January 18.

Malinowski, B. 1927, *Sex and Repression in Savage Society.* London: Routledge & Kegan Paul.

Mallinger, K. 1990. "The American Family: History and Development," in P. Bomar, ed. *Nurses and Family Health Promotion.* Philadelphia: Saunders.

Maraldo, J. C. 1976. *Buddhism in the Modern World.* New York: Collier Books.

Marketplace. 1998. National Public Radio, September 25.

Marquand, R. 1998. "How Islam Extremism Can Dissolve Old Borders." *Christian Science Monitor,* August 20.

Marquis, J. 1999. "Smog Study of Children Yields Ominous Results." *Los Angeles Times,* March 18.

Marshall, T., and C. J. Williams. 1993. "A Time to Build, a Time to Destroy." *Los Angeles Times,* January 26.

Martin, R., R. J. Mutchnick, and W. T. Austin. 1990. *Criminological Thought: Pioneers Past and Present.* New York: Macmillan.

Martin, T. Castro, and L. L. Bumpass. 1989. "Recent Trends in Marital Disruption." *Demography* 6:37.

Martindale, D. 1981. *The Nature and Types of Sociological Thought.* Boston: Houghton Mifflin.

Martinkus, J. 1999. "Martial law imposed in East Timor." *San Diego Union-Tribune,* September 7.

———. 1998. "Russians Find Becoming a Latvian Isn't Easy." *Christian Science Monitor,* April 21.

Marx, K. 1970, original 1844. *Critique of Hegel's 'Philosophy of Right.'* J. O'Malley, ed. Cambridge: Cambridge University Press.

Marx, K., and F. Engels. 1955, original 1848. *The Communist Manifesto.* S. H. Beer, ed. New York: Appleton-Century-Crofts.

Masland, T. 1994. "Will It Be Peace or Punishment?" *Newsweek* (August 1):37.

Massey, D. S. 1996. "Concentrating Poverty Breeds Violence." *Population Today* (June/July):5.

Masters, R. 1997. "Straight Talk . . . About Biology and Psychopathology." *Crime Times* 3(3):2.

Masters, W. H., V. E. Johnson, and R. C. Kolodny. 1988. *Human Sexuality.* Chicago: Scott Foresman/Little, Brown.

Mathews, J. 1992. "Americans Can Learn from Asia's Educational Systems." *Japan Times Weekly International Edition,* December 14–20.

Matloff, J. 1995. "Crime in South Africa Cuts Across Racial, Economic Lines." *Christian Science Monitor,* November 13, p. 1c.

Matthews, J. 1989. "Rescue Plan for Africa." *World Monitor* (May):28–36.

Mattox, W. R. 1997. "Adding Healthy New Meaning to the Term 'Marital Bliss.'" *San Diego Union-Tribune,* January 23, p. B7.

Maugh III, T. 1996. "Worldwide Study Finds Big Shift in Causes of Death." *Los Angeles Times,* September 16, p. A14.

Maugh, T. H., II, and N. Zamichow. 1991. "Study Ties Part of Brain to Men's Sexual Orientation." *Los Angeles Times,* August 30.

Maugh, T. H., II. 1991. Survey of Identical Twins Links Biological Factors with Being Gay." *Los Angeles Times,* December 15.

———. 1993. "Genetic Component Found in Lesbianism, Study Says." *Los Angeles Times,* March 12.

Maykuth, A. 1998. "S. African Women, Once Deprived, Become Entrepreneurs." *San Diego Union-Tribune,* August 25.

McCaghy, C. H. and T. A., Capron. 1994. *Deviant Behavior: Crime, Conflict, and Interest Groups, Third Edition.* New York: Macmillan.

McDonnell, P. J. 1998a. "Mexican Arrivals Seek New Frontiers." *Los Angeles Times,* January 1, p. A26.

———. 1998b. "Mexican Immigration—Now Surging—Has Ebbed and Flowed for a Century." *Los Angeles Times,* January 1, p. A26.

McFalls, J. A. 1998. "Population: A Lively Introduction." *Population Bulletin* 53(3). Washington, DC: Population Reference Bureau.

McGeary, J., and M. Michaels. 1998. "Africa Rising." *Time* (March 30):34–46.

McGee, T. G. 1977. "The Persistence of the Proto-Proletariat: Occupational Structures and Planning of the Future of Third World Cities." In *Third World Urbanization,* J. Abu-Lughod and R. Hay Jr., eds. Chicago: Maaroufa Press.

McGuire, S. 1988. "A Compromised Election: Despite Cries of Fraud, Mexico's Ruling Party Claims a Close Victory." *Newsweek* (July 18):36–37.

McKaughan, S. 1997. "Land Reform in Brazil: A Framework for Policy Formulation." In *Policymaking in a Redemocratized Brazil.* Austin, Texas: Lyndon B. Johnson School of Public Affairs (Policy Research Report No. 119).

McKusick, L., W. Horstman, and T. J. Coates. 1985. "AIDS and Sexual Behavior Reported by Gay Men in San Francisco." *American Journal of Public Health* 75:493–496.

McLanahan, S., and G. Sandefur. 1994. *Growing Up with a Single Parent: What Hurts, What Helps.* Cambridge MA: Harvard University Press.

McLaughlin, A. 1998. "Testing Put to the Test." *Christian Science Monitor,* November 25.

McLaughlin, A., and G. R. Chaddock. 1998. "The Perils of Testing Teachers." *Christian Science Monitor,* July 3.

McNeal, C., and P. R. Amato. 1998. "Parents' Marital Violence—Long-Term Consequences for Children." *Journal of Family Issues* (March):123–139.

Mead, C. 1985. *Champion: Joe Louis.* New York: Charles Scribner's Son.

Mead, G. H. 1934. *Mind, Self, and Society.* Chicago: University of Chicago Press.

Mead, M. 1963, original 1935. *Sex and Temperament in Three Primitive Societies.* New York: William Morrow.

Meadows, D. 1992. "We Can't Keep Stealing from the Future." *Los Angeles Times,* April 27.

Meckler, L. 1998. "Blacks in America Get Sick More Than Whites, Die Sooner." *San Diego Union-Tribune,* November 27.

"The Media Violence Story in Canada." 1997. < http://www. media-awareness.ca/eng/issues/violence/viostory.htm > Accessed August 27, 1999.

Meisler, S. 1992. "Third World Finds 'Free' Markets Closed." *Los Angeles Times,* April 24.

Menen, C. 1998. "Enter Argentina." *Harvard International Review* (Summer):18–20.

Merida, K. 1995. "A Middle Class That Still Doesn't Feel It's Made It." *Washington Post National Weekly Edition,* October 16–22.

Merrick, T. W. 1986. "World Population in Transition." *Population Bulletin* 41(2).

Merrifield, D. B. 1992. "Was This Recession Really Necessary?" *World Monitor* (September):29–33.

Merton, R. 1957. *Social Theory and Social Structure.* New York: Free Press.

———. 1968. *Social Theory and Social Structure,* enlarged edition. New York: Free Press.

Metha, A., B. Weber, and D. Webb. 1998. "Youth Suicide Prevention: A Survey and Analysis of Policies and Efforts in the 50 States." *Suicide and Life Threatening Behavior* 28(Summer):150–164.

Mexico's New Frontier." 1997. *Economist* (February, 8):41–42.

Middleton, A. 1990. "How Did the Maquiladora Industry Begin?" *San Diego Business Journal.*

Mieszkowski, P., and E. S. Mills. 1993. "The Causes of Metropolitan Suburbanization." *Journal of Economic Perspectives* (Summer):135–147.

Mifflin, L. 1999. "Pediatricians Prescribe Strict TV Rationing." *San Diego Union-Tribune,* August 4.

Milbank, D. 1995. "Old Flaws Undermine New Poverty-Level Data." *Wall Street Journal,* October 5.

Milgram, S. 1963. "Behavioral Study of Obedience." *Journal of Abnormal and Social Psychology* 67:371–378.

———. 1965. "Some Conditions of Obedience and Disobedience to Authority." *Human Relations* 18 (February):57–76.

Miller, A. G. 1986. *The Obedience Experiments: A Case of Controversy in Social Science.* New York: Praeger.

Miller, E. M. 1991. "Prostitution." *The American Encyclopedia,* electronic edition. Danbury, CT: Grolier.

Miller, J. 1998. "The United Kingdom Is Being Divided." *Washington Post National Weekly Edition,* October 26, p. 23.

Miller, L. 1999. "The Age of Divine Diversity." *Wall Street Journal,* February 10.

Miller, M. 1992. "Salinas Accused of Doctoring the Books on Mexico's History." *Los Angeles Times,* September 22.

Miller, R. R. 1985. *Mexico: A History.* Norman: University of Oklahoma Press.

Mills, C. W. 1956. *The Power Elite.* London: Oxford University Press.

Minerbrook, S. 1994. "A Generation of Stone Killers" *U.S. News and World Report,* January 17, pp. 33–35

"Ministry Backs More-Nationalistic Textbooks." 1991. *Japan Times Weekly International Edition,* July 8–14.

Moffett, G. 1994. "Reining in the World's Galloping Population." *Christian Science Monitor,* August 17, p. 7.

Molidor, C. 1996. "Female Gang Members: A Profile of Aggression and Victimization." *Social Work* (May):251–256.

Montagu, A. 1980. "Introduction," in A. Montagu, ed. *Sociobiology Examined.* New York: Oxford University Press.

Montalbano, W. D. 1994. "Italian Baby Boom Goes Bust." *Los Angeles Times,* June 24, p. A1.

Montgomery, L. 1999. "Serbs Reportedly Using Rape as Weapon of Terror, Shame." *San Diego Union-Tribune,* April 13.

Morgan, S. 1999. "Riverside Struggles with Infamous Image." *San Diego Union-Tribune,* May 16.

Morin, R. 1995. "Across the Racial Divide." *Washington Post National Weekly Edition,* October 16–22.

———. 1998a. "Keeping the Faith." *Washington Post National Weekly Edition,* January 12, p. 37.

———. 1998b. "Breaking the Divorce Cycle." *Washington Post National Weekly Edition,* September 7, p. 35.

———. 1998c. "What Makes A 'Bad' American." *Washington Post National Weekly Edition,* November 20, p. 25.

———. 1999. "Have the People Lost Their Voice?" *Washington Post National Weekly Edition,* June 28, p. 34.

Morley. R. 1994. "Wife Beating and Modernization: The Case or Papua New Guinea " *Journal of Comparative Family Studies* 25(1): 25–52.

Morse, J. 1999. "The Test of Their Lives." *Time* (February 15).

Mosher, S. W. 1997. "Too Many People? Not by a Long Shot." *Wall Street Journal,* February 10, p. A18.

Ms. 1993. "Action Alert: International News" (January— February):12–13.

Murdock, D. 1995. "Let's Derail Uncle Sam's Corporate Gravy Train." *San Diego Union-Tribune,* March 16.

Murphy, K. 1992. "There's No Housing in Cairo at All; People Are Living in Tombs." *Los Angeles Times,* May 26.

———. 1994. "Cairo Conferences Linking Growth, Environment." *Los Angeles Times,* September 12, p. A6.

Murr, A. 1998. "Secrets in the Desert" *Newsweek* (August 10):37.

Murray, G. 1992. "Studies Blast Japanese Management in Britain." *Japan Times Weekly International Edition,* July 27—August 2.

"Mutatations May Have Foiled Plague." 1998. *San Diego Union-Tribune,* May 9, p. A10.

Mwangi, G. 1999. "Poverty has Kenyans begging for answers." San Diego Uttioll-Tribune, May 8.

Mydans, S. 1998. "In Jakarta, Reports of Numerous Rapes Of Chinese in Riots." New York Times, June 10.

———. 1999. "Violence Accompanies East Timor Tally." *San Diego Union-Tribune,* September 2.

Nadon, S. M., C. Koverola, and E. H. Schludermann. 1998. "Antecedents to Prostitution." *Journal of Interpersonal Violence* (April):206–221.

Nagpaul, H. 1988. "India's Giant Cities." In M. Dogan and J. D. Kasarda (Eds.) *A World of Giant* Cities—The Metropolis Era. Newbury Park, CA: Sage Vol 1 pp. 252–290.

Nakada, T. 1992. "When *Sumimasen* Seems to be the Hardest Word." *Japan Times Weekly International Edition,* March 30— April 5.

Nanda, S., and R. L. Warms. 1998. *Cultural Anthropology* Belmont CA: Wadsworth.

Nasar, S. 1992. "Fed Report Gives New Data on Gains by Richest in 80s." *New York Times,* April 21.

Nass, G., and M. Fisher. 1988. *Sexuality Today.* Boston: Towes and Bartlett.

National Advisory Commission on Civil Disorders. 1968. *Report of the National Advisory Commission on Civil Disorders.* Washington DC: U.S. Government Printing Office.

National Catholic Educational Association. 1999. "Catholic School Highlights." NCEA News Release, January 8. Washington, DC: National Catholic Educational Association.

National Center for Education Statistics. 1999. *The Condition of Education, 1999.* Washington, DC: U.S. Department of Education, National Center for Education Statistics.

National Commission on Excellence in Education. 1993. *A Nation at Risk: The Imperative for Educational Reform.* Washington, DC: U.S. Government Printing Office.

National Institute of Mental Health. 1982. *Television and Behavior: Ten Years of Scientific Progress and Implications of Behavior.* Washington, DC: U.S. Government Printing Office.

National Public Radio. 1991a. "Sunday Morning: Report on Brazil." May 12.

———. 1991b. *All Things Considered,* November 4.

———. 1999. *Morning News,* January.

Navarrette, R., Jr. 1992. "Life in the Academic Fast Track." *Los Angeles Times,* April 12.

Nelan, B. W. 1998. "Better Than Nothing." *Time* (September 21):74–76.

"Neo-Nazis' numbers growing in Germany." *San Diego Union-Tribune,* February 28.

Neumark, Y. D., J. Delva, and J. C. Anthony. 1998. "The Epidemiology of Adolescent Inhalant Drug Involvement." *Archives of Pediatric and Adolescent Medicine* (August):781–786.

Newcomb, A. 1999. "State Woos Teachers with a (Big) Bonus." *Christian Science Monitor,* February 9.

Newland, K. 1980. *City Limits: Emerging Constraints of Urban Growth.* Washington, DC: Population Institute.

Newsweek. 1990. "Perspectives." (July 16):17.

Nichols, R. 1996. "Experts Gather to Ask if the World Could Feed Three Billion More People." *San Diego Union-Tribune,* November 13, p. A2.

Niebuhr, G. 1998. "Southern Baptists Declare Wife Should 'Submit' to Her Husband." *New York Times,* June 10.

Nietschmann, B. 1988. "Third World War: The Global Conflict over the Rights of Indigenous Nations." *Utne Reader* (November—December):84–90.

"1989 Berlin Wall." 1999. *NOVA Online.* < http://novaonline. nv.cc.va.us/eli/evans/his135/MODULES/Events/berlinwall89. htm > Accessed August 31, 1999.

"1961 Berlin Wall." 1999. *NOVA Online.* < http://novaonline. nv.cc.va.us/eli/evans/hisl35/MODULES/Events/Berlinwall6l. htm > Accessed August 31, 1999.

Nisbet, E. 1974. *The Sociology of Emile Durkheim.* New York: Oxford University Press.

Nishimura, Y. 1991. "Company Recruits Gear Up for Tough Training Programs." *Japan Times Weekly International Edition,* February 11–17.

Nishizawa, J. 1995. "Lost Souls: Aum and Japan's Exam Hell." *Japan Times Weekly International Edition,* May 29—June 4.

Nordland, R. 1993. "The Mullahs vs. Modernization." *Newsweek* (March 1):53.

"A 'Normal' Poland." 1997. *New York Times,* December 12, p. A10.

Norton, A. J., and P. C. Glick. 1986. "One Parent Families: A Social and Economic Profile." *Family Relations* 35:9–17.

Novartis Foundation for Sustainable Development. 1999. " 'Street Children' in Brazil." < http://www.foundation.novartis.com/brazilian_street_children.htm > Accessed September 3, 1999.

Nullis, C. 1992. "Contraceptive Use Increases, WHO Finds in Report on Health." *Los Angeles Times,* June 27.

Nye, J. S., Jr. 1992. "Explosion of Tribalism Demonstrates Self-Determination Has Limitations." *Buffalo Times,* December 27.

O'Connor, M. L. 1998. "The Number of Abortions Among U.S. Women Fell 5 percent in 1994, Continuing a Decline Begun in the Early 1990s." *Family Planning Perspectives* (March/April): 101–102.

O'Hare, W. P. 1992. "America's Minorities—The Demographics of Diversity." *Population Bulletin,* 47(4, December).

Oakes, J, 1985. *Keeping Track: How Schools Structure Inequality.* New Haven, CT: Yale University Press.

Obiora, A. L. 1997. Bridges and Barricades: Rethinking Polemics and Intransigence in the Campaign Against Female Circumcision." *Case Western Reserve Law Review* 47(2):275–325.

Ogburn, W. F. 1950. *Social Change.* New York: Viking Press.

Olin, P., and B. N. Tandon. 1994. "An International Perspective on Child Day-Care Health." *Pediatrics* 94(6):1085–1087.

Olshansky, S. J., B. Carnes, R. G. Rogers, and L. Smith. 1997. *Infectious Diseases: New and Ancient Threats to World Health.* Population Reference Bureau. Washington, DC: Population Reference Bureau.

Olson, E. 1998. "U. N. Urges Fiscal Accounting Include Sex Trade" *New York Times,* August 2O, p. A11.

"150,000 besiege Belgrade." 1999. *San Diego Union-Tribune,* August 20.

Ono, T. 1992. "More Young People Quitting Jobs for Freedom." *Japan Times Weekly International Edition,* March 2–8.

Orcutt, J. A. 1973. "Societal Reaction and the Response to Deviation in Small Groups." *Social Forces* 52:259–267.

Orlebeke, J. F., D. L. Knol, and F. C. Verhulst. 1997. "Increase in Child Behavior Problems Resulting from Maternal Smoking During Pregnancy." *Archives of Environmental Health* (July/August):317–321.

Orme, Jr., W. A. 1999. "Water Stress Poses an Ongoing Threat to Mideast's Well-Being." *San Diego Union-Tribune,* April 1.

Oropesa, R. S. 1997. "Development and Marital Power in Mexico." *Social Forces* (June):1291–1317.

Ouchi, W. G. 1981. *Theory Z: How American Business Can Meet the Japanese Challenge.* Reading, MA: Addison-Wesley.

Pacher, S. 1987. "The World According to Lester Brown." *Utne Reader* (September—October): 84–93.

Packard, W. 1988. *Evangelism in America.* New York: Paragon House.

———. 1992. "Tijuana's Midnight Express." *Newsweek* (November 23):41.

Painter, E., and D. L. Weisel. 1997. "Crafting Local Responses to Gang Problems: Case Studies From Five Cities." *Public Management* (July):4–7.

Palen, J. J. 1992. *The Urban World* New York: McGraw-Hill.

Palmer, L. 1999. "Abortion Losing Its Appeal to Women of Gen X." *San Diego Union-Tribune,* September 5.

Pappas, B., and J. Levine. 1998. "Boppa Um Mao Mao." *Forbes* 161(2):39.

Parachini, A. 1986. "Drug Abuse Afflicts U.S. in Cycles." *Los Angeles Times,* July 31.

Parenti, M. 1989. "Imperialism Causes Third World Poverty," in J. Rohr, ed. *The Third World—Opposing View Points.* San Diego, CA: Greenhaven Press, pp. 17–24.

"Parents Who Kill Their Children." 1995. *U.S. News & World Report* (May 5):14.

Park, R. E., and E. W. Burgess. 1921. *Introduction to the Science of Sociology.* Chicago: University of Chicago Press.

Parker, J. H. 1982. *Principles of Sociology.* Lanham, MD: University Press of America.

Parrillo, V. N. 2000. *Strangers to These Shores,* 6th ed. Boston: Allyn & Bacon.

Parsons, T. 1954. *Essays in Sociological Theory.* New York: Free Press.

———. 1966. *Societies: Evolutionary and Comparative Perspectives.* Englewood Cliffs, NJ: Prentice Hall.

———. 1971. *The System of Modern Societies.* Englewood Cliffs, NJ: Prentice Hall.

Parsons, T., and N. J. Smelser. 1956. *Economy and Society.* New York: Free Press.

Parsons, T., and R. F. Bales. 1955. *Family, Socialization, and Interaction Processes.* New York: Free Press.

"The Patriot Movement." 1998. *Intelligence Report* (Spring):6–7.

Paxton, M. 1992. "Low Awareness in Japan—Still 'Nothing to Do with Me.' " *Japan Times Weekly International Edition,* March 30—April 5.

Pear, R. 1995. "Sweeping Revisions Proposed in the Way U.S. Poverty Is Defined." *San Diego Union-Tribune,* April 30.

Pearce, D. 1978. "The Feminization of Poverty: Women, Work, and Welfare." *Urban and Social Change Review* (Winter—Spring):28–36.

———. 1990. "The Feminization of Poverty." *Journal for Peace and Justice Studies* 2(1):1–20.

Pearl, D. 1999. "Why Ethnic Cleansing, Once Under Way, Is So Difficult to Reverse." *Wall Street Journal,* April 22.

Pearlman, D. N. 1998. "Slipping Through the Safety Net: Implications for Women's Health." *Journal of Health Care for the Poor and Underserved* (August):217–221.

Pearlstein, S. 1995. "The Rich Get Richer and . . . " *Washington Post National Weekly Edition,* June 12–18.

Peele, S. 1989. *The Diseasing of America—Addiction Treatment Out of Control.* Lexington, MA: D.C. Heath.

———. 1999. *Diseasing of America: How We Allowed Recovery Zealots and the Treatment Industry to Convince Us We Are All Out of Control.* New York: Jossey-Bass Publishers.

Peeno, L. 1998. "Patients Are the Losers When Medical Practice Is Free of Liability." *Los Angeles Times,* October 9, p. B9.

Pehrson, J. 1998. "Disgruntled Chinese Workers Miss the 'Iron Rice Bowl.' " *Christian Science Monitor,* March 13, p. 14.

Pesic, V. 1996. *Serbian Nationalism and the Origins of the Yugoslav Crisis.* Washington, DC: United States Institute of Peace.

Peterson, Janice. 1987. "The Feminization of Poverty." *Journal of Economic Issues* 21(March):329–337.

Peterson, S. 1998. "For Iraq's Educated Elite: Tales of Stock Market, Kitch Market." *Christian Science Monitor,* March 6, p. 7.

Pfister, A. "Not for kids." 1995. *Cover Story* (September).

Pfohl, S. J. 1994. *Images of Deviance and Social Control.* Second Edition. New York: McGraw-Hill.

Phillips, A. 1997. "The English-Only Debate." *Maclean's* (May 5):42.

Phillips, K. 1969. *The Emerging Republican Majority.* New Rochelle, NY: Arlington.

———. 1990a. "In the '80s, the Rich Got a Lot Richer, but with New Taxes That Could Change." *Los Angeles Times,* June 24.

———. 1990b. *The Politics of Rich and Poor.* New York: Random House.

Philo Kim, B. L. 1992. *Two Koreas in Development.* Publishers, New Brunswick, NJ: Transaction.

"Physician Group's Unprecedented Study Calls Taliban War on Women a Health and Human Rights Crisis in Afghanistan." 1998. Boston: Physicians for Human Rights, August 5.

Piaget, J. 1929. *The Child's Conception of the World.* New York: Harcourt, Brace.

———. 1932. *The Moral Judgment of the Child.* New York: Free Press.

Piatt, G. 1997. "Foreign Automakers Flock to Poland." *Christian Science Monitor,* October 25, p. 3.

Pines, M. 1981. "The Civilization of Genie." *Psychology Today* 15(September):28–34.

Platt, K. 1998. " 'Titanic' Cultural Invasion Hits China." *Christian Science Monitor,* April 20, p. 1, and 6.

Platt, K. 1998. "China Prepares to Issue 4 Million Pink Slips." *Christian Science Monitor,* March 31.

Plotkin, H. 1991. "Capitalism." *The New Grolier Electronic Encyclopedia.* Danbury, CT: Grolier Electronic Publishing.

"A Poll Jay Leno Would Love." 1998. *Christian Science Monitor,* September 8.

Pollack, A. 1997. "Dioxin Rates Give Japan Doubt on Trash-Burning." *New York Times,* April 21.

Pollard, K. M. 1999. "Outlook Mixed for America'a Children." *Population Today* (October):3–4.

Pope, H. 1999. "Kurdish Dilemma Is Far from over for U.S., Turkey." *Wall Street Journal,* February 25.

Popenoe, D. 1988. *Disturbing the Nest Family Change and Decline in Modern Societies.* New York: Aldine De Gruyter.

———. 1991. "Family Decline in the Swedish Welfare State." *Public Interest* 101 (Winter): 65–77.

———. 1992. "Family Decline: A Rejoinder." *Public Interest* Fall (109):117–122.

Popline, 1990. "India's Program Stresses Role of Women." March—April, p. 3.

Population Action International. 1992. *International Human Suffering Index.* Washington, DC: Population Action International.

Population Crisis Committee. 1989. "Population Pressures—Threat to Democracy." Washington, DC: Population Crisis Committee.

Population Institute. 1988. "A Continent in Crisis—Building a Future for Africa in the 21st Century." Report to the 101st Congress, pp. 23–24. Special report from the series *Toward the 21st Century.*

Population Reference Bureau. 1986. *Population in Perspective: Regional Views.* Washington, DC: Population Reference Bureau.

Portes, A. 1976. "On the Sociology of Development, Theories and Issues." *American Journal of Sociology* (July):55–85.

Porubcansky, M. J. 1993. "Czechs, Slovaks Part as Friends After a Marriage Lasting 74 Years." *San Diego Union-Tribune,* January 1.

Post, T. 1993. "A Pattern of Rape." *Newsweek* (January 4):32–36.

Postel, S. 1994. "Carrying Capacity: Earth's Bottom Line," in L. Starke, ed. *State of the World 1994.* New York: W. W. Norton, pp. 3–21.

———. 1996. *Dividing the Waters: Food Security, Ecosystem Health, and the New Politics of Scarcity.* Worldwatch Paper 132. Washington, DC: Worldwatch Institute.

Power, C. 1998. "The New Islam." *Newsweek,* March 18.

Power, J. 1992. "Forgotten Women." *San Diego Union-Tribune,* February 18.

Pratap, A. 1996. "Who are the Taliban of Afghanistan?" *CNN Interactive World News,* October 5. < http://www.cnn.com/WORLD/96/10/05/taleban/ > Accessed August 16, 1999.

Pratt, W. 1984. *Understanding U.S. Fertility: Findings from the National Survey of Family Growth, Cycle III.* Washington, DC: Population Reference Bureau.

Press, R. M. 1994. "U. N. Investigator Cites Preplanned Genocide in Rwanda." *Christian Science Monitor,* July 1.

Preston, S. H. 1986. "The Decline of Fertility in Non-European Countries." *Population and Development Review* 12:26–47.

Prince, C. J. 1998. "After Some Success, a New Effort to Broaden Women's Rights." *Christian Science Monitor,* March 13.

Progress. 1989. *Social Policy* (Fall): 75–76.

Prusher, I. R. 1998a. "Water Lies At Heart Of Mideast Land Fight." *Christian Science Monitor,* April 17.

———. 1998b. "Inside an African Famine." *Christian Science Monitor* (October 9):7–9.

———. 1998c. "Spotlight on Killing of Women for 'Family Honor.' " *Christian Science Monitor,* October 23.

Pugh, T. 1999. "Police Forces Heed Public's Call for Reform." *San Diego Union-Tribune,* April 10.

Purvis, A. 1997. "The Global Epidemic." *Time* (January 6):76–78.

Puryear, J. M. 1997. *Education in Latin America: Problems and Challenges.* Partnership for Educational Revitalization in the Americas, No. 7, < http://www.iadialog.org/preal7en.html > Accessed 1999 September 3.

Qena, N. 1999. "Burying The Hatchet?" *Balkan Crisis Reports,* August 11.

Queen, S., R. W. Habenstein, and J. S. Quadagno. 1985. *The Family in Various Cultures.* New York: Harper & Row.

Quinney, R. 1970. *The Social Reality of Crime.* Boston: Little, Brown.

———. 1977. *Class State and Crime—On the Theory and Practice of Criminal Justice.* New York: McKay.

Radosevich, L. 1998. "Zero In on Europe." *InfoWorld* (July 13):1–3.

———. 1998c. "Russia's Robber Barons." *Washington Post National Weekly,* January 12, p. 15.

———. 1998b. "Russia's Industrial Black Hole." *Washington Post National Weekly,* December 15–22, p. 14.

Ramo, J. C., H. Beech, and F. Gibney. 1998. "When Cultures Collide." *Time* (August 8):56–58.

Rangarajan, A., and P. Gleason. 1998. "Young Unwed Fathers of AFDC Children: Do They Provide Support?" *Demography* (May):175–186.

Rangel, C. 1989. "Imperialism Does Not Cause Third World Poverty," in J. Rohr, ed. *The Third World—Opposing View Points.* San Diego, CA: Greenhaven Press, pp. 25–31.

Ransdell, E. 1995. "The World's Most Dangerous Country." *U.S. News & World Report* (August 21):44.

Raschke, H. J. 1988. "Divorce," in M. B. Sussman and S. K. Steinmetz, eds. *Handbook of Marriage and the Family.* New York: Plenum Press, pp. 597–615.

Rattner, S. 1995. "GOP Ignores Income Inequality." *Wall Street Journal,* May 23.

"Reaching Out, If He Can." 1998. *Economist* (August 8):41.

Rebeck, G. 1990. "Gay Families Begin to Win Recognition." *Utne Reader* (September—October): 34.

Reckless, W. C. 1967. *The Crime Problem.* New York: Meredith.

"Resentment Mounts in Brazil Over Severe Economic Reforms" (1998) *San Diego Union-Tribune, November 2,* p. A11.

Rezende, F. 1998. "The Brazilian Economy: Recent Developments and Future Prospects." *International Affairs* 732(3):563–575.

Rhode, C. 1992. "Unceasing Abuses: Human Rights Crimes Go Unpunished in Mexico." *Human Rights Watch Quarterly Newsletter* (Winter):6–7.

Rich, J. L. 1999. "Brazil's 'Street Children' Suffer Still." MSNBC, June 23.

Richardson, L. 1988. *The Dynamics of Sex and Gender. A Sociological Perspective,* 3rd ed. New York: Harper & Row.

Richburg, K. B. 1997. *Out of America.* New York: Basic Books.

Ricklefs, R. 1998. "Canada Fights to Fend off American Tastes and Tunes." *Wall Street Journal,* September 24.

Riesman, D. 1961. *The Lonely Crowd.* New Haven, CT: Yale University Press.

Ritzer, G. 1996. *The McDonaldization of Society.* Revised Edition. Thousand Oaks, CA: Pine Forge Press.

Robberson, T. 1995c. "Another Kind of Uprising in Chiapas." *Washington Post National Weekly Edition,* October 2–8.

Robbins, C. A., with R. Knight, D. Stanglin, J. Impoco, and S. V. Lawrence. 1992–1993. "From Russia to South Africa, Democracy Fights an Uphill Battle." *U.S. News & World Report,* December 28—January 4.

Robbins, T. 1976. In Thomas Robbins et al., eds. "The Last Civil Religion: Reverend Moon and the Unification Church." *Sociological Analysis* 37(2): 111–125.

Roberts, S. V., with K. Hetter, T. Gest, J. Popkin, D. McGraw, and J. Eddings. 1995. "The Religious Right: Church Meets State." *U.S. News & World Report* (April 24):26–30.

Robertson, R. 1989. "Globalization, Politics, and Religion," in J. A. Beckford and T. Luckman, eds. *The Changing Face of Religion.* Newbury Park, CA: Sage.

Robinson, P. H. 1994. "A Failure of Moral Leadership?" *The Public Interest* (Fall):40–48.

Rodman, H. 1963. "The Lower Class Value Stretch." *Social Forces* 42(2):205–215.

Rodriguez, C. 1992. "Mexico's Most Polluted City." *Los Angeles Times,* April 21.

Roethlisberger, F. J., and W. J. Dickson. 1964, original 1939. *Management and the Worker.* Cambridge, MA: Harvard University Press.

Rogers, A. B. 1988. "Does Biology Constrain Culture?" *American Anthropologist* 90 (December):819–831.

Rohde, D. 1994a. "Developing Nations Win More Investment." *Christian Science Monitor,* August 31, p. 4.

———. 1994b. "More Violence Against Kids by Parents Than Strangers." *Christian Science Monitor,* November 9, p. 3.

———. 1995. "A New Curtain Rises Behind Ex-Iron Curtain." *Christian Science Monitor,* February 27, p. 6.

Rohlen, T. P. 1986. " 'Spiritual Education' in a Japanese Bank," in T. S. Lebra and W. P. Lebra, eds. *Japanese Culture and Behavior.* Honolulu: University of Hawaii Press, pp. 307–335.

Roos, P. A. 1985. *Gender & Work: A Comparative Analysis of Industrial Societies.* Albany: State University of New York Press.

Roos, P. A., and B. F. Reskin. 1984. "Institutional Factors Contributing to Sex Segregation in the Workplace," in B. F. Reskin, ed. *Sex Segregation in the Workplace: Trends, Explanations, Remedies.* Washington, DC: National Academy Press, pp. 235–260.

Rose, J. J. 1993. "Divorce Rate Is Higher for Low Income." *San Diego Union-Tribune,* January 16, p. A10.

Rose, R. 1997. "Evaluating Election Turnout." Stockholm: International IDEA.

Rose, S. J. 1992. *Social Stratification in the United States: The American Profile Poster Revised and Expanded.* New York: New Press.

Rosenberg, H. 1991. "Channel 7 Doesn't Hear the Voices of Dissent." *Los Angeles Times,* February 26.

Rosenthal, E. 1998. "China Officially Lifts Filter on Staggering Pollution Data." *New York Times,* June 14.

Rosenthal, M. 1994. "Single Mothers in Sweden: Work and Welfare in the Welfare State." *Social Work* Vol 39(3):270–278.

Ross, E. A. 1922. *The Social Trend.* New York: Century.

Rossi, A. 1984. "Gender and Parenthood." *American Sociological Review* 49:1–19.

Rossides, D. W. 1990. *Comparative Societies: Social Types and Their Interrelations.* Englewood Cliffs, NJ: Prentice Hall.

Rotella, S. 1994. "Both Sides of the Mexico Drug Wars Adore Stolen 4´4s." *Los Angeles Times,* May 22, p. A1.

Rozen, L. 1999. "Minority At Risk." *Balkan Crisis Reports,* August 13.

Rubin, B. A. 1996. "Afghanistan: The Forgotten Crisis." WRITENET Country Papers, February. < http://enterprise. aacc.cc.md.us/~ haq/Txt.crisis.html > Accessed August 21, 1999.

Rudd, D. M. 1989. "The Prevalence of Suicidal Ideation Among College Students." *Suicide and Life Threatening Behavior* 19(2)(Summer):173–183.

Rudo, Z. H., and D. S. Powell. 1998. "The Effects of Violence in the Home on Children's Emotional, Behavioral, and Social Functioning: A Review of the Literature." *Journal of Emotions and Behavioral Disorders* (Summer):94–103.

Rundle, R. H. 1998. "HMOs Brace Themselves for 'Avalanche' of New Laws." *Wall Street Journal,* February 20, p. B4.

Rusher, W. A. 1993. "The Shadow of Ross Perot Still Chases President Clinton." *San Diego Union-Tribune,* February 21.

Russell, C., and M. Ambry. 1993. *Official Guide to American Incomes.* Ithaca, NY: New Strategist Publications.

Russell, J. W. 1994. *After the Fifth Sun: Class and Race in North America.* Englewood Cliffs, NJ: Prentice Hall.

"RVP Regional Updates." 1998. *Journal of Property Management* (January/February):11–19.

Ryan, T. 1993. "Indian Crusader Seeks to Halt Child Slavery." *Far Eastern Economic Review* (July 8):62.

Sachs, A. 1993. "AIDS Orphans: Africa's Lost Generation." *World Watch* (September—October):10–11.

Sachs, S., G. Palumbo, and R. Ross. 1987. "The Cold City: The Winter of Discontent?" in G. Gappert, ed. *The Future of Winter Cities.* Beverly Hills, CA: Sage, pp. 13–34.

Sacirbey, 0. 1998a. "German Women Create Their Jobs By Starting Their Own Businesses." *Christian Science Monitor,* March 13.

———. 1998b. "German Green Party Meets Values Shock." *Christian Science Monitor,* August 14.

Salholz, E. 1987. "Do Colleges Set Asian Quotas?" *Newsweek* 109(February 9):60.

Salholz, E., E. Clift, K. Springer, and P. Johnson. 1990. "Women Under Assault." *Newsweek* (July 16): 23–24.

Samuelson, R. J. 1998. "The Global Economy's Next Threat." *San Diego Union-Tribune,* November 19, p. B12.

San Diego Tribune. 1991. "Zaire Capital on Brink of AIDS Disaster." November 4.

San Diego Union-Tribune. 1992a. "World Grows by 97 Million People a Year." April 30.

———. 1992b. "Next Century Could See One-Fifth World Infected, Says Expert." December 16.

San Diego Union. 1990a. "Rich Grew Richer in '80s, but Most Americans Just Treaded Water." January 11.

———. 1990b. "Babies in Womb Learn Language, Researcher Says." August 13.

Sanchez, R. 1998. "Cracking Down on Campus Drinking." *Washington Post National Weekly Edition,* May 18, p. 29.

Sanchez, T. 1994/1995. "Apartheid in Americas." *CrossRoads* (December/January).

Sanchez-Klein, J. 1998. "Single Currency to Drive European Commerce." *InfoWorld* (July 27):56.

Sanders, S. 1989. *Mexico—Chaos on Our Doorstep.* Lantham, NY: Madison Books.

Sanders, W. 1983. *Criminology.* Reading, MA: Addison-Wesley.

———. 1994. *Gangbangs and Drive-bys: Grounded Culture and Juvenile Gang Violence.* New York: Aldine de Gruyter.

Santoro, L. 1998. "Echo of 1994 Genocide: Rwanda Slayings Persist." *Christian Science Monitor,* March 3.

———. 1999. "Congo: Playing the Ethnic Card." *Christian Science Monitor,* January 4.

Satchell, M. 1994. "Deadly Trade in Toxics." *U.S. News & World Report (March 7).*

Saunders, D. G. 1986. "When Battered Women Use Violence: Husband Abuse or Self Defense?" *Violence and Victims* 1:47–60.

Savage, D. G. 1990. "Asians, Latinos Surge in U.S. Growth Rates." *Los Angeles Times,* March 2.

Savitz, L. D. 1972. "Introduction to the Reprint Edition," in G. Lombroso-Ferrero, ed. *Lombroso's Criminal Man.* Montclair, NY: Patterson Smith.

Schaefer, R. T. 1990. *Racial and Ethnic Groups,* 4th ed. Glenview, IL: Scott, Foresman/Little, Brown Higher Education.

Schell, O. 1997. "The Coming of Mao Zedong Chic." *Newsweek* 129(20):42–43.

Scheper-Hughes, N. and D. Hoffman. 1994a. "Kids Out of Place (Part 1). *NACLA Report on the Americas,* May/June.

———. 1994b. "Kids Out of Place (Part 2). *NACLA Report on the Americas,* May/June.

Schlesinger, J. M. 1998. "Rise in Inequality of Wealth in 1980s Slowed in Early 1990s, IRS Study Shows." *Wall Street Journal,* March 27.

Schmidt, S. 1999. "Small Town's Horror Hard to Forget." *San Diego Union-Tribune,* May 23.

Schmit, J. 1999. "Japan Shifts to Merit Pay." *USA Today,* July 23, p. 5B.

Schreiber, M. 1995. "A Nation Without Guns," in M. I. White and S. Barnet, eds. *Comparing Cultures—Readings on Contemporary Japan for American Writers.* Boston: Bedford Books of St. Martin's Press, pp. 386–392.

Schroeder, S. A. and M. P. Beachler. 1995. "Physician Shortage in Rural America." *Lancet* (April):1001–1002.

Scott, D. C. 1992a. "Mexico City Police Strike over Corruption Ranks." *Christian Science Monitor,* March 16.

——. 1992b. "Mexico's Public-Works Program Bolsters President as It Aids the Poor." *Christian Science Monitor,* September 16.

——. 1992c. "Mexican Opposition Denounces Politics of New School Texts." *Christian Science Monitor,* September 21.

——. 1992d. "Mexico Finalizes Restoration of Ties to Catholic Church." *Christian Science Monitor,* September 28.

——. 1993. "Public Anger Spurs Mexican Anti-Drug Efforts." *Christian Science Monitor,* June 10.

——. 1995. "Free Trade Winners Praise the Pact, But Will Kudos Last?" *Christian Science Monitor,* January 3.

Scott, J. 1992. "Why Do You Act That Way?" *Los Angeles Times,* April 18.

Scott, W. R. 1995. *Organizations: Rational, Natural, and Open Systems,* 3rd ed. Englewood Cliffs, NJ: Prentice Hall.

Segelken, R. 1998. "40% of World Deaths Caused by Environmental Pollution." < http://www.ecomall.com/greenshopping/cornell.htm > Accessed August 2, 1999.

Seid, R. 1993. "Human Side of NAFTA Helps Mexico." *San Diego Union-Tribune,* January 10.

Seidman, S., and D. G. Wagner. 1992. *Postmodernism and Social Theory.* Oxford: Blackwell.

Seligman, J. 1993. "Husbands No, Babies Yes." *Newsweek* (July 26):53.

Sender, H. 1998. "The Devil to Pay," in *Crash of '97,* Dan Biers, ed. Hong Kong: Review.

Senser, R. A. 1994. "The Crime of Child Slavery—Child Labor in South Asia." *Current* (March—April):29–34.

Serulnikov, S. 1994. "When Looting Becomes a Right—Urban Poverty and Food Riots in Argentina." *Latin American Perspectives* (21, Summer):69–89.

Seward, D. 1999. "Death Knell for Some Currency Exchangers." *Buffalo News,* January 6, p. B7.

Sewell, W. H., and V. P. Shah. 1967. "Socioeconomic Status, Intelligence, and the Attainment of Higher Education." *Sociology of Education* 40(Winter):1–23.

Shannon, T. R. 1989. *Urban Problems in Sociological Perspective.* Prospect Heights, IL: Waveland Press.

Shannon, T. R., N. Kleniewski, and W. M. Cross. 1997. *Urban Problems in Sociological Perspective* Inc. Prospect Heights, IL: Waveland Press.

Shapiro, J. P., R. L. Dorman, C. J. Welker, and J. B. Cough. 1998. "Youth Attitudes Towards Guns and Violence: Relations With Sex, Age, Ethnic Group, and Firearm Exposure." *Journal of Clinical Child Psychology* (March):98–106.

Shapiro, L. 1990. "Guns and Dolls." *Newsweek* (May 28):56–65.

Sharpe, A. 1997. "The Operation was a Success; the Bill was Quite a Mess." *Wall Street Journal,* September 17, p. 1.

Shaw, D. 1990. "Asian-Americans Chafe Against Stereotype of 'Model Citizen.'" *Los Angeles Times,* December 11.

Shelley, L. 1981. *Crime and Modernization—The Impact of Industrialization and Urbanization.* Carbondale: Southern Illinois University Press.

Shepard, J. M. 1987. *Sociology.* St. Paul, MN: West.

Sheppard, D. 1999. "Strategies to Reduce Gun Violence." OJJDP Fact Sheet, February, No. 93. U.S. Department of Justice, Washington, DC: U.S. Government Printing Office.

Sherrill, R. 1997. "A Year in Corporate Crime." *Nation,* February 7, pp. 11–17.

Shultz, S. 1998. "AIDS: No More Silver Bullet." *U.S. News and World Report,* July 13, pp. 20–21.

Shur, E. M. 1979. *Interpreting Deviance—A Sociological Introduction.* New York: Harper & Row.

Sidhva, S. 1998. "India: Back to Slow Growth." *Far Eastern Economic Review* (June 18):67.

Siegel, L. 1998. *Criminology.* St. Paul: West.

Siegel, L. J. 1998. *Criminology.* Belmont, CA: West Wadsworth Publishing.

Silva, M. 1999. "Bush Signature Makes Florida First with Statewide School Voucher Plan." *Miami Herald,* June 22.

Silver, M., and D. Geller. 1978. "On the Irrelevance of Evil: The Organization and Individual Action." *Journal of Social Issues* 34:125–136.

Simmel, G. 1950, original 1908. *The Sociology of Georg Simmel.* Kurt Wolff, ed. Glencoe, IL: Free Press.

Simon, J. 1994. *The Terrorist Trap: America's Experience with Terrorism.* Bloomington, IN: Indiana University Press.

Simpson, G. E., and J. M. Yinger. 1985. *Racial and Cultural Minorities: An Analysis of Prejudice and Discrimination,* 5th ed. New York: Plenum Press.

Singer, H. 1992. "International Aid Can Reduce Famine," in C. Wekesser and C. Pierce, eds. *Africa: Opposing Viewpoints.* San Diego: Greenhaven Press, pp. 100–107.

Sissell, K. 1998a. "Sustainable Development: Can Industry Make It Pay?" *Chemical Week,* May 13, p. 56.

——. 1998b. "Mexico's Economy Shows Steady Growth." *Chemical Week* (June 24):S3–S4.

Sivard, R. 1985. *Women—A World Survey.* Washington, DC: World Priorities.

——. 1993. *World Military and Social Expenditures.* Washington, DC: World Priorities.

Sizer, T. R. 1984. *Horace's Compromise: The Dilemma of the American High School.* Boston: Houghton Mifflin.

——. 1992. "What's Missing." *World Monitor* (November): 20–27.

Slutske, W., A. Heath, S. Dinwiddle, P. Madden, K. Bucholz, M. Dune, D. Statham, and N. Martin. 1997. "Modeling Genetic and Environmental Influences in the Etiology of Conduct Disorder: A Study of 2,683 Twin Pairs." *Journal of Abnormal Psychology* 106(2):266–279.

Smelser, N. 1973. "Toward a Theory of Modernization," in A. Etzioni and E. Etzioni-Halvey, eds. *Social Change—Sources, Patterns and Consequences.* New York: Basic Books, pp. 268–284.

Smith, B. C. 1998. "Globalization and the Independent Company." *Automotive Manufacturing and Production* (July):14–15.

Smith, C. 1990. "Officeless Ladies." *Far Eastern Economic Review* 147(7, February 15):12–13.

Smith, C., and C. A. Visher. 1980. "Sex and Involvement in Deviance/Crime: A Quantitative Review of the Literature." *American Sociological Review* 45:691–701.

Smith, D. E. 1971. *Religion, Politics, and Change in the Third World.* New York: Free Press.

Smith, F. 1997. "A Synthetic Framework and a Heuristic for Integrating Multiple Perspectives on Sustainability," in F. Smith, ed. *Environmental Sustainability: Practical and Global Implications.* Boca Raton, FL: St. Lucie Press.

Smith, G. 1992. "International Aid Worsens Famines," in C. Wekesser and C. Pierce, eds. *Africa: Opposing Viewpoints.* San Diego: Greenhaven Press, pp. 108–115.

Smith, G., and E. Malkin. 1998a. "Feeling the Squeeze in Mexico." *Business Week* (September 21):34–35.

——. 1998b. "Mexican Makeover." *Business Week* (December 21):50–52.

Sneider, D. 1995. "Ethnic Conflict in Ex-Soviet Region Keeps Riches Out of Reach." *Christian Science Monitor,* June 1.

Snyder, T. 1999. *Digest of Education Statistics, 1998.* Washington, DC: U.S. Department of Education, National Center for Education Statistics.

So, A. Y. 1990. *Social Change and Development.* Newbury Park, CA: Sage.

Sobieraj, S. 1998. "Clinton Aims to Cure Inbalance in Health Care." *San Diego Union-Tribune,* February 22, p. A2.

"A Social Profile." 1998. *Economist,* March 28, pp. 27–28.

Society for Threatened Peoples. 1998. "Kosovo: War, Mass Expulsion, Deportation, Massacre." Report. August.

Soldo, B. I., and E. M. Agree. 1988. *America's Elderly.* Washington, DC: Population Reference Bureau.

Sorenson, S. B. 1991. "Suicide Among the Elderly: Issues Facing Public Health." *American Journal of Public Health* 81(9): 1109–1110.

Soroka, G. 1999. Conversation with Gabrielle Soroka, Vice President for Governmental Affairs, Waste Management, Inc. August 13.

Soros, G. 1998. "The Crisis of Global Capitalism." *Newsweek* (December 7):78–82.

South, S. J. and K. D. Crowder. 1997. "Residential Mobility Between Cities and Suburbs: Race, Suburbanization, and Back-to-the-City Moves." *Demography* (November):525–538.

———. 1998. *Exploring Social Change: America and the World* Upper Saddle River, NJ: Prentice Hall.

Southern Poverty Law Center. 1999a. "The Toll of Hate." *Intelligence Report,* Issue 93 (Winter).

———. 1999b. "The Year in Hate." *Intelligence Report,* Issue 93 (Winter).

Sowell, T. 1983. "Second Thoughts About the Third World." *Harpers* (November):34–42.

Spaeth, A. 1996. "Peace That Terrifies." *Time International Magazine,* 148(16).

Spakes, P. 1992. "National Family Policy: Sweden Versus the United States." *Affilia: Journal of Women and Social Work* 7(1):44–60.

Sparrow, M. K. 1996. *License to Steal: Why Fraud Plagues America's Health Care System.* Boulder, CO: Westview Press.

Spates, J., and J. Macionis. 1987. *Sociology of Cities.* New York: St. Martin's Press.

"Speaking of Water." 1993. *Los Angeles Times,* December 4.

Spence, J. A. 1990. *The Search for Modern China.* New York: W. W. Norton.

Spicer, K. 1995. "A Canadian Agenda for Children's Television." Ottawa: CRTC Public Affairs.

Spradley, J. P., and D. W. McCurdy. 1989. *Anthropology—The Cultural Perspective.* Prospect Heights, IL: Waveland Press.

Sprey, J. 1966. "Family Disorganization: Toward a Conceptual Clarification." *Journal of Marriage and the Family* 28:398–406.

———, 1969. "The Family as a System of Conflict." *Journal of Marriage and the Family* 31:699–706.

Stanley, A. 1994b, "From Repression to Respect, Russian Church in Comeback." *New York Times,* October 3.

Starr, P. 1994. *The Logic of Health Care Reform.* New York: Whittle Books in Association with Penguin Books.

"Statistical Projections/Trends." 2000. *Centers for Disease Control http://www.cdgov/nchstp/hiv_aids/hivinfo/vfax/260210.htm*

Steele, C. M. 1992. "Race and the Schooling of Black Americans." *Atlantic Monthly* (April):68–78.

Steffensmeier, D., and E. Allan. 1995. "Criminal Behavior: Gender And Age," in J. P. Sheley, ed. *Criminology: A Contemporary Handbook.* Belmont CA: Wadsworth.

Stegman, M. A., and M. A. Turner. 1996. "The Future of Urban America in the Global Economy." *Journal of the American Planning Association* (Spring):157–164.

Steinzor, N. 1994. "The Baby Express." *ZPG Reporter* (August):1–4.

Stevens, W. K. 1997. "Kyoto Accord Only a Start in War Against Global Warming." *San Diego Union-Tribune,* June 7.

Stohr, K. 1998. " 'One Nation' Divides Australia." *Christian Science Monitor,* July 23.

"Stop Gender Apartheid in Afghanistan." 1999. The Feminist Majority Foundation Online. < http://www.feminist.org/afghan/facts.html > Accessed August 16, 1999.

Stork's Return. 1991. *Economist* April 13, p. 47.

Strauss, M. A., and R. Gelles. 1990. "How Violent Are American Families? Estimates from the National Family Violence Resurvey and Other Studies," in M. A. Strauss and R. J. Gelles, eds. *Physical Violence in American Families: Risk Factors and Adaptations to Violence in 8,145 Families.* New Brunswick, NJ: Transaction.

Strauss, M. A., and R. J. Gelles. 1986. "Societal Change and Change in Family Violence from 1975 to 1985 as Revealed in Two National Surveys." *Journal of Marriage and the Family* (August):465–479.

Strauss, M. A., R. J. Gelles, and S. K. Steinmetz. (1980). *Behind Closed Doors.* Garden City, NY: Anchor Books, Doubleday.

Stromquist, N. P. 1996. *Gender and Democracy in Education in Latin Latin America.* New York: Council on Foreign Relations Working Group on Educational Reform.

"Suicide Among Black Youths: United States, 1980–1995" 1998. *Journal of the American Medical Association* (May 13):279.

Sumner, W. G. 1883. *What Social Classes Owe to Each Other.* New York: Harper and Brothers.

———. 1960, original 1906. *Folkways.* New York: New American Library.

Superville, D. 1995. "The Glass Ceiling Report: Women, Minorities Still Lack Top Jobs." *San Diego Union-Tribune,* March 16.

"Supreme Court Rules CDA Unconstitutional." 1997. Citizens Internet Empowerment Coalition, June 26. < http://www.ciec.org/ > Accessed September 4, 1999.

Suro, R. 1994. "American Success Stories." *Washington Post National Weekly Edition,* April 25—May 1.

Sutherland, E. H., and D. R. Cressey. 1970. *Criminology.* Philadelphia: Lippincott.

Sykes, G. M., and D. Matza. 1957. "Techniques of Neutralization: A Theory of Delinquency." *American Sociological Review* 22:664–670.

Szulc, T. 1982. "What Indira Gandhi Wants You to Know." *Parade* (July 25):4–6.

Szymanski, A. 1981. *The Logic of Imperialism.* New York: Praeger.

Tönnies, F. 1963, original 1887. *Community and Society.* New York: Harper & Row.

"Taiwan and Korea—Two Paths to Prosperity." 1990. *Economist* (July 14):19–22.

"Taliban defends its policies toward women." 1998. *The Minnesota Daily,* March 9.

"Taliban Impose New Roles on Women." 1998. *Associated Press* < http://www.rawa.org/bus.htm > Accessed August 16, 1999.

"The Taliban's War on Women: A Health and Human Rights Crisis in Afghanistan. Executive Summary." 1998. Boston: Physicians for Human Rights.

Tamburri, R. 1998a. "Canada Considers New Stand Against American Culture." *Wall Street Journal,* February 4.

———. 1998b. "Canadians Clash Over Cost of Diversity." *Wall Street Journal,* April 1.

Tannenbaum, F. 1938. *Crime and the Community.* New York: Ginn.

Tasker, P. 1987. *The Japanese.* New York: Truman Talley Books.

Tavares, R. 1995. "Land and Democracy: Reconsidering the Agrarian Question." *NACLA Report on the Americas,* May/June.

Teachman, J. D. 1987. "Family Background, Educational Resources, and Educational Attainment." *American Sociological Review* 52:548–557.

Tefft, S. 1994. "Islam's Radical Twist in Indonesia." *Christian Science Monitor,* April 5, p. 4a.

Thanos, P. 1998. "Israel Faces New Economy and Challenges at 50." *Business America* (September):15–17.

Theodorson, G. A., and A. Theodorson. 1969. *A Modern Dictionary of Sociology.* New York: Barnes & Noble.

"They're Not Writing Either." 1999. *San Diego Union-Tribune,* April 19.

Thollander, J. 1997. "Public Education and the Secular Purposes of the Ten Commandments." *NeoPolitique* (December).

Thomas, P. 1994. "Getting to the Bottom Line of Crime." *Washington Post National Review Edition,* July 18–24, p. 31.

Thomas, R. 1992. "Please, Don't Bother Me." *Newsweek* (July 20):46–47.

Thomas, W. I. 1967, original 1923. *The Unadjusted Girl.* New York: Harper & Row.

Thomas, W. I., with D. Swaine Thomas. 1928. *The Child in America.* New York: Knopf.

Thompson, D. 1999. "Capitol Hill Meltdown." *Time,* (August 9).

Thompson, J. J. 1998. "Plugging the Kegs." *U.S. News & World Report* (January 26):63–67.

Thomspon, M., J. Graff, and S. C. Gwynne. 1997. "Fatal Neglect." *Time* (October 27):34–38.

Thornton, A. 1985. "Changing Attitudes Toward Separation and Divorce: Causes and Consequences." *American Journal of So-*

ciology 90:856–872.

"3,000 Immigrants Each Day." 1994. *Popline* (September—October):2–4.

"Threats to Earth, Air and Water." 1992. *Washington Spectator,* 18(19).

"3 Acquitted of Killing Brazilian Street Children." 1996. *CNN World News Story Page,* December 10.

Tittle, C. R., W. J. Villemez, and D. A. Smith. 1978. "The Myth of Social Class and Criminality: An Empirical Assessment of the Empirical Evidence." *American Sociological Review* 43: 643–656.

Tjaden, P., and N. Thoennes 1998. "Stalking in America: Findings from the National Violence Against Women Survey." *National Institute of Justice Centers for Disease Control and Prevention.* Research brief, April.

"Tobacco's Toll on America." 1989. New York: American Lung Association.

Tobin, J. J., D. Y. H. Wu, and D. H. Davidson. 1989. "How Three Key Countries Shape Their Children." *World Monitor* (April):36–45.

Toch, T., with B. Wagner, K. Glastris, N. Linnon, M. Daniel, J. Sieder, M. Jennings, and M. Tharp. 1993. "The Perfect School." *U.S. News & World Report* (January 11):46–61.

Todaro, M. P., and J. Stilkind. 1981. *City Bias and Rural Neglect: The Dilemma of Urban Development.* New York: Population Council.

Toffler, A. 1990. "Toffler's Next Shock." *World Monitor* (November):33–44.

Tong, L. 1998. "Consumerism Sweeps the Mainland." *Marketing Management* (Winter):32–35.

"Too Busy To Hate." 1997. *Intelligence Report: The Face of Terrorism* (Winter) Issue 47. A Project of the Southern Poverty Law Center, pp. 17–18.

"Trends in the HIV and AIDS Epidemic, 1998." 1998. *Centers for Disease Control http://www.cdcnpin.org/geneva98/trends/start/htm*

Trost, J. 1996. "Family Studies in Sweden." *Marriage and Family Review* 23(3/4):723–744.

Trout, M. E. 1994. "The Price of Health Care Reform: Two Sides of the Same Story." *UCSD Perspective* (4):11–13.

Tuchman, G. 1978. *Making News: A Study in the Construction of Reality.* New York: Free Press.

Tucker, N. 1999. "Court Ruling Wipes Out Women's Rights in Zimbabwe." *San Diego Union-Tribune,* April 14.

Tudge, C. 1997. "Reltive Danger." *Natural History* (September):28–31.

Tumin, M. M. 1953a. "Some Principles of Stratification: A Critical Analysis." *American Sociological Review* 18(4):387–394.

———. 1953b. "Reply to Kingsley Davis." *American Sociological Review* 18(6):672–673.

———. 1985. *Social Stratification: The Forms and Functions of Inequality,* 2nd ed. Englewood Cliffs, NJ: Prentice Hall.

Turner, J. H. 1997. *The Institutional Order: Economy, Kinship, Religion, Polity, Law, and Education in Evolutionary and Comparative Perspective.* New York: Addison Wesley Longman.

Turner, J. H., and A. Maryanski. 1979. *Functionalism.* Menlo Park, CA: Benjamin/Cummings.

Tyson, A. S. 1994. "Asian Americans Spurn Image as Model Minority." *Christian Science Monitor,* August 26.

U.N. Development Program 1995. *Human Development Report 1995.* New York: Oxford University Press.

———. 1998. *Human Development Report 1998.* New York: Oxford University Press.

U.S. Agency of International Development. 1992. "Western Aid Reforms Can Strengthen Africa's Economies," in C. Wekesser and C. Pierce, eds. San Diego: Greenhaven Press, pp. 116–122.

U.S. Bureau of the Census. 1998a. "Money Income in the United States: 1997." *Current Population Reports,* P60-200. Washington, DC: U.S. Government Printing Office.

———. 1998b. "Poverty in the United States: 1997." *Current Population Reports,* P60-201. Washington, DC: U.S. Government Printing Office.

———. 1998c. *Statistical Abstract of the United States: 1998.* Washington, DC: U.S. Government Printing Office.

———. 1999a. "Money Income in the United States: 1998." *Current Population Reports,* P60-206. Washington, DC: U.S. Government Printing Office.

———. 1999b. "Poverty in the United States: 1998." *Current Population Reports,* P60-207. Washington, DC: U.S. Government Printing Office.

U.S. Department of Justice 1992. "Drilling for Oil in Russia." December 7:54.

U.S. Department of State. 1998. "Background Notes: Brazil, March 1998."

U.S. Environmental Protection Agency. 1999. *1997 Toxics Release Inventory.* Washington, DC: U.S. Environmental Protection Agency.

"U.S. Leads World in Violent Crimes." 1991. *San Diego Union,* March 13, p. A12.

Udall, B. 1998. "The Lonely Polygamist." *Esquire* (February): 44–47.

Ueda, T. 1992a. "New Textbooks May Help Young Face up to Japan's Past." *Japan Times Weekly International Edition,* July 27—August 2.

Umberson, D., K. Anderson, J. Glick, and A. Shapiro. 1998. "Domestic Violence, Personal Control, and Gender." *Journal of Marriage and the Family* (May):442–452.

"U.N. Agencies Join Against FGM/FC." 1997. *Public Heath Reports* 113(1):6.

Universal Almanac 1993. "Switzerland." Kansas City: Andrews & McMeel, p. 464.

"The Unpunished Extermination of Teenagers and Children." 1998. *O Globo,* November 8.

Urquhart, J., and C. J. Chipello. 1998. "A Unilateral Quebec Secession Is Barred." *Wall Street Journal,* August 12, p. A12.

USA Today. 1993. "Health-Care Costs." January 5.

Useem, M. and J. Karabel. 1986. "Pathways to Corporate Management." *American Sociological Review* 51(2):184–200.

Utsunomiya, Y. 1992. "Agencies Fear Cocaine May Become the No. 1 Habit." *Japan Times Weekly International Edition,* November 4–10.

Van Kempen, R., and P. Marcuse. 1997. "A New Spatial Order in Cities?" *American Behavioral Scientist* (Nov/Dec):285–298.

Van Slambrouck, P. 1998. "America's Power Base Tilts Toward the Rockies." *Christian Science Monitor,* September 28, p. 1.

Vander Zanden, J. W. 1983. *American Minority Relations,* 4th ed. New York: Plenum Press.

Venkataraman, N. S. 1998. "India Faces Economic Aggression in 1998." *Chemical Business* (January):13–15.

Violence by Intimates. 1998. U.S. Department of Justice. Washington, DC: U.S. Government Printing Office.

Violent Relationships: Battering and Abuse Among Adults. 1997. Wylie, TX: Information Plus.

Vittachi, N. 1995. "Bad Taste." *Far Eastern Economic Review,* August 3, p. 34.

Vobejda, B. 1995. "The Known Factor in Rape." *Washington Post Weekly Review,* August 21–27, p. 37.

Voelker, R. 1997. "Battered Men." *Journal of the American Medical Association* (August 27):620.

Vujacic, V. 1995. "Serbian Nationalism, Slobodan Milosevic and the Origins of the Yugoslav War." *The Harriman Review* 8(4).

Wade, N. 1995. "Microbes into Infinity." *New York Times.* May 15.

Wakin, D. J. 1999. "Ethnic Albanian Leader Skips Inaugural Kosovo Council Meeting." *San Diego Union-Tribune,* July 19.

Walinsky, A. 1995. "The Crisis of Public Order." *Atlantic Monthly* (July):39–74.

Walker, R. 1998. " 'New Quebeckers' an Unseen Force." *Christian Science Monitor,* October 30.

Walker, S. L. 1993. "Mexico Addresses Smog with a Cover Up." *San Diego Union-Tribune,* February 5.

Walker, S. L. 1999. "Southern Exposure." *San Diego Union-Tribune,* September 5.

Walker, T. "Chinese Men Embrace Divorce." *World Press Review* (October 1993):40.

Wallace, C. P. 1994. "Asia's Tigers Flex Their Muscles." *Los Angeles Times,* May 28, p. A1.

———. 1994b. "Asians Power Up the Private Sector." *Los Angeles Times,* November 29, H2.

Wallerstein, I. 1996. "National Development and the World System at the End of the Cold War," in A. Inkles and M. Sasaki, eds. *Comparing Nations and Cultures—Readings in a Cross-Disciplinary Perspective.* Englewood Cliffs, NJ: Prentice Hall, pp. 484–497.

Wallerstein, J. S., and J. Lewis. 1998. "The Long-Term Impact of Divorce on Children." *Family and Conciliation Courts Review* (July):368–383.

Walsh, M. W. 1997. "The Nation with Too Much Cash." *Los Angeles Times,* October 9, p. A1.

Walsh, S. 1998. "Targeting the Future." *Washington Post National Weekly Review,* April 6, p. 29.

Walters, D. K. H. 1993. "Global Food Shortage Looms, Experts Say." *Los Angeles Times,* January 30.

Walters, L. S. 1994. "Goals 2000 Act Broadens Federal Role." *Christian Science Monitor,* April 11.

———. 1996. "Classroom Issues to Play Key Role in '96 Election." *Christian Science Monitor,* January 30.

Ward, D. A., T. J. Carter, and R. D. Perrin. 1994. *Social Deviance Being, Behaving, and Branding.* Boston: Allyn and Bacon.

Ward, D., and G. G. Kassebaum. 1965. *Women's Prison: Sex and Social Structure.* Chicago: Aldine.

Warner, W. L., and L. Srole. 1945. *The Social Systems of American Ethnic Groups.* New Haven, CT: Yale University Press.

Warren, D. 1991. "Education in the United States." *The Academic American Encyclopedia,* electronic version. Danbury, CT.: Grolier.

Warshaw, S. 1988a. *India Emerges.* Berkeley, CA: Diablo Press.

———. 1988b. *Japan Emerges.* Berkeley, CA: Diablo Press.

"Water's Scarcity in the Mideast and World." 1998. *Die Welt*/German Newspaper News Service, in *Christian Science Monitor,* April 17.

Watson, D. 1997. "Indigenous People and the Global Economy." *Current History* (November)389–391.

Watson, R., with M. G. Warner, R. Nordland, and K. Breslau. 1992. "Ethnic Cleansing." *Newsweek* (August 17):16–20.

Waud, R. N. 1980. *Economics.* New York: Harper & Row.

"We Are Witnessing a Transformation of Society and Civilization." 1997. *UNESCO Courier* (November):47–50.

Webb, E. J., D. T. Campbell, R. D. Schwartz, and L. Sechrest. 1966. *Unobtrusive Measures: Nonreactive Research in the Social Sciences.* Chicago: Rand McNally.

Weber, M. 1946, original 1919. "Bureaucracy," in H. H. Gerth and C. Wright Mills, eds. *From Max Weber: Essays in Sociology.* New York: Oxford University Press, pp. 196–244.

———. 1946. "Class, Status, Party," in H. H. Gerth and C. Wright Mills, eds. *From Max Weber: Essays in Sociology.* New York: Oxford University Press.

———. 1958, original 1904. *The Protestant Ethic and the Spirit of Capitalism.* New York: Scribner's.

———. 1978, original 1921. *Economy and Society.* G. Roth and C. Wittich, eds. Berkeley: University of California Press.

Weeks, J. R. 1999. *Population—An Introduction to Concepts and Issues, 7th ed.* Belmont, CA: Wadsworth.

Weiner, E. 1994. "Muslim Radicals and Police Hunt Feminist Bangladeshi Writer." *Christian Science Monitor,* July 26, p. 6.

Weinstein, J. 1991. "Urban Growth in India: Demographic and Sociocultural Propects." *Studies in Comparative International Development* 26(4):29–34.

Weinstein, M. M. 1998. "Unlike Russia, Poland Kept Clear of Economic Quagmire." *San Diego Union-Tribune,* October 9, p. A26.

Weir, F. 1998. "Despite it All, Russian Firms Do Well." *Christian Science Monitor,* December 3, p. 6.

Weis, L., ed. 1988. *Class, Race, and Gender in American Education.* Albany: State University of New York Press.

Weisberger, B. A. 1996. "What Makes A Marriage?" *American Heritage* (November):14–15.

"Welcome to Teacher Testing." 1998. *Washington Post National Weekly Edition,* July 20–27.

Welsh, B. W. W., and P. Butorin. 1990. *Dictionary of Development—Third World Economy, Environment, Society.* New York: Garland Publishing.

Wessel, D. 1998a. "Again, the Rich Get Richer, but This Time They Pay More Taxes." *Wall Street Journal,* April 2.

———. 1998b. "Who Will Teach Johnny to Read?" *Wall Street Journal,* November 9.

Westerman, M. 1989. "Death of the Frito Bandito." *American Demographics* (March):28–32.

Weston, D. M. 1999. "Bill Gates' $90 Billion Tops World's Working Rich." *San Diego Union-Tribune,* June 21.

Wheeler, D. L. 1995. "A Growing Number of Scientists Reject the Concept of Race." *Chronicle of Higher Education,* February 17.

White, J. S. 1998. "How Provider Fraud Flattens Corporate Profits." *Business and Health* (March):28–35.

Whiting, R. 1992. "Japan's Version of Hardball." *San Diego Union-Tribune,* October 8.

"Whose Language Is It?" 1996. *ABA Journal* (November):44.

"Why Do Serbs Care?" < http://www.zoran.net/afp/text/background/why_do_serbs_care.htm > Accessed August 24, 1999.

Whyte, W. 1988. *City. Rediscovering the Center.* New York: Doubleday.

Wickman, P. M. 1974. "Social Norms," in *Encyclopedia of Sociology.* Guilford, CT: Dushkin Publishing Group, p. 199.

Wienk, R. E., C. E. Reid, J. C. Simonson, and F. J. Eggers. 1979. "Measuring Racial Discrimination in American Housing Markets: The Housing Market Practices Survey." Washington. DC: U. S Government Printing Office.

Wilgoren, J. 1998. "State Outpaces U.S. in Population Gain." *Los Angeles Times,* January 1, p. A1.

Wilkerson, I. 1994. "Growing Peril on South African Roads: Wave of Carjackings." *New York Times,* September 27, p. A3.

———. 1997. "Cry, The Crime-Ridden Country" *Business Week* (October 20):30D–31D.

Willen, H., and H. Montgomery. 1996. "The Impact of Wish for Children and Having Children on Attainment and Importance of Life Values." *Journal of Comparative Family Studies* 27(3):499–518.

Williams, D. 1998. "Ukraine, at the Fork in the Road." *Washington Post National Weekly Edition,* October 26, p. 15.

Williams, F. P., III, and M. D. McShane. 1988. *Criminological Theory.* Englewood Cliffs, NJ: Prentice Hall.

Williams, L., and M. Otto. 1999. "Fruits of Labor in U.S. Are Only Sweet for Some." *San Diego Union-Tribune,* September 4.

Williams, P. W. 1989. *Popular Religion in America,* reprint edition. Urbana: University of Illinois Press.

Williams, R. M., Jr. 1970. *American Values—A Sociological Perspective.* New York: Knopf, pp. 452–502.

Williamson, J. B., A. Munley, and L. Evans. 1980. *Aging and Society.* New York: Holt, Rinehart and Winston.

Willie, C. W. 1978. "The Inclining Significance of Race." *Society* 15(July–August):10, 12–13.

———. 1979. *The Caste and Class Controversy.* Bayside, NY: General Hall.

Wilson, D. 1997. "South Africa Is Engaged in a Race for Economic Growth." *New Statesmen* 126(4359):15.

———. 1997. "Apartheid's Feared Police Prove Inept and Corrupt." *New York Times,* March 25, p. A1.

Wilson, E. O. 1978a. *On Human Nature.* Cambridge, MA: Harvard University Press.

———. 1978b. "What Is Sociobiology?" *Society* (September—October):10–14.

Wilson, J. F., and W. R. Clark. 1989. *Religion: A Preface.* Englewood Cliffs, NJ: Prentice Hall.

Wilson, J. J. 1994. Fact Sheet #2. < http://aspensys.aspensys.com.209/RO-127-range/ncjrs/data/gangsfs.txt >

Wilson, J. Q., and R. Herrnstein. 1985. *Crime and Human Nature—The Definitive Study of the Causes of Crime.* New York: Simon & Schuster.

Wilson, S. L. 1989. *Mass Media/Mass Culture: An Introduction.* New York: Random House.

Wilson, W. J. 1978. *The Declining Significance of Race.* Chicago: University of Chicago Press.

———. 1987. *The Truly Disadvantaged: The Inner City, the Underclass, and Public Policy.* Chicago: University of Chicago Press.

———. 1989. *The Ghetto Underclass*. Newbury Park, CA: Sage.

Winner, K. 1995. "Q&A—Ernesto Zedillo Ponce de Leon." *San Diego Union-Tribune,* July 23, p. G5.

Winslow, R. 1998. "Health-Care Inflation Kept in Check Last Year." *Wall Street Journal,* January 20, p. B1.

Wirth, L. 1938. "Urbanism as a Way of Life." *American Journal of Sociology* 44:1–24.

Witkin, G. 1998. "The Crime Bust." *U.S. News & World Report* (May 25):28–37.

"Women Gaining Few Seats in Parliament." 1997. *San Diego Union-Tribune,* March 17.

"Women in Afghanistan: The Violations Continue." 1997. *Amnesty International Report,* June.

"Women of Our World." 1998. Population Reference Bureau, Washington, D. C: Population Reference Bureau.

"Women's Access to Land Still Restricted by Tradition." 1996. *Women's International News Network* (Autumn):12–14.

Wood, D. B. 1998a. "Arizona's Big Stakes in Charter Schools." *Christian Science Monitor,* June 2.

———. 1998b. "War Between States Over Gambling." *Christian Science Monitor,* September 8.

———. 1999. "California's Big Test: Holding Students Back." *Christian Science Monitor,* February 5.

Woodall, J. 1997. "Stalking the Next Epidemic: ProMED Tracks Emerging Diseases." *Public Health Reports* (Jan/Feb):78–82.

Woodard, C. 1998. "When Rote Learning Fails Against the Test of Global Economy." *Christian Science Monitor,* April 15, p. 7.

Woolard, D. and R. M. Edwards. 1997. "Female Circumcision: An Emerging Concern in College Healthcare." *Journal of American College Health* 45(5):230–232.

World Bank. 1999a. *1999 World Development Indicators.* New York: Oxford University Press.

———. 1999c. *World Development Report 1998/99: Knowledge for Development.* New York: Oxford University Press.

"World Health Organization: Women's Health and Family Violence." 1997. *Women's International Network News,* March 1, p. 54.

World Population Data Sheet—1998. 1998. Population Reference Bureau. Washington, DC: Polulation Reference Bureau.

World Urbanization Prospects: The 1996 Revision (1997) United Nations Secretariat, Department of Economics and Social Affairs, Population Division, New York.

Wright, E. O. 1985. *Classes.* New York: McGraw-Hill.

Wright, J. W., ed. 1998. *The New York Times 1999 Almanac.* New York: Penguin Reference Books.

Wright, J. W., general ed. 1992. *The Universal Almanac 1993.* Kansas City, MO: Andrews & McMeel.

Wright, R. 1992a. "Poverty's Shadow Haunting New Democracies." *Los Angeles Times,* February 25.

———. 1992b. "Global Alliances Shifting from Political to Economic." *Los Angeles Times,* March 3.

———. 1992c. "69% of Mankind Called Free; Ethnic Strife Clouds Gains." *Los Angeles Times,* December 18.

———. 1994. "Rich and Poor Gap Widens Around the Globe." *Los Angeles Times,* June 14.

Wrong, D. H. 1961. "The Oversocialized Conception of Man in Modern Sociology." *American Sociological Review* 26(April):183–193.

Yinger, J. 1995. *Closed Doors, Opportunities Lost: The Continuing Costs of Housing Discrimination.* New York: Russell Sage Foundation.

"Young and Abused." 1996. *U.S. News & World Report* (September 30):24.

Young, J. 1993. "Asia's Rapid Urbanization Brings Economic Fruits." *Christian Science Monitor,* April 20, p. 9.

Young, K. 1954. *Isn't One Wife Enough?* New York: Henry Holt.

"Yugoslavia and the Balkans." 1999. *BBC News History File.*

Zakaria, F. 1999. "The Beginning of the End?" *Newsweek* (July 26).

Zaldivar, R. A. 1995. " 'Middle Class' Is in the Eye of the Beholder." *Buffalo News,* January 12.

Zastrow, C., and L. Bowker. 1984. *Social Problems: Issues and Solutions.* Chicago: Nelson-Hall.

Zellner, W. P. 1995. *Counter Cultures—A Sociological Analysis.* New York: St. Martin's Press.

Zha, J. 1995. *China Pop: How Soap Operas, Tabloids, and Bestsellers Are Transforming China.* New York: The New Press.

Zierler, S., L. Feingold, D. Laufer, P. Velentga, I. Kantrowitz-Gordon, and K. Meyer. 1991. "Adult Survivors of Childhood Sexual Abuse and Subsequent Risk of HIV Infection." *American Journal of Public Health* 81(5):572–575.

Zucker, A. 1997. "Law and Ethics." *Death Studies* (May/June):319–322.

Zuckerman, M. B. 1998. "Land of the Rising Sun?" *U.S. News & World Report* (July):64.

Name Index

Kaplan, R. D., 352
Karabel, J., 223
Karp, J., 257
Kassebaum, G. G., 178
Kastenbaum, B., 16
Kastenbaum, R., 16
Katz, L. F., 201
Kaylor, R., 326
Kemps, D., 275
Kennedy, J., 131
Kennedy, P., 251, 257, 260
Kephart, W. M., 208
Kepp, M., 15
Kerbo, H. R., 93, 99, 103, 221
Key, K., 326
Kifner, J., 125
Kim, L., 70
Kinsella, K., 288
Kinsey, A. C., 178
Kinsman, M., 344
Kirchner, J. T., 190
Kirp, D. L., 155
Kirvo, L. J., 319
Klein, M., 182
Kleniewski, N., 319
Knestout, B., 281
Knickerbocker, B., 305
Knodel, J., 353
Knol, D. L., 166
Koch, K., 44
Kochanek, S. A., 256
Kohen, S., 240
Kolata, G., 186
Korman, S. B., 199
Korman, S. K., 197
Koss, M., 180
Kottak, C., 121
Koverola, C., 177
Krieger, L. M., 281
Kronholz, J., 228, 229, 231
Krueger, A., 184
Kwong, J., 46, 47

L
La Franchi, H., 143, 225, 226, 227, 258
Ladd, G. W., 81
LaFee, S., 35
Lampman, J., 50
Landes, J. B., 196
Landler, M., 116
Lane, C., 256
Lanier, C. A., 180
Lardner, J., 111, 172, 279
Larkin, R. P., 7, 314
LaRocco, L., 208
Larson, D., 198
Lash, S., 343
Laslett, B., 171
Lau, G., 298
Lauer, J., 198
Lauer, R. H., 198, 329
Lauritsen, J., 179, 180
Layng, A., 145, 146
Leaming, J., 218, 350, 351
Lederman, D., 228
Lee, C. S., 254
Leeds, A., 33

Leek, M., 193
Lefkowitz, J. P., 231
Lehman, S., 258
Lemert, E. M., 171
Lenski, G., 67, 233, 270, 300
Lenski, G. E., 98
Lenski, J., 67, 233, 270
Leslie, G. R., 197, 199
Leung, S., 316
Levin, M., 183
Levine, J., 48
Levine, S. B., 223
Levy, F., 104
Levy, J. R., 305
Lewis, F., 150
Lewis, J., 202, 203
Lewis, O., 41
Lewis, P., 139
Li, C., 48
Lichter, D. T., 207
Light, I., 313
Lin, J., 177
Lindner, E. W., 235
Lipset, S. M., 269
Little, C. B., 163, 176, 177, 178
Liu, J., 255
Livingston, J., 180
Lloyd, J., 237
Logan, J. R., 316
Logan, M., 318
Lombroso, C., 164
Lombroso-Ferrero, G., 165, 166
Longman, P., 250
Lott, J. R. Jr., 182
Loup, J., 294
Louw, A., 187, 188, 189
Lozada, M., 181
Lublin, J. S., 150
Luckenbill, D. F., 179
Lutz, W., 36
Lyman, P., 188
Lynch, J., 208

M
MacFarquhar, R., 46
Macionis, J., 315, 322
Mackenzie, H., 295
Macleod, L., 16
MacNeil, J., 306
Madge, J., 16
Madrid, A., 37
Madsen, C. F., 41
Magnuson, E., 168
Makowsky, M., 11, 12, 13, 16
Malinowski, B., 42
Malkin, E., 258
Mallinger, K., 194, 195
Malthus, T., 292-293
Mann, M., 146
Manning, W. D., 207
Maraldo, J. C., 240
Marcuse, P., 9
Marquand, R., 240
Marquis, J., 303
Marshall, T., 260
Martin, C. E., 178
Martin, R., 167

Martindale, D., 329
Martinkus, J., 352
Marx, K., 12, 18-19, 98-100, 146, 233-234, 292-293
Maryanski, A., 13, 18
Masland, T., 127
Massey, D. S., 176
Masters, R., 166
Mathews, J., 230
Matloff, J., 118, 187, 189
Matthews, J., 259
Mattox, W. R., 199
Matza, D., 184
Maugh, T. H. II, 178
Maykuth, A., 348
Mazari-Hirriart, M., 311
McCurdy, D. W., 39
McDonnell, P. J., 285
McFalls, J. A., 278, 279, 282, 283, 285, 286, 287, 288
McGaghy, C. H., 166
McGeary, J., 259
McGee, T. G., 326
McKaughan, S., 110
McKim, P. C., 35, 39
McLanahan, S., 207
McLaughlin, A., 232
McNeal, C., 212
McShane, M. D., 168
Mead, C., 39
Mead, G. H., 20, 79-80
Mead, M., 142
Meadows, D., 306
Meckler, L., 128
Meidlinger, L. R., 175, 176
Meier, R. F., 162, 164, 176
Menen, C., 258
Merida, K., 128
Merrick, T. W., 288
Merton, R., 17, 63, 168, 169
Messerschmidt, J., 175
Meyer, G., 41
Meyer, M. W., 63
Michaels, M., 259
Mieszkowski, P., 316
Mifflin, L., 344
Milbank, D., 134
Milgram, S., 27-28
Miller, E. M., 176
Miller, J., 271
Miller, L., 238
Miller, M., 221
Mills, C. W., 264-265
Mills, E. S., 316
Minerbrook, S., 161
Moffet, G., 295
Molidor, C., 182
Montagu, A., 33
Montalbano, W. D., 290
Montgomery, H., 204, 205
Montgomery, L., 125
Moore, W. E., 97-98
Morgan, S., 115
Morin, R., 128, 203, 229, 238, 268
Morley, R., 214
Morse, J., 231, 232
Munley, A., 143
Murdock, D., 105

Murphy, K., 288, 306, 322
Murr, A., 209
Murray, G., 65
Mutchnick, R. J., 167
Mwangi, G., 95
Mydans, S., 116, 352

N
Nadon, S. M., 177
Nagpaul, H., 325
Nanda, S., 3, 196
Nasar, S., 105
Nass, G., 178
Navarrette, R., Jr., 223
Nelan, B. W., 261
Neumark, Y. D., 186
Newcomb, A., 232
Nichols, R., 295
Niebuhr, G., 347
Nietschmann, B., 270, 271
Nisbet, E., 167
Nishizawa, J., 230
Nolan, P., 67, 233, 270
Nordland, R., 240
Norton, A. J., 207
Notesien, F., 293
Nye, J. S. Jr., 271

O
Oakes, J., 221
Obiora, A. L., 31
O'Connor, M. L., 277
Ogburn, W., 49
O'Hare, W. P., 118
Olin, P., 205
Olms, 8
Olshansky, S. J., 353
Olson, E., 177
Orcutt, J. A., 170
Orlebeke, R. S., 166
Orme, W. A. Jr., 301
Oropesa, R. S., 215
Otto, M., 346
Ouchi, W. G., 64-65

P
Painter, E., 182
Pakulski, J., 343
Palchikoff, K., 280
Palen, J. J., 311
Palmer, L., 348
Pappas, B., 48
Parachini, A., 185
Parenti, M., 335
Park, R. E., 313
Parker, J. H., 315
Parrillo, 120, 127, 131
Parsons, T., 17, 144-145, 246, 263
Pear, R., 134
Pearce, D., 150
Pearl, D., 126
Pearlstein, S., 266
Pedrick-Cornell, C., 211, 213
Peele, S., 164, 171
Peeno, L., 299
Pehrson, J., 256
Perrin, R. D., 177
Pesic, V., 123, 124

Subject Index

individualism in, 46-48
population of, 289
suicide rates in, 15
Cities. See also Urban areas
central business district of, 314
concentric zone model of, 314, 315
history of, in United States, 315-317
human ecology and, 313-316
megacities, 322, 324, 325-327
models of, 314-315
modernization of, 312-313
multiple-nuclei model of, 314-315
sector model of, 314, 315
suburbanization, 316-317
sunbelt, 317-319
urbanization, 313
winter, 319
Class. See Social class
Class conflict theory. See Conflict theory
Clinton, William Jefferson, 228, 236-237
Closed-class system, 101, 102-103
ascription, 102
endogamy, 102
Coercive organizations, 62
Cognitive development
concrete operational stage of, 78
formal operational stage of, 78
maturation and, 77-78
preoperational stage of, 78
sensorimotor stage of, 78
socialization as, 77-78
Collectivities. See Groups
Colombia, suicide rates in, 15
Colonialism, 334-335
Columbine High School, 84, 344
Communal (gemeinschaft) relations, 66
Comte, Auguste, 5, 10, 11, 12, 13, 329
Concentric zone model, 314, 315
Conception variables, 277
Concrete operational stage, 78
Condition, inequality of, 92
Conflict, role, 57
Conflict management

functionalist theory of, 220
socialization as, 77
Conflict theory, 18-20
bourgeoisie, 18
class, 98-100
of economy, 246
of education, 220-223
of families, 196
gender and, 145-146, 157
materialistic determinism, 99
mode of production, 99
objective classes, 99
political education and, 221
of politics, 263-264
proletariat, 18
religion and, 233-234
stratification and, 221-223
subjective classes, 99
substructure, 99
superstructure, 99, 221
Conformity, 163
anglo-, 120-121
Constructs, 23
Continued subjugation, 126-127
Control, social, 348-349
language as, 36-37
socialization and, 89
Control groups, 27
Cooley, Charles H., 20, 78-79
Core, 332
Core values, 39
Corporate capitalism, 248
Corporate crime, 184
Corporations, 248
Coser, Lewis, 19-20
Costa Rica, suicide rates in, 15
Countercultures, 45, 48-49
African National Congress as, 48-49
Ku Klux Klan as, 45, 48
in Poland, 48
religion in, 235-236
Solidarity as, 48
in South Africa, 48-49
in United States, 45, 48
Covert participant observation, 26
Crime, 348-349. See also Deviance; Laws
age and, 175
anomie theory of, 168-169
biological factors of, 164-166
corporate, 184
deviance and, 163
differential association theory of, 169-170

drug abuse, 185-186, 189-190
drug trafficking, 185
ethnicity and, 175-176
firearms, 182-183
functionalist theory of, 166-168
gender and, 175
health care and, 298
illegal immigration, 185, 284-285
labeling theory of, 170-171
murder, 179
occupational, 183
offenders, 174-176
organizational, 184
pornography, 185
prostitution, 176-177, 185
race and, 175-176
rape, 155-156, 180
robbery, 179-180, 185
social class and, 176
in South Africa, 187-189
stalking, 180-181
statistics, 172-176
stratification and, 112
street gangs, 181-182
in sunbelt cities, 318
theories of, 164-172
violence, 178-179, 181-182
white-collar, 183-184, 185
Criminal behavior. See Crime
Criminal justice. See Crime; Laws
Cross-cultural research, 5
Crude birth rate, 277
Crude death rate, 281
Cuba, controlling fertility in, 294
Cultural anthropology, 5
Cultural assimilation, 119
Cultural diversity, 44-45, 48-50
countercultures (See Countercultures)
cultural lag, 49-50
in India, 45
in Poland, 48
in South Africa, 48-49
subcultures, 44-45
in United States, 45, 48
Cultural lag, 49-50
Cultural relativism, 43-44
Cultural storage, 220
Culture, 342-343
behavior, 32-34
biological basis of, 32-34
defined, 31-32
imitation perspective of, 34

innateness hypothesis of, 35
language and, 34-37, 36-37
material, 37-38
nonmaterial, 37-38
popular, 38-39
of poverty, 41
reinforcement theory of, 34-35
roots of, 32-39
Sapir-Whorf hypothesis of, 35-36
Culture shock, 44
Custodial care, 220
Czech Republic, economy of, 261

D
Dahrendorf, Ralf, 19
Darwin, Charles, 96, 164
Darwinism, social, 95-97
Davis-Moore theory, 97-98
De facto racism, 126
De jur racism, 126
Debunking, 9-10
Decentralization, in education, 227-228
Definition of the situation, 20
Democracy and economy, 247-248
Democratic socialist economy, 247
Democratization and education, 227
Demographic transition theory, 293-294
Demography, 276
Denmark
economy of, 262
political participation in, 266
Denominations, religious, 235
Dependent variable data, 22
Descent
bilineal, 197
matrilineal, 197
patrilineal, 197
Descriptive research, 23-24
Desertification, 301
Desocialization, 75
Determinism, materialistic, 99
Developed countries, 94
LDCs defined, 6
Developing countries, 94
economic growth in, 250
families in, 215
nationalism in, 269-271
urban areas in, 322-324, 328
women in, 337-339

Deviance, 162-164, 348-349. See also Crime
  absolutist perspective of, 162
  alcohol abuse as, 185-186, 189-190
  anomie theory of, 168-169
  biological factors of, 164-166
  conforming behavior and, 163
  criminal behavior and, 163
  differential association theory of, 169-170
  drug abuse as, 185-186, 189-190
  functionalist theory of, 166-168
  homosexuality, 177-178
  labeling theory of, 170-171
  normative perspective of, 162
  pornography as, 185
  primary, 171
  prostitution as, 176-177, 185
  reactive perspective of, 162-163
  secondary, 171
  sexual, 176-178
  street gangs, 181-182
  theories of, 164-172
  violence as, 178-179, 181-182
Devolution and nationalism, 270-271
Differential association theory, 169-170
Discrimination, 117
Displacement, goal, 63-64
Divorce. See also Families; Marriage
  African Americans and, 199, 200
  age and, 199
  children and, 202-203, 206
  duration of marriage and, 200
  Hispanic Americans and, 199, 200
  laws re, 200
  race and, 199, 200
  rates of, 202
  religion and, 200
  social class and, 199-200
  in United States, 199-203, 206
Dominican Republic, suicide rates in, 15
Dowry deaths, 337-338
Drug abuse, 185-186, 189-190

Drug trafficking, 185
Dual-labor market, 149
Durkheim, Emile, 11-12, 66, 67, 69, 329, 330. See also Functionalist theory
Dyad groups, 61
Dynamics, social, 11

E
Economic inequality, 104-106
  dimensions of, 93
  global, 94
  wealth, 105-106
Economic substructure, 99
Economy/economic systems, 351-352
  in Africa, 258-260
  in Asia, 250-257
  capitalist, 234, 247, 248
  central business district, 314
  conflict theory of, 246
  corporate capitalism, 248
  corporations, 248
  democracy and, 247-248
  in Europe, 260-262
  European Economic Union, 261, 262
  fall of Soviet Union and, 260
  functionalist theory of, 246
  gross national product, 247
  growth of, in developing world, 250
  income (See Income)
  international marketplace, 249-251, 254-262
  International Monetary Fund, 252-254
  internationalization of, 249
  in Latin America, 257-258
  in Middle East, 259-260
  North American Free Trade Agreement, 258
  political, 245
  postindustrialization of, 248-249
  poverty and, 249-250
  segmentation and, 248
  as social institution, 245-251, 254-262
  socialist, 247
  supply and demand, 245-246
  theories of, 246
  types of, 246-248
  underemployment and, 249-250

unemployment and, 249-250
Ecuador, suicide rates in, 15
Education, 350-351. See also Children; Schools
  Asian model of, 230
  bureaucratization in, 228
  charter schools, 231
  conflict theory of, 220-223
  decentralization in, 227-228
  democratization and, 227
  functionalist theory of, 219-220
  illiteracy and, 229
  income and, 222
  inequality in, 226
  in Latin America, 224-227
  models of, 225-226
  political, 221
  school choice plans, 230-231
  school vouchers, 230-231
  as social institution, 219-223, 227-232
  Standards Movement in, 231-232
  stratification and, 221-223
  student performance levels, 229
  as superstructure, 221
  theories of, 219-223
  in United States, 223, 227-232
  voting and, 267
Egalitarian authority, 197
Ego, 77
Egoistic suicide, 14-15
Empirical data, 22
Employment issues
  dual-labor market, 149
  gender and, 147-150
  segmented-labor market, 149
Endogamy, 102, 197
Engels, Friedrich, 99, 145, 146, 196
English economy, 262
Environmental issues, 300-307, 352-354
  addressing, 305-306
  air pollution, 302-303
  carrying capacity, 300
  desertification, 301
  fossil fuel depletion, 302
  global warming, 303-304
  greenhouse effect, 303-304
  land/soil depletion, 301
  nonrenewable resources, 300

pollution, 302-305
  radioactive waste disposal, 305
  renewable resources, 300
  resource depletion, 300-302
  solid waste disposal, 304
  sustainable development, 306-307
  toxic waste disposal, 304-305
  waste disposal, 304-305
  water shortages, 300-301
Equality. See also inequality
  gender and, 156-158, 157-158
  of opportunity, 92
  strategies of, 157-158
Eritrea, economy of, 259
Ethics, 23
  Milgram Experiment, 27-28
Ethiopia
  controlling fertility in, 294
  population of, 289
Ethnicity/ethnic relations, 116-119, 118-119, 119-121, 125-127, 346-347. See also Race/race relations
  African Americans (See African Americans)
  anglo-conformity, 120-121
  Asian Americans, 130, 132
  assimilation, 119-121
  continued subjugation, 126-127
  crime and, 175-176
  discrimination, 117
  ethnic group defined, 118
  extermination and, 127
  genocide and, 127
  Hispanic Americans (See Hispanic Americans)
  legal protection of minorities, 121
  majority groups, 116-117
  Melting Pot, 119-120
  minority groups, 116-117
  Native Americans, 130-132, 342-343
  pluralism and, 121
  population transfer, 125-126
  poverty and, 132-135
  prejudice, 117
  scapegoating, 126-127
  in United States, 127-128
Ethnocentrism, 42-43
Ethnography, 321

392

Subject Index

Societal development,
     continued
  mechanical solidarity, 66
  organic solidarity, 66
  societies defined, 65-66
Societies, defined, 65-66
Sociocultural
     considerations of
     gender, 140
Socioeconomic class. See
     Economic inequality;
     Social class
Sociology
  defined, 3
  modernization of, 5-8
Soil depletion, 301
Solid waste disposal, 304
Solidarity
  as counterculture, 48
  mechanical, 66
  organic, 66
South Africa
  counterculture in, 48-49
  crime in, 187-189
  end of apartheid in, 187-
     189
South America. See Latin
     America
South Korea
  economy of, 251, 252-
     254
  International Monetary
     Fund and, 252-254
  population of, 289
  suicide rates in, 15
  women in, 338
Southern countries, 94
Soviet Union, fall of, 260,
     268-269, 280, 283
Spain, economy of, 262
Spencer, Herbert, 13, 329,
     330
Spousal abuse, 211, 212-
     214
SR, 285
Stalking, 180-181
Standards Movement in
     education, 231-232
State, defined, 270
Statics, social, 11
Status, 55-56
  achieved, 55-56
  ascribed, 55
  master, 56
Stereotypes, 43
  gender, 140-142
Storage, cultural, 220
Strain, role, 56-57
Stratification, 95-101, 101-
     104, 345-346. See also
     Inequality
  assessing, 93-95
  closed-class system, 101,
     102-103
  conflict theory of, 98-100
  crime and, 112

Davis-Moore theory of,
     97-98
  education and, 221-223
  functionalist theory of,
     97-98
  gender and, 140, 146-
     151, 155-158
  income and, 148-150
  materialistic
     determinism, 99
  mental health and, 107,
     111
  multiple-hierarchies
     model of, 100-101
  natural superiority
     theory of, 95-97
  open-class system, 101-
     102
  physical health and, 107,
     111
  political involvement
     and, 111-112
  social, 93, 106-107, 111-
     112
  social class, 106
  social Darwinism and,
     95-97
  social mobility and, 103-
     104
  in United States, 104-106
  work and, 147-148
Stratum, 100
Street gangs, 181-182
Streetwise (Anderson),
     321-322
Structural assimilation, 119
Structural-functional
     theory. See
     Functionalist theory
Structural mobility, 103-104
Subcultures, 44-45
Subgroup differences, 157
Subjective classes, 99
Subjective social class, 106
Subjectivistic orientation,
     20
Subjectivistic perspective,
     20-21
Subjugation, 126-127
Substructure, economic, 99
Suburbanization, 316-317
Sudan, economy of, 259
Suicide, 14-17
  altruistic, 14
  anomic, 15
  egoistic, 14-15
  fatalistic, 15-16
  rates of, 15-16, 278
Sunbelt cities, 317-319
Superego, 77
Superstructure
  conflict theory, 99
  education as, 221
Supply and demand, 245-
     246
Survey research, 25

Sustainable development,
     306-307
Sweden
  economy of, 262
  families in, 204-206
  political participation in,
     266
Switzerland, political
     participation in, 266
Symbolic interaction, 20-
     21, 157
Symbols, significant, 21

T
Taiwan, economy of, 251
Tanzania
  economy of, 259
  international migration
     and, 284
Taxes in sunbelt cities, 318
Television and religion,
     237-238
Terrorism, political, 244
Thailand, AIDS in, 280
Theological stage of
     development, 10
Theories. See also
     Hypothesis; Models
  anomie, 168-169
  conflict (See Conflict
     theory)
  of crime, 164-172
  Davis-Moore, 97-98
  defined, 12
  demographic transition,
     293-294
  of deviance, 164-172
  differential association,
     169-170
  of economy, 246
  of education, 219-223
  on families, 195-196
  functionalist (See
     Functionalist theory)
  of gender, 144-146, 156-
     158
  grand, 12
  labeling, 170-171
  middle-range, 12-13
  of modernization, 329-
     331
  multiple-hierarchies
     model, 100-101
  natural superiority, 95-
     97
  of politics, 263-264
  of population, 293-294
  Protestant ethic, 234
  reinforcement, 34-35
  on religion, 233-234
  social Darwinism, 95-97
  of socialization, 77-80
  symbolic interactionism,
     20-21
  unilinear theories of
     change, 330

of urban areas, 319-322
  world system (See World
     system theory)
Third World
  controlling fertility in,
     294
  defined, 6, 7
  mortality rates in, 281
  urban areas in, 322-324,
     328
  women in, 337-339
Thomas, William Isaac, 20
Tocqueville, Alexis de, 40
Tönnies, Ferdinand, 66,
     67, 69, 329
Total institutions, 85, 88
Toxic waste disposal, 304-
     305
Traditional authority, 268
Transformation, social, 220
Triad, 61
Typologies, defined, 57

U
Uganda
  AIDS in, 280
  economy of, 259
Ukraine
  AIDS in, 280
  economy of, 261
Underemployment, 249-
     250
Unemployment, 249-250
Unilinear theories of
     change, 330
Unions in sunbelt cities,
     318
United Arab Emirates,
     economy of, 259
United Kingdom, 266. See
     also individual
     countries, e.g.
     England
United States
  African Americans in,
     127-128
  AIDS in, 279-280
  Asian Americans in, 130
  cities in, 312, 313
  counterculture in, 45, 48
  divorce in, 199-203, 206
  economic system in,
     248-249
  education in, 223, 227-
     232
  ethnicity/ethnic
     relations, 127-132
  families in, 194-195
  Hispanic Americans in,
     128-130
  history of cities in, 315-
     317
  illegal immigration to,
     284-285
  illiteracy in, 229
  inequality in, 104-106